CyberReader

◆ **Victor J. Vitanza**

UNIVERSITY OF TEXAS AT ARLINGTON

ALLYN AND BACON

Boston London Toronto Sydney Tokyo Singapore

Vice President, Humanities: Joseph Opiela
Production Coordinator: Susan Brown
Editorial-Production Service: Matrix Productions
Designer: Seventeenth Street Studios
Cover Administrator: Linda Knowles
Composition Buyer: Linda Cox
Manufacturing Buyer: Aloka Rathnam
Acknowledgments appear on pages 310–312,
which constitutes a continuation of the copyright page.

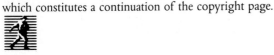

Library of Congress Cataloging-in-Publication Data

Vitanza, Victor J.
    CyberReader / Victor J. Vitanza.
        p.   cm.
    Includes bibliographical references (p.).
    ISBN 0-205-19779-5
    1. Internet (Computer network) 2. World Wide Web (Information
    retrieval system) I. Title.
TK5105.875.I57V58   1996
302.23—dc20   95-47815
                                                          CIP

Printed in the United States of America
10 9 8 7 6 5 4 3 2 1   99   98   97   96

■ CONTENTS

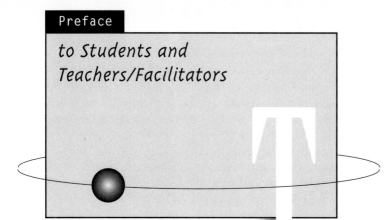

to Students and Teachers/Facilitators

he purpose of this book is to introduce you to the Internet (the Net) and the World Wide Web (WWW). Unlike many such books on the market, however, *CyberReader* invites you to reflect on the technology that has made available this new mode of information and the rapid changes that come with it. More simply put, this book is about *change*—about how technology is extending our lives and everything around us geometrically. Exponentially.

Years ago, my family and I were invited next door to watch television. Our neighbors were the first on our block to purchase what was much later to be called the "boob tube." The screen was 9 inches across and the image had a green tint. Every few minutes our neighbor had to jump up and adjust the rabbit ears (the antennae). We were all blown away. It was magic. It was as if our neighbor were pulling images out of a hat! For days on end, I gave my family no peace: we had to have a TV and that was all there was to it. But my parents kept saying that they thought it best to wait until television "was perfected." I noticed that the phrase was being repeated by a lot of people. Just about all of us were waiting for things to be perfected! (The same argument was used a few years later about color television.)

There's no doubt that things have changed and are changing so rapidly that anyone waiting for anything technological to be perfected would miss model after new improved model and perhaps the thing itself morphing into something totally different. Morphing equals metamorphosis equals "a transformation, as by magic or sorcery." Speed!

In the computer business there is "Moore's Law," which states that microcompressors double their power (speed and overall capability) and get twice as cheap (assuming the absence of a monopoly) every eighteen months. Figure out the math on that one: Where will we be technologically in five years, ten years, or twenty years?

A few years ago, I thought about getting a fax machine when I heard about the students in China during the Tiananmen Square revolt using that technology to communicate to the outside world. I never bought one. The other day, I bought a new modem with a baud rate of 28,000 and with it I was given some extra software that allows faxing. My computer (an LCIII, an outdated Mac) now has the capability to fax and to download information at a rate that seems like a blink of an eye on my black-and-white 19″ monitor. Shortly after purchasing my new modem, however, I read in the newspaper a long article on a new service known as ISDN (integrated services digital network) that would eventually be available in our area. I was crushed when the author of the article wrote: "I put an impressive Pipeline 50 router on my PC and connected to my Internet service provider at speeds up to 128 kilobits per second, nearly nine times faster than a 14.4 modem"! I read on to find exactly how much it was going to cost me to have this new thing: hundreds of $$$$. I called my service provider for my personal PPP connection (to the Internet and WWW) to inquire whether or not the company could provide this service. A representative said yes and for hundreds of $$$$, but to wait a few months and it would only cost hundreds of ¢¢¢. I decided to wait for things to be perfected! After all, I had just jumped from a 2400 baud rate to 28,000 rate! I could wait. Sure I could! And be momentarily satisfied with the speed that I had.

(As I write this, I am mocking myself. I am well aware of the stupidity of all this. At the same time, however, I am aware, as John Perry Barlow says, that there is no way to stop any of this technology and the speed it generates. If I were to say, like a good neo-Luddite, that it could be and ought to be stopped, I would equally have to mock myself for believing that I could stop with a sword what amounts to a tidal wave. I am well aware that a single human being stopped a line of tanks in Tiananmen Square, but I am also aware that technology broadcasted this event to the world over. Speaking, writing, books, fax machines, television, the Internet—all are technologies that determine our lives. As Marshall McLuhan said: the medium is the message.)

But all these examples of speed and change are child's play in comparison to other things technological. This book, at times, will introduce many readers to the bizarre or weird or what is also called the "edge" or "fringe." Besides inviting you to think about some of the most basic concepts such as freedom of expression and how to realize it on the Internet, this book will also introduce you to such fringe philosophies and sciences as

- extropianism and transhumanism

- nanotechnology

- crash culture

- cyberpunks

- hackers and crackers

- cyberdelics

- teledildonics, and so on

It can get even more bizarre, strange, and for many people wonderful (as in full of wonder). All of this wonderment (and yes, at times, hype) is the result of breathtaking speed.

It is this kind of speed—approaching that of light and beyond—that makes such a book very difficult to write and to edit. I have been painfully aware that any article or topic/theme I select may be obsolete as soon as the book appears. After all, the production of this book takes a long time—not only for me to write, edit, and get permissions from publishers and authors to reprint their work, but also for the publisher to produce the physical thing we call a "book," what you are holding in your hands. To complicate matters further, this book is about what is out on the World Wide Web, about particular websites or packets of digitized information on the WWW, which change so rapidly. Essentially, this book with all its URLs (Uniform Resource Locators, telephone numbers) is somewhat comparable to a telephone directory of the world that has millions of residents listed in it who, as a way of life, are *nomadic* and constantly disconnecting and reconnecting their services and telephone numbers. Here today; gone and morphed into something else tomorrow! That's speed and change.

Are there any constants?

I would like to think that our discussions about this technology, as manifested in the articles that I have selected and on the WWW itself, do have some "constants." The articles deal with basic historicized issues such as time and space, the actual and the virtual, freedom of access to information versus censorship, identity and privacy, sex and gender and the like. Our different takes on each of these may change, but as issues they have remained pretty much constant. Our URLs or e-mail addresses (eddresses) may change, but the search engines (directories) for locating our new ones only change in their increased abilities to locate the new addresses.

Therefore, while this has not been an easy book to put together, my publisher and editor and I have worked hard at anticipating problems and solving them before they arise. That is why we have decided to make this book not only an actual book in print but also a virtual, updated set of news and notes about the book at our Website <http://www.abacon.com/~cyber>. That's right: with the support of and Allyn & Bacon, I will be able to update this book constantly. When new articles that supplement or complement those that I have included here come out, I can cite them or, if possible with permission, place them out at the *CyberReader* website and make links to articles that are newly on the WWW. Likewise, when URLs no longer reach their destination, I can put in the new URLs, if available, and constantly update the list with still newer sites on the WWW. Though the actual book is fixed within each edition, the virtual part of the book on the WWW will constantly change as required.

But there is another reason for having made this anthology both an actual book and a virtual, updated set of news and notes about the book. Books are not obsolete. Someday they may very well be in museums, but not in the foreseeable future. (This issue is discussed in Chapter 4.) Books have become audiotapes and may become—and of course already are—compact disks (CDs), but magazines and books will still be around for a long while. (There is speed, but there is nostalgia. And there is the impulse toward differences and choices.) But a book that is actual and virtual at the same time can be of great value because it allows us to see the differences between books on paper and on monitors, books with words as atoms of ink and as bits of pixels; because it allows us to see the differences among a flat presentation of words/text (as in this book itself), a simulated version of hypertext (as we have attempted in a few cases in this book, say, with the introductions and other sections), and a virtual hypertext on the WWW (which we have done by placing the introduction to this book at our website, the medium of the Web itself).

To be sure, we will have not thought of everything, and that's why we have also placed out on the *CyberReader* website the means for you to communicate with us, to leave us a message, to tell us what you would like to see in forthcoming editions or on the website. We hope that you enjoy the book and its virtual updates.

■ FAQS (FREQUENTLY ASKED QUESTIONS):

1. What if I know absolutely nothing about computers, e-mail, and all that? What should I do?

Well, you have done the first thing by signing up for a course. (If you are reading this book without benefit of a teacher/facilitator and a course, then you might find such a course.) What you should do is—simply put—*ask for help.* Ask your instructor/facilitator or someone in your class. There is, however, often a gender bias built into our cultural attitudes about things technological: men are supposed to know, women are not. (This issue is discussed in Chapter 3.) Therefore, if you are male and another male or a female asks for help, *help that person!* Help both yourself and others in creating an actual and a virtual community. At times, it can be very difficult to ask for help, but you must. When I wanted to learn about the Internet, I asked one of my female graduate students and she became my facilitator. In the spirit of freeware and shareware, share what you know.

2. What if we have only Lynx as a browsing program at our university and therefore only text without graphics or sound?

The book is written on the assumption that most people with access to the Web at various universities have only *Lynx.* If, however, you have access via a *Mosaic* or *Netscape* browser, then all this will be much easier for you. Instead of using the arrow keys (→ ↓ ↑ ←) to navigate by way of the hot links (boldface type), all you have to do is point at the icons or underlined words and click. If you still are on *Lynx,* think of it this way: the best way to learn how to drive an automobile is with a stick or standard transmission. Thereafter, when an automatic transmission is available, driving (browsing) will be a snap. Or at least that's what I told myself when I started out with *Lynx*! To research this book, I used both *Lynx* and *Netscape* 1.1.

3. How should we or I read CyberReader?

We suggest that you look through the table of contents and then skim the book. If you are already familiar with the Internet (sending e-mail) and the WWW, then you might want to just skim Appendix A (CyberSearch). If not, then perhaps you might want to read through this section first. After that, you can read the book from top to bottom or read the chapters in the order that interests you. (There are two possible exceptions: you might want to begin with Chapter 1 and you might want to read and work on Chapters 2 and 3 in succession.) The sequence that you follow in reading the book will, of course, give you a different impression of *CyberReader*. Also, you should try to read all of the material in one chapter or section together. Again, these are only suggestions; at times you may want to surf intuitively from one interest to another.

4. What is the intended relationship among the individual introductions to each chapter, the readings themselves, and the closing sections entitled "Further Questions and Suggestions"?

As usual, the introductions are there to establish a context for the readings. The articles were selected because they are part of a conversation on a set of issues; you will note, when reading, many cross-references within and among the articles. The closing sections are designed to open up the Internet and the WWW to you in the light of the readings. After reading about, say, William Gibson, you are then directed to his homepage (his virtual residence), or to other specific work by or about him, or to the search engines that will allow you to find additional information about Gibson or things Gibsonian. Having said all this, however, I would remind you again to feel free to surf.

5. What should I do if I keep finding words (jargon) I don't understand?

Every attempt has been made to define terms, or at least to suggest, especially about elusive ones, what they might mean. But if you still find yourself at a loss when reading, we suggest you try Appendix B (the Glossary). If you do not find any help there, then you might try some of the URLs that we have supplied for dictionaries or glossaries on the WWW.

6. Is there a website on the Net where I can find FAQs about FAQs?

Yes, it's *World Wide Web FAQs* <http://sunsite.unc.edu/boutell/faq/www_faq.html>. And we will have a FAQs link on the Allyn & Bacon *(CyberReader)* website that will extend those already begun here. Just point your browser to <http://www.abacon.com/~cyber>, and we'll see you there.)>=

■ ACKNOWLEDGMENTS

I would like to thank Collin Brooke, Douglas Brown, Philip Cohen, Robert Cook, Diane Davis, Cynthia Haynes-Burton, Mathew Levy, Thomas Rickert, David Rieder, Alan Taylor, David Vitanza, and Nancy Wood for their suggestions and, in general, for their help. I would especially like to thank my wife, Toni, for the four months of hyperpatience while I completed this cyberbook and all of her assistance in seeing it get to press. And I would like to thank RAV(e), too. I am appreciative of the assistance given me by John Perry Barlow, Julian Dibbell, Donna Haraway, Michael Heim, Queen Mu, Susan Herring, Chris Goggins, Senator James Exon, James Harrington, Howard Rheingold, Douglas Rushkoff, Benjamin Woolley, Ted Nelson, and many, many others. Similarly, I would like to thank Joe Opiela (my editor), Susannah Davidson, Susan Brown, Merrill Peterson, and everyone at Allyn & Bacon.

—Victor J. Vitanza

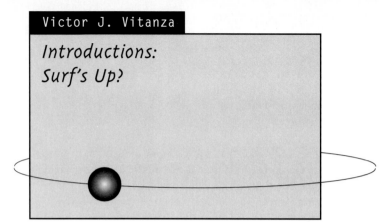

Victor J. Vitanza

Introductions: Surf's Up?

John Dewey worked to restore education to its primitive, pre-print phase. He wanted to get the student out of the passive role of consumer of uniformly packaged learning. In fact, Dewey in reacting against passive print culture was surf-boarding along on the new electronic wave.

—Marshall McLuhan, *The Gutenberg Galaxy*

Cyberia is frightening to everyone. Not just to technophobes, rich businessmen, midwestern farmers, and suburban house-wives, but, most of all, to the boys and girls hoping to ride the crest of the informational wave.
　Surf's up.

—Douglas Rushkoff, *Cyberia*

Hi, call me Sophist@utarlg.uta.edu. I have many signatures such as R. U. Rhetoricus?, R. U. Sophisticus?, or Vic Vit, Rotciv, saVVy, vvictor, Victa Nyanza, vEager, v///ger, Vaud-Ville, and so on.

I am writing two introductions here: one for the traditional reader, who wants just the basic, safe, vanilla approach to using *CyberReader;* another for the off-the-wall reader, who wants to take risks and see this book in different ways. (This introduction can be found on the Allyn & Bacon website, under *CyberReader,* and in hypertext format, html.)

Let's call the first introduction the "Bill Gates" way; the second, the "Timo-thy Leary" way.

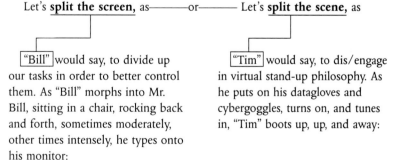

Let's **split the screen,** as————or———— Let's **split the scene,** as

"Bill" would say, to divide up our tasks in order to better control them. As "Bill" morphs into Mr. Bill, sitting in a chair, rocking back and forth, sometimes moderately, other times intensely, he types onto his monitor:

Just think of this book that you have in your hands right now as

"Tim" would say, to dis/engage in virtual stand-up philosophy. As he puts on his datagloves and cybergoggles, turns on, and tunes in, "Tim" boots up, up, and away:

Just don't think of this actual book that you have in your hands right

CyberReader 96+. It will provide you with everything you could ever need or desire to begin thinking about the subjects of cyberspace, virtual reality, and hyper-reality—the three main concepts that *CR 96+* introduces and elaborates on. Though these concepts overlap, there are some distinguishing characteristics, which are examined in Chapter 1 of the readings. However, here's a very quick notion of how the three differ:

Cyberspace, according to William Gibson who coined the phrase, is "consensual hallucination";

Virtual Reality (VR), according to Jaron Lanier, who coined the phrase, is "post-symbolic communication"; and

hyperreal(ity) is—who coined this word?—"more real than real."

These phrases probably tell you very little at this point, but they will begin to tell you perhaps more and more of what the future holds for all of us as you proceed through the readings and make forays on the World Wide Web (WWW or W3). And all with my help. Just follow my directions after the readings and you will take a step into a world that will transform you!

The purpose of *CR 96+* is to introduce you to the crucial issues that are associated with each of these concepts, to introduce you specifically to a multifaceted set of "readings" on each topic, and to send you out to the WWW to discover more of that conversation but in a virtual community that grows by the thousands everyday.

now as a book at all; think of it as a surfboard.

Now climb on top and catch this big wave I'm sending your way.

Back in the Sixties, lots of us were, so to speak, a little *leery* of technology, except that which produced better things through chemistry. We were called the counterculture. Now, I don't remember much else about the Sixties. But today we Sixties people live on. Now many of us take in large doses of electricity: ecstatic electricity. We drop pixels of electronic LSD. But I wander.

I want to introduce *CyberReader* so that all of you who read and study this book can become cybernauts.

Back in the Sixties, we of the counterculture knew we were embarking on an important trip into the future. If you look at the history of the development of consciousness, earlier generations moved like snails across the centuries. They surfed tiny waves. It took about a century and a half for earlier generations to move from cave drawings to handwriting. Today we surf tidal waves. In this century alone we have advanced from black & white television to color TVs (with colors more real than real) to virtual reality. Whereas we used to watch TV, it now watches us! While we used to sit in front of the TV, we now "sit" in it. We are capable of being in its virtual space. (We are beaming ourselves up and down and all over the virtualscape.) Soon we will evolve into cyborgs, a hybrid of half protoplasm and half silicon.

Back before the Sixties, after WW2—oh, say, between 1950 and 1965—there were the *Beats,* who were "low-tech, but early psychedelic explorers." After that generation, between

Think of *CR 96+* as your Gateway to cyberspace. Or think of it as your book-to-human-to-computer interface. Think of it as sort of a "Holodeck" (as you might remember from *Star Trek: The Next Generation*), a library room of a book that you enter that leads you to virtuality and increases your virtuosity as a reader of actual books and a surfer of virtual ones.

On deck, you will find seven chapters and three Appendices. Before reading any of the chapters, you might want to start with the preface and then read very quickly the appendices, both of which will give you an additional sense of what to expect.

Here are the rooms:

Introductions: "Surf's Up?"

Chapter 1: CyberSpace (Virtual Reality, Hyperreality)

Chapter 2: Freedom/Censorship (Security/Hackers)

Chapter 3: Cyberwars (FlameWars, Sexual Politics, and Netsex/"Porn"/ Violence)

Chapter 4: HyperText (Virtual Books, Multimedia)

Chapter 5: Virtual Libraries (and Copyright vs. Copyleft)

Chapter 6: CyberPunk/Cyborgs

Chapter 7: MUDs/MOOs

Appendix A: CyberSearch (The Search Engines)

Appendix B: CyberGlossary

Appendix C: Bibliography of Cyberspace

So this is pretty cool, huh? If it's a little intimidating,

1965 and 1975, there were the *Hippies,* who were, as I said, "psychedelic, but anti-high-tech." After that high wave, between 1975 and 1990, there were the *Cyberpunks,* who were "high-tech electronic." Now we are getting to your generation, the biggest wave to date in the history of the development of human consciousness. Between 1990 and 2005, there are you whom I call the *"New Breed"* and who are "psyche-delic [cyberdelic], super high-tech, with interest in smart drugs, brain machines, and the Internet."

Well, this is how I survey recent history in my book *Chaos and Cyber Culture.* VV includes a selection from that book here in *CyberReader* for you to read.

Excuse me, I keep forgetting that I am supposed to be introducing VV's *CyberReader*! Actually and virtually, it is the phirst of its kind. It's a smart book! VV nudges especially those of you who are incipiently of the "New Breed"—from books as well as TV to simulated books to virtual books out to the W3. Each wave that you are asked to surf gets a little bigger—perhaps a little more frightening.

But remember, you are the New Breed! What VV wants you to do, what your own generation wants, just as recent generations did, is to TFYQA.

Think for Yourself; Question Authority! So when you read and surf with this book . . . TFYQA. Live up to that code not only in your everyday lives but especially while reading the authors in this book, many of whom themselves (by now) represent authority *because* they questioned authority. Now you must question them just as you must question me! Surfing and questing and hacking are what we cybernauts are remember: Don't be afraid, I'm here to help. Just think of me as your friendly lifeguard making the superhighway safe for you and others. So go ahead and paddle out because the surf's up and ready for you to enjoy.

about. Extend (hyper-) your mind and if you think all this is only hype, then, surf with that thought. TFYQA! Make VVaves!

—"Bill"
(8-o

—"Tim"

Unsplitting the page (monitor), for a moment, let us think of other personages who would radically reintroduce and recombine ways of thinking about *CyberReader*. How about:

Ned Ludd?

Sandy Stone?

Christopher Columbus?

Winona Ryder?

HAL?

R2D2?

Any of the replicants in *Bladerunner*?

And let's insist on You! and your (actual/virtual/elite) Class!

Etc.?

CyberSpace

(Virtual Reality, Hyperreality):

Benjamin Woolley ◈ "Cyberspace"

Michael Heim ◈ "The Essence of vr"

Douglas Rushkoff ◈ "Seeing Is Beholding"

Umberto Eco ◈ "Enchanted Castles"

> The sky above the port was the
> color of television, tuned to a
> dead channel.
>   —William Gibson, *Neuromancer*

We need first to feel comfortable—but not too comfortable, as if we ever could—with three puzzling terms:

cyberspace,

virtual reality, and

hyperreality

Before we can understand these terms and how other authors think about them, we must grasp the ancient distinction made by Plato among *ideal, actual,* and *sham* (virtual). Briefly put, Plato assumes a realm of ideal forms for all things. His example in Book 10 of the *Republic* is a bed: there is "bedness" (as an abstraction, an ideal, the "really real") before there can be an actual bed made by a carpenter. An actual bed, therefore, is once removed from an ideal bed. For Plato, a painting of a bed is twice removed and hence it is a sham bed, a simulated bed, a virtual bed—and of no value except to confuse matters. Consequently, Plato would allow the carpenter into his utopia, but not the painter.

Now the term *cyberspace* (A.K.A. psyberspace). There is agreement that this word was coined and popularized by William Gibson in his novel *Neuromancer.* For Gibson, it means "consensual hallucination." (Note how problematic the term *hallucination* is!) But let's ask: Where does this consensual hallucination occur in most of our lives? Gibson and others would most likely answer that it occurs in the "matrix" and would offer the example of the telephone system (i.e., the wires, cables, satellites). In other words, when we speak over the phone, our conversation is *in* the matrix. It does not matter where we are when we phone, for we can phone from just about anywhere now, especially since cellular phones are available on a larger scale in our society. As subtle as this distinction may sound, it has a profound impact on us. Plato would definitely not like the telephone any more than he liked writing as a substitute for face-to-face (F2F) dialogue. Both the telephone and writing are substitutes for actual communication, which would be only once removed from the ideal, which Plato believed only the philosopher was capable of knowing. In this Platonic point of view, then, cyberspace can be seen as sham space.

Setting this term aside for a while, let's look at the next term, *virtual reality* (VR), which was coined by Jaron Lanier. Whereas the term *cyberspace* may have had its origins in cyberpunk science fiction, Howard Rheingold suggests that VR had its origins in science. It is a matter of actual technology. Science, wanting to deal with and understand the actual world, stumbled over the virtual world. Lanier speaks of VR as "postsymbolic communication." A person can put on cybergloves (A.K.A. datagloves), head-mounted displays, and (sometimes) body suits and be in VR. With these articles on, a person can be convinced or persuaded that he or she is elsewhere. However, it is not necessary to don the gloves and helmet; stepping into a flight simulator, which many student and seasoned pilots do everyday, can give a person the same perception of being in VR. In great part, postsymbolic communication has to do with a consensual hallucination between at least two or more people who are willing to agree on imaginary (possible) worlds. This is postsymbolic communication because the possible worlds and objects created in them are not created with words or necessarily, as Michael Heim tells us, with "Real-world references."

The easy difference between cyberspace and virtual reality is that we can actually believe we are *in* virtual reality. When I am talking on the telephone, I have no sense of being *in* the matrix; when I wear a VR glove and helmet, I have a sense of being *in* another place that I previously was not in. Notice that I said in the first sentence "actually . . .*in* [VR]." Herein lies a confusion of not only terms but realities. While in a sense my body is in the glove and helmet, my mind is in the matrix, telling me that my body is there also. For many, including Plato and even Aristotle, this is not a good state to be in. When we are actually in VR, we are not imitating a real action but are in a *virtual* (simulated) reality that spills over, not only in this oxymoronic term, but also into what we have taken to be reality—that is, *real* reality! And it spills over with an (apparent) vengeance! Today more than before, because of our technologies, we have not Reality but realities—hence not only such phrases as "consensual reality" but also "designer realities" and "electronic LSD."

But what about SIMNET, the global war game simulator? When the Gulf War was fought in 1991, it was waged on monitors of various sorts, like fighting done in video games; the reporting of this war was mostly imparted with footage from these "games." Soldiers actually present in the field, wearing night goggles or not, spoke of the battlefield as surreal, unearthly, simulated. When a reporter caught in the war asked his colleagues afterwards what the war was like, they were astonished because he was actually in it. For him, however, being in the Gulf War did not constitute actually seeing it on TV, which is *where* the war took place, in that consensual hallucination. (Some, such as Jean Baudrillard, maintain that the war never "actually" took place! What could Baudrillard possibly mean by such a statement?)

From cyberspace to VR, let's turn now to *hyperreality,* which is no less confusing a term. What adds to the confusion is that hyperreality is often used to mean virtual reality. Initially, however, I would venture this distinction: virtual reality is brought about immediately by a mechanistic environment (e.g., television, video games, VR gloves, and helmet); hyperreality consists of the long-term consequences of these trips into virtuality. There is a residual effect when we move from reality to VR and back again—namely, the "reality effect," with so-called "real reality" or the "actual" becoming merely one among countless virtual realities. (*Hyper-* means to extend.) According to Baudrillard, reality is now *hyper*reality; we have passed completely out of one reality and into extended realities. And most devastatingly, hyperreality is *more* real than reality and, for many of us, more attractive. This new reality, or realities, contains paradoxically fewer (everyday) polar distinctions—whether they be between the real and the not real, or among cyberspace, virtual reality, and hyperreality—than the old reality. As Baudrillard says, there is an "implosion—an absorption of . . . the differential mode of determination, with its positive and negative charge—an implosion of meaning. *That is where simulation begins.*" Again, where? Where there is a loss of traditional distinctions (real vs. fiction, war vs. peace, truth vs. lie, good vs. evil, male vs. female)? Has life turned into a dead channel on a television set?

Many critics argue that because we are losing such distinctions, we must put the brakes on VR; others exclaim, however, that there are no brakes to apply. Still other critics argue that VR is liberating, allowing us to steer ourselves clear of would-be philosopher-kings. (The Greek root *cyber-* means "steersman" or "pilot.") However, while the technology—whether it be speaking, writing, typing, word processing, simulating, or the like—enables or, as we say, "empowers" us in many wonderful and helpful ways, it does also drive us. But in what direction, when we have lost in postsymbolic communication our traditional notion of "where" as an actual place! Space and time seem to be imploding, collapsing differences, as Baudrillard and others suggest. Where has "where" gone? Have we passed through the looking glass? Can we ever find our way back to where and who we were? Do we even want to?

I leave these questions along with others for your consideration after you have read the following articles. They are difficult concepts, to be sure, but crucial to your understanding of what has been and still is *taking place.*

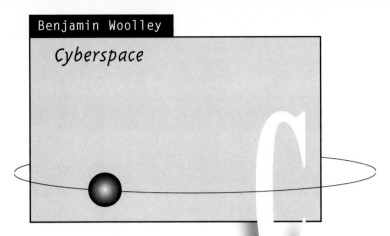

Benjamin Woolley

Cyberspace

"Cyberspace...
is presently
inhabited
almost
exclusively by
mountain men,
desperados and
vigilantes, kind
of a rough
bunch," said
John Perry
Barlow. "And, as
long as that's
the case, it's
gonna be the
Law of the Wild
in there. . . ."

yberspace has a nice buzz to it," said William Gibson, recalling his use of the term in his fiction, "it's something that an advertising man might of thought up, and when I got it I knew that it was slick and essentially hollow and that I'd have to fill it up with meaning."[1] By the beginning of the 1990s it was so full of meaning, it was fit to burst. In his original use of the term in *Neuromancer*, Gibson had famously described it as a "consensual hallucination"—a term he left ill defined. It was, he later said, meant to suggest "the point at which media [flow] together and surround us. It's the ultimate extension of the exclusion of daily life. With cyberspace as I describe it you can literally wrap yourself in media and not have to see what's really going on around you."

It was a fictional rendition of Ivan Sutherland's original concept of the "ultimate display," a form of display that presented information to all the senses in a form of total immersion. However, Gibson had extended Sutherland's idea of a "looking glass into a mathematical wonderland" to embrace the entire universe of information: "A graphic representation of data abstracted from the banks of every computer in the human system. Unthinkable complexity. Lines of light ranged in the nonspace of the mind, clusters and constellations of data. Like city lights receding."[2]

In the rhetoric of the virtual realists, this "nonspace" was not simply a mathematical space nor a fictional metaphor but a new frontier, a very real one that was open to exploration and, ultimately, settlement. "Cyberspace . . . is presently inhabited almost exclusively by mountain men, desperados and vigilantes, kind of a rough bunch," said John Perry Barlow. "And, as long as that's the case, it's gonna be the Law of the Wild in there. . . . Whenever you make a financial transaction, really it involves electronic data representing money. So we feel that the way to minimize anxiety, and to make certain that the freedoms we have in the so-called real world stay intact in the virtual world, is to make it inhabitable by ordinary settlers. You know, move the homesteaders in."[3] To do this, Barlow had even set up the Electronic Frontier Foundation with Mitch Kapor, the founder of the software house Lotus, one of the most successful companies to emerge out of the personal computer era and one, ironically, roundly condemned by the hacker radical Richard Stallman for its illiberal policy towards copyright.

In the twilight of the space age, cyberspace was becoming the new final frontier, and virtual reality was the Enterprise. NASA's key role in the development of the technology, right at the time of the *Challenger* and *Hubble* humiliations, when the agency no longer commanded the emblematic heights (or generous financial backing) it had enjoyed during the 1960s, was heavily symbolic. Like astronomical space, cyberspace was only dimly perceived by ordinary people, but there was a promise that technology would one day provide them with access to it. Day trips to the moon having proved unfeasible, attention was turning to mystery tours of the digital domain.

What, then, is cyberspace? The actual term is technically unimportant. Other phrases are used synonymously: cyberia, virtual space, virtual worlds, dataspace, the digital domain, the electronic realm, the information sphere. One can examine its etymological entrails for meaning—"cyber," meaning steersman, coming from "cybernetics," the study of control mechanisms—but that yields very little. A more productive strategy is to try to discover why the terms have acquired such currency. How did a word that Gibson had thrown into his work almost casually when he coined it acquire, within a few years, such value?

One interpretation of cyberspace is that it concerns the annihilation of space. "As electrically contracted," wrote Marshall McLuhan in 1964, "the globe is no more than a village."[4] "After three thousand years of explosion, by means of fragmentary and mechanical technologies, the Western world is imploding. During the mechanical ages we had extended our bodies in space. Today, after more than a century of electric technology, we have extended our central nervous system itself in a global embrace, abolishing both space and time as far as our planet is concerned."

Neglected in the 1970s, when the world was probably too diverted by shortages of energy to concern itself with ideas of electrical contraction, this concept of the global village began to become fashionable again in the 1980s. It was seen as the perfect expression of the new era of world finance and international telephone networks. In the 1980s, the financial system had migrated onto computer and communications networks, satellite and cable links that spanned the globe, capable of carrying data and voice, creating the conditions that produced the October 1987 stock market crash, where a fall in the New York stock exchange precipitated a collapse in prices that tripped off markets around the world within hours. "In principle," wrote Mark Poster, a Californian professor of history, in 1990, "information is now instantly available all over the globe and may be stored and retrieved as long as electricity is available. Time and space no longer restrict the exchange of information. McLuhan's 'global village' is technically feasible."[5]

The imagery of the "global village" is seductive, suggesting that the technology of communications will collapse dispersed urban alienation into the cosy confines of a pre-industrial age. It suggests the emergence of a whole new type of working environment, the "telecottage," set in rural surroundings, far away from the jams yet part of the world's information traffic. Telecommunications companies have even started setting up such cottages in remote areas such as the Scottish Highlands. Certain white-collar jobs, claim the global villagers, entail nothing more than the exchange of information—meetings, paperwork, taking decisions—all of which can easily be communicated over the telephone network. As a result, a teleworker's attachment to the job becomes a factor of his or her connection to the network rather than proximity to the company office.

But Marshall McLuhan expected more from the idea of the global village than a new type of post-industrial working environment. He saw technology as an extension of the body. Just as the wheel is an extension of the foot, the telescope an extension of the eye, so the communications network is an extension of the nervous system. So, as the communications network has spread across the globe, so has our neural network. Television has become our eyes, the telephone our mouths and ears; our brains are the interchange for a nervous system that stretches across the whole world—we have breached the terminating barrier of the skin.

Marshall McLuhan saw technology as an extension of the body. Just as the wheel is an extension of the foot, the telescope an extension of the eye, so the communications network is an extension of the nervous system.

The technology that has made this possible is the network. Networks are not new: there have, presumably, been social ones since the dawn of society. What is new is the technology of communication that has enabled information of any type to be carried from one place to another regardless of their distance. Such networks are electronic, and carry their messages instantly by wire, by optical fibre, by radio and microwave. In computing, it is the network that is seen as providing the next great step in the technology's inevitable progress. Personal computing will become what Steve Jobs has dubbed "interpersonal computing."

Networks first found their way into computing via the development of a system to connect computers deployed in projects funded by the American Advanced Research Projects Agency, ARPA. This ARPAnet was originally designed to allow ARPA researchers to share data, but was increasingly used to exchange messages, which in turn helped develop a sense of community between the geographically scattered centres they worked in. This was, in a sense, the world's first "virtual" community, existing only in its interaction over ARPAnet.

ARPAnet developed in two directions: it grew outwards, to span the entire globe, coming to be called Internet. Internet is, for many, the model of what virtual communities can be like. Geography is irrelevant—so there are no "backwaters," no "provinces" excluded by the central metropolis. Hierarchy is irrelevant, because everyone has equal access to the network, and everyone is free to communicate with as few or as many people as they like.

ARPAnet also contracted, inspiring the development of the world's first "local area" network, "Ethernet." As the word "local" implies, geography has not quite been rendered irrelevant by telecommunication networks. The more information there is to carry and the further it has to go, the more it costs to carry it. Local area networks (LANs) were designed to carry a great deal of information across short distances—the distance between computers in the same office. Because of their carrying capacity—their "bandwidth"—they are able to create a much richer form of communication between the individual users, so rich, in fact, that on well-implemented local area networks, the distinction between each user's personal system and the network begins to blur. What belongs to whom in terms of files and facilities depends not on its physical location inside any particular machine, but upon the way it is organized across the LAN. In 1991, NeXT, the computer company set up by Steven Jobs after his departure from Apple, announced "Zilla," a program that enables a network of NeXT computers to act as a single, virtual supercomputer. A network of 100 NeXT machines was, according to Zilla's designer Richard Crandall, as powerful as a Cray 2, then the most powerful supercomputer in the world. A Zilla computer could, furthermore, have its power distributed between offices across the globe. With the development of optical fibre, which offers almost limitless bandwidth, as an alternative to wire, the possibility arose that this new form of "interpersonal" computing would truly render geography irrelevant and allow new forms of social as well as commercial interaction to emerge.

In the mid-1980s, NASA's Human Factors Research Division began working on developing what it provocatively called "telepresence." Telepresence was originally promoted as a way of controlling robots. Since it is better to send machines than humans into hazardous environments like space, the NASA research team aimed to provide a wrap-around technology that would give the machine operator the feeling of "being" in the place of the machine being operated. If, for example, a robot was being used to repair an external component on a shuttle or space station, the robot's cameras would be connected to a head-mounted display so that the wearer could see what he or she would see if actually there. Similarly, a glove or exoskeleton (that is, a series of hinges and struts clamped to the body, like an articulated splint) could be used to reproduce the wearer's movements in the robot's arm and hand or to provide tactile feedback, resisting the wearer's movements in accordance with the pressure exerted on the robot's limbs when it picks up an object. A sufficiently rich communication between the operator and the robot would, the NASA team hoped, result in the robot essentially becoming the operator's body; he or she would be "telepresent," instantly transported to wherever the robot was working.

Since the communication between robot and operator is via an information link, perhaps you could be telepresent anywhere. Just plug the helmet and some sort of sensory bodysock into the telephone and television network and you would be away, literally, discovering the true meaning of McLuhan's limitless sensorium. No more watching television, but, as William Gibson put it, "doing" television. We could climb through the window of the world.

Is this, then, cyberspace? Is there really some sort of space, some sort of independent realm created by the interconnection of the world's information systems? Is this a metaphorical space or a real one?

Conventionally, we think of networks as transparent, as systems for conveying messages from one human being to another without in any way shaping their meaning. McLuhan's other great contribution to the media age was the phrase: "The medium is the message." What he meant was that networks (or media—in other words, systems for carrying information) are not transparent. Television is not a window on the world, it does not simply show its audience pictures of events that happen to be taking place elsewhere. Rather, it actually has a role in determining what the audiences see and how they make sense of it. A game show or soap opera is not a natural event; it has been created specifically for the cameras, and only makes sense if seen on TV. (Studio audiences, one might think, are watching the event "for real," but in fact they need the prompting of an army of studio managers and warm-up artists to make up for what is, in fact, a very unreal event, constantly interrupted by retakes, filmed inserts and cutaways.)

No more watching television, but, as William Gibson put it, "doing" television. We could climb through the window of the world. Is this, then, cyberspace?

On July 20, 1989, Wes Thomas, publicist for the magazine *Mondo 2000,* claimed that he had "unleashed the world's first media virus."[6] An unspecified source had told him of the spread of a particularly dangerous computer virus, variously called "October 12," "Datacrime" and "Columbus Day." A computer virus is extraordinarily like a biological one. A biological virus is a small strand of genetic code that uses the host organism's replicating mechanism to produce copies of itself, which are then spread to other host organisms via whatever medium they are able to use—say, the exchange of body fluids, as seems to be the case with HIV. A computer virus is similarly a strand of code, a computer program, that uses the computer's replicating mechanism to produce copies of itself, which are then spread to other host computers via whatever medium they are able to use, usually via floppy disks and the public networks used by enthusiasts to exchange software. The most significant difference between a computer virus and a biological one is that the former is written by a computer programmer for mischievous purposes, whereas the latter arises spontaneously in nature.

Thomas sent a note via electronic mail to two journalists alerting them to news of the computer virus, which he subsequently discovered would activate on October 12 in any year and wipe out the host computer's disk drives on the 13th, which in 1989 happened to fall on a Friday. As soon as the story appeared in the *San Francisco Examiner,* it was picked up by the world's press agencies. According to Thomas, the CNN cable news service (often described as the global village's local TV station) announced that "all PC computers would be wiped out at 12:01 a.m. on October 13th." The British tabloid, *Daily Star,* even featured the story on the front page of its October 5 issue, anticipating the spread of a "doomsday computer bug," and the BBC carried a news item on October 13 on the anticipated epidemic, which, as it turned out, amounted to no more than an outbreak of irregular behavior on a computer at the Royal National Institute for the Blind.

The interesting feature of the Friday the 13th virus was, of course, the way that the reporting of its spread was as much a feature of its epidemiology as the spread of the program itself. Thomas had released a story that was evidently highly contagious. Besides being a date of Christian significance (13 being the number at the Last Supper, and Friday the day of the Crucifixion), Friday the 13th had far more popular significance as the name of a successful series of Hollywood horror movies. The AIDS scare had also increased awareness of the threat of viruses. In the era of antibiotics and vaccines, the public perception of infection in countries like Britain and America had been that it was basically controllable, despite the continuous background presence of venereal disease. Few people realized just how little control medicine had over viral disease. AIDS changed all that. It also disinterred old attitudes about the links between disease and sin. The term "virus" was no longer simply a medical term, like "bacteria"; it had suddenly acquired a moral resonance. It was a resonance that was easily transferred to the computer virus. Like AIDS, we were all threatened with being tainted by the hacker's lack of moral hygiene. Infection was guilt.

The technological as well as the social climate provided the Friday the 13th virus with perfect breeding conditions. Since the international acceptance of the IBM Personal Computer as a technical standard, the vast majority of personal computers had become functionally identical: a homogeneous "species" had, in other words, emerged with very little variation to protect it from opportunistic infection. Worse, this technological monoculture was both dispersed, used across the Western world by the self-employed and the multinational alike, and highly connected by computer networks and dial-up computer services such as bulletin boards. The release of a virus capable of efficient reproduction in such an environment genuinely threatened widespread damage.

But not *that* much damage. Because the story had such mythical potency, the technical threat of the computer virus was wildly overstated by the news coverage. The world portrayed as under the greatest threat, the world of the corporate computer user, was in fact under the least threat, because most corporations get most of their software from authorized channels. The most vulnerable users were those who regularly swapped illicit software—the hackers, in other words, who were best able to spot any signs of infection and deal with them, and who in many people's eyes would be the deserving victims of any damage they caused.

More significant than the impact of the Friday the 13th virus was the increasing awareness, expressed by writers like Thomas, that the international media network was, like the computer network, not merely a passive communications system but an environment that, in many respects, had a life of its own. The virus story was a global village phenomenon. AIDS, a global village disease spread by international travel and the exchange of blood products, had created the conditions for its spread. It was introduced into an environment which was increasingly homogenized by global capitalism, and that, thanks to the sheer speed of turnover of the news agenda, was unable to build resistance. It was, in other words, evidence of the emergence of an artificial environment—something that McLuhan himself anticipated.

According to Richard Dawkins, a zoologist at Oxford University and the author of *The Selfish Gene*,[7] a feature common to all forms of life is the replicator, a mechanism that can store information and replicate it. The replicator for natural life is the gene, made up of DNA. An important distinction needs to be established in order to understand the concept of the replicator. There is the information to be replicated, called the genotype, and the product of that information being "expressed," the phenotype. The information encoded in the gene is the genotype. The organism it produces is the phenotype. The phenotype can be thought of as a set of tools which are there to make copies of the genotype. Our bodies, along with their reproductive apparatus, are the most obvious phenotypic expression of our genes. Dawkins called his book *The Selfish Gene* because, from a zoological perspective, living organisms are the product and servant of their genes. The genes that produce the most effective phenotypes for reproduction do best, because they spread. Those that do badly disappear.

Computer viruses are, like biological viruses, replicators in a special sense, because they are parasitical, they do not come packaged with the means of phenotypic expression. Nevertheless, it is easy to imagine a refinement of the computer virus that fits in exactly with the genotype/phenotype model. The virus program can be thought of as the genotype, and the effect it has on the computer when it is executed can be thought of as the phenotypic expression. The program might even be miscopied, and the result might be a new version of the original computer virus program that, when executed, produces a phenotype that copies the virus more efficiently. The result would be the beginnings of evolution.

The unfolding scenario is a threatening one: the artificial environment created by computers will become host to a new, evolving lifeform, one that could spread uncontrolled through the world's networks. We should not, however, reassure ourselves with the thought that such a lifeform will confine itself to the realm of computers. Let us extrapolate further by introducing one of the most powerful of Dawkins's ideas: that of the extended phenotype.

The phenotypic effect of a gene is usually thought of as the body that carries the gene. But why stop there? Surely, argues Dawkins, anything that results from the gene's expression can be regarded as the phenotype.[8] Even something as large and inanimate as a beaver's dam is a genetic effect, one that contributes to the beaver gene's chances of reproduction. By the same token, could not a computer virus evolve some sort of extended phenotype? Suppose, for example, that a mutated virus caused the host system to behave in a way that prompted the computer user to indulge in some particularly vigorous file copying (perhaps it causes the system to crash a couple of times, which encourages the user to make more backup copies of infected files). Such a virus could spread further, and would do so because it, unlike other viruses, had evolved a mechanism for manipulating the world beyond the computer.

On the same day that Wes Thomas's media virus swept the globe, an event occurred that did seem to confirm that something mysterious was spreading through the global village.

There is no reason to suppose that evolution would stop there. Human users provide a perfect means of acquiring new reproductive resources. They are influenced by the computers—otherwise they would not use them—and could therefore be used in any way that escapes obvious detection to aid a particular virus's spread. This does not mean that viruses would turn computer users into mindless servants, any more than biological viruses that use us, as they surely do, to spread, have turned us into mindless servants. The point is that replicators are almost by definition opportunistic. Successful ones will take any opportunity they can to spread; that is what made them successful and is the reason they, unlike all the unsuccessful ones, have survived and evolved.

Although there is very little evidence that such replicators have yet colonized our computer systems, on the same day that Wes Thomas's media virus swept the globe, an event occurred that did seem to confirm that something mysterious was spreading through the global village.

On Friday, October 13, 1989 Wall Street went into free fall, throwing the world's financial markets into a state of chaos which, for many dealers, chillingly recalled the dark days of October 1987. The strange aspect of the 1989 crash was, however, the total absence of any apparent cause: the world economy was in pretty good shape and the European, Far Eastern as well as U.S. stock markets, until that point, appropriately stable. "Explanations abound," reported *Financial World*. "An isolated sequence, driven by events perhaps? An illogical fall with a fast return to reason? Or, a chilling thought, the reverse?"[9]

There was no possibility that the trigger was the computer virus. Computers had been implicated in the 1987 crash, when falling prices triggered systems programmed to sell shares that passed a particular price threshold, which in turn caused prices to fall further, which pushed share prices past yet lower thresholds, which triggered off yet more selling. This time, however, the computing equivalent of fire breaks should have ensured that such automatic trading systems were under control.

One possible cause, however, that the markets did not contemplate—perhaps could not contemplate—was that the 1989 crash was evidence that the world stock markets were, in effect, beyond human control. It has been increasingly hard to relate the movement of the markets to real economic conditions. Japan's Nikkei index, for example, suffered terrible falls in following years, despite the country's robust economic performance. Similarly, the British stock market reached new highs while a persistently weak economy went through one of its periodic slumps.

Though stock markets have always behaved unpredictably, the new electronic, computerized, globally networked markets are far more volatile. There seems to be a diminishing relationship between the value of a company's shares and its actual performance. The "casino economy," as leftist critics labelled it, was becoming a computer game that was under the control of no one player. Like the patterns in the computer Game of Life, unexpected patterns such as sudden rises and falls in the markets seemed to be the result of the interaction of capital, "emergent" properties of a complex system rather than the whim of individuals acting according to their best interests.

It was 1930, the year Gödel's famous paper undermining the certainties of mathematics was published, that Britain was forced off the gold standard by increasing instability of the pound, then a major world currency.

It was 1930, the year Gödel's famous paper undermining the certainties of mathematics was published, that Britain was forced off the gold standard by increasing instability of the pound, then a major world currency. This total breakdown of the system had only happened twice before since its adoption in the early eighteenth century: during the Napoleonic and the First World Wars.[10] This time it was gone for good, killed off by the world depression that followed the first Wall Street crash of October 1929.

The gold standard was a stabilizing measure designed to provide a fixed measure of money's value by relating it to a fixed quantity of gold. It meant that the purely symbolic nature of paper money was anchored in something that was regarded as having inherent material value. However, for economic reasons, this was a system that the British government could not sustain while the economic order collapsed around it. One might have thought this was the time when something as fixed and certain as gold was worth its weight as a form of security. But, as it turned out, gold itself had no intrinsic value; it, too, could not escape the vagaries of supply and demand on the international marketplace.

The abandonment of the gold standard has turned money into a purely abstract quantity, a symbol. A deficit is no different to a surplus, except that the mathematical sign for one is a minus, for the other a plus. Exchange has become an arithmetical correlation: if my balance goes up by so much, yours must come down by the same amount. Currencies "float," their level being set by their relationship to all other currencies. There exists no material means of distinguishing "my" money from anyone else's, no need for physical possession, no stash of gold or even cash in my bank's vaults that increases or diminishes according to how much I earn or spend. In the global village, this process of abstraction has reached its purest expression. Junk bonds, paper billionaires, credit ratings—money is just a parameter in a process running on a global computer, part of the reason that for many it is now meaningless, even worthless, a form of pure abstract symbolism that bears no relation to productive effort or material rewards. It exists in another realm, the same realm as the media virus—in cyberspace.

Perhaps cyberspace, then, is—literally—where the money is. Perhaps it is also the place where events increasingly happen, where our lives and fates are increasingly determined; a place that has a very direct impact on our material circumstances—a blip in the money markets can raise bank lending rates, a blip in a multinational's productivity can close factories and throw economies into depression, a blip in the TV ratings can wipe out an entire genre of programming, a blip in an early warning system can release a missile.

Perhaps cyberspace, then, is— literally—where the money is.

The power of this realm comes from its connectedness. It is a continuum, not a series of discrete systems that act independently of each other. Blips are not isolated events. Accelerated and amplified by electronics, they are the result of the subtle interactions of the millions of bits of data that flow through the world's networks. Furthermore, anyone connected to these networks, be they a humble telephone subscriber or TV viewer, participates in such events. No one can avoid becoming active citizens of cyberspace.

To people who have been involved in computing, and in particular personal computing, in the 1980s, such citizenry is no mere matter of theoretical speculation, it is very real. In 1982, I visited California for the weekly computer trade newspaper *Datalink*. The magazine's editor, Guy Kewney, and I decided to use the trip as an opportunity to try out a new way of communicating text that would avoid the delay and inconvenience of reading the articles over the phone (this was at a time when faxes were still relatively rare, even in California).

I typed up my articles on an Osborne-1 portable microcomputer. About the size of my tightly packed suitcase, and almost as heavy, it would have probably been easier to lug around an IBM golfball typewriter, but I needed to have my text in "machine-readable," word-processed form, not typed on paper, because I was going to send it back to Britain in that form. To do this, I used a modem—a device that turns the electronic signals generated by a computer into the sort of signals carried by a telephone line—and dialed up an "electronic mail" system in the UK called "Gold." Once connected, I sent the file that contained the text of my article down the line to Gold, which filed it away in its own computer for retrieval by colleagues at the office.

The result was instant, international communication, and, in the following few years, it became a standard means for reporters to file their copy, particularly so as the weight of portable computers decreased. It was just one of a growing number of ways that computers and telecommunications combined to change working practices. Academics used the ever-spreading networks to communicate with their peers by electronic mail. Businesses began to dial up databases of stock market prices, press cuttings or company accounts. Indeed, by the late 1980s, a whole new multi-billion dollar "value added services" communications market had emerged. Businesses like AT&T were no longer telephone companies, they were "telecommunications" companies, their networks were no longer just for voice, they were for any kind of data.

Computer users were plugged straight into this growth in telecommunications. Many linked up to the ever-increasing number of electronic services at their disposal: bulletin boards, online databases, home banking, teleshopping. The experience of using such services powerfully reinforced the collective imagination of computer users that there was another "world," a world where much of their social intercourse might take place, where much of their information would come from. They also knew that it was linked into the networks of international finance, commerce and government—as demonstrated by the growing number of stories about hackers gaining unauthorized access to company and defence systems using the same basic equipment. And it was the world infected by the computer virus, spread by the exchange of pirated and "homebrew" software deposited on bulletin boards and conferencing systems.

It was the excitement of being part of this world that stoked up the computing community's interest in virtual reality. Could this be where the denizens of the global village truly belonged? Could this be a *new* reality?

■ NOTES

1. Interview with the author, *Late Show,* BBC 2, September 26, 1990.

2. William Gibson, *Neuromancer,* London: Grafton, 1986, p. 67.

3. David Gans and R. U. Sirius, "Civilizing the electronic frontier," *Mondo 2000,* 3, Winter 1991, p. 49.

4 Marshall McLuhan, *Understanding Media: the extensions of man,* London: Routledge, 1964, p. 5.

5. Mark Poster, *The Mode of Information: poststructuralism and social context,* Cambridge: Polity Press, 1990, p. 2.

6. Wes Thomas, "How I created a media virus," *Mondo 2000,* 2, Summer 1990, p. 137.

7. Richard Dawkins, *The Selfish Gene,* 2nd edition, Oxford: Oxford University Press, 1989.

8. Richard Dawkins, *The Extended Phenotype,* Oxford: Oxford University Press, 1982, p. 200.

9. Stephen Kindel and Amy Barrett, "The crash that wasn't . . . or was it?," *Financial World,* November 14, 1989, 158 (23), p. 26.

10. E. J. Hobsbawm, *Industry and Empire,* London: Penguin, 1969, p. 236.

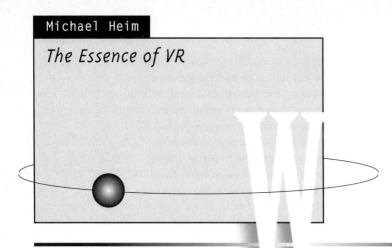

The Essence of VR

What is virtual reality?

A simple enough question.

We might answer: "Here, try this arcade game. It's from the Virtuality series created by Jonathan Waldern. Just put on the helmet and the datagloves, grab the control stick, and enter a world of computer animation. You turn your head and you see a three-dimensional, 360-degree, color landscape. The other players see you appear as an animated character. And lurking around somewhere will be the other animated warriors who will hunt you down. Aim, press the button, and destroy them before they destroy you. Give it a few minutes and you'll get a feel for the game, how to move about, how to be part of a virtual world. That's virtual reality!"

Suppose the sample experience does not satisfy the questioner. Our questioner has already played the Virtuality game. Suppose the question is about virtual reality in general.

Reach for a dictionary. *Webster's* states:

Virtual: *"being in essence or effect though not formally recognized or admitted"*
Reality: *"a real event, entity, or state of affairs"*

We paste the two together and read: "Virtual reality is an event or entity that is real in effect but not in fact."

Not terribly enlightening. You don't learn nuclear physics from dictionaries. We need insight, not word usage.

The dictionary definition does, however, suggest something about VR. There is a sense in which any simulation makes something seem real that in fact is not. The Virtuality game combines head-tracking device, glove, and computer animation to create the "effect" on our senses of "entities" moving at us that are "not in fact real."

But what makes VR distinctive? "What's so special," our questioner might ask, "about these computer-animated monsters? I've seen them before on television and in film. Why call them 'virtual realities'?"

The questioner seeks not information, but clarification.

Pointing to the helmet and gloves, we insist: "Doesn't this feel a lot different from watching TV? Here you can interact with the animated creatures. You

shoot them down or hide from them or dodge their ray guns. And they interact with you. They hunt you in three-dimensional space just as you hunt
them. That doesn't happen in the movies, does it? Here you're the central
actor, you're the star!"

Our answer combines hands-on demonstration with a reminder of other
experiences. We draw a contrast, pointing to something that VR is not. We
still have not said what it is.

To answer what VR is, we need concepts, not samples or dictionary phrases
or negative definitions.

OK, so what is it?

Our next reply must be more informed: "Go to the source. Find the origi-
nators of this technology; ask them. For twenty years, scientists and engineers
have been working on this thing called *virtual reality*. Find out exactly what
they have been trying to produce."

When we look to the pioneers, we see virtual reality going off in several
directions. The pioneers present us with at least seven divergent concepts currently guiding VR research. The different views have built camps that fer-
vently disagree as to what constitutes virtual reality.

Here is a summary of the seven:

■ SIMULATION

Computer graphics today have such a high degree of realism that the
sharp images evoke the term *virtual reality*. Just as sound systems were once
praised for their high fidelity, present-day imaging systems now deliver virtual reality. The images have a shaded texture and light radiosity that pull the
eye into the flat plane with the power of a detailed etching. Landscapes produced on the GE Aerospace "visionics" equipment, for instance, are photoreal-
istic real-time texture-mapped worlds through which users can navigate.
These dataworlds spring from military flight simulators. Now they are being
applied to medicine, entertainment, and education and training.

The realism of simulations applies to sound as well. Three-dimensional
sound systems control every point of digital acoustic space, their precision
exceeding earlier sound systems to such a degree that three-dimensional audio
contributes to virtual reality.

■ INTERACTION

Some people consider virtual reality any electronic representation with
which they can interact. Cleaning up our computer desktop, we see a graphic
of a trash can on the computer screen, and we use a mouse to drag a junk file
down to the trash can to dump it. The desk is not a real desk, but we treat it
as though it were, virtually, a desk. The trash can is an icon for a deletion
program, but we use it as a virtual trash can. And the files of bits and bytes
we dump are not real (paper) files, but function virtually as files. These are

virtual realities. What makes the trash can and the desk different from cartoons or photos on TV is that we can interact with them as we do with metal trash cans and wooden desktops. The virtual trash can does not have to fool the eye in order to be virtual. Illusion is not the issue. Rather, the issue is how we interact with the trash can as we go about our work. The trash can is real in the context of our absorption in the work, yet outside the computer work space we would not speak of the trash can except as a virtual trash can. The reality of the trash can comes from its handy place in the world woven by our engagement with a project. It exists through our interaction.

Defined broadly, virtual reality sometimes stretches over many aspects of electronic life. Beyond computer-generated desktops, it includes the virtual persons we know through telephone or computer networks. It includes the entertainer or politician who appears on television to interact on the phone with callers. It includes virtual universities where students attend classes on line, visit virtual classrooms, and socialize in virtual cafeterias.

■ ARTIFICIALITY

As long as we are casting our net so wide, why not make it cover everything artificial? On first hearing the term *virtual reality,* many people respond immediately: "Oh, sure, I live there all the time." By this they mean that their world is largely a human construct. Our environment is thoroughly geared, paved, and wired—not quite solid and real. Planet Earth has become an artifice, a product of natural and human forces combined. Nature itself, the sky with its ozone layer, no longer escapes human influence. And our public life has everywhere been computerized. Computer analysis of purchasing habits tells supermarkets how high and where to shelve the Cheerios. Advertisers boast of "genuine simulated walnut."

But once we extend the term *virtual reality* to cover everything artificial, we lose the force of the phrase. When a word means everything, it means nothing. Even the term *real* needs an opposite.

■ IMMERSION

Many people in the VR industry prefer to focus on a specific hardware and software configuration. This is the model set for virtual reality by Sutherland, Fisher, Furness, and Brooks, before whom the term *virtual reality* did not exist, since no hardware or software claimed that name.

The specific hardware first called VR combines two small three-dimensional stereoscopic optical displays, or "eye-phones"; a Polhemus head-tracking device to monitor head movement; and a dataglove or hand-held device to add feedback so the user can manipulate objects perceived in the artificial environment. Audio with three-dimensional acoustics can support the illusion of being submerged in a virtual world. That is, the illusion is immersion.

According to this view, virtual reality means sensory immersion in a virtual environment. Such systems, known primarily by their head-mounted displays

(HMD) and gloves, were first popularized by Jaron Lanier's VPL (Virtual Programming Language) Incorporated. The HMD cuts off visual and audio sensations from the surrounding world and replaces them with computer-generated sensations. The body moves through artificial space using feedback gloves, foot treadmills, bicycle grips, or joysticks.

A prime example of immersion comes from the U.S. Air Force, which first developed some of this hardware for flight simulation. The computer generates much of the same sensory input that a jet pilot would experience in an actual cockpit. The pilot responds to the sensations by, for instance, turning a control knob, which in turn feeds into the computer, which again adjusts the sensations. In this way, a pilot can get practice or training without leaving the ground. To date, commercial pilots can upgrade their licenses on certain levels by putting in a certain number of hours on a flight simulator.

Computer feedback may do more than readjust the user's sensations to give a pseudoexperience of flying. The feedback may also connect to an actual aircraft, so that when the pilot turns a knob, a real aircraft motor turns over or a real weapon fires. The pilot in this case feels immersed and fully present in a virtual world, which in turn connects to the real world.

When you are flying low in an F-16 Falcon at supersonic speeds over a mountainous terrain, the less you see of the real world, the more control you can have over your aircraft.

When you are flying low in an F-16 Falcon at supersonic speeds over a mountainous terrain, the less you see of the real world, the more control you can have over your aircraft. A virtual cockpit filters the real scene and represents a more readable world. In this sense, VR can preserve the human significance of an overwhelming rush of split-second data. The heads-up display in the cockpit sometimes permits the pilot to view the real landscape behind the virtual images. In such cases, the simulation is an augmented rather than a virtual reality.

The offshoots of this technology, such as the Waldern arcade game, should not distract us—say the immersion pioneers—from the applications being used in molecular biology (docking molecules by sight and touch), airflow simulation, medical training, architecture, and industrial design. Boeing Aircraft plans to project a flight controller into virtual space, so that the controller floats thousands of feet above the airport, looking with an unobstructed view in any direction (while actually seated in a datasuit on the earth and fed real-time visual data from satellite and multiple camera viewpoints).

A leading model of this research has been the workstation developed at NASA–Ames, the Virtual Interface Environment Workstation (VIEW). NASA uses the VIEW system for telerobotic tasks, so that an operator on earth feels immersed in a remote but virtual environment and can then see and manipulate objects on the moon or Mars through feedback from a robot. Immersion research concentrates on a specific hardware and software configuration. The immersive tools for pilots, flight controllers, and space explorers are a much more concrete meaning of VR than is the vague generalization "everything artificial."

■ TELEPRESENCE

Robotic presence adds another aspect to virtual reality. To be present somewhere yet present there remotely is to be there virtually (!). Virtual reality shades into telepresence when you are present from a distant location—"present" in the sense that you are aware of what's going on, effective, and able to accomplish tasks by observing, reaching, grabbing, and moving objects with your own hands as though they were close up. Defining VR by telepresence nicely excludes the imaginary worlds of art, mathematics, and entertainment. Robotic telepresence brings real-time human effectiveness to a real-world location without there being a human in the flesh at that location. Mike McGreevy and Lew Hitchner walk on Mars, but in the flesh they sit in a control room at NASA–Ames.

Telepresence medicine places doctors inside the patient's body without major incisions. Medical doctors like Colonel Richard Satava and Dr. Joseph Rosen routinely use telepresence surgery to remove gall bladders without the traditional scalpel incisions. The patient heals from surgery in one-tenth the usual time because telepresence surgery leaves the body nearly intact. Only two tiny incisions are needed to introduce the laparoscopic tools. Telepresence allows surgeons to perform specialist operations at distant sites where no specialist is physically present.

By allowing the surgeon to be there without being there, telepresence is a double-edged sword, so to speak. By permitting immersion, telepresence offers the operator great control over remote processes. But at the same time, a psychotechnological gap opens up between doctor and patient. Surgeons complain of losing hands-on contact as the patient evaporates into a phantom of bits and bytes.

■ FULL-BODY IMMERSION

About the same time that head-mounted displays appeared, a radically different approach to VR was emerging. In the late 1960s, Myron Krueger, often called "the father of virtual reality," began creating interactive environments in which the user moves without encumbering gear. Krueger's is come-as-you-are VR. Krueger's work uses cameras and monitors to project a user's body so it can interact with graphic images, allowing hands to manipulate graphic objects on a screen, whether text or pictures. The interaction of computer and human takes place without covering the body. The burden of input rests with the computer, and the body's free movements become text for the computer to read. Cameras follow the user's body, and computers synthesize the user's movements with the artificial environment.

I see a floating ball projected on a screen. My computer-projected hand reaches out and grabs the ball. The computer constantly updates the interaction of my body and the synthetic world that I see, hear, and touch.

In Krueger's Videoplace, people in separate rooms relate interactively by mutual body painting, free-fall gymnastics, and tickling. Krueger's Glowflow, a light-and-sound room, responds to people's movements by lighting phosphorescent tubes and issuing synthetic sounds. Another environment, Psychic Space, allows participants to explore an interactive maze in which each footstep corresponds to a musical tone, all produced with live video images that can be moved, scaled, and rotated without regard to the usual laws of cause and effect.

■ NETWORKED COMMUNICATIONS

Pioneers like Jaron Lanier accept the immersion model of virtual reality but add equal emphasis to another aspect that they see as essential. Because computers make networks, VR seems a natural candidate for a new communications medium. The RB2 (Reality Built for Two) System from VPL highlights the connectivity of virtual worlds. In this view, a virtual world is as much a shared construct as a telephone is. Virtual worlds, then, can evoke unprecedented ways of sharing, what Lanier calls "post-symbolic communication." Because users can stipulate and shape objects and activities of a virtual world, they can share imaginary things and events without using words or real-world references.

Virtual worlds, then, can evoke unprecedented ways of sharing, what Lanier calls "post-symbolic communication."

Accordingly, communication can go beyond verbal or body language to take on magical, alchemical properties. A virtual-world maker might conjure up hitherto unheard-of mixtures of sight, sound, and motion. Consciously constructed outside the grammar and syntax of language, these semaphores defy the traditional logic of verbal and visual information. VR can convey meaning kinetically and even kinesthetically. Such communication will probably require elaborate protocols as well as lengthy time periods for digesting what has been communicated. Xenolinguists will have a laboratory for experiment when they seek to relate to those whose feelings and world views differ vastly from their own.

"All right, enough!" shouts our questioner, bleary eyed with information overload.

"I've taken your virtual-reality tour, listened to the pioneers, and now my head is spinning. These pioneers do indeed explore in different directions. There's a general drift here but no single destination. Should I go home feeling that the real virtual reality does not exist?"

Let's not lose stamina now. We cannot let the question fizzle. Too much depends on searching for the true virtual reality.

We should not get discouraged because a mention of reality, virtual or otherwise, opens several pathways in the clearing.

Let us recall for a moment just how controversial past attempts were to define the term *reality*. Recall how many wars were fought over it.

People today shy away from the *R*-word. *Reality* used to be the key to a person's philosophy. As a disputed term, *reality* fails to engage scientific minds because they are wary of any speculation that distracts them from their specialized work. But a skeptical attitude will fall short of the vision and direction we need.

Here's a brief sidebar on how controversial the *R*-word has been throughout Western history:

Plato holds out ideal forms as the "really real" while he denigrates the raw physical forces studied by his Greek predecessors. Aristotle soon demotes Plato's ideas to a secondary reality, to the flimsy shapes we abstract from the really real—which, for Aristotle, are the individual substances we touch and feel around us. In the medieval period, real things are those that shimmer with symbolic significance. The biblical-religious symbols add superreal messages to realities, giving them permanence and meaning, while the merely material aspects of things are less real, merely terrestrial, defective rubbish. In the Renaissance, things counted as real that could be counted and observed repeatedly by the senses. The human mind infers a solid material substrate underlying sense data but the substrate proves less real because it is less quantifiable and observable. Finally, the modern period attributed reality to atomic matter that has internal dynamics or energy, but soon the reality question was doomed by the analytical drive of the sciences toward complexity and by the plurality of artistic styles.

If for two thousand years Western culture has puzzled over the meaning of reality, we cannot expect ourselves in two minutes, or even two decades, to arrive at the meaning of virtual reality.

This reminder of metaphysics should fortify us for the long haul. If for two thousand years Western culture has puzzled over the meaning of reality, we cannot expect ourselves in two minutes, or even two decades, to arrive at the meaning of virtual reality.

The reality question has always been a question about direction, about focus, about what we should acknowledge and be concerned with. We should not therefore be surprised when VR proves controversial and elusive. Creating a new layer of reality demands our best shot, all our curiosity and imagination, especially since for us, technology and reality are beginning to merge.

When we look for the essence of a technology, we are engaging in speculation, but not in airy speculation. Our speculation involves where we plant our feet, who we are, and what we choose to be. Behind the development of every major technology lies a vision. The vision gives impetus to developers in the field even though the vision may not be clear, detailed, or even practical. The vision captures the essence of the technology and calls forth the cultural energy needed to propel it forward. Often a technological vision taps mythic consciousness and the religious side of the human spirit.

Consider for a moment the development of space technology. (Keep in mind that an inner connection exists between outer space and cyberspace, as I will point out later.) The U.S. space program enjoyed its most rapid development in the 1960s, culminating in the moon walk in 1969. What was the vision behind it?

The U.S. space program was a child of the cold war. The May 1961 speech by President John F. Kennedy that set NASA's goals incorporated traditional elements of myth: heroic struggle, personal sacrifice, and the quest for national prominence. Yet the impetus for Kennedy's speech came largely from without. What launched the U.S. space program was the fear of being surpassed by the Soviets, who had made a series of bold advances in human space travel. The goal of the moon landing was for the United States an attempt not to be overtaken by the Soviet developments in manned space exploration.

Few Americans know about the vision of their Russian competitors in space exploration. Everyone knows, of course, that the Communist revolution in 1917 froze Russian public goals in the hackneyed single-party language of a Marxist-Leninist agenda. Some historians know the name of the great Russian rocket pioneer Konstantin Tsiolkovsky (1857–1935), who stands with the American Robert H. Goddard (1882–1945) and the German-born Hermann Oberth (b. 1894). But less is known about the background of Tsiolkovsky's thinking and the visionary philosophy that influenced the first generation of Soviet space explorers.

The U.S. space program was a child of the cold war.

What lay behind the energetic push to send human beings into outer space? The Russians to this day have gathered far more data on human survival in outer space. The need for information was more than curiosity or a vague lust for new frontiers; it was a moral mission, a complex and imaginative grasp of human destiny in the cosmos. The early Russian rocket pioneers, who gave the impetus to the program, felt there was an essence to their space technology, a deep inner fire that inspired and directed the research. They felt an existential imperative that drew on the religious and cultural traditions coming down through the main stream of Russian history. This essence was not itself technological, and so we might call it the esoteric essence of space technology, the hidden core of ideas that in themselves are not technological. In fact, the ideas behind the first space exploration were lofty, awe inspiring, and even mystical.

The visionary ideas fueling Tsiolkovsky and the early Russian explorers came from N. F. Fedorov. Nikolai Fedorovich Fedorov (1828–1903) was a powerful inspiration to Soloviev, Dostoevsky, Tolstoy, and a whole generation of Russians who sought to understand how modernization connects with traditional religion and culture. Even the engineers of the Trans-Siberian Railway came often to sit at the feet of the famous sage. Fedorov lived an intensely spiritual life, dedicated exclusively to ideas and learning. His profound vision applied certain strands of Russian Orthodox spirituality to the harnessing of modern technology.

Sketching a national vision, Fedorov drew large. He argued that Russia should marshal its military and national strength toward a single goal: the conquest of nature. Conquering nature meant regulating the earth as a harmonious system. It meant controlling the weather so that harvests would be plentiful. It meant balancing nature so that all life-forms could thrive together in harmony. In his vision, Fedorov saw armies producing solar energy and harnessing the electromagnetic energy of the earth, using the energy to regulate the earth's motion in space, turning the earth into a vessel for cosmic cruises. Overpopulation would cease to be a problem as humanity colonized other planets.

Sketching a national vision, Fedorov drew large. He argued that Russia should marshal its military and national strength toward a single goal: the conquest of nature. Conquering nature meant regulating the earth as a harmonious system.

Unique to Fedorov's vision is its guiding moral spark. Instead of basing the conquest of nature on dominance, aggression, and egoism, Fedorov shunned the notion that humans should rule the cosmos out of a selfish desire for material wealth and abundance. Instead, he envisioned the conquest of nature as an act of altruism. But being generous to future generations can be less than purely altruistic, for they can return the favor by their acclaim of our deeds. We must regulate the forces of nature, he believed, so altruistically that we serve those who cannot possibly return our favors: we must conquer nature in order to resurrect our ancestors, the ultimate act of altruism.

The resurrection of all our dead ancestors, and it alone, provides a lofty enough ideal to mobilize humanity to explore the entire universe, including outer space. Fedorov found this thought in Russian Orthodox Christianity. According to Christian belief, the dead will rise again so that Christ, in a final judgment, will reorganize and completely redeem the world. The bodies of all human beings will one day rise again, and this resurrection, according to Fedorov, will take place through the work of human beings who carry out the divine plan. The long-range goal of human cooperation must be to discover the laws of nature to such a depth that we can eventually reconstitute the bodies of past human beings from their remaining physical particles still floating about in the universe.

Fedorov's strategy was to channel science and technology toward the reunion of all humanity. He decried the heartless positivism that builds on the sufferings and corpses of previous generations, instead seeking a purely idealistic motive. Without such a high aim, a heartless science would ultimately turn against society. For him, and for the many Soviet scientists inspired by him, the ultimate aim of the space program was, quite literally, nothing less than resurrecting the dead.

Contrast this sublime—and to us incredible and bizarre—vision of the space program with current U.S. public policy. "The commercialization of space," as promoted by administrations since the late 1970s, offers civilian entrepreneurs new opportunities for investment. To cover this naked self-interest, a mythic notion from U.S. history adds the sense of a new frontier. As a mere resource for commerce, space holds little allure, but a new frontier beyond earth adds adventure to the hope for personal gain. The vision even draws on the California gold rush in the nineteenth century, the spirit of enterprise.

In fact, this last word, *enterprise,* shows us where the commercialization of space falls short. Commercialization fails to touch the essence of space exploration, for commercial interests will neglect the long-range research needed for space science. Commercialization also drives up the cost of information derived from space exploration so that the data from space will not be available to small businesses, university scientists, farmers, state and local governments, and developing countries. In short, this kind of exploration envisions no future, only short-range profit.

But for NASA, for space enthusiasts, and for the Pentagon people, enterprise has a capital E. The word refers to a spirit of business adventure.

But for NASA, for space enthusiasts, and for the Pentagon people, *enterprise* has a capital E. The word refers to a spirit of business adventure, but it also, in many minds, has another important meaning. Many technical people today also take *enterprise* to be the proper name in a science fiction myth, that of the starship *Enterprise* in *Star Trek,* the popular science fiction television series about twenty-first-century space travelers. *Star Trek* contributed the code word, the handshake, the common inspiration for space exploration in the United States. (Shake hands informally with someone at the Pentagon or NASA and be prepared with an answer to the query "Are you a Trekkie?") For hundreds of technicians, the space program flies on the imaginative wings of Gene Roddenberry's brainchild, born on September 8, 1966, when the TV show was first aired. But Roddenberry was no Fedorov. The sage of Pasadena created no unifying vision to direct humanity "where no one has gone before." His fictional productions treated only a motley collection of profound moral questions pertaining to human behavior at any time, any place. But despite the limits of its lineage, *Star Trek* showed us more truly the esoteric essence, the real meaning, of space exploration than did government statements on the commercialization of space. The essence of the American space program, its heart and soul, comes from *Star Trek.*

Where in VR is a counterpart to the space program's esoteric essence? What is the essence of VR, its inner spirit, the cultural motor that propels the technology? When the first conferences met on cyberspace and on virtual reality in 1989 and 1990, respectively, two threads of shared vision ran through the diverse groups of participants. One was the cyber punk writings of William Gibson, known to both technical and literary types as the coiner of the term *cyberspace*. The other was the Holodeck from *Star Trek: The Next Generation*.

Along with its cargo bay of imaginative treasures, the starship *Enterprise* brought the Holodeck. The Holodeck is familiar furniture in the vocabulary of virtual-reality pioneers. For most people, the Holodeck portrays the ideal human-computer interface. It is a virtual room that transforms spoken commands into realistic landscapes populated with walking, talking humanoids and detailed artifacts appearing so lifelike that they are indistinguishable from reality. The Holodeck is used by the crew of the starship *Enterprise* to visit faraway times and places such as medieval England and 1920s America. Generally, the Holodeck offers the crew rest and recreation, escape and entertainment, on long interstellar voyages.

The Holodeck is familiar furniture in the vocabulary of virtual-reality pioneers.

While not every VR pioneer explicitly agrees on goals, the Holodeck draws the research onward. Publicly, researchers try to maintain cool and reasonable expectations about VR. Hyperbole from the media often stirs grandiose expectations in the public; when presented with actual prototypes, the public turns away with scorn. So researchers play down talk of the Holodeck. At the MIT Media Lab, leaders such as David Zeltzer avoid the term *virtual reality* not only because of the specter of metaphysics it evokes, but also because of the large promises it raises. The term seems to make greater claims than do terms like *virtual environments* (preferred at MIT and NASA) and *virtual worlds* (preferred at the universities of North Carolina and Washington). But when speaking at a VR conference for the Data Processing Management Association in Washington, D.C., on June 1, 1992, Zeltzer made an intriguing aside, one that touches, I think, on the highest possibilities of virtual reality, on its esoteric essence.

Did I say "esoteric essence"? How can we expect to give our young questioner an answer to "What is virtual reality?" when we have left the public, exoteric world of clear explanations and have embarked on a search for the esoteric essence of VR, its underlying vision? Well, our questioner seems to have gotten lost some time ago, most likely during the sidebar on the history of reality. I think I see someone off in the distance pulling avidly on the trigger of the Virtuality game. Maybe more time spent in VR will eventually deliver better answers than any verbal speculation. At any rate, on to the esoteric essence . . .

Zeltzer's remark went something like this: "True virtual reality may not be attainable with any technology we create. The Holodeck may forever remain fiction. Nonetheless, virtual reality serves as the Holy Grail of the research."

"Holy Grail?" Holy Grail!

Now when Zeltzer made this reference, he was not deliberately invoking a Jungian archetype. His remark expressed modesty and diffidence rather than alchemical arrogance. Still, archetypes do not have to hit us in the nose to wield their peculiar power. They work most powerfully at the back of the

subconscious mind, and therein lies their magic. An effective archetype works
its magic subtly.

David Zeltzer was calling up a mythic image far more ancient and infinitely more profound than *Star Trek. Star Trek* has, after all, become the stuff
of trivia: *Star Trek* ties and boxer shorts, *Star Trek* vinyl characters and mugs
("Fill them with a hot beverage and watch Kirk and Spock beam up to an
unknown world"). *Star Trek* lost any sublimity it may have had when it came
to occupy Kmart shelves along with electric flyswatters and noisemaker
whoopee cushions.

The Holy Grail, though, sums up the aspirations of centuries. It is an
image of the Quest. From Tennyson's romantic *Idylls of the King* to Malory's
King Arthur and the Knights of the Round Table, the ancient Grail legend
reaches back to Christian and pre-Christian times. The Grail has always been
a symbol of the quest for a better world. In pre-Christian times, the Grail was
the cup that holds a cure for an ailing king who, suffering from his own
wounds, sees his country turning into a wasteland. Christians believed the
Grail to be both the chalice of Jesus' Last Supper and the cup that caught the
Savior's blood at the Crucifixion. Medieval legend links the spear that pierced
Jesus' side on the cross with the sacred cup that held his blood. Later works
of art, from T. S. Eliot's *The Wasteland* to Richard Wagner's *Parsifal,* have preserved the Grail story as a symbol of spiritual quest and lofty aspiration.

Perhaps the essence of VR ultimately lies not in technology but in art, perhaps art of the highest order. Rather than control or escape or entertain or
communicate, the ultimate promise of VR may be to transform, to redeem our
awareness of reality—something that the highest art has
attempted to do and something hinted at in the very label *virtual reality,* a label that has stuck, despite all objections, and
that sums up a century of technological innovation. VR
promises not a better vacuum cleaner or a more engrossing
communications medium or even a friendlier computer interface. It promises the Holy Grail.

> VR *promises not*
> *a better vacuum*
> *cleaner or a*
> *more engrossing*
> *communications*
> *medium or even*
> *a friendlier*
> *computer*
> *interface. It*
> *promises the*
> *Holy Grail.*

We might learn something about the esoteric essence of VR
by thinking about Richard Wagner's *Parsifal.* Wagner himself
was searching for a Holodeck, though he did not know it. By
the time he finished *Parsifal,* his final opera, Wagner no longer
considered his work to be opera. He did not want it called
opera or music or theater or even "art," and certainly not
entertainment. By the time he finished his last work, Wagner
realized he was trying to create another reality, one that
would in turn transform ordinary reality. The term he came to
use was "a total work of art," by which he meant a seamless
union of vision, sound, movement, and drama that would
sweep the viewer to another world, not to escape but to be
changed. Nor could the viewer be a mere spectator. Wagner created a specially designed building in Bayreuth, Germany, well off the beaten track,
where the audience would have to assemble after a long journey because he

forbade the performance of *Parsifal* in any other building. The audience would have to prepare itself well ahead of time by studying the libretto, because *Parsifal* was long, mysterious, and full of complex, significant details. (Wagner's *Ring* cycle takes over fifteen hours to present a related myth.) Looking for the right terms to express his intent, Wagner called *Parsifal* "a festival play for consecrating the stage" *(ein Bühnenweihfestspiel)*. The Bayreuth theater would become the site for a solemn, nearly liturgical celebration. The mythmaker would create a counter-reality, one reminiscent of the solemn mass of the Catholic church, which appeals to all the senses with its sights, sounds, touch, drama, even appealing to smell with incense and candles. The audiences at Bayreuth were to become pilgrims on a quest, immersed in an artificial reality.

The drama *Parsifal,* like a mysterious dream, resists easy summary, and it eludes interpretation. But the general story outline is clear. The protectors of "correct values" (the Knights) inevitably paint themselves into the corner of righteousness. Paralyzed, unable to act, their leadership suffers intense internal pain (Amfortas). They can regain the power of the Grail that they protect only through the intervention of someone who is still innocent of right and wrong, someone who is by all standards a fool. The innocent fool (Arabic, *fal parsi*) can clean out the sclerotic righteous society only after passing a test and learning to feel the sufferings of others. Once the innocent fool has acquired compassion for others and sensitivity to life's complexity, he can bring the power (the Spear) back to the righteous Knights of the Holy Grail. The Grail Knights then come to understand more deeply what the work of the Holy Grail, and their mission, means. The Grail grants its full power only to those who can be touched by compassion.

Wagner's Holodeck presents a Parsifal who mirrors the individual audience members at Bayreuth. Wagner shaped the drama with story and music so that strong sensations would engulf the audience and pierce them to the heart. Each listener begins as a naive spectator and is then gradually touched by the painful actions on stage until the listener becomes transformed into a more sensitive and compassionate member, ready to bring to a sick society some measure of healing and renewal.

Wagner hoped to do more than make music and theater; he believed that his music dramas could transform society by imparting new feelings and attitudes. This goal he shared with traditional religion; and religion returns the competition with distrust and the accusation of heterodoxy. For this reason, Wagner's work remains to this day controversial among religious people, including many artists and musicians who have strong religious faith.

How well did Wagner succeed? One of the most telling tributes to the success of Wagner's *Parsifal* comes from a Jesuit priest, Father Owen Lee, who in a radio broadcast intermission feature from the Metropolitan Opera in New York City said:

I watched as usual from the least expensive seat under the roof, hovering there with an unearthly feeling for long half-hours floating in an immense space, suffused with a sense of what Baudelaire felt listening to Wagner: "A sense of being suspended in an ecstasy compounded of joy and insight." I can remember staggering out of theaters after Parsifal, hardly aware of people applauding, the music streaming through me, carried out of myself, seeing my experience—indeed, feeling that I was seeing all experience—at a higher level of awareness, put in touch with a power greater than myself, a kind of holy fool.[1]

Another holy fool was the Finnish composer Jan Sibelius, who wrote: "Heard *Parsifal.* Nothing else in all the world has made so overwhelming an impression on me. All my heartstrings throbbed." The German composer Max Reger wrote: "Heard *Parsifal.* Cried for two weeks, then decided to become a composer."

Someday VR will elicit similar rave reviews, not mere thrills, but insight into experience. As it evolves its art form, VR will have certain advantages over Wagner's "total work of art." Certain disadvantages might also plague it where Wagnerian solutions might help.

▪ ACTIVITY/PASSIVITY

VR systems, as Jaron Lanier points out, can reduce apathy and the couch-potato syndrome simply by requiring creative decisions. Because computers make VR systems interactive, they also allow the artist to call forth greater participation from users. Whereas traditional art forms struggle with the passivity of the spectator, the VR artist finds a controlled balance between passivity and activity. The model of user navigation can be balanced by the model of pilgrimage and sacred awe.

▪ MANIPULATION/RECEPTIVITY

Some observers date the advent of VR to the moment when the dataglove appeared on the computer screen. At that moment, the user became visible as an active, involved force in the digital world. This implies that VR has a tilt toward manipulation, even a latent tendency toward aggressive, first-person attitudes. The VR artist will need strategies for inducing a more receptive atmosphere, so that the user can be open in all directions, receiving signals from and having empathy for other beings. The user must be able to be touched, emotionally moved, by non-first-person entities in the virtual world. The spear of manipulation must join the cup of sensitivity. If simulators serve to train hand-eye and other coordination skills, VR may take a further step and become a training tool to enhance receptivity.

▪ REMOTE PRESENCE

The visual bias of current VR brings out a possible detachment in the user's sense of the world. Seeing takes place at a distance, whereas hearing and the other senses are more intimate to our organic life. The visual bias increases the detachment of telepresence. Some VR versions stress the "looking-at" factor, such as David Gelernter's Mirror Worlds, in which, in real-time, users can zoom in on miniature shoe-box worlds containing local homes, businesses, cities, governments, or nations. VR offers the opportunity to shift the Western philosophy of presence. From Pythagoras to Aristotle, from Berkeley to Russell, our philosophical sense of presence has relied on vision, consequently putting us in the position of spectators. To be touched, we need to introduce more sensory awareness. VR may develop a kind of feedback in which presence includes an openness and sensitivity of the whole body.

■ A U G M E N T E D   R E A L I T Y

VR will enhance the power of art to transform reality. The picture frame, the proscenium, the movie theater all limit art by blocking it off as a section of reality. VR, with its augmented reality, allows a smoother, more controlled transition from virtual to real and back. This capability, which may frighten psychologists, will offer artists an unprecedented power to transform societies.

VR will enhance the power of art to transform reality

These are a few of the differences that make virtual reality different from traditional art forms. They belong to the essence of VR, its Holy Grail. This goal means that we need a different breed of artist as well. And where will we find these new cybersages, these virtual-world makers? I see our young questioner smiling broadly now as yet another wounded pterodactyl drops from the pink sky of Waldern's arcade game. Plenty of fledgling enthusiasm here, and a society that needs healing and renewal.

■ N O T E

1. Father Owen Lee, "Metropolitan Opera Broadcast Intermission Feature," March 28, 1992.

Seeing Is Beholding

erence McKenna—considered by many the successor to Tim Leary's psychedelic dynasty—couldn't make it to Big Heart City Friday night for the elder's party. The bearded, lanky, forty-somethingish Irishman was deep into a Macintosh file, putting the finishing touches on his latest manuscript about the use of mind-altering plants by ancient cultures. But by Saturday evening he was ready to descend from his small mountaintop ranch house to talk about the virtual reality that has his fans so excited.

We're backstage with McKenna at a rave where he'll be speaking about drugs, consciousness, and the end of time. He's gotten famous, on the West Coast at least, as a sort of public relations manager for the plant kingdom. Part human, part gnome, and part mushroom, McKenna speaks from experience. This experience just happens to be an intimate connection with mind-altering vegetation, so his words sprawl like kudzu over the consciousness. If you listen to McKenna, that is, really listen, you can't help but get wrapped up in his rap. The luckiest of friends and mentees hang out with him in his dressing room as he prepares to go on.

"VR really is like a trip," one boy offers McKenna in the hopes of launching the Celtic Bard into one of his lyrical diatribes. Terence ponders a moment and then he's off.

> "VR *really is like a trip*," *one boy offers McKenna in the hopes of launching the Celtic Bard into one of his lyrical diatribes. Terence ponders a moment and then he's off.*

"I link virtual reality to psychedelic drugs because I think that if you look at the evolution of organism and self-expression and language, language is seen to be some kind of process that actually tends toward the visible." McKenna strings his thoughts together into a breathless oral continuum. "The small mouth-noise way of communicating is highly provisional; we may be moving toward an environment of language that is beheld rather than heard."

Still, the assembled admirers hang on McKenna's every word, as if each syllable were leaving a hallucinatory aftervision on the adrenal cortex. They too dream of a Cyberia around the corner, and virtual reality is the closest simulation of what a world free of time, location, or even a personal identity might look like. Psychedelics and VR are both ways of creating a new, nonlinear reality, where self-expression is a community event.

"You mean like ESP?"

Terence never corrects anyone—he only interpolates their responses. "This would be like a kind of telepathy, but it would be much more than that: A world of visible language is a world where the individual doesn't really exist in the same way that the print-created world sanctions what we call 'point of view.' That's really what an ego is: it's a consistently defined point of view within a context of narrative. Well, if you replace the idea that life is a narrative with the idea that life is a vision, then you displace the linear progression of events. I think this is technically within reach."

To Terence, the invention of virtual reality, like the resurgence of psychoactive drugs, serves as a kind of technological philosopher's stone, bringing an inkling of the future reality into the present. It's both a hint from our hyperdimensional future and an active, creative effort by cyberians to reach that future.

"I like the concept of the philosopher's stone. The next messiah might be a machine rather than a person. The philosopher's stone is a living stone. It is being made. We are making it. We are like tunnelers drilling toward something. The overmind is drilling toward us, and we are drilling toward it. And when we meet, there will be an enormous revelation of the true nature of being. I think every person who takes five or six grams of psilocybin mushrooms in silent darkness is probably on a par with Christ and Buddha, at least in terms of the input."

So, according to McKenna, the psychedelic vision provides a glimpse of the truth cyberians are yearning for. But have psychedelics and virtual reality really come to us as a philosopher's stone, or is it simply that our philosopher's stoned?

■ MORPHOGENETIC FIELDS FOREVER

Cyberians share a psychedelic common ground. To them, drugs are not simply a recreational escape but a conscious and sometimes daring foray into new possible realities. Psychedelics give them access to what McKenna is calling the overmind and what we call Cyberia. However stoned they might be when they get there, psychedelic explorers are convinced that they are experiencing something real, and bringing back something useful for themselves and the rest of us.

Psychedelic exploration, however personal, is thought to benefit more than the sole explorer. Each tripper believes he is opening the door between humanity and hyperspace a little wider. The few cyberians who haven't taken psychedelics still feel they have personally experienced and integrated the psychedelic vision through the trips of others, and value the role of these chemicals in the overall development of Cyberia. It is as if each psychedelic journey completes another piece of a universal puzzle.

But, even though they have a vast computer net and communications infrastructure at their disposal, psychedelic cyberians need not communicate their findings so directly. Rather, they believe they are each sharing and benefiting from a collective experience. As we'll see, one of the most common realizations of the psychedelic trip is that "all is one." At the euphoric peak of a trip, all people, particles, personalities, and planets are seen as part of one great entity or reality—one big fractal.

Cyberians share a psychedelic common ground. To them, drugs...give them access to what McKenna is calling the overmind and what we call Cyberia.

It may have been that realization that led Cambridge biologist Rupert Sheldrake to develop his theory of morphogenetic fields, now common knowledge to most cyberians. From *morph,* meaning "forms," and *genesis,* meaning "birth," these fields are a kind of cumulative record of the past behaviors of species, groups, and even molecules, so that one member of a set can learn from the experience of all the others.

A failed animal-behavior test is still one of the best proofs of Sheldrake's idea. Scientists were attempting to determine if learned skills could be passed on from parents to children genetically. They taught adult mice how to go through a certain maze, then taught their offspring, and their offspring, and so on for twenty years and fifty generations of mice. Indeed, the descendants of the taught mice knew how to get through the maze very quickly without instruction, but so did the descendants of the control group, who had never seen the maze at all! Later, a scientist decided to repeat this experiment on a different continent with the same mouse species, but they already knew how to go through the maze, too! As explained by morphic resonance, the traits need not have been passed on genetically. The information leak was due not to bad experimental procedure but to the morphogenetic field, which stored the experience of the earlier mice from which all subsequent mice could benefit.

Sheldrake's picture of reality is a vast fractal of resonating fields. Everything, no matter how small, is constantly affecting everything else.

Similarly, if scientists are developing a new crystalline structure, it may take years to "coax" atoms to form the specific crystal. But once the crystal is developed in one laboratory, it can be created instantly in any other laboratory in the world. According to Sheldrake, this is because, like the mice, the atoms are all "connected" to one another through morphogenetic fields, and they "learn" from the experiences of other atoms.

Sheldrake's picture of reality is a vast fractal of resonating fields. Everything, no matter how small, is constantly affecting everything else. If the tiniest detail in a fractal pattern echoes the overall design of the entire fractal, then a change to (or the experience of) this remote piece changes the overall picture (through the principles of feedback and iteration). Echoing the realizations of his best friends, Ralph Abraham and Terence McKenna, Sheldrake is the third member of the famous "Trialogues" at Esalen, where the three elder statesmen (by cyberian standards) discuss onstage the ongoing unfolding of reality before captivated audiences of cyberians. These men are, quite consciously, putting into practice the idea of morphogenetic fields. Even if these Trialogues were held in private (as they were for years), Cyberia as a whole would benefit from the intellectual developments. By pioneering the new "headspace," the three men leave their own legacy through morphic resonance, if not direct communication through their publishing, lectures, or media events.

Likewise, each cyberian psychedelic explorer feels that by tripping he is leaving his own legacy for others to follow, while himself benefiting from the past psychedelic experiences of explorers before him. For precisely this reason, McKenna advises using only organic psychedelics, which have well-developed morphogenetic fields: "I always say there are three tests for a drug. It should occur in nature. That gives it a morphogenetic field of resonance to the life of the planet. It should have a history of shamanic usage [which gives it a morphogenetic field of resonance to the consciousness of other human beings]. And it should be similar to or related to neurotransmitters in the brain. What's interesting about that series of filters, is that it leaves you with the most powerful hallucinogens there are: psilocybin, DMT, ayahuasca, and, to some degree, LSD."

From the principle of morphogenesis, cyberians infer that psychedelic substances have the ability to reshape the experience of reality and thus—if observer and observed are one—the reality itself.

These are the substances that stock the arsenal of the drug-using cyberian. Psychedelics use among cyberians has developed directly out of the drug culture of the 1960s. The first tripsters—the people associated with Leary on the East Coast, and Ken Kesey on the West Coast—came to startling moral and philosophical conclusions that reshaped our culture. For today's users, drugs are part of the continuing evolution of the human species toward greater intelligence, empathy, and awareness.

From the principle of morphogenesis, cyberians infer that psychedelic substances have the ability to reshape the experience of reality and thus—if observer and observed are one—the reality itself. It's hardly disputed that, even in a tangible, cultural sense, the introduction of psychedelics into our society in the 1960s altered the sensibilities of users and nonusers alike. The trickle-down effect through the arts, media, and even big business created what can be called a postpsychedelic climate, in which everything from women's rights, civil rights, and peace activism to spirituality and the computer revolution found suitable conditions for growth.

As these psychoactive plants and chemicals once again see the light of day, an even more self-consciously creative community is finding out about designer reality. While drugs in the 1960s worked to overcome social, moral, and intellectual rigidity, drugs now enhance the privileges of the already free. Cyberians using drugs do not need to learn that reality is arbitrary and manipulable, or that the landscape of consciousness is broader than normal waking-state awareness suggests. They have already learned this through the experiences of men like Leary and Kesey. Instead, they take chemicals for the express purpose of manipulating that reality and exploring the uncharted regions of consciousness.

■ INTEGRATING THE BELL CURVE

LSD was the first synthesized chemical to induce basically the same effect as the organic psychedelics used by shamans in ancient cultures. Psychedelics break down one's basic assumptions about life, presenting them instead as arbitrary choices on the part of the individual and his society. The tripper feels liberated into a free-form reality, where his mind and point of view can alter his external circumstances. Psychedelics provide a way to look at life unencumbered by the filters and models one normally uses to process reality. (Whether psychedelics impose a new set of their own filters is irrelevant here. At least the subjective experience of the trip is that the organizing framework of reality has been obliterated.)

Nina Graboi, the author of *One Foot in the Future,* a novel about her own spiritual journey, was among the first pioneers of LSD in the 1960s. Born in 1918 and trained as an actress, she soon became part of New York's bohemian subculture, and kept company with everyone from Tim Leary to Alan Watts. She now works as an assistant to mathematician Ralph Abraham, and occasionally hosts large conferences on psychedelics. She spoke to me at her Santa Cruz beach apartment, over tea and cookies. She believes from what she has seen over the past seven decades that what psychedelics do to an indi-vidual, LSD did to society, breaking us free of cause-and-effect logic and into an optimistic creativity.

"Materialism really was at its densest and darkest before the sixties and it did not allow us to see that anything else existed. Then acid came along just at the right time—I really think so. It was very important for some people to reach states of mind that allowed them to see that there is more, that we are more than just these physical bodies. I can't help feeling that there were forces at work that went beyond anything that I can imagine. After the whole LSD craze, all of a sudden, the skies opened up and books came pouring down and wisdom came. And something started happening. I think by now there are enough of us to have created a morphogenetic field of awareness, that are open to more than the materialists believe."

But Graboi believes that the LSD vision needs to be integrated into the experience of America at large. It's not enough to tune in, turn on, and drop out. The impulse now is to recreate reality consciously—and that happens both through a morphogenetic resonance as well as good old-fashioned work.

"I don't think we have a thing to learn from the past, now. We really have to start creating new forms, and seeing real ways of being. This was almost like the mammalian state coming to a somewhat higher octave in the sixties, which was like a quantum leap forward in consciousness. It was a gas. The end of a stage and the beginning of a new one. So right now there are still these two elements very much alive: the old society wanting to pull backward and keep us where we were, and the new one saying, 'Hey, there are new frontiers to conquer and they are in our minds and our hearts.'"

Nina does not consider herself a cyberian, but she does admit she's part of the same effort, and desperately hopes our society can reach this "higher octave." As with all psychedelics, "coming down" is the hardest part. Most would prefer simply to "bring up" everything else . . . to make the rest of the world conform to the trip.

The acid experience follows what can be called a bell curve: the user takes the drug, goes up in about an hour, stays up for a couple of hours, then comes down over a period of three or four hours. It is during the coming-down time—which makes up the majority of the experience—that the clarity of vision or particular insight must be integrated into the normal waking-state consciousness. Like the Greek hero who has visited the gods, the tripper must figure out how the peak of his Aristotelian journey makes sense. The integration of LSD into the sixties' culture was an analogous process. The tripping community had to integrate the truth of their vision into a society that could not grasp such concepts. The bell curve of the sixties touched ground in the form of political activism, sexual liberation, the new age movement, and new scientific and mathematical models.

While cyberians usually surf the waves of consciousness for no reason but fun, they take acid because there's work to be done.

Cyberians today consider the LSD trip a traditional experience. Even though there are new psychedelics that more exactly match the cyberian checklist for ease of use, length of trip, and overall intensity, LSD provides a uniquely epic journey for the tripper, where the majority of time and energy in the odyssey is spent bringing it all back home. While cyberians usually surf the waves of consciousness for no reason but fun, they take acid because there's work to be done.

When Jaida and Cindy, two twenty-year-old women from Santa Cruz, reunited after being away from each other for almost a year, they chose LSD because they wanted to go through an intense experience of reconnection. Besides, it was the only drug they could obtain on short notice. They began by smoking some pot and hitch hiking to a nearby beachtown. By the time they got there, the girls were stoned and the beach was pitch black. They spent the rest of the night talking and sleeping on what they guessed was a sand dune, and decided to "drop" at dawn. As the sun rose, the acid took effect.

When the girls stood up, Jaida accidentally stepped on a crab claw that was sticking out of the sand. Blood flowed out of her foot. As she describes it now:

"The pain was just so . . . incredible. I could feel the movement of the pain all the way up to my brain, going up the tendrils, yet it was very enjoyable. And blood was coming out, but it was incredibly beautiful. At the same time, there was still the part of me that said 'you have to deal with this,' which I was very grateful for."

Once Jaida's foot was bandaged, the girls began to walk together. As they walked and talked, they slipped into a commonly experienced acid phenomenon: shared consciousness. "It's the only time I've ever been psychic with Cindy. It's like one of those things that you can't believe . . . there's no evidence or anything. Whatever I was thinking, she would be thinking. We were making a lot of commentary about the people we were looking at, and there'd be these long stretches of silence and I would just be sort of thinking along, and then she would say word for word what I was thinking. Like that. And then I would say something and it would be exactly what she was thinking. And we just did that for about four or five hours. She's a very different physical type from me, but it reached the point where I could feel how she felt in her body. I had the very deep sensation of being inside her body, hearing her think, and being able to say everything that she was thinking. We were in a reality together, and we shared the same space. Our bodies didn't separate us from each other. We were one thing."

But then came the downside of the bell curve. The girls slowly became more "disjointed." They began to disagree about tiny things—which way to walk, whether to eat. "There was this feeling of losing it. I could feel we were moving away from it with every step. There was a terrible disappointment that set in. We couldn't hold on to that perfect attunement."

By the time the girls got back to their campsite on the sand dune, their disillusionment was complete. The sand dune was actually the local trash dump. As they climbed the stinking mound of garbage to gather their sleeping bags, they found the "crab claw" on which Jaida had stepped. It was really a used tampon and a broken bottle. And now Jaida's foot was beginning to smart.

Jaida's reintegration was twofold: She could no more bring back her empathic ability than she could the belief that she had stepped on a crab claw. What Jaida retained from the experience, though, came during the painful crash landing. She was able to see how it was only her interpretation that made her experience pain as bad, or the tampon and glass as less natural than a crab claw. As in the experience of a Buddha, the garbage dump was as beautiful as a sand dune . . . until they decided it was otherwise. Losing her telepathic union with her friend symbolized and recapitulated the distance that had grown between them over the past year. They had lost touch, and the trip had heightened both their friendship and their separation.

Most acid trippers try to prolong that moment on the peak of the bell curve, but to do so is futile. Coming down is almost inevitably disillusioning to some degree. Again, though, like in a Greek tragedy, it is during the reintegration that insight occurs, and progress is made—however slight—toward a more all-encompassing or cyberian outlook. In order to come down with a minimum of despair and maximum of progress, the tripper must guide his own transition back to normal consciousness and real life while maintaining the integrity of whatever truths he may have gleaned at the apogee of his journey. The LSD state itself is not an end in itself. While it may offer a brief exposure to post-paradigm thinking or even hyperdimensional abilities, the real value of the LSD trip is the *change* in consciousness, and the development of skills in the user to cope with that change. Just as when a person takes a vacation, it is not that the place visited is any better than where he started. It's just different. The traveler returns home changed.

Eugene Schoenfeld, M.D., is the Global Village Town Physician. A practicing psychologist, he wrote the famous "Dr. Hip" advice column in the sixties; he now treats recovering drug addicts. It's easy to see why he has become such a trusted friend and counselor to Cyberia's many chemical casualties. His rich eyes seem to absorb the anxiety of whoever stares into them. One gentle nod of his large, shiny head shows he understands. This man has been there. This man groks. The doctor believes that the desire to alter consciousness, specifically psychedelically, is a healthy urge.

On the way back, the tripper realizes that reality itself has been arbitrarily arranged.

"I think what happens is that it allows people to sense things in a way that they don't ordinarily sense them because we couldn't live that way. If our brains were always the way that they are under the influence of LSD, we couldn't function. Perhaps it is that when babies are born—that's the way they perceive things. Gradually they integrate their experience because we cannot function if we *see music,* for example. We can't live that way.

"Part of the reason why people take drugs is to change their sense of reality, change their sensation, change from the ordinary mind state. And if they had *that* state all the time, they would seek to change *it.* It seems that humans need to change their minds in some way. There's a reason why people start talking about 'tripping.' It's related to trips people take when they physically change their environment. I'm convinced that if there were a way to trip all the time on LSD, they would want to change their reality to something else. That is part of the need."

The sense of being on a voyage, of "tripping," is the essence of a classic psychedelic experience. The user is a traveler, and an acid or mushroom trip is a heroic journey or visionquest through unexplored regions, followed by a reentry into mundane reality. Entry to the psychedelic realm almost always involves an abandonment of the structures by which one organizes reality, and a subsequent shedding of one's ego—usually defined by those same organizational structures. On the way back, the tripper realizes that reality itself has been arbitrarily arranged. The voyager sees that there may be such a thing as an objective world, but whatever it is we're experiencing as reality on a mass scale sure isn't it. With the help of a psychedelic journey, one can come back and consciously choose a different reality from the one that's been agreed upon by the incumbent society. This can be manifest on a personal, theoretical, political, technological, or even spiritual level.

As Dr. Schoenfeld, who once served as Tim Leary's family physician and now shares his expertise with cyberians as co-host of the DRUGS conference on the WELL, explains, "that quality—that non-judgmental quality could be carried over without the effects of the drug. After all, one hopes to learn something from a drug experience that he can use afterward. (All this interest in meditation and yoga, all these various disciplines, it all began with people taking these drugs and wanting to recreate these states without drugs.) So, to the extent that they can, that is a useful quality. And this nonjudgmental quality is something I think that can be carried over from a drug experience."

■ O V E R   T H E R E

So, the use of psychedelics can be seen as a means toward experiencing free-flowing designer reality: the goal, and the fun, is to manipulate intentionally one's objectivity in order to reaffirm the arbitrary nature of all the mind's constructs, revealing, perhaps, something truer beneath the surface, material reality. You take a trip on which you go nowhere, but everything has changed anyway.

The place people "go" on a trip— the psychedelic corridors of Cyberia—may even be a real space.

To some, though, it is not just the change of consciousness that makes psychedelics so appealing, but the qualitative difference in the states of awareness they offer. The place people "go" on a trip—the psychedelic corridors of Cyberia—may even be a real space. According to Terence McKenna's frontline correspondence from that place, it is quite different from normal waking-state consciousness:

The voyager journeys "into an invisible realm in which the causality of the ordinary world is replaced with the rationale of natural magic. In this realm, language, ideas, and meaning have greater power than cause and effect. Sympathies, resonances, intentions, and personal will are linguistically magnified through poetic rhetoric. The imagination is invoked and sometimes its forms are beheld visibly. Within the magical mind-set of the shaman, the ordinary connections of the world and what we call natural laws are deemphasized or ignored."

As McKenna describes it, this is not just a mindspace but more of a netherworld, where the common laws of nature are no longer enforced. It is a place where cause-and-effect logic no longer holds, where events and objects function more as icons or symbols, where thoughts are beheld rather than verbalized, and where phenomena like morphic resonance and the fractal reality become consciously experienced. This is the description of Cyberia.

As such, this psychedelic world is not something experienced personally or privately, but, like the rest of Cyberia, as a great group project. The psychedelic world each tripper visits is the same world, so that changes made by one are felt by the others. Regions explored by any traveler become part of the overall map. This is a hyperdimensional terrain on which the traditional solo visionquest becomes a sacred community event.

This feeling of being part of a morphogenetic unfolding is more tangible on psilocybin mushrooms than on LSD. McKenna voices Cyberia's enchantment with the ancient organic brain food: "I think that people should grow mushrooms. They are the real connector back into the archaic, even more so than LSD, which was largely psychoanalytical. It didn't connect you up to the greeny engines of creation. Psilocybin is perfect."

Like LSD, mushrooms provide an eight-hour, bell-curve trip, but it is characterized by more physical and visual "hallucinations" and a much less intellectual edge. Users don't overanalyze their experiences, opting instead to revel in them more fully. Mushrooms are thought to have their own morphogenetic field, which has developed over centuries of their own evolution and their use by ancient cultures. The mushroom trip is much more predictable, cyberians argue, because its morphogenetic field is so much better established than that of acid, which has only been used for a couple of decades, and mostly by inexperienced Western travelers.

Students at U.C. Santa Cruz have developed a secret section of woods dedicated to mushroom tripping called Elf Land (the place just behind Ralph Abraham's office).

As a result, mushroom experiences are, in many ways, less intensely disorienting than LSD trips; the "place" one goes on mushrooms is more natural and user-friendly than the place accessed on acid or other more synthetic psychedelics. Likewise, 'shroomers feel more tangibly a part of the timeless, locationless community of other users, or even animals, fairies, or the "greeny engines" of the spirit of Nature herself.

For this feeling of morphic community and interconnection with nature to become more tangible, groups of 'shroomers often choose to create visionquest hot spots. Students at U.C. Santa Cruz have developed a secret section of woods dedicated to mushroom tripping called Elf Land (the place just behind Ralph Abraham's office). Some students believe that fairies prepared and maintain the multidimensional area of the woods for 'shroomers. Others even claim to have found psilocybin mushrooms—which these fairies are said to leave behind them—growing in Elf Land. Most of all, Elf Land serves as a real-world reference plane for the otherworldly, dimensionless mushroom plane. And, like the morphogenetic mushroom field, Elf Land is shared and modified by everyone who trips there, making the location a kind of cumulative record of a series of mushroom trips.

Mariah is tripping in Elf Land for the first time. A sophomore at U.C. Santa Cruz, the English major had heard of Elf Land since she began taking mushrooms last year, but never really believed in it as a real, physical place. She eats the mushrooms in her dorm with her friends Mark and Rita, then the trio head out to the woods. It's still afternoon, so the paths are easy to follow, but Rita—a much more plugged-in, pop-cultural, fashion-conscious communications major than one would expect to find tripping in the woods of Santa Cruz—suddenly veers off into a patch of poison oak.

Mark, a senior mathematics major and Rita's boyfriend, grabs Rita by the arm, afraid that she's stoned and losing her way.

"It's a pathless path, Mariah," Rita assures the younger girl, with- out even looking at Mark. Rita knows that Mariah's fears are the most pressing, and that Mark's concerns will be answered by these indirect means. Rita has made it clear that this trip is for Mariah.

"It's the perfect place to trip." Rita puts her arm around Mariah. "People continually put things there. Some of it's very subtle, too. Every time you go there, there's different stuff there. And it's all hidden in the trees up past the fire trails, up in the deep woods there." She points a little farther up the hill.

Then Mariah sees something—a little rock on the ground with an arrow painted on it. "Lookee here!" She stops, picks it up, and turns it over. Painted on the back are the words "This way to Elf Land."

"Someone left this for me?" Mariah asks, the mushrooms taking full effect now, and the fluorescent words on the gray rock beginning to vibrate.

"Just for you, Mariah," Rita whispers, "and for everyone. Come on."

"Here's another one!" Mark is at an opening to the deeper woods, standing next to another sign, this one carved into the side of a tree: "Welcome to Elf Land."

As the three pass through the opening, they walk into another world. It's a shared state of consciousness, not just among the three trippers but among them and everyone else who has ever tripped in Elf Land or anywhere else.

Mariah is thinking about her name; how she got it, how it's shaped her, how it's like the name Mary from the Bible, but changed somehow, too. Updated. At the same moment as these thoughts, she comes upon a small shrine that has been set up in a patch of ferns between two tall trees. The two-foot statue is of the Virgin Mary, but she has been decorated—updated— with a Day-Glo costume.

"How'd that get there?" Mariah wonders out loud.

Meanwhile, Mark has wandered off by himself. He's been disturbed about his relationship with Rita. She seems so addicted to popular culture—not the die-hard Deadhead he remembers from their freshman year. Should they stay together after graduation? Get married, even?

He stands against a tree and leans his head against its trunk, looking up into the branches. He looks at the way each larger branch splits in two. Each smaller branch then splits in two, and so and so on until the branches become leaves. Each leaf, then, begins with a single vein, then splits, by two, into smaller and smaller veins. Mark is reminded of chaos math theory, in which ordered systems, like a river flowing smoothly, become chaotic through a process called bifurcation, or dividing by twos. A river splits in two if there's a rock in its path, the two separate sections preserving—between the two of them—the order and magnitude of the original. A species can bifurcate into two different mutations if conditions require it. And a relationship can break up if . . .

As Mark stares at the bifurcated pairs of branches and leaves, he realizes that bifurcation is the nature of decision making. He's caught in the duality of a painful choice, and the tree is echoing the nature of decision-making itself.

"Making a decision?" Mariah asks innocently. She has read the small sign nailed into the side of the tree: "Tree of Decision."

"I wonder who left that there?" Mark wonders aloud.

"Doesn't matter," answers Rita, emerging from nowhere. "Someone last week, last year. A tripper, an elf . . . whoever."

As if on a visionquest, Mark and Mariah were presented with a set of symbols in material form that they could analyze and integrate into a pattern. They were "beholding" their thoughts in physical form. The reality of their trip was confirmed not just by their fantasies but by the totems and signs left for them by other trippers experiencing the same things at different times.

Mushrooms very often give users the feeling of being connected with the past and the future. Whether the 'shroomers know about morphogenetic fields, they do feel connected with the spirit of the woods, and everyone who has traveled before in the same space. Going up is the voyage to that space, peaking is the unself-conscious experience of the new world, and coming down is the reintegration during which the essence of the peak experience is translated into a language or set of images a person can refer to later, at baseline reality.

Enchanted Castles

nd so we set out on a journey, holding on to the Ariadne-thread, an open-sesame that will allow us to identify the object of this pilgrimage no matter what form it may assume. We can identify it through two typical slogans that pervade American advertising. The first, widely used by Coca-Cola but also frequent as a hyperbolic formula in every-day speech, is "the real thing"; the second, found in print and heard on TV, is "more"—in the sense of "extra." The announcer doesn't say, for example, "The program will continue" but rather that there is "More to come." In America you don't say, "Give me another coffee"; you ask for "More coffee"; you don't say that cigarette A is longer than cigarette B, but that there's "more" of it, more than you're used to hav-ing, more than you might want, leaving a surplus to throw away—that's prosperity.

American imagination demands the real thing and, to attain it, must fabricate the absolute fake.

This is the reason for this journey into hyperreality, in search of instances where the American imagination demands the real thing and, to attain it, must fabricate the absolute fake; where the boundaries between game and illusion are blurred, the art museum is contaminated by the freak show, and falsehood is enjoyed in a situation of "fullness," of *horror vacui*. . . .

Winding down the curves of the Pacific coast between San Francisco, Tortilla Flat, and Los Padres National Park, along shores that recall Capri and Amalfi, as the Pacific Highway descends toward Santa Barbara, you see the castle of William Randolph Hearst rise, on the gentle Mediterranean hill of San Simeon. The traveler's heart leaps, because this is the Xanadu of *Citizen Kane,* where Orson Welles brought to life his protagonist, explicitly modeled on the great news-paper magnate, ancestor of the unfortunate Symbionese Patricia.

Having reached the peak of wealth and power, Hearst built here his own Fortress of Solitude, which a biographer has described as a combination of palace and museum such as had not been seen since the days of the Medicis. Like someone in a René Clair movie (but here reality far outstrips fiction), Hearst bought, in bits or whole, palaces, abbeys, and convents in Europe, had them dismantled brick by numbered brick, packaged and shipped across the ocean, to be reconstructed on the enchanted hill, in the midst of free-ranging wild animals. Since he wanted not a museum but a Renaissance house, he complemented the original pieces with bold imitations, not bothering to distinguish the genuine from the copy. An incontinent collectionism, the bad taste of the nouveau riche, and a thirst for prestige led him to bring the past down to the level of today's life; but he conceived of today as worth living only if guaranteed to be "just like the past."

Amid Roman sarcophagi, and genuine exotic plants, and remade baroque stairways, you pass Neptune's Pool, a fantasy Greco-Roman temple peopled with classical statues including (as the guidebook points out with fearless candor) the famous Venus rising from the water, sculpted in 1930 by the Italian sculptor Cassou, and you reach the Great House, a Spanish-Mexican–style cathedral with two towers (equipped with a thirty-six-bell carillon), whose portal frames an iron gate brought from a sixteenth-century Spanish convent, surmounted by a Gothic tympanum with the Virgin and Child. The floor of the vestibule encloses a mosaic found in Pompeii, there are Gobelins on the walls, the door into the Meeting Hall is by Sansovino, the great hall is fake Renaissance presented as Italo-French. A series of choir stalls comes from an Italian convent (Hearst's agents sought the scattered pieces through various European dealers), the tapestries are seventeenth-century Flemish, the objects—real or fake—date from various periods, four medallions are by Thorvaldsen. The Refectory has an Italian ceiling "four hundred years old," on the walls are banners "of an old Sienese family." The bedroom contains the authentic bed of Richelieu, the billiard room has a Gothic tapestry, the projection room (where every night Hearst forced his guests to watch the films he produced, while he sat in the front row with a handy telephone linking him with the whole world) is all fake Egyptian with some Empire touches; the Library has another Italian ceiling, the study imitates a Gothic crypt, and the fireplaces of the various rooms are (real) Gothic, whereas the indoor pool invents a hybrid of the Alhambra, the Paris Métro, and a Caliph's urinal, but with greater majesty.

The striking aspect of the whole is not the quantity of antique pieces plundered from half of Europe, or the nonchalance with which the artificial tissue seamlessly connects fake and genuine, but rather the sense of fullness, the obsessive determination not to leave a single space that doesn't suggest something, and hence the masterpiece of bricolage, haunted by *horror vacui,* that is here achieved. The insane abundance makes the place unlivable, just as it is hard to eat those dishes that many classy American restaurants, all darkness and wood paneling, dotted with soft red lights and invaded by nonstop music, offer the customer as evidence of his own situation of "affluence": steaks four inches thick with lobster (and baked potato, and sour cream and melted butter, and grilled tomato and horseradish sauce) so that the customer will have "more and more," and can wish nothing further.

An incomparable collection of genuine pieces, too, the Castle of Citizen Kane achieves a psychedelic effect and a kitsch result not because the Past is

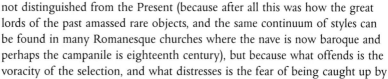

not distinguished from the Present (because after all this was how the great lords of the past amassed rare objects, and the same continuum of styles can be found in many Romanesque churches where the nave is now baroque and perhaps the campanile is eighteenth century), but because what offends is the voracity of the selection, and what distresses is the fear of being caught up by this jungle of venerable beauties, which unquestionably has its own wild flavor, its own pathetic sadness, barbarian grandeur, and sensual perversity, redolent of contamination, blasphemy, the Black Mass. It is like making love in a confessional with a prostitute dressed in a prelate's liturgical robes reciting Baude- laire while ten electronic organs reproduce the *Well-Tempered Clavier* played by Scriabin.

An incomparable collection of genuine pieces, too, the Castle of Citizen Kane achieves a psychedelic effect and a kitsch result.

But Hearst's castle is not an *unicum,* not a *rara avis:* It fits into the California tourist landscape with perfect coherence, among the waxwork Last Suppers and Disneyland. And so we leave the castle and travel a few dozen miles, toward San Luis Obispo. Here, on the slopes of Mount San Luis, bought entirely by Mr. Madonna in order to build a series of motels of disarming pop vulgarity, stands the Madonna Inn.

The poor words with which natural human speech is pro- vided cannot suffice to describe the Madonna Inn. To convey its external appearance, divided into a series of constructions, which you reach by way of a filling station carved from Dolomitic rock, or through the restau- rant, the bar, and the cafeteria, we can only venture some analogies. Let's say that Albert Speer, while leafing through a book on Gaudí, swallowed an over- generous dose of LSD and began to build a nuptial catacomb for Liza Min- nelli. But that doesn't give you an idea. Let's say Arcimboldi builds the Sagrada Familia for Dolly Parton. Or: Carmen Miranda designs a Tiffany locale for the Jolly Hotel chain. Or D'Annunzio's Vittoriale imagined by Bob Cratchit, Calvino's *Invisible Cities* described by Judith Krantz and executed by Leonor Fini for the plush-doll industry, Chopin's Sonata in B flat minor sung by Perry Como in an arrangement by Liberace and accompanied by the Marine Band. No, that still isn't right. Let's try telling about the rest rooms. They are an immense underground cavern, something like Altamira and Luray, with Byzantine columns supporting plaster baroque cherubs. The basins are big imitation-mother-of-pearl shells, the urinal is a fireplace carved from the rock, but when the jet of urine (sorry, but I have to explain) touches the bot- tom, water comes down from the wall of the hood, in a flushing cascade something like the Caves of the Planet Mongo. And on the ground floor, in keeping with the air of Tyrolean chalet and Renaissance castle, a cascade of chandeliers in the form of baskets of flowers, billows of mistletoe surmounted by opalescent bubbles, violet-suffused light among which Victorian dolls swing, while the walls are punctuated by art-nouveau windows with the col- ors of Chartres and hung with Regency tapestries whose pictures resemble the garish color supplements of the Twenties. The circular sofas are red and gold, the tables gold and glass, and all this amid inventions that turn the whole into

a multicolor Jell-O, a box of candied fruit, a Sicilian ice, a land for Hansel and
Gretel. Then there are the bedrooms, about two hundred of them, each with a
different theme: for a reasonable price (which includes an enormous bed—
King or Queen size—if you are on your honeymoon) you can have the Prehistoric Room, all cavern and stalactites, the Safari Room (zebra walls and
bed shaped like a Bantu idol), the Kona Rock Room (Hawaiian), the California Poppy, the Old-Fashioned Honeymoon, the Irish Hills, the William Tell,
the Tall and Short, for mates of different lengths, with the bed in an irregular
polygon form, the Imperial Family, the Old Mill.

   The Madonna Inn is the poor man's Hearst Castle; it has no artistic or
philological pretensions, it appeals to the savage taste for the amazing, the
overstuffed, and the absolutely sumptuous at low price. It says to its visitors:
"You too can have the incredible, just like a millionaire."

   This craving for opulence, which goads the millionaire as it does the
middle-class tourist, seems to us a trademark of American behavior, but it is
much less widespread on the Atlantic coast, and not because there are fewer
millionaires. We could say that the Atlantic millionaire finds no
difficulty in expressing himself through the means of essential
modernity, by building in glass and reinforced concrete, or by
restoring an old house in New England. But the house is

*The Madonna
Inn is the poor
man's Hearst
Castle.*

already there. In other words, the Atlantic coast yearns less for
Hearstian architectural expression because it has its own architecture, the historical architecture of the eighteenth century
and the modern, business-district architecture. Baroque
rhetoric, eclectic frenzy, and compulsive imitation prevail where
wealth has no history. And thus in the great expanses that were
colonized late, where the posturban civilization represented by Los Angeles is
being born, in a metropolis made up of seventy-six different cities where alley-
ways are ten-lane freeways and man considers his right foot a limb designed
for pressing the accelerator, and the left an atrophied appendix, because cars
no longer have a clutch—eyes are something to focus, at steady driving speed,
on visual-mechanical wonders, signs, constructions that must impress the mind
in the space of a few seconds. In fact, we find the same thing in California's
twin-state, Florida, which also seems an artificial region, an uninterrupted continuum of urban centers, great ramps of freeways that span vast bays, artificial
cities devoted to entertainment (Disneyland and Disney World are in California
and Florida, respectively, but the latter—a hundred and fifty times bigger than
the former—is even more pharaonic and futuristic).

   In Florida, south of St. Petersburg, crossing a series of bridges suspended
over inlets of the sea and proceeding along water-level highways that link two
cities across a bay as marvelous as it is useless for human beings without car,
boat, and private marina, you come to Sarasota. Here the Ringling dynasty (of
circus magnates) has left substantial memories of itself. A circus museum, a
painting and sculpture museum complete with Renaissance villa, the Asolo
Theater, and finally the "Ca' d'Zan." The words, as the guidebook explains,
mean "House of John in Venetian dialect," and in fact the Ca' is a palazzo, or

rather a section of Grand Canal façade which opens on a garden of overwhelming botanical beauty, where, for example, a banyan tree, its multiple exposed roots spilling to the ground, creates a wild gazebo inhabited by a bronze statue; and at the rear, there is an only slightly Venetian terrace where, following a path punctuated by a Cellini, or a Giovanni da Bologna, fake, but with the proper patina and mold in all the right places, you gaze out on one of the bayous of Florida, once the paradise of early explorers or the blessed land of Little Jody, where he wept and followed Flag, the immortal yearling.

Ca' d'Zan is a Venetian palazzo that could be used for an architecture course's final exam: Describe a Venetian palazzo, symbol of the pomp and historical destiny of the Doges, meeting place of Latin civilization and Moorish barbarism. Obviously, the student aiming at an "A" emphasizes the bright colors, the Oriental influences, and produces a result that would be more pleasing to Othello than to Marco Polo. About the interior there can't be a moment's doubt: It's the Hotel Danieli. The architect Dwight James Baum deserves (in the sense that Eichmann does) to go down in history. Also because, not content with the Danieli, he overdid. He engaged an unknown Hungarian decorator to paint a coffered ceiling in a barroom-naïf style, he lavished terracottas, docked gondolas, Murano-style glass of pink, amethyst, and blue; but to be double-sure he decked it all with Flemish and English tapestries, French trumeaux, art-nouveau sculpture, Empire chairs, Louis XV beds, Carrara marbles (with labels guaranteeing origin), as usual carved by artisans brought specially from Venice; and into the bargain he made extra certain that the bar would have leaded glass panels, brought—note the archeological refinement—from the Cicardi Winter Palace of St. Louis. And this, to tell the truth, seems to me the maximum of sincere effort. Here again the authentic pieces, which would make Sotheby's ecstatic, are numerous, but what prevails is the connective tissue, totally reconstructed with arrogant imagination, though explanatory labels are quick to tell you that the good is good, arriving even at certain catalogue naïvetés like the legend stuck on a Dutch porcelain clock in the form of a medieval castle, which says, "Dutch, 1900 ca.?" The portraits of the proprietors, husband and wife, now happily deceased and assumed into history, dominate the whole. For the prime aim of these wild Xanadus (as of every Xanadu) is not so much to live there, but to make posterity think how exceptional the people who did live there must have been. And, frankly, exceptional gifts would be required—steady nerves and a great love of the past or the future—to stay in these rooms, to make love, to have a pee, eat a hamburger, read the newspaper, button your fly. These eclectic reconstructions are governed by a great remorse for the wealth that was acquired by methods less noble than the architecture that crowns them, a great will to expiatory sacrifice, a desire for posterity's absolution.

But it is hard to apply punishing irony to these pathetic ventures, because other powerful people have thought to assert their place in history through the

> *Ca' d'Zan is a Venetian palazzo that could be used for an architecture course's final exam.*

Nuremberg Stadium or the Foro Mussolini, and there is something disarming about this search for glory via an unrequited love for the European past. We are tempted to feel sorry for the poor history-less millionaire who, to recreate Europe in desolate savannahs, destroys the genuine savannah and turns it into an unreal lagoon. But surely this hand-to-hand battle with history, pathetic as it may be, cannot be justified, because history will not be imitated. It has to be made, and the architecturally superior America shows this is possible.

The Wall Street area in New York is composed of skyscrapers, neo-Gothic cathedrals, neoclassical Parthenons, and primary cubelike structures. Its builders were no less daring than the Hearsts and the Ringlings, and you can also find here a Palazzo Strozzi, property of the Federal Reserve Bank of New York, complete with rustication and all. Built in 1924 of "Indiana limestone and Ohio sandstone," it ceases its Renaissance imitation at the third floor, rightly, and continues with eight more stories of its own invention, then displays Guelph battlements, then continues as skyscraper. But there is nothing to object to here, because lower Manhattan is a masterpiece of living architecture, crooked like the lower line of Cowboy Kate's teeth; skyscrapers and Gothic cathedrals compose what has been called a jam session in stone, certainly the greatest in the history of mankind. Here, moreover, the Gothic and the neoclassical do not seem the effect of cold reasoning; they illustrate the revivalist awareness of the period when they were built, and so they aren't fakes, at least no more than the Madeleine is, in Paris, and they are not incredible, any more than the Victor Emmanuel monument is, in Rome. Everything is integrated in a now homogeneous urban landscape, because real cities redeem, in their context, even what is architectonically ugly. And perhaps in New York the Ca' d'Zan of Sarasota would be acceptable, just as in Venice, on the Grand Canal, so many sibling-palazzos of the Ca' d'Zan are acceptable.

In fact, a good urban context and the history it represents teach, with a sense of humor, even kitsch how to live, and thus exorcise it. On the way between San Simeon and Sarasota I stopped in New Orleans. I was coming from the recreated New Orleans of Disneyland, and I wanted to check my reactions against the real city, which represents a still intact past, because the Vieux Carré is one of the few places that American civilization hasn't remade, flattened, replaced. The structure of the old Creole city has remained as it was, with its low houses, its cast-iron balconies and arcades, reasonably rusted and worn, its tilting buildings that mutually support one another, like buildings you see in Paris or Amsterdam, repainted perhaps, but not too much. Storyville is gone; there is no Basin Street left, no red-light district, but there are countless strip joints with doors open onto the street, in the racket of bands, of circulating tourists, strolling idlers. The Vieux Carré isn't the least like the entertainment district of an American city; it is more

The Wall Street area in New York is composed of skyscrapers, neo-Gothic cathedrals, neoclassical Parthenons, and primary cubelike structures. Its builders were no less daring than the Hearsts and the Ringlings.

like a cousin of Montmartre. In this corner of pretropical Europe there are still restaurants inhabited by *Gone with the Wind* characters, where waiters in tails discuss with you the alterations in sauce béarnaise due to the impact of local spices. Other places, strangely similar to a Milanese *brasera,* know the mysteries of *bollito* with green sauce (shamelessly presented as Creole cuisine).

On the Mississippi you can take a six-hour trip on a paddle-steamer, obviously fake, constructed according to the latest mechanical criteria, but still it transports you along wild shores inhabited by alligators as far as Barataria, where Jean Lafitte and his pirates hid before joining up with Andrew Jackson to fight the British. So in New Orleans, history still exists and is tangible, and under the porch of the Presbythère there stands, a forgotten archeological item, one of the first submarines in the world, with which Confederate sailors attacked Yankee vessels during the Civil War. Like New York, New Orleans knows its own fakes and historicizes them: In various patrician houses in Louisiana, for example, there exist copies of Ingres's portrait of Napoleon enthroned, because many French artists came here in the nineteenth century saying they were pupils of the great painter, and they distributed copies, more or less reduced, and more or less successful, but this was in a time when oil copies were the only way of knowing the original, and local historiography celebrates these copies as the documentation of their own "coloniality." The fake is recognized as "historical," and is thus garbed in authenticity.

> On the Mississippi you can take a six-hour trip on a paddle-steamer, obviously fake.

Now in New Orleans, too, there is a wax museum, devoted to the history of Louisiana. The figures are well made, the costumes and furnishings are honestly precise. But the atmosphere is different; the circus feeling, the magic aura are absent. The explanatory panels have an undertone of skepticism and humor; when an episode is legendary, it is presented as such, and perhaps with the admission that it is more fun to reconstruct legend than history. The sense of history allows an escape from the temptations of hyperreality. Napoleon, seated in his bathtub, discussing the sale of Louisiana, according to the memoirs of the period should spring up and spatter water on the others present; but the Museum explains that costumes are very expensive and apologizes for not attempting absolute verisimilitude. The waxworks refer to legends that have left their traces in the streets of the neighborhood: the colony, the aristocrats, the Creole beauties, the prostitutes, the pitiless swordsmen, the pirates, the riverboat gamblers, jazz, the Canadians, Spanish, French, English. New Orleans is not in the grip of a neurosis of a denied past; it passes out memories generously like a great lord; it doesn't have to pursue "the real thing."

> The fake is recognized as "historical," and is thus garbed in authenticity.

Elsewhere, on the contrary, the frantic desire for the Almost Real arises only as a neurotic reaction to the vacuum of memories; the Absolute Fake is offspring of the unhappy awareness of a present without depth.

Chapter 1

Questions and Suggestions for Further Study on the Net/WWW

■ QUESTIONS BASED ON THE READINGS:

1. My brief introduction to this chapter begins with a quotation (the first lines) from William Gibson's cyberpunk novel *Neuromancer*. I allude to this quote only in passing. Now that you have finished reading the articles included here, what do you take this description to mean?

If you have not read *Neuromancer*, you might want to, because it is all about this opening quote and all about the topic/theme of this chapter (also see Chapter 6 on cyberpunk/cyborgs). Here's another Gibson quote from the same novel:

Cyberspace. A consensual hallucination experienced daily by billions of legitimate operators, in every nation, by children being taught mathematical concepts. . . . A graphical representation of data abstracted from the banks of every computer in the human system. Unthinkable complexity. Lines of light ranged in the non-space of the mind, clusters and constellations of data. Like city lights, receding.

2. Benjamin Woolley artfully dodges making a definition of cyberspace. He is interested instead in why Gibson's term became common currency. Woolley refers to McLuhan's discussion of *explosion* (fragmentation of societies) and *implosion* (global village). What do these terms/images mean in this context? Or in relation to my brief introduction to this chapter? What does Woolley/McLuhan mean by extending our bodies—as, for example, by television becoming our eyes? What does Woolley mean when he uses the word *network*? What is ARPAnet? Summarize Woolley's account of the development of the Net from LANs (local area networks) to the World Wide Web (WWW). How are all these questions connected? What do they add up to—most important, in relation to cyberspace?

What is *telepresence*? What is the difference between "watching" and "doing" television? What is meant by McLuhan's notion, "The medium is the message [or massage]"? What does Woolley give as an explanation for the studio audience that doesn't see a real-life event as opposed to the at-home viewers who don't see a real-life event? After all, doesn't a studio audience actually see real people?

What is a computer virus? And why does Woolley discuss it? In other words, what is its relevance to a general discussion on cyberspace? What does

Woolley (and Thomas, the writer he refers to) think the Friday the 13th virus told us about the news media itself? (Are there parallels among a virus passing through the human system, the personal computer system, and the media, or mediascape? If so, what are these parallels and their significance? It might help you to find out what the word *meme* means.) Was the hacker who released the virus saying something to us or just being mischievous or reckless?

What does the discussion of replicators, genotypes, and phenotypes have to do with cyberspace? What is Woolley driving at with his detailed exposition of Dawkins's discussion of a phenotypic effect of a gene? What do Dawkins and Woolley mean when they talk about the virus manipulating the world around it? Is this science fiction with virus monsters, or is it reality—or can we tell the difference any more? Why does Woolley tease us with a connection between the Friday the 13th virus and the stock market crash of 1989? Why does he include a discussion of the gold standard in Great Britain?

Finally, Woolley says: "Perhaps cyberspace, then, is—literally—where the money is. Perhaps it is also the place where events increasingly happen, where our lives and fates are increasingly determined; a place that has a very direct impact on our material circumstances—a blip" can change everything. We, in *cyberspace,* are now subject to blips (viruses and their manipulations). What does Woolley possibly mean when he says it is our "connectedness" that contributes to our being subject to blips?

After reading Woolley, what do you know? Fear? Not understand?

3. Michael Heim, like Woolley, struggles with the task of defining virtual reality. Finally, he turns to seven different current views of VR. What are they? Why does Heim use the framing device of the person wanting to know about VR? After listening to the seven explanations of VR, the questioner finally exclaims: "There's a general drift here but no single destination. Should I go home feeling that the real virtual reality does not exist?" Why does Heim shift from a discussion of VR to one of reality, the *R*-word? (Note that he inserts a sidebar on Plato.)

Heim makes an extended comparison between the U.S. space program and the former Soviet Union's visionary ideas. Why this comparison? What is the significance of the word *enterprise?* How does the television program *Star Trek* fit into the discussion?

Explain Heim's distinction between esoteric and exoteric essences. What does he mean when he says, "VR . . . promises the Holy Grail"? Or: "VR will enhance the power of art to transform reality"?

4. Why does Douglas Rushkoff entitle his essay "Seeing Is Beholding"?

Rushkoff begins his take on VR with an anecdote about Terence McKenna, the "philosopher" of the psychedelic plant world. Why does Rushkoff begin with this discussion? Can you tell from Rushkoff's tone (i.e., the author's voice or attitude) what his purpose might be? What is the analogy or parallel, as Rushkoff reports it, between psychedelic (mind-expanding) drugs and VR or cyberspace?

What do McKenna and his cohorts believe is beneficial in their taking drugs? What scientific experiments does Rushkoff cite that might explain the benefits? (How would you compare Woolley's views of VR and cyberspace with McKenna's view? With Rushkoff's view of McKenna's view?) What is the "unity" that Rushkoff talks about? The morphogenetic field? How do taking drugs and, by analogy, trekking in cyberspace change reality?

In discussing Nina Graboi's views of LSD, Rushkoff reports that the so-called bell curve of intelligence improves when a person takes psychedelic drugs; most notably, the bell curve dramatically improved and manifested its upward movement in the 1960s and 1970s in political protests against the war in Vietnam, sexual liberation, concern for the environment, and new mathematical systems and designs (fractals). What is Rushkoff suggesting by relating the story of Jaida and Cindy? What is your overall assessment of Rushkoff's account?

5. If taking psychedelic drugs is one way to (go on a) trip, what does Umberto Eco have in mind when he asserts that inhabitants of the U.S. travel in hyperreality? What, in other words, does Eco mean when he writes: "There is an America of furious hyperreality. . . . There is another, more secret America . . . and it creates somehow *a network of references and influences* that finally spread also to the products of high culture and the entertainment industry" [emphasis mine]? Why does Eco cite and discuss the "enchanted castles" (the Hearst Castle, the Madonna Inn, the "Ca' d'Zan")? Can you think of similar "enchanted" places that you have traveled to?

What does Eco mean when he says: "The frantic desire for the Almost Real arises only as a neurotic reaction to the vacuum of memories; the Absolute Fake is offspring of the unhappy awareness of a present without depth"? Can "the real thing" be found in the United States or, as far as that goes, elsewhere? If it can, then why hypertravel? As opposed to Disneyland in Anaheim, are Hollywood and South Central Los Angeles "the real thing"? As opposed to the Hearst Castle, is the Golden Gate Bridge or the Grand Canyon "the real thing"? (This is a tricky question. How many times have you seen the bridge and the canyon represented in various media before you "actually" saw them?—if you have ever seen them! Think of McLuhan's notion of the medium is the message.)

Jean Baudrillard writes in *Simulacra and Simulation:* "Disneyland exists in order to hide that it is the 'real' country, all of 'real' America that is Disneyland. . . . Disneyland is presented as imaginary in order to make us believe that the rest is real, whereas all of Los Angeles and the America that surrounds it are no longer real, but belong to the hyperreal order and to the order of simulation. It is no longer a question of a false representation of reality (ideology) but of concealing the fact that the real is no longer real, and thus of saving the reality principle." Does this quote help in thinking about some of the questions?

6. Is it time to panic? (See *Panic Encyclopedia* below, and search for "Panic Cyberspace.")

■ FURTHER STUDY ON THE NET/WWW

A computer search for any one of our three terms in this section—say, *cyberspace*—will give you more cybernoise than you can begin to deal with. I say "noise" because of the sheer amount of hits you will get. But it can be fun and will garner items of information you would never think of searching for.

Let's surf and search through the noise. If you search for the term *cyberspace* (at, say, *WebCrawler* <http://webcrawler.com/>), you might find this website, which in many ways is a good one to begin with:

• *Cyberspace: The New Frontier* <http://www.cs.uidaho.edu/lal/cyberspace/ cyberspace.html>. There are links to many very basic and important themes such as the Electronic Frontier Foundation, John Perry Barlow, the Internet, Cyberpunk, Virtual Reality, and many others.

• Further searching: If you try again (say, at *Yahoo* <http://www.yahoo. com/>) under the term *hyperreal* (not *hyperreality,* which will not get you much, if anything here, at least when I tried it), you will get a few very interesting hits in relation (or similar) to

Entertainment:Music:Genres:Rave and Techno
Hyperreal—the Techno/Ambient/Rave Archive
Texas Raves—serving all those Texas Ravers out there!
Transeform
Vrave—the online virtual rave, an interactive text-based vir-
tual environment for the discussion of aspects of raves and
raving, music, and other related subjects

Entertainment:Music:Genres:Rave and Techno:Artists
Aphex Twin—Hardcore/ambient

Entertainment:Music:Instruments
The Analogue Heaven—a mailing list for people interested in
playing, collecting, modifying, and designing analog musical
equipment.

Entertainment:Television:Shows:Music
Cyberia—featuring computer animation and techno music video

At this point in your search, you should begin to get the idea that the categories *cyberspace, virtual reality,* and *hyperreal* are often associated with lots of "weird" topics, or rather they are associated with topics that are considered to be on the edge or fringe. Therefore, be aware, as I said in the preface, when you study cyberspace, you will touch on what might appear to you as some pretty *phr*eaky subjects. Especially look at:

• *Hyperreal* <http://www.hyperreal.com/>. (This site has numerous links to other sites. From this site, you might try the link to . . .)

- *Island World* <http://www.hyperreal.com/island/>. (This one is based on Aldous Huxley's utopian novel *Island.*)

If you search more specifically, this time, for something from Rushkoff's piece—say, for Terence McKenna (at *WebCrawler* <http://webcrawler. com/>)—you can get a few hits, one of which is

- *Terence McKenna Land* <http://www.intac.com/~dimitri/dh/mckenna. html>.

Each of these computer searches on the Web can help you to supplement and complement what you have read.

If you search for something from Heim's article—say, for Jaron Lanier (at Lycos <http://lycos.cs.cmu.edu/>)—you will get a few hits, some of which are

- a *Brief Biography of Jaron Lanier* <http://www.well.com/Community/ Jaron.Lanier/general.html>

- *Lanier's homepage* <http://www.well.com/Community/Jaron.Lanier/ index.html>

- *Technology of Cyberspace* (Lanier) <http://mmm.dartmouth.edu/ pages/engs4/engs4.html>

You could continue this kind of searching by using a variety of search engines, specifically in relation to Heim's book. For example, you could search for Heim's key terms *artificiality, immersion, telepresence, full-body immersion,* and *networked communications,* further expanding your knowledge. What you have been doing, therefore, is reading an article and searching and browsing through what you find as a means—let's say—of extended reading, or hyperreading, or just plain old research in a new environment. You will do more of this as you proceed from chapter to chapter of this book.

For other interesting sites, try

- *The Encyclopedia of Virtual Environments* (EVE) <http://www.cs.umd.edu/ projects/eve/eve-main.html>. (This was developed by a group of students like you for a class. Spend some time browsing this site; later you will have reason to return to it.)

- *The Voice of the Shuttle: The Technology of Writing* <http://humanitas.ucsb. edu/shuttle/techwrit.html#composition>. (Check out such topics as VRML, virtual reality markup language.)

- *Hot Virtual Reality Sites* <http://nemo.ncsl.nist.gov/~sressler/hotvr.html>. Loads of exciting stuff here.

- *Nanotechnology on the WWW* <http://galaxy.einet.net/galaxy/Engineering- and-Technology/Mechanical-Engineering/Nanotechnology/Nano.html>. (*Nano-* is a prefix meaning a billionth. Right now, this is considered a fringe science. Eric Drexler coins the term and discusses this future tech- nology in *Engines of Creation.* The implications of a technology of engines the size of a virus are staggering. These micromachines, once injected into the human body, could completely rebuild it by, for example, clearing away arteries of plaque deposits, correcting errant cell behavior, and so on. Check out this website and take a glimpse at the future.)

- *EnviroLink* <http://envirolink.org/envirowebs.html>. (With all this talk about technology, we should not forget the *other* environment. EnviroLink is the best and most complete list about the environment and has links to other webpages. Be sure to visit this site regularly.)

■ H E R E   A R E   S O M E   A D D I T I O N A L   O N - L I N E   N E T W O R K S (W E B S I T E S ,   W I T H   A R C H I V E S ,   A N D   N E W S G R O U P S) :

Let's now visit some of the homepages of the authors we have been reading:

- *Michael Heim: Project Metaphysics Home Page* <http://www.jovanet.com/~mheim/index.htm/>. (This site includes seminars on virtual reality taught by Heim, a list of Heim's books [*Electric Language* and *The Metaphysics of Virtual Reality*], and an article and interview.)

- *Benjamin Woolley, Welcome to Ben's Home Page* <http://www.bbcnc.org.uk/tv/the_net/ben/>. (This site has the appearance of being managed by someone other than the author. But visit the links—say, the music links (from Gregorian chant to the Stones) or other links, which will surely change from time to time.)

- *Howard Rheingold* <http://www.well.com/user/hlr/>. (This is an interesting site, very personalized. Be sure to check out *What's New & Rheingoldian?*)

- *Douglas Rushkoff's Home Page* <http://www.interport.net/~rushkoff/>. (What you will find here immediately are some links to information about Rushkoff's books: *Cyberia, The GenX Reader,* and *Media Virus.* When you click on *Cyberia,* you will get the preface to the book.)

- *FutureCulture* <http://www.uio.no/~mwatz/futurec/>.

The FutureCulture mailing list has to be one of the better known lists on what could be termed the Alternative Circuit on the Net. Started by Andy Hawks, it has survived net.death several times and continues to evolve with a sense of real community.

FutureCulture is deliberately broad in scope when it comes to the topics discussed, but a quick list might include:
Technoculture/new edge/cyberculture
Cyberspace & the Internet
Virtual reality
The computer underground
Cyberpunk (literary and cultural movements)
Raves and rave culture

Media (music/movies/books/magazines) that are relevant
Virtual communities
Social and public policy issues

However, be warned that FutureCulture is not just another
generic KOOL cyberpunk discussion list, but rather a community. Sometimes we discuss Artificial Life and nanotech,
sometimes we discuss the future of monogamy and the misery of
breaking up. We're cyborgs, but we're also humans.

FutureCulture info
FutureCulture introduction
The FutureCulture FAQ, from March 1993 (Note that this FAQ is
not updated as to reflect the current state of the list,
which naturally has a focus somewhat different from what it
had two years ago...)
Archives of messages on the list, starting October 7th 1994
FutureCulture people's homepages
The **introductions thread** from September 1994, in which a
lot of FC people introduced themselves. Kindly supplied by
Gregory H. Ritter.

- *Newsgroups* (Usenet):
  alt.cyberspace
  alt.mtv.sucks
  alt.newbie
  alt.newbies
  alt.music.techno
  alt.rave

■ MORE REFERENCES FOR SURFING THE
  WEB (THAT SUPPLEMENT THE READINGS):

- *Transcripts of Recent Roundtables* <http://www.irsociety.com/recent.htm>.
  (Lots to read here about the themes of VR, cyberspace, hyperreal[ity].)

- *Panic Encyclopedia* <http://english-www.hss.cmu.edu/ctheory/
  panic/panic_contents.html>. (The entire book, from which "Panic Cyberspace" comes, is available on line. Browse it at your leisure and compare it to
  The Encyclopedia of Virtual Environments [EVE]. This virtual book can be found
  in the index at *The English Server* [CMU] <http://english-
  server.hss.cmu.edu/>. And be sure to read the entry for "Panic Cyberspace.")

- *Disney Sites* <http://www.best.com/~dijon/disney/parks/
  waltdisneyworld/>

- MTV <http://mtv.com/>

- *Star Trek* <http://www.cosy.sbg.ac.at/rec/startrek/index.htm>

- *Star Trek: The Next Generation* <http://198.147.111.30/~werdna/
  sttng/>

- *Star Wars Multimedia www* <http://bantha.pc.cc.cmu.edu:1138/StarWars/Pictures/SW_STILLS.html>. (Lots of movie stills [JPEG Gallery]. You will need a Mosaic or Netscape browser.)

- *NASA Scientific and Technical Information Server* <http://www.sti.nasa.gov/STI-homepage.html>

- *Committee Report on VR.5* <http://www.microserve.net/~server/vr5/>. (About the television show *VR.5*.)

- *Extropians and Other Transhumans* <http://www.c2.org/~arkuat/extr/>. Here you will discover:

Extropian interests include **transhumanism**, futurist philosophy, **life extension**, **cryonics**, **robotics and artificial intelligence**, **smart drugs**, intelligence-intensifying technologies, **personality uploading**, and other practical applications of **neuroscience**, **artificial life**, nanocomputers and molecular **nanotechnology**, **memetics** (ideas as replicating agents), experimental **free communities** in **space**, on the **oceans**, and in **cyberspace**, effective thinking, information filtering, life management, self-transformative psychology, **spontaneous order** (**free markets**, **neural networks**, **evolutionary processes**, genetic algorithms, etc), **cryptography** and other privacy technologies, **electronic markets**, **digital cash**, critical analysis of environmentalism, and explorations of the ultimate limits of physics, among other things.

The boldface type, as you find it on the Net, is a hot link to an extended text or hypertext. In Netscape, however, links are underlined.)

■ MORE REFERENCES FOR READING:

Abraham, Ralph H. *Chaos Gaia Eros.* New York: HarperCollins, 1994.

Barlow, John Perry, Sven Birkerts, Kevin Kelly, and Mark Slouka. "What Are We Doing On-line?" *Harper's Magazine* (August 1995): 35–46.

Baudrillard, Jean. *Simulacra and Simulation.* Trans. Sheila Faria Glaser. Ann Arbor: University of Michigan Press, 1994.

Brand, Stewart. *The Media Lab: Inventing the Future at MIT.* New York: Viking, 1987.

Dawkins, Richard. *The Selfish Gene.* 2nd ed. Oxford: Oxford University Press, 1989.

Heim, Michael. *The Metaphysics of Virtual Reality.* New York: Oxford University Press, 1993.

Holtzman, Steven R. *Digital Mantras: The Languages of Abstract and Virtual Worlds.* Cambridge, MA: MIT Press, 1994.

Kroker, Arthur, Marilouise Kroker, David Cook. *Panic Encyclopedia: The Definitive Guide to the Postmodern Scene.* New York: St. Martin's Press, 1989.

Online. *The English Server* (CMU). Internet. 22 August 1995. Available: <http://english-www.hss.cmu.edu/ctheory/panic/panic_contents.html>.

McLuhan, Marshall. *The Gutenberg Galaxy.* Toronto: University of Toronto Press, 1965.

McLuhan, Marshall. *Understanding Media: The Extensions of Man.* London: Routledge, 1964.

McLuhan, Marshall, and Quentin Fiore. *The Medium is the Massage.* New York: Bantam, 1967.

The McLuhan Program in Culture and Technology. Online. Internet. 22 August 1995. Available: <http://www.mcluhan.toronto.edu/Welcome.html>.

Mitchell, William J. *City of Bits: Space, Place, and the Infobahn.* Cambridge, MA: MIT Press, 1995. (Mitchell says that every day more and more of what we have taken to be physical atoms and protoplasm are being converted into bits. According to Mitchell, all of our so-called existence is becoming bits [zeros and ones, which are distinctions only in VR]. It is as if we are being imploded into a black hole, where no light follows. Where? In the "Bit-sphere.") As I state in the preface to *CyberReader,* everything changes on the Net, but while I write, *City of Bits* can be found on line. MIT Press. Internet. 20 July 1995. Available: <http://www-mitpress.mit.edu/>.

Moore, Dinty W. *The Emperor's Virtual Clothes: The Naked Truth About Internet Culture.* Chapel Hill, NC: Algonquin, 1995.

Negroponte, Nicholas. *Being Digital.* New York: Knopf, 1995. Browse through the "Being Digital" Cyberdock. Online. Internet. 22 August 1995. Available: <http://www.obs-us.com/obs/english/books/nn/bdintro.html/>.

Poster, Mark. *The Mode of Information.* Cambridge, MA: Polity Press, 1990.

Rheingold, Howard. *Virtual Reality.* New York: Simon & Schuster, 1991.

Rosenberg, Michael S. "Virtual Reality: Reflections of Life, Dreams, and Technology: An Ethnography of a Computer Society." 16 March 1992. *Xerox Parc.* Online. Internet. 22 August 1995. Available: <ftp://parcftp.xerox.com/pub/MOO/papers/ethnography.txt>. Includes an excellent glossary.

Rushkoff, Douglas. *Cyberia: Life in the Trenches of Hyperspace.* New York: HarperCollins, 1995.

Slouka, Mark. *War of the Worlds: Cyberspace and the High-Tech Assault on Reality.* New York: Basic Books, 1995.

Stoll, Clifford. *Silicon Snake Oil: Second Thoughts on the Information Highway.* New York: Doubleday, 1995.

Thomas, Wes. "NanoCyborgs (A Conversation with Charles Ostman)." *Mondo 2000,* 12 (1994): 16–29.

Woolley, Benjamin. *Virtual Worlds: A Journey in Hype and Hyperreality.* New York: Penguin, 1993.

Freedom/Censorship

(Security/Hackers):

I n this chapter as well as the next, for the most part we will be reading indirectly about the U.S. Constitution: a document written a couple of centuries ago whose principles and laws have spread from New England all across what is known today as the United States. As our map grew from colonies to territories to states, so grew the reach of the Constitution. As we attempt today, however, to stretch our map to include cyberspace, so grows our confusion. Geographical colonization, we are finding out, is not at all comparable to the colonization of cyberspace. The principles of the *actual* world are difficult, if not finally impossible, to apply to the *virtual* world. And yet many legislators and citizens are trying to apply the Constitution to virtual world(s).

In a recent issue of *Newsweek* ("TechnoMania," February 27, 1995), the editors write: "The revolution has only just begun, but already it's starting to overwhelm us. It's outstripping our capacity to cope, antiquating our laws, transforming our mores, reshuffling our economy, reordering our priorities, redefining our workplaces." We are, the editors say, in the "Bit Bang"—not the Big Bang of creation, but the Bang of a terminal revolution that challenges us with problems we have no idea how to deal with. The major problem is applying the Constitution to the New Virtual World. For many citizens of the actual world, this is not a problem; they say, just apply the Constitution as we do to the actual world. For others, however, this kind of thinking is part of the problem; just applying it to a virtual world, they argue, is an unjust application that *really,* in the long run, cannot be implemented. They remind us further that applying the Constitution to the actual world itself has been no easy, uncontested task.

The media have touted the problem as "Crimes of the 'Net.'" Some argue, however, that the term *criminal activity* is too broadly applied and gives the state and federal governments a pretext to extend their powers over those people living in the Internet communities. The issue has become, therefore, one of freedom of expression versus censorship on the Internet, of private versus public, of freedom on the virtual range versus being fenced in and restricted by legislation that would post actual and virtual signs warning of "illegal" trespassing.

In our first group of readings, published in *Newsweek* and *The New York Times,* we will see how events as they occur on the Net are reported as outright crimes and how, finally, we are told the days of the Wild West on the cyberrange are coming to an end. Juxtaposed with these two stories is a manifesto published in the electronic publication *Phrack* by a hacker who calls himself "Mentor" and offers a challenge to anyone who would call him a criminal. What hackers in general challenge us with is an ethic, as Steven Levy in his *Hackers* phrases it, that says "information wants to be free." Hackers, as Bruce Sterling depicts them, "are absolutely soaked through with heroic antibureaucratic sentiment. Hackers long for recognition as a praiseworthy cultural archetype, the postmodern electronic equivalent of the cowboy and mountain man." What was considered "theft," as the *Newsweek* story points out, can be reconsidered by a hacker *in some cases* as "sharing" (hence the term *shareware*). Many hackers say that they are not "crackers" (thieves) and that the popular media and the government (or strong economical forces such as telephone or communications and software companies) want to blur the difference between the two so as to curb freedom of expression and to centralize authority. In other words, it is claimed that these centralized economic forces want to stretch the term *cracker* to hackers in order to widen surveillance in cyberspace. Whatever the case, the ethic of sharing is a major challenge to what we, in constitutional and economic terms, have considered the very concept of *property* or *proprietary goods* to be. (We will return to this issue in a later chapter on the difference between copyright and copyleft.)

The next group of readings deals with what Sterling has called the "hacker crackdown" in his book of the same title. A truncated version of the crackdown story goes like this: There was much concern shown by John Perry Barlow (associated with the Grateful Dead) and hackers across the country about the number of federal crackdowns, and in December 1989 they were invited by *Harper's Magazine* to discuss the issue on the WELL (Whole Earth 'Lectronic Link), a Bulletin Board System in the San Francisco Bay Area. Such hackers (crackers?) as "Phiber Optik" and "Acid Phreak" made their appearance to discuss such questions as whether or not there is a "hacker ethic" and whether hacking is a crime. Shortly thereafter, on January 24, 1990, the federal government and New York State police raided the homes of Phiber Optik, Acid Phreak, and another hacker. Optik (Mark Abene) was not charged in this raid until a year later and then only with a misdemeanor. The raids escalated: March 1, 1991 has come to be known as the day of "Steve Jackson Games" raid, in Austin, Texas—specifically, on "Mentor" and others— then, on May 7–9, came the "Operation Sundevil" raids all across the country.

These raids make up the hacker crackdown; in June of the same year, they led to the creation of the Electronic Freedom Foundation by Barlow and Mitchell Kapor. Barlow's zany yet serious manifesto, "Crime and Puzzlement," is the founding document of the EFF. Shortly thereafter, the EFF began defending hackers in the courtroom. (In "Further Suggestions" we will go to the EFF website and check out their activities and archives.)

So, then, what does a cracker look like? Do we have a candidate? After reading these articles and others, we will want to know; after all, we do need to distinguish between the two so that we can defend ourselves against criminals. We will end (or rebegin?) our readings here with the story of Kevin D. Mitnick as it is presented in two *New York Times* stories and elsewhere. But the story is not only about Mitnick but also Tsutomu Shimomura! We will return to these two men in "Further Suggestions," for instead of easily making clearcut distinctions for us, their stories only further complicate a very intractable problem. (The issue of freedom of expression is continued in Chapter 3.)

Michael Meyer with Anne Underwood

Crimes of the "Net"

Software: Hackers call it "sharing." But theft on the Internet is costing companies billions, and the high-tech industry is struggling to stop it.

ay Curci is an earnest, diligent guy. He spends days off with his wife, but works from home every weekend. One recent Saturday he settled himself in front of the computer in his den—and noticed something odd. Dozens of people were logging on to a seldom-used computer that Curci, a systems administrator, runs at Florida State University. More puzzling was that most of the users were from abroad. And, once logged in, they seemed to just . . . disappear.

Hackers, Curci realized. Quickly, he tracked the intruders to their destination—a so-called invisible directory, or data bank lacking any identifiable name or listing. He was astonished by what he found: a vast cache of proprietary software, including test versions of Windows 95 and OS/2, the new operating systems being developed by Microsoft Corp. and IBM. He had no idea who secreted it within the university's computers. But it was obviously a pirate's treasure trove. There were games and word-processing programs, even "tools" to help hackers break passwords and conceal their digital trespasses. Curci scrambled the purloined programs to make them unusable, even as a dozen hackers swarmed to download copies. But, he guesses, hundreds of cybersurfers beat him to the punch. Many more are still trying.

Such is the dark side of the Internet, the ubiquitous electronic web linking as many as 40 million computers worldwide. As anyone not wholly techno-illiterate knows by now, the Net is growing gangbusters. It's our new frontier, a digital Wild West. As befits such a rough-and-ready place, it's populated by lots of bad guys. Want the latest computer games from Broderbund or 3DO? Interested in previewing Microsoft's vaunted Windows 95, nine months before it hits a store near you? Tap into the Net, find the right bulletin board, and you can probably secure a free copy. Telephone credit cards, copyrighted music, even digital *Playboy* centerfolds are being electronically pilfered, too. Hackers call it "sharing." Others consider it theft, pure and simple. "It's like shoplifting," says Bruce Lehman, U.S. commissioner of patents and trademarks, no different from letting your fingers do the walking at your local CD store.

It's hard to gauge the scope of the phenomenon or its economic impact. But numbers tell part of the story. By some estimates, roughly $2 billion worth of software was stolen over the Internet last year, a growing portion of the total $7.4 billion the Software Publishers Association reckons was lost to piracy in 1993. Just last month the leader of an international piracy ring operating out of Majorca, Spain, pleaded guilty to a brand of fraud destined to become commonplace. According to U.S. investigators, the racketeers stole 140,000 telephone credit-card numbers, then sold them to computer bulletin boards in the United States and Europe. Hackers used the numbers to make a whopping $140 million worth of long-distance phone calls—sometimes merely to pay for their time online, other times to tap into remote computers and download hijacked software. Who ate the loss? GTE Corp., AT&T, Bell Atlantic and MCI, among others.

It was not an isolated incident. Police have arrested half a dozen bulletin-board operators in recent months on charges of illegally distributing software over the Internet. "This is only the tip of the iceberg," says Sandra Sellers of the Software Publishers Association. The association has identified 1,600 bulletin boards carrying bootleg software, she claims. Last week authorities in North Carolina indicted nine alleged members of a nationwide piracy ring, known digitally by code names like Phone Stud, Major Theft and Killerette. Like the hackers of the Majorca network, they have been charged with stealing as many as 100,000 telephone credit-card numbers—as well as pirating an array of software. The cost to the phone companies has been estimated at $50 million.

The thievery isn't likely to stop with software and phone cards. Not so far in the future, the Internet will become a well-traveled avenue of commerce.

Theft on the Infohighway

October 1994 Hackers bust into computers at Florida State University and upload pirated versions of a dozen new programs, including Windows 95.

September 1994 Max Louarn, 22, is arrested for masterminding a plot to sell 140,000 pilfered phone-card numbers in the United States and abroad via computer bulletin boards. He later pleads guilty.

August 1994 Richard D. Kenadek, 43, is indicted for reportedly allowing pirated programs to be traded on his bulletin board, Davey Jones Locker.

April 1994 David LaMacchia, 20 and a student at MIT, is indicted for conspiracy to commit wire fraud, after allegedly permitting the distribution of more than $1 million worth of copyrighted software over the Internet.

December 1993 Playboy wins its suit against George Frena, who allowed copyrighted nude photos to be distributed on his computer billboard.

November 1993 Frank Music Corp. files a class-action suit against CompuServe for allegedly permitting subscribers to post more than 500 copyrighted songs, including Frank's "Unchained Melody."

Already retailers are using it to hawk everything from computer parts to flowers and teddy bears. Since anyone with a modem and a computer can go into business, the possibilities for abuse are almost endless. *Playboy* magazine, for instance, has sued half a dozen bulletin boards over the last two years for baring its Bunny pix. CompuServe, the major online information service, has been sued by 140 music publishers for allegedly permitting subscribers to download popular songs. Cybertheft as yet accounts for an indiscernible share of the $400 million lost annually to record piracy, but that's partly because of technical difficulties. Taping a popular single takes only a few moments; pirating a digital version can require anywhere from 30 minutes to several hours, depending on your equipment. But that will change as digital transmission technology improves. Before long, says David Leibowitz at the Recording Industry Association of America, "you will be able to download an entire album in seconds." Then, watch out.

Businesses are moving to protect themselves. Perhaps because it's so obviously part of a trend, the Florida break-in provoked an unusually tough response. Microsoft posted a $10,000 bounty for information leading to the arrest and conviction of the perpetrators. DeScribe Inc., a computer-software company whose new word-processing program was found among the pirated software, offered a $20,000 reward. IBM is investigating, in cooperation with federal authorities. But tracking the cybercrooks won't be easy. The Internet is a chaotic place. Hackers go from computer to computer, vaulting borders and leaving few traces. Before entering a computer at Florida State University, they might pass through another computer in Finland, say, that strips any names or addresses from their communications. Even when uncovered, pirates can disavow wrongdoing. For instance, many of the Florida intruders hailed from Asia, where piracy is not always considered a crime.

Legality collides with practicality when battling cybertheft. As part of its plan for a "national information infrastructure," the Clinton administration proposes tightening the federal Copyright Act to explicitly cover transmissions over the Internet. New laws would also make it clear that electronic property rights are as sacrosanct as any other. But to what effect? The rules of commerce and fair play that govern real-world business are alien to the anarchic "Wild West" culture of the Internet. There, the prevailing ethic is "shareware." Knowledge is to be disseminated. Anything found in etherspace is widely considered to be "mine" as well as "yours"—"ours," in other words. Digital socialism rules the Net, not copyrightable capitalism. Few Interneters would disagree that stealing and reselling software or credit cards is wrong. But fewer still would feel guilty about copying the latest game version of Doom, or some such, rather than forking out $39.95. Unfortunately, that often admirable ethos makes it easier for genuine crooks to perpetrate—and justify—their crimes.

Peter H. Lewis

No More "Anything Goes": Cyberspace Gets Censors

reedom of expression has always been the rule in the fast-growing web of public and private computer networks known as cyberspace. But even as thousands of Americans each week join the several million who use computer networks to share ideas and "chat" with others, the companies that control the networks and sometimes individual users are beginning to play the role as censor.

Earlier this month, the American Online network shut several feminist discussion forums, saying it was concerned that the subject matter might be inappropriate for young girls who would see the word "girl" in the forum's headline and "go in there looking for information about their Barbies," a spokeswoman said.

Users on other networks have been banished, censored or censured this year for the widespread posting of messages like "Jesus Is Coming," "Your Armenian Grandfathers Are Guilty of Genocide." The third case brought to cyberspace the long conflict between Turks and Armenians, and, according to some network users, produced a counterattack by an unknown Armenian sympathizer who programmed his or her computer to sniff out any message on the system containing the word "turkey" and substitute "genocide," even in forums discussing Thanksgiving meals.

On Prodigy, the country's largest commercial network, with more than two million users, supervisors have been expanding the use of what they call "George Carlin software," which finds messages with certain objectionable words and warns those who sent them to erase them or their messages will be censored. The nickname refers to the comedian who does a monologue about censorship in broadcasting titled "Seven Dirty Words." Prodigy's list of offending words has grown into the dozens.

A University of Florida student's access to the giant network known as the Internet was revoked this month after the student used university computers to repeatedly post copies of a political polemic. Outrage and calls for censorship arose among users of the Usenet network after racist messages appeared on forums set up to discuss O. J. Simpson's arrest on murder charges.

Then there is the case of Arnt Gulbrandsen, a 25-year-old Norwegian computer programmer who was enraged earlier this month when he saw that a Phoenix law firm, Canter & Siegel, was once again advertising its services over the worldwide Usenet computer network, despite pleas from many users to cease and desist. From his keyboard halfway around the world, Mr. Gulbrandsen launched the electronic equivalent of a Patriot missile: each time the law firm sent out an electronic advertisement, his computer automatically sent out a message that caused the network system to intercept and destroy the firm's transmissions.

"I was somewhat surprised that I only got positive feedback," Mr. Gulbrandsen said. "I expected more than a little 'flaming,'" as personal attacks and complaints, transmitted electronically, are known among networks users.

■ TROUBLESOME ISSUES

Even longtime networks users who applaud such a use of what they call a "cancelbot" acknowledge that the situation raises broad and troubling issues about censorship in cyberspace.

But because the wide use of computer networks is so new, no established case law moderates the debate over censorship in such cases, the way it does for publishing, broadcasting and speech.

For some networks, the legal questions hinge on whether they are to be considered common carriers, much like telephone companies or even bookstores, which are not responsible for the content of the messages they carry, or to be regarded as private networks that have the right to establish and enforce standards of language and ethics for all users.

In recent court cases involving the computer network Compuserve, a division of the H&R Block Company, the network has argued that it is protected as a common carrier. But that raises the question of whether Compuserve has been right to enforce its own standards for content.

■ NO ONE SOURCE

The responsibility for any censorship rests not with a central authority but with the administrators of the thousands of private and public computer networks. Many of those administrators offer guidelines for users, but enforcement is usually left to peer pressure—criticism from others using the network. While some networks will act to stop a potentially objectionable message before it is distributed, others will take action only after a message is posted and users complain about it.

Because of their international nature, the networks operate outside the framework of First Amendment protections familiar to most Americans. "What First Amendment?" Wolfgang Schelongowski, a Usenet user in Bochum, Germany, transmitted during a network debate on such issues. "No such thing here, or in any country besides the U.S.A."

Laurence A. Canter and Martha S. Siegel, the lawyers who are Mr. Gulbrandsen's target, said his actions amounted to censorship. "What does this mean, that everyone on Usenet will have to meet the standards of this Gulbrandsen guy or he will take it upon himself to cancel their messages?" Ms. Siegel asked. "If anything is going to bring down the net, it'll be things like robot cancelers and self-styled censors."

The conflict is most intense on Usenet, a cooperative anarchy of private and public computers comprising more than 8,000 discussion groups, used by an estimated six million people worldwide. Usenet is most commonly reached through the Internet, an even larger web that links some 25 million people worldwide.

■ A SHIFT IN PURPOSE

The technology that enables messages to be canceled was built into Usenet originally to allow an individual to withdraw a message he or she had written. As a safeguard, the command was designed so that only the writer could withdraw a message. In practice, however, canceling was occasionally used by computer system administrators to remove offensive or outdated messages.

Canceling someone else's message is controversial, said Ron Newman, a programmer who helped develop a technology used on many Internet computers, "because the person who issues the cancel message has to write a message claiming, falsely, to be the sender of the original message." In other words, the canceler must commit electronic forgery.

"The cancel facility was not intended to be used this way, and it could easily be abused by people who want to set themselves up as censors," Mr. Newman said.

Mr. Gulbrandsen and Internet technical experts acknowledged that it would be easy to create "cancelbots" that wipe out messages from a given company, or even a certain country.

But even with its potential for abuse, Mr. Gulbrandsen's action against Canter & Siegel seems to have met with popular support among users, many of whom object to advertising on the network. "C. & S. illustrates a potential vulnerability of the net," Mike Godwin, legal counsel for the Electronic Frontier Foundation, a lobbying group in Washington, said of the law firm. "They are pushing it to the extreme. If everyone did what they did," the system would be clogged with unwanted messages and there would be "nothing worth reading."

Mr. Godwin added: "The EFF believes very strongly that censorship is the wrong way to approach net problems. But we also believe there are rules of the road that limit what you can do on the net, rules that don't amount to censorship."

Daniel P. Dern of Newton Center, Mass., author of *The Internet Guide for New Users,* said even well-intentioned action could drift into censorship.

"There is a danger of the cancel wars shifting from inappropriate resource use to canceling based on 'I don't like your opinion,'" he said. "At what point does somebody say, 'I don't like this person, and I'm going to cancel them'?"

To most users of the Internet, unbridled freedom, even anarchy, are guiding principles.

"Usenet has principles, it has a social structure, but it has no government," said Brad Templeton, publisher at the Clarinet Communications Corporation, an electronic-newspaper company in San Jose, California. "People who study such things have said that a real anarchy, like a commune, starts breaking down at about 100 people. Somehow we have managed to grow a community of several million people. Now people see the fringes of that system breaking down. Is the answer to impose a government, or is the answer to be found within the system? The idea of a cancelbot is actually something working within the system."

Hacker's Manifesto, or
The Conscience of a Hacker

The following was written
shortly after my arrest,
January 8, 1986

Another one got caught today, it's all over the papers. "Teenager Arrested in Computer Crime Scandal", "Hacker Arrested after Bank Tampering"...

Damn kids. They're all alike.

But did you, in your three-piece psychology and 1950's technobrain, ever take a look behind the eyes of the hacker? Did you ever wonder what made him tick, what forces shaped him, what may have molded him?

I am a hacker, enter my world...

Mine is a world that begins with school... I'm smarter than most of the other kids, this crap they teach us bores me...

Damn underachiever. They're all alike.

I'm in junior high or high school. I've listened to teachers explain for the fifteenth time how to reduce a fraction. I understand it. "No, Ms. Smith, I didn't show my work. I did it in my head..."

Damn kid. Probably copied it. They're all alike.

I made a discovery today. I found a computer. Wait a second, this is cool. It does what I want it to. If it makes a mistake, it's because I screwed it up. Not because it doesn't like me...

Or feels threatened by me...

Or thinks I'm a smart ass...

Or doesn't like teaching and shouldn't be here...

Damn kid. All he does is play games. They're all alike.

And then it happened... a door opened to a world... rushing through the phone line like heroin through an addict's veins, an electronic pulse is sent out, a refuge from the day-to-day incompetencies is sought... a board is found.

"This is it... this is where I belong..."

I know everyone here... even if I've never met them, never talked to them, may never hear from them again... I know you all...

Damn kid. Tying up the phone line again. They're all alike...

You bet your ass we're all alike . . . we've been spoon-fed baby food at school when we hungered for steak . . . the bits of meat that you did let slip through were pre-chewed and tasteless. We've been dominated by sadists, or ignored by the apathetic. The few that had something to teach found us willing pupils, but those few are like drops of water in the desert.

This is our world now . . . the world of the electron and the switch, the beauty of the baud. We make use of a service already existing without paying for what could be dirt-cheap if it wasn't run by profiteering gluttons, and you call us criminals. We explore . . . and you call us criminals. We seek after knowledge . . . and you call us criminals. We exist without skin color, without nationality, without religious bias . . . and you call us criminals. You build atomic bombs, you wage wars, you murder, cheat, and lie to us and try to make us believe it's for our own good, yet we're the criminals.

Yes, I am a criminal. My crime is that of curiosity. My crime is that of judging people by what they say and think, not what they look like. My crime is that of outsmarting you, something that you will never forgive me for.

I am a hacker, and this is my manifesto. You may stop this individual, but you can't stop us all . . . after all, we're all alike.

—The Mentor

Is Computer Hacking a Crime?

he image of the computer hacker drifted into public awareness in the mid-Seventies, when reports of Chinese-food-consuming geniuses working compulsively at keyboards began to issue from MIT. Over time, several of these impresarios entered commerce, and the public's impression of hackers changed: They were no longer nerds but young, millionaire entrepreneurs.

The most recent news reports have given the term a more felonious connotation. Early this year, a graduate student named Robert Morris, Jr. went on trial for releasing a computer program known as a worm into the vast Internet system, halting more than 6,000 computers. The subsequent public debate ranged from the matter of proper punishment for a mischievous kid to the issue of our rapidly changing notion of what constitutes free speech—or property—in an age of modems and data bases. In order to allow hackers to speak for themselves, *Harper's Magazine* recently organized an electronic discussion and asked some of the nation's best hackers to "log on," discuss the protean notions of contemporary speech, and explain what their powers and talents are.

The following forum is based on a discussion held on the WELL, a computer bulletin-board system based in Sausalito, California. The forum is the result of a gradual accretion of arguments as the participants—located throughout the country—opined and reacted over an eleven-day period. *Harper's Magazine* senior editor Jack Hitt and assistant editor Paul Tough served as moderators.

ADELAIDE is a pseudonym for a former hacker who has sold his soul to the corporate state as a computer programmer.

BARLOW is John Perry Barlow, a retired cattle rancher, a former Republican county chairman, and a lyricist for the Grateful Dead, who currently is writing a book on computers and consciousness entitled *Everything We Know Is Wrong.*

BLUEFIRE is Dr. Robert Jacobson, associate director of the Human Interface Technology Laboratory at the University of Washington and a former information-policy analyst with the California legislature.

BRAND is Russell Brand, a senior computer scientist with Reasoning Systems, in Palo Alto, California.

CLIFF is Clifford Stoll, the astronomer who caught a spy in a military computer network and recently published an account of his investigation entitled *The Cuckoo's Egg.*

DAVE is Dave Hughes, a retired West Pointer who currently operates his own political bulletin board.

DRAKE is Frank Drake, a computer-science student at a West Coast university and the editor of *W.O.R.M.,* a cyberpunk magazine.

EDDIE JOE HOMEBOY is a pseudonym for a professional software engineer who has worked at Lucasfilm, Pyramid Technology, Apple Computer, and Autodesk.

EMMANUEL GOLDSTEIN is the editor of 2600, the "hacker's quarterly."

HANK is Hank Roberts, who builds mobiles, flies hang gliders, and proofreads for the *Whole Earth Catalog.*

JIMG is Jim Gasperini, the author, with TRANS Fiction Systems, of Hidden Agenda, a computer game that simulates political conflict in Central America.

JRC is Jon Carroll, daily columnist for the *San Francisco Chronicle* and writer-in-residence for the Pickle Family Circus, a national traveling circus troupe based in San Francisco.

KK is Kevin Kelly, editor of the *Whole Earth Review* and a cofounder of the Hacker's Conference.

LEE is Lee Felsenstein, who designed the Osborne-1 computer and cofounded the Homebrew Computer Club.

MANDEL is Tom Mandel, a professional futurist and an organizer of the Hacker's Conference.

RH is Robert Horvitz, Washington correspondent for the *Whole Earth Review.*

RMS is Richard Stallman, founder of the Free Software Foundation.

TENNEY is Glenn Tenney, an independent-systems architect and an organizer of the Hacker's Conference.

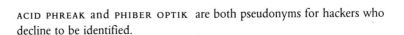

ACID PHREAK and PHIBER OPTIK are both pseudonyms for hackers who decline to be identified.

■ THE DIGITAL FRONTIER

HARPER'S [Day 1, 9:00 A.M.]: When the computer was young, the word *hacking* was used to describe the work of brilliant students who explored and expanded the uses to which this new technology might be employed. There was even talk of a "hacker ethic." Somehow, in the succeeding years, the word has taken on dark connotations, suggesting the actions of a criminal. What is the hacker ethic, and does it survive?

ADELAIDE [Day 1, 9:25 A.M.]: The hacker ethic survives, and it is a fraud. It survives in anyone excited by technology's power to turn many small, insignificant things into one vast, beautiful thing. It is a fraud because there is nothing magical about computers that causes a user to undergo religious conversion and devote himself to the public good. Early automobile inventors were hackers too. At first the elite drove in luxury. Later practically everyone had a car. Now we have traffic jams, drunk drivers, air pollution, and suburban sprawl. The old magic of an automobile occasionally surfaces, but we possess no delusions that it automatically invades the consciousness of anyone who sits behind the wheel. Computers are power, and direct contact with power can bring out the best or the worst in a person. It's tempting to think that everyone exposed to the technology will be grandly inspired, but, alas, it just ain't so.

BRAND [Day 1, 9:54 A.M.]: The hacker ethic involves several things. One is avoiding waste; insisting on using idle computer power—often hacking into a system to do so, while taking the greatest precautions not to damage the system. A second goal of many hackers is the free exchange of technical information. These hackers feel that patent and copyright restrictions slow down technological advances. A third goal is the advancement of human knowledge for its own sake. Often this approach is unconventional. People we call crackers often explore systems and do mischief. They are called hackers by the press, which doesn't understand the issues.

KK [Day 1, 11:19 A.M.]: The hacker ethic went unnoticed early on because the explorations of basement tinkerers were very local. Once we all became connected, the work of these investigators rippled through the world. Today the hacking spirit is alive and kicking in video, satellite TV, and radio. In some fields they are called chippers, because they modify and peddle altered chips. Everything that was once said about "phone phreaks" can be said about them too.

DAVE [Day 1, 11:29 A.M.]: Bah. Too academic. Hackers hack. Because they want to. Not for any higher purpose. Hacking is not dead and won't be as long as teenagers get their hands on the tools. There is a hacker born every minute.

ADELAIDE [Day 1, 11:42 A.M.]: Don't forget ego. People break into computers because it's fun and it makes them feel powerful.

BARLOW [Day 1, 11:54 A.M.]: Hackers hack. Yeah, right, but what's more to the point is that humans hack and always have. Far more than just opposable thumbs, upright posture, or excess cranial capacity, human beings are set apart from all other species by an itch, a hard-wired dissatisfaction. Computer hacking is just the latest in a series of quests that started with fire hacking. Hacking is also a collective enterprise. It brings to our joint endeavors the simultaneity that other collective organisms—ant colonies, Canada geese—take for granted. This is important, because combined with our itch to probe is a need to *connect.* Humans miss the almost telepathic connectedness that I've observed in other herding mammals. And we want it back. Ironically, the solitary sociopath and his 3:00 A.M. endeavors hold the most promise for delivering species reunion.

EDDIE JOE HOMEBOY [Day 1, 4:44 P.M.]: Hacking really took hold with the advent of the personal computer, which freed programmers from having to use a big time-sharing system. A hacker could sit in the privacy of his home and hack to his heart's and head's content.

LEE [Day 1, 5:17 P.M.]: "Angelheaded hipsters burning for the ancient heavenly connection to the starry dynamo in the machinery of night" (Allen Ginsberg, "Howl"). I still get an endorphin rush when I go on a design run—my mind out over the edge, groping for possibilities that can be sensed when various parts are held in juxtaposition with a view toward creating a whole object: straining to get through the epsilon-wide crack between What Is and What Could Be. Somewhere there's the Dynamo of Night, the ultra-mechanism waiting to be dreamed, that we'll never get to in actuality (think what it would *weigh!*) but that's present somehow in the vicinity of those mental wrestling matches. When I reemerge into the light of another day with the design on paper—and with the knowledge that if it ever gets built, things will never be the same again—I know I've been where artists go. That's hacking to me: to transcend custom and to engage in creativity for its own sake, but also to create objective effects. I've been around long enough to see the greed creeps take up the unattended reins of power and shut down most of the creativity that put them where they are. But I've also seen things change, against the best efforts of a stupidly run industry. We cracked the egg out from under the Computer Priesthood, and now everyone can have omelets.

RMS [Day 1, 5:19 P.M.]: The media and the courts are spreading a certain image of hackers. It's important for us not to be shaped by that image. But there are two ways that it can happen. One way is for hackers to become part of the security-maintenance establishment. The other, more subtle, way is for a hacker to become the security-breaking phreak the media portray. By shaping ourselves into the enemy of the establishment, we uphold the establishment. But there's nothing wrong with breaking security if you're accomplishing something useful. It's like picking a lock on a tool cabinet to get a screwdriver to fix your radio. As long as you put the screwdriver back, what harm does it do?

ACID PHREAK [Day 1, 6:34 P.M.]: There is no one hacker ethic. Everyone has his own. To say that we all think the same way is preposterous. The hacker of old sought to find what the computer itself could do. There was nothing illegal about that. Today, hackers and phreaks are drawn to *specific,* often corporate, systems. It's no wonder everyone on the other side is getting mad. We're always one step ahead. We were back then, and we are now.

CLIFF [Day 1, 8:38 P.M.]: RMS said, "There's nothing wrong with breaking security if you're accomplishing something useful." Huh? How about, There's nothing wrong with entering a neighbor's house if you're accomplishing something useful, just as long as you clean up after yourself. Does my personal privacy mean anything? Should my personal letters and data be open to anyone who knows how to crack passwords? If not my property, then how about a bank's? Should my credit history be available to anyone who can find a back door to the private computers of TRW, the firm that tracks people's credit histories? How about a list of AIDS patients from a hospital's data bank? Or next week's prime interest rate from a computer at the Treasury Department?

A Hacker's Lexicon

Back door: A point of entry into a computer system—often installed there by the original programmer—that provides secret access.

Bomb: A destructive computer program, which, when activated, destroys the files in a computer system.

Chipper: A hacker who specializes in changing the programming instructions of computer chips.

Cracker: A hacker who breaks illegally into computer systems and creates mischief; often used pejoratively. The original meaning of *cracker* was narrower, describing those who decoded copyright-protection schemes on commercial software products either to redis-tribute the products or to modify them; sometimes known as a software pirate.

Hacker: Originally, a compulsive computer programmer. The word has evolved in meaning over the years. Among computer users, *hacker* carries a positive connotation, meaning anyone who creatively explores the operations of computer systems. Recently, it has taken on a negative connotation, primarily through confusion with *cracker.*

Phone phreak: One who explores the operations of the phone system, often with the intent of making free phone calls.

Social engineering: A nontech-nical means of gaining informa-tion simply by persuading people to hand it over. If a hacker wished to gain access to a computer system, for example, an act of *social engineering* might be to contact a system operator and to convince him or her that the hacker is a legitimate user in need of a pass-word; more colloquially, a con job.

Virus: A program that, having been introduced into a system, replicates itself and attaches itself to other programs, often with a variety of mischievous effects.

Worm: A destructive program that, when activated, fills a computer system with self-replicating information, clogging the system so that its operations are severely slowed, sometimes stopped.

BLUEFIRE [Day 1, 9:20 P.M.]: Computers are everywhere, and they link us together into a vast social "cybernetia." The grand skills of the hackers, formidable though they may have been, are incapable of subverting this automated social order. The networks in which we survive are more than copper wire and radio waves: They are *the* social organization. For every hacker in revolt, busting through a security code, ten thousand people are being wired up with automatic call-identification and credit-checking machines. Long live the Computer Revolution, which died aborning.

JRC [Day 1, 10:28 P.M.]: We have two different definitions here. One speaks of a tinkerer's ecstasy, an ecstasy that is hard to maintain in the corporate world but is nevertheless at the heart of Why Hackers Hack. The second is political, and it has to do with the free flow of information. Information should flow more freely (how freely is being debated), and the hacker can make it happen because the hacker knows how to undam the pipes. This makes the hacker ethic—of necessity—antiauthoritarian.

EMMANUEL GOLDSTEIN [Day 2, 2:41 A.M.]: It's meaningless what we call ourselves: hackers, crackers, techno-rats. We're individuals who happen to play with high tech. There is no *hacker community* in the traditional sense of the term. There are no leaders and no agenda. We're just individuals out exploring.

BRAND [Day 2, 9:02 A.M.]: There are two issues: invariance and privacy. Invariance is the art of leaving things as you found them. If someone used my house for the day and left everything as he found it so that there was *no way* to tell he had been there, I would see no problem. With a well-run computer system, we can assure invariance. Without this assurance we must fear that the person picking the lock to get the screwdriver will break the lock, the screwdriver, or both. Privacy is more complicated. I want my medical records, employment records, and letters to *The New Republic* private because I fear that someone will do something with the information that is against my interests. If I could trust people not to do bad things with information, I would not need to hide it. Rather than preventing the "theft" of this data, we should prohibit its collection in the first place.

HOMEBOY [Day 2, 9:37 A.M.]: Are crackers really working for the free flow of information? Or are they unpaid tools of the establishment, identifying the holes in the institutional dike so that they can be plugged by the authorities, only to be tossed in jail or exiled?

DRAKE [Day 2, 10:54 A.M.]: There is an unchallenged assumption that crackers have some political motivation. Earlier, crackers were portrayed as failed revolutionaries; now Homeboy suggests that crackers may be tools of the establishment. These ideas about crackers are based on earlier experiences with subcultures (beats, hippies, yippies). Actually, the contemporary cracker is often middle-class and doesn't really distance himself from the "establishment." While there are some anarcho-crackers, there are even more right-wing crackers. The hacker ethic crosses political boundaries.

MANDEL [Day 2, 11:01 A.M.]: The data on crackers suggests that they are either juvenile delinquents or plain criminals.

BARLOW [Day 2, 11:34 A.M.]: I would far rather have *everyone* know my most intimate secrets than to have noncontextual snippits of them "owned" by TRW and the FBI—and withheld from me! Any cracker who is entertained by peeping into my electronic window is welcome to the view. Any institution that makes money selling rumors of my peccadilloes is stealing from me. Anybody who wants to inhibit that theft with electronic mischief has my complete support. Power to the techno-rats!

EMMANUEL [Day 2, 7:09 P.M.]: Calling someone on the phone is the equivalent of knocking on that person's door, right? Wrong! When someone answers the phone, you are *inside* the home. You have already been *let in.* The same with an answering machine, or a personal computer, if it picks up the phone. It is wrong to violate a person's privacy, but electronic rummaging is not the same as breaking and entering. The key here is that most people are unaware of *how easy it is* for others to invade their electronic privacy and see credit reports, phone bills, FBI files, Social Security reports. The public is grossly underinformed, and that's what must be fixed if hackers are to be thwarted. If we had an educated public, though, perhaps the huge—and now common—data bases would never have been allowed to exist. Hackers have become scapegoats: We discover the gaping holes in the system and then get blamed for the flaws.

HOMEBOY [Day 2, 7:41 P.M.]: Large, insular, undemocratic governments and institutions need scapegoats. It's the first step down the road to fascism. *That's* where hackers play into the hands of the establishment.

DAVE [Day 2, 7:55 P.M.]: If the real criminals are those who leave gaping holes in their systems, then the real criminals in house burglaries are those who leave their windows unlatched. Right? Hardly. And Emmanuel's analogy to a phone being answered doesn't hold either. There is no security protection in making a phone call. A computer system has a *password,* implying a desire for security. Breaking into a poorly protected house is still burglary.

CLIFF [Day 2, 9:06 P.M.]: Was there a hacker's ethic and does it survive? More appropriately, was there a vandal's ethic and does it survive? As long as there are communities, someone will violate the trust that binds them. Once, our computers were isolated, much as eighteenth-century villages were. Little was exchanged, and each developed independently. Now we've built far-flung electronic neighborhoods. These communities are built on trust: people believing that everyone profits by sharing resources. Sure enough, vandals crept in, breaking into systems, spreading viruses, pirating software, and destroying people's work. "It's okay," they say. "I can break into a system because I'm a hacker." Give me a break!

BARLOW [Day 2, 10:41 P.M.]: I live in a small town. I don't have a key to my house. Am I asking for it? I think not. Among the juvenile delinquents in my town, there does exist a vandal's ethic. I know because I once was one. In a real community, part of a kid's rite of passage is discovering what walls can be breached. Driving 110 miles per hour on Main Street is a common symptom of rural adolescence, publicly denounced but privately understood. Many teenagers die in this quest—two just the night before last—but it is basic to our culture. Even rebellious kids understand that risk to one's safety is one thing, wanton vandalism or theft is another. As a result, almost no one locks anything here. In fact, a security system is an affront to a teenage psyche. While a kid might be dissuaded by conscience, he will regard a barricade as an insult and a challenge. So the CEOs who are moving here (the emperor of PepsiCo and the secretary of state among them) soon discover that over the winter people break into their protected mansions just to hang out. When systems are open, the community prospers, and teenage miscreants are satisfied to risk their own lives and little else. When the social contract is enforced by security, the native freedom of the adolescent soul will rise up to challenge it in direct proportion to its imposition.

HANK [Day 2, 11:23 P.M.]: Barlow, the small town I grew up in was much like yours—until two interstate highways crossed nearby. The open-door style changed in one, hard summer because our whole *town* became unlocked. I think Cliff's community is analogous to my little town—confronted not by a new locked-up neighbor who poses a challenge to the local kids but by a sudden, permanent opening up of the community to many faceless outsiders who owe the town no allegiance.

EMMANUEL [Day 3, 1:33 A.M.]: Sorry, I don't buy Dave's unlatched-window analogy. A hacker who wanders into a system with the ease that it's done today is, in my analogy, walking into a house without walls—and with a cloaking device! Any good hacker can make himself invisible. If housebreaking were this easy, people would be enraged. But we're missing the point. I'm not referring to accessing a PC in someone's bedroom but about accessing credit reports, government files, motor vehicle records, and the megabytes of data piling up on each of us. Thousands of people legally can see and use this ever-growing mountain of data, much of it erroneous. Whose rights are we violating when we peruse a file? Those of the person we look up? He doesn't even know that information exists, that it was compiled without his consent, and that it's not his property anymore! The invasion of privacy took place long before the hacker ever arrived. The only way to find out how such a system works is to break the rules. It's not what hackers do that will lead us into a state of constant surveillance; it's allowing the authorities to impose on us a state of mock crisis.

MANDEL [Day 3, 9:27 A.M.]: Note that the word *crime* has no fixed reference in our discussion. Until recently, breaking into government computer systems wasn't a crime; now it is. In fact, there is some debate, to be resolved in the courts, whether what Robert Morris, Jr. did was actually a crime [see "A Brief History of Hacking"]. *Crime* gets redefined all the time. Offend enough people or institutions and, lo and behold, someone will pass a law. That is partly what is going on now: Hackers are pushing buttons, becoming more visible, and that inevitably means more laws and more crimes.

ADELAIDE [Day 3, 9:42 A.M.]: Every practitioner of these arts knows that at minimum he is trespassing. The English "country traveler ethic" applies: The hiker is always ethical enough to close the pasture gates behind him so that no sheep escape during his pastoral stroll through someone else's property. The problem is that what some see as gentle trespassing others see as theft of service, invasion of privacy, threat to national security—take your pick.

BARLOW [Day 3, 2:38 P.M.]: I regard the *existence* of proprietary data about me to be theft—not just in the legal sense but in a faintly metaphysical one, rather like the belief among aborigines that a photograph steals the soul. The crackers who maintain access to that data are, at this level, liberators. Their incursions are the only way to keep the system honest.

"The virus could become an instrument of freedom. At the risk of sounding like some digital posse comitatus, I say: Fear the Government That Fears Your Computer."

RMS [Day 3, 2:48 P.M.]: Recently, a tough anti-hacker measure was proposed in England. In *The Economist* I saw a wise response, arguing that it was silly to treat an action as worse when it involves a computer than when it does not. They noted, for example, that physical trespassing was considered a civil affair, not a criminal one, and said that computer trespassing should be treated likewise. Unfortunately, the U.S. government was not so wise.

BARLOW [Day 3, 3:23 P.M.]: The idea that a crime is worse if a computer is involved relates to the gathering governmental perception that computer viruses and guns may be related. I know that sounds absurd, but they have more in common than one might think. For all its natural sociopathy, the virus is not without philosophical potency—like a gun. Here in Wyoming guns are part of the furniture. Only recently have I observed an awareness of their political content. After a lot of frothing about prying cold, dead fingers from triggers, the sentiment was finally distilled to a bumper sticker I saw on a pickup the other day: "Fear the Government That Fears Your Gun." Now I've read too much Gandhi to buy that line without misgivings, but it would be hard to argue that Tiananmen Square could have been inflicted on a populace capable of shooting back. I don't wholeheartedly defend computer viruses, but one must consider their increasingly robust deterrent potential. Before it's over, the War on Drugs could easily turn into an Armageddon between those who love liberty and those who crave certainty, providing just the excuse the control freaks have been waiting for to rid America of all that constitutional molly-coddling called the Bill of Rights. Should that come to pass, I will want to use every available method to vex and confuse the eyes and ears of surveillance. The virus could become the necessary instrument of our freedom. At the risk of sounding like some digital *posse comitatus,* I say: Fear the Government That Fears Your Computer.

TENNEY [Day 3, 4:41 P.M.]: Computer-related crimes are more feared because they are performed remotely—a crime can be committed in New York by someone in Los Angeles—and by people not normally viewed as being criminals—by teenagers who don't look like delinquents. They're very smart nerds, and they don't look like Chicago gangsters packing heat.

BARLOW [Day 4, 12:12 A.M.]: People know so little of these things that they endow computers and the people who *do* understand them with powers neither possesses. If America has a religion, its ark is the computer and its covenant is the belief that Science Knows. We are mucking around in the temple, guys. It's a good way to catch hell.

DAVE [Day 4, 9:18 A.M.]: Computers *are* the new American religion. The public is in awe of—and fears—the mysteries and the high priests who tend them. And the public reacts just as it always has when faced with fear of the unknown—punishment, burning at the stake. Hackers are like the early Christians. When caught, they will be thrown to the lions before the Roman establishment: This year the mob will cheer madly as Robert Morris is devoured.

KK [Day 6, 11:37 A.M.]: The crackers here suggest that they crack into systems with poor security *because* the security is poor. Do more sophisticated security precautions diminish the need to crack the system or increase it?

ACID [Day 6, 1:20 P.M.]: If there was a system that we knew was uncrackable, we wouldn't even try to crack it. On the other hand, if some organization boasted that its system was impenetrable and we knew that was media hype, I think it would be safe to say we'd have to "enlighten" them.

EMMANUEL [Day 6, 2:49 P.M.]: Why do we insist on cracking systems? The more people ask those kinds of questions, the more I want to get in! Forbid access and the demand for access increases. For the most part, it's simply a mission of exploration. In the words of the new captain of the starship *Enterprise,* Jean-Luc Picard, "Let's see what's out there!"

BARLOW [Day 6, 4:34 P.M.]: Tell us, Acid, *is* there a system that you know to be uncrackable to the point where everyone's given up?

ACID [Day 6, 8:29 P.M.]: CICIMS is pretty tough.

PHIBER OPTIK [Day 7, 2:36 P.M.]: Really? CICIMS is a system used by Bell operating companies. The entire security system was changed after myself and a friend must have been noticed in it. For the entire United States, there is only one such system, located in Indiana. The new security scheme is flawless *in itself,* and there is no chance of "social engineering," i.e., bullshitting someone inside the system into telling you what the passwords are. The system works like this: You log on with the proper account and password; then, depending on who you are, the system asks at random three of ten questions that are unique to each user. But the system *can* be compromised by entering forwarding instructions into the phone company's switch for that exchange, thereby intercepting every phone call that comes in to the system over a designated period of time and connecting the call to your computer. If you are familiar with the security layout, you can emulate its appearance and fool the caller into giving you the answers to his questions. Then you call the system yourself and use those answers to get in. There are other ways of doing it as well.

BLUEFIRE [Day 7, 11:53 P.M.]: I can't stand it! Who do you think pays for the security that the telephone companies must maintain to fend off illegal use? I bet it costs the ratepayers around $10 million for this little extravaganza. The cracker circus isn't harmless at all, unless you don't mind paying for other people's entertainment. Hackers who have contributed to the social welfare should be recognized. But cracking is something else—namely, fun at someone else's expense—and it ain't the folks who own the phone companies who pay; it's us, me and you.

BARLOW [Day 8, 7:35 A.M.]: I am becoming increasingly irritated at this idea that you guys are exacting vengeance for the sin of openness. You seem to argue that if a system is dumb enough to be open, it is your moral duty to violate it. Does the fact that I've never locked my house—even when I was away for months at a time—mean that someone should come in and teach me a good lesson?

ACID [Day 8, 3:23 P.M.]: Barlow, you leave the door open to your house? Where do you live?

BARLOW [Day 8, 10:11 P.M.]: Acid, my house is at 372 North Franklin Street in Pinedale, Wyoming. Heading north on Franklin, go about two blocks off the main drag before you run into a hay meadow on the left. I'm the last house before the field. The computer is always on. But do you really mean to imply what you did with that question? Are you merely a sneak looking for easy places to violate? You disappoint me, pal. For all your James Dean-on-Silicon rhetoric, you're not a cyberpunk. You're just a punk.

EMMANUEL [Day 9, 12:55 A.M.]: No offense, Barlow, but your house analogy doesn't stand up, because your house is far less interesting than a Defense Department computer. For the most part, hackers don't mess with individuals. Maybe we feel sorry for them; maybe they're boring. Institutions are where the action is, because they are compiling this mountain of data—without your consent. Hackers are not guardian angels, but if you think we're what's wrong

A Brief History of Hacking

September 1970 John Draper takes as his alias the name Captain Crunch after he discovers that the toy whistle found in the cereal of the same name perfectly simulates the tone necessary to make free phone calls.

March 1975 The Homebrew Computer Club, an early group of computer hackers, holds its first meeting in Menlo Park, California.

July 1976 Homebrew members Steve Wozniak, twenty-six, and Steve Jobs, twenty-one, working out of a garage, begin selling the first personal computer, known as the Apple.

June 1980 In one week, errors in the computer system operating the U.S. air-defense network cause two separate false reports of Soviet missile launches, each prompting an increased state of nuclear readiness.

December 1982 Sales of Apple personal computers top one billion dollars per year.

November 1984 Steven Levy's book *Hackers* is published, popu-larizing the concept of the "hacker ethic": that "access to computers, and anything that might teach you something about the way the world works, should be unlimited and total." The book inspires the first Hacker's Conference, held that month.

January 1986 The "Pakistani Brain" virus, created by a software distributor in Lahore, Pakistan, infects IBM computers around the world, erasing data tiles.

June 1986 The U.S. Office of Technology Assessment warns that massive, cross-indexed government computer records have become a "de facto national data base containing personal information on most Americans."

March 1987 William Gates, a Harvard dropout who founded Microsoft Corporation, becomes a billionaire.

November 1988 More than 6,000 computers linked by the nationwide Internet computer network are infected by a destructive computer program known as a worm and are crippled for two days. The worm is traced to Robert Morris, Jr., a twenty-four-year-old Cornell University graduate student.

December 1988 A federal grand jury charges Kevin Mitnick, twenty-five, with stealing computer programs over telephone lines. Mitnick is held without bail and forbidden access to any telephones without supervision.

March 1989 Three West German hackers are arrested for entering thirty sensitive military computers using home computers and modems. The arrests follow a three-year investigation by Clifford Stoll, an astronomer at the Lawrence Berkeley Laboratory who began tracing the hackers after finding a seventy-five-cent billing error in the lab's computer system.

January 1990 Robert Morris, Jr. goes on trial in Syracuse, New York, for designing and releasing the Internet worm. Convicted, he faces up to five years in prison and a $250,000 fine.

with the system, I'd say that's precisely what those in charge want you to believe. By the way, you left out your zip code. It's 82941.

BARLOW [Day 9, 8:34 A.M.]: Now that's more like it. There is an ethical distinction between people and institutions. The law makes little distinction. We pretend that institutions are somehow human because they are made of humans. A large bureaucracy resembles a human about as much as a reef resembles a coral polyp. To expect an institution to have a conscience is like expecting a horse to have one. As with every organism, institutions are chiefly concerned with their own physical integrity and survival. To say that they have some higher purpose beyond their survival is to anthropomorphize them. You are right, Emmanuel. The house analogy breaks down here. Individuals live in houses; institutions live in mainframes. Institutions are functionally remorseless and need to be checked. Since their blood is digital, we need to be in their bloodstreams like an infection of humanity. I'm willing to extend limitless trust to other human beings. In my experience they've never failed to deserve it. But I have as much faith in institutions as they have in me. None.

OPTIK [Day 9, 10:19 A.M.]: In other words, Mr. Barlow, you say something, someone proves you wrong, and then you agree with him. I'm getting the feeling that you don't exactly chisel your views in stone.

HANK [Day 9, 11:18 A.M.]: Has Mr. Optik heard the phrase "thesis, antithesis, synthesis"?

BARLOW [Day 10, 10:48 A.M.]: Optik, I do change my mind a lot. Indeed, I often find it occupied by numerous contradictions. The last time I believed in absolutes, I was about your age. And there's not a damn thing wrong with believing in absolutes at your age either. Continue to do so, however, and you'll find yourself, at my age, carrying placards filled with nonsense and dressing in rags.

ADELAIDE [Day 10, 6:27 P.M.]: The flaw in this discussion is the distorted image the media promote of the hacker as "whiz." The problem is that the one who gets caught obviously isn't. I haven't seen a story yet on a true genius hacker. Even Robert Morris was no whiz. The genius hackers are busy doing constructive things or are so good no one's caught them yet. It takes no talent to break into something. Nobody calls subway graffiti artists geniuses for figuring out how to break into the yard. There's a difference between genius and ingenuity.

BARLOW [Day 10, 9:48 P.M.]: Let me define my terms. Using *hacker* in a mid-spectrum sense (with crackers on one end and Leonardo da Vinci on the other), I think it does take a kind of genius to be a truly productive hacker. I'm learning PASCAL now, and I am constantly amazed that people can spin those prolix recursions into something like PageMaker. It fills me with the kind of awe I reserve for splendors such as the cathedral at Chartres. With crackers like Acid and Optik, the issue is less intelligence than alienation. Trade their modems for skateboards and only a slight conceptual shift would occur. Yet I'm glad they're wedging open the cracks. Let a thousand worms flourish.

OPTIK [Day 10, 10:11 P.M.]: You have some pair of balls comparing my talent with that of a skateboarder. Hmm. . . . This was indeed boring, but nonetheless: [*Editors' Note: At this point in the discussion, Optik—apparently having hacked into TRW's computer records—posted a copy of Mr. Barlow's credit history. In the interest of Mr. Barlow's privacy—at least what is left of it—Harper's Magazine has not printed it.*] I'm not showing off. Any fool knowing the proper syntax and the proper passwords can look up a credit history. I just find your high-and-mighty attitude annoying and, yes, infantile.

HOMEBOY [Day 10, 10:17 P.M.]: Key here is "any fool."

ACID [Day 11, 1:37 P.M.]: For thirty-five dollars a year anyone can have access to TRW and see his or her own credit history. Optik did it for free. What's wrong with that? And why does TRW keep files on what color and religion we are? If you didn't know that they kept such files, who would have found out if it wasn't for a hacker? Barlow should be grateful that Optik has offered his services to update him on his personal credit file. Of course, I'd hate to see my credit history up in lights. But if you hadn't made our skins crawl, your info would not have been posted. Everyone gets back at someone when he's pissed; so do we. Only we do it differently. Are we punks? Yeah, I guess we are. A punk is what someone who has been made to eat his own words calls the guy who fed them to him.

■ HACKING THE CONSTITUTION

HARPER'S [Day 4, 9:00 A.M.]: Suppose that a mole inside the government confirmed the existence of files on each of you, stored in the White House computer system, PROFS. Would you have the right to hack into that system to retrieve and expose the existence of such files? Could you do it?

TENNEY [Day 4, 1:42 P.M.]: The proverbial question of whether the end justifies the means. This doesn't have much to do with hacking. If the file were a sheet of paper in a locked cabinet, the same question would apply. In that case you could accomplish everything without technological hacking. Consider the Pentagon Papers.

EMMANUEL [Day 4, 3:55 P.M.]: Let's address the hypothetical. First, I need to find out more about PROFS. Is it accessible from off site, and if so, how? Should I update my 202-456 scan [a list of phone numbers in the White House's exchange that connect incoming calls to a computer]? I have a listing

for every computer in that exchange, but the scan was done back in 1984. Is
PROFS a new system? Perhaps it's in a different exchange? Does anybody
know how many people have access to it? I'm also on fairly good terms with
a White House operator who owes me a favor. But I don't know what to ask
for. Obviously, I've already made up my mind about the *right* to examine this
material. I don't want to debate the ethics of it at this point. If you're with
me, let's do something about this. Otherwise, stay out of the way. There's
hacking to be done.

ACID [Day 4, 5:24 P.M.]: Yes, I would try to break into the PROFS system. But
first I'd have someone in the public eye, with no ties to hacking, request the
info through the Freedom of Information Act. Then I'd hack in to verify the
information I received.

DRAKE [Day 4, 9:13 P.M.]: Are there a lot of people involved in this anti-
hacker project? If so, the chances of social engineering data out of people
would be far higher than if it were a small, close-knit group. But yes, the simple truth is, if the White House has a dial-up line, it can be hacked.

EMMANUEL [Day 4, 11:27 P.M.]: The implication that a trust has been
betrayed on the part of the government is certainly enough to make me want
to look a little further. And I know I'm doing the right thing on behalf of
others who don't have my abilities. Most people I meet see me as an ally who
can help them stay ahead of an unfair system. That's what I intend to do
here. I have a small core of dedicated hackers who could help. One's specialty
is the UNIX system, another's is networks, and another's is phone systems.

TENNEY [Day 5, 12:24 A.M.]: PROFS is an IBM message program that runs on
an operating system known as VM. VM systems usually have a fair number of
holes, either to gain access or to gain full privileges. The CIA was working
on, and may have completed, a supposedly secure VM system. No ethics here,
just facts. But a prime question is to determine what system via what phone
number. Of course, the old inside job is easier. Just find someone who owes a
favor or convince an insider that it is a moral obligation to do this.

BARLOW [Day 5, 2:46 P.M.]: This scenario needs to be addressed in four
parts: ethical, political, practical I (from the standpoint of the hack itself), and
practical II (disseminating the information without undue risk).
  Ethical: Since World War II, we've been governed by a paramilitary
bureaucracy that believes freedom is too precious to be entrusted to the people. These are the same folks who had to destroy the village in order to save
it. Thus the government has become a set of Chinese boxes. Americans who
believe in democracy have little choice but to shred the barricades of secrecy
at every opportunity. It isn't merely permissible to hack PROFS. It is a moral
obligation.
  Political: In the struggle between control and liberty, one has to avoid
action that will drive either side to extreme behavior. The basis of terrorism,

remember, is excess. If we hack PROFS, we must do it in a way that doesn't become a pretext for hysterical responses that might eventually include zero tolerance of personal computers. The answer is to set up a system for entry and exit that never lets on we've been there.

Practical I: Hacking the system should be a trivial undertaking.

Practical II: Having retrieved the smoking gun, it must be made public in such a way that the actual method of acquisition does not become public. Consider Watergate: The prime leaker was somebody whose identity and information-gathering technique is still unknown. So having obtained the files, we turn them over to the *Washington Post* without revealing our own identities or how we came by the files.

EMMANUEL [Day 5, 9:51 P.M.]: PROFS is used for sending messages back and forth. It's designed *not* to forget things. And it's used by people who are not computer literate. The document we are looking for is likely an electronic-mail message. If we can find out who the recipient or sender is, we can take it from there. Since these people frequently use the system to communicate, there may be a way for them to dial into the White House from home. Finding that number won't be difficult: frequent calls to a number local to the White House and common to a few different people. Once I get the dial-up, I'll have to look at whatever greeting I get to determine what kind of system it is. Then we need to locate someone expert in the system to see if there are any built-in back doors. If there aren't, I will social engineer my way into a working account and then attempt to break out of the program and explore the entire system.

BRAND [Day 6, 10:06 A.M.]: I have two questions: Do you believe in due process as found in our Constitution? And do you believe that this "conspiracy" is so serious that extraordinary measures need to be taken? If you believe in due process, then you shouldn't hack into the system to defend our liberties. If you don't believe in due process, you are an anarchist and potentially a terrorist. The government is justified in taking *extreme* action to protect itself and the rest of us from you. If you believe in the Constitution but also that this threat is so extreme that patriots have a duty to intercede, then you should seek one of the honest national officials who can legally demand a copy of the document. If you believe that there is no sufficiently honest politician and you steal and publish the documents, you are talking about a revolution.

ACID [Day 6, 1:30 P.M.]: This is getting too political. Who says that hacking has to have a political side? Generalizing does nothing but give hackers a false image. I couldn't care less about politics, and I hack.

LEE [Day 6, 9:01 P.M.]: Sorry, Acid, but if you hack, what you do is inherently political. Here goes: Political power is exercised by control of information channels. Therefore, any action that changes the capability of someone in power to control these channels *is* politically relevant. Historically, the one in power has been not the strongest person but the one who has convinced the goon squad to do his bidding. The goons give their power to him, usually in exchange for free food, sex, and great uniforms. The turning point of most successful revolutions is when the troops ignore the orders coming from above and switch their allegiance. Information channels. Politics. These days, the cracker represents a potential for making serious political change if he coordinates with larger social and economic forces. Without this coordination, the cracker is but a techno-bandit, sharpening his weapon and chuckling about how someday. . . . Revolutions often make good use of bandits, and some of them move into high positions when they're successful. Bur most of them are done away with. One cracker getting in won't do much good. Working in coordination with others is another matter—called politics.

JIMG [Day 7, 12:28 A.M.]: A thought: Because it has become so difficult to keep secrets (thanks, in part, to crackers), and so expensive and counterproductive (the trade-off in lost opportunities is too great), secrets are becoming less worth protecting. Today, when secrets come out that would have brought down governments in the past, "spin-control experts" shower the media with so many lies that the truth is obscured despite being in plain sight. It's the information equivalent of the Pentagon plan to surround each real missile with hundreds of fake ones, rendering radar useless. If hackers managed to crack the White House system, a hue and cry would be raised—not about what the hackers found in the files but about what a threat hackers are to this great democracy of ours.

"I don't want any Congressional King George treading on my cursor. We must continue to have absolute freedom of electronic speech!"

HARPER'S [Day 7, 9:00 A.M.]: Suppose you hacked the files from the White House and a backlash erupted. Congressmen call for restrictions, arguing that the computer is "property" susceptible to regulation and not an instrument of "information" protected by the First Amendment. Can we craft a manifesto setting forth your views on how the computer fits into the traditions of the American Constitution?

DAVE [Day 7, 5:30 P.M.]: If Congress ever passed laws that tried to define what we do as "technology" (regulatable) and *not* "speech," I would become a rebellious criminal immediately—and as loud as Thomas Paine ever was. Although computers are part "property" and part "premises" (which suggests a need for privacy), they are supremely instruments of *speech*. I don't want any congressional King Georges treading on my cursor. We must continue to have *absolute* freedom of electronic speech!

BARLOW [Day 7, 10:07 P.M.]: Even in a court guided by my favorite oxymoron, Justice Rehnquist, this is an open-and-shut case. The computer is a printing press. Period. The only hot-lead presses left in this country are either in museums or being operated by poets in Vermont. The computer cannot fall under the kind of regulation to which radio and TV have become subject, since computer output is not broadcast. If these regulations amount to anything more than a fart in the congressional maelstrom, then we might as well scrap the whole Bill of Rights. What I am doing with my fingers right now is "speech" in the clearest sense of the word. We don't need no stinking manifestos.

JIMG [Day 8, 12:02 A.M.]: This type of congressional action is so clearly unconstitutional that "law hackers"—everyone from William Kunstler to Robert Bork—would be all over it. The whole idea runs so completely counter to our laws that it's hard to get worked up about it.

ADELAIDE [Day 8, 9:51 A.M.]: Not so fast. There used to be a right in the Constitution called "freedom from unreasonable search and seizure," but, thanks to recent Supreme Court decisions, your urine can be demanded by a lot of people. I have no faith in the present Supreme Court to uphold any of my rights of free speech. The complacent reaction here—that whatever Congress does will eventually be found unconstitutional—is the same kind of complacency that led to the current near-reversals of *Roe* v. *Wade.*

JRC [Day 8, 10:05 A.M.]: I'd forgo the manifestos and official explanations altogether: Fight brushfire wars against specific government incursions and wait for the technology to metastasize. In a hundred years, people won't have to be told about computers because they will have an instinctive understanding of them.

KK [Day 8, 2:14 P.M.]: Hackers are not sloganeers. They are doers, take-things-in-handers. They are the opposite of philosophers: They don't wait for language to catch up to them. Their arguments are their actions. You want a manifesto? The Internet worm was a manifesto. It had more meaning and symbolism than any revolutionary document you could write. To those in power running the world's nervous system, it said: Wake up! To the underground of hackers, crackers, chippers, and techno-punks, it said: You have power; be careful. To the mass of citizens who find computers taking over their telephone, their TV, their toaster, and their house, it said: Welcome to Wonderland.

BARLOW [Day 8, 10:51 P.M.]: Apart from the legal futility of fixing the dam after it's been breached, I've never been comfortable with manifestos. They are based on the ideologue's delusion about the simplicity, the figure-outability, of the infinitely complex thing that is Life Among the Humans. Manifestos take reductionism for a long ride off a short pier. Sometimes the ride takes a very long time. Marx and Engels didn't actually crash until last year.

Manifestos fail because they are fixed and consciousness isn't. I'm with JRC: Deal with incursions when we need to, on our terms, like the guerrillas we are. To say that we can outmaneuver those who are against us is like saying that honeybees move quicker than Congress. The future is to the quick, not the respectable.

RH [Day 8, 11:43 P.M.]: Who thinks computers can't be regulated? The Electronic Communications Privacy Act of 1986 made it a crime to own "any electronic, mechanical, or other device [whose design] renders it primarily useful for the purpose of the surreptitious interception of wire, oral, or electronic communication." Because of the way Congress defined "electronic communication," one could argue that even a modem is a surreptitious interception device (SID), banned by the ECPA and subject to confiscation. It's not that Congress intended to ban modems; it was just sloppy drafting. The courts will ultimately decide what devices are legal. Since it may not be possible to draw a clear bright line between legal and illegal interception devices, the gray area—devices with both legitimate and illegitimate uses—may be subject to regulation.

BARLOW [Day 9, 8:52 A.M.]: I admit with some chagrin that I'm not familiar with the ECPA. It seems I've fallen on the wrong side of an old tautology: Just because all saloon keepers are Democrats, it doesn't follow that all Democrats are saloon keepers. By the same token, the fact that all printing presses are computers hardly limits computers to that function. And one of the other things computers are good at is surreptitious monitoring. Maybe there's more reason for concern than I thought. Has any of this stuff been tested in the courts yet?

RH [Day 9, 10:06 P.M.]: My comments about surreptitious interception devices are not based on any court cases, since there have not been any in this area since the ECPA was enacted. It is a stretch of the imagination to think that a judge would ever find a stock, off-the-shelf personal computer to be a "surreptitious interception device." But a modem is getting a little closer to the point where a creative prosecutor could make trouble for a cracker, with fallout affecting many others. An important unknown is how the courts will apply the word *surreptitious*. There's very little case law, but taking it to mean "by stealth; hidden from view; having its true purpose physically disguised," I can spin some worrisome examples. I lobbied against the bill, pointing out the defects. Congressional staffers admitted privately that there was a problem, but they were in a rush to get the bill to the floor before Congress adjourned. They said they could patch it later, but it is a pothole waiting for a truck axle to rumble through.

JIMG [Day 10, 8:55 A.M.]: That's sobering information, RH. Yet I still think that this law, if interpreted the way you suggest, would be found unconstitutional, even by courts dominated by Reagan appointees. Also, the economic cost of prohibiting modems, or even restricting their use, would so outweigh conceivable benefits that the law would never go through. Finally, restricting modems would have no effect on the phreaks but would simply manage to slow everybody else down. If modems are outlawed, only outlaws will have modems.

RH [Day 10, 1:52 P.M.]: We're already past the time when one could wrap hacking in the First Amendment. There's a traditional distinction between words—expressions of opinions, beliefs, and information—and deeds. You can shout "Revolution!" from the rooftops all you want, and the post office will obligingly deliver your recipes for nitroglycerin. But acting on that information exposes you to criminal prosecution. The philosophical problem posed by hacking is that computer programs transcend this distinction: They are pure language that dictates action when read by the device being addressed. In that sense, a program is very different from a novel, a play, or even a recipe: Actions result automatically from the machine reading the words. A computer has no independent moral judgment, no sense of responsibility. Not yet, anyway. As we program and automate more of our lives, we undoubtedly will deal with more laws: limiting what the public can know, restricting devices that can execute certain instructions, and criminalizing the possession of "harmful" programs with "no redeeming social value." Blurring the distinction between language and action, as computer programming does, could eventually undermine the First Amendment or at least force society to limit its application. That's a very high price to pay, even for all the good things that computers make possible.

HOMEBOY [Day 10, 11:03 P.M.]: HACKING IS ART. CRACKING IS REVOLUTION. All else is noise. Cracks in the firmament are by nature threatening. Taking a crowbar to them is revolution.

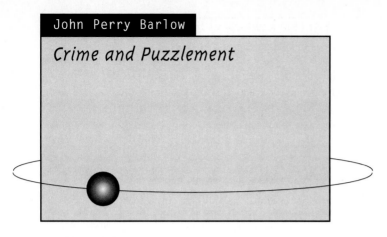

John Perry Barlow

Crime and Puzzlement

■ DESPERADOS OF THE DATASPHERE

So me and my sidekick Howard, we was sitting out in front of the 40 Rod Saloon one evening when he all of a sudden says, "Lookee here. What do you reckon?" I look up and there's these two strangers riding into town. They're young and got kind of a restless, bored way about 'em. A person don't need both eyes to see they mean trouble . . .

Well, that wasn't quite how it went. Actually, Howard and I were floating blind as cave fish in the electronic barrens of the WELL, so the whole incident passed as words on a display screen:

HOWARD: Interesting couple of newusers just signed on. One calls himself acid and the other's optik.

BARLOW: Hmmm. What are their real names?

HOWARD: Check their finger files.

And so I typed !finger acid. Several seconds later the WELL's Sequent computer sent the following message to my Macintosh in Wyoming:

```
Login name: acid                        In real life: Acid Phreak
```

By this, I knew that the WELL had a new resident and that his corporeal analog was supposedly called Acid Phreak. Typing !finger optik yielded results of similar insufficiency, including the claim that someone, somewhere in the real world, was walking around calling himself Phiber Optik. I doubted it.

However, associating these sparse data with the knowledge that the WELL was about to host a conference on computers and security rendered the conclusion that I had made my first sighting of genuine computer crackers. As the arrival of an outlaw was a major event to the settlements of the Old West, so was the appearance of crackers cause for stir on the WELL.

The WELL (or Whole Earth 'Lectronic Link) is an example of the latest thing in frontier villages, the computer bulletin board. In this kind of small town, Main Street is a central minicomputer to which (in the case of the WELL) as many as 64 microcomputers may be connected at one time by phone lines and little blinking boxes called modems.

In this silent world, all conversation is typed. To enter it, one forsakes both body and place and becomes a thing of words alone.

You can see what your neighbors are saying (or recently said), but not what either they or their physical surroundings look like. Town meetings are continuous and discussions rage on everything from sexual kinks to depreciation schedules.

There are thousands of these nodes in the United States, ranging from PC clone hamlets of a few users to mainframe metros like CompuServe, with its 550,000 subscribers. They are used by corporations to transmit memoranda and spreadsheets, universities to disseminate research, and a multitude of factions, from apiarists to Zoroastrians, for purposes unique to each.

Cyberspace, in its present condition, has a lot in common with the 19th Century West.

Whether by one telephonic tendril or millions, they are all connected to one another. Collectively, they form what their inhabitants call the Net. It extends across that immense region of electron states, microwaves, magnetic fields, light pulses and thought which sci-fi writer William Gibson named Cyberspace.

Cyberspace, in its present condition, has a lot in common with the 19th Century West. It is vast, unmapped, culturally and legally ambiguous, verbally terse (unless you happen to be a court stenographer), hard to get around in, and up for grabs. Large institutions already claim to own the place, but most of the actual natives are solitary and independent, sometimes to the point of sociopathy. It is, of course, a perfect breeding ground for both outlaws and new ideas about liberty.

Recognizing this, *Harper's Magazine* decided in December 1989 to hold one of its periodic Forums on the complex of issues surrounding computers, information, privacy, and electronic intrusion or "cracking." Appropriately, they convened their conference in Cyberspace, using the WELL as the "site."

Harper's invited an odd lot of about 40 participants. These included: Clifford Stoll, whose book *The Cuckoo's Egg* details his cunning efforts to nab a German cracker. John Draper or "Cap'n Crunch," the grand- daddy of crackers whose blue boxes got Wozniak and Jobs into consumer electronics. Stewart Brand and Kevin Kelly of Whole Earth fame. Steven Levy, who wrote the seminal *Hackers*. A retired Army colonel named Dave Hughes. Lee Felsenstein, who designed the Osborne computer and was once called the "Robespierre of computing." A UNIX wizard and former hacker named Jeff Poskanzer. There was also a score of aging techno-hippies, the crackers, and me.

What I was doing there was not precisely clear since I've spent most of my working years either pushing cows or song-mongering, but I at least brought to the situation a vivid knowledge of actual cow-towns, having lived in or around one most of my life.

That and a kind of innocence about both the technology and morality of Cyberspace which was soon to pass into the confusion of knowledge.

At first, I was inclined toward sympathy with Acid 'n' Optik as well as their colleagues, Adelaide, Knight Lightning, Taran King, and Emmanuel. I've always been more comfortable with outlaws than Republicans, despite having more certain credentials in the latter camp.

These kids were fractious, vulgar, immature, amoral, insulting, and too damned good at their work.

But as the *Harper's* Forum mushroomed into a boom-town of ASCII text (the participants typing 110,000 words in 10 days), I began to wonder. These kids were fractious, vulgar, immature, amoral, insulting, and too damned good at their work.

Worse, they inducted a number of former kids like myself into Middle Age. The long feared day had finally come when some gunsel would yank my beard and call me, too accurately, an old fart.

Under ideal circumstances, the blind gropings of bulletin board discourse force a kind of Noh drama stylization on human commerce. Intemperate responses, or "flames" as they are called, are common even among conference participants who understand one another, which, it became immediately clear, the cyberpunks and techno-hippies did not.

My own initial enthusiasm for the crackers wilted under a steady barrage of typed testosterone. I quickly remembered I didn't know much about who they were, what they did, or how they did it. I also remembered stories about crackers working in league with the Mob, ripping off credit card numbers and getting paid for them in (stolen) computer equipment.

The techno-hippies were of the unanimous opinion that, in Dylan's words, one "must be honest to live outside the law."

And I remembered Kevin Mitnik. Mitnik, now 25, recently served federal time for a variety of computer and telephone related crimes. Prior to incarceration, Mitnik was, by all accounts, a dangerous guy with a computer. He disrupted phone company operations and arbitrarily disconnected the phones of celebrities. Like the kid in *Wargames,* he broke into the North American Defense Command computer in Colorado Springs.

Unlike the kid in *Wargames,* he is reputed to have made a practice of destroying and altering data. There is even the (perhaps apocryphal) story that he altered the credit information of his probation officer and other enemies. Digital Equipment claimed that his depredations cost them more than $4 million in computer downtime and file rebuilding. Eventually, he was turned in by a friend who, after careful observation, had decided he was "a menace to society."

His spectre began to hang over the conference. After several days of strained diplomacy, the discussion settled into a moral debate on the ethics of security and went critical.

The techno-hippies were of the unanimous opinion that, in Dylan's words, one "must be honest to live outside the law." But these young strangers apparently lived by no code save those with which they unlocked forbidden regions of the Net.

They appeared to think that improperly secured systems deserved to be violated and, by extension, that unlocked houses ought to be robbed. This latter built particular heat in me since I refuse, on philosophical grounds, to lock my house.

Civility broke down. We began to see exchanges like:

DAVE HUGHES: Clifford Stoll said a wise thing that no one has commented on. That networks are built on trust. If they aren't, they should be.

ACID PHREAK: Yeah. Sure. And we should use the "honor system" as a first line of security against hack attempts.

JEFF POSKANZER: This guy down the street from me sometimes leaves his back door unlocked. I told him about it once, but he still does it. If I had the chance to do it over, I would go in the back door, shoot him, and take all his money and consumer electronics. It's the only way to get through to him.

ACID PHREAK: Jeff Poskanker (Puss? Canker? yechh) Anyway, now when did you first start having these delusions where computer hacking was even *remotely* similar to murder?

Presented with such a terrifying amalgam of raw youth and apparent power, we fluttered like a flock of indignant Babbitts around the Status Quo, defending it heartily. One former hacker howled to the *Harper's* editor in charge of the forum, "Do you or do you not have names and addresses for these criminals?" Though they had committed no obvious crimes, he was ready to call the police.

They finally got to me with:

ACID: Whoever said they'd leave the door open to their house . . . where do you live? (the address) Leave it to me in mail if you like.

I had never encountered anyone so apparently unworthy of my trust as these little nihilists. They had me questioning a basic tenet, namely that the greatest security lies in vulnerability. I decided it was time to put that principle to the test . . .

BARLOW: Acid. My house is at 372 North Franklin Street in Pinedale, Wyoming. If you're heading north on Franklin, you go about two blocks off the main drag before you run into hay meadow on the left. I've got the last house before the field. The computer is always on . . .

And is that really what you mean? Are you merely just the kind of little sneak that goes around looking for easy places to violate? You disappoint me, pal. For all your James Dean-on-silicon rhetoric, you're not a cyberpunk. You're just a punk.

ACID PHREAK: Mr. Barlow: Thank you for posting all I need to get your credit information and a whole lot more! Now, who is to blame? ME for getting it or YOU for being such an idiot?! I think this should just about sum things up.

BARLOW: Acid, if you've got a lesson to teach me, I hope it's not that it's idiotic to trust one's fellow man. Life on those terms would be endless and brutal. I'd try to tell you something about conscience, but I'd sound like Father O'Flannigan trying to reform the punk that's about to gutshoot him. For no more reason than to watch him die.

But actually, if you take it upon yourself to destroy my credit, you might do me a favor. I've been looking for something to put the brakes on my burgeoning materialism.

I spent a day wondering whether I was dealing with another Kevin Mitnik before the other shoe dropped:

BARLOW: . . . With crackers like acid and optik, the issue is less intelligence than alienation. Trade their modems for skateboards and only a slight conceptual shift would occur.

OPTIK: You have some pair of balls comparing my talent with that of a skateboarder. Hmmm . . . This was indeed boring, but nonetheless:

At which point he downloaded my credit history.

Optik had hacked the core of TRW, an institution which has made my business (and yours) their business, extracting from it an abbreviated (and incorrect) version of my personal financial life. With this came the implication that he and Acid could and would revise it to my disadvantage if I didn't back off.

> *Optik had hacked the core of TRW, an institution which has made my business (and yours) their business, extracting from it an abbreviated (and incorrect) version of my personal financial life.*

I have since learned that while getting someone's TRW file is fairly trivial, changing it is not. But at that time, my assessment of the crackers' black skills was one of superstitious awe. They were digital brujos about to zombify my economic soul.

To a middle-class American, one's credit rating has become nearly identical to his freedom. It now appeared that I was dealing with someone who had both the means and desire to hoodoo mine, leaving me trapped in a life of wrinkled bills and money order queues. Never again would I call The Sharper Image on a whim.

I've been in redneck bars wearing shoulder-length curls, police custody while on acid, and Harlem after midnight, but no one has ever put the spook in me quite as Phiber Optik did at that moment. I realized that we had problems which exceeded the human conductivity of the WELL's bandwidth. If someone were about to paralyze me with a spell, I wanted a more visceral sense of him than could fit through a modem.

I e-mailed him asking him to give me a phone call. I told him I wouldn't insult his skills by giving him my phone number and, with the assurance conveyed by that challenge, I settled back and waited for the phone to ring. Which, directly, it did.

In this conversation and the others that followed I encountered an intelligent, civilized, and surprisingly principled kid of 18 who sounded, and continues to sound, as though there's little harm in him to man or data. His cracking impulses seemed purely exploratory, and I've begun to wonder if we wouldn't also regard spelunkers as desperate criminals if AT&T owned all the caves.

The terrifying poses which Optik and Acid had been striking on screen were a media-amplified example of a human adaptation I'd seen before: One becomes as he is beheld. They were simply living up to what they thought we, and, more particularly, the editors of *Harper's,* expected of them. Like the televised tears of disaster victims, their snarls adapted easily to mass distribution.

Months later, *Harper's* took Optik, Acid and me to dinner at a Manhattan restaurant which, though very fancy, was appropriately Chinese. Acid and Optik, as material beings, were well-scrubbed and fashionably clad. They looked to be dangerous as ducks. But, as *Harper's* and the rest of the media have discovered to their delight, the boys had developed distinctly showier personae for their rambles through the howling wilderness of Cyberspace.

Months later, Harper's took Optik, Acid and me to dinner at a Manhattan restaurant.

Glittering with spikes of binary chrome, they strode past the klieg lights and into the digital distance. There they would be outlaws. It was only a matter of time before they started to believe themselves as bad as they sounded. And no time at all before everyone else did.

In this, they were like another kid named Billy, many of whose feral deeds in the pre-civilized West were encouraged by the same dime novelist who chronicled them. And like Tom Horn, they seemed to have some doubt as to which side of the law they were on. Acid even expressed an ambition to work for the government someday, nabbing "terrorists and code abusers."

There is also a frontier ambiguity to the "crimes" the crackers commit. They are not exactly stealing VCRs. Copying a text file from TRW doesn't deprive its owner of anything except informational exclusivity. (Though it may be said that information has monetary value only in proportion to its containment.)

There was no question that they were making unauthorized use of data channels. The night I met them, they left our restaurant table and disappeared into the phone booth for a long time. I didn't see them marshalling quarters before they went.

And, as I became less their adversary and more their scoutmaster, I began to get "conference calls" in which six or eight of them would crack pay phones all over New York and simultaneously land on my line in Wyoming. These deft maneuvers made me think of sky-diving stunts where large groups convene geometrically in free fall. In this case, the risk was largely legal.

Their other favorite risky business is the time-honored adolescent sport of trespassing. They insist on going where they don't belong.

Their other favorite risky business is the time-honored adolescent sport of trespassing. They insist on going where they don't belong. But then teen-age boys have been proceeding uninvited since the dawn of human puberty. It seems hard-wired. The only innovation in the new form of the forbidden zone is the means of getting in it.

In fact, like Kevin Mitnik, I broke into NORAD when I was 17. A friend and I left a nearby "woodsie" (as rustic adolescent drunks were called in Colorado) and tried to get inside the Cheyenne Mountain. The chrome-helmeted Air Force MP's held us for about 2 hours before letting us go. They weren't much older than us and knew exactly our level of national security threat. Had we come cloaked in electronic mystery, their alert status certainly would have been higher.

Whence rises much of the anxiety. Everything is so ill-defined. How can you guess what lies in their hearts when you can't see their eyes? How can one be sure that, like Mitnik, they won't cross the line from trespassing into another adolescent pastime, vandalism? And how can you be sure they pose no threat when you don't know what a threat might be?

And for the crackers some thrill is derived from the metamorphic vagueness of the laws themselves. On the Net, their effects are unpredictable. One never knows when they'll bite.

This is because most of the statutes invoked against the crackers were designed in a very different world from the one they explore. For example, can unauthorized electronic access be regarded as the ethical equivalent of old-fashioned trespass? Like open range, the property boundaries of Cyberspace are hard to stake and harder still to defend.

Is transmission through an otherwise unused data channel really theft? Is the trackless passage of a mind through TRW's mainframe the same as the passage of a pickup through my Back 40? What is a place if Cyberspace is everywhere? What are data and what is free speech? How does one treat property which has no physical form and can be infinitely reproduced? Is a computer the same as a printing press? Can the history of my business affairs properly belong to someone else? Can anyone morally claim to own knowledge itself?

If such questions were hard to answer precisely, there are those who are ready to try. Based on their experience in the Virtual World, they were about as qualified to enforce its mores as I am to write the Law of the Sea. But if they lacked technical sophistication, they brought to this task their usual conviction. And, of course, badges and guns.

■ OPERATION SUN DEVIL

Recently, we have witnessed an alarming number of young people who, for a variety of sociological and psychological reasons, have become attached to their computers and are exploiting their potential in a criminal manner. Often, a progression of criminal activity occurs which involves telecommunications fraud (free long distance phone calls), unauthorized access to other computers (whether for profit, fascination, ego, or the intellectual challenge), credit card fraud (cash advances and unauthorized purchases of goods), and then move on to other destructive activities like computer viruses.

Our experience shows that many computer hacker suspects are no longer misguided teenagers mischievously playing games with their computers in their bedrooms. Some are now high tech computer operators using computers to engage in unlawful conduct.
>   —excerpts from a statement by Garry M. Jenkins,
>   Assistant Director, U.S. Secret Service

The right of the people to be secure in their persons, houses, papers, and effects, against unreasonable searches and seizures, shall not be violated, and no warrants shall issue but upon probable cause, support by oath or affirmation, and particularly describing the place to be searched, and the persons or things to be seized.
>   —Amendment IV, U.S. Constitution

On January 24, 1990, a platoon of Secret Service agents entered the apartment which Acid Phreak shares with his mother and 12-year-old sister. The latter was the only person home when they burst through the door with guns drawn. They managed to hold her at bay for about half an hour until their quarry hap-pened home.

By then, they were nearly done packing up Acid's worldly goods, including his computer, his notes (both paper and magnetic), books, and such dubiously dangerous tools as a telephone answering machine, a ghetto blaster and his complete collection of audio tapes. One agent asked him to define the real purpose of the answering machine and was frankly skeptical when told that it answered the phone. The audio tapes seemed to contain nothing but music, but who knew what dark data Acid might have encoded between the notes...

When Acid's mother returned from work, she found her apartment a scene of apprehended criminality. She asked what, exactly, her son had done to deserve all this attention and was told that, among other things, he had caused the AT&T system crash several days earlier. (Previously AT&T had taken full responsibility.) Thus, the agent explained, her darling boy was thought to have caused over a billion dollars in damage to the economy of the United States.

On January 24, 1990, a platoon of Secret Service agents entered the apartment which Acid Phreak shares with his mother and 12-year-old sister.

This accusation was never turned into a formal charge. Indeed, no charge of any sort was filed against Mr. Phreak then and, although the Secret Service maintained resolute possession of his hardware, software, and data, no charge had been charged four months later.

Across town, similar scenes were being played out at the homes of Phiber Optik and another colleague code-named Scorpion. Again, equipment, notes, disks both hard and soft, and personal effects were confiscated. Again no charges were filed.

Thus began the visible phase of Operation Sun Devil, a two-year Secret Service investigation which involved 150 federal agents, numerous local and state law enforcement agencies, and the combined security resources of PacBell, AT&T, Bellcore, Bell South MCI, U.S. Sprint, Mid-American, Southwestern Bell, NYNEX, U.S. West and American Express.

The focus of this impressive institutional array was the Legion of Doom, a group which never had any formal membership list but was thought by the members with whom I spoke to number less than 20, nearly all of them in their teens or early twenties.

I asked Acid why they'd chosen such a threatening name. "You wouldn't want a fairy kind of thing like Legion of Flower Pickers or something. But the media ate it up too. Probing the Legion of Doom like it was a gang or something, when really it was just a bunch of geeks behind terminals."

Sometime in December 1988, a 21-year-old Atlanta-area Legion of Doomster named The Prophet cracked a Bell South computer and downloaded a three-page text file which outlined, in bureaucrat-ese of surpassing opacity, the administrative procedures and responsibilities for marketing, servicing, upgrading, and billing for Bell South's 911 system.

A dense thicket of acronyms, the document was filled with passages like:

In accordance with the basic SSC/MAC strategy for provisioning, the SSC/MAC will be Overall Control Office (OCO) for all Notes to PSAP circuits (official services) and any other services for this customer. Training must be scheduled for all SSC/MAC involved personnel during the pre-service stage of the project.

And other such.

At some risk, I too have a copy of this document. To read the whole thing straight through without entering coma requires either a machine or a human who has too much practice thinking like one. Anyone who can understand it fully and fluidly has altered his consciousness beyond the ability to ever again read Blake, Whitman, or Tolstoy. It is, quite simply, the worst writing I have ever tried to read.

Since the document contains little of interest to anyone who is not a student of advanced organizational sclerosis . . . that is, no access codes, trade secrets, or proprietary information . . . I assume The Prophet only copied this file as a kind of hunting trophy. He had been to the heart of the forest and had returned with this coonskin to nail to the barn door.

Furthermore, he was proud of his accomplishment, and since such trophies are infinitely replicable, he wasn't content to nail it to his door alone. Among the places he copied it was a UNIX bulletin board (rather like the WELL) in Lockport, Illinois called Jolnet.

It was downloaded from there by a 20-year-old hacker and pre-law student (whom I had met in the *Harper's* Forum) who called himself Knight Lightning. Though not a member of the Legion of Doom, Knight Lightning and a friend, Taran King, also published from St. Louis and his fraternity house at the University of Missouri a worldwide hacker's magazine called *Phrack.* (From phone phreak and hack.)

When Knight Lightning got hold of the Bell South document, he thought it would amuse his readers and reproduced it in the next issue of Phrack.

Phrack was an unusual publication in that it was entirely virtual. The only time its articles hit paper was when one of its subscribers decided to print out a hard copy. Otherwise, its editions existed in Cyberspace and took no physical form.

When Knight Lightning got hold of the Bell South document, he thought it would amuse his readers and reproduced it in the next issue of *Phrack.* He had little reason to think that he was doing something illegal. There is nothing in it to indicate that it contains proprietary or even sensitive information. Indeed, it closely resembles telco reference documents which have long been publicly available.

However, Rich Andrews, the systems operator who oversaw the operation of Jolnet, thought there might be something funny about the document when he first ran across it in his system. To be on the safe side, he forwarded a copy of it to AT&T officials. He was subsequently contacted by the authorities, and he cooperated with them fully. He would regret that later.

On the basis of the foregoing, a grand jury in Lockport was persuaded by the Secret Service in early February to hand down a seven-count indictment against The Prophet and Knight Lightning, charging them, among other things, with interstate transfer of stolen property worth more than $5,000. When The Prophet and two of his Georgia colleagues were arrested on February 7, 1990, the Atlanta papers reported they faced 40 years in prison and a $2 million fine. Knight Lightning was arrested on February 15.

The property in question was the aforementioned blot on the history of prose whose full title was "A Bell South Standard Practice (BSP) 660-225-104SV-Control Office Administration of Enhanced 911 Services for Special Services and Major Account Centers, March, 1988."

And not only was this item worth more than $5,000.00, it was worth, according to the indictment and Bell South, precisely $79,449.00. And not a penny less. We will probably never know how this figure was reached or by whom, though I like to imagine an appraisal team consisting of Franz Kafka, Joseph Heller, and Thomas Pynchon . . .

In addition to charging Knight Lightning with crimes for which he could go to jail 30 years and be fined $122,000.00, they seized his publication, *Phrack,* along with all related equipment, software and data, including his list of subscribers, many of whom would soon lose their computers and data for the crime of appearing on it.

I talked to Emmanuel Goldstein, the editor of *2600,* another hacker publication which has been known to publish purloined documents. If they could shut down *Phrack,* couldn't they as easily shut down *2600?*

He said, "I've got one advantage. I come out on paper and the Constitution knows how to deal with paper."

In fact, nearly all publications are now electronic at some point in their creation. In a modern newspaper, stories written at the scene are typed to screens and then sent by modem to a central computer. This computer composes the layout in electronic type and the entire product is transmitted electronically to the presses. There, finally, the bytes become ink.

Phrack merely omitted the last step in a long line of virtual events. However, that omission, and its insignificant circulation, left it vulnerable to seizure based on content. If the 911 document had been the Pentagon Papers (another proprietary document) and *Phrack* the *New York Times,* a completion of the analogy would have seen the government stopping publication of the *Times* and seizing its every material possession, from notepads to presses.

Not that anyone in the newspaper business seemed particularly worried about such implications. They, and the rest of the media who bothered to report Knight Lightning's arrest, were too obsessed by what they portrayed as actual disruptions of emergency service and with marvelling at the sociopathy of it. One report expressed relief that no one appeared to have died as a result of the "intrusions."

Meanwhile, in Baltimore, the 911 dragnet snared Leonard Rose, aka Terminus. A professional computer consultant who specialized in UNIX, Rose got a visit from the government early in February. The G-men forcibly detained his wife and children for six hours while they interrogated Rose about the 911 document and ransacked his system.

Rose had no knowledge of the 911 matter. Indeed, his only connection had been occasional contact with Knight Lightning over several years . . . and admitted membership in the Legion of Doom. However, when searching his hard disk for 911 evidence, they found something else. Like many UNIX consultants, Rose did have some UNIX source code in his possession. Furthermore, there was evidence that he had transmitted some of it to Jolnet and left it there for another consultant.

UNIX is a ubiquitous operating system, and though its main virtue is its openness to amendment at the source level, it is nevertheless the property of AT&T. What had been widely distributed within businesses and universities for years was suddenly, in Rose's hands, a felonious possession.

Finally, the Secret Service rewarded the good citizenship of Rich Andrews by confiscating the computer where Jolnet had dwelt, along with all the e-mail, read and unread, which his subscribers had left there. Like the many others whose equipment and data were taken by the Secret Service subsequently, he wasn't charged with anything. Nor is he likely to be. They have already inflicted on him the worst punishment a nerd can suffer: data death.

Andrews was baffled. "I'm the one that found it, I'm the one that turned it in. . . . And I'm the one that's suffering," he said.

One wonders what will happen when they find such documents on the hard disks of CompuServe. Maybe I'll just upload my copy of Bell South Standard Practice (BSP) 660-225-104SV and see . . .

In any case, association with stolen data is all the guilt you need. It's quite as if the government could seize your house simply because a guest left a stolen VCR in an upstairs bedroom closet. Or confiscate all the mail in a post office upon finding a stolen package there. The first concept of modern jurisprudence to have arrived in Cyberspace seems to have been Zero Tolerance.

Rich Andrews was not the last to learn about the Secret Service's debonair new attitude toward the 4th Amendment's protection against unreasonable seizure.

Early on March 1, 1990, the offices of a role-playing game publisher in Austin, Texas called Steve Jackson Games were visited by agents of the United States Secret Service. They ransacked the premises, broke into several locked filing cabinets (damaging them irreparably in the process) and eventually left carrying three computers, two laser printers, several hard disks, and many boxes of paper and floppy disks.

Later in the day, callers to the Illuminati BBS (which Steve Jackson Games operated to keep in touch with role-players around the country) encountered the following message:

Early on March 1, 1990, the offices of a role-playing game publisher in Austin, Texas, called Steve Jackson Games were visited by agents of the United States Secret Service.

So far we have not received a clear explanation of what the Secret Service was looking for, what they expected to find, or much of anything else. We are fairly certain that Steve Jackson Games is not the target of whatever investigation is being conducted; in any case, we have done nothing illegal and have nothing whatsoever to hide. However, the equipment that was seized is apparently considered to be evidence in whatever they're investigating, so we aren't likely to get it back any time soon. It could be a month, it could be never.

It's been three months as I write this and, not only has nothing been returned to them, but, according to Steve Jackson, the Secret Service will no longer take his calls. He figures that, in the months since the raid, his little company has lost an estimated $125,000. With such a fiscal hemorrhage, he can't afford a lawyer to take after the Secret Service. Both the state and national offices of the ACLU told him to "run along" when he solicited their help.

He tried to go to the press. As in most other cases, they were unwilling to raise the alarm. Jackson theorized, "The conservative press is taking the attitude that the suppression of evil hackers is a good thing and that anyone who happens to be put out of business in the meantime . . . well, that's just their tough luck."

In fact, *Newsweek* did run a story about the event, portraying it from Jackson's perspective, but they were almost alone in dealing with it.

What had he done to deserve this nightmare? Role-playing games, of which Dungeons and Dragons is the most famous, have been accused of creating obsessive involvement in their nerdy young
players, but no one before had found it necessary to prevent their publication.

It seems that Steve Jackson had hired the wrong writer. The managing editor of Steve Jackson Games is a former cracker, known by his fellows in the Legion of Doom as The Mentor. At the time of the raid, he and the rest of Jackson staff had been working for over a year on a game called GURPS Cyberpunk, High-Tech Low-Life Role-Playing.

At the time of the Secret Service raids, the game resided entirely on the hard disks they confiscated. Indeed, it was their target. They told Jackson that, based on its author's background, they had reason to believe it was a "handbook on computer crime." It was therefore inappropriate for publication, 1st Amendment or no 1st Amendment.

I got a copy of the game from the trunk of The Mentor's car in an Austin parking lot. Like the Bell South document, it seemed pretty innocuous to me, if a little inscrutable. Borrowing its flavor from the works of William Gibson and Austin sci-fi author Bruce Sterling, it is filled with silicon brain implants, holodecks, and gauss guns.

It is, as the cover copy puts it, "a fusion of the dystopian visions of George Orwell and Timothy Leary." Actually, without the gizmos, it describes a future kind of like the present its publisher is experiencing at the hands of the Secret Service.

An unbelievably Byzantine world resides within its 120 large pages of small print. (These role-players must be some kind of idiots savants . . .) Indeed, it's a thing of such complexity that I can't swear there's no criminal information in there, but then I can't swear that Grateful Dead records don't have satanic messages if played backwards. Anything's possible, especially inside something as remarkable as Cyberpunk.

The most remarkable thing about Cyberpunk is the fact that it was printed at all. After much negotiation, Jackson was able to get the Secret Service to let him have some of his data back. However, they told him that he would be limited to an hour and a half with only one of his three computers. Also, according to Jackson, "They insisted that all the copies be made by a Secret Service agent who was a two-finger typist. So we didn't get much."

In the end, Jackson and his staff had to reconstruct most of the game from neural rather than magnetic memory. They did have a few very old backups, and they retrieved some scraps which had been passed around to game testers. They also had the determination of the enraged.

Despite government efforts to impose censorship by prior restraint, Cyberpunk is now on the market. Presumably, advertising it as "the book that was seized by the U.S. Secret Service" will invigorate sales. But Steve Jackson Games, the heretofore prosperous publisher of more than a hundred role-playing games, has been forced to lay off more than half of its employees and may well be mortally wounded.

On May 8, 1990, Operation Sun Devil, heretofore an apparently random and nameless trickle of Secret Service actions, swept down on the Legion of Doom and its ilk like a bureaucratic tsunami.

Any employer who has heard this tale will think hard before he hires a computer cracker. Which may be, of course, among the effects the Secret Service desires.

On May 8, 1990, Operation Sun Devil, heretofore an apparently random and nameless trickle of Secret Service actions, swept down on the Legion of Doom and its ilk like a bureaucratic tsunami. On that day, the Secret Service served 27 search warrants in 14 cities from Plano, Texas, to New York, New York.

The law had come to Cyberspace. When the day was over, transit through the wide open spaces of the Virtual World would be a lot trickier.

In a press release following the sweep, the Secret Service boasted having shut down numerous computer bulletin boards, confiscated 40 computers, and seized 23,000 disks. They noted in their statement that "the conceivable criminal violations of this operation have serious implications for the health and welfare of all individuals, corporations, and United States Government agencies relying on computers and telephones to communicate."

It was unclear from their statement whether "this operation" meant the Legion of Doom or Operation Sun Devil. There was room to interpret it either way.

Because the deliciously ironic truth is that, aside from the 3-page Bell South document, the hackers had neither removed nor damaged anyone's data. Operation Sun Devil, on the other hand, had "serious implications" for a number of folks who relied on "computers and telephones to communicate." They lost the equivalent of about 5.4 million pages of information. Not to mention a few computers and telephones.

And the welfare of the individuals behind those figures was surely in jeopardy. Like the story of the single mother and computer consultant in Baltimore whose sole means of supporting herself and her 18-year-old son was stripped away early one morning. Secret Service agents broke down her door with sledge hammers, entered with guns drawn, and seized all her computer equipment. Apparently her son had also been using it . . .

I was about to have an experience which would restore both my natural sense of unreality and my unwillingness to demean the motives of others. I was about to see firsthand the disorientation of the law in the featureless vastness of Cyberspace.

Or the father in New York who opened the door at 6:00 AM and found a shotgun at his nose. A dozen agents entered. While one of them kept the man's wife in a choke-hold, the rest made ready to shoot and entered the bedroom of their sleeping 14-year-old. Before leaving, they confiscated every piece of electronic equipment in the house, including all the telephones.

It was enough to suggest that the insurance companies should start writing policies against capricious governmental seizure of circuitry.

In fairness, one can imagine the government's problem. This is all pretty magical stuff to them. If I were trying to terminate the operations of a witch coven, I'd probably seize everything in sight. How would I tell the ordinary household brooms from the getaway vehicles?

But as I heard more and more about the vile injustices being heaped on my young pals in the Legion of Doom, not to mention the unfortunate folks nearby, the less I was inclined toward such temperate thoughts as these. I drifted back into a 60's-style sense of the government, thinking it a thing of monolithic and evil efficiency and adopting an up-against-the-wall willingness to spit words like "pig" or "fascist" into my descriptions.

In doing so, I endowed the Secret Service with a clarity of intent which no agency of government will ever possess. Despite almost every experience I've ever had with federal authority, I keep imagining its competence.

For some reason, it was easier to invest the Keystone Kapers of Operation Sun Devil with malign purpose rather than confront their absurdity straight on. There is, after all, a twisted kind of comfort in political paranoia. It provides one such a sense of orderliness to think that the government is neither crazy nor stupid and that its plots, though wicked, are succinct.

I was about to have an experience which would restore both my natural sense of unreality and my unwillingness to demean the motives of others. I was about to see firsthand the disorientation of the law in the featureless vastness of Cyberspace.

■ IN SEARCH OF NUPROMETHEUS

I pity the poor immigrant . . .

—Bob Dylan

Sometime last June, an angry hacker got hold of a chunk of the highly secret source code which drives the Apple Macintosh. He then distributed it to a variety of addresses, claiming responsibility for this act of information terrorism in the name of the Nu Prometheus League.

Apple freaked. NuPrometheus had stolen, if not the Apple crown jewels, at least a stone from them. Worse, NuPrometheus had then given this prize away. Repeatedly.

All Apple really has to offer the world is the software which lies encoded in silicon on the ROM chip of every Macintosh. This set of instructions is the cyber-DNA which makes a Macintosh a Macintosh.

Worse, much of the magic in this code was put there by people who not only do not work for Apple any longer, but might only do so again if encouraged with cattle prods. Apple's attitude toward its ROM code is a little like that of a rich kid toward his inheritance. Not actually knowing how to create wealth himself, he guards what he has with hysterical fervor.

Time passed, and I forgot about the incident. But one recent May morning, I learned that others had not. The tireless search for the spectral heart of NuPrometheus finally reached Pinedale, Wyoming, where I was the object of a two-hour interview by Special Agent Richard Baxter, Jr. of the Federal Bureau of Investigation.

Poor Agent Baxter didn't know a ROM chip from a Vise-grip when he arrived, so much of that time was spent trying to educate him on the nature of the thing which had been stolen. Or whether "stolen" was the right term for what had happened to it.

You know things have rather jumped the groove when potential suspects must explain to law enforcers the nature of their alleged perpetrations.

I wouldn't swear Agent Baxter ever got it quite right. After I showed him some actual source code, gave a demonstration of e-mail in action, and downloaded a file from the WELL, he took to rubbing his face with both hands, peering up over his fingertips and saying, "It sure is something, isn't it," or, "Whooo-ee."

Or, "My 8-year-old knows more about these things than I do." He didn't say this with a father's pride so much as an immigrant's fear of a strange new land into which he will be forcibly moved and in which his own child is a native. He looked across my keyboard into Cyberspace and didn't like what he saw.

We could have made it harder for one another, but I think we each sensed that the other occupied a world which was as bizarre and nonsensical as it could be. We did our mutual best to suppress immune response at the border.

You'd have thought his world might have been a little more recognizable to me. Not so, it turns out. Because in his world, I found several unfamiliar features, including these:

1. The Hacker's Conference is an underground organization of computer out-laws with likely connections to, and almost certainly sympathy with, the NuPrometheus League. (Or as Agent Baxter repeatedly put it, the "New Prosthesis League.")

2. John Draper, the aforementioned Cap'n Crunch, in addition to being a known member of the Hacker's Conference, is also CEO and president of Autodesk, Inc. This is of particular concern to the FBI because Autodesk has many top-secret contracts with the government to supply Star Wars graphics imaging and "hyperspace" technology. Worse, Draper is thought to have Soviet contacts.

He wasn't making this up. He had lengthy documents from the San Francisco office to prove it. And in which Autodesk's address was certainly correct.

On the other hand, I know John Draper. While, as I say, he may have once distinguished himself as a cracker during the Pleistocene, he is not now, never has been, and never will be CEO of Autodesk. He did work there for a while last year, but he was let go long before he got in a position to take over.

Nor is Autodesk, in my experience with it, the Star Wars skunk works which Agent Baxter's documents indicated. One could hang out there a long time without ever seeing any gold braid.

Their primary product is something called AutoCAD, by far the most popu-lar computer-aided design software but generally lacking in lethal potential. They do have a small development program in Cyberspace, which is what they call Virtual Reality. (This, I assume is the "hyperspace" to which Agent Baxter's documents referred.)

However, Autodesk had reduced its Cyberspace program to a couple of programmers. I imagined Randy Walser and Carl Tollander toiling away in the dark and lonely service of their country. Didn't work. Then I tried to describe Virtual Reality to Agent Baxter, but that didn't work either. In fact, he tilted. I took several runs at it, but I could tell I was violating our border agreements. These seemed to include a requirement that neither of us try to drag the other across into his conceptual zone.

I fared a little better on the Hacker's Conference. Hardly a conspiracy, the Hacker's Conference is an annual convention originated in 1984 by the Point Foundation and the editors of *Whole Earth Review.* Each year it invites about a hundred of the most gifted and accomplished of digital creators. Indeed, they are the very people who have conducted the personal computer revolution. Agent Baxter looked at my list of Hacker's Conference attendees and read their bios.

Agent Baxter looked at my list of Hacker's Conference attendees and read their bios. "These are the people who actually design this stuff, aren't they?" He was incredulous. Their corporate addresses didn't fit his model of outlaws at all well.

"These are the people who actually design this stuff, aren't they?" He was incredulous. Their corporate addresses didn't fit his model of outlaws at all well.

Why had he come all the way to Pinedale to investigate a crime he didn't understand which had taken place (sort of) in five different places, none of which was within 500 miles?

Well, it seems Apple has told the FBI that they can expect little cooperation from Hackers in and around the Silicon Valley, owing to virulent anti-Apple sentiment there. They claim this is due to the Hacker belief that software should be free combined with festering resentment of Apple's commercial success. They advised the FBI to question only those Hackers who were as far as possible from the twisted heart of the subculture.

They did have their eye on some local people, though. These included a couple of former Apple employees, Grady Ward and Water Horat, Chuck Farnham (who has made a living out of harassing Apple), Glenn Tenney (the purported leader of the Hackers), and, of course, the purported CEO of Autodesk.

Other folks Agent Baxter asked me about included Mitch Kapor, who wrote Lotus 1-2-3 and was known to have received some of this mysterious source code. Or whatever. But I had also met Mitch Kapor, both on the WELL and in person. A less likely computer terrorist would be hard to come by.

Actually, the question of the source code was another area where worlds but shadow-boxed. Although Agent Baxter didn't know source code from Tuesday, he did know that Apple Computer had told his agency that what had been stolen and disseminated was the complete recipe for a Macintosh computer. The distribution of this secret formula might result in the creation of millions of Macintoshes not made by Apple. And, of course, the ruination of Apple Computer.

In my world, NuPrometheus (whoever they, or more likely, he might be) had distributed a small portion of the code which related specifically to Color QuickDraw. QuickDraw is Apple's name for the software which controls the Mac's on-screen graphics. But this was another detail which Agent Baxter could not capture. For all he knew, you could grow Macintoshes from floppy disks.

I explained to him that Apple was alleging something like the ability to assemble an entire human being from the recipe for a foot, but even he knew the analogy was inexact. And trying to get him to accept the idea that a corporation could go mad with suspicion was quite futile. He had a far different perception of the emotional reliability of institutions.

When he finally left, we were both dazzled and disturbed. I spent some time thinking about Lewis Carroll and tried to return to writing about the legal persecution of the Legion of Doom. But my heart wasn't in it. I found myself suddenly too much in sympathy with Agent Baxter and his struggling colleagues from Operation Sun Devil to get back into a proper sort of pig-bashing mode.

Given what had happened to other innocent bystanders like Steve Jackson, I gave some thought to getting scared. But this was Kafka in a clown suit. It wasn't precisely frightening. I also took some comfort in a phrase once applied to the administration of Frederick the Great: "Despotism tempered by incompetence."

Of course, incompetence is a double-edged banana. While we may know this new territory better than the authorities, they have us literally out-gunned. One should pause before making well-armed paranoids feel foolish, no matter how foolish they seem.

■ THE FEAR OF WHITE NOISE

Neurosis is the inability to tolerate ambiguity.
                    —Sigmund Freud, appearing to me in a dream

I'm a member of that half of the human race which is inclined to divide the human race into two kinds of people. My dividing line runs between the people who crave certainty and the people who trust chance.

You can draw this one a number of ways, of course, like Control vs. Serendipity, Order vs. Chaos, Hard answers vs. Silly questions, or Newton, Descartes & Aquinas vs. Heisenberg, Mandelbrot & the Dalai Lama. Etc.

Large organizations and their drones huddle on one end of my scale, busily trying to impose predictable homogeneity on messy circumstance. On the other end, freelancers and ne'er-do-wells cavort about, getting by on luck if they get by at all.

However you cast these poles, it comes down to the difference between those who see life as a struggle against cosmic peril and human infamy and those who believe, without any hard evidence, that the universe is actually on our side. Fear vs. Faith.

I am of the latter group. Along with Gandhi and Rebecca of Sunnybrook Farm, I believe that other human beings will quite consistently merit my trust if I'm not doing something which scares them or makes them feel bad about themselves. In other words, the best defense is a good way to get hurt.

I'm a member of that half of the human race which is inclined to divide the human race into two kinds of people.

In spite of the fact that this system works very reliably for me and my kind, I find we are increasingly in the minority. More and more of our neighbors live in armed compounds. Alarms blare continuously. Potentially happy people give their lives over to the corporate state as though the world were so dangerous outside its veil of collective immunity that they have no choice.

I have a number of theories as to why this is happening. One has to do with the opening of Cyberspace. As a result of this development, humanity is now undergoing the most profound transformation of its history. Coming into the Virtual World, we inhabit Information. Indeed, we become Information. Thought is embodied and the Flesh is made Word. It's weird as hell.

Beginning with the invention of the telegraph and extending through television into Virtual Reality, we have been, for over a century, experiencing a terrifying erosion in our sense of both body and place. As we begin to realize the enormity of what is happening to us, all but the most courageous have gotten scared.

And everyone, regardless of his psychic resilience, feels this overwhelming sense of strangeness. The world, once so certain and tangible and legally precise, has become an infinite layering of opinions, perceptions, litigation, camera-angles, data, white noise, and, most of all, ambiguities. Those of us who are of the fearful persuasion do not like ambiguities.

Indeed, if one were a little jumpy to start with, he may now be fairly humming with nameless dread. Since no one likes his dread to be nameless, the first order of business is to find it some names.

For a long time here in the United States, Communism provided a kind of catch-all bogeyman. Marx, Stalin and Mao summoned forth such a spectre that, to many Americans, annihilation of all life was preferable to the human portion's becoming Communist. But as Big Red wizened and lost his teeth, we began to cast about for a replacement.

Finding none of sufficient individual horror, we have draped a number of objects with the old black bunting which once shrouded the Kremlin. Our current spooks are terrorists, child abductors, AIDS, and the underclass. I would say drugs, but anyone who thinks that the War on Drugs is not actually the War on the Underclass hasn't been paying close enough attention.

There are a couple of problems with these Four Horsemen. For one thing, they aren't actually very dangerous. For example, only seven Americans died in worldwide terrorist attacks in 1987. Fewer than 10 (out of about 70 million) children are abducted by strangers in the U.S. each year. Your chances of getting AIDS if you are neither gay nor a hemophiliac nor a junkie are considerably less than your chances of getting killed by lightning while golfing. The underclass is dangerous, of course, but only, with very few exceptions, if you are a member of it.

The perfect bogeyman for Modern Times is the Cyberpunk!

The other problem with these perils is that they are all physical. If we are entering into a world in which no one has a body, physical threats begin to lose their sting.

And now I come to the point of this screed: The perfect bogeyman for Modern Times is the Cyberpunk! He is so smart he makes you feel even more stupid than you usually do. He knows this complex country in which you're perpetually lost. He understands the value of things you can't conceptualize long enough to cash in on. He is the one-eyed man in the Country of the Blind.

In a world where you and your wealth consist of nothing but beeps and boops of micro-voltage, he can steal all your assets in nanoseconds and then make you disappear.

He can even reach back out of his haunted mists and kill you physically. Among the justifications for Operation Sun Devil was this chilling tidbit:

"Hackers had the ability to access and review the files of hospital patients. Furthermore, they could have added, deleted, or altered vital patient information, possibly causing life-threatening situations."

Perhaps the most frightening thing about the Cyberpunk is the danger he presents to The Institution, whether corporate or governmental. If you are frightened, you have almost certainly taken shelter by now in one of these collective organisms, so the very last thing you want is something which can endanger your heretofore unassailable hive.

And make no mistake, crackers will become to bureaucratic bodies what viruses presently are to human bodies. Thus, Operation Sun Devil can be seen as the first of many waves of organizational immune response to this new antigen. Agent Baxter was a T-cell. Fortunately, he didn't know that himself and I was very careful not to show him my own antigenic tendencies.

I think that herein lies the way out of what might otherwise become an Armageddon between the control freaks and the neo-hip. Those who are comfortable with these disorienting changes must do everything in our power to convey that comfort to others. In other words, we must share our sense of hope and opportunity with those who feel that in Cyberspace they will be obsolete eunuchs for sure.

It's a tall order. But, my silicon brothers, our self-interest is strong. If we come on as witches, they will burn us. If we volunteer to guide them gently into its new lands, the Virtual World might be a more amiable place for all of us than this one has been.

Of course, we may also have to fight.

Defining the conceptual and legal map of Cyberspace before the ambiguophobes do it for us (with punitive overprecision) is going to require some effort. We can't expect the Constitution to take care of itself. Indeed, the precedent for mitigating the Constitutional protection of a new medium has already been established. Consider what happened to radio in the early part of this century.

Under the pretext of allocating limited bandwidth, the government established an early right of censorship over broadcast content which still seems directly unconstitutional to me. Except that it stuck. And now, owing to a large body of case law, looks to go on sticking.

New media, like any chaotic system, are highly sensitive to initial conditions. Today's heuristical answers of the moment become tomorrow's permanent institutions of both law and expectation. Thus, they bear examination with that destiny in mind.

In over-reaching as extravagantly as they did, the Secret Service may actually have done a service for those of us who love liberty.

Earlier in this article, I asked a number of tough questions relating to the nature of property, privacy, and speech in the digital domain. Questions like: "What are data and what is free speech?" or "How does one treat property which has no physical form and can be infinitely reproduced?" or "Is a computer the same as a printing press?" The events of Operation Sun Devil were nothing less than an effort to provide answers to these questions. Answers which would greatly enhance governmental ability to silence the future's opinionated nerds.

In overreaching as extravagantly as they did, the Secret Service may actually have done a service for those of us who love liberty. They have provided us with a devil. And devils, among their other galvanizing virtues, are just great for clarifying the issues and putting iron in your spine. In the presence of a devil, it's always easier to figure out where you stand.

While I previously had felt no stake in the obscure conundra of free telecommunication, I was, thanks to Operation Sun Devil, suddenly able to plot a trajectory from the current plight of the Legion of Doom to an eventual constraint on opinions much dearer to me. I remembered Martin Neimoeller, who said:

In Germany they came first for the Communists, and I didn't speak up because I wasn't a Communist. Then they came for the Jews, and I didn't speak up because I wasn't a Jew. They came for the trade unionists, and I didn't speak up because I wasn't a trade unionist. Then they came for the Catholics, and I didn't speak up because I was a Protestant. Then they came for me, and by that time no one was left to speak up.

I decided it was time for me to speak up.

The evening of my visit from Agent Baxter, I wrote an account of it which I placed on the WELL. Several days later, Mitch Kapor literally dropped by for a chat.

Also a WELL denizen, he had read about Agent Baxter and had begun to meditate on the inappropriateness of leaving our civil liberties to be defined by the technologically benighted. A man who places great emphasis on face-to-face contact, he wanted to discuss this issue with me in person. He had been flying his Canadair bizjet to a meeting in California when he realized his route took him directly over Pinedale.

We talked for a couple of hours in my office while a spring snowstorm swirled outside. When I recounted for him what I had learned about Operation Sun Devil, he decided it was time for him to speak up, too.

He called a few days later with the phone number of a civil libertarian named Harvey Silverglate, who, as evidence of his conviction that everyone deserves due process, is currently defending Leona Helmsley. Mitch asked me to tell Harvey what I knew, with the inference that he would help support the costs which are liable to arise whenever you tell a lawyer anything.

I found Harvey in New York at the offices of that city's most distinguished constitutional law firm, Rabinowitz, Boudin, Standard, Krinsky, and Lieberman. These are the folks who made it possible for the *New York Times* to print the Pentagon Papers. (Not to dwell on the unwilling notoriety which partner Leonard Boudin achieved back in 1970 when his Weathergirl daughter blew up the family home . . .)

As of today (in early June of 1990), Mitch and I are legally constituting the Electronic Frontier Foundation.

In the conference call which followed, I could almost hear the skeletal click as their jaws dropped. The next day, Eric Lieberman and Terry Gross of Rabinowitz, Boudin met with Acid Phreak, Phiber Optik, and Scorpion.

The maddening trouble with writing this account is that *Whole Earth Review,* unlike, say, *Phrack,* doesn't publish instantaneously. Events are boiling up at such a frothy pace that anything I say about current occurrences surely will not obtain by the time you read this. The road from here is certain to fork many times. The printed version of this will seem downright quaint before it's dry.

But as of today (in early June of 1990), Mitch and I are legally constituting the Electronic Frontier Foundation, a two (or possibly three) man organization which will raise and disburse funds for education, lobbying, and litigation in the areas relating to digital speech and the extension of the Constitution into Cyberspace.

Already, on the strength of preliminary stories about our efforts in the *Washington Post* and the *New York Times,* Mitch has received an offer from Steve Wozniak to match whatever funds he dedicates to this effort. (As well as a fair amount of abuse from the more institutionalized precincts of the computer industry.)

The Electronic Frontier Foundation will fund, conduct, and support legal efforts to demonstrate that the Secret Service has exercised prior restraint on publications, limited free speech, conducted improper seizure of equipment and data, used undue force, and generally conducted itself in a fashion which is arbitrary, oppressive, and unconstitutional.

In addition, we will work with the Computer Professionals for Social Responsibility and other organizations to convey to both the public and the policy-makers metaphors which will illuminate the more general stake in liberating Cyberspace.

Not everyone will agree. Crackers are, after all, generally beyond public sympathy. Actions on their behalf are not going to be popular no matter who else might benefit from them in the long run.

Nevertheless, in the litigations and political debates which are certain to follow, we will endeavor to assure that their electronic speech is protected as certainly as any opinions which are printed or, for that matter, screamed. We will make an effort to clarify issues surrounding the distribution of intellectual property. And we will help to create for America a future which is as blessed by the Bill of Rights as its past has been.

John Markoff

A Most-Wanted Cyberthief Is Caught in His Own Web

aleigh, NC, February 15 [1995]—After a search of more than two years, a team of F.B.I. agents early this morning captured a 31-year-old computer expert accused of a long crime spree that includes the theft of thousands of data files and at least 20,000 credit card numbers from computer systems around the nation.

The arrest of Kevin D. Mitnick, one of the most wanted computer criminals, followed a 24-hour stakeout of an apartment building here.

A convicted computer felon on the run from Federal law enforcement officials since November 1992, Mr. Mitnick has used his sophisticated skills over the years to worm his way into many of the nation's telephone and cellular telephone networks and vandalize government, corporate and university computer systems. Most recently, he had become a suspect in a rash of break-ins on the global Internet computer network.

"He was arguably the most wanted computer hacker in the world," said Kent Walker, an assistant United States attorney in San Francisco who helped run the investigation, "He allegedly had access to corporate trade secrets worth millions of dollars. He was a very big threat."

But Federal officials say Mr. Mitnick's confidence in his hacking skills may have been his undoing. On Christmas Day, he broke into the home computer of a computer security expert, Tsutomu Shimomura, a researcher at the federally financed San Diego Supercomputer Center.

Mr. Shimomura then made a crusade of tracking down the intruder, a pursuit that led to today's arrest. Mr. Shimomura, working from a monitoring post in San Jose, Calif., determined last Saturday that Mr. Mitnick was operating through a computer modem connected to a cellular telephone somewhere near Raleigh, North Carolina.

Mr. Shimomura was present today at Mr. Mitnick's prearraignment hearing at the Federal courthouse here. At the end of the hearing, Mr. Mitnick, who now has shoulder-length brown hair and was wearing a black sweat suit and handcuffs, turned to Mr. Shimomura, whom he had never met face to face.

"Hello, Tsutomu," Mr. Mitnick said. "I respect your skills."

Mr. Shimomura, who is 30 and also has shoulder-length hair, nodded solemnly.

Mr. Shimomura had flown on Sunday morning to Raleigh, where he helped telephone company technicians and Federal investigators use cellular-frequency scanners to home in on Mr. Mitnick.

Mr. Mitnick was arrested at 2 o'clock this morning in his apartment in the Raleigh suburb of Duraleigh Hills, after F.B.I. agents used their scanners to determine that Mr. Mitnick, in keeping with his nocturnal habits, had connected once again to the Internet.

Mr. Mitnick, already wanted in California for a Federal parole violation, was charged today with two Federal crimes. The first, illegal use of a telephone access device, is punishable by up to 15 years in prison and a $250,000 fine. The second charge, computer fraud, carries potential penalties of 20 years in prison and a $250,000 fine. Federal prosecutors said they were considering additional charges related to Mr. Mitnick's reported Internet spree.

Federal officials say Mr. Mitnick's motives have always been murky. He was recently found to have stashed thousands of credit card numbers on computers in the San Francisco Bay area—including the card numbers of some of the best-known millionaires in Silicon Valley. But there is no evidence yet that Mr. Mitnick had attempted to use those credit card accounts.

Indeed, frequently ignoring the possibility of straightforward financial gain from the information he has stolen, Mr. Mitnick has often seemed more concerned with proving that his technical skills are better than those whose job it is to protect the computer networks he has attacked.

Federal officials say the arrest of Mr. Mitnick does not necessarily solve all the recent Internet crimes, because his trail of electronic mail has indicated that he may have accomplices. One of them is an unknown computer operator, thought to be in Israel, with whom Mr. Mitnick has corresponded electronically and boasted of his Internet exploits, investigators said.

Still, the capture of Mr. Mitnick gives the F.B.I. custody of a notoriously persistent and elusive computer break-in expert. Raised in the San Fernando Valley near Los Angeles by his mother, Mr. Mitnick has been in and out of trouble with the law since 1981. It was then, as a 17-year-old, that he was placed on probation for stealing computer manuals from a Pacific Bell telephone switching center in Los Angeles.

Those who know Mr. Mitnick paint a picture of a man obsessed with the power inherent in controlling the nation's computer and telephone networks. The recent break-ins he is accused of conducting include forays into computer systems at Apple Computer Inc. and Motorola Inc. and attacks on commercial services that provide computer users with access to the Internet, including the Well in Sausalito, California, Netcom in San Jose, California, and the Colorado Supernet, in Boulder, Colorado.

To make it difficult for investigators to determine where the attacks were coming from, Mr. Mitnick is said to have used his computer and modem to manipulate a local telephone company switch in Raleigh to disguise his whereabouts.

In recent weeks, as an elite team of computer security experts tightened an invisible electronic net around the fugitive, Mr. Mitnick continued to taunt his pursuers, apparently unaware of how close they were to capturing him. About 10 days ago, for example, someone whom investigators believe to have been Mr. Mitnick left a voice-mail message for Mr. Shimomura, a Japanese citizen. The message reprimanded Mr. Shimomura for converting the intruder's earlier voice-mail messages into computer audio files and making them available on the Internet.

"Ah Tsutomu, my learned disciple," the taunting voice said. "I see that you put my voice on the Net. I'm very disappointed, my son."

But the continued attempts at one-upmanship simply gave the pursuers more electronic evidence.

"He was a challenge for law enforcement, but in the end he was caught by his own obsession," said Kathleen Cunningham, a deputy marshal for the United States Marshals Service who has pursued Mr. Mitnick for several years.

Mr. Mitnick first came to national attention in 1982 when, as a teenage prank, he used a computer and a modem to break into a North American Air Defense Command computer. He subsequently gained temporary control of three central offices of telephone companies in Manhattan and all the phone switching centers in California. This gave him the ability to listen in on calls and pull pranks like reprogramming the home phone of someone he did not like so that each time the phone was picked up, a recording asked for a deposit of a coin.

Overconfidence may have undone a high-tech felon.

But the break-ins escalated beyond sophomoric pranks. For months in 1988, Mr. Mitnick secretly read the electronic mail of computer security officials at MCI Communications and the Digital Equipment Corporation, learning how their computers and phone equipment were protected. Officials at Digital later accused him of causing $4 million in damage to computer operations at the company and stealing $1 million of software. He was convicted in July 1989 and sentenced to a year in a low-security Federal prison in Lompoc, California.

One of his lawyers convinced the court that Mr. Mitnick had an addiction to computers. In July 1989, after his release from prison, he was placed in a treatment program for compulsive disorders, the Beit T'shuvah center in Los Angeles. During his six months there, he was prohibited from touching a computer or modem.

That restriction was a condition of his probation when he was released in mid-1990, and it was for reportedly violating this condition that Federal officials were pursuing him when he dropped out of sight in November 1992.

In September 1993, the state police in California also issued a warrant for his arrest. The warrant stated that Mr. Mitnick had wiretapped calls from agents of the Federal Bureau of Investigation to the California Department of Motor Vehicles. He then used law-enforcement access codes obtained by eavesdropping on the agents to gain illegal access to the drivers' license data base in California.

John Markoff

Hacker and Grifter Duel on the Net

an Francisco—My first inkling that Kevin Mitnick might be reading my electronic mail came more than a year ago. I found a document posted on a public electronic bulletin board containing a personal message that could only have been obtained by someone reading my mail.

At the time, I suspected it might be Mr. Mitnick, a convicted computer felon who was being sought by the F.B.I. for violation of probation, but I simply shrugged and stopped using that e-mail account for anything important. I'd been around the Internet long enough to believe that true computer security is a fleeting illusion. In cyberspace, many people have become inured to the dangers of living in a world of swashbuckling electronic pirates.

But the exploits of rogue technophiles that once made people fatalistic about privacy have also brought about a kind of backlash. If some citizens of cyberspace are blasé about the likelihood of electronic intrusion, a growing number of others react to the filching of computer files with the feelings of outrage and violation normally provoked by a burglar's rifling their home. What once seemed like a misguided spirit of adventure seems more and more like garden-variety vandalism.

Last month, when I learned that my accounts were again among those vandalized, I was less tolerant than I had been a year ago. I was not alone. The electronic intruder had also rifled the files from the home computer of Tsutomu Shimomura, a researcher at the San Diego Supercomputer Center, and left taunting messages. Mr. Shimomura, who has a deeply felt sense of right and wrong, abandoned a cross-country skiing vacation to spend the next two weeks on little sleep, tracking down the person who, he believed, had done it.

Mr. Shimomura and a team of three other computer experts came to believe that their suspect was Mr. Mitnick, who was being hunted by the F.B.I. for various crimes, including the theft of some 20,000 credit card numbers from computer systems around the country. They let me know he was probably responsible for a second intrusion into my e-mail account. Mr. Shimomura began cooperating with the F.B.I. to track him down. Using sophisticated surveillance software in Sausalito and San Jose, California, he watched his suspect type out messages that seemed to reflect Mr. Mitnick's thoughts, worries and complaints.

I had to agree that Mr. Mitnick seemed to be the typist. One day this month, I watched Mr. Shimomura's computer screen as the suspect wrote a message to an acquaintance complaining that I had put his picture on the front page of *The New York Times*. There were only two people who could have written this, and of the two, Mr. Mitnick was the only plausible suspect. So I too became enmeshed in the digital manhunt for the nation's most wanted computer outlaw.

The technical sophistication of the pursued and his pursuer, Mr. Shimomura, was remarkable. But underneath the technological paraphernalia—the tracking software and the radio homing devices carried by the pursuer, the baffling telephone switching manipulations used by the pursued to cover his tracks—there was the interplay of two opposing personalities, who had little in common beside their considerable skills.

Their meeting was a collision of two dramatically different minds that happen to share a fascination for cyberspace. One is an intense scientist who is a master at manipulating computers, the other is a chameleon-like grifter who is a master at manipulating human beings.

Mr. Mitnick seemed to believe he was an equal of the man who finally caught him. At his pre-trial hearing in Federal District Court in Raleigh, North Carolina last week where he faced charges of computer fraud and illegal use of a telephone access device, he greeted Mr. Shimomura saying, "Hi, Tsutomu. I respect your skills."

The feeling wasn't mutual. In Mr. Shimomura's eyes, Mr. Mitnick's history of break-ins was a simple violation of the tight-knit community of computer users who have built and maintained the Internet. "This kind of behavior is unacceptable," Mr. Shimomura said. And so, he decided to put a stop to it.

It didn't take long. Using different tools, including his own homebrew software program, which permits a video-like reconstruction of individual users' computer sessions, and cellular telephone scanning equipment, he had narrowed down the location of the suspect.

Early Monday morning, two weeks after he began his hunt, Mr. Shimomura was pointing to a cluster of apartment buildings in Raleigh, North Carolina and telling F.B.I. agents, whom he had been in regular contact with, that they would find their target inside. Two days later, the F.B.I. knocked on an apartment door and arrested Mr. Mitnick.

■ LISTEN FAST

Mr. Shimomura's technical skills are obvious. He himself is almost impossible to classify. Although he studied under the physicist Richard Feynman at the California Institute of Technology, he has no college degree. What he does have is an uncanny ability to solve complex technical problems in the manner of *Star Trek*'s Vulcan Mr. Spock. After meeting Mr. Shimomura for the first time in Sausalito, California, two weeks ago, an F.B.I. agent turned to Assistant United States Attorney Kent Walker and shook his head saying, "He talks at 64,000 bits-per-second but I can only listen at 300 bits-per-second."

Mr. Shimomura also has what Neal Stephenson, the author of the novel *Snowcrash,* calls "kneejerk iconoclasticism," a willingness to question every-thing. He seems to embody the very essence of the original hacker ethic—writing programs to create something elegant, not for gain—as described by Steven Levy, the author of *Hackers: Heros of the Computer Revolution.* "Tsutomu's very much into the culture of sharing," Mr. Levy said.

Mr. Mitnick was not. I wrote my first article about Mr. Mitnick in the early 1980's after he was arrested in Southern California for breaking into a Pacific Bell central office and stealing the telephone company's technical manuals. At the time he was a teenager.

Since then Mr. Mitnick has been arrested three more times. In 1987, he was convicted of unauthorized access to a computer for electronically break-ing into the computers at the Santa Cruz Operation. He was sentenced to probation. In 1988, he was charged with stealing software electronically from the Digital Equipment Corporation. He was convicted a year later and sen-tenced to a year in prison and six months of counseling for what his attorney termed his addiction to computers. The third arrest came last week. He is in Wade County jail in western North Carolina, awaiting trial.

Mr. Mitnick is the archetype of the cyberpunk antihero. He feels as if he's living in a post-Orwellian world, where outlaw street culture merges with high technology. Read William Gibson's novel *Neuromancer* or watch Ridley Scott's movie *Bladerunner,* and you will understand a world populated by superfast computers and shady characters who blend high-tech skills with an outlaw sensibility.

If anything, Mr. Mitnick's real "darkside" brilliance comes not from his computer skills, but from his insight into people. He understands how organi-zations keep information and he knows how to trick people into giving the information to him.

Mr. Mitnick is not a hacker in the original sense of the word. Mr. Shimo-mura is. And when their worlds collided, it was obvious which one of them had to win.

Chapter 2

Questions and Suggestions for Further Study on the Net/WWW

■ QUESTIONS BASED ON THE READINGS:

1. Is there such a thing as a cybercommunity? A cybercitizen (or cyberzen)? If there is, what are its implications? If not, then why not?

2. The readings include much discussion of the U.S. Constitution and the First Amendment as well as other amendments. Since the Internet moves beyond the boundaries of the United States, what does the Constitution have to do with how cybercitizens discourse with each other and move about on the Web?

3. What are the differences among CompuServe, Arnt Gulbrandsen, and the U.S. government when each interferes (by way of, so to speak, a "cancel-bot") with the free passage of information?

4. What does "Mentor" mean when he writes: "We make use of a service already existing without paying for what could be dirt-cheap if it wasn't run by profiteering gluttons, and you call us criminals"? Do you agree with him? If so, why? If not, why not? Do you find Meyer's distinction (in "Crimes of the 'Net'") between "digital socialism" and "copyrightable capitalism" helpful? How so?

5. In terms of upstaging others, which hackers come out ahead in "Is Computer Hacking a Crime" (the exchange over the WELL)? What are your criteria for making this decision? What is your attitude toward Phiber Optik when he discloses Barlow's credit history before all online? After reading the exchange from beginning to end, what do you think the hacker's ethic is? State specific examples in the transcript for *why* you think what you think about their exchange on ethics.

6. What is Barlow's attitude toward the hackers in the *Harper's* forum when he writes of them in "Crime and Puzzlement"? Does his attitude remain the same throughout? Toward the end of his article, Barlow refers to the Pentagon Papers. What are they and what is their relevance?

7. Kevin D. Mitnick is referred to intermittently throughout the articles in this section. (The last two articles by Markoff are exclusively devoted to Mitnick.) What is Mitnick's function when he is cited? Do you have a sense that Mitnick functions as a sort of *baseline* by which each author is

able to distinguish good from bad, hacker from cracker? If not, what sense do you get? Reread the conclusion of the second article by Markoff. To get a better sense of who Mitnick is, research him as fully as you can in the library and on the Net, and write about what you find. This could be a group or a class project that could be put on a website for others to visit from all over the world. This, too, would be a kind of sharing. (See the two additional articles on Mitnick by Jeff Goodell and by Katie Hafner below.)

■ FURTHER STUDY ON THE NET/WWW (SEE "FURTHER SUGGESTIONS" IN CHAPTER 3, FOR FEDERAL GOVERNMENT WEBSITES):

Let's take a detailed look at the website for the Electronic Frontier Foundation, <http://www.eff.org/>. (For basic instructions on how to access a URL, see Appendix A.) Once you are at the website (or homepage) for EFF, you will see

EFF—The Electronic Frontier Foundation
A non-profit civil liberties organization working in the public interest to protect privacy, free expression, and access to online resources and information.
EFF Info
Alerts
Current Newsletter
Archives

Pointing down with the ↓ key, you will eventually get to:

EFF SERVICES, FORUMS & PUBLICATIONS
EFF Document & File Archives—a Web, Gopher & FTP Online Library
EFF's (Extended) Guide to the Internet—EEGttI
EFFector Online EFF Newsletter—Backissues & Index
EFF News and Discussion via Usenet
EFF- and Net-Related Images, Animations and Sounds
The EFF Virtual World Tour of Cyberspace, featuring Aerosmith
Other Publications and Material of Interest
EFF BOARD, STAFF & VOLUNTEER HOMEPAGES

Scrolling or pointing up with the ↑ key, let's take a look at the Archives with the → key. Here you will find

The Main Archive
EFF WWW Archive Topical Index—See a list of subjects in the EFF document and file library, each topic linked to a directory of files and anchors to other, related sites and net-resources

EFF WWW-Enhanced **FTP Archive Top Level**—The root of the EFF online library directory tree, with links to on- and off-site relevant material & resources

EFF **Gopher Archive** For those who prefer gopher: the EFF document library accessed via gopher.eff.org

Special Collections

The Frontier Files Collection—A diskette-full of some of the more important material on our site: a "Best of EFF" compilation—available in several formats.

The Computers & Academic Freedom (CAF) Online Library—Volunteer-maintained collection featuring academic acceptable usage policies, information on intellectual freedom, collections of state and foreign computer crime laws, and more.

The Computer underground Digest (CUD) E-Zine Archive—Volunteer-maintained collection of electronic publications related to hacking, security, privacy, and the technical side of networking and computing.

Let's take a closer look at the *archives*. When in them, you will find an alphabetized list of a wide variety of political interests such as

CMU Censorship
Caller ID
Canadian Censorship
Canadian Legal Cases
Canadian Legal Issues
Canadian Medical Privacy
Canadian Privacy
Censorship—Hate-speech & Discrimination
Censorship—Terrorism & Militias
Censorship and Child Porn
Censorship/Exon bill
Chain Letter
Church of Scientology v the Net
Civil Liberties (Misc)
Clipper/EES/Capstone/Tessera/Key Escrow
Congressional Committee
Congressional Reform
Consciousness in Cyberia
Crypto Tools
Crypto/Privacy/Security

As usual, embedded hypertextually in each of these is another list with further information. If you continue, however, to scroll or point down ↓ the list you will eventually get to

Hackers

Pointing → from there, you get to

EFF HACKERS ARCHIVE

and eventually, you will find

DISCLAIMER: Material not authored by EFF does not necessarily represent the opinions, views, or policies of EFF.
a_little_perspective_please—A Little Perspective, Please by Mitch Kapor
blake_hackers_in_the_mist—Hackers in the Mist by Roger Blake
bloodaxe-goggans_94.interview—Excerpts from interview with Chris Goggans
can_hackers_be_sued_for_damages—Can hackers be sued for damages caused by computer viruses? by Pamala Samuelson
cellhackers.article—Cellular Phreaks and Code Dudes by John Markhoff
chomsky_on_the_net.interview—
computer_crime_laws_by_state—Computer Crime Laws by State
denning_hackers.speech—Concerning Hackers Who Break into Computer Systems by Dorothy Denning
hackers_and_your_privacy.paper—
hacking.faq—2600 Hacking FAQ by Voyager
hackers_with_cause.paper—Computer Hackers: Rebels With a Cause by Tanja S. Rosteck
hacking%3acivil_liberties_or_cr—Civil Liberties in Cyberspace: When does hacking turn from an exercise of civil liberties into crime? by Mitchell Kapor
hackers_retaliate_by_leaking_m—Hackers retaliate by leaking manual By Keay Davidson
hlywd_hacker.article—Hollywood Hacker by Jim Thomas
hypermedia.biblio—
masterkey_clipper.story—MASTER KEY by Infocalypse
mitnik_pioneer_award_joke.article—
nexus.faq—
old_and_new_hackers—Old Hackers, New Hackers: What's the Difference? by Steve Mizrach
password_is_loopholes_quittner—

phiber_jailed.article–The Prisoner: Phiber Optik Goes Directly
to Jail by Julian Dibbel
reflections_on_hacker_sentencin–Reflections On Hacker Sentenc-
ing by John F. McMullen

There is more in this archive, but notice some of the titles and names. Do
you find some that you recognize? At this point, you might want to begin
looking at some of these articles and perhaps printing them to your screen
and downloading them. (For help downloading a copy, see Appendix A.)

As you continue on down the list under Hackers, you will notice

The Hacker Crackdown by Bruce Sterling
Hacker Policies
Technical
Hacker Publications

Here you find the entire and electronically updated copy of Sterling's book
The Hacker Crackdown and other invaluable information and sites for research.
There is much out on the Net that is totally free—information wants to be
free—but be very careful to read all the warnings concerning copyright
notices, what can and cannot be distributed, and how it can be distributed!
For example, read what Sterling has to say about your use of his book! (We
will discuss this issue of copyright later in Chapter 5 and in Appendix A.)
Continuing to move down the electronic page, you will find:

Links to Related Off-Site Resources
Defcon II Information
EFF's System Security Archives
CLM Hacker Page
Phrack Magazine Homepage
Cypherpunks Homepage
Randy King's Homepage
LoPht
CPSR's Computer Crime Archive

Notice *Phrack*! Following your pointer at that location you will get to the
electronic journal's history and archives. (Notice how its homepage begins
and that you can subscribe free.)

■ HERE ARE SOME ADDITIONAL ON-LINE NETWORKS
(WEBSITES, WITH DISCUSSION LISTS MENTIONED)
FOR AND ON FREEDOM, CENSORSHIP, AND HACKERS
(SEE "QUESTIONS AND SUGGESTIONS" IN CHAPTER
3):

- *Steven Levy's homepage* <http://www.echonyc.com/~steven/
  Steven.Levy.html>.

Here you will find a link to his book *Hackers.* Levy says:

My first book and probably the most popular, even ten years
after publication. *Hackers* gets into the mindset of those
people who push the computer past the envelopes of expectations—sitting at the keyboard these are artists, pioneers,
explorers. It is here that I introduced the concept of The
Hacker Ethic:
*Access to computers should be unlimited and total. Always
yield to the Hands-On Imperative. All information should be
free. Mistrust authority—promote decentralization. Hackers
should be judged by their hacking. You can create art and
beauty on a computer. Computers can change your life for the
better.*

- *Netwatchers Cyberzine* <http://www.ionet.net/~mdyer/front.shtml> ("A
  monthly cyberzine covering legal developments in cyberspace and the
  online community.")

- *The Phrack Home Page:* <http://freeside.com/phrack.html>. (Check out the
  full archives.)

- *Steve Jackson's Games:* <http://www.io.com/sjgames/>. (Here you will find
  current releases [games] and specifically the game "GURPS," which so
  excited the federal government into raiding this company in Austin, Texas.)

- *Newsgroups* (Usenet):
  alt.censorship
  alt.hackers
  alt.fan.Kevin-Mitnick
  alt.politics.datahighway
  alt.privacy
  alt.society.civil-liberty

Using WebCrawler: We have only skimmed the surface by looking into the
EFF sight. As a research project, look through the archives, read what interests
you, and begin to formulate what the difference might be between a hacker
and a cracker, at least, from this body of literature found on EFF. In order to
find other positions, you might want to do some searching by way of
WebCrawler, <http://webcrawler.com/>. (For additional information on using
WebCrawler and other search engines, see Appendix A.) Once you get to
WebCrawler, all you have to do is type, in the search space, what you think
might be the appropriate key words such as *hacker* or *cracker* or particular
names such as *Phiber Optik* or *Kevin Mitnick* or *Tsutomu Shimomura,* and wait to
see what information is available on the Web.

Using a library database (GENL): Search for key terms or names such as the
authors of the articles you read in this section—Michael Meyer, Mitchell
Kapor, John Perry Barlow, or John Markoff. Take a look, for example, at the

different articles that have been written about Kevin Mitnick and try to discover what differences in storyline, and especially in motive, are assigned to Mitnick for hacking/cracking.

Using Lycos <http://lycos.cs.cmu.edu/>: As you did in your library's database, search for the same names but add Kevin Mitnick.

- *On litigation and hackers,* point to this Gopher site (just as you type in URLs): <gopher://oss.net/00/oss/oss93/cyberlaw.txt>. (Here you will find discussed the problematic word *Cyberlaw.)*

- *The WELL (Whole Earth 'Lectronic Link*): This costs money to subscribe to, but it's well worth it; the WELL is the BBS in the Bay Area on which the *Harper's Magazine* discussion took place among the hackers: <http://www.well.com/>

- *John Perry Barlow's Home(stead)Page:* <http://www.eff.org/~barlow/barlow.html>. (Here you will find, among many other works, "Crime and Puzzlement Part Two.")

- *Mitchell Kapor's Homepage:* <http://www.kei.com:80/homepages/mkapor/>

- *The Grateful Dead* (for you Deadheads!): <http://www.cs.cmu.edu/afs/cs.cmu.edu/user/mleone/web/dead.html> (On August 8th, 1995, as I was finishing this book, Jerry Garcia died. *All I know is something like a bird within him sang, All I know he sang a little while and then flew on.*)

- . . . and other bands and musicians to be found on *The Ultimate Band List:* <http://american.recordings.com/wwwofmusic/ubl/ubl.shtml>. (This is a website of bands—a full range of Western to New Age—with links to each band and also to newgroups, mailing lists, FAQ files, lyrics, guitar tablatures, and digitized songs.)

■ MORE REFERENCES FOR READING
AND FOR SURFING THE WEB:

Goodell, Jeff. "The Samurai and the Cyberthief." *Rolling Stone* (May 4, 1995): 40–44, 46–47, 71.

Hafner, Katie, and John Markoff. *Cyberpunk: Outlaws and Hackers on the Computer Frontier.* New York: Simon & Schuster, 1991. (Part 1 is devoted to "Kevin [Mitnick]: The Dark-Side Hacker.")

Hafner, Katie. "Kevin Mitnick, Unplugged." *Esquire* (August 1995): 81–88.

Levy, Steven. *Hackers: Heroes of the Computer Revolution.* Garden City, NJ: Anchor/Doubleday, 1984. Online: Steven Levy's homepage. Internet. 20 July 1995. Available: <http://www.echonyc.com/~steven/Steven.Levy.html>

Shapiro, Andrew L. "Cyberscoop!" *The Nation* (March 20, 1995): 369–370. (By way of multiperspectives, Shapiro raises some questions about John Markoff's reporting on Kevin Mitnick. A must read!)

Slatalla, Michelle, and Joshua Quittner. *Masters of Deception: The Gang that Ruled Cyberspace.* New York: HarperCollins, 1995. (See a chapter, "Gang War in Cyberspace," reprinted in *Wired* [December 1994]: 146–51, 200–05. Online: HotWired. Internet. 22 August 1995. Available: <http://vip.hotwired.com/wired/2.12/features/hacker.html>.)

Steele, Guy L. et al., ed. *The Hacker's Dictionary: A Guide to the World of Computer Wizards.* Harper & Row, 1983; *The New Hacker's Dictionary,* MIT Press. Online: The Jargon File. Internet. 27 August 1995. Available: <http://www.ccil.org/jargon/jargon.html>.

Sterling, Bruce. *The Hacker Crackdown: Law and Disorder on the Electronic Frontier.* New York: Bantam, 1992. Online: Fric's Home Page. Internet. 27 August 1995. Available as hypertext version: <http://home.eznet.net/~frac/crack.html>; or Online. The English Server (CMU). Internet. 27 August 1995. Available as plain text version: <gopher://english.hss.cmu.edu:70/0F-2%3A1576%3AThe%20Hacker %20Crackdown>. See the discussion of EFF above for another on-line site.

Wired magazine—at its on-line counterpart, *HotWired* <http://www.hotwired.com/>—features an "Index of Privacy Resources," which has a considerable number of links to information about issues of civil liberties on the Net.

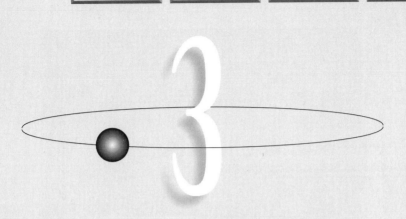

CyberWars

(Flame Wars, Sexual Politics, and Netsex/"Porn"/Violence)

There is a growing concern about gender differences in cyberspace. When on line, it is argued—whether someone on a BBS or newsgroup or even on academic lists or especially at a MOO—gender stereotypes are greatly amplified. (MOO is short for mud object oriented and is a virtual place where people can talk by typing to each other in real time; it is comparable to Inter Relay Chat "rooms" provided by some commercial on-line services.) Males tend to dominate the talk or make sexual advances toward females (or those whom they take to be females). Females tend to lurk on lists or to be annoyed—and understandably so—when males hit on them at MOOS. In cyberspace, it is generally thought, males are active and females are passive. Males tend to flame, while females tend to be silenced publicly, causing them either to unsubscribe from the discussion list or post to each other privately. There are exceptions to this general claim, of course, but many who study exchanges on the Net insist that these exceptions are few and far between. Though we may not especially like stereotypes, we human beings tend to live by them in a major way in cyberspace. This raises the question of whether or not the two sexes are predisposed to active/passive or agonistic/nurturing roles by biology or culture, by gene or scene.

For Barbara Kantrowitz, men and women are not biologically determined in this way, which means, then, that women are not naturally passive in respect to things computerized, but culturally passive. Kantrowitz works from the presumption that while males at an early age are generally encouraged to be aggressive, assertive, and interested in things mechanical, females at the same age are culturally encouraged to be passive and invested in things nonmechanical. Kantrowitz argues that males generally learn to play Nintendo games, while females are encouraged to play with Barbie: "Computer culture is created, defined and controlled by men. Women often feel about as welcome as a system crash." For Kantrowitz, this difference can and must be corrected. Ada Lovelace, she points out, was the "very first computer programmer."

In "Gender Gap in Cyberspace," Deborah Tannen supports Kantrowitz's position, but she approaches the problem of the gender gap by explaining how she differs from Ralph (her colleague and neighbor) in respect to the way she thinks about and utilizes her computer. Says Tannen, "Men want to force computers to submit. Women just want computers to work." In "Bringing Familiar Baggage to the New Frontier: Gender Differences in Computer-Mediated Communication," Susan Herring reports on her empirical study of several discussion lists, giving representative examples and statistics to back up her claim—very similar to Kantrowitz's and Tannen's—that males dominate the Net.

Sexual differences lead both to discussions of sexual politics in cyberspace and to attempts to legislate laws against sexual harassment and pornography and to enforce them. As we have seen in Chapter 2, the Internet has been like the Wild West before law and order was brought to it. We are at that juncture now when Congress is talking in very specific terms about putting a stop to "cyberporn" on the Net, not only to protect women but also children or "the family." Senator James Exon (D-Nebraska) and James Harrington (of the American Civil Liberties Union) take pro and con positions on the issue, which they divide in terms of *protecting the family* versus *protecting freedom of expression.* At the time that I write, Exon has drafted a bill (generally known as the "Communications Decency Act") that would outlaw all sexual harassment and porn. However, many senators and representatives oppose the bill on the grounds that it would not prevent the problems and would be unenforceable and even unconstitutional; alternative bills are being drafted. (More information on this issue is available in Further Suggestions at the close of this chapter.) There have been many other spinoffs from this issue as took place, on Cable News Network, in part because of the Jake Baker case. (Baker was an undergraduate student at the University of Michigan, Ann Arbor, who wrote and posted a sexual fantasy with violence in it toward one of his female classmates, whose actual name he uses in the story.) Though a bill may very well become law soon, the issue will continue to be a crucial one.

Moving from the very general to the specific, we find in the two remaining articles different takes on the problem of sexual politics on the Net. One solution, put forth by Howard Rheingold, is not for the banning of sex but for its legitimization in terms of "Teledildonics" (an extension of Ted Nelson's word *dildonics*). In discussing various aspects of the technology, Rheingold writes: "The tool that I am suggesting is much more than a fancy vibrator, but I suggest we keep the archaic name. A more sober formal description of the technology would be 'interactive tactile telepresence.' " Less interested in the technological side, Gerard Van Der Leun places "digital sex" in a necessary historical context, reminding us that sex and technology together are not a new problem. And yet, when sex moves into all things cyber, we are confronted with serious human problems. We will return to this issue when we read about MUDs and MOOs in Chapter 7.

Barbara Kantrowitz

Men, Women, Computers

Cyberspace, it turns out, isn't much of an Eden after all. It's marred by just as many sexist ruts and gender conflicts as the Real World.

As a longtime *Star Trek* devotee, Janis Cortese was eager to be part of the Trekkie discussion group on the Internet. But when she first logged on, Cortese noticed that these fans of the final frontier devoted megabytes to such profound topics as whether Troi or Crusher had bigger breasts. In other words, the purveyors of this *Trek* dreck were all *guys*. Undeterred, Cortese, a physicist at California's Loma Linda University, figured she'd add perspective to the electronic gathering place with her own momentous questions. Why was the male cast racially diverse while almost all the females were young, white and skinny? Then, she tossed in a few lustful thoughts about the male crew members.

After those seemingly innocuous observations, "I was chased off the net by rabid hounds," recalls Cortese. Before she could say "Fire phasers," the Trekkies had flooded her electronic mailbox with nasty messages—a practice called "flaming." Cortese retreated into her own galaxy by starting the all-female Starfleet Ladies Auxiliary and Embroidery/Baking Society. The private electronic forum, based in Houston, now has more than 40 members, including psychologists, physicians, students and secretaries. They started with Trek-talk, but often chose to beam down and go where no man had ever wandered before—into the personal mode. When Julia Kosatka, a Houston computer scientist, got pregnant last year, she shared her thoughts with the group on weight gain, sex while expecting and everything else on her mind. Says Kosatka: "I'm part of one of the longest-running slumber parties in history."

From the Internet to Silicon Valley to the PC sitting in the family room, men and women often seem like two chips that pass in the night. Sure, there are women who spout techno-speak in their sleep and plenty of men who think a hard drive means four hours on the freeway. But in general, computer culture is created, defined and controlled by men. Women often feel about as welcome as a system crash.

About a third of American families have at least one computer, but most of those are purchased and used by males. It may be new technology, but the old rules still apply. In part, it's that male-machine bonding thing, reincarnated in the digital age. "Men tend to be seduced by the technology itself," says Oliver Strimpel, executive director of The Computer Museum in Boston.

"They tend to get into the faster-race-car syndrome," bragging about the size of their discs or the speed of their microprocessors. To the truly besotted, computers are a virtual religion, complete with icons (on-screen graphics), relics (obsolete programs and machines) and prophets (Microsoft's Bill Gates, outlaw hackers). This is not something to be trifled with by mere . . . females, who seem to think that machines were meant to be *used,* like the microwave oven or the dishwasher. Interesting and convenient on the job but not worthy of obsession. Esther Dyson, editor of *Release 1.0,* an influential software-industry newsletter, has been following the computer field for two decades. Yet when she looks at her own computer, Dyson says she still doesn't "really care about its innards. I just want it to work."

Men tend to be seduced by the technology. . . . Women are much more practical, much more interested in the machine's utility.

Blame (a) culture (b) family (c) schools (d) all of the above. Little boys are expected to roll around in the dirt and explore. Perfect training for learning to use computers, which often requires hours in front of the screen trying to figure out the messy arcanum of a particular program. Girls get subtle messages—from society if not from their parents—that they should keep their hands clean and play with their dolls. Too often, they're discouraged from taking science and math—not just by their schools but by parents as well (how many mothers have patted their daughters on the head and reassured them: "Oh, I wasn't good at math, either").

The gender gap is real and takes many forms.

■ BARBIE VS. NINTENDO

Girls' technophobia begins early. Last summer, Sarah Douglas, a University of Oregon computer-science professor, took part in a job fair for teenage girls that was supposed to introduce them to nontraditional occupations. With great expectations, she set up her computer and loaded it with interesting programs. Not a single girl stopped by. When she asked why, the girls "told me computers were something their dads and their brothers used," Douglas sadly recalls. "Computer science is a very male profession . . . When girls get involved in that male world, they are pushed away and belittled. Pretty soon, the girls get frustrated and drop out."

Computer games usually involve lots of shooting and dying. Boy stuff. What's out there for girls? "If you walk down the street and look in the computer store, you will see primarily male people as sales staff and as customers," says Jo Sanders, director of the gender-equity program at the Center for Advanced Study in Education at the City University of New York Graduate Center.

Boys and girls are equally interested in computers until about the fifth grade, says University of Minnesota sociologist Ronald Anderson, who coauthored the recent report "Computers in American Schools." At that point, boys' use rises significantly and girls' use drops, Anderson says, probably because sex-role identification really kicks in. Many girls quickly put computers on the list of not-quite-feminine topics, like car engines and baseball batting averages. It didn't have to be this way. The very first computer programmer was a woman, Ada Lovelace, who worked with Charles Babbage on his mechanical computing machines in the mid-1800s. If she had become a role model, maybe hundreds of thousands of girls would have spent their teenage years locked in their bedrooms staring at screens. Instead, too many are doing their nails or worrying about their hair, says Marcelline Barron, an administrator at the Illinois Mathematics and Science Academy, a publicly funded coed boarding school for gifted students. "You're not thinking about calculus or physics when you're thinking about that," says Barron. "We have these kinds of expectations for young girls. They must be neat, they must be clean, they must be quiet."

Despite great strides by women in other formerly male fields, such as law and medicine, women are turning away from the computer industry. Men earning computer-science degrees outnumber women 3 to 1 and the gap is growing, according to the National Science Foundation. Fifteen years ago, when computers were still new in schools, they hadn't yet been defined as so exclusively male. But now girls have gotten the message. It's not just the technical and cultural barrier. Sherry Turkle, a Massachusetts Institute of Technology sociologist who teaches a course on women and computers, says that computers have come to stand for "a world without emotion," an image that seems to scare off girls more than boys.

The vast majority of videogame designers are men: they make games they want to play. Why do you think it's called Game Boy?

In the past decade, videogames have become a gateway to technology for many boys, but game manufacturers say few girls are attracted to these small-screen shoot-'em-ups. It's not surprising that the vast majority of videogame designers are men. They don't call it Game *Boy* for nothing. Now some manufacturers are trying to lure girls. In the next few months, Sega plans to introduce "Berenstein Bears," which will offer players a choice of boy or girl characters. A second game, "Crystal's Pony Tale," involves coloring (there's lots of pink in the background). Neither game requires players to "die," a common videogame device that researchers say girls dislike. Girls also tend to prefer nonlinear games, where there is more than one way to proceed. "There's a whole issue with speaking girls' language," says Michealene Cristini Risley, group director of licensing and character development for Sega. The company would like to hook girls at the age of 4, before they've developed fears of technology.

Girls need freedom to explore and make mistakes. Betsy Zeller, a 37-year-old engineering manager at Silicon Graphics, says that when she discovered computers in college, "I swear I thought I'd seen the face of God." Yet she had to fend off guys who would come into the lab and want to help her work through problems or, worse yet, do them for her. "I would tell them to get lost," she says. "I wanted to do it myself." Most women either asked for or accepted proffered help, just as they are more likely to ask for directions when lost in a strange city. That may be the best way to avoid driving in circles for hours, but it's not the best way to learn technical subjects.

Schools are trying a number of approaches to interest girls in computers. Douglas and her colleagues are participating in a mentorship program where undergraduate girls spend a summer working with female computer scientists. Studies have shown that girls are more attracted to technology if they can work in groups: some schools are experimenting with team projects that require computers but are focused on putting out a product, like a newspaper or pamphlet. At the middle and high-school level, girls-only computer classes are increasingly popular. Two months ago Roosevelt Middle School in Eugene, Ore., set up girls-only hours at the computer lab. Games were prohibited and artists were brought in to teach girls how to be more creative with the computer. Students are also learning to use e-mail, which many girls love. Says Debbie Nehl, the computer-lab supervisor: "They see it as high-tech note-passing."

■ POWER NETWORKS

As a relatively new industry, the leadership of computerdom might be expected to be more gender-diverse. Wrong: few women have advanced beyond middle-management ranks. According to a study conducted last year by the *San Jose Mercury News,* there are no women CEOs running major computer-manufacturing firms and only a handful running software companies. Even women who have succeeded say they are acutely conscious of the differences between them and their male coworkers. "I don't talk the same as men," says Paula Hawthorn, an executive at Montage Software, in Oakland, California. "I don't get the same credibility." The difference, she says, "is with you all the time."

Women who work in very technical areas, such as programming, are often the loneliest. Anita Borg, a computer-systems researcher, remembers attending a 1987 conference where there were so few women that the only time they ran into each other was in the restroom. Their main topic of discussion: why there were so few women at the conference. That bathroom cabal grew into Systers, an on-line network for women with technical careers. There are now 1,740 women members from 19 countries representing 200 colleges and universities and 150 companies. Systers is part mentoring and part consciousness-raising. One graduate student, for example, talked about how uncomfortable she felt sitting in her shared office when a male graduate student and a professor put a picture of a nude woman on a computer. The problem was resolved when a couple of female faculty members, also on the Systers network, told their offending colleagues that the image was not acceptable.

Women have been more successful in developing software, especially when their focus is products used by children. Jan Davidson, a former teacher, started Davidson & Associates, in Torrance, California, with three programs in 1982. Now it's one of the country's biggest developers of kids' software, with 350 employees and $58.6 million in revenues. Multimedia will bring new opportunities for women. The technology is so specialized that it requires a team—animators, producers, scriptwriters, 3-D modelers—to create state-of-the-art products. It's a far cry from the stereotype of the solitary male programmer, laboring long into the night with only takeout Chinese food for company. At Mary Cron's Rymel Design Group in Palos Verdes, California, most of the software artists and designers are women, Cron says, "It's like a giant puzzle," she adds. "We like stuff we can work on together."

As more women develop software, they may also help create products that will attract women consumers—a huge untapped market. Heidi Roizen, a college English major, cofounded T/Maker Co. in Mountain View, California, a decade ago. She says that because women are often in charge of the family's budget, they are potential consumers of personal-finance programs. Women are also the most likely buyers of education and family-entertainment products, a fast-growing segment of the industry. "Women are more typically the household shopper," Roizen says. "They have tremendous buying power."

■ WIRED WOMEN

The Infobahn—a.k.a. the Information Superhighway—may be the most hyped phenomenon in history—or it could be the road to the future. In any case, women want to get on. But the sign over the access road says CAUTION. MEN WORKING. WOMEN BEWARE. Despite hundreds of thousands of new users in the last year, men still dominate the Internet and commercial services such as Prodigy or CompuServe. The typical male conversation on line turns off many women. "A lot of time, to be crude, it's a pissing contest," says Lisa Kimball, a partner in the Meta Network, a Washington, D.C., on-line service that is 40 percent female. Put-downs are an art form. When one woman complained recently in an Internet forum that she didn't like participating because she didn't have time to answer all her e-mail, she was swamped with angry responses, including this one (from a man): "Would you like some cheese with your whine?"

Many men on the net aren't out to win sensitivity contests.

Some men say the on-line hostility comes from resentment over women's slowly entering what has been an almost exclusively male domain. Many male techno-jocks "feel women are intruding into their inner sanctum," says André Bacard, a Silicon Valley, California, technology writer. They're not out to win sensitivity contests. "In the computer world, it's 'Listen, baby, if you don't like it, drop dead'," says Bacard. "It's the way men talk to guys. Women aren't used to that."

Even under more civilized circumstances, men and women have different conversational styles, says Susan Herring, a University of Texas at Arlington professor who has studied women's participation on computer networks. Herring found that violations of long-established net etiquette—asking too many basic questions, for example—angered men. "The women were much more tolerant of people who didn't know what they were doing," Herring says. "What really annoyed women was the flaming and people boasting. The things that annoy women are things men do all the time."

Like hitting on women. Women have learned to tread their keyboards carefully in chat forums because they often have to fend off sexual advances that would make Bob Packwood blush. When subscribers to America Online enter one of the service's forums, their computer names appear at the top of the screen as a kind of welcome. If they've chosen an obviously female name, chances are they'll soon be bombarded with private messages seeking detailed descriptions of their appearance or sexual preferences. "I couldn't believe it," recalls 55-year-old Eva S. "I said, 'Come on, I'm a grandmother'."

More and more women are signing on to networks that are either coed and run by women, or are exclusively for women. Stacy Horn started ECHO (for East Coast Hang Out) four years ago because she was frustrated with the hostility on line. About 60 percent of ECHO's 2,000 subscribers are men; among ECHO's 50 forums, only two are strictly for women. "Flaming is nonexistent on ECHO," Horn says. "New women get on line and they see that. And then they're much more likely to jump in." Women's Wire in San Francisco, started in January, has 850 subscribers, only 10 percent of them men—the reverse of most on-line services. "We wanted to design a system in which women would help shape the community from the floor up," says cofounder Ellen Pack. The official policy is that there is no such thing as a dumb question—and no flaming.

Male subscribers say Women's Wire has been a learning experience for them, too. Maxwell Hoffmann, a 41-year-old computer-company manager, says that many men think that only women are overly emotional. But men lose it, too. A typical on-line fight starts with two guys sending "emotionally charged flames going back and forth" through cyberspace (not on Women's Wire). Then it expands and "everybody starts flaming the guy. They scream at each other and they're not listening."

If only men weren't so *emotional,* so *irrational,* could we all get along on the net?

■ T O Y S   A N D   T O O L S

In one intriguing study by the Center for Children and Technology, a New York think tank, men and women in technical fields were asked to dream up machines of the future. Men typically imagined devices that could help them "conquer the universe," says Jan Hawkins, director of the center. She says women wanted machines that met people's needs, "the perfect mother."

Someday, gender-blind education and socialization may render those differences obsolete. But in the meantime, researchers say both visions are useful. If everyone approached technology the way women do now, "we wouldn't be pushing envelopes," says Cornelia Bruner, associate director of the center. "Most women, even those who are technologically sophisticated, think of machines as a means to an end." Men think of the machines as an extension of their own power, as a way to "transcend physical limitations." That may be why they are more likely to come up with great leaps in technology, researchers say. Without that vision, the computer and its attendant industry would not exist.

Men typically imagine devices that could help them conquer the universe. . . . Women want machines that meet people's needs, the perfect mother.

Ironically, gender differences could help women. "We're at a cultural turning point," says MIT's Turkle. "There's an opportunity to remake the culture around the machine." Practicality is now as valued as invention. If the computer industry wants to put machines in the hands of the masses, that means women—along with the great many men who have no interest in hot-rod computing. An ad campaign for Compaq's popular Presario line emphasizes the machine's utility. After kissing her child good night, the mother in the ad sits down at her Presario to work. As people start to view their machines as creative tools, someday women may be just as comfortable with computers as men are.

Deborah Tannen

Gender Gap in Cyberspace

Men want to force computers to submit. Women just want computers to work.

I was a computer pioneer, but I'm still something of a novice. That paradox is telling.

I was the second person on my block to get a computer. The first was my colleague Ralph. It was 1980. Ralph got a Radio Shack TRS-80; I got a used Apple II+. He helped me get started and went on to become a maven, reading computer magazines, hungering for the new technology he read about, and buying and mastering it as quickly as he could afford. I hung on to old equipment far too long because I dislike giving up what I'm used to, fear making the wrong decision about what to buy and resent the time it takes to install and learn a new system.

My first Apple came with videogames: I gave them away. Playing games on the computer didn't interest me. If I had free time I'd spend it talking on the telephone with friends.

Ralph got hooked. His wife was often annoyed by the hours he spent at his computer and the money he spent upgrading it. My marriage had no such strains—until I discovered e-mail. Then I got hooked. E-mail draws me the same way the phone does: it's a souped-up conversation.

E-mail deepened my friendship with Ralph. Though his office was next to mine, we rarely had extended conversations because he is shy. Face to face he mumbled so, I could barely tell he was speaking. But when we both got on e-mail, I started receiving long, self-revealing messages: we poured our hearts out to each other. A friend discovered that e-mail opened up that kind of communication with her father. He would never talk much on the phone (as her mother would), but they have become close since they both got on line.

Why, I wondered, would some men find it easier to open up on e-mail? It's a combination of the technology (which they enjoy) and the obliqueness of the written word, just as many men will reveal feelings in dribs and drabs while riding in the car or doing something, which they'd never talk about sitting face to face. It's too intense, too bearing-down on them, and once you start you have to keep going. With a computer in between, it's safer.

It was on e-mail, in fact, that I described to Ralph how boys in groups often struggle to get the upper hand whereas girls tend to maintain an appearance of cooperation. And he pointed out that this explained why boys are more likely to be captivated by computers than girls are. Boys are typically motivated by a social structure that says if you don't dominate you will be dominated. Computers, by their nature, balk: you type a perfectly appropriate command and it refuses to do what it should. Many boys and men are incited by this defiance: "I'm going to whip this into line and teach it who's boss! I'll get it to do what I say!" (and if they work hard enough, they always can). Girls and women are more likely to respond, "This thing won't cooperate. Get it away from me!"

Although no one wants to think of herself as "typical"—how much nicer to be sui generis—my relationship to my computer is—gulp—fairly typical for a woman. Most women (with plenty of exceptions) aren't excited by tinkering with the technology, grappling with the challenge of eliminating bugs or getting the biggest and best computer. These dynamics appeal to many men's interest in making sure they're on the top side of the inevitable who's-up-who's-down struggle that life is for them. E-mail appeals to my view of life as a contest for connections to others. When I see that I have 15 messages I feel loved.

I once posted a technical question on a computer network for linguists and was flooded with long dispositions, some pages long. I was staggered by the generosity and expertise, but wondered where these guys found the time— and why all the answers I got were from men.

Like coed classrooms and meetings, discussions on e-mail networks tend to be dominated by male voices, unless they're specifically women-only, like single-sex schools. On line, women don't have to worry about getting the floor (you just send a message when you feel like it), but, according to linguists Susan Herring and Laurel Sutton, who have studied this, they have the usual problems of having their messages ignored or attacked. The anonymity of public networks frees a small number of men to send long, vituperative, sarcastic messages that many other men either can tolerate or actually enjoy, but turn most women off.

The anonymity of networks leads to another sad part of the e-mail story: there are men who deluge women with questions about their appearance and invitations to sex. On college campuses, as soon as women students log on, they are bombarded by references to sex, like going to work and finding pornographic posters adorning the walls.

■ TAKING TIME

Most women want one thing from a computer—to work. This is significant counterevidence to the claim that men want to focus on information while women are interested in rapport. That claim I found was often true in casual conversation, in which there is no particular information to be conveyed. But with computers, it is often women who are more focused on information, because they don't respond to the challenge of getting equipment to submit.

Once I had learned the basics, my interest in computers waned. I use it to write books (though I never mastered having it do bibliographies or tables of contents) and write checks (but not balance my checkbook). Much as I'd like to use it to do more, I begrudge the time it would take to learn.

Ralph's computer expertise costs him a lot of time. Chivalry requires that he rescue novices in need, and he is called upon by damsel novices far more often than knaves. More men would rather study the instruction booklet than ask directions, as it were, from another person. "When I do help men," Ralph wrote (on e-mail, of course), "they want to be more involved. I once installed a hard drive for a guy, and he wanted to be there with me, wielding the screwdriver and giving his own advice where he could." Women, he finds, usually are not interested in what he's doing: they just want him to get the computer to the point where they can do what they want.

Which pretty much explains how I managed to be a pioneer without becoming an expert.

Susan Herring

Bringing Familiar Baggage to the New Frontier: Gender Differences in Computer-Mediated Communication

■ INTRODUCTION

Although research on computer-mediated communication (CMC) dates back to the early days of computer network technology in the 1970s, researchers have only recently begun to take the gender of users into account.[1] This is perhaps not surprising considering that men have traditionally dominated the technology and have comprised the majority of users of computer networks since their inception, but the result is that most of what has been written about CMC incorporates a very one-sided perspective. However, recent research has been uncovering some eye-opening differences in the ways men and women interact "on-line," and it is these differences that I will address here.

My basic claim has two parts: first, that women and men have recognizably different styles in posting electronic messages to the Internet, contrary to claims that CMC neutralizes distinctions of gender, and second, that women and men have different communication ethics—that is, they value different kinds of on-line interactions as appropriate and desirable. I illustrate these differences—and some of the problems that arise because of them—with specific reference to the phenomenon of "flaming."

■ BACKGROUND

Since 1991 I've been lurking (or what I prefer to call "carrying out ethnographic observation") on various computer-mediated discussion lists, downloading electronic conversations and analyzing the communicative behaviors of participants. I became interested in gender shortly after subscribing to my first discussion list, LINGUIST-L, an academic forum for professional linguists. Within the first month after I began receiving messages, a conflict arose on the list (what I would later learn to call a "flame war") in which the two major theoretical camps within the field became polarized around an issue of central interest. My curiosity was piqued by the fact that very few women were contributing to this important professional event; they seemed to be sitting on the sidelines while men were airing their opinions and getting all the attention. In an attempt to understand the women's silence, I made up an anonymous survey which I sent to LINGUIST-L asking subscribers what they thought of the discussion and, if they hadn't contributed, why not.

■ INITIAL OBSERVATIONS

The number one reason given by both men and women for not contributing to the LINGUIST discussion was "intimidation"—as one respondent commented, participants were "ripping each other's lungs out." Interestingly, however, men and women responded differently to feeling intimidated. Men seemed to accept such behavior as a normal feature of academic life, making comments to the effect that "Actually, the barbs and arrows were entertaining, because of course they weren't aimed at me." In contrast, many women responded with profound aversion. As one woman put it: "That is precisely the kind of human interaction I committedly avoid. . . . I am dismayed that human beings treat each other this way. It makes the world a dangerous place to be. I dislike such people and I want to give them WIDE berth."

When I analyzed the messages in the thread itself, another gender difference emerged, this time relating to the linguistic structure and rhetoric of the messages. A daunting 68 percent of the messages posted by men made use of an adversarial style in which the poster distanced himself from, criticized, and/or ridiculed other participants, often while promoting his own importance. The few women who participated in the discussion, in contrast, displayed features of attenuation—hedging, apologizing, asking questions rather than making assertions—and a personal orientation, revealing thoughts and feelings and interacting with and supporting others.

One respondent commented, participants were "ripping each other's lungs out."

It wasn't long before I was noticing a similar pattern in other discussions and on other lists. Wherever I went on mixed-sex lists, men seemed to be doing most of the talking and attracting most of the attention to themselves, although not all lists were as adversarial as LINGUIST. I started to hear stories about and witness men taking over and dominating discussions even of women-centered topics on women-centered lists.[2] In contrast, on the few occasions when I observed women attempting to gain an equal hearing on male-dominated lists, they were ignored, trivialized, or criticized by men for their tone or the inappropriateness of their topic.[3] It wasn't until I started looking at lists devoted to women's issues, and to traditionally "feminized" disciplines such as women's studies, teaching English as a second language, and librarianship, that I found women holding forth in an amount consistent with their numerical presence on the list. I also found different interactional norms: little or no flaming, and cooperative, polite exchanges.

■ D I F F E R E N T   S T Y L E S

As a result of these findings, I propose that women and men have different characteristic on-line styles. By characteristic styles, I do not mean that all or even the majority of users of each sex exhibit the behaviors of each style, but rather that the styles are recognizably—even stereotypically—gendered. The male style is characterized by adversariality: putdowns, strong, often contentious assertions, lengthy and/or frequent postings, self-promotion, and sarcasm. Below are two examples, one from an academic list (LINGUIST) and the other from a nonacademic list (POLITICS).[4]

1. [Jean Linguiste's] proposals towards a more transparent morphology in French are exactly what he calls them: a farce. Nobody could ever take them seriously—unless we want to look as well at pairs such as *pe`re - me`re*, *coq - poule* and defigure the French language in the process.

[strong assertions ("exactly," "nobody"), putdowns ("JL's proposals are a farce"; implied: "JL wants to defigure the French language")]

The male style is characterized by adversariality: putdowns, strong, often contentious assertions, lengthy and/or frequent postings, self-promotion, and sarcasm.

2. >yes, they did . . . This is why we must be allowed to remain armed . . .
   >who is going to help us if our government becomes a tyranny?
   >no one will.

oh yes we *must* remain armed. anyone see day one last night abt charlestown where everyone/s so scared of informing on murderers the cops have given up? where the reply to any offense is a public killing? knowing you/re not gonna be caught cause everyone/s to afraid to be a witness?

yeah, right, twerp.

>—[RON) "THE WISE"—

what a joke.

[sarcasm, name calling, personal insults]

The second example would be characterized as a "flame" by most readers because of its personally offensive nature. Less exclusively male-gendered but still characteristic of male postings is an authoritative, self-confident stance whereby men are more likely than women to represent themselves as experts, e.g., in answering queries for information. The following example is from NOTIS-L.

3. The NUGM Planning meeting was cancelled before all of this came up. It has nothing to do with it. The plans were simply proceeding along so well that there was no need to hold the meeting. That is my understanding from talking to NOTIS staff just last week.

[authoritative tone, strong assertions ("nothing," "simply," "just")]

The female-gendered style, in contrast, has two aspects which typically co-occur: supportiveness and attentuation. "Supportiveness" is characterized by expressions of appreciation, thanking, and community-building activities that make other participants feel accepted and welcome. "Attenuation" includes hedging and expressing doubt, apologizing, asking questions, and contributing ideas in the form of suggestions. The following examples from a nonacademic list (WOMEN) and an academic list (TESL-L) illustrate each aspect:

4. >[AILEEN],

>

>I just wanted to let you know that I have really enjoyed all

>your posts about Women's herstory. They have been

>extremely informative and I've learned alot about the

>women's movement. Thank you!

>

>—[ERIKA]

DITTO!!!! They are wonderful!

Did anyone else catch the first part of a Century of Women? I really enjoyed it. Of course, I didn't agree with everything they said. . . . but it was really informative.

[ROBERTA]~~~~~~~~~~~~~~~~~~~~~~~~~~~~~

[appreciates, thanks, agrees, appeals to group]

5. [. . .] I hope this makes sense. This is kind of what I had in mind when I realized I couldn't give a real definitive answer. Of course, maybe I'm just getting into the nuances of the language when it would be easier to just give the simple answer. Any response?

[hedges, expresses doubt, appeals to group]

The female style takes into consideration what the sociologist Erving Goffman called the "face" wants of the addressee—specifically, the desire of the addressee to feel ratified and liked (e.g., by expressions of appreciation) and her desire not to be imposed upon (e.g., by absolute assertions that don't allow for alternative views). The male style, in contrast, confronts and threatens the addressee's "face" in the process of engaging him in agonistic debate.

Although these styles represent in some sense the extremes of gendered behavior, they have symbolic significance above and beyond their frequency of use. For example, other users regularly infer the gender of message posters on the basis of features of these styles, especially when the self-identified gender of a poster is open to question. Consider the following cases, the first involving a male posting as a female, the second a suspected female posting as a male:

i. A male subscriber on SWIP-L (Society for Women in Philosophy list) posted a message disagreeing with the general consensus that discourse on SWIP-L should be nonagonistic, commenting, "There's nothing like a healthy denunciation by one's colleagues every once in a while to get one's blood flowing, and spur one to greater subtlety and exactness of thought." He signed his message with a female pseudonym, however, causing another (female) subscriber to comment later, "I must confess to looking for the name of the male who wrote the posting that [Suzi] sent originally and was surprised to find a female name at the end of it." The female subscriber had (accurately) inferred that anyone actively advocating "denunciation by one's colleagues" was probably male.

ii. At a time when one male subscriber had been posting frequent messages to the WOMEN list, another subscriber professing to be a man posted a message inquiring what the list's policy was towards men participating on the list, admitting, "I sometimes feel guilty for taking up bandwidth." The message, in addition to showing consideration for the concerns of others on the list, was very attenuated in style and explicitly appreciative of the list: "I really enjoy this list (actually, it's the best one I'm on)." This prompted another (female) subscriber to respond, "Now that you've posed the question . . . how's one to know you're not a woman posing this question as a man?" Her suspicion indicates that on some level she recognized that anyone posting a message expressing appreciation and consideration for the desires of others was likely to be female.

The existence of gendered styles has important implications, needless to say, for popular claims that CMC is anonymous, "gender blind," and hence inherently democratic. If our on-line communicative style reveals our gender, then gender differences, along with their social consequences, are likely to persist on computer-mediated networks.[5]

Entire lists can be gendered in their style as well. It is tacitly expected that members of the nondominant gender will adapt their posting style in the direction of the style of the dominant gender. Thus men on women's special interest lists tend to attenuate their assertions and shorten their messages, and women, especially on male-dominated lists such as LINGUIST and PAGLIA-L, can be contentious and adversarial. Arguably, they must adapt in order to participate appropriately in keeping with the norms of the local list culture. Most members of the nondominant gender on any given list, however, end up style mixing, that is, taking on some attributes of the dominant style while preserving features of their native style—for example, with men often preserving a critical stance and women a supportive one at the macro-message level. This suggests that gendered communication styles are deeply rooted—not surprising, since they are learned early in life—and

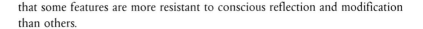

that some features are more resistant to conscious reflection and modification than others.

DIFFERENT COMMUNICATION ETHICS

The second part of this essay concerns the value systems that underlie and are used to rationalize communicative behavior on the net. In particular, I focus on the phenomenon of flaming, which has been variously defined as "the expression of strong negative emotion," use of "derogatory, obscene, or inappropriate language," and "personal insults." A popular explanation advanced by CMC researchers[6] is that flaming is a by-product of the medium itself—the decontextualized and anonymous nature of CMC leads to "disinhibition" in users and a tendency to forget that there is an actual human being at the receiving end of one's emotional outbursts. However, until recently CMC research has largely overlooked gender as a possible influence on behavior, and the simple fact of the matter is that it is virtually only men who flame. If the medium makes men more likely to flame, it should have a similar effect on women, yet if anything the opposite appears to be the case. An adequate explanation of flaming must therefore take gender into account.

Why do men flame? The explanation, I suggest, is that women and men have different communication ethics, and flaming is compatible with male ethical ideals. I stumbled upon this realization recently as a result of a survey I conducted on politeness on the Internet. I originally hypothesized that the differences in the extremes of male and female behavior online—in particular, the tendency for women to be considerate of the "face" needs of others while men threaten others' "face"—could be explained if it turned out that women and men have different notions of what constitutes appropriate behavior. In other words, as a woman I might think adversarial behavior is rude, but men who behave adversarially might think otherwise. Conversely, men might be put off by the supportive and attenuated behaviors of women.

In the survey, I asked subscribers from eight Internet discussion lists to rank their like or dislike for 30 different on-line behaviors, including "flaming," "expressing thanks and appreciation," and "overly tentative messages," on a scale of 1 (like) to 5 (dislike). The survey also asked several open-ended questions, including most importantly: "What behaviors bother you most on the net?"

My initial hypothesis turned out to be both correct and incorrect. It was incorrect in that I found no support whatsoever for the idea that men's and women's value systems are somehow reversed. Both men and women said they liked expressions of appreciation (avg. score of 2), were neutral about tentative messages (avg. about 3), and disliked flaming (although women expressed a stronger dislike than men, giving it a score of 4.3 as compared with only 3.9 for men). This makes male flaming behavior all the more puzzling. Should we conclude, then, that men who flame are deliberately trying to be rude?

The answers to the open-ended questions suggest a different explanation. These answers reveal a gender contrast in values that involves politeness but cannot be described in terms of politeness alone. It seems women place a high value on consideration for the wants and needs of others, as expressed in the following comment by a female net user:

If we take responsibility for developing our own sensitivities to others and controlling our actions to minimize damage—we will each be doing [good deeds] for the whole world constantly.

Men, in contrast, assign greater value to freedom from censorship (many advocate absolute free speech), forthright and open expression, and agonistic debate as a means to advance the pursuit of knowledge. Historically, the value on absolute freedom of speech reflects the civil libertarian leanings of the computing professionals who originally designed the net and have con-tributed much of the utopian discourse surrounding it; the value on agonistic debate is rooted in the western (male) philosophical tradition.

These ideals are stirringly evoked in the following quote from R. Hauben (1993) praising the virtues of the Usenet system, on which 95 percent of the contributors are estimated to be male:

The achievement of Usenet News demonstrates the importance of facilitating the develop-ment of uncensored speech and communication—there is debate and discussion—one person influences another—people build on each other's strengths and interests, differ-ences, etc.

One might think that uncensored speech if abused could cause problems, but M. Hauben (1993) explains that there is a democratic way of handling this eventuality:

When people feel someone is abusing the nature of Usenet News, they let the offender know through e-mail. In this manner . . . people fight to keep it a resource that is helpful to society as a whole.

In daily life on the Internet, however, the ideal of "people fight[ing] to keep [the net] a resource that is helpful to society as a whole" often translates into violent action. Consider, for example, the response of a male survey respon-dent to the question: "What behaviors bother you most on the net?" (typos are in the original):

As much as I am irritated by [incompetent posters], I don't want imposed rules. I would prefer to "out" such a person and let some public minded citi-zen fire bomb his house to imposing rules on the net. Letter bombing a annoying individual's feed is usually preferable to building a formal heirarchy of net cops.

Another net vigilante responds graphically as follows:

I'd have to say commercial shit. Whenever someone advertises some damn get-rich-quick scheme and plasters it all over the net by crossposting it to every newsgroup, I reach for my "gatling gun mailer crasher" and fire away at the source address.

These responses not only evoke an ideal of freedom from external authority, they provide an explicit justification for flaming—as a form of self-appointed regulation of the social order, a rough and ready form of justice on the virtual frontier. Thus a framework of values is constructed within which flaming and other aggressive behaviors can be interpreted in a favorable (even prosocial) light. This is not to say that all or even most men who flame have the good of net society at heart, but rather that the behavior is in principle justifiable for men (and hence tolerable) in ways that it is not for most women.

◼ NETIQUETTE

Further evidence that flaming is tolerated and justified within a system of male values comes from the content of written rules of network etiquette, or "netiquette," such as are available on many public FTP sites and in introductory messages to new members of some discussion lists. I analyzed the content of netiquette rules from six lists, along with those found in the guidelines for Usenet and in the print publication *Towards an Ethics and Etiquette for Electronic Mail,* by Norman Shapiro and Robert Anderson (1985). What do netiquette rules have to say about flaming?

The answer is: remarkably little, given that it is one of the most visible and frequently complained about "negatives" cited about the Internet. One might even say there is a striking *lack* of proscription against flaming, except on a few women-owned and women-oriented lists. And in the rare instances where flaming is mentioned, it is implicitly authorized. Thus the guidelines for new subscribers to the POLITICS list prohibit "flames of a personal nature," and Shapiro and Anderson advise, "Do not insult or criticize third parties without giving them a chance to respond." While on the surface appearing to oppose flaming, these statements in fact implicitly authorize "flames other than of a personal nature" (for example, of someone's ideas or values) and "insulting or criticizing third parties" (provided you give them a chance to respond!). Normative statements such as these are compatible with male values and male adversarial style; the intimidating rhetoric on LINGUIST and many other lists is not a violation of net etiquette according to these rules.[7] Yet these are behaviors that female survey respondents say intimidate them and drive them away from lists and newsgroups. Can the Internet community afford to tolerate behaviors that intimidate and silence women? This is a question that urgently needs to be raised and discussed net wide.

◼ CONCLUSIONS

To sum up, I have argued that women and men constitute different discourse communities in cyberspace—different cultures, if you will—with differing communicative norms and practices. However, these cultures are not "separate but equal," as recent popular writing on gender differences in communication has claimed. Rather, the norms and practices of masculine net culture, codified in netiquette rules, conflict with those of the female culture in ways that render cyberspace—or at least many "neighborhoods" in cyberspace—inhospitable to women. The result is an imbalance whereby men control a disproportionate share of the communication that takes place via computer networks.

This imbalance must be redressed if computer-mediated communication is ever to live up to its much-touted democratic potential. Fortunately, there are ways in which women can promote their concerns and influence the discourse of the net;[8] I will mention three here. First and foremost is to participate, for example in women-centered lists. Such lists provide supportive fora for women on line and are frequently models of cooperative discourse whose norms can spread if subscribers participate in other lists as well. But separatism has its disadvantages, among them the risk of ghettoization. Women must not let themselves be driven by flame throwers away from mainstream, mixed-sex fora, but rather should also actively seek to gain influence there, individually and collectively, especially in fora where metadiscourse about the net itself takes place.

The second way to promote women's interests netwide is to educate online communities about the rhetorical strategies used in intimidating others, and to call people on their behavior and its consequences when they use such strategies.[9] This is already happening on some women-centered lists such as WMST-L and SWIP-L—aware of the tendency for a single man or group of men to dominate discussions, female subscribers call attention to this behavior as soon as they realize it is happening; interestingly, it is happening less and less often on these lists. Group awareness is a powerful force for change, and it can be raised in mixed-sex fora as well.

Finally, women need to contribute in any way they can to the process that leads to the encoding of netiquette rules. They need to instigate and participate persuasively in discussions about what constitutes appropriate and inappropriate behavior on line—seeking to define in concrete terms what constitutes "flaming," for instance, since women and men are likely to have different ideas about this. They must be alert to opportunities (or make their own opportunities) to write out guidelines for suggested list protocol (or modifications to list protocol if guidelines already exist) and post them for discussion. No greater power exists than the power to define values, and the structure of the Internet—especially now, while it is still evolving and seeking its ultimate definition—provides a unique opportunity for individual users to influence the normative process.

Indeed, it may be vital that we do so if women's on-line communication styles are to be valued along with those of men, and if we are to insure women the right to settle on the virtual frontier on their own—rather than on male-defined—terms.

■ N O T E S

This essay was originally delivered as a speech to the American Library Association as part of a panel entitled "Making the Net*Work*: Is there a Z39.50 in gender communication?", Miami, June 27, 1994. Copyright rests with the author.

1. A notable exception to this generalization is the work of Sherry Turkle in the 1980s on how women and men relate to computers.

2. For an extreme example of this phenomenon that took place on the soc.feminism Usenet newsgroup, see Sutton (1994).

3. Herring, Johnson, and DiBenedetto (1992, in press).

4. All names mentioned in the messages are pseudonyms.

5. This problem is discussed in Herring (1993a).

6. For example, Kiesler et al. (1984), Kim and Raja (1990), and Shapiro and Anderson (1985).

7. The discussion of politeness and communication ethics here is an abbreviated version of that presented in Herring (In press a, In press b).

8. For other practical suggestions on how to promote gender equality in networking, see Kramarae and Taylor (1993).

9. Cases where this was done, both successfully and unsuccessfully, are described in Herring, Johnson & DiBenedetto (In press).

■ R E F E R E N C E S

Hauben, Michael. 1993. "The social forces behind the development of Usenet News." Electronic document. (FTP weber.ucsd.edu, directory /pub/usenet.hist)

Hauben, Ronda. 1993. "The evolution of Usenet News: The poor man's ARPANET." Electronic document. (FTP weber.ucsd.edu, directory /pub/usenet.hist)

Herring, Susan. 1992. "Gender and participation in computer-mediated linguistic discourse." Washington, DC: ERIC Clearinghouse on Languages and Linguistics, document no. ED345552.

Herring, Susan. 1993a. "Gender and democracy in computer-mediated communication." *Electronic Journal of Communication* 3(2), special issue on Computer-Mediated Communication, T. Benson, ed. Reprinted in R. Kling (ed.), *Computerization and Controversy*, 2nd ed. New York: Academic (In press).

Herring, Susan. 1993b. "Men's language: A study of the discourse of the Linguist list." In A. Crochetihre, J. -C. Boulanger, and C. Ouellon (eds.), *Les Langues Menacies: Actes du XVe Congres International des Linguistes,* Vol. 3. Quebec: Les Presses de l'Université Laval, 347–350.

Herring, Susan. In press a. "Politeness in computer culture: Why women thank and men flame." In M. Bucholtz, A. Liang and L. Sutton (eds.), *Communicating In, Through, and Across Cultures: Proceedings of the Third Berkeley Women and Language Conference.* Berkeley Women and Language Group.

Herring, Susan. In press b. "Posting in a different voice: Gender and ethics in computer-mediated communication." In C. Ess (ed.), *Philosophical Perspectives on Computer-Mediated Communication.* Albany: SUNY Press.

Herring, Susan. In press c. "Two variants of an electronic message schema." In S. Herring (ed.), *Computer-Mediated Communication: Linguistic, social, and cross-cultural perspectives.* Amsterdam/Philadelphia: John Benjamins.

Herring, Susan, Deborah Johnson, and Tamra DiBenedetto. 1992. "Participation in electronic discourse in a 'feminist' field." In M. Bucholtz, K. Hall, and B. Moonwomon, eds., *Locating Power: Proceedings of the Second Berkeley Women and Language Conference.* Berkeley Women and Language Group.

Herring, Susan, Deborah Johnson, and Tamra DiBenedetto. In press d. "'This discussion is going too far!' Male resistance to female participation on the Internet." In M. Bucholtz and K. Hall, eds., *Gender Articulated: Language and the Socially-Constructed Self.* New York: Routledge.

Kiesler, Sara, Jane Seigel, and Timothy W. McGuire. 1984. "Social psychological aspects of computer-mediated communication." *American Psychologist,* 39, 1123–1134.

Kim, Min-Sun and Narayan S. Raja. 1990. "Verbal aggression and self-disclosure on computer bulletin boards." ERIC document (ED334620).

Kramarae, Cheris and H. Jeanie Taylor. 1993. "Women and men on electronic networks: A conversation or a monologue?" In Taylor, Kramarae and Ebben, eds., *Women, Information Technology and Scholarship,* 52–61. Urbana, IL: Center for Advanced Study.

Rheingold, Howard. 1993. *The Virtual Community: Homesteading on the Electronic Frontier.* Reading, MA: Addison-Wesley.

Seabrook, John. 1994. "My first flame." *The New Yorker,* June 6, 1994, 70–79.

Shapiro, Norman Z. and Robert H. Anderson. 1985. *Toward an Ethics and Etiquette for Electronic Mail.* The Rand Corporation.

Sutton, Laurel. 1994. "Using USENET: Gender, power, and silencing in electronic discourse." *Proceedings of the 20th Annual Meeting of the Berkeley Linguistics Society* (BLS-20). Berkeley: Berkeley Linguistics Society, Inc.

Turkle, Sherry. 1984. *The Second Self: Computers and the Human Spirit.* London: Granada.

Keep Internet Safe for Families

hen a youngster logs onto a computer terminal, he or she is welcomed into a vast new world of information that will revolutionize how we all learn and work in the future. This worldwide web of computer connections represents an information explosion unprecedented in world history. This information revolution may rival the invention of the printing press and broadcasting in terms of how it will affect our daily lives.

The evolving telecommunications infrastructure known as the Internet will link homes, businesses, schools, hospitals and libraries to each other and to a vast array of electronic information resources. Imagine a student in Hastings, Nebraska, being able to tap into the computer database of a University in Budapest, Hungary, more easily than walking down to the local library.

But there are some dark side roads on the information super highway that contain material that would be considered unacceptable by any reasonable standard.

The U.S. Senate will consider my proposal, the Communications Decency Amendment, to lay down some basic guidelines on the information superhighway. I want to make this exciting new highway as safe as possible for kids and families to travel. Just as we have laws against dumping garbage on the interstate, we ought to have similar laws for the information superhighway.

My amendment to the Telecommunications Reform Bill will toughen penalties for people who actively "transmit" pornographic and harassing material, boosting the maximum fine from $50,000 to $100,000 and increasing the maximum jail sentence from six months to two years. We need this added deterrent so that those who would pervert the network will think twice. We already have laws to prohibit obscenity over the telephone or pornography through the mail. My amendment extends to computer users the very same protections against obscenity or harassment that now partially protect telephone users.

The legislation does not make innocent "carriers" of electronic messages liable for inappropriate messages, nor does it by any stretch of the imagination require system operators to "eavesdrop" on electronic messages. To do so would be the equivalent of holding the mailman liable for the packages he delivers.

Many critics say that on the Internet, anything should go, no matter how outrageous. I say the framers of the Constitution never intended for the First Amendment to protect pornographers and pedophiles.

There are documented cases of computer misuse all over the country. These include incidents of electronic stalking, inappropriate contact with children and computer breaking and entering.

Last summer, the *Los Angeles Times* reported that a computer at the Lawrence Livermore National Laboratory in California was being used to store and distribute hard-core pornography. Despite the lab's elaborate security precautions, investigators found more than 1,000 pornographic pictures. The computer was shut down and the FBI called in.

The *Washington Post* reported on a case where a group of investigators signed on to a major computer service with false identifications and pretended to be children. They posted a few innocuous messages on teen bulletin boards and the next day they had "solicitations for nude pictures, phone sex and offers to meet in person for sex."

Computers are a unique medium because children often have much more knowledge about how they operate than their parents. My amendment would pass the standard outlined by the U.S. Supreme Court that Congress may take action to protect children from obscenity, pornography and indecency in areas like radio or television broadcasts where youngsters have unique access.

Does anyone really think that a parent can stand over their child's shoulder and monitor them all of their waking hours of every day? If anyone thinks that this material is hard for youngsters to come by, they don't know youngsters.

We have laws against murder and we have laws against speeding. We still have murder and we still have speeding. But I think most reasonable people would agree that we very likely would have more murders and more speeders if we didn't have laws as a deterrent.

In a recent newspaper article, a computer "hacker" who viewed some of this pornography on the Internet said 98 percent of it is no worse than you might find in an "adult video rental store." That weird admission makes my point. Is material that is okay for an adult video store okay for kids to see on their home computers?

To those who are critical of my suggestions I say, "Come, let us reason together." Nothing is etched in stone and I am open to any constructive proposals. I have suggested, for example, a parental lock-out mechanism as a possible solution to make certain areas of the Internet inaccessible to youngsters.

We are talking about our most important and precious commodity—our children. We cannot simply throw up our hands and say a solution is impossible or the First Amendment is so sacrosanct that we must stand idly by while our children are inundated with pornography and smut on the Internet. The public needs to be aware of the problem and direct its correction.

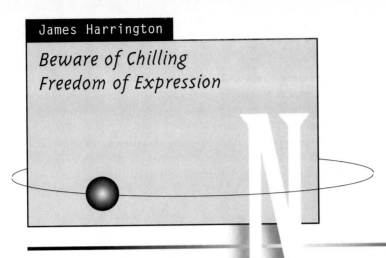

James Harrington

Beware of Chilling Freedom of Expression

one of our founders who gathered together more than 200 years ago to write the Constitution and eventually author its Bill of Rights could have imagined an electronic communication system such as the Internet. Yet, even if the drafters could have peered into the future, they probably would not have framed the First Amendment any differently. They would apply the principles in the First Amendment with as much vitality to today's debate about obscenity, children and access to the Internet, as they did to King George's suppression of colonial newspapers.

Today's debate comes courtesy of U.S. Sen. J. James Exon (D-Neb.). Mr. Exon is sponsor of the Communications Decency Amendment that could punish electronic communicators who transmit 'obscene, lewd, lascivious, filthy, or indecent' language and images—rather broad and vague terms that could apply to what most of us might speak or write to another. The new law, if passed, would punish Internet use of the "seven dirty words" we might speak in daily life; the penalty is a $100,000 fine and/or two years jail time.

This attempt to censor cyberspeech raises two major constitutional problems: Can the government limit access to sexually explicit information on the Internet to adults who want it, and, if so, who decides what is "offensive" and thus punishable?

The Internet can bring to our homes instantly accessible art, literature, music, science and just general communication from around the globe; the Internet also can be a conduit for obscenity, and for children who know how to find it. Not that obscenity is new to human existence, even for minors. Nor is salacious and vulgar material easy to locate on the Internet; ferreting it out requires a certain adeptness, even for seasoned Internet surfers. Its availability alone should not set the stage for cybercensorship.

Three general philosophical arguments support strong constitutional guarantees of free speech, assembly and press. The most favored is the concept of full and unlimited access to the "marketplace of ideas." If an idea has value, then arguments in its favor will carry the day by the force of their logic. On the other hand, ideas of no (or bad) consequence will fall of their own dead weight. Democracy strengthens itself through this intellectual free market. Government intervention is counterproductive because it impedes communication; and, since people naturally resent repressive measures, state censorship undercuts political legitimacy.

Self-development is a second rationale for the constitutional communication protections: Absent causing real harm to another person, individuals should live unfettered by government and free to develop the kind of autonomous character they desire. That, after all, is one purpose of a democracy, and often the wellspring of culture and scientific advance.

Freedom to criticize government at will is the third reason for constitutionally protected speech and press. We rarely see government move against the press these days, the last memorable time being its failed attempt during the Vietnam War to block publication of the Pentagon Papers. Lack of government activity in this area is due in part to the shallow critical and analytical quality of today's print and electronic media.

The Internet has expanded the "marketplace of ideas" beyond the wildest imaginations of Thomas Jefferson who had to wait months for learned books from Europe. Now, he could surf around the world, in minutes admiring museum art in Sydney, Australia, or accessing the human rights law library at the University of Genoa. Imagine how Internet could have fueled Benjamin Franklin's creativity and might have fed his prurient interests as well. This latter choice, though, Mr. Franklin would have argued, was his, not the government's.

If an adult wants to access sexual materials on the Internet, that right belongs to the adult. Individuals have the liberty to define their own personal autonomy and development; they may err, even seriously, but the mistake is theirs, not ours. We simply don't trust the government making private decisions for us and what we may read or freely say to each other.

The Internet has made the obscenity problem more difficult, however; and the media have played it up because of its uniqueness. Many facets of the Internet operate as repositories ("billboards" or "mail boxes") of communications and materials that other users may "visit" and from which they may take an item at will and even download it.

Obviously, because of the country's diversity, something stored on a personal billboard might be viewed as "indecent" in Waco, Texas, but not in Los Angeles. Yet Mr. Exon's bill would allow prosecution of the originator of alleged indecency (which includes using the "f" word) in any jurisdiction where the electronic mail is downloaded. Thus, an Internet user in rural Tennessee may visit the billboard of a Hollywood Internetter, take and download some "lascivious" material, and thus make the billboard owner criminally liable.

This leads to the second problem. Mr. Exon's proposed Communications Decency Amendment not only punishes offensive sexual material, but it allows the most conservative community in the nation to hold the rest of the country hostage to its very narrow definitions of "obscene, lewd, lascivious, filthy or indecent."

This frightening scenario has occurred already under another obscenity law. A Tennessee jury convicted a couple in Milpitas, California, on 11 counts of obscenity. They now face 55 years in prison and a $2.75 million fine, thanks to a Memphis postal inspector, who found out they stored sexually explicit material on their electronic billboard and set out to prosecute them halfway across the country.

Mr. Exon's proposal also could punish us for writing a racy Internet love note to a spouse, even though we would speak the words on the telephone without fear, and whether what we write is offensive might be judged by a jury a thousand miles away from us.

A few years back the U.S. Supreme Court ruled that prevailing community standards should measure what is, and is not, obscene in a given locale. That case sought to protect rural and conservative communities from imposition of standards acceptable in large urban communities such as New York. Mr. Exon's bill, however, enforces the converse; it allows rural, conservative communities to set standards for the rest of the nation.

As to the problem of children possibly finding scatological material on the Internet, efforts would be better directed toward technology, such as filters and bowdlerizers that parents can use if needed. Some technology already exists: university Internet systems lock out pornographic materials; and commercial on-line services can do the same. All in all, though, parental guidance is key; there is no effective substitute. For some reason, cybercensors find this alternative uncomfortable.

We ought to exult in the explosion of Internet's unrestrained expression; the passionate desire to convey ideas and expand creativity is a hundred times better than commercial media's suffocating programs, milquetoast news and boring sound-bites.

Mr. Exon's misguided proposal would send a message to Internet users around the world that the United States is more interested in being a cyber-cop rather than fostering a global marketplace of ideas where all can speak without fear and in the hope of bettering the human condition.

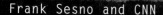

Panelists Debate
Electronic Privacy Issues

NN, February 13, 1995 21:00 Eastern Time

FRANK SESNO, Anchor: The U.S. government is going after a Michigan college student on a felony charge involving sexual fantasy and violence. It all started with a trip down the information highway with a detour into a murky, unregulated area. Using "Jake Baker" as his computer name, 20-year-old Abraham Jacob Alkhabaz posted stories in the Internet fraught with sexual violence using the real name of a woman classmate. An example of his work—"I yanked her up by the hair and force her hands behind her back. I quickly get them restrained with duct tape. Her little body struggles against me as she screams for help." He also described the theme of his work—"rape is romance."

(HIGHLIGHT:
A Michigan
student faces
criminal charges
for transmitting
sexually explicit,
violent fiction
over the
Internet. Privacy
advocate Marc
Rotenberg and
Democratic
Senator James
Exon of
Nebraska
debate the
issue.)

Last week, the student was suspended from the University of Michigan. Now he faces a federal felony charge of threatening to injure.

SAUL GREEN, U.S. Attorney: There were transmissions back and forth between people who received this transmission and this story that discussed and described, perhaps, how to actually fulfill some of the things that are outlined in the story.

DAVID CAHILL, Alkhabaz's Attorney: He never bothered her. He never contacted her at all. He had a class with her last semester, remembered her name, and then when he wrote the story used her name.

FRANK SESNO: The American Civil Liberties Union believes Alkhabaz is protected under the First Amendment. Last Friday, a U.S. district judge ordered him held without bond pending his trial. He's scheduled to be back in court on Friday for an appeal hearing on the bond issue. The federal charge has a maximum prison sentence of five years.

Now joining us to discuss the Michigan case and some of the legal issues involved, Democratic Senator James Exon of Nebraska, who joins us from

Capitol Hill, and Marc Rotenberg, director of the Electronic Privacy Information Center in Washington. Thanks very much to both of you. Senator, let me
start with you. Was the law broken in the case out of Michigan?

SEN. JAMES EXON: I don't know enough about that case, and I'm not a
lawyer, but I'm glad to see that somebody's starting to get into this. Basically
what we're trying to do with our law is to simply apply the laws that are now
enforced on telephones over to and on to the new information superhighway.
I think young people, especially small children, should be able to cruise that
superhighway without being endangered by a whole series of smut, pornography, call it what you will. There's been many cases of this. At least I hope
that this one case may set a precedent, and I hope that the action that we
plan to take in the United States Senate will simply clear out some of the
smut, some of the pornography, while not interfering with the legitimate
rights of any citizen.

FRANK SESNO: All right. Let's come back to the Senate measure in just a
minute. Marc Rotenberg, was the law broken?

MARC ROTENBERG, Electronic Privacy Information Center: I think that
will have to be determined by the court, Frank. It's a difficult case. It's a test
case, and what you see here is federal prosecutors trying to respond to a public concern about offensive speech.

FRANK SESNO: Senator . . . in your news release just last week . . . your bill is
described as the "Communications Decency Act," and it says here it would
extend and strengthen protections against obscene and indecent material to
cover these computers and emerging technologies. Now, how exactly would
you accomplish that?

SEN. JAMES EXON: We would simply accomplish that, and what this is
designed to do is to give more enforcement law to the prosecutors and also to
the judges for increasing the sentences for people that are found guilty of
promoting smut and pornography.

FRANK SESNO: What's wrong with that, Marc Rotenberg?

MARC ROTENBERG: Well, I'm sympathetic to the senator's concern, but I
think it would be a mistake to try to regulate Internet communications as we
currently regulate the telephone network. It's clear that this is a very different
type of communications environment, and I think the proposal will raise a
whole host of problems.

FRANK SESNO: Such as?

MARC ROTENBERG: Well, I think the breadth of the proposal in particular—
in this instance, it would penalize not just the person who speaks the words
that might be found to be offensive, but also the companies and universities
and other service providers that transmit the information. We have never

previously penalized people operating as common carriers in that setting, and I think it would be a mistake to do so here.

SEN. JAMES EXON: Marc, I think you're overreacting. That is not the intent of our legislation at all. If you or others want to come in and help us out to better define this—we're not trying to penalize the universities. Clearly that is not the wording of the legislation, but it's part of the hoopla that goes on any time anyone tries to take any action to clean up portions of our society that myself and others believe are bringing great injury, particularly to our young people. You just cited some very legitimate legal considerations that I would like to talk with you about and work with you on. I am very fearful, though, that what you and others that are very much concerned about the First Amendment to the Constitution are saying, "It's wrong to have the laws that we have now in place with regard to telephone. It's wrong, for example, to have laws with regard to the U.S. mails." I would simply say to you that— And you talk about the universities and others being part of this, that [it's] like saying we're going to put the mailman who delivers the smut in jail. That is not our intent at all.

MARC ROTENBERG: Well, I'm very pleased to hear you say that, Senator, and we would be happy to work with you. The bill as currently drafted, I'm afraid, does create these problems. It speaks, for example, of penalizing the transmission of speech which may be found to be lewd or obscene. That's new ground in this area of law. I think we need to look at that. I also think we need to look at the question of whether you really want to penalize speech that's considered to be harassing. You know, it's a problem, of course, harassment, but if you begin to penalize speech between people who know each other—I mean, do you want to penalize the people who call us at home? It's really going to be open season, I'm afraid, on the Internet, and it's something that really requires careful study.

FRANK SESNO: Gentlemen, is this about the First Amendment? Is this about freedom of speech and expression, or is it about a new technology and trying to get your arms around it?

MARC ROTENBERG: Well, Frank, I think it's about both. Clearly our country has very strong respect for open speech, and at times we pay a bit of a price—we hear things we don't want to hear—but I agree with the senator. Certainly we should be prepared to punish things that actually cause harm to people, and we don't disagree about that. But it is also a new technology, and new technologies pose new issues, pose new challenges, and we have to find ways to respond appropriately.

SEN. JAMES EXON: I agree with you, Marc. It poses new opportunities, new challenges and also new dangers, and that's the part that I'm trying to address. I certainly like your attitude. I think maybe we can work together on this. It seems to me, from what you're saying, that you agree there's a problem, but you don't think the action that I have taken so far is the right way to go. I say come together. Let's talk. And maybe we can work out something that is agreeable to all and stop smut and pornography from overpowering this new system—

FRANK SESNO: Senator, how much smut and pornography do you think there is on the Internet?

SEN. JAMES EXON: From what I have read from many sources, from some universities you've had to take down certain links because there is so much smut and so much pornography that it was even embarrassing to universities, which are usually pretty open on this.

FRANK SESNO: Mr. Rotenberg, how do you respond to that? Because, in fact, there is a lot of that stuff out there.

MARC ROTENBERG: Well, that's true, Frank. There are problems, and the university is responding. The on-line service providers are responding. I think people—

FRANK SESNO: They can't police every terminal in the lab.

MARC ROTENBERG: Well, they can police their own terminals, and I think that's an important point also. We need to develop—

FRANK SESNO: In a university, for example, many of the students have computers in every room.

MARC ROTENBERG: I think the point here is that we want the university policing its own community, and we want the on-line service providers policing its own community. The risk, and frankly it's a serious risk, is that the federal government will intervene and say, "We want this standard applied to the universities, to the on-line service providers and to everybody else." And I think that outcome won't leave anybody very happy.

FRANK SESNO: Senator, before we break here, what's the course for your proposed legislation?

SEN. JAMES EXON: Well, let me say this—the first thing everyone should recognize is that right now there is a bulletin board that almost anyone can check into. It lists different subjects. It goes into sex. You can plug into that, and you can get all kind of lewd, obscene smut material. I think we've got to take some action now before this gets out of hand, and I want to work with Marc and others who are very much concerned about the First Amendment, as I am. But I think we can get something done if we work together instead of just throwing up our hands and saying this is so big we can't do anything about it.

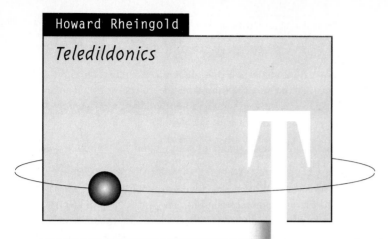

Howard Rheingold

Teledildonics

he first fully functional teledildonics system will be a communication device, not a sex machine. You probably will *not* use erotic telepresence technology in order to have sexual experiences with machines. Thirty years from now, when portable telediddlers become ubiquitous, most people will use them to have sexual experiences with other *people,* at a distance, in combinations and configurations undreamed of by precybernetic voluptuaries. Through a marriage of virtual reality technology and telecommunication networks, you will be able to reach out and touch someone—or an entire population—in ways humans have never before experienced. Or so the scenario goes.

The word "dildonics" was coined in 1974 by that zany computer visionary Theodore Nelson (inventor of hypertext and designer of the world's oldest unfinished software project, appropriately named "Xanadu"™), to describe a machine (patent #3,875,932) invented by a San Francisco hardware hacker by the name of How Wachspress, a device capable of converting sound into tactile sensations. The erotogenic effect depends upon where you, the consumer, decide to interface your anatomy with the tactile stimulator. VR raises the possibility of a far more sophisticated technology.

The word "dildonics" was coined in 1974 by that zany computer visionary Theodor Nelson

Picture yourself a couple of decades hence, dressing for a hot night in the virtual village. Before you climb into a suitably padded chamber and put on your 3D glasses, you slip into a lightweight (eventually, one would hope, diaphanous) bodysuit, something like a body stocking, but with the kind of intimate snugness of a condom. Embedded in the inner surface of the suit, using a technology that does not yet exist, is an array of intelligent sensor-effectors—a mesh of tiny tactile detectors coupled to vibrators of varying degrees of hardness, hundreds of them per square inch, that can receive and transmit a realistic sense of tactile presence, the way the visual and audio displays transmit a realistic sense of visual and auditory presence.

You can reach out your virtual hand, pick up a virtual block, and by running your fingers over the object, feel the surfaces and edges, by means of the

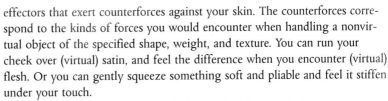

effectors that exert counterforces against your skin. The counterforces correspond to the kinds of forces you would encounter when handling a nonvir-
tual object of the specified shape, weight, and texture. You can run your
cheek over (virtual) satin, and feel the difference when you encounter (virtual)
flesh. Or you can gently squeeze something soft and pliable and feel it stiffen
under your touch.

Now, imagine plugging your whole sound-sight-touch telepresence system
into the telephone network. You see a lifelike but totally artificial visual representation of your own body and of your partner's. Depending on what numbers you dial and which passwords you know and what you are willing to
pay (or trade or do), you can find one partner, a dozen, a thousand, in various
cyberspaces that are no farther than a telephone number. Your partner(s) can
move independently in the cyberspace, and your representations are able to
touch each other, even though your physical bodies might be continents

*Now, imagine
plugging your
whole sound-
sight-touch
telepresence
system into
the telephone
network.*

apart. You will whisper in your partner's ear, feel your partner's breath on your neck. You run your hand over your partner's clavicle, and 6000 miles away, an array of effectors are
triggered, in just the right sequence, at just the right frequency, to convey the touch exactly the way you wish it to be
conveyed. If you don't like the way the encounter is going, or
someone requires your presence in physical reality, you can
turn it all off by flicking a switch and taking off your virtual
birthday suit.

Before plunging into questions about whether it is ethical
to build or moral to use teledildonic technology, it pays to ask
how far today's technology seems to be from achieving such
capabilities, because the answer appears to be: very far.
Fiberoptic networks will be required to handle the very high
bandwidth that tactile telepresence requires, perhaps including
the kind of hybrid circuit and packet-switched technology

NTT is installing in Japan as "broadband ISDN"; fortuitously, it looks like the
world is going to be webbed with fiberoptic bundles for other reasons. Carrying information back and forth across town, continent, or hemisphere in large
amounts, fairly quickly, will not be a problem. Until the speed of light barrier
is broken, the physical size of the planet precludes a truly instantaneous online shared cyberspace; the larger your cyberspace is distributed geographically, the larger your system lag time is likely to be. The computation load
generated by such a system is definitely a problem, too, a show-stopper, in
fact, in terms of today's computing capabilities. The most serious technical
obstacles that make teledildonics an early-to-mid-twenty-first-century technology rather than next year's fad lie in the extremely powerful computers
needed to perform the enormous number of added calculations required to
monitor and control hundreds of thousands of sensors and effectors. Every
nook and protuberance, every plane and valley and knob of your body's surface, will require its own processor.

Transducers are a real problem, as well. It will take decades to develop the mesh of tiny, high-speed, safe but powerful tactile effectors: today's vibrators are in the ENIAC era. The engineering problems in building the transducers, the parts of the system that communicate in a form that people can squeeze and scratch, stroke and probe, may be formidable, but they are already the subject of focused effort on three continents. Hennequin with his pneumatics and Johnson with his shape memory alloy are not the only ones. The researchers who were showing me their demonstrations at ATR in Japan were very interested in the transmission of touch. Researchers in Italy may have just made a big step toward the kind of intimate cybergarment described above. A very crude prototype of the light weight sensor-effector mesh has already been developed, according to these passages quoted from a 1990 article by Shawna Vogel, "Smart Skin":

One of the most sophisticated approaches to this goal is being developed at the University of Pisa by Italian engineer Danilo De Rossi, who has closely modeled an artificial skin on the inner and outer layers of human skin: the dermis and epidermis. His flexible, multi-layered sheathing even has the same thickness as human skin—roughly that of a dime.

De Rossi's artificial dermis is made of a water-swollen conducting gel sandwiched between two layers of electrodes that monitor the flow of electricity through the squishy middle. Like the all-natural human version, this dermis senses the overall pressure being exerted on an object. As pressure deforms the gel, the voltage between the electrodes changes; the harder the object being pressed, the greater the information. By keeping tabs on how the voltage is changing, a skin-clad robot could thus distinguish between a rubber ball and a rock.

For resolving the finer details of surface structure, De Rossi has created an epidermal layer of sensor-studded sheets of plastic placed between thin sheets of rubber. The sensors are pinhead-size disks made of piezoelectric substances, which emit an electric charge when subjected to pressure. These disks can sense texture as fine as the bumps on a braille manuscript.

These scientific frontiers provide the jumping-off point for the VR sex fantasy: Put together a highly refined version of "smart skin" with enough computing power, cleverly designed software, some kind of effector system, and a high-speed telecommunication network, and you have a teledildonics system. The tool I am suggesting is much more than a fancy vibrator, but I suggest we keep the archaic name. A more sober formal description of the technology would be "interactive tactile telepresence."

Teledildonics seems to be a thought experiment that got out of control. The quantum physicists had used this technique of imagining a certain set of conditions as a kind of mental scenario, a *gedankenexperiment,* a "thought experiment." The idea is to induce people to put themselves into an appropriate mindset for seeing the implications of a new discovery. I made the mistake of performing my gedankenexperiment on my local node of the Worldnet.

I wrote a short riff on teledildonics, not too different in content from this chapter, and posted it on the WELL; I used my modem to send the electronic version of that essay from my home computer to the larger computer a few miles from my home that stores the electronic record of conversations and publications that constitute the WELL. It's a cheap way of getting instant feedback from a few dozen respondents out of a local readership of a couple of thousand people. Anybody whose home computer is communicating with the WELL a moment after I post it, or in the middle of the night, or six months later, can tell me what they think publicly in the public conversation, or privately via e-mail. People can also do other things, like copy documents and send them places. I thought that my piece would stimulate discussion that could help me think through the various implications of sex at a distance. The weird part came when I started receiving electronic mail from around the country within hours of posting that essay. I did not take special measures to prevent anybody from duplicating the file.

Teledildonics seems to be a thought experiment that got out of control.

Apparently, one of the several thousand people who had access to the WELL had sent my teledildonics riff elsewhere via electronic mail; it only takes a few keystrokes to send an existing file on your host computer to any other computer in the Worldnet.

The piece seems to have struck a nerve. I noticed that an editor who interviewed me in Tokyo for one of Japan's largest computer magazines had a printed copy. I got calls from London and Amsterdam. People seemed to skip over all of my verbal qualifications and descriptions of technical difficulties, and almost all the people who contacted me for information seemed to believe that such a device actually exists somewhere and that I've seen it or tested it in some fulsome way. Among the other experiences my thought experiment led me into was a dinner with a German journalist. A young reporter for *Der Spiegel,* one of Germany's two largest news magazines, was traveling in search of the next computer revolution, and that had led him to VR. After our dinner, he wrote an article; it was published several months later. My name was mentioned. There was a photo. My agent sent me a very rough translation, which apparently was too rough, or else I failed to read it thoroughly enough. A month after that, I got a call from a woman in Augsburg, Germany, who was quite insistent that I should come to address a convention for NCR, within a few days. She persuaded me to speak, as specifically or vaguely as I wanted, about "future prospects for virtual reality." When I arrived in Augsburg, I was immediately whisked to a reception given by the mayor at the splendidly gilded, restored Augsburg City Hall. Then we retired to the municipal ratskeller for beer, sausage, and an interminable bilingual skit about Augsburg's history. It was at this point that NCR's German marketing communications director told me that I was a hot commodity in Germany at that time, because of what *Der Spiegel*'s story had said, or what they thought it said.

"What do you mean?" I asked.

"The part where they said you were experimenting with ways to have sex with computers," the marketing communications director replied.

No wonder the vice presidents who introduced themselves to me were smiling the way they were when they told me they were looking forward to my talk. So I opened my presentation with John von Neumann's limerick.

The teledildonics story was also published in *Mondo 2000,* an avant-garde, technology-oriented "mutazine." I got even more weird phone calls after that. I can't help believing, from the reaction I've received in response to an essay I wrote in ten minutes, for fun, that the interest in this possibility will remain high. When people seem to want a technology to develop, to literally lust for a possible new toy, that need can take on a force of its own, especially given the rates of progress in the enabling technologies and the enormous market-driven forces that will be unleashed when sex at a distance becomes possible. Yes, teledildonics is a titillating fantasy, far from the serious human realities of medical imaging or teleoperated machine guns. But once you start thinking about sex at a distance, it's amazing how many other questions about future possibilities present themselves, questions about big changes that might be in store for us. Given the rate of development of VR technologies, we don't have a great deal of time to tackle questions of morality, privacy, personal identity, and even the prospect of a fundamental change in human nature. When the VR revolution really gets rolling, we are likely to be too busy turning into whatever we are turning into to analyze or debate the consequences.

One side effect of technological power seems to be that human culture is growing more mechanized. We wake up and eat and sleep and arrange our days according to the dictates of the machines that make our lives easier—or at least difficult in different ways—than our grandparents' lives. At the same time, human desires have been progressively stimulated, confused, and ultimately numbed by the barrage of provocative images, sounds, words thrown our way via electronic media; McLuhan didn't tell us that the global village would be experienced primarily by most people as an overdose of beautifully crafted advertisements, based largely on sexual innuendo, for the products of multinational corporations. Electronic media have been used thus far by a few to manipulate the desires of many, resulting in unprecedented financial profit. It is possible that telepresence technology, if linked with an inherently distributed network system such as the telecommunications infrastructure, will give this power to many, rather than reserving it for a few. Whether that is true and whether it is a good idea are both questions that remain to be settled.

To many, the idea of literally "embracing technology" seems repugnant. Computer ethicist Joseph Weizenbaum, author of *Computing Power and Human Reason,* I am sure, would consider it antihuman. And perhaps it is. We should think about those deep moral reservations of a few less than optimistic prophets very hard and very long. But there is no doubt that people everywhere in the world are fascinated by the prospect. And why not? Contemporary philosophers have pointed to progressive mechanization of human culture and the future of sexual expression as the site of a potential cultural collision of immense dimensions.

Think about a few fundamental assumptions about the way things are that might have to change if teledildonics becomes practical. If everybody can look as beautiful, sound as sexy, and feel as nubile and virile as everybody else, then what will become the new semiotics of mating? What will have erotic meaning? In the area of sexual-cultural coding, much can be learned by the way people seem to be using other electronic communication technologies to construct artificial erotic experience. "Telephone sex," in which paying customers are metered for the number of minutes they have a conversation about their choice of sexually charged topics, with a real human of the gender of their choice, might offer clues. So says Allucquére Rosanne Stone, a scholar of such matters. I met her on the net, and we knew each other's opinions pretty well by the time we met "ftf" ("face to face"), as the computer conferencing habituees say. Stone had been spending her time interviewing VR programmers, telephone sex workers, and amputees, because they all shared the experience of disembodiment and of feeling sensations from a body that does not exist physically.

"Telephone sex," in which paying customers are metered for the number of minutes they have a conversation about their choice of sexually charged topics, . . . might offer clues.

When she found out about my quest into all the odd corners of VR research, Stone made contact with me via e-mail. In an electronic mail exchange, Stone sent me some provocative observations about telephone sex, part of a work-in-progress named "Sex and Death Among the Disembodied," which seemed to have direct bearing on the idea that people might use the telecommunication infrastructure for erotic gratification:

Phone sex is the process of constructing desire through a single mode of communication. In the process, participants draw on a repertoire of cultural codes to construct a scenario that compresses large amounts of information into a very small space. The worker verbally codes for gesture, appearance, and proclivity, and expresses these as tokens, sometimes in no more than a word. The client uncompresses the tokens and constructs a dense, complex interactional image. In these interactions desire appears as a product of the tension between embodied reality and the emptiness of the token, in the forces that maintain the preexisting codes for body in the modalities that are not expressed in the token; that is, tokens in phone sex are purely verbal, and the client uses cues in the verbal token to construct a multimodal object of desire with attributes of shape, tactility, etc. This act is thoroughly individual and interpretive; out of a highly compressed token of desire the client constitutes meaning that is dense, locally situated, and socially particular.

The secondary social effects of technosex are potentially revolutionary. If technology enables you to experience erotic frissons or deep physical, social, emotional communion with another person with no possibility of pregnancy or sexually transmitted disease, what then of conventional morality, and what of the social rituals and cultural codes that exist solely to enforce that morality? Is disembodiment the ultimate sexual revolution and/or the first step toward abandoning our bodies? Whenever I think of the vision of billions of earthlings of the future, all plugged into their home reality sets, I think of

E. M. Forster's dystopia of a future in which people remain prisoners of their cubicles, entranced by their media, not even aware of the possibility of physical escape. And then I think that it is good to beware of looking at the future through the moral lens of the present: in a world of tens of billions of people, perhaps cyberspace is a better place to keep most of the population relatively happy, most of the time.

Back to thought-provocative implications of telesex. If you can map your hands to your puppet's legs, and let your fingers do the walking through cyberspace, as it is possible to do in a crude way with today's technology, there is no reason to believe you won't be able to map your genital effectors to your manual sensors and have direct genital contact by shaking hands. What will happen to social touching when nobody knows where anybody else's erogenous zones are located?

Privacy and identity and intimacy will become tightly coupled into something we don't have a name for yet. In Unix computer systems, such as those used by the host computers of Worldnet, files (documents, data bases, graphics, encoded sounds and programs) and categories of users who have access to those files can be grouped into nested hierarchies by a system of "permissions," like hiding information behind doors of encryption that can be opened only by those who know the key. People who use Unix systems today often have publicly accessible file areas, in which everyone with access to the computer system has the key (a secret combination of numbers and letters and punctuation marks) to read and copy these files, and private areas for which only a small group of associates or one trusted partner knows the key. In cyberspace, if a parallel structure emerges, your most public persona—the way you want the world to see you—will be "universally readable," in Unix terms. If you decide to join a group at a collegial or peer level, or decide to become informationally intimate with an individual or group of individuals, you will share the public keys to your identity permission access codes. It might be that the physical commingling of genital sensations will come to be regarded as a less intimate act than the sharing of the data structures of your innermost self-representations.

Potential psychosocial effects of present state-of-the-art VR technology were cannily anticipated thirty years ago by Marshall McLuhan in *Understanding Media*, which seems to make more sense in the 1990s than it did at the time it was published. But future cyberspace spinoffs are getting into territory beyond the McLuhan horizon. With all those layers of restricted access to self-representations that may differ radically from layer to layer, what happens to the self? Where does identity lie? What new meanings will "intimacy" and "morality" accrete? And with our information machines and our bodily sensations so deeply "intertwingled," as Theodore Nelson might say, will our communication devices be regarded as "it"s or will they be part of "us"?

Gerard Van Der Leun

"This Is a Naked Lady"

Sex is a virus that infects new technology.

Back in the dawn of online when a service called The Source was still in flower, a woman I once knew used to log on as "This is a naked lady." She wasn't naked of course, except in the minds of hundreds of young and not-so-young males who also logged on to The Source. Night after night, they sent her unremitting text streams of detailed wet dreams, hoping to engage her in online exchanges known as "hot chat"—a way of engaging in a mutual fantasy typically found only through 1-900 telephone services. In return, "The Naked Lady" egged on her digital admirers with leading questions larded with copious amounts of double entendre.

When I first asked her about this, she initially put it down to "just fooling around on the wires."

"It's just a hobby," she said. "Maybe I'll get some dates out of it. Some of these guys have very creative and interesting fantasy lives."

At the start, The Naked Lady was a rather mousy person—the type who favored gray clothing of a conservative cut—and was the paragon of shy and retiring womanhood. Seeing her on the street, you'd never think that her online persona was one that excited the libidos of dozens of men every night.

At the start, The Naked Lady was a rather mousy person.

But as her months of online flirtations progressed, a strange transformation came over her: She became (through the dint of her blazing typing speed) the kind of person that could keep a dozen or more online sessions of hot chat going at a time. She got a trendy haircut. Her clothing tastes went from Peck and Peck to tight skirts slit up the thigh. She began regaling me with descriptions of her expanding lingerie collection. Her speech became bawdier, her jokes naughtier.

In short, she was becoming her online personality—lewd, bawdy, sexy, a man-eater.

The last I saw of her, The Naked Lady was using her online conversations to cajole dates and favors from those men foolish enough to fall into her clutches.

The bait she used was an old sort—sex without strings attached, sex without love, sex as a fantasy pure and simple. It's an ancient profession whose costs always exceed expectations and whose pleasures invariably disappoint. However, the "fishing tackle" was new: online telecommunications.

In the eight years that have passed since The Naked Lady first appeared, a number of new wrinkles have been added to the text-based fantasy machine. Groups have formed to represent all sexual persuasions. For a while, there was a group on the Internet called, in the technobabble that identifies areas on the net, alt.sex.bondage.golden.showers.sheep. Most people thought it was a joke, and maybe it was.

But as her months of online flirtations progressed, a strange transformation came over her.

Online sex stories and erotic conversations consume an unknown and unknowable portion of the global telecommunications bandwidth. Even more is swallowed by graphics. Now, digitized sounds are traveling the nets, and digital deviants are even "netcasting" short movie clips. All are harbingers of things to come.

It is as if all the incredible advances in computing and networking technology over the past decades boil down to the ability to ship images of turgid members and sweating bodies everywhere and anywhere at anytime. Looking at this, it is little wonder that whenever this is discovered (and someone, somewhere, makes the discovery about twice a month), a vast hue and cry resounds over the nets to root-out the offending material and burn those who promulgated it. High tech is being perverted to low ends, they cry. But it was always so.

There is absolutely nothing new about the prurient relationship between technology and sexuality.

Sex, as we know, is a heat-seeking missile that forever seeks out the newest medium for its transmission. William Burroughs, a man who understands the dark side of sexuality better than most, sees it as a virus that is always on the hunt for a new host—a virus that almost always infects new technology first. Different genders and psyches have different tastes, but the overall desire seems about as persistent over the centuries as the lust for bread and salvation.

We could go back to Neolithic times when sculpture and cave painting were young. We could pick up the prehistoric sculptures of females with pendulous breasts and very wide hips—a theme found today in pornographic magazines that specialize in women of generous endowment. We could then run our flashlight over cave paintings of males whose members seem to exceed the length of their legs. We could travel forward in time to naughty frescos in Pompeii, or across continents to where large stones resembling humongous erections have for centuries been major destinations to pilgrims in India, or to the vine-choked couples of the Black Pagoda at Ankor Wat where a Mardi Gras of erotic activity carved in stone has been on display for centuries. We could proceed to eras closer to our time and culture, and remind people that movable type not only made the Gutenberg Bible possible, but that it also made cheap broadsheets of what can only be called "real smut in

Elizabethan English" available to the masses for the very first time. You see, printing not only made it possible to extend the word of God to the educated classes, it also extended the monsters of the id to them as well.

Printing also allowed for the cheap reproduction and broad distribution of erotic images. Soon, along came photography; a new medium, and one that until recently did more to advance the democratic nature of erotic images than all previous media combined. When photography joined with photolithography, the two together created a brand new medium that many could use. It suddenly became economically feasible and inherently possible for lots of people to enact and record their sexual fantasies and then reproduce them for sale to many others. Without putting too fine a point on it, the Stroke Book was born.

There is absolutely nothing new about the prurient relationship between technology and sexuality.

Implicit within these early black-and-white tomes (which featured a lot of naked people with Lone Ranger masks demonstrating the varied ways humans can entwine their limbs and conceal large members at the same time) were the vast nascent publishing empires of *Playboy, Penthouse,* and *Swedish Erotica.*

The point here is that all media, when they are either new enough or become relatively affordable, are used by outlaws to broadcast unpopular images or ideas. When a medium is created, the first order of business seems to be the use of it in advancing religious, political, or sexual notions and desires. Indeed, all media, if they are to get a jump-start in the market and become successful, must address themselves to mass drives—those things we hold in common as basic human needs.

But of all these: food, shelter, sex and money; sex is the one drive that can elicit immediate consumer response. It is also why so many people obsessed with the idea of eliminating pornography from the earth have recently fallen back on the saying "I can't define what pornography is, but I know it when I see it."

They're right. You can't define it; you feel it. Alas, since everyone feels it in a slightly different way and still can't define it, it becomes very dangerous to a free society to start proscribing it.

And now we have come to the "digital age" where all information and images can be digitized; where all bits are equal, but some are hotter than others. We are now in a land where late-night cable can make your average sailor blush. We live in an age of monadic seclusion, where dialing 1-900 and seven other digits can put you in intimate contact with pre-op transsexuals in wet suits who will talk to you as long as the credit limit on your MasterCard stays in the black.

If all this pales, the "adult" channels on the online service CompuServe can fill your nights at $12.00 an hour with more fantasies behind the green screen than ever lurked behind the green door. And that's just the beginning. There are hundreds of adult bulletin board systems offering God Knows What to God Knows Who, and making tidy profits for plenty of folks.

Sex has come rocketing out of the closet and into the terminals of anyone smart enough to boot up FreeTerm. As a communications industry, sex has transmogrified itself from the province of a few large companies and individuals into a massive cottage industry.

It used to be, at the very least, that you had to drive to the local (or not-so-local) video shop or "adult" bookstore to refresh your collection of sexual fantasies. Now, you don't even have to leave home. What's more, you can create it yourself, if that's your pleasure, and transmit it to others.

It is a distinct harbinger of things to come that "Needless to say . . ." letters now appearing online are better than those published in Penthouse Forum, or that sexual images in binary form make up one of the heaviest data streams on the Internet, and that "amateur" erotic home videos are the hottest new category in the porn shops.

Progress marches on. In time, robotics will deliver household servants and sex slaves.

Since digital sex depends on basic stimuli that is widely known and understood, erotica is the easiest kind of material to produce. Quality isn't the primary criteria. Quality isn't even the point. Arousal is the point, pure and simple. Everything else is just wrapping paper. If you can pick up a Polaroid, run a Camcorder, write a reasonably intelligible sentence on a word processor or set up a bulletin board system, you can be in the erotica business. Talent has very, very little to do with it.

The other irritating thing about sex is that like hunger, it is never permanently satisfied. It recurs in the human psyche with stubborn regularity. In addition, it is one of the drives most commonly stimulated by the approved above-ground media (Is that woman in the Calvin Klein ads coming up from a stint of oral sex, or is she just surfacing from a swimming pool?) Mature, mainstream corporate media can only tease. New, outlaw media delivers. Newcomers can't get by on production values, because they have none.

Author Howard Rheingold has made some waves recently with his vision of a network that will actually hook some sort of tactile feedback devices onto our bodies so that the fantasies don't have to be so damned cerebral. He calls this vision "dildonics," and he has been dining out on the concept for years. With it, you'll have virtual reality coupled with the ability to construct your own erotic consort for work, play, or simple experimentation.

Progress marches on. In time, robotics will deliver household servants and sex slaves.

I saw The Naked Lady about three months ago. I asked her if she was still up to the same old games of online sex. "Are you kidding?" she told me. "I'm a consultant for computer security these days. Besides, I have a kid now. I don't want that kind of material in my home."

Chapter 3

Questions and Suggestions for Further Study on the Net/WWW

■ QUESTIONS BASED ON THE READINGS:

1. If you are male, discuss with your class (males alone or with the whole class) what your attitude has been and presently is either (a) toward women *and* technology, or (b) more specifically, women *and* computers. Have you found yourself refusing to help women who have no background in how computers or their programs work? If you have helped women, how have you gone about helping them? Be introspective about the *how*.

2. If you are female, discuss with your class (females alone or with the whole class) what your attitude has been and presently is (a) toward technology in general and (b) computers in particular. Have you found yourself shying away from them because to use them and demonstrate your comfort in using them might be "unfeminine"? How have you asked a male, if you initiated the asking, for help with a computer? Why did you ask? How have males responded to your asking?

   (I pretty much taught myself how to use a computer and specific word-processing programs, but other males showed me how to use complicated desktop publishing programs. When it came to the Internet, however, a female graduate student taught me and is still teaching me about various aspects of the technology—ranging from how to work within a vax system and send e-mail to how to function in a MOO environment.)

3. If you are a male and have had some experience posting to discussion groups and going to MOOs, how have you responded to those whom you have thought to be female? If you post to them privately or approach them at a MOO, how do you begin a conversation? Does it differ from how you begin one in real life and time? Is it the same? (If you have never gone to a MOO and would like to, see Questions and Suggestions in Chapter 7. If you know someone who knows how, have that person give you instructions and a helping hand when you both arrive from your separate terminals.)

4. If you are male, attend a MOO and take the gender and name of a female when you sign on. How do people talk to you, publicly and privately? Do you find, after a while, that your mascarade is transparent? Do you find

yourself feeling uneasy about how people are talking to you? Do two men discussing an issue ignore you or sexually harass you? (You can do the same, in certain circumstances, on a discussion list.)

5. What conceptual parallels do you see, on one hand, between Kantrowitz's presumption that technology is determined by acculturation and not by biological gender and, on the other hand, Harrington's presumption that standards of decency are not universal but should be determined by local standards (i.e., that people in rural and urban areas should decide locally for themselves about what counts as decency)? If Senator Exon's amendment to the Telecommunications Reform Act of 1995 or any comparable bill is passed, is it enforceable? If the amendment is deemed enforceable, how specifically would such a policy be implemented? (For more information on Exon's bill, see Further Study below.)

6. Keeping Tannen's comparison between her friend Ralph and herself in mind, make similar comparisons between yourself and another person of the opposite gender who uses computers. Do you see similarities or differences? What does the use of a computer mean to you? To others you know?

7. Herring's study is in part statistical. Try keeping a log of how males in your class discussions, a newsgroup, a discussion list on line, or a MOO respond to females and vice versa, and what the ratio might be between males and females posting. (To be sure, on a newgroup or at a MOO it is difficult to tell about someone's gender if the person does not use a regularly identifiable name, but again study how the person posts, i.e., uses language on line.) Add any other comments to your log that you think are pertinent to the issue of gender differences.

8. "Sex is in the mind" has become a commonplace among some people. What could such a statement possibly mean? What might this commonplace have to do with sex in cyberspace or virtual reality? Does Harold Rheingold, in "Teledildonics," help you understand what experiencing VR might be like? What is the relationship between sex and technology as Gerard Van Der Leun describes it? (The issues of sex and gender will take on further significance in Chapters 6 and 7.)

■ F U R T H E R   S T U D Y   O N   T H E   N E T / W W W :

Kantrowitz points to a number of "wired women" who have developed on-line networks for women such as Systers, ECHO, and Women's Wire. If you were to find the names of groups or discussion lists such as these and needed to know more about them, one way is to use the *WebCrawler* <http://webcrawler.com/>. (If you are having difficulties following these instructions, then please see Appendix A.) Once you get to *WebCrawler*, all you have to do is type, in the appropriate space, the key word *Syster* and make a search. This will give you *WebCrawler Search Results*:

The query "Syster" found 8 documents and returned 6:

1000 Groups Relating to Women in Computer Science/Computing
0123 WICS Home Page
0028 ftp://nic.umass.edu/pub/ednet/educatrs.1st

```
0028   Web-sters' Net-Work: Women in Info Technology
0020   European Satellite Information
0008   SLIDERS FAQ Web Page
```

At this point, you can type ↑ or ↓ (or click) and scroll up or down the list and type → on your keyboard and you will be on your way to a few websites that have a great deal of information about women and technology on the Internet. (As more and more sites for women are put out on the Net, the number of items retrieved in the search will of course increase.)

If you recall, Kantrowitz refers to Ada Lovelace as the first programmer. You can make a search for more information by typing in the search area *Ada Lovelace* and then execute the search. When done, you will be told:

```
The query "Ada Lovelace" found 16 documents and returned 13:
```

```
1000   Lovelace Ada Tutor Home Page
0314   User Guide to Mklesson—Home Page
0157   ftp://sw-eng.falls-church.va.us/public/AdaIC/pol-
       hist/history/lady-lov.txt
0134   Home of the Brave Ada Programmers
0070   Past Notable Women of Computing
0058   ftp://cpsr.org/cpsr/gender/clark/Lewis.Judith
0054   Languages and System
0032   Home page of HPDR
0022   The Ada-Belgium Organization
0017   THE HISTORY OF COMPUTING
0017   Communications Manifestos
0005   DSP Jargon File
0001   BABEL: A Glossary of Computer Related Abbreviations and
       Acronyms
```

One point to remember is that not all these hits are about the Ada we are searching for; only a few are. Moving the arrow button up and down and then to the right for a search, you will find some interesting information. For example, you will discover a tutorial for a program language called ADA, a website called "Home of the Brave Ada Programmers" (with a tremendous amount of information) and another called "Past Notable Women of Computing" with a number of names listed, including

```
*Ada Byron King, Countess of Lovelace, 1815-1852
```

which, when searched, gives you a brief bibliography. If you search "Communications Manifestos" and move down the list, you will find

```
*Catch up on your computer history and read about Augusta Ada
Lovelace, the inventor of computer programing.
```

While you were arrowing or scrolling down, you probably noticed other titles that interested you such as

```
*Doctress Neutopia: The Feminization of Cyberspace*
```

```
*Ellen Balka: Women's Access to On-line Discussions About
Feminism.
```

There are still others, but we are now away from our specific search for Ada Lovelace.

■ HERE ARE SOME ADDITIONAL
  WEBSITES, FOR AND ABOUT WOMEN:

- *Women-oriented sites on the Web* <http://www.rpi.edu/~schmel/ FRED/gender.html>. (There are about five pages of sites, which close with:

```
*The Geekgirl homepage—Tank Girl's byte-savvy sister
*Here's the Webgrrl's site
*And, the Cybergrrl goes Surfing! site
*The Female Bodybuilder home page
*Men's Issues page
*Finally, a link to the Women's Wire gopher
```

Notice the link to the Men's Issues page.)

- *Women Homepage* <http://www.mit.edu:8001/people/sorokin/women/ index.html#mymess>

- *Feminist Use of Cyberspace* <ftp://english.hss.cmv.edu/English.Server/ Feminism/Feminist./.20Use./.20of./.20Cyberspace>. (Notice that this is an ftp site. What you will find is Ellen Balka's "Women's Access to On-Line Discussions about Feminism," an invaluable, well-researched article.)

- *Groups Relating to Women in Computer Science/Computing* <http:// www.cs.yale.edu:80/HTML/YALE/CS/HyPlans/tap/cs-women- groups.html>. (I found this one while searching through *WebCrawler.*)

- *Web-sters' Net-Work: Women in Info Technology* <http://lucien. berkeley.edu/women_in_it.html>. (Same as above.)

- *TAP: The Ada Project* <http://www.cs.yale.edu/HTML/YALE/CS/ HyPlans/tap/tap.html>

- *Electronic Frontier Foundation* <http://www.eff.org/>. (For the information on women, you must get to the EFF *Archives.* Then you must go to *Topical Index.* Once in the index, go to the topic *Cyberlinguistics.* If you scroll down, you will notice *Gender in Cyberia,* both of which have loads of information, many sites, and papers on various subjects. (Often files get shifted around at EFF, so you may have to look through the archives.)

- *I'm NOT Miss Manner's of the Internet* <http://rs6000.adm.fau.edu/ rinaldi/netiquette.html>. (Here you will find Arlene Rinaldi's *Netiquette Home Page,* which has valuable resources on the issue of netiquette.)

■ S O M E   W E B S I T E S   W H E R E   M O R E   I N F O R M A T I O N   A B O U T
F R E E D O M   O F   E X P R E S S I O N   C A N   B E   F O U N D   (A L O N G
W I T H   A G E N C I E S   O F   T H E   F E D E R A L   G O V E R N M E N T   A N D
A   F E W   N E W S G R O U P S) :

> Though the piece of legislation generally known as Exon's "Communications Decency Act" may be eventually passed with further amendments by Congress and signed (or vetoed) by the President, the law will most likely be contested in the judicial branch. Even if it is not passed and new bills take its place, contestation will continue. The sites below will mostly keep this information in their databanks because it is history being made and, hence, will continue to be a focus for research. There will simply be more information added to these sites and under the same general rubric: *Freedom in Cyberspace.* Just today (July 1, 1995), I received from *HotFlash* (2.25, *Wired* magazine's on-line newsletter) the following statement:

> The Exon language that eventually passed the full Senate (84-16) was far removed from the original. And while the tricked-up version looks better on paper, it's still a poison-pen for free speech.

- (Return to) *Electronic Frontier Foundation* <http://www.eff.org/>. (At the website, you will see an index, which includes *Alerts* and *Archives.* Under *Alerts* you will find references, at present, to the Exon bill or any future bills on communication that the Foundation is monitoring. When you get into the *Topical Index,* the first listed will be the yearly legislation, under which you will find a great deal of information. As you arrow or scroll down the index, you will find other relevant material.)

- *American Civil Liberties Union* (gopher server) <gopher://aclu.org:6601/> and<gopher://gopher.nyc.pipeline.com/11/society/aclu/issues/cyberspace>

- *The Center for Democracy and Technology* <http://www.cdt.org/>

- *Christian Coalition Main Menu* <http://www.cc.org/>

- *Stop the 1995 Communications Decency Act!* <http://www.panix.com/vtw/exon/exon.html>

- *Government Affairs* <http://www.ema.org/ema/html/govtaffr.htm#CurrPubl>

- *Supreme Infotrainschedule* <http://www.dorsai.org/~adamn/congress.html> (The House, the Senate, the White House).

- *THOMAS: Legislative Information on the Internet* <http://thomas.loc.gov/>. (Full texts of legislation, with their versions, as well as of the Congressional Record, Senate Gopher, House Gopher, C-SPAN Gopher, and much more.)

- *Newsgroups*
  alt.censorship
  alt.feminism
  alt.internet.media-coverage

■ T H E   D I S C U S S I O N   A B O U T   J A K E   B A K E R :

- *The Michigan Telecommunications and Technology Law Review* <http://www.umich.edu/~umlaw/mttlr.html>. (The page is also entitled: *Policing the Internet: Jake Baker and beyond.* It is volume 1.1 of *MTTLR* and includes a debate with opening statements and eleven questions answered by some notable authorities on the law and free speech. By the time *CyberReader* is in print, this page will be relocated in the archives of *MTTLR*.)

- *MIT Student Association for Freedom of Expression (SAFE) Home Page* <http://www.mit.edu:8001/activities/safe/home.html>. (Includes various writings on freedom of expression issues, case archives, notable results of certain policies, various policies and reports, satire and humor, resources for fighting back, selected legal decisions. See *The files in this archive,* then *The Case Archives,* where you will find: *The "Jake Baker" story: Fantasy or Threat.*)

- *Sex, Censorship, and the Internet* <http://www.eff.org/CAF/cafuiuc.html>. (Deals with such questions as "Should the University carry newsgroup 'alt.sex'?" and "Should students be punished for using vulgarities on the Net?" The index has a number of legal cases and mountains of information. As you can see from the URL, this page is located at the Electronic Freedom Foundation website.)

- *Legal Pitfalls in Cyberspace: Defamation on Computer Networks* <http://www.kbs.citri.edu.au/law/defame.html>. (Lots of links to cyberspace and the law.)

  Be sure to go to <http://www.abacon.com/ncyber> the Allyn & Bacon website and directly to the *CyberReader* section for additional information on the Baker case.

■ M O R E   R E F E R E N C E S   F O R   R E A D I N G
   A N D   F O R   S U R F I N G   T H E   W E B :

- "Cyberporn" (cover story) *Time* (July 3, 1995). Shortly after this issue appeared, *Wired* magazine ran a series of responses in its on-line *HotWired* indicating that *Time* magazine had portrayed the whole issue of cyberporn and children's access to it much like a scandal sheet would. To see it, point to: <http://www.hotwired.com/special/pornscare/>. You should signup for *HotWired* so that you can start receiving its newsletter *HotFlash* and have access to its usenet: <http://www.hotwired.com/Login/>. You will be asked to supply a name and password; simply follow the instructions. The largest and best collection of articles and discussions on this issue of *Time* is *The Cyberporn Report* <http://www.cybernothing.org/cno/reports/cyberporn.html>. What you find here is essentially a casebook (anthology) on the subject. See *Time* magazine: <http://www.pathfinder.com/@@W@OD1QAAAAAAK77/time/timehomepage.html>.

- Dery, Mark, ed. *Flame Wars: The Discourse of Cyberculture.* Durham, NC: Duke University Press, 1994.

- *The English Server* (Carnegie Mellon Univ.) <http://english-www.hss.cmu.edu/>. (You're on your own here. By now, you can pick out the relevant topics in the index for this section of your readings. This is a very popular site, so do not be surprised if you find it busy. Just keep trying; it's worth it.)

- *Howard Rheingold* <http://www.well.com/user/hlr/>. (The author of *Virtual Reality* and *The Virtual Community,* editor of *Whole Earth Review* and editor-in-chief of *The Millennium Whole Earth Catalog* also writes a column on virtual reality and communities. Check out his website for his articles and other things Rheingoldian.)

- Kramarae, C., ed. *Technology and Women's Voices: Keeping in Touch.* New York: Routledge, 1988.

- McCormack, Michael. "Tell It to the Judge." *Net* (British version) 9 (August 1995): 60–62.

- Stone, Allucqukre Rosanne. *The War of Desire and Technology at the Close of the Mechanical Age.* Cambridge, MA: MIT Press, 1995.

- Tannen, Deborah. *You Just Don't Understand: Women and Men in Conversation.* New York: William Morrow, 1990.

- Wajcman, J. *Feminism Confronts Technology.* University Park, PA: Pennsylvania State University Press, 1991.

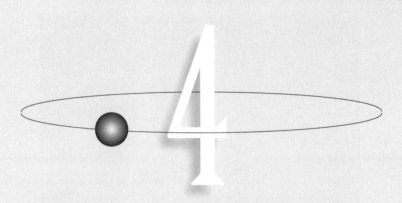

HyperText

(Virtual Books, Multimedia):

T he title of this chapter can be misleading and needs some immediate explanation. I am not using the term *hypertext* in any exclusive sense. Let me simplify matters and say that I have, at east, two senses in mind: on the one hand, the *death* of the actual book and the *birth* of the virtual book and, on the other, that form of writing (i.e., hypertextual writing) which has no sense of a beginning or ending as we commonly experience such conventions in narratives (whether they be in books or films or our so-called everyday life). Notice how the first sense speaks of *beginning* and *ending* (birth/death) and the second, by implication, speaks of *only middles* and everywhere middles.

This distinction is abstract (just as the difference between *actual* and *virtual* is), but it can be understood if we explore the readings in this section.

First we have Neil Postman speaking for books and Camille Paglia speaking for TV, or so the title of the exchange leads us to believe! Upon closer examination of the "printed" transcript of the dinner conversation, we can see otherwise: Postman favors books over television; Paglia, however, favors both the book and the television and other media and *all simultaneously.* She says: "When I wrote my book, I had earphones on, blasting rock music or Puccini and Brahms. The soap operas—with the sound turned down—flickered on my TV. I'd be talking on the phone at the same time." (She explains this difference with Postman in terms of being born before or after World War II.)

Now juggle these two images—of being in tune with one thing versus being in tune with many things—while we go on to Sven Birkerts. (If you were born after WWII, you should be able to juggle these images!) Birkerts makes a distinction among

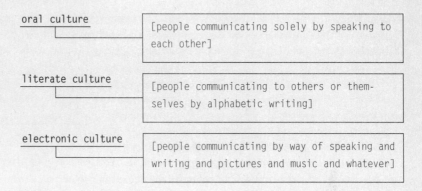

oral culture   [people communicating solely by speaking to each other]

literate culture   [people communicating to others or themselves by alphabetic writing]

electronic culture   [people communicating by way of speaking and writing and pictures and music and whatever]

He further distinguishes literate (print) culture in terms of

linear thinking,

logic/concepts, and

vertically cumulative

and electronic culture as not an unbroken line or thread of thought but a

network (a web), not logical but

impressionistic and **imagistic** (television commercials), not

vertically cumulative but

laterally associative. . . .

What am I doing? Has this not become a joke (an irony, a paradox)? Here I am in a book (literate culture), trying to explain hypertext, virtual books, multimedia (electronic culture)! Notice how in the previous paragraph I (and the people who helped me produce this book) tried to create a simulation of electronic culture while explaining it. That is, we, as so many other authors/ publishers before us—such as in *Wired* magazine, or MONDO 2000 or *.Net* or even special Issues of *Time* and *Newsweek*—tried to fool your eyes and brain into believing you were *actually* reading a *virtual* text, *hypertext*. What's being simulated is the World Wide Web (WWW). The simulation is an attempt to create what is called a hot link [Link] followed by a linked text that would replace the previous text on the screen; the printed page, however, would feature a virtual box of text out in the margin. A perfect example of this effect is found in the Introduction to this book with its two split monologues; other examples of this kind of formatting are found in *MONDO 2000: A User's Guide to the New Edge.*

In this book we can only simulate hypertext, of course. Is our attempt at simulation to be criticized? Perhaps. As you will see when you read Birkerts and others, however, we readers are not yet in an electronic culture as much as we are in a literate culture. Birkerts calls the period we are in "proto-electronic," which will "not require a transition period of two centuries" as did the transition from oral culture into literate culture. He says: "Fifty years, I'm sure, will suffice." Until we pass over into electronic culture, we will talk about such a culture and about hypertext itself by way of literate culture. But in order to have our book and eat hypertext too, each chapter of this book begins with traditional, literate introductions to the readings but ends with information to get you out into electronic culture . . .

In that light, then, I ask again: *What is hypertext?* You will find it in the WWW. When you are out on the Web, you are in the conditions of an electronic culture, in hypertext, which has no beginning or ending, but is all middle. You can jump in anywhere and move in the direction of your interests from one site to another. It's not like picking up a book and reading it the way that we traditionally have been taught to, from beginning to end. When you begin to do research out on the Web—when you are supposed to be focused toward a particular goal—you will discover that your interests may change quickly and capriciously and, more important, that the technology of hypertext allows you to pursue those interests easily. Hypertext, to be hypertext, does not have to follow the logic of linear thought but can follow (and some insist *should* follow) associative thought. (Linear, discursive, propositional thought, we say in terms of brain hemisphericity, comes from the left brain; associative thought comes from the right brain.) *What is a virtual book?* In its grandest form, it is the Web. (Other examples are forthcoming in the readings.) *What is multimedia?* If you are using the program *Lynx* as your means of browsing the Web, you will get only text (i.e., words); if you are using *Mosaic* or *Netscape,* you will get not only text but also pictures (graphics) and sound (voice, music, etc.). *Lynx* gives you only hypertext; *Mosaic* and *Netscape* and whatever the next browser program is will give you multimedia (which is, again, hypertext plus pictures and sound). Just a few weeks ago, I saw *Hot Java,* a program that allows for three dimensionality and higher levels of interaction!

As you *read* (back to the irony) Jay David Bolter, you will better understand, in a bookish-linear sense, what hypertext can be. As you read the four brief remaining selections about William Gibson's (Dennis Ashbaugh's, and Kevin Begos's) *Agrippa: A Book of the Dead* (the electronic book that can be read only once, because it is consumed by a virus as you read it!), you might come to understand how the death of the book is the death of death and a bursting forth of lifeeeeeeeeeeee.

Neil Postman and Camille Paglia

She Wants Her TV!
He Wants His Book!

hat I see as dangerous here," he said "is the discontinuity of emotion that television promotes, its unnatural evocation, every five minutes, of different and incompatible emotions."

"You leave a restaurant," she said, "and get killed by a falling air conditioner. A tornado hits a picnic. There is no sense to reality. Television is actually closer to reality than anything in books. The madness of TV is the madness of human life."

So went the conversation between two cultural critics, Neil Postman and Camille Paglia, taking up an argument that has vexed nearly everyone in this century—the struggle for preeminence between words and pictures, today between books and television. This conflict is uniquely American—debate so dense with prejudices that it has turned almost all of us into liars: "I don't watch TV" is now so common a dissembling among those who read that it has become a kind of mantra. And "I read that book" is a euphemism acceptable among recent generations to mean simply that one has heard of the title.

Neil Postman is one of the most original writers in defense of the book. A professor of communication arts at New York University and the author of *Amusing Ourselves to Death: Public Discourse in the Age of Show Business,* Postman is a scholar, raised in the pretelevision world, whose eloquence owes much to the classical declarative prose of Strunk and White. He argues that reading is an ordered process requiring us to sit at a table, consume ideas from left to right, and make judgments of truth and falsehood. By its nature, reading teaches us to reason. Television, with its random unconnected images, works against this linear tradition and breaks the habits of logic and thinking. Postman has said that the two most dangerous words in this century are "Now . . . this"—that strange verbal doo dad uttered by television anchors to ease the transition from a report on a natural disaster to a commercial about your need—desperate need in fact—for an electric toothbrush.

Those who argue from the other side usually make a weak and unconvincing case. With the possible exception of Marshall McLuhan, anyone writing about television has done so with apologies. Recently, a new critic has emerged named Camille Paglia. She is a professor of humanities at the Philadelphia College of the Arts and is currently finishing a critical history of culture that ranges from the cave paintings of Altamira to the Rolling

Stones concert at Altamont. Volume One, entitled *Sexual Personae: Art and Decadence from Nefertiti to Emily Dickinson,* was recently nominated for a National Book Critics Circle Award. Paglia was born after World War II, an accident to which she ascribes great significance. To hear her talk is to confirm her theory about the influence of the modern media: She speaks in a rush of images, juxtapositions, and verbal jump cuts. She argues that instead of criticizing television, most academics and other cultural critics simply turn up their noses dismissively at its enormous power—a kind of intellectual denial. Television, Paglia says, is the culture. And, she asks, by what and whose criteria is the latest Madonna any less meaningful an icon than the last? To those who argue that kids who watch television can't recall any of the facts mentioned on it, she wonders whether we have ever watched television. Perhaps we are doing something else when we stare at the screen; perhaps the remembrance of facts has nothing to do with television's significance or effect.

Since no two thinkers have in recent time made such compelling cases, *Harper's Magazine* decided to introduce them. We sent each author a copy of the other's book and asked each to read it. One cold winter night in December, we asked them to dine in the Private Tasting Room of New York City's Le Bernardin restaurant—a small, glass room located inside the kitchen of Chef Gilbert Le Coze. Throughout the conversation Bruno Jourdaine served a *menu dégustation* beginning with seviche of black bass and poured glasses of St. Veran Trenel (1988). We began the dinner with a blessing in the form of two readings from the Bible.

```
Thou shalt not make unto thee any graven image.
```
—Exodus 20:4

```
In the beginning was the Word, and the Word was with God, and
the Word was God.
```
—John 1:1

CAMILLE PAGLIA: But John got it all wrong. "In the beginning was nature." That's the first sentence of *my* book. Nature—violent, chaotic, unpredictable, uncontrollable—predates and stands in opposition to the ordered, structured world created by the word, by the law, by the book-centered culture of Judeo-Christianity. The image—which is pagan and expressive of nature's sex and violence—was outlawed by Moses in favor of the word. That's where our troubles began.

Remember that when the Ten Commandments were handed down on Mount Sinai, Moses had just led the Jews out of Egypt. They had followed Joseph down there several hundred years before and had become resident workers, then slaves. Over time, Judaism had gotten a little mixed up with the local Egyptian cults—a syncretism not unlike Santería in the Caribbean, with its blend of voodoo and Catholicism. When Moses tried to get his people to leave Egypt, there was resistance: "What are we *doing?* Moses, you're crazy. What homeland are you talking about?" The Ten Commandments were an attempt to clarify what is Hebrew, what is Jewish.

The Second Commandment implies that the Hebrew God has no shape, that He is pure spirit. Egyptian gods often appeared in animal form. The pagan cults of Egypt, Babylon, and Canaan worshiped such idols—for example, the Golden Calf. So Moses is saying, "We do not worship the gods of nature but a God who is above nature, a God who *created* nature. The ultimate God."

And the prohibition against images didn't forbid just pagan idols. It banned *all* visual imagery, of anything on earth or in the heavens. Moses knew that once a people begin to make images of any kind, they fall in love with them and worship them. Historically, the Second Commandment diverted Jewish creative energy away from the visual arts and into literature, philosophy, and law.

NEIL POSTMAN: It is curious that of the first three, so-called establishing commandments, two of them concern communications: the prohibitions against making graven images and taking the Lord's name in vain. Yet this makes sense if you think about the problems of constructing an ethical system 3,000 years ago. It was critical to tell the members of the tribe how to symbolize their experience. That is why Moses chose writing—using a phonetic alphabet, which the Jews no doubt borrowed from the Egyptians—to conceptualize this nonvisual, nonmaterial God. Writing is the perfect medium because, unlike pictures or an oral tradition, the written word is a symbol system *of* a symbol system, twice removed from reality and perfect for describing a God who is also far removed from reality: a nonphysical, abstracted divinity. Moses smartly chose the right communications strategy. With the Second Commandment, Moses was the first person who ever said, more or less, "Don't watch TV; go do your homework."

Most important, the written word allows for the development of a God who is, above all things, *mobile.* To invent a God who exists only in the word and through the word is to make a God that can be taken anyplace. Just as writing is portable speech, Moses' God is a portable God, which is fitting for a people setting forth on a long journey.

PAGLIA: That is why Jewish culture is one of the founts of Western tradition and why Western culture is so intellectually developed. Jewish thought is highly analytical, as is Greco-Roman philosophy. Both are very Apollonian. But the Greco-Roman tradition is also one of pagan idolatry. Early Christianity, which first proselytized among the poor, outcast, and unlearned, needed to use visual imagery, which became more and more pronounced in the Middle Ages and early Renaissance. Out of this came the renegade priest Martin Luther, who correctly diagnosed a lapse from authentic early Christianity in medieval Catholicism. Catholics are never told to read the Bible. Instead, they have to listen to the priest commenting on excerpts from the Bible, usually just the New Testament.

POSTMAN: Luther called the invention of the printing press the "supremist act of grace by which the Gospel can be driven forward." And it was. As a result of Luther's Reformation, the intellectual geography of Europe flipped. Until then Venice, in the south of Europe, was the leading printing center and one of the world's intellectual capitals. Then the Catholic Church got nervous about it, because of the possibilities of further heresy, and began to restrict the printing press. And then, within a year of each other, Galileo died and Newton was born. The intellectual power of Europe moved from the south to the north. England, Scandinavia, Germany became the realm of the word, and the south returned to spectacle. Catholicism resorted increasingly to ornament and beautiful music and painting. To this day we think of Spain, Italy, and southern France as centers of great visual arts, from the Escorial to the Sistine Chapel. The north, home of the austere Protestant, concentrated on the word, until it found its greatest fulfillment here in the first political system built on the word alone: no divine right of kings, no mysticism, just a few pages of written text, the American Constitution.

PAGLIA: The polarity in Europe got more and more rigid. In the north, book, book, book; but in the Counter-Reformation of southern Europe, unbelievably lurid images—like Bernini's St. Teresa having a spiritual orgasm. My first child-hood memories are of images, fantastic images, created by the Catholic Church. The statues are polychromatic, garish. In my church stood a statue of St. Sebastian, nude, arrows piercing his flesh, red blood dripping down. Who can wonder where *my* mind came from? Here were spectacular pagan images standing right next to the altar. In the beginning, you see, were sex and violence.

Early Christianity was very masculine. Just two male gods and a neuter—the Father, the Son, and the Holy Ghost. But the popular imagination couldn't tolerate that, so in the Middle Ages it added the Virgin Mary. Go reread the Bible and see how small a role Mary plays in the Gospels. Almost none. She is a survivor of the great goddess cults of antiquity. I interpret the most essential elements of Italian Catholicism as pagan. Martin Luther saw the latent paganism of the Catholic Church and rebelled against it. The latest atavistic discoverer of the pagan heart of Catholicism is Madonna. This is what she's up to. She doesn't completely understand it herself. When she goes on *Nightline* and makes speeches about celebrating the body, as if she's some sort of Woodstock hippie, she's way off. She needs *me* to tell her. But this is what she's doing—revealing the eroticism and sadomasochism, the pagan ritualism and idolatry in Italian Catholicism.

Protestantism today continues to be based on the word and the book. That's why Protestant ministers in church or on television always stress the Bible. They shout, "*This* is all you need." And they wave it, they flap it, they even slam it around. The Protestant needs no priest, no hierarchy. There is nothing between you and God. Protestants want a close and chatty relationship with Jesus: "Have you accepted Christ as your *personal* Savior?" And they sing, "He walks with you and He talks with you." For Protestants, Jesus is a friend, the Good Shepherd.

The Italian Catholic Jesus can't speak. He's either preliterate—a baby in the arms of Mary—or comatose—a tortured man on a cross. The period when Christ is literate, when he can speak, is edited out of southern Catholicism.

■ . . . B A K E D   S E A   U R C H I N . . .

POSTMAN: It helps to understand your point if we remember what happens every time Moses leaves. He comes back and the whole tribe has lapsed into idol worship. He is always complaining to Aaron, "What the hell did you do while I was gone?" The image is so seductive. Catholics are known for keeping little images on the dashboard of their cars, and nowadays you find them among Jews as well. Many reform temples now have more and more interesting visual designs. The Second Commandment held for a long time. Jews weren't known for their achievements in the visual arts until this century.

This proves my point about the life of the word and the image: Humans are not biologically programmed to be literate. In John Locke's essay on education, he insists that the body must become a slave to the mind. One of my students, upon hearing that quotation, said, "I know just what he means." And she told me how she can only read lying on her side while holding the book against the wall and, as a result, only reads the right-hand page of any book. This is the challenge of literacy: to get children accustomed to sitting still, to abiding in a realm that is unnaturally *silent.* That is the world of the word. How can silence compete with television?

This is the challenge of literacy: to get children accustomed to sitting still, to abiding in a realm that is unnaturally silent.

PAGLIA: But, Neil, people who are naturally disposed to reading may not be as physically active as others. There is an important difference here. I teach dancers. They are sometimes poor readers or even dyslexic. But they are brilliant at other, older forms of feeling and expression. Some people are inclined to the sedentary life that reading requires, others are not. That is why the entire discourse on sex and gender in academe and in the media is so off, because teachers and writers are not nearly as athletic or rambunctious as others.

POSTMAN: The literate person does pay a price for literacy. It may be that readers become less physically active and not as sensitive to movement, to dance, and to other symbolic modes. That's probably true. It's a Faustian bargain. Literacy gives us an analytic, delayed response in perceiving the world, which is good for pursuits such as science or engineering. But we do lose some part of the cerebral development of the senses, the sensorium.

PAGLIA: And some people have more developed sensoriums than others. I've found that most people born before World War II are turned off by the modern media. They can't understand how we who were born after the war can read a book and watch TV at the same time. But we *can.* When I wrote my book, I had earphones on, blasting rock music or Puccini and Brahms. The soap operas—with the sound turned down—flickered on my TV. I'd be talking on the phone at the same time. Baby boomers have a multilayered, multitrack ability to deal with the world. I often use the metaphor of a large restaurant stove to describe the way the mind works. There are many burners, and only one of them is the logical, analytical burner. And, Neil, I think we agree that our contemporary education system neglects it.

One reason American academic feminism is so mediocre is that these women can't think their way out of a wet paper bag. They have absolutely no training in logic, philosophy, or intellectual history, so they're reduced to arguing that we should throw out Plato and Aristotle because they're dead white males, or some such nonsense. That's so dopey and ignorant. People born before World War II can't understand those of us raised in the fragmented, imagistic world of TV. We can shut off one part of the brain and activate another. Scientists, psychologists, and IQ testers haven't caught up with these new ways of perception.

"With the commandment forbidding graven images, Moses became the first to say, 'Don't watch TV; do your homework.'"

POSTMAN: Camille, I think we actually agree on the evidence. Only you think it is all just fine and will be a liberating development. Television and the other visual media will enlarge the sensorium and give people a fuller repertoire of means of expression. Marshall McLuhan used to refer to people like me and others as POBS: Print-Oriented Bastards—literates who had their right hemispheres amputated or atrophied. You should adopt the term, Camille; your analysis is absolutely correct. Only I tend to see this development as ominous.

Bertrand Russell used to utter a lovely phrase. He said that the purpose of education was to teach each of us to defend ourselves against the "seductions of eloquence." In the realm of the word, we learn the specific techniques used to resist these seductions: logic, rhetoric, and literary criticism. What worries me is that we have not yet figured out how to build defenses against the seductions of imagery. The Nazi regime was only the most recent example of seducing, through words and images, one of the most *literate* populations on earth. I remember Hitler's rantings. Now, I won't ask you how old you are.

PAGLIA: I'm forty-three. I was born in 1947. And you graduated from college in 1953. I checked! I wanted to know, because I think this information is absolutely critical to how one views the mass media. I graduated from college in 1968. There are only fifteen years between us, but it's a critical fifteen years, an unbridgeable chasm in American culture.

■ . . .   S H R I M P   A N D   B A S I L   B E I G N E T S   . . .

POSTMAN: I remember the imagery of the 1940s, when an entire political machine was pressed into the service of imagistic propaganda. In America it is somewhat different. There *is* a machine producing such images, but it is capitalism, and the output is the commercial. The process is the same. Have you seen the commercial for Hebrew National frankfurters? It shows Uncle Sam while a narrator declares how good and healthy frankfurters are because

Uncle Sam maintains such high standards. Then Uncle Sam looks up as the narrator adds that Hebrew Nationals are even better than other frankfurters because they must answer to a higher authority.

PAGLIA: I love that ad! It's wonderful. Hilarious.

POSTMAN: Here is what bothers me. Symbols *are* infinitely repeatable, but they are not inexhaustible. If you use God to sell frankfurters, or if you use the face of George Washington to sell discount car tires, you drain the symbol of the very meanings, Camille, that you so astutely discover and explicate in your book. You look at a painting and analyze its levels of meaning, its ambiguities, its richness. But what happens if people see the same image a thousand times, and always to sell tight jeans?

PAGLIA: I would argue exactly the opposite. In the Hebrew National ads the invocation of Uncle Sam and God reinforces their symbolic meaning and helps young people have a historical perspective on their own culture.

Ads shaped the imagination of my generation. The Hebrew National image of Jehovah—that he's invisible, a voice inspiring his children to high standards—is faithful to tradition. It's a fabulous ad. And, by the way, it's true—kosher franks *are* better! I believed this ad and bought the franks! I love ads as an art form. To me, there is no degradation in this particular ad at all.

POSTMAN: Perhaps you're not taking it seriously enough, Camille. By age twenty, the average American has seen 800,000 television advertisements, about 800 a week. I am not talking about radio, print, or any other kind of advertisement. I am referring only to television advertisements. Television commercials are now the most powerful source of socialization, and the schools ought to take them seriously.

Some advertisements are good, of course. I don't think Madonna would serve too well. But I think of Jimmy Stewart selling soup. In that advertisement, the producers used his voice only because that voice is sufficient to symbolize what he stands for—the embodiment of the thoroughly decent American. So the use of that imagery is fine. But in the Hebrew National advertisement, a sense of the sacred is being eliminated, or exploited by redirecting it to the profane world.

PAGLIA: If Jehovah had never expressed Himself about table manners, I would support you. But the Bible shows that Jehovah instructed the Jews at great length about what foods to eat and how to prepare and serve them.

POSTMAN: And, of course, Jehovah also forbade shellfish—everything we're eating tonight!

PAGLIA: This is the point. Kosher ritual preparation is dictated by the Bible. Nothing in the Hebrew National ad distorts or lies about Jewish tradition.

POSTMAN: Suppose you saw a commercial that showed Jesus looking at a bottle of Gallo wine and saying, "When I turned the water into wine in Cana, it wasn't nearly as good as this Gallo Pinot Noir." What does that do to the meaning of Jesus Christ for Christians? You seem very enthusiastic about the use of these images, but I think the *secularization* of these symbols and religious icons is dangerous.

PAGLIA: To you, coming from the Judeo-Christian tradition, this looks secular. If you look at it from my perspective, popular culture is an eruption of paganism—which is also a sacred style. In your book, you skip from 1920 to television. I think you leap over a critical period—the great studio era of Hollywood movies in the 1930s and 1940s. Cinema then was a pagan cult full of gods and goddesses, glamour and charisma. It was a style devoted to the sacred and the numinous. So it's not that the sacred has been lost or is being trivialized. We are steeped in idolatry. The sacred is everywhere. I don't see any secularism. We've returned to the age of polytheism. It's a rebirth of the pagan gods.

What I argue in my book is that Judeo-Christianity never defeated paganism but rather drove it underground, from which it constantly erupts in all kinds of ways. Ancient Greco-Roman culture harnessed the dynamic duality of the Apollonian and the Dionysian principles. We've inherited the Apollonian element of the Greco-Roman tradition. The history of Western civilization has been a constant struggle between these two impulses, an unending tennis match between cold Apollonian categorization and Dionysian lust and chaos.

That's why you can always tell whether a critic was born before or after World War II by the way he or she speaks of the twentieth century. To you who grew up knowing life as narrative exposition and who saw the end of an era with Fitzgerald and Hemingway—and you're right, there was a great shift, and the novel is now dead as a doornail—it's the Age of Anxiety. But the death of the novel was also the beginning of movies. I date the modern age from the first sound pictures in 1928. I call the twentieth century the Age of Hollywood.

There's a huge generational difference here. For those of us born after the war, our minds were formed by TV. Take Susan Sontag, born in 1933. There are fourteen years between her and me. It doesn't seem like much, but it's like an abyss between us. In the 1960s she was writing briefly about popular culture, but then she backed off and has spent the rest of her life saying, "I'm serious, I'm serious. Gotta find that ultimate Eastern European writer!" A few years ago, she boasted in *Time* that she had no TV and had to rent one when a guest came to visit. My TV is constantly fluttering. It's a hearth fire in the modern home. TV is not something you *watch;* it is simply on, all the time.

■ .   .   .   S E A R E D   S C A L L O P S   I N   T R U F F L E   V I N A I G R E T T E   .   .   .

POSTMAN: If you keep this up, Camille, I'm going to need either more wine or a cigarette. Do you mind if I smoke?

PAGLIA: Not at all. Neil, in your book you mentioned tests in which people didn't remember any facts from a news program they had watched thirty minutes earlier on TV. But they weren't testing the right part of the brain. Watching TV has nothing to do with thought or analysis. It's a passive but highly efficient process of storing information to be used later. The proper analogy is to interstate driving or football. You know, baseball was *the* sport of the pre–World War II era. Academics love it. It's the ultimate academic sport—linear, logical, slow. Football, especially as *remade* for TV with slow motion and replays, is the sport of my generation. There's a lot of writing about baseball but hardly any good stuff about football. When a quarterback pulls back from the line and quickly checks out the field, he's not thinking, he's *scanning,* the very thing we do when we watch TV. It's like the airline pilot sweeping his eyes across his bank of instruments or the driver cruising down the interstate at high speed, always scanning the field, looking for the drunk, the hot rod, the police, or the slow old lady in the Cadillac—watch out for *her.* None of these people—the quarterback, the pilot, the driver—is thinking. They're only reading the field and working by instinct, deciding in an instant where to throw the ball or steer the jet or car. The decision is made by intuition, not by ratiocination.

POSTMAN: It's called pattern recognition.

PAGLIA: Oh, really? Perfect! And that's why you can't picture Susan Sontag driving a car. You know what I mean? Can you imagine Susan Sontag behind the wheel? Forget it. It's like a *New Yorker* cartoon: *Susan Sontag buys her first car!*

POSTMAN: Of course, I agree: Reading a book and "reading" television are two completely different cerebral activities. I can remember hearing print-oriented people complain that the problem with a show like *Charlie's Angels* is that it didn't honor the Aristotelian unities of time, place, and action. Or that it didn't have any *true* character development.

PAGLIA: You liked *Charlie's Angels?*

POSTMAN: As a matter of fact, I did, but I am bringing it up as an example of how people misread television. Print-oriented people can't understand such a show because they try to judge it by the measures of literature. I came to understand *Charlie's Angels* when I realized that the entire show was about *hair.*

Do you remember that at the end of the show there was a two-minute segment in which the disembodied voice of Charlie explained to the angels *what the entire show had been about.* I imagine that the show was written by a bunch of former English majors. And I see them confounded by the fact that they have just written a show that is basically about hair and doesn't fit any of the categories that they have been taught count. So at the end, they shoehorn in a vestigial narrative. Once I saw an episode in which, in order to explain everything, the voice at the end had to mention characters and action that hadn't even been *in* the program: "She killed him because years ago he had stolen money and given it to a third person . . ." Those sixty seconds before the credits—when the show was actually already over—were meant to give a show about hair a sense of logic or coherence.

PAGLIA: *TV Guide* once said about the actresses on *Knots Landing*—my favorite prime-time show—that "they act with their hair." I love it! Soap operas also are mainly about hair, you know. Very pagan—the worship of beauty. And do you realize that the Farrah Fawcett hairdo of *Charlie's Angels* can still be seen today in every shopping mall in America? Though that show has been off the air for ten years, it has this incredible ongoing influence. Farrah herself has moved on to battered-wife roles, but her old Seventies hairstyle is still the dominant look for boy-crazy girls in American high schools. Awesome, really.

"Print-oriented people judged Charlie's Angels by the measures of literature, but it was a show entirely about hair."

POSTMAN: We agree on the influence of popular culture as expressed through visual images. Everyone has a right to defend his or her own culture, and I feel sure there will be a cost to the kind of culture I value. It may be that your sensorium has been enlivened while mine has atrophied. But let's look at my tradition and see what it has accomplished. Consider that in 1776 Thomas Paine sold, by the most conservative estimates, 300,000 copies of *Common Sense.* That is the equivalent of selling 30,000,000 copies—a feat attainable only today by Danielle Steel or Tom Wolfe. Camille, do you think we will pay a price for this more fully developed sensorium?

PAGLIA: In your book you say that there was a high literacy rate during the American Revolution. But does that mean people actually *read* books? Political and literary books? Or was it that they could just sign their names? Your portrait of the highly literate nineteenth century also sort of ignores the trashy sentimental novels, ladies' fashion magazines, and the dime western. I agree with you that our country was founded as an Enlightenment experiment. The framers of the American Constitution were true intellectuals. But I think your book puts undue stress on that period, which was, as I see it, a kind of privileged moment. Comparing our period with that one—when there was a high degree of cultural awareness and political activity—makes us think we're slipping into a decline. But maybe we're just returning to the norm. I think the world as it is now is the way it always was.

■   .   .   .   BLACK BASS IN CORIANDER NAGE   .   .   .

POSTMAN: I'm not certain it was only a privileged moment, although you are right in suggesting that a high literacy rate creates a somewhat abstracted view of the world. Our culture paid a price for literacy, and it will pay a price for its transformation into a visual culture. We are, for example, rapidly losing any sense of sacrality. The reason the Ayatollah Khomeini struck most Americans as either a complete riddle or a lunatic is that he was actually a *truly religious person.* And we can no longer understand what such a person is like.

PAGLIA: Exactly. Whenever Qaddafi would spend days in his tent, the Western media would sneer and ridicule him. I couldn't believe it. Does no one understand the ethical meaning of the desert in Bedouin culture? It's like our Walden Pond. Hasn't the media ever seen *Lawrence of Arabia?* There are two lessons in the Salman Rushdie case. First, artistic freedom is a value only in the democratic Western tradition. Second, to millions of people in the world, religion is a matter of life and death.

POSTMAN: Camille, I think these observations support my argument that what I call the secularization of imagery depletes religious symbolism: not only the frequency of the image but also the ignominious tie between the image and commercialization. That is why we in the West can't understand why someone would risk his life in an attempt to kill Salman Rushdie. To us, it's crazy. To the martyr, it is the path to heaven.

PAGLIA: Rather than your total secularization, I see the repaganization of Western culture. In the realm of politics, I think pop culture—the vehicle of the pagan eruption—plays a crucial role. Popular culture has the function of purging politics of many of its potential demagogues. Elvis Presley, an enormously charismatic figure, was able to build his empire in the politically neutral realm of pop culture.

POSTMAN: Are you saying that Hitler might have been a Hollywood star in America?

PAGLIA: Today, you have other ways for extraordinarily charismatic people to create their worlds. There are other ways to rule the universe. Before popular culture, the only realm that allowed that kind of power of personality was politics.

POSTMAN: I see the confluence between television and politics a little differently. The first television president was, obviously, John Kennedy. But the first *image* president was Ronald Reagan. They were very different figures. Kennedy, Jimmy Carter, even Mario Cuomo are very much identified with regions of the country. They were and are developed personalities that play well on television.But Reagan and even Bush are different. Remember how no one knows what state Bush is from and how Reagan's being from California seemed irrelevant. These are personalities onto whom a full spectrum of voters are able to project their personal image of a president. Whatever a president is supposed to be, then that is what Reagan or Bush is.

PAGLIA: As a television persona, Reagan was avuncular and nostalgic—a return to the happy, innocent, pre-World War II era of baseball, before the chaos and disasters of the Sixties. He was simple, kindly, even-tempered, sometimes goofy. He got into his pajamas right after dinner. He ate jelly beans. He called his wife "Mommy." He never aged. His hair never got gray. To liberal writers and academics, these things seemed stupid and ludicrous.

They were off reading his policy papers, missing the whole point of his popularity. Our president is both the political and the symbolic head of our government, serving in jobs that in England, for example, are separately represented by the prime minister and the queen. The president symbolizes the nation in psychodramatic form.

POSTMAN: A nation as heterogeneous as ours gropes to find comprehensive symbols and icons to pull us together. Ronald Reagan was such an image. Every Christmas you hear people say, "Happy Holidays." We try to be so polite and inclusive. We are a fragile polity desperate for unifying images. But, paradoxically, we can destroy ourselves by exhausting the available icons.

PAGLIA: Another such image is the national weather map, which is shown, naturally, on TV. Here's this patchwork country of Chinese and Chicanos and African-Americans and Jews and Italians, and then there's this map with beautifully sweeping curved lines of air pressure stretching from sea to shining sea, pulling us together. The weatherman and the president are our two titular heads.

These images and their meaning become obvious once you know how to read TV. One more example. Remember, during the 1988 election, how everyone was calling George Bush a wimp? And he *was* a wimp, constantly trotting after Reagan and in his shadow. What a ninny, I would think; he'll never win the election. Then came the day when Ronald Reagan made his last visit to the Republican convention, and Bush named Dan Quayle as his running partner for vice president. It was the most stunning moment of TV transformation I've ever seen, but no one in the media picked it up. After Reagan left, remember the outdoor scene when Bush named Quayle? The press hysterically rushed off to report the story of how silly, stupid, and rich Quayle was. But the story was not that George had picked a jerk. The story was that George Bush, emerging as a new man, had picked a *son*. Bush had made a complete *rite de passage* on television and for television. Remember how Quayle was jumping around acting like a puppy—even grabbing Bush by the shoulder? Later that day at the indoor press conference, Bush was amazingly stern and confident. He cut reporters off, he was completely in charge. He was this totally new person, a man no one had seen before. It was then I knew he was going to be president. I called people up and told them, but no one believed me. If you didn't know how to read TV or weren't watching, you missed it completely.

POSTMAN: And my point, Camille, which you are overlooking, is that Roger Ailes engineered that entire effect. We were all manipulated into having just that very perception.

PAGLIA: What I am talking about is nothing that Roger Ailes could have created. It was a side of Bush that predated Roger Ailes. We all have many personas, and we can pick and choose which to make public. But we cannot create them. Roger Ailes could not have saved Michael Dukakis.

■ . . . R O A S T   M O N K F I S H   O N   S A V O Y   C A B B A G E . . .

POSTMAN: Granted. If you read Bush's résumé, it is one of the most macho documents of recent times—first baseman at Yale, youngest Navy pilot, shot down in combat, head of the CIA. But when Ailes saw him acting like a ninny on television—and television does have a way of showing the authentic soul—I agree, he went to work on the indecisive wimp and promoted the image of the macho guy so that you and others would pick it up. And then that image was repeated and repeated, washing away any memory of a past impression.

PAGLIA: In your book you speak of television as being a medium of flashing images with only an eternal present and no past. I disagree. It's just the opposite. TV is a genre of reruns, a formulaic return to what we already know. Everything is familiar. Ads and old programs are constantly recycled. It's like mythology, like the Homeric epics, the oral tradition, in which the listener hears pasages, formulae, and epithets repeated over and over again. There is a joy in repetition, as children know when they say, "Mommy, tell me that story again." TV is a medium that makes us feel "at home."

"Pop culture purges politics of demagogues: A charismatic figure such as Elvis could build his empire in the pop realm."

If you go back to the Fifties, when movies lost their cultural centrality to TV, you'll see that the great sacred images—the huge, cold images of cinema—were being miniaturized, familiarized, and domesticated by the television screen. The box became part of the family, and the shows reflected it: *Father Knows Best* and *Leave it to Beaver*. Ads are the same way. I put one of my favorite ads in my book—Luciana Avedon crooning, "Camay has coconut-enriched lather." I adored that ad! Of course, ads you hate are like torture. You want to die.

So TV is about repetition and compulsion. It's like prayer, like the Catholic Rosary, repeated over and over again. That's what ads are: soothing litanies that make us feel safe and familiar and at home in the strange modern world.

POSTMAN: So idolatry has triumphed. I think Luther would join Moses in saying that the cult of the word is defenseless in the face of the image.

PAGLIA: Moses got his people out of Egypt, out of the land of the pagan image. That was the only way. Judaism could not have flourished in Egypt. Today, either you live in a cabin in northern Canada or you try to control TV. And I believe we *should* try to control it, by the way. Liberals are wrong when they say, "Parents should just turn off the TV set." You can't. TV is everywhere. It's bigger than politics. It's bigger than the Church.

POSTMAN: This is where education comes in, Camille. I believe that educational theory should be what I call "ecological"; that is, education should supply what the rest of the culture is not supplying. In this case, I think the only defense against the seductions of imagery is a literate education. If children are educated in the traditions of the word, then perhaps they will be able to make discriminating choices in the chaotic realm of the image.

PAGLIA: To me the ideal education should be rigorous and word-based—logocentric. The student must learn the logical, hierarchical system. Then TV culture allows the other part of the mind to move freely around the outside of that system. This is like the talent you need for internal medicine. An internist has to be intuitive. He knows there are about a half dozen different systems in the body, all interrelated. His mind has to weave in and out and around them and more or less guess what's wrong. This is the mental flexibility that a word-based education and a TV-based culture can develop. All parents should read to their children, from infancy on. Education is, by definition, repressive. So if you're going to repress, then repress like hell. I don't believe in the Dewey or Montessori methods—"We want to make this pleasant." There is nothing pleasant about learning to read or to think. The teachers used to shake me and yell at me to stay in line or sit still in my seat. I didn't like it, but I recommend it.

PAGLIA: *Well, Neil, that's life.*

POSTMAN: *That's insanity.*

PAGLIA: *Not to me.*

POSTMAN: In *Aspects of the Novel,* E. M. Forster wrote that if you say the king died and the queen died, you don't have a story. But if you say that the king died *because* the queen died, you have a story. I find that television undermines these simple word-based connections. The whole idea of language is to provide a world of intellectual and emotional continuity and predictability. But many of my students no longer understand, for example, the principle of contradiction. I was talking to one student the other day about a paper in which he asserted one thing to be true in the first paragraph and the exact opposite to be true three paragraphs later. He said, "What's the problem?"

This habit derives from television, which tells you that there was a rape in New York and then it tells you there was an earthquake in Chile and then it tells you that the Mets beat the Cardinals.

PAGLIA: Well, Neil, that's life.

POSTMAN: That's insanity.

PAGLIA: Not to me. In your book you say TV is Dadaist in its random, nihilistic compilation of unrelated events. I say it's surrealist—because *life* is surreal! You leave a restaurant and get killed by a falling air conditioner. A tornado hits a picnic. There's no sense to reality. It simply happens. Television is actually closer to reality than anything in books. The madness of TV is the madness of human life.

POSTMAN: Here is what I would like: When our young student is watching Dan Rather say that 5,000 people died in an earthquake in Chile and then Dan says, "We'll be right back after this word from United Airlines," I would like our student to say, "Hey, wait a second, how could he ask me to make such an emotional switch?"

PAGLIA: My answer is this: Buddha smiles. He sees the wheel of reincarnation and accepts the disasters of the universe. That's the way it should be. There's no way we can possibly extend our compassion to 5,000 dead people. By juxtaposing such jarring images, TV is creating a picture of the world that is simply true to life. We are forced to contemplate death the way farmers do— as just another banal occurrence, no big deal. Nature can crack the earth open and swallow thousands, and then the sun shines and the birds sing. It's like going from an airplane crash to a hemorrhoids ad. In TV, as in nature, all have equal weight.

■ . . . C A R O U S E L   O F   C A R A M E L   D E S S E R T S

POSTMAN: What I am focusing on is our emotional response to those things. We all know that nurses who work in hospitals make jokes. They see the absurdity of death routinely. But they don't see anywhere near the number of deaths the television viewer sees. What I see as dangerous here is a discontinuity of emotion that television promotes, its unnatural evocation, every five minutes, of different and incompatible emotions.

PAGLIA: By moving from disaster to commercial, TV creates the effect of Greek tragedy: emotion, then detachment; contemplation of loss, then philosophical perspective. At the end of *Hamlet,* there are four corpses strewn all over the stage.

POSTMAN: But no one is laughing—although I will admit that in the graveyard scene, when Hamlet makes the "Alas, poor Yorick" speech, he *is* laughing. But my point is, just after Horatio's final soliloquy, at least on television, we would then see the Hebrew National spot, or perhaps a commercial for Danish pastry.

"Jesus was a brilliant Jewish stand-up comedian, a phenomenal improvisor. His parables are great one-liners."

PAGLIA: To make that radical switch from disaster to detachment is, I think, a maturing process. If you fully responded emotionally to every disaster you saw, you'd be a mess. In fact, you'd be a perpetual child, a psychological cripple. Wisdom by definition is philosophical detachment from life's disasters.

POSTMAN: Injecting humor into otherwise insane catastrophes is comic relief. It is what we must do unless we want to go mad. But the effect I am talking about on the television news is different.

PAGLIA: I know that you see "amusement" as a bad thing wherever it shows up. You said in your book that teaching has finally been reduced to a branch of popular entertainment and that students won't sit still for anything that's not as funny as Big Bird on Sesame Street. And you cite Plato, Cicero, and Locke as educational philosophers who would insist on seriousness. I respectfully disagree. Plato's dialogues, which follow the Socratic method, a conversational give-and-take such as we're having here, are in fact very entertaining. There's a lot of comedy in Plato. Socrates is always pretending to be the most ignorant person there, and so on.

I think Jesus was a brilliant Jewish stand-up comedian, a phenomenal improvisor. His parables are great one-liners. When an enemy, trying to trap him, asks him about paying taxes, Jesus says, "Show me the coin of the tribute. Whose image is on it?" "Caesar's," the guy replies. "Then render unto Caesar the things that are Caesar's and unto God the things that are God's." I think that line got applause and laughs.

POSTMAN: You studied with Harold Bloom too long.

PAGLIA: Bloom used to say, "Teaching's a branch of show biz!" One last point—there are the koans, the teachings of the great Buddhist masters. They often took the form of slapstick. The novice comes in and says, "Tell me about life, master," and the elder whacks him on the head. Or says something surreal, like "Beanstalk!" So we do have many examples of teaching by great sages using humor or stand-up improv—Plato, Jesus, Buddha.

POSTMAN: *You studied with Harold Bloom too long.*

PAGLIA: *Bloom used to say, "Teaching's a branch of show biz!"*

POSTMAN: No one is saying not to use humor in the classroom. I guess we are talking about magnitude. It is one thing to use humor to reveal an idea you are developing. But now it is used simply to win the student's attention. Consequently, drawing an audience—rather than teaching—becomes the focus of education, and that is what television does. School is the one institution in the culture that should present a different worldview: a different way of knowing, of evaluating, of assessing. What worries me is that if school becomes so overwhelmed by entertainment's metaphors and metaphysics, then it becomes not content-centered but attention-centered, like television, chasing "ratings" or class attendance. If school becomes that way, then the game may be lost, because school is using the same approach, epistemologically, as television. Instead of being something different from television, it is reduced to being just another *kind* of television.

PAGLIA: Our dialogue has reached one major point of agreement. I want schools to stress the highest intellectual values and ideals of the Greco-Roman and Judeo-Christian traditions. Nowadays, "logocentric" is a dirty word. It comes from France, where deconstruction is necessary to break the stranglehold of centuries of Descartes and Pascal. The French *have* something to deconstruct. But to apply Lacan, Derrida, and Foucault to American culture is absolutely idiotic. We are born into an imagistic and pagan culture ruled by TV. We don't need any more French crap from ditsy Parisian intellectuals and their American sycophants. Neil, we agree on this: We need to reinforce the logocentric and Apollonian side of our culture in the schools. It is time for enlightened repression of the children.

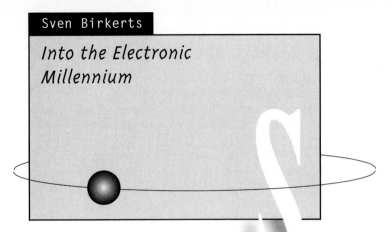

Into the Electronic Millennium

Some years ago, a friend and I comanaged a used and rare book shop in Ann Arbor, Michigan. We were often asked to appraise and purchase libraries—by retiring academics, widows, and disgruntled graduate students. One day we took a call from a professor of English at one of the community colleges outside Detroit. When he answered the buzzer I did a double take—he looked to be only a year or two older than we were. "I'm selling everything," he said, leading the way through a large apartment. As he opened the door of his study I felt a nudge from my partner. The room was wall-to-wall books and as neat as a chapel.

The professor had a remarkable collection. It reflected not only the needs of his vocation—he taught nineteenth- and twentieth-century literature—but a book lover's sensibility as well. The shelves were strictly arranged, and the books themselves were in superb condition. When he left the room we set to work inspecting, counting, and estimating. This is always a delicate procedure, for the buyer is at once anxious to avoid insult to the seller and eager to get the goods for the best price. We adopted our usual strategy, working out a lower offer and a more generous fallback price. But there was no need to worry. The professor took our first offer without batting an eye.

As we boxed up the books, we chatted. My partner asked the man if he was moving. "No," he said, "but I am getting out." We both looked up. "Out of the teaching business, I mean. Out of books." He then said that he wanted to show us something. And indeed, as soon as the books were packed and loaded, he led us back through the apartment and down a set of stairs. When we reached the basement, he flicked on the light. There, on a long table, displayed like an exhibit in the Space Museum, was a computer. I didn't know what kind it was then, nor could I tell you now, fifteen years later. But the professor was keen to explain and demonstrate.

While he and my partner hunched over the terminal, I roamed to and fro, inspecting the shelves. It was purely a reflex gesture, for they held nothing but thick binders and paperbound manuals. "I'm changing my life," the ex-professor was saying. "This is definitely where it's all going to happen." He told us that he already had several good job offers. And the books? I asked. Why was he selling them all? He paused for a few beats. "The whole profession represents a lot of pain to me," he said. "I don't want to see any of these books again." The scene has stuck with me. It is now a kind of marker in my mental life. That afternoon I got my first serious inkling that all was not well in the world of print and letters. All sorts of corroborations followed. Our professor was by no means an isolated case. Over a period of two years we met with several others like him. New men and new women who had glimpsed the future and had decided to get out while the getting was good. The selling off of books was sometimes done for financial reasons, but the need to burn bridges was usually there as well. It was as if heading to the future also required the destruction of tokens from the past.

A change is upon us—nothing could be clearer. The printed word is part of a vestigial order that we are moving away from—by choice and by societal compulsion. I'm not just talking about disaffected academics, either. This shift is happening throughout our culture, away from the patterns and habits of the printed page and toward a new world distinguished by its reliance on electronic communications.

A change is upon us— nothing could be clearer. The printed word is part of a vestigial order that we are moving away from—by choice and by societal compulsion.

This is not, of course, the first such shift in our long history. In Greece, in the time of Socrates, several centuries after Homer, the dominant oral culture was overtaken by the writing technology. And in Europe another epochal transition was effected in the late fifteenth century after Gutenberg invented movable type. In both cases the long-term societal effects were overwhelming, as they will be for us in the years to come.

The evidence of the change is all around us, though possibly in the manner of the forest that we cannot see for the trees. The electronic media, while conspicuous in gadgetry, are very nearly invisible in their functioning. They have slipped deeply and irrevocably into our midst, creating sluices and circulating through them. I'm not referring to any one product or function in isolation, such as television or fax machines or the networks that make them possible. I mean the interdependent totality that has arisen from the conjoining of parts—the disk drives hooked to modems, transmissions linked to technologies of reception, recording, duplication, and storage. Numbers and codes and frequencies. Buttons and signals. And this is no longer "the future," except for the poor or the self-consciously atavistic—it is now. Next to the new technologies, the scheme of things represented by print and the snail-paced linearity of the reading act looks stodgy and dull. Many educators say that our students are less and less able to read, or analyze, or write with clarity and purpose. Who can blame the students? Everything they meet with in the world around them gives the signal: That was then, and electronic communications are now.

Do I exaggerate? If all this is the case, why haven't we heard more about it? Why hasn't somebody stepped forward with a bow tie and a pointer stick to explain what is going on? Valid questions, but they also beg the question. They assume that we are all plugged into a total system—

where else would that "somebody" appear if not on the screen at the communal hearth?

Media theorist Mark Crispin Miller has given one explanation for our situation in his discussions of television in *Boxed In: The Culture of TV.* The medium, he proposes, has long since diffused itself throughout the entire system. Through sheer omnipresence it has vanquished the possibility of comparative perspectives. We cannot see the role that television (or, for our purposes, all electronic communications) has assumed in our lives because there is no independent ledge where we might secure our footing. The medium has absorbed and eradicated the idea of a pretelevision past; in place of what used to be we get an ever-new and ever-renewable present. The only way we can hope to understand what is happening, or what has already happened, is by way of a severe and unnatural dissociation of sensibility.

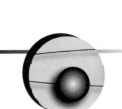

Do I exaggerate?

To get a sense of the enormity of the change, you must force yourself to imagine—deeply and in nontelevisual terms—what the world was like a hundred, even fifty, years ago. If the feat is too difficult, spend some time with a novel from the period. Read between the lines and reconstruct. Move through the sequence of a character's day and then juxtapose the images and sensations you find with those in the life of the average urban or suburban dweller today.

Inevitably, one of the first realizations is that a communications net, a soft and pliable mesh woven from invisible threads, has fallen over everything. The so-called natural world, the place we used to live, which served us so long as the yardstick for all measurements, can now only be perceived through a scrim. Nature was then; this is now. Trees and rocks have receded. And the great geographical Other, the faraway rest of the world, has been transformed by the pure possibility of access. The numbers of distance and time no longer mean what they used to. Every place, once unique, itself, is strangely shot through with radiations from every other place. "There" was then; "here" is now.

One of the first realizations is that a communications net, a soft and pliable mesh woven from invisible threads, has fallen over everything.

Think of it. Fifty to a hundred million people (maybe a conservative estimate) form their ideas about what is going on in America and in the world from the same basic package of edited images—to the extent that the image itself has lost much of its once-fearsome power. Daily newspapers, with their long columns of print, struggle against declining sales. Fewer and fewer people under the age of fifty read them; computers will soon make packaged information a custom product. But if the printed sheet is heading for obsolescence, people are tuning in to the signals. The screen is where the information and entertainment wars will be fought. The communications conglomerates are waging bitter takeover battles in their zeal to establish global empires. As Jonathan Crary has written in "The Eclipse of the Spectacle," "Telecommunications is the new arterial network, analogous in part to what railroads were for capitalism in the nineteenth century. And it is this electronic substitute for geography that corporate and national entities are now carving up." Maybe one reason why the news of the change is not part of the common currency is that such news can only sensibly be communicated through the more analytic sequences of print.

To underscore my point, I have been making it sound as if we were all abruptly walking out of one room and into another, leaving our books to the moths while we settle ourselves in front of our state-of-the-art terminals. The truth is that we are living through a period of overlap; one way of being is pushed athwart another. Antonio Gramsci's often-cited sentence comes inevitably to mind: "The crisis consists precisely in the fact that the old is dying and the new cannot be born; in this interregnum a great variety of morbid symptoms appears." The old surely is dying, but I'm not so sure that the new is having any great difficulty being born. As for the morbid symptoms, these we have in abundance.

The overlap in communications modes, and the ways of living that they are associated with, invites comparison with the transitional epoch in ancient Greek society, certainly in terms of the relative degree of disturbance. Historian Eric Havelock designated that period as one of "proto-literacy," of which his fellow scholar Oswyn Murray has written:

To him [Havelock] the basic shift from oral to literate culture was a slow process; for centuries, despite the existence of writing, Greece remained essentially an oral culture. This culture was one which depended heavily on the encoding of information in poetic texts, to be learned by rote and to provide a cultural encyclopedia of conduct. It was not until the age of Plato in the fourth century that the dominance of poetry in an oral culture was challenged in the final triumph of literacy.

Our historical moment, which we might call "proto-electronic," will not require a transition period of two centuries . . . .

That challenge came in the form of philosophy, among other things, and poetry has never recovered its cultural primacy. What oral poetry was for the Greeks, printed books in general are for us. But our historical moment, which we might call "proto-electronic," will not require a transition period of two centuries. The very essence of electronic transmissions is to surmount impedances and to hasten transitions. Fifty years, I'm sure, will suffice. As for what the conversion will bring— and *mean*—to us, we might glean a few clues by looking to some of the "morbid symptoms" of the change. But to understand what these portend, we need to remark a few of the more obvious ways in which our various technologies condition our senses and sensibilities.

I won't tire my reader with an extended rehash of the differences between the print orientation and that of electronic systems. Media theorists from Marshall McLuhan to Walter Ong to Neil Postman have discoursed upon these at length. What's more, they are reasonably commonsensical. I therefore will abbreviate.

The order of print is linear, and is bound to logic by the imperatives of syntax. Syntax is the substructure of discourse, a mapping of the ways that the mind makes sense through language. Print communication requires the active engagement of the reader's attention, for reading is fundamentally an act of translation. Symbols are turned into their verbal referents and these are in turn interpreted. The print engagement is essentially private. While it does represent an act of communication, the contents pass from the privacy of the sender to the privacy of the receiver. Print also posits a time axis; the turning of pages, not to mention the vertical descent down the page, is a forward-moving succession, with earlier contents at every point serving as a ground for what follows. Moreover, the printed material is static—it is the reader, not the book, that moves forward. The physical arrangements of print are in accord with our traditional sense of history. Materials are layered; they lend themselves to rereading and to sustained attention. The pace of reading is variable, with progress determined by the reader's focus and comprehension.

The electronic order is in most ways opposite. Information and contents do not simply move from one private space to another, but they travel along a network. Engagement is intrinsically public, taking place within a circuit of larger connectedness. The vast resources of the network are always there, potential, even if they do not impinge on the immediate communication. Electronic communication can be passive, as with television watching, or interactive, as with computers. Contents, unless they are printed out (at which point they become part of the static order of print) are felt to be evanescent. They can be changed or deleted with the stroke of a key. With visual media (television, projected graphs, highlighted "bullets") impression and image take precedence over logic and concept, and detail and linear sequentiality are sacrificed. The pace is rapid, driven by jump-cut increments, and the basic movement is laterally associative rather than vertically cumulative. The presentation structures the reception and, in time, the expectation about how information is organized.

Further, the visual and nonvisual technology in every way encourages in the user a heightened and ever-changing awareness of the present. It works against historical perception, which must depend on the inimical notions of logic and sequential succession. If the print medium exalts the word, fixing it into permanence, the electronic counterpart reduces it to a signal, a means to an end.

Transitions like the one from print to electronic media do not take place without rippling or, more likely, *reweaving* the entire social and cultural web. The tendencies outlined above are already at work. We don't need to look far to find their effects. We can begin with the newspaper headlines and the millennial lamentations sounded in the op-ed pages: that our educational systems are in decline; that our students are less and less able to read and comprehend their required texts, and that their aptitude scores have leveled off well below those of previous generations. Tag-line communication, called "bite-speak" by some, is destroying the last remnants of political discourse; spin doctors and media consultants are our new shamans. As communications empires fight for

control of all information outlets, including publishers, the latter have suc-
cumbed to the tyranny of the bottom line; they are less and less willing to
publish work, however worthy, that will not make a tidy profit. And, on every
front, funding for the arts is being cut while the arts themselves appear to be
suffering a deep crisis of relevance. And so on.

Every one of these developments is, of course, overdetermined, but there
can be no doubt that they are connected, perhaps profoundly, to the transition
that is underway.

Certain other trends bear watching. One could argue, for instance, that the
entire movement of postmodernism in the arts is a consequence of this same
macroscopic shift. For what is postmodernism at root but an aesthetic that
rebukes the idea of an historical time line, as well as previously uncontested
assumptions of cultural hierarchy. The postmodern artifact manipulates its
stylistic signatures like Lego blocks and makes free with combinations from
the formerly sequestered spheres of high and popular art. Its combinatory
momentum and relentless referencing of the surrounding culture mirror perfectly the associative dynamics of electronic media.

One might argue likewise, that the virulent debate within academia over
the canon and multiculturalism may not be a simple struggle between the
entrenched ideologies of white male elites and the forces of formerly disenfranchised gender, racial, and cultural groups. Many of those who would
revise the canon (or end it altogether) are trying to outflank the assumption
of historical tradition itself. The underlying question, avoided by many, may
be not only whether the tradition is relevant, but whether it might not be too
taxing a system for students to comprehend. Both the traditionalists and the
progressives have valid arguments, and we must certainly have sympathy for
those who would try to expose and eradicate the hidden assumptions of bias
in the Western tradition. But it also seems clear that this debate could only
have taken the form it has in a society that has begun to come loose from its
textual moorings. To challenge repression is salutary. To challenge history
itself, proclaiming it to be simply an archive of repressions and justifications,
is idiotic.*

Then there are the more specific sorts of developments. Consider the
multibillion-dollar initiative by Whittle Communications to bring commercially sponsored education packages into the classroom. The underlying

---

*The outcry against the modification of the canon can be seen as a plea for old reflexes and
routines. And the cry for multicultural representation may be a last-ditch bid for connection to
the fading legacy of print. The logic is simple. When a resource is threatened—made scarce—
people fight over it. In this case the struggle is over textual power in an increasingly nontextual
age. The future of books and reading is what is at stake, and a dim intuition of this drives the
contending factions.

As Katha Pollitt argued so shrewdly in her much-cited article in The Nation: If we were a
nation of readers, there would be no issue. No one would be arguing about whether to put Toni
Morrison on the syllabus because her work would be a staple of the reader's regular diet anyway.
These lists are suddenly so important because they represent, very often, the only serious works
that the student is ever likely to be exposed to. Whoever controls the lists comes out ahead in the
struggle for the hearts and minds of the young.

premise is staggeringly simple: If electronic media are the one thing that the young are at ease with, why not exploit the fact? Why not stop bucking television and use it instead, with corporate America picking up the tab in exchange for a few minutes of valuable airtime for commercials? As the *Boston Globe* reports:

Here's how it would work:

Participating schools would receive, free of charge, $50,000 worth of electronic paraphernalia, including a satellite dish and classroom video monitors. In return, the schools would agree to air the show.

The show would resemble a network news program, but with 18- to 24-year-old anchors.

A prototype includes a report on a United Nations Security Council meeting on terrorism, a space shuttle update, a U2 music video tribute to Martin Luther King, a feature on the environment, a "fast fact" ('Arachibutyrophobia is the fear of peanut butter sticking to the roof of your mouth') and two minutes of commercial advertising.

"You have to remember that the children of today have grown up with the visual media," said Robert Calabrese (Billerica School Superintendent]. "They know no other way and we're simply capitalizing on that to enhance learning."

A collective change of sensibility may already be upon us. We need to take seriously the possibility that the young truly "know no other way," that they are not made of the same stuff that their elders are.

Calabrese's observation on the preconditioning of a whole generation of students raises troubling questions: Should we suppose that American education will begin to tailor itself to the aptitudes of its students, presenting more and more of its materials in newly packaged forms? And what will happen when educators find that not very many of the old materials will "play"—that is, capture student enthusiasm? Is the *what* of learning to be determined by the *how*? And at what point do vicious cycles begin to reveal their viciousness?

A collective change of sensibility may already be upon us. We need to take seriously the possibility that the young truly "know no other way," that they are not made of the same stuff that their elders are. In her *Harper's* magazine debate with Neil Postman, Camille Paglia observed:

Some people have more developed sensoriums than others. I've found that most people born before World War II are turned off by the modern media. They can't understand how we who were born after the war can read and watch TV at the same time. But we can. When I wrote my book, I had earphones on, blasting rock music or Puccini and Brahms. The soap operas—with the sound turned down—flickered on my TV. I'd be talking on the phone at the same time. Baby boomers have a multilayered, multitrack ability to deal with the world.

I don't know whether to be impressed or depressed by Paglia's ability to disperse her focus in so many directions. Nor can I say, not having read her book, in what ways her multitrack sensibility has informed her prose. But I'm baffled by what she means when she talks about an ability to "deal with the world." From the context, "dealing" sounds more like a matter of incessantly repositioning the self within a barrage of onrushing stimuli.

Paglia's is hardly the only testimony in this matter. A *New York Times* article on the cult success of Mark Leyner (author of *I Smell Esther Williams* and *My Cousin, My Gastroenterologist*) reports suggestively:

His fans say, variously, that his writing is like MTV, or rap music, or rock music, or simply like everything in the world put together: fast and furious and intense, full of illusion and allusion and fantasy and science and excrement.

Larry McCaffery, a professor of literature at San Diego State University and co-editor of Fiction International, *a literary journal, said his students get excited about Mr. Leyner's writing, which he considers important and unique: "It speaks to them, somehow, about this weird milieu they're swimming through. It's this dissolving, discontinuous world." While older people might find Mr. Leyner's world bizarre or unreal, Professor McCaffery said, it doesn't seem so to people who grew up with Walkmen and computers and VCR's, with so many choices, so much bombardment, that they have never experienced a sensation singly.*

The article continues:

There is no traditional narrative, although the book is called a novel. And there is much use of facts, though it is called fiction. Seldom does the end of a sentence have any obvious relation to the beginning. "You don't know where you're going, but you don't mind taking the leap," said R. J. Cutler, the producer of "Heat," who invited Mr. Leyner to be on the show after he picked up the galleys of his book and found it mesmerizing. "He taps into a specific cultural perspective where thoughtful literary world view meets pop culture and the TV generation."

My final exhibit—I don't know if it qualifies as a morbid symptom as such—is drawn from a *Washington Post Magazine* essay on the future of the Library of Congress, our national shrine to the printed word. One of the individuals interviewed in the piece is Robert Zich, so-called "special projects czar" of the institution. Zich, too, has seen the future, and he is surprisingly candid with his interlocutor. Before long, Zich maintains, people will be able to get what information they want directly off their terminals. The function of the Library of Congress (and perhaps libraries in general) will change. He envisions his library becoming more like a museum: "Just as you go to the National Gallery to see its Leonardo or go to the Smithsonian to see the Spirit of St. Louis and so on, you will want to go to libraries to see the Gutenberg or the original printing of Shakespeare's plays or to see Lincoln's hand-written version of the Gettysburg Address."

Zich is outspoken, voicing what other administrators must be thinking privately. The big research libraries, he says, "and the great national libraries and their buildings will go the way of the railroad stations and the movie palaces of an earlier era which were really vital institutions in their time . . . Somehow folks moved away from that when the technology changed."

And books? Zich expresses excitement about Sony's hand-held electronic book, and a miniature encyclopedia coming from Franklin Electronic Publishers. "Slip it in your pocket," he says. "Little keyboard, punch in your words and it will do the full text searching and all the rest of it. Its limitation, of course, is that it's devoted just to that one book." Zich is likewise interested in the possibility of memory cards. What he likes about the Sony product is the portability: one machine, a screen that will display the contents of whatever electronic card you feed it.

I cite Zich's views at some length here because he is not some Silicon Valley research and development visionary, but a highly placed executive at what might be called, in a very literal sense, our most conservative public institution. When men like Zich embrace the electronic future, we can be sure it's well on its way.

Others might argue that the technologies cited by Zich merely represent a modification in the "form" of reading, and that reading itself will be unaffected, as there is little difference between following words on a pocket screen or a printed page. Here I have to hold my line. The context cannot but condition the process. Screen and book may exhibit the same string of words, but the assumptions that underlie their significance are entirely different depending on whether we are staring at a book or a circuit-generated text. As the nature of looking—at the natural world, at paintings—changed with the arrival of photography and mechanical reproduction, so will the collective relation to language alter as new modes of dissemination prevail.

Whether all of this sounds dire or merely "different" will depend upon the reader's own values and priorities. I find these portents of change depressing, but also exhilarating—at least to speculate about. On the one hand, I have a great feeling of loss and a fear about what habitations will exist for self and soul in the future. But there is also a quickening, a sense that important things are on the line. As Heraclitus once observed, "The mixture that is not shaken soon stagnates." Well, the mixture is being shaken, no doubt about it. And here are some of the kinds of developments we might watch for as our "proto-electronic" era yields to an all-electronic future:

1. *Language erosion.* There is no question but that the transition from the culture of the book to the culture of electronic communication will radically alter the ways in which we use language on every societal level. The complexity and distinctiveness of spoken and written expression, which are deeply bound to traditions of print literacy, will gradually be replaced by a more telegraphic sort of "plainspeak." Syntactic masonry is already a dying art. Neil Postman and others have already suggested what losses have been incurred by the advent of telegraphy and television—how the complex discourse patterns of the nineteenth century were flattened by the requirements of communication over distances. That tendency runs riot as the layers of mediation thicken. Simple linguistic prefab is now the norm, while ambiguity, paradox, irony, subtlety, and wit are fast disappearing. In their place, the simple "vision thing" and myriad other "things." Verbal intelligence, which has long been viewed as suspect as the act of reading, will come to seem positively conspiratorial. The

greater part of any articulate person's energy will be deployed in dumbing-down her discourse.

Language will grow increasingly impoverished through a series of vicious cycles. For, of course, the usages of literature and scholarship are connected in fundamental ways to the general speech of the tribe. We can expect that curricula will be further streamlined, and difficult texts in the humanities will be pruned and glossed. One need only compare a college textbook from twenty years ago to its contemporary version. A poem by Milton, a play by Shakespeare—one can hardly find the text among the explanatory notes nowadays.

Language will grow increasingly impoverished through a series of vicious cycles.

Fewer and fewer people will be able to contend with the so-called masterworks of literature or ideas. Joyce, Woolf, Soyinka, not to mention the masters who preceded them, will go unread, and the civilizing energies of their prose will circulate aimlessly between closed covers.

2. *Flattening of historical perspectives.* As the circuit supplants the printed page, and as more and more of our communications involve us in network processes—which of their nature plant us in a perpetual present—our perception of history will inevitably alter. Changes in information storage and access are bound to impinge on our historical memory. The depth of field that is our sense of the past is not only a linguistic construct, but is in some essential way represented by the book and the physical accumulation of books in library spaces. In the contemplation of the single volume, or mass of volumes, we form a picture of time past as a growing deposit of sediment; we capture a sense of its depth and dimensionality. Moreover, we meet the past as much in the presentation of words in books of specific vintage as we do in any isolated fact or statistic. The database, useful as it is, expunges this context, this sense of chronology, and admits us to a weightless order in which all information is equally accessible.

If we take the etymological tack, history (cognate with "story") is affiliated in complex ways with its texts. Once the materials of the past are unhoused from their pages, they will surely *mean* differently. The printed page is itself a link, at least along the imaginative continuum, and when that link is broken, the past can only start to recede. At the same time it will become a body of disjunct data available for retrieval and, in the hands of our canny dream merchants, a mythology. The more we grow rooted in the consciousness of the now, the more it will seem utterly extraordinary that things were ever any different. The idea of a farmer plowing a field—an historical constant for millennia—will be something for a theme park. For, naturally, the entertainment industry, which reads the collective unconscious unerringly, will seize the advantage. The past that has slipped away will be rendered ever more glorious, ever more a fantasy play with heroes, villains, and quaint settings and props. Small-town American life returns as "Andy of Mayberry"—at first enjoyed with recognition, later accepted as a faithful portrait of how things used to be.

3. *The waning of the private self.* We may even now be in the first stages of a process of social collectivization that will over time all but vanquish the ideal of the isolated individual. For some decades now we have been edging away from the perception of private life as something opaque, closed off to the world; we increasingly accept the transparency of a life lived within a set of systems, electronic or otherwise. Our technologies are not bound by season or light—it's always the same time in the circuit. And so long as time is money and money matters, those circuits will keep humming. The doors and walls of our habitations matter less and less—the world sweeps through the wires as it needs to, or as we need it to. The monitor light is always blinking; we are always potentially on-line.

I am not suggesting that we are all about to become mindless, soulless robots, or that personality will disappear altogether into an oceanic homogeneity. But certainly the idea of what it means to be a person living a life will be much changed. The figure-ground model, which has always featured a solitary self before a background that is the society of other selves, is romantic in the extreme. It is ever less tenable in the world as it is becoming. There are no more wildernesses, no more lonely homesteads, and, outside of cinema, no more emblems of the exalted individual.

I am not suggesting that we are all about to become mindless, soulless robots, or that personality will disappear altogether into an oceanic homogeneity.

The self must change as the nature of subjective space changes. And one of the many incremental transformations of our age has been the slow but steady destruction of subjective space. The physical and psychological distance between individuals has been shrinking for at least a century. In the process, the figure-ground image has begun to blur its boundary distinctions. One day we will conduct our public and private lives within networks so dense, among so many channels of instantaneous information, that it will make almost no sense to speak of the differentiations of subjective individualism.

We are already captive in our webs. Our slight solitudes are transected by codes, wires, and pulsations. We punch a number to check in with the answering machine, another to tape a show that we are too busy to watch. The strands of the web grow finer and finer—this is obvious. What is no less obvious is the fact that they will continue to proliferate, gaining in sophistication, merging functions so that one can bank by phone, shop via television, and so on. The natural tendency is toward streamlining: The smart dollar keeps finding ways to shorten the path, double-up the function. We might think in terms of a circuit-board model, picturing ourselves as the contact points. The expansion of electronic options is always at the cost of contractions in the private sphere. We will soon be navigating with ease among cataracts of organized pulsations, putting out and taking in signals. We will bring our terminals, our modems, and menus further and further into our former privacies; we will implicate ourselves by degrees in the unitary life, and there may come a day when we no longer remember that there was any other life.

While I was brewing these somewhat melancholy thoughts, I chanced to read in an old *New Republic* the text of Joseph Brodsky's 1987 Nobel Prize acceptance speech. I felt as though I had opened a door leading to the great vault of the nineteenth century. The poet's passionate plea on behalf of the book at once corroborated and countered everything I had been thinking. What he upheld in faith were the very ideals I was saying good-bye to. I greeted his words with an agitated skepticism, fashioning from them something more like a valediction. Here are four passages:

If art teaches anything . . . it is the privateness of the human condition. Being the most ancient as well as the most literal form of private enterprise, it fosters in a man, knowingly or unwittingly, a sense of his uniqueness, of individuality, of separateness—thus turning him from a social animal into an autonomous "I."

The great Baratynsky, speaking of his Muse, characterized her as possessing an "uncommon visage." It's in acquiring this "uncommon visage" that the meaning of human existence seems to lie, since for this uncommonness we are, as it were, prepared genetically.

Aesthetic choice is a highly individual matter, and aesthetic experience is always a private one. Every new aesthetic reality makes one's experience even more private; and this kind of privacy, assuming at times the guise of literary (or some other) taste, can in itself turn out to be, if not a guarantee, then a form of defense, against enslavement.

In the history of our species, in the history of Homo sapiens, the book is an anthropological development, similar essentially to the invention of the wheel. Having emerged in order to give us some idea not so much of our origins as of what that sapiens is capable of, a book constitutes a means of transportation through the space of experience, at the speed of a turning page. This movement, like every movement, becomes flight from the common denominator . . . This flight is the flight in the direction of "uncommon visage," in the direction of the numerator, in the direction of autonomy, in the direction of privacy.

Brodsky is addressing the relation between art and totalitarianism, and within that context his words make passionate sense. But I was reading from a different vantage. What I had in mind was not a vision of political totalitarianism, but rather of something that might be called "societal totalism"—that movement toward deindividuation, or electronic collectivization, that I discussed above. And from that perspective our era appears to be in a headlong flight *from* the "uncommon visage" named by the poet.

Trafficking with tendencies—extrapolating and projecting as I have been doing—must finally remain a kind of gambling. One bets high on the validity of a notion and low on the human capacity for resistance and for unpredictable initiatives. No one can really predict how we will adapt to the transformations taking place all around us. We may discover, too, that language is a hardier thing than I have allowed. It may flourish among the beep and the click and the monitor as readily as it ever did on the printed page. I hope so, for language is the soul's ozone layer and we thin it at our peril.

Jay David Bolter

The Computer as a New Writing Space

Consider this simple example of electronic writing. (See Fig. 1.) The text is a continuous prose paragraph, displayed on the computer screen for the reader to read in the traditional way. Some of the words are in boldface; the style indicates that there is a note on that word or phrase, something more to be said. To retrieve the note, the reader points with the cursor at the text in boldface and presses a button. A second window then opens on the screen and presents a new paragraph for the reader to consider. The reader examines the note and may then return to the original paragraph.

In one sense this is simply the electronic equivalent of the footnote used in printed books for hundreds of years. Instead of looking to the bottom of the page or the end of the book, the reader aims the cursor and the computer retrieves and displays the reference. The machine is merely handling the

FIGURE 1

(a) To examine a note, the reader points to and activates a phrase in boldface. (b) A new window appears and presents the associated text, which contains boldface phrases of its own.

Nature of writing

Writing has been called "visible language." The name suggests that the spoken word is the primary human experience and that writing merely visualizes speech. **Eric Havelock carries this suggestion to its extreme when he insists that writing should be reduced to a functional minimum.** To insist upon pure phonetic writing is to ignore the possibility that visible signs may convey messages that cannot be spoken. A broader definition of writing would include any system of visual symbols—even systems like those of **mathematics or computer programming,** which are hard to speak, and **picture writing,** which does not immediately correspond to spoken language

---

Nature of writing

Note

"Strictly speaking, written orthography should behave solely as the servant of the spoken tongue, reporting its sounds as accurately and swiftly as possible. It need not and should not have a nature of its own.... [T]he artistic fascination of the Chinese with the **calligraphy of the ideogram** has had its counterpart in the development of scripts and their elaboration in European and Arabic countries. This visual development of the written signs has nothing to do with the purpose of language, namely **instantaneous communication** between members of a human group." (Eric A. Havelock, <u>The Literate Revolution in Greece and its Cultural Consequences</u>, 53).

mechanics of reading footnotes. But there is this important difference: the second window can also contain boldface phrases that in turn lead the reader to other paragraphs. The process can continue indefinitely as the reader moves from one window to another through a space of paragraphs. The second paragraph is not necessarily subordinate to the first. A phrase in boldface may lead the reader to a longer, more elaborate paragraph. One paragraph may be linked to many and serve in turn as the destination for links from many others. In a printed book, it would be intolerably pedantic to write footnotes to footnotes. But in the computer, writing in layers is quite natural, and reading the layers is effortless. All the individual paragraphs may be of equal importance in the whole text, which then becomes a network of interconnected writings. The network is designed by the author to be explored by the reader in precisely this peripatetic fashion.

Such a network is called a *hypertext,* and, as we shall see, it is the ability to create and present hypertextual structures that makes the computer a revolution in writing. The computer as hypertext invites us to write with symbols that have both an intrinsic and extrinsic significance. That is, the symbols have a meaning that may be explained in words, but they also have meaning as elements in a larger structure of verbal gestures. Both words and structures are visible, writeable, and readable in the electronic space.

■ WRITING PLACES

With or without the computer, whenever we write, we write topically. We conceive of our text as a set of verbal gestures, large and small. To write is to do things with topics—to add, delete, and arrange them. The computer changes the nature of writing simply by giving visual expression to our acts of conceiving and manipulating topics. A writer working with a word processor spends much of the time entering words letter by letter, just as he or she does at a typewriter. Revising is a different matter. With most word processors, writers can delete or replace an entire word; they can highlight phrases, sentences, or paragraphs. They can erase a sentence with a single keystroke; they can select a paragraph, cut it from its current location, and insert it elsewhere, even into another document. In using these facilities, the writer is thinking and writing in terms of verbal units or topics, whose meaning transcends their constituent words. The Greek word *topos* meant literally a place, and ancient rhetoric used the word to refer to commonplaces, conventional units or methods of thought. In the Renaissance, topics became headings that could be used to organize any field of knowledge, and these headings were often set out in elaborate diagrams. (See Ong, 1958, pp. 104–130.) Our English word *topic* is appropriate for the computer because its etymology suggests the spatial character of electronic writing: topics exist in a writing space that is not only a visual surface but

With or without the computer, whenever we write, we write topically. To write is to do things with topics—to add, delete, and arrange them.

also a data structure in the computer. The programmers who designed word processors recognized the importance of topical writing, when they gave us operations for adding or deleting sentences and paragraphs as units. They did not, however, take the further step of allowing a writer to associate a name or a visual symbol with such topical units. This important step lends the unit a conceptual identity. The unit symbol becomes an abiding element in the writer's thinking and expression, because its constituent words or phrases can be put out of sight.

On a printed or typed page, we indent and separate paragraphs to indicate the topical structure. Within each paragraph, however, we have only punctuation, occurring in the stream of words, to mark finer structure. A better representation of topical writing is the conventional outline, in which major topics are designated by Roman numerals, subtopics by capital letters, sub-subtopics by Arabic numerals, and so on. Each point of an outline serves to organize and situate the topics subordinate to it, and the outline as a whole is a static representation, a snapshot, of the textual organization. The conventions of outlining turn the writing surface into a tiered space in which the numbering and indentation of lines represent the hierarchy of the author's ideas. A paragraphed text is the flattening or linearization of an outline.

The word processor, which imitates the layout of the typed page, also flattens the text.

The word processor, which imitates the layout of the typed page, also flattens the text. It offers the writer little help in conceiving the evolving structure of the text. Although the word processor allows the writer to define a verbal unit in order to move or delete it, the definition lasts only until the operation is complete. But if the word processor offers the writer only temporary access to his or her structure, another class of programs called outline processors makes structure a permanent feature of the text. An outline processor sets the traditional written outline in motion. A writer can add points to an electronic outline in any order, while the computer continually renumbers to reflect additions or deletions. The writer can promote minor points to major ones, and the computer will again renumber. The writer can collapse the outline in order to see only those points above a certain level, an action that gives an overview of the evolving text. In short the writer can think globally about the text: one can treat topics as unitary symbols and write with those symbols, just as in a word processor one writes with words. (See Fig. 2.)

Writing in topics is not a replacement for writing with words; the writer must eventually attend to the details of his or her prose. The outline processor contains within it a conventional word processor, so that the writer can attach text to each of the points in the outline. But in using an outline processor, writers are not aware of a rigid distinction between outlining and prose writing: they move easily back and forth between structure and prose. What is new is that the points of the outline become functional elements in the text, because when the points move, the words move with

(a)   (b)

Electronic Writing Space   Electronic Writing Space

  I. Introduction   I. Introduction
                                      A. Example
  II. Writing places   1. Figure 1
                                      B. Footnote
  III. Electronic trees   C. Hypertext
                                   II. Writing places
  IV. Hypertext   A. Topos
                                      B. Print format
  V. Hypermedia   C. Word processor
                                         1. Conventional
  VI. The First Hypertext   2. Desktop publishing
                                      D. Outline processor
  VII. Writers and Readers   1. Figure 2
                                      E. Topical writing
                                         1. With the computer
(c)   2. In print

  II. Writing places
     A. Topos

| With or without the computer, whenever we write, we write topically. We conceive of our text as a set of verbal gestures, large and small. To write is to do things with topics—to add, delete, and arrange them. The computer changes the nature of writing simply by giving visual expression to our acts of conceiving and manipulating topics. A writer working with a word processor spends much of his time entering words letter by letter, just as he does at a typewriter. Revising is a different matter. With most word processors, the |

     B. Print format

| On a printed or typed page, we indent and separate paragraphs to indicate the topical structure. Within each paragraph, however, we have only punctuation, occurring in the stream of words, to mark finer structure. A better representation of topical writing is the conventional outline, in which major topics are designated by Roman numerals, subtopics by capital letters, sub-subtopics by Arabic numerals, and so on. Each point of an outline serves to organize and situate the topics subordinate to it, and the outline as a whole is a |

     C. Word processor

| The word processor, which imitates the layout of the typed page, also flattens the text. It offers the writer little help in conceiving the evolving structure of his text. Although the word processor allows |

FIGURE 2
An outline processor can reveal or hide detail as the writer requires. It may show only the major points (a), the full outline (b), or the prose paragraph attached to each point of the outline (c).

them. In this way the computer makes visible and almost palpable what writers have always known: that the identifying and arranging of topics is itself an act of writing. Outline processing is writing at a different grain, a replication on a higher level of the conventional act of writing by choosing and arranging words. The symbols of this higher writing are simply longer and more complicated "words," verbal gestures that may be whole sentences or paragraphs.

In an outline processor, then, the prose remains, but it is encased in a formally operative structure. With a pen or typewriter, writing meant literally to form letters on a page, figuratively to create verbal structures. In an electronic writing system, the figurative process becomes a literal act. By defining topical symbols, the writer can, like the programmer or the mathematician, abstract himself or herself temporarily from the details of the prose, and the value of this abstraction lies in seeing more clearly the structural skeleton of the text. It is not possible or desirable that the prose writer should become a mathematician or that human language should be reduced to a system of logical symbols. The result of giving language wholeheartedly over to formalism would simply be the impoverishment of language. On the other hand, the electronic medium can permit us to play creatively with formal structures in our writing without abandoning the richness of natural language.

▪ ELECTRONIC TREES

It is no accident that the computer can serve as an outline processor. The machine is designed to create and track such formal structures, which are important for all its various uses. The computer's memory and central processing unit are intricate hierarchies of electronic components. Layers of software in turn transform the machine's physical space of electronic circuits into a space of symbolic information, and it is in this space that a new kind of writing can be located. Like the space of the modern physicist, the space of the computer is shaped by the objects that occupy it. The computer programmer forms his or her space by filling it with sym-bolic elements and then by connecting these elements as the program requires. Any symbol in the space can refer to another symbol by using its numerical address. Pointers hold together the structure of computer programs, and programming itself may be defined as the art of building symbolic structures in the space that the com-puter provides—a definition that makes programming a species of writing.

One such programming structure, which represents hierarchy, is called a *tree*. Trees (and their relatives such as *lists, stacks,* and *net-works*) are ubiquitous in programs that must record and track large bodies of information or information subject to frequent change. Tree diagrams, in which elements are connected by branches as in a genealogical tree, have a long history in writing as well. They date back at least to the early Middle Ages and are not uncommon in medieval and Renaissance books, where they served for the spatial arrangement of topics (Ong, 1958, pp. 74–83, 199–202, 314–318). The traditional outline is a strict hierarchy that can just as easily be represented by a tree diagram. Part of the outline that we saw earlier (Fig. 2) is represented by the following tree (Fig. 3).

Both the tree and the outline give us a better reading of structure than does ordinary paragraphing, because they mold the visual space of the text in a way that reflects its structure. A printed page of paragraphs is by comparison a flat and uninteresting space, as is the window of a word processor. A writer can use a word processor to type an outline, and, if the word processor permits graphics, the writer can insert a tree diagram into the text. But the outline or diagram will then be stored as a picture, a sequence of bits to be shown on the screen; the picture will not be treated as a data structure and will not inform the space in which the writer is working. The writer will not be able to change the structure by manipulating the outline, as he or she can in an outline processor, and that ability is necessary for true electronic writing. In using an outline processor, the writer can intervene at any level of the evolving structure. And if the writer gives the reader a diskette rather than a printed version, then the reader too gains immediate access to that structure. All this is possible, because the writing space itself has become a tree, a hierarchy of topical elements.

The electronic writing space is extremely malleable. It can be fashioned into one tree or into a forest of hierarchical trees. A hierarchy defines a strict order of subordination: each point in an outline is arranged under exactly one heading; each topical unit in a tree diagram (except the root) has exactly one

FIGURE 3
A tree diagram represents hierarchical relationships among elements.

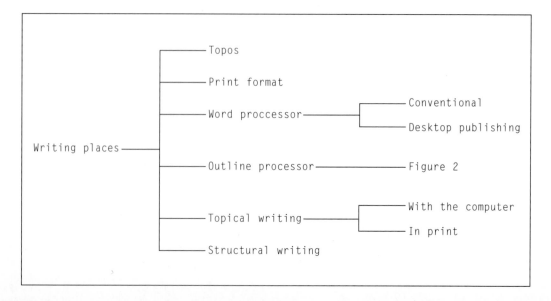

incoming arrow. In any printed or written text, one such hierarchical order always precludes others. The static medium of print demands that the writer settle on one order of topics, although the writer may find that the topics could be arranged equally well in, say, three orders corresponding to three electronic outlines. Unlike the space of the printed book, the computer's writing space can represent any relationships that can be defined as the interplay of pointers and elements. Multiple relationships pose no special problem. A writer could therefore maintain three outlines, each of which deployed the same topics in a different order. These outlines may all reside in the computer's memory at the same time, each activated at the writer's request. The writer may choose to examine topics from any of the three vantage points and then switch to another; he or she may alter one outline while leaving the others intact; he or she may alter any of the outlines themselves without revising the text in any one of the topics. The structure of an electronic text is in this sense abstracted from its verbal expression.

The electronic writing space is extremely malleable. It can be fashioned into one tree or into a forest of hierarchical trees.

This multiplicity and abstraction already render the electronic writing space more flexible than its predecessors. And if all writing were only hierarchical, then the outline processor itself would be revolutionary in its freeing of writing from the frozen structure of the printed page. But there is one further step to be taken in liberating the text.

■ HYPERTEXT

The goal of conventional writing is to create a perfect hierarchy, but it is not always easy to maintain the discipline of such a structure. All writers have had the experience of being overwhelmed with ideas as they write. The act of writing itself releases a flood of thoughts—one idea suggesting another and another, as the writer struggles to get them down in some form before they slip from his or her conscious grasp. "I only wish I could write with both hands," noted Saint Teresa, "so as not to forget one thing while I am saying another." (See Peers, 1972, vol. 2, p. 88.) Romantics like Carlyle founded their psychology of literature upon this experience. The experience is not limited to saints and poets: many, perhaps most, writers begin their work with a jumble of verbal ideas and only a vague sense of how these ideas will fit together. The writer may start by laying out topics in an arrangement less formal than an outline: he or she may organize by association rather than strict subordination. Teachers of writing often encourage their students to begin by sketching out topics and connecting them through lines of association, and they call this activity "prewriting." What students create in prewriting is a network of elements— exactly what computer programmers mean by the data structure they call a network. The computer can maintain such a network of topics, and it can reflect the writer's progress as he or she trims the network by removing connections and establishing subordination until there is a strict hierarchy. In the world of print, at least in nonfiction, associative writing is considered only a preliminary.

Association is not really prior to writing, as the term "prewriting" suggests. Association is always present in any text: one word echoes another; one sentence or paragraph recalls others earlier in the text and looks forward to still others. A writer cannot help but write associatively: even if he or she begins with and remains faithful to an outline, the result is always a network of verbal elements. The hierarchy (in the form of paragraphs, sections, and chapters) is an attempt to impose order on verbal ideas that are always prone to subvert that order. The associative relationships define alternative organizations that lie beneath the order of pages and chapters that a printed text presents to the world. These alternatives constitute subversive texts-behind-the-text.

"I only wish I could write with both hands," noted Saint Teresa, "so as not to forget one thing while I am saying another."

Previous technologies of writing, which could not easily accommodate such alternatives, tended to ignore them. The ancient papyrus roll was strongly linear in its presentation of text. The codex, especially in the later Middle Ages, and then the printed book have made better efforts to accommodate association as well as hierarchy. In a modern book the table of contents (listing chapters and sometimes sections) defines the hierarchy, while the indices record associative lines of thought that permeate the text. An index permits the reader to locate passages that share the same word, phrase, or subject and so associates passages that may be widely separated in the pagination of the book. In one sense the index defines other books that could be constructed from the materials at hand, other themes that the author could have formed into an analytical narrative, and so invites the reader to read the book in alternative ways. An index transforms a book from a tree into a network, offering multiplicity in place of a single order of paragraphs and pages. There need not be any privileged element in a network, as there always is in a tree, no single topic that dominates all others. Instead of strict subordination, we have paths that weave their way through the textual space. Thus, the outline and tree that we saw earlier (Figs. 2 and 3) can become the network shown in Fig. 4. If all texts are ultimately networks of verbal elements, the computer is the first medium that can record and present these networks to writers and readers. Just as the outline processor treats text as a hierarchy, other computer programs can fashion the text into a general network or hypertext.

Hypertext has only recently become a discipline in computer science. (See Smith & Weiss, 1988.) The term "hypertext" was coined two decades ago by Ted Nelson. Working with mainframe computers in the 1960s, Nelson had come to realize the machine's capacity to create and manage textual networks for all kinds of writing. "Literature," he wrote, "is an ongoing system of interconnecting documents." By literature he meant not only belles-lettres but also scientific and technical writing: any group of writings on a well-defined sub-

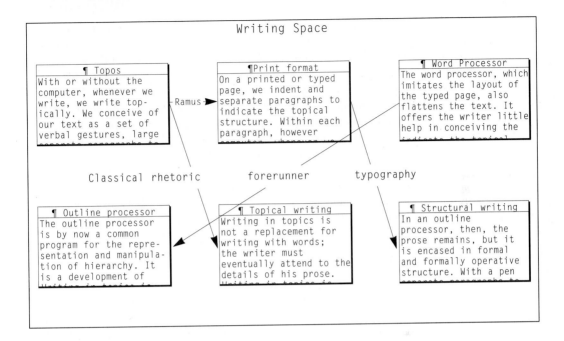

Writing Space

¶ Topos
With or without the computer, whenever we write, we write top-ically. We conceive of our text as a set of verbal gestures, large

←Ramus→

¶Print format
On a printed or typed page, we indent and separate paragraphs to indicate the topical structure. Within each paragraph, however

¶ Word Processor
The word processor, which imitates the layout of the typed page, also flattens the text. It offers the writer little help in conceiving the

Classical rhetoric   forerunner   typography

¶ Outline processor
The outline processor is by now a common program for the repre-sentation and manipula-tion of hierarchy. It is a development of

¶ Topical writing
Writing in topics is not a replacement for writing with words; the writer must eventually attend to the details of his prose.

¶ Structural writing
In an outline processor, then, the prose remains, but it is encased in formal and formally operative structure. With a pen

FIGURE 4
A hypertext is a network of textual elements and connections.

ject. "A literature is a system of interconnected writings. We do not offer this as our definition, but as a discovered fact" (Nelson, 1984, p. 2/7; see also Nelson, 1974 and Conklin, 1987, pp. 22–23). Actually this "fact" had been discovered independent of and long before the computer, but the machine has provided Nelson and others in the last two decades with the technology needed to realize and indeed to reify writing as a network. Even before Nelson, the scientist and engineer Vannevar Bush had envisioned using electro-mechanical technology as a hypertextual reading and writing system. In 1945 Bush proposed (but never built) what he called a "memex," a device that would serve as an interactive encyclopedia or library. The reader of the memex would be able to display two texts on a screen and then create links between passages in the texts. These links would be stored by the memex and would be available for later display and revision; collectively they would define a network of interconnections. Because electronic storage was not yet capacious or reliable, Bush chose microfilm as the storage medium for his memex. Fortunately the development of electromagnetic and optical disks has rendered microfilm obsolete for this purpose. But computer technology was already far enough advanced for Bush to see the possibility of hypertext and to express himself enthusiastically. His article proclaims nothing less than "a new relationship between thinking man and the sum of knowledge" (see Bush, 1945, p. 101).

Whether realized on microfilm or in computer memory, a hypertext con-sists of topics and their connections, where again the topics may be para-graphs, sentences, individual words, or indeed digitized graphics. A hypertext is like a printed book that the author has attacked with a pair of scissors and cut into convenient verbal sizes. The difference is that the electronic hypertext does not simply dissolve into a disordered bundle of slips, as the printed book must. For the author also defines a scheme of electronic connections to indicate relationships among the slips. In fashioning a hypertext, a writer might begin with a passage of continuous prose and then add notes or glosses on important words in the passage. As we suggested earlier (Fig. 1), the glosses themselves could contain glosses, leading the reader to further texts. A hypertextual network can extend indefinitely, as a printed text cannot.

A computer hypertext might serve, for example, to collect scholars' notes on complex texts such as Joyce's *Ulysses* and *Finnegans Wake*. The computer can record and update the collective work of many scholars who continue today adding to, refining, and revising the glosses; it can connect notes to other notes as appropriate. Such exegesis, currently recorded in books and journals, would be both easier to use and more appropriate as a hypertext, because *Ulysses* and particularly *Finnegans Wake* are themselves hypertexts that have been flattened out to fit on the printed page. But an author does not have to be as experimental as Joyce to profit from hypertext. A historian might choose to write an essay in which each paragraph or section is a topic in a hypertextual network. The connections would indicate possible orders in which topics could be assembled and read, and each order of reading might produce a different literary and analytic result. A mathematician might choose to write a hypertextbook that could tailor itself to different students with differing degrees of mathematical proficiency. Hypertext can serve for all sorts of more popular materials as well: directories, catalogues, how-to-manuals—wherever the reader wishes to move through the text in a variety of orders. In fact thousands of such hypertexts are already available, written for display by Hypercard, a program for the Apple Macintosh computer.

In general, the connections of a hypertext are organized into paths that make operational sense to author and reader. Each topic may participate in several paths, and its significance will depend upon which paths the reader has traveled in order to arrive at that topic. In print, only a few paths can be suggested or followed. In an electronic version the texture of the text becomes thicker, and its paths can serve many functions. Paths can, as in a tree structure, indicate subordination. They can also remind the writer of relationships among topics that had to be sacrificed for the sake of an eventual hierarchy. They can express cyclic relationships among topics that can never be hierarchical. They can categorize topics for later revision: the writer might wish to join two paths together or intersect two paths and preserve only those elements common to both. In the electronic medium, hierarchical and associative thinking may coexist in the structure of a text, since the computer can take care of the mechanics of maintaining and presenting both networks and trees. In the medium of print, the writer may use an index to show alternatives, but these alternatives must always contend with the fixed order of the pages of the book. The canonical order is defined by the book's pagination, and all other suggested orders remain subordinate. A hypertext has no canonical order. Every path defines an equally convincing and appropriate reading, and in that simple fact the reader's relationship to the text changes radically. A text as a network has no univocal sense; it is a multiplicity without the imposition of a principle of domination.

In place of hierarchy, we have a writing that is not only topical: we might also call it "topographic." The word "topography" originally meant a written description of a place, such as an ancient geographer might give. Only later did the word come to refer to mapping or charting—that is, to a visual and mathematical rather than verbal description. Electronic writing is both a visual and verbal description. It is not the writing of a place, but rather a writing with places, spatially realized topics. Topographic writing challenges the idea that writing should be merely the servant of spoken language. The writer and reader can create and examine signs and structures on the computer screen that have no easy equivalent in speech. The point is obvious when the text is a collection of images stored on a videodisk, but it is equally true for a purely verbal text that has been fashioned as a tree or a network of topics and connections.

A text as a network has no univocal sense; it is a multiplicity without the imposition of a principle of domination.

Topographic writing as a mode is not even limited to the computer medium. It is possible to write topographically for print or even in manuscript. Whenever we divide our text into unitary topics and organize those units into a connected structure and whenever we conceive of this textual structure spatially as well as verbally, we are writing topographically. As we shall see in a later chapter, many literary artists in the 20th century have adopted this mode of writing. Although the computer is not necessary for topographic writing, it is only in the computer that the mode becomes a natural, and therefore also a conventional, way to write.

■ HYPERMEDIA

The first generation of personal computers could only display about one or two hundred different signs—the letters of the alphabet, numerals, punctuation, and some special characters. The writer had to choose from those shapes and therefore symbols that were wired into the displays or into their interface cards. Now the advent of inexpensive, bit-mapped graphics has removed that limitation. With bit-mapping, each pixel, each tiny square or rectangle on the screen, is under programmed control: permissible shapes are no longer frozen into the hardware. The letters of the alphabet themselves are defined by software, so that the system can provide not only the Roman alphabet in pica, but other styles, type fonts, and sizes as well. Images can be represented on the screen as easily as letters of the alphabet. These machine images have the same advantage of dynamic control as do the letter forms, and they suffer from the same problem of graininess, since the images too consist of a finite number of pixels.

Some word processors already permit the writer to insert diagrams and pictures directly into the text. But in word processing the graphic image is not really part of the text; it is merely allowed to coexist with the verbal text. As we have seen in the figures presented earlier, the computer has the capacity to integrate word and image more subtly, to make text itself graphic by representing its structure graphically to the writer and the reader. The computer can even dissolve the distinction between the standardized letter forms and symbols of the writer's own making. True electronic writing is not limited to verbal text: the writeable elements may be words, images, sounds, or even actions that the computer is directed to perform. The writer could use his or her network to organize pictures on videodisk or music and voices on an audio playback device. Instead of moving from paragraph to paragraph in a verbal text, the reader might be shown videotaped scenes of a play in a variety of orders. The reader might move through an aural landscape created by various recorded sounds or walk through a city by viewing photographs of various buildings. (Such was the Aspen project. See Brand, 1987, pp. 141–142.) Any combination of these elements is possible. The same computer screen might display verbal text below or beside a video image; it might combine sound and verbal writing. These combinations have come to be called *hypermedia* and are already quite sophisticated.

The introduction of video images might seem to turn electronic writing into mere television.

The introduction of video images might seem to turn electronic writing into mere television. Television itself often displays words on the screen, but it robs the displayed words of their cognitive value. Text on television is mere ornamentation; words appear most often to reinforce the spoken message or to decorate the packages of products being advertised. In fact, hypermedia is the revenge of text upon television (Joyce, 1988, p. 14). In television, text is absorbed into the video image, but in hypermedia the televised image becomes part of the text. This incorporation is literally true in MIT's Project Athena, in which the reader can run a videotape in a window on his computer screen. The video image therefore sits among the other textual elements for the reader to examine. (For a description of Project Athena, see Balkovich, Lerman, & Parmelee, 1985.) The Intermedia system developed at Brown University is another instance, in which texts and images are read and written in the same computer environment. (See Yankelovich, Haan, Meyrowitz, & Drucker, 1988.) Once video images and sound are taken into the computer in this fashion, they too become topical elements. Writers can fashion these elements into a structure. They can write with images, because they can direct one topical image to refer to another and join visual and verbal topics in the same network (see Fig. 5). A journalist might select examples from a library of digitized still pictures and form them into a pictorial essay. An art historian might take images of Renaissance painting and attach explanatory comments. In fact, one can link the comments not only to the whole painting, but also to given areas of the image. The eyes of one portrait may refer to a comment, which may in

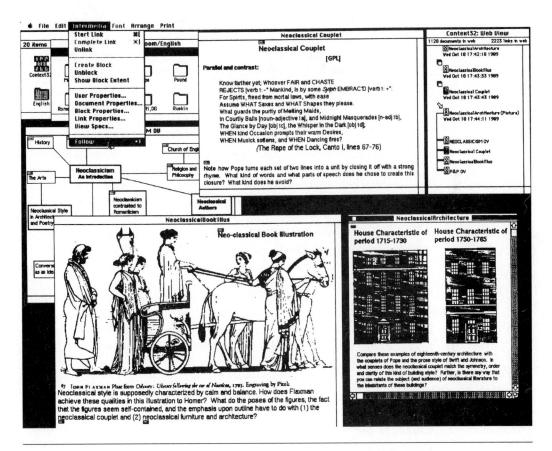

FIGURE 5

In the Intermedia project at Brown University, text and graphics can be combined into a single hypertextual web. Here, in a complex set of windows on the Macintosh computer screen, a passage from Pope is related to examples of Neoclassical architecture and book illustration. The link icon is a small box that contains a right pointing arrow. Wherever that icon occurs, the reader can choose to follow the links to another element in the hypertext. Reprinted with the kind permission of Professor George P. Landow.

turn link to eyes of other portrait examples. Other parts of the painting would lead to other comments and other examples. The reader would begin with the first picture and then choose to read the network of examples and explanations in a variety of orders, based on an interest in hands, eyes, or other elements of Renaissance technique. In each case the elements of the pictures have themselves become signs that refer to verbal topics and to other pictures. The image is functioning symbolically within the writer's text.

Such multimedia texts are by no means the death of writing. A hypermedia display is still a text, a weaving together of elements treated symbolically. Hypermedia simply extends the principles of electronic writing into the domain of sound and image. The computer's control of structure promises to create a synaesthesia in which anything that can be seen or heard may contribute to the texture of the text. These synaesthetic texts will have the same qualities as electronic verbal texts. They too will be flexible, dynamic, and interactive; they too will blur the distinction between writer and reader.

■ THE FIRST HYPERTEXT

Although experiments have been conducted since the 1960s, workable hypertext systems such as Intermedia are relatively recent. It was not until the advent of personal computers and workstations that hypertext could be made available to a large audience of writers and readers. On the other hand, the principle of hypertext has been implicit in computer programming for much longer. Hypertext is the interactive interconnection of a set of symbolic elements, and many kinds of computer programs (databases, simulation programs, even programs for artificial intelligence) are special cases of that principle. Hypertext shows how programming and conventional prose writing can combine in the space provided by the computer. It puts at the disposal of writers data structures (trees and networks) that have been used for decades by programmers. Conversely, it makes us realize that the programmer's data structures are formalized versions of the textual strategies that writers have exploited for centuries.

At any one moment the network holds a vast text of interrelated writings—the intersection of thousands of messages on hundreds of topics. It is a hypertext that no one reader can hope to encompass, one that changes moment by moment as messages are added and deleted.

Important anticipations of hypertext can be found in the computerized communications networks, such as ARPANET or BITNET, put in place in the 1960s and 1970s. Such a network constitutes the physical embodiment of hypertext. Each element or *node* in the network is a computer installation, while the connections among these elements are cables and microwave and satellite links. Each computer node serves dozens or hundreds of individual subscribers, and these subscribers both produce and read messages created by others within their computing facility, around the nation, or around the world. Some messages travel a single path through the communications links until they reach their marked destination, while general messages spread out to all the elements in the net. At any one moment the network holds a vast text of interrelated writings—the intersection of thousands of messages on hundreds of topics. It is a hypertext that no one reader can hope to encompass, one that changes moment by moment as messages are added and deleted.

Subscribers use these networks both for personal mail and to conduct ongoing discussions in so-called "newsgroups." When one subscriber in a newsgroup "publishes" a message, it travels to all the dozens or hundreds of others who belong to that group. The message may elicit responses, which in turn travel back and forth and spawn further responses. The prose of these messages is almost as casual as conversation, precisely because publication in this medium is both easy and almost unrestricted. The transition from reader to writer is completely natural. The reader of one message can with a few keystrokes send off a reply. Readers may even incorporate part of the original message in the reply, blurring the distinction between their own text and the text to which they are responding. There is also little respect for the conventions of the prior medium of print. Subscribers often type newspaper articles or excerpts from books into their replies without concern for copyright. The notion of copyright seems faintly absurd, since their messages are copied and relayed automatically hundreds of times in a matter of hours.

Writing for such a network is by nature topographical: relatively small units of prose are sent and received. The medium itself encourages brevity, since two correspondents can send and receive several messages in one day. And the addresses of the messages provide a primitive system of links. To reply to a given message is to link your text to the earlier one, and both message and reply may then circulate for days around the network provoking other responses. No user is bound to read or reply to anything; instead, any message can refer to any other or ignore all previous messages and strike out in a new direction. A communications network is therefore a hypertext in which no one writer or reader has substantial control, and because no one has control, no one has substantial responsibility. The situation is different for hypertext systems for microcomputers, where there is one author and one reader. There the twin issues of control and responsibility are paramount.

■ WRITERS AND READERS OF HYPERTEXT

When we receive a written or typed letter, we hold in our own hands the paper that the sender also has handled. We see and touch the inkmarks that he or she has made. With electronic mail we receive bits of information that correspond to the tapping of keys on the writer's keyboard. We read this information as patches of light on our computer screen, and we touch nothing that the writer has touched. Like all other kinds of writing, electronic writing is an act of postponement or deferral. As writers, we defer our words by setting them down on a writing surface for later reading by ourselves or by others. The reader's task is to reactivate the words on the page and to devise for them a new context, which may be close to or far removed from the author's original context. There is always a gulf between author and reader, a gap that the technique of writing first creates and then mediates. In one sense the computer opens a particularly wide gap because of the abstract nature of electronic technology. On the other hand, the author has a unique opportunity to control the procedure of reading, because he or she can program restrictions into the text itself.

Computer-assisted instruction, for example, is nothing other than a hypertext in which the author has restricted the ways in which the student/reader

can proceed. In typical computer-assisted instruction the program poses a question and awaits an answer from the student. If the student gives the correct answer, the program may present another question. If the student's answer is wrong, the program may explain the student's error. If the student makes the same error repeatedly, the program may present a review of the point that the student has failed to grasp. In most cases, these questions and explanations are texts that the teacher/programmer has composed and stored in advance. However, good programming can make these simple programs seem uncannily clever in replying to the student. In fact such a program takes on a persona created for it by the teacher/programmer, as it transfers the teacher's words into the new context of the student's learning session. In general, the reader of an electronic text is made aware of the author's simultaneous presence in and absence from the text, because the reader is constantly confronting structural choices established by the author. If the program allows the reader to make changes in the text or to add new connections (as some hypertext systems do), then the game becomes still more complex. As readers we become our own authors, determining the structure of the text for the next reader, or perhaps for ourselves in our next reading.

As readers we become our own authors, determining the structure of the text for the next reader, or perhaps for ourselves in our next reading.

Electronic text is the first text in which the elements of meaning, of structure, and of visual display are fundamentally stable. Unlike the printing press or the medieval codex, the computer does not require that any aspect of writing be determined in advance for the whole life of a text. This restlessness is inherent in a technology that records information by collecting for fractions of a second evanescent electrons at tiny junctions of silicon and metal. All information, all data, in the computer world is a kind of controlled movement, and so the natural inclination of computer writing is to change, to grow, and finally to disappear. Nor is it surprising that these constant motions place electronic writing in a kaleidoscope of relationships with the earlier technologies of typewriting, printing, and handwriting.

■ REFERENCES

Balkovich, E., Lerman, S., and Parmelee, R.P. (1985). Computing in higher education: The Athena Project. *Computer,* 18 (10), 112–125.

Brand, Stewart. (1987). The media lab: Inventing the future at M.I.T. New York: Penguin Books.

Bush, Vannevar. (1945). As we may think. *Atlantic Monthly,* 176 (1), 101–108.

Conklin, J. (1987). Hypertext: An introduction and survey. *I.E.E.E. Computer,* 20 (9), 17–41.

Joyce, Michael. (1988). Siren shapes: Exploratory and constructive hypertexts. *Academic Computing,* 3 (4), 10–14, 37–42.

Nelson, Ted H. (1974). *Dream machines.* Theodor H. Nelson.

Nelson, Ted H. (1984). *Literary machines.* Theodor H. Nelson.

Ong, Walter J. (1958). *Ramus, method, and the decay of dialogue: From the art of discourse to the art of reason.* Cambridge, MA: Harvard University Press.

Peers, E. Allison (Trans.). (1972). *Complete works of St. Teresa of Jesus.* (Vols. 1–3). London: Sheed and Ward.

Smith, John B., and Weiss, Stephen F. (Eds.). (1988). Hypertext [Special Issue]. *Communications of the ACM,* 31 (7).

Yankelovich, Nicole, Haan, Bernard J., Meyrowitz, Norman K., and Drucker, Steven M. (1988). Intermedia: the concept and the construction of a seamless information environment. *Computer,* 21 (1), 81–96.

John F. Baker

Electronic Art Book . . . For One Read Only

One of the more unusual book concepts to come our way was shown in rough form recently at the ABA convention and will be available this month to a very limited number of buyers. And even those buyers will not be able to read it for very long.

Enough of the mystery. The work in question is called *Agrippa (A Book of the Dead)*. It is the collaborative effort of Vancouver-based science fiction "cyberpunk" writer William Gibson and New York artist Dennis Ashbaugh, and published by Kevin Begos Jr., Manhattan publisher of limited edition art books. The unique element is that, at its heart, *Agrippa* is an electronic book programmed to disappear as soon as it is read.

At the center of *Agrippa,* which is housed in an elaborate binding that looks as if it has been much worn by time and burned in the bargain, is a computer disc that can be played on IBM or Apple machines. This contains Gibson's text, a poetic effusion about his father, who died when he was very young. It is only the length of a short story, and takes about 15 minutes to scroll by. But as it does so, the text disappears, never to be retrieved. It has been specially encrypted with a program that destroys it even as it is being read. Related etchings by Ashbaugh of genetic codes, printed in the book housing the disc, have been done in special inks that mutate when exposed to the light, so that they subtly change over time, appearing and disappearing. The whole creation is thus in the process of alteration, like human perception and memory.

"This isn't really like me," says Begos. "I hate computers. But I have to say that there are very exciting elements to electronic publishing, and I wanted to take a look at the medium and what it means to publishing. I guess I see a disappearing book as a sort of satire on collecting."

Gibson—although a kind of guru to countless computer hackers and nerds with such books as *Neuromancer (*Ace*), Count Zero* (Ace) and *Mona Lisa Overdrive* (Bantam)—confesses that he is not technologically very adept. "When they meet me, my fans are always disappointed by my lack of expertise," he told *Publishers Weekly.* "But then they were never my target audience." As for the *Agrippa* project, "it's hermetic and willfully eccentric. It seems pointless, but it may lead somewhere." (His next venture into electronics is with his

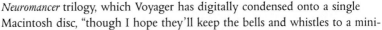
Neuromancer trilogy, which Voyager has digitally condensed onto a single Macintosh disc, "though I hope they'll keep the bells and whistles to a minimum. I'm just a writer, though I seem to be participating actively in the end of print!")

It is only the length of a short story, and takes about 15 minutes to scroll by. But as it does so, the text disappears, never to be retrieved.

Gibson and Begos both scoff at the notion, offered in some published reports and as a rumor making the hacker rounds, that their creation is a kind of computer virus that will create havoc in the computers on which it plays. "Gibson only got a computer a couple of years ago," says Begos. "He couldn't write a computer program to save his life."

Begos, who is creating only 455 copies of *Agrippa*, 95 special editions at $1500 each and 350 limited editions at $450, expects his sales to be mostly to museums and computer freaks anxious to see if they can break the encrypting code and capture Gibson's story permanently. He is making one daring experiment in broad-scale publishing, however—once again of an entirely new kind. At a date to be announced, probably some time in October, Gibson's text will be given a one-time fiberoptic "transmission" via modem, which could theoretically be picked up on millions of computer bulletin boards around the world. Even then, if all goes well, its appearance will be evanescent.

Why *Agrippa*? It turns out that this is the brand name of a photograph album put out by Kodak in Gibson's father's youth, in which he placed family pictures the author discovered on a recent pilgrimage to his childhood home in Virginia.

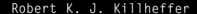

Robert K. J. Killheffer

The Shape of Books to Come:
A collaborative book(?)
challenges ideas about
the immortality of art

When we think about art and literature, we often think of huge granite and marble libraries and vast museums like the Metropolitan or the Louvre. We tend to place high emphasis on the permanence of these twin pillars of our culture. Libraries spend millions maintaining their collections, and museums likewise on restoration and cleaning.

But one of the functions of art and literature is to challenge our assumptions. Now cyberpunk guru William Gibson and artist Dennis Ashbaugh have collaborated on *Agrippa: A Book of the Dead,* an elaborately conceived marriage of antique bookcraft and modern computer technology that may alter our conceptions of the immortality of artworks.

Agrippa was published last September by art-book publisher Kevin Begos, Jr. A 95-copy edition costs $1,500. (The ten deluxe copies go for $7,500 each, while a simpler 350-copy edition is priced at $450 each.) At its heart is a diskette containing the text of Gibson's story. Ashbaugh created a weighty, worn-looking book to house the disk, illustrated with his copperplate engravings. The oversized book's pages feature an alphabetic representation of a strand of DNA—a continuous series of the letters A, C, G, and T, standing for the four basic building blocks of DNA: adenine, cytosine, guanine, and thymine.

Sounds interesting, you say, but what's so special? There's a catch: An encryption program on disk devours the text as you read it, so you can only read it once. And Ashbaugh's etchings mutate when exposed to light—some of the ink vanishes while other images appear. So for all the care that went into its production, *Agrippa* will not "survive" a single reading intact.

Reactions to this audacious project have ranged from excitement to outrage. Begos says at least one person insisted, "It's not a book," but most have reacted with "a combination of admiration and discomfort." Begos likes the idea of challenging people's perceptions: "Our assumptions about books and bookmaking are in some ways like all our romantic ideas about life," and therefore worth questioning.

Ashbaugh, somewhat facetiously, calls *Agrippa* "the most important book since the Gutenberg Bible." That, he admits, may be overstatement, but it *has* been a long time since any project challenged bookmaking concepts so strongly. Electronic books have been threatening to force this sort of reevaluation for years, and perhaps now, with *Agrippa* and the recent release of the Sony "Bookman," they will finally do so. But *Agrippa* challenges perceptions on a number of levels. The book feels like an ancient volume: It's oversized, to be read at a lectern not on the subway; its pages are heavy rag, its binding handsewn, and its page design reminiscent of the earliest printed books. Yet the text is not words but DNA code, and Ashbaugh's "book" is actually a container for the book of the future, a floppy diskette. In fact, *Agrippa* is more art object than book—the arbitrary division between art and literature is wholly erased.

One further twist was added to the *Agrippa* project on December 9 when the text of Gibson's story was broadcast via modem to viewing sites across the country and in Japan and Germany. Venues varied from the turn-of-the-century charm of the Americas Society in New York to a room in the University of Tallahassee's art department. Such an event is an open invitation to computer hackers to tap in and acquire Gibson's story free, but *Agrippa*'s makers don't see that as a draw-back. As Ashbaugh puts it, "They only get the text." They miss all the context, which is a vital part of the impact of *Agrippa*. And that hijacked text will still contain the encryption program, which few computer pirates will be able to defeat. Says Begos, "You'd have to hit it with a lot of brute mathematical force. Anyone with access to a supercomputer would have a chance, but you couldn't do it with a PC."

Where will it all lead? No one can say, least of all Begos, Ashbaugh, and Gibson. But *Agrippa* raises issues about the shape of books to come, issues we'll all be confronting, like it or not, in the very near future.

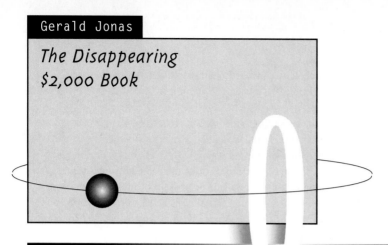

Gerald Jonas

The Disappearing $2,000 Book

Once upon a time storytellers perpetuated the tales of the tribe by memorizing them. With the invention of books, memory became less important: if you forgot something, you could look it up. Then came the computer; to access its electronic memory, all you had to remember was which key to press. Now this evolution has come full circle with a story-on-a-disk that destroys itself as you read it, leaving nothing but the memory of words glimpsed briefly on a computer screen.

The author of the self-sabotaging story is William Gibson, whose 1984 novel *Neuromancer* gave birth to the terms "cyberpunk" and "cyberspace." Cyberpunk is science fiction with an attitude; it imagines a future in which people use the latest technology to do nasty things to one another. Mr. Gibson's characters, who spend the better part of their lives literally plugged into supercomputers, experience electronic data-flow as sensory input; they live in a "consensual hallucination" that Mr. Gibson has dubbed cyberspace.

His ambivalence about the brave new world of the future is exemplified in the booby-trapped art book that Mr. Gibson has created along with the painter Dennis Ashbaugh and the publisher Kevin Begos Jr. The entire project—entitled *Agrippa (A Book of the Dead)*—is designed to challenge conventional notions about books and art while extracting money from collectors of both.

The deluxe edition of *Agrippa* comes in a 16-by-21½-inch metal mesh case sheathed in Kevlar, the polymer that bulletproof vests are made of. Sheltered inside the case is a book of 93 rag-paper pages bound in singed and stained linen that appears to have survived a fire. The last 60 pages have been fused together to form a block; cut into the block is a four-inch square that holds a computer disk; encrypted on this disk is the text of *Agrippa (A Book of the Dead)*, a short story by Mr. Gibson. The encryption process entails a computer "virus" programmed by a team of anonymous hackers. Because of the virus, the story cannot be viewed normally on a computer screen or printed out at will. The first time the disk is inserted in a computer, the words of the story begin scrolling up the screen at a preset speed as if the computer and not the reader were scanning the text. The first "reading" is also the last. As the sentences scroll by, the virus is silently corrupting all the data on the disk. When the last word vanishes from the screen, the disk is no longer usable.

The text of Mr. Gibson's story appears nowhere in the book itself. Thirty-two pages contain long sequences of the letters G, A, T, C. This is another kind of code; the letters represent the four building blocks of the DNA double-helix molecule, and the sequences were excerpted from real human genetic material. Seven pages of the book are devoted to copperplate etchings—brownish blobs on greenish backgrounds—by Mr. Ashbaugh. These were inspired by laboratory-generated images of human genetic material, known as "gene scans" or "DNA footprints." Six of the etchings have been overprinted with early 20th-century advertisements for gadgets like telephones and cameras; a special ink was used so that these reproductions literally wipe off the page at the slightest touch.

Mr. Ashbaugh's etchings remain, although buyers of *Agrippa* are assured that the plates used to make these images will be destroyed or defaced as soon as the 95th impression is pulled. Only 95 copies of *Agrippa* are being offered, at $2,000 apiece, to serious collectors.

The challenge for collectors who buy *Agrippa* is how to protect their investment while savoring the object. To read Mr. Gibson's story is to destroy it. Even turning the pages of the book to look at the pictures is to risk altering the book irreversibly. Collectors will not be entirely unfamiliar with this problem, says Mr. Begos, who once published books under the auspices of the Limited Editions Club and who now works out of 61 East Eighth Street, Box 146, New York, N.Y. 10003. The erasable ink and the self-erasing story are extreme cases, but according to Mr. Begos, collectors rarely open their fine art books for fear of damaging the expensive goods. "If you pay thousands of dollars for a limited edition, you're not likely to curl up in bed with it," he said.

Dennis Ashbaugh, who was an admirer of Mr. Gibson's science fiction before they met, relishes the sense of discomfort that *Agrippa* induces in book lovers and art lovers alike. He found that working with Mr. Gibson confirmed his own discomfort with purely abstract paintings. "I was completely bored with the paintings I was doing," Mr. Ashbaugh said. "They had nothing to do with being alive today. I'm keen on making paintings that exist maybe 15 minutes into the future."

When *Agrippa (A Book of the Dead)* was exhibited in May at the Center for Book Arts on lower Broadway in Manhattan, Marshall Blonsky, who teaches literary theory at New York University and the New School, gave a lecture on analyzing the text, which he had received in readable form only six hours earlier. After making apologies for the necessarily sketchy nature of his remarks, Mr. Blonsky went on to link the *Agrippa* project to the work of "at least two writers, Maurice Blanchot, in particular 'The Absence of the Book,' and Stéphane Mallarmé," the 19th-century poet whose obsessions presaged "the 1960's-70's runaway adventure first called semiology and then semiotics and deconstruction. . . . The collaborators in *Agrippa* are responding to a historical condition of language, a modern skepticism about it."

Asked to comment on this, Mr Gibson said (by telephone from his home in Vancouver, British Columbia), "Honest to God, these academics who think it's all some sort of big-time French philosophy—that's a scam. Those guys worship Jerry Lewis, they get our pop culture all wrong." Although Mr. Gibson did a cameo appearance as the godfather of cyberspace on the first epsiode of the television series *Wild Palms,* he disclaims any special expertise in computers or virtual reality. He wrote *Neuromancer* on a 1927 Hermes portable typewriter; he got his notion of cyberspace from watching the body language of children playing video games in an arcade.

Nowadays Mr. Gibson writes on a Macintosh SE30 computer; his newest novel, *Virtual Light,* has just been published. He lives with his wife, Deborah, and their two children, Claire, 10, and Graeme, 15, in a cedar-shingled house overlooking Vancouver harbor. Although the self-destroying encryption of the *Agrippa* disk was supposed to be unbreakable, Mr Gibson was not at all surprised to learn that the international legion of computer hackers had broken the code within a few days of its appearance and that the full text had been posted on the network of electronic bulletin boards that function as primitive precursors to Mr. Gibson's imagined cyberspace. (This global network, which includes the Whole Earth 'Lectronic Link, or WELL, on the West Coast, and the East Coast Hang Out, or ECHO, based in New York, as well as the world-spanning Internet, is the model for the Clinton Administration's proposed "information superhighway.")

Fans of Mr. Gibson's science fiction who read *Agrippa* on their computer screens may be disappointed to find that it bears no resemblance to the hopped-up style and frenetically paced action of his cyberpunk novels. The self-destroying story turns out to be a sweetly sentimental prose poem about the fragility of memory, triggered by Mr. Gibson's discovery of his father's old photograph album (a string-bound, loose-leaf album sold by Kodak in the early 1920's under the name Agrippa). Only one section, set in the "old bus station" in Mr. Gibson's hometown of Wytheville, Va., refers even tangentially to the world of *Neuromancer.*

When the colored restroom
was no longer required
they knocked open the cinderblock
and extended the magazine rack
to new dimensions,
a cool fluorescent cave of dreams
smelling faintly and forever of disinfectant . . .
There it was I was marked out as a writer
                of science fiction,
having discovered in that alcove
copies of certain magazines
esoteric and precious.

Peter Schwenger

Agrippa, Or,
The Apocalyptic Book

All techniques meant to
unleash forces are techniques
of disappearance.

—Paul Virilio

lack box recovered from some unspecified disaster, the massive case opens to reveal the textures of decay and age. Yellowed newspaper, rusty honeycombing, fog-colored cerement enveloping a pale book. On the book's cover, a burned-in title: *Agrippa (A Book of the Dead)*. Within it, page after page printed with cryptic letters.

TGTGG
CCATA
AATAT
TACGA
GTTTG

These are the combinatory possibilities of genetic codes, as re-coded by scientists. The pages are singed at their edges; more fragments of old newspaper are interspersed. And at intervals, engravings by New York artist Dennis Ashbaugh reproduce the commercial subjects of a previous generation, subjects that will later acquire a fuller meaning: a telephone ad ("Tell Daddy we miss him"), a diagram for the assembly of a pistol, an advertised magnesium gun "for nighttime photography." Black patches like burns smudge these images. With exposure to light the images gradually fade; the black patches reveal themselves to be the rhythmic chains of the DNA molecule as captured in microphotography). Embedded in the last pages of the book is a computer disk containing a text by cyberpunk novelist William Gibson. When activated, it runs once; then a built-in computer virus destroys the text, leaving a blank disk.

No matter, for now, what the evanescent content of that disk may be. Its specific content is less important than the fact of its disappearance. In a jibe at the art world's commercialism, publisher Kevin Begos, Jr., suggested to Ashbaugh that "what we should do is put out an art book on computer that vanishes." Ashbaugh took him seriously, took him further; Gibson was enlisted shortly after. For all its complex resonances as an object, then, *Agrippa* is based on this one idea: a book disappears.

The idea has precedents. Maurice Blanchot's essay on "The Absence of the Book" argues from writerly experience that a work always becomes something other than what it is intended to be—what it is intended to be being, of course, a book. But the book (icon of law, presence, textual-cultural wholeness) is always betrayed by what Blanchot calls "the disaster." This disaster has to do with the necessary falling short of a work's concept at the same time that an unexpected otherness beyond the work is evoked. A book never real-

Agrippa is based on this one idea: a book disappears.

izes its desired full presence; its realization occurs only and paradoxically through absence—"the prior deterioration of the book, the game of dissidence it plays with reference to the space in which it is inscribed; the preliminary dying of the book."[1] In the end the original concept, and even the very idea of "concept" must be exploded, Blanchot argues, citing Mallarmé's curious statement that "there is no explosion but a book."

Mallarmé also said that "the world exists in order to be put into a book." And he made this book—Le Livre— the ongoing preoccupation and project of his last twenty years, a project which came to nothing. Le Livre never appeared; its absence may have been the very point of it. The book's nonappearance is linked to the disappearance of the world, a crucial component of Mallarmé's art—so Sartre argues.

Meaning is a second silence deep within silence; it is the negation of the world's status as a thing. This ever unspoken meaning, which would disappear if one ever attempted to speak it . . . is quite simply the absence *of certain objects. What is involved here is not the mere absence of a particular being but a "resonant disappearance."*[2]

Sartre is here quoting Mallarmé's "disparition vibratoire," which was for him the condition of any possible meaning or truth. Speaking of his own writing, Mallarmé said that "whatever truth emerged in the process did so with the loss of an impression which, after flaring up for a brief instant, burned itself out."[3]

Kevin Begos has acknowledged the influence of both Mallarmé's book and Blanchot's "Absence of the Book." One more book was needed to catalyze *Agrippa*, however—an old photograph album discovered by Gibson on a trip back to his home town of Wytheville, Virginia. His computerized text reproduces its commercial title page:

ALBUMS
C. A. AGRIPPA
Order extra leaves by letter and name

The print is dim, scrawled over with something indecipherable. The opening words of Gibson's text describe the opening of the album:

I hesitated
before untying the bow
that bound the book together
A Kodak album of time-harmed
black construction paper

These words describing a hesitation themselves hesitate before they begin scrolling past. Then, one by one, the old photographs are rendered in words, each with its caption—though these captions are sometimes indecipherable, their obscurity described along with the rest of the book's "time-harmed" textures. This electronic book, book of the future, evokes through its words the ghost of antiquated pages.

That this ghostly book is a photo album means that it is already a book of the dead.

That this ghostly book is a photo album means that it is already a book of the dead. In the photographs a whole world of people and objects is depicted in intense specificity: shadows cast over the brim of straw hats, grass that needs cutting, electric wires strung over street intersections. Yet all these things fall into a Mallarméan absence. Viewing a photograph, Roland Barthes says, "I shudder . . .*over a catastrophe which has already occurred.* Whether or not the subject is already dead, every photograph is this catastrophe."[4] The black box of the camera is a temporal mechanism; Gibson speaks of the fall of the shutter as dividing time.

The description of the album's discovery is followed by the recollection of an earlier discovery by Gibson: As a boy he opened a drawer to find another mechanism of disappearance, his father's pistol. He took it out of the drawer and it unexpectedly discharged; when he dropped it, it went off again. Beyond the biographical fact, there may be a link here to another pair of explosions half a world away: Gibson's father worked on the Manhattan Project. Another possible disappearance of the world is adumbrated, not literary but literal; the singed, disastrous look of the black box's contents takes on a new significance. This "relic from the future," as Begos has called it, replicates a typical pattern of nuclear-war fiction. Relic of a past event which is yet to take place in the future, the nuclear narrative is transmitted backward to us in the present, which is that future's past. The paradoxes shuttle and blur into "time no more," as announced by the angel of the apocalypse; and that "no more" is echoed in the last resonances of a disappearing world.

The men who moved the world closer to disappearance have, most of them, themselves disappeared; Gibson's father died when his son was six. To the degree that *Agrippa* is a memoir of Gibson's father, its irreversible passing is like his life, or any life. We can reread a human life only in memory. We can, of course, *write* of a human life, write "in memory of." When we do, we inhabit a paradoxical space, according to Jacques Derrida:

[D]oes the expression "in memory of" mean that the name is "in" our memory—supposedly a living capacity to recall images or signs from the past, etc.? Or that the name is in itself, out there somewhere, like a sign or symbol, a monument, epitaph, stele or tomb, a memorandum, aide-mémoire, a memento, an exterior auxiliary set up "in memory of"? Both, no doubt; and here lies the ambiguity of memory, the contamination which troubles us, troubles memory and the meaning of "memory."[5]

Following a distinction in Hegel, Derrida suggests that there are two kinds of memory: mechanical memorization (*Gedächtnis*), associated with writing, and interiorized recollection (*Erinnerung*), associated with mourning. For Derrida, these are at odds with each other: "[T]he inscription of memory [is] an effacement of interiorizing recollection, of the 'living remembrancing.' "[6] Or, as Paul de Man puts it, art "*materially* inscribes, and thus forever forgets, its ideal content."[7] But the process can be reversed: writing that disappears can make another kind of memory appear. This is an *un*forgetting, in Heidegger's terms—the return from Lethe—*aletheia* or truth, a version akin to Mallarmé's truth. To lose the text commemorating a loss is not, then, to redouble loss; it is to move away from the loss that is always inherent in memory's textual mechanism. It is once again to take into one's keeping the memory that is interiorized recollection.

What I have just said may give the impression that Gibson's text is exclusively past-bound, father-oriented, in one way or another an act of mourning. This is not so. At a certain point in the album, and in his own book, the photographed small-town streets which are his father's memories fuse with Gibson's own memories. He then detaches himself from those past streets, remembers the process of forgetting them. By way of the draft board office on the town's main street, Gibson recalls his one-way trip to the Canadian border; when he crosses that border, time is divided as if by a shutter. He describes the unfamiliar feel, the texture, of his first days in Toronto. Finally, a leap into an even stranger future, so remote from these that it might be a scene from one of Gibson's own novels. In a Far Eastern city, a typhoon speeds "horizontal rain" at the speaker's face. Yet this destructive future elicits neither mourning nor fear. In the last words to scroll by, the speaker is "laughing in the mechanism."

What mechanism? The word "mechanism" is repeated at intervals in *Agrippa*, and the idea is implicit throughout it.

—The camera is a mechanism for dividing time.

—The gun, when it discharges, enforces in the silence that follows an "awareness of the mechanism."

—Behind the gun, the bomb—and a mechanism extending beyond the bomb casing to the Manhattan Project and the forces that produced it.

—On a still night in Wytheville, the boy can hear the clicking as traffic lights change a block away, and this too is described as an awareness of the mechanism. How far away does the mechanism extend?

—The photograph album is referred to as a mechanism; any book is a mechanism.

—Language is a mechanism; for Jacques Lacan, it is the mechanism we are born into, the set of the structuring principles of our lives.

—An affinity between chains of signifiers and chromosomal chains. If we are born into the mechanism of language, we are born *out of* a genetic mechanism—out of which we cannot move, for it composes us.

—The mechanisms of our genes and our nervous systems, insofar as they are mechanisms, are linked to those of the computer in a cybernetic field.

When the disk has run its course, everything in the text—book, camera, gun, explosion, father, town, time, memory—is encrypted into a mechanized code much like that on Ashbaugh's pages, before it contorts and vanishes. Always, and in all its versions, the mechanism is involved with absence and its ultimate end is disappearance.

That disappearance is apocalyptic: I am using the word not only in its sense of overwhelming destruction, but also in its original Greek sense of revelation. The last book of the Bible has forever linked destruction with revelation—as Blanchot does, as Mallarmé does. Moreover, it does so repeatedly through a *book*. The Book of the Apocalypse describes the opening of a book; that opening, seal by seal, unleashes a series of terrible endings. The Last Judgment is initiated when the Book of the Dead is opened. And finally the sky disappears "as a scroll when it is rolled together." Microcosmic apocalypse, *Agrippa* too is destroyed by being opened, its images fading, its text scrolling past us into irreversible emptiness. But if there can be no rereading, the reading we have finished may not be finished with us. After the final destruction of heaven and earth in the Bible a new heaven and earth come to pass; and something like this comes to pass in reading, even if what is read can never be read again. Blanchot has said that writing is "the opaque, empty opening into that which is when there is no more world, when there is no world yet."[8] He hovers here between "no more" and "not yet," between loss and potential: the emptiness is apocalyptic, in both its senses. Through the necessary destruction of the text (all texts), something comes to pass. Though the question of what comes to pass is ultimately beyond us, the question of *how* it comes to pass is not.

A book, says Blanchot, is "a ruse by which writing goes towards *the absence of the book*."[9] The ruse in *Agrippa,* as in other books, has to do with framing. The final disappearance of *Agrippa* takes place within multiple frames, some literal, some literary: the black box, the corroded coffin in which the shrouded book is laid; the book's cover and title; the time-bound pages of newspaper, commercial images, genetic codes; the embedded disk of magnetic code; the code of language; rhythm and recurrence—all that I have articulated of what this work articulates, and more. All of these are mechanisms which, rightly combined, explode into revelation, the immanence of something *beyond*. But in the revelation of what lies between or beyond these framing elements, they are annihilated. For what is apprehended is exactly what is other than these separate elements, a sum that exceeds these parts. We move

4:/HyperText 244

In the very act of disappearing, then, Agrippa makes something appear.

toward the famous conclusion of Wittgenstein's *Tractatus*—a tautology that is saved from the "intense inane" by being itself framed, the product of a certain process in time. At the end of the process that is *Agrippa* we are left not merely with emptiness, but with our awareness of that process both in and beyond the mechanism. Knowing that there *has been* a process in time, the blank page (as in Isak Dinesen's tale) may be the most eloquent text. "The most beautiful and perfect book in the world," says Ulises Carrión, "is a book with only blank pages, in the same way that the most complete language is that which lies beyond all that the words of man can say."[10] In the very act of disappearing, then, *Agrippa* makes something appear.

■ NOTES

This work was supported by the Social Sciences and Humanities Research Council of Canada. Special thanks to Veronica Hollinger and Sasha Sergejewski.

1. Maurice Blanchot, "The Absence of the Book," in *The Gaze of Orpheus and Other Literary Essays,* ed. P. Adams Sitney, trans. Lydia Davis (Barrytown, NY, 1981), 151.

2. Jean-Paul Sartre, *Mallarmé, or the Poet of Nothingness,* trans. Ernest Sturm (University Park, PA, 1988), 140.

3. Letter from Mallarmé to Eugène Lefébvre, 17 May 1867, in *Stéphane Mallarmé: Correspondance, 1862–1871,* ed. Henri Mondor (Paris, 1959), 245–46.

4. Roland Barthes, *Camera Lucida: Reflections on Photography,* trans. Richard Howard (New York, 1981), 96.

5. Jacques Derrida, *Mémoires: For Paul de Man,* trans. Cecile Lindsay, Jonathan Culler, and Eduardo Cadava (New York, 1986), 50.

6. Ibid., 56.

7. Paul de Man, "Sign and Symbol in Hegel's *Aesthetics,*" *Critical Inquiry* 8 (1982): 773; cited in Derrida, *Mémoires,* 67.

8. Maurice Blanchot, *The Space of Literature,* trans. Ann Smock (Lincoln, NE, 1982), 33.

9. Blanchot, "Absence of the Book," 147.

10. Ulises Carrión, quoted in *Artists' Books: A Critical Anthology and Sourcebook,* ed. Joan Lyons and Gibbs M. Smith (Rochester, 1985), 38.

Chapter 4

Questions and Suggestions for Further Study on the Net/WWW

■ Q U E S T I O N S   B A S E D   O N   T H E   R E A D I N G S :

1. What is the significance of beginning the dinner discussion between Neil Postman and Camille Paglia with two passages as "a blessing" from the Bible? (Did you notice that the meal is punctuated with fish courses?) Map out the step-by-step images and analogies that Paglia uses as she proceeds during the opening pages of the discussion. How does Postman respond to these images? (Perhaps you might want to concentrate first on the adver-tisement for Hebrew National Frankfurters and then work your way back.) Trace how Postman and Paglia both weave in and out of the discussion and how, occasionally, Postman will say, "Camille, I think these [your] observations support my argument" about "secularization." And then Paglia talks about "repaganization." What's the difference? What does Paglia mean by the logocentric and Apollonian side of Western culture and its Dionysian side? Paglia points to her agreement with Postman at the very end ("enlightened repression of the children"), but what leads to their dif-ferences (Postman's favoring books and Paglia's favoring all media includ-ing books)? How do you respond to Paglia's attitude that terrible things happen to human beings and we just have to learn to live with them? Would you charge her with political quietism (indifference to suffering) when she makes this kind of statement?

2. When you wake up in the morning or arrive home, do you turn on the television right away? Do you do your homework with the television on? With music blasting? With TV on and music blasting?

3. Birkerts's article is actually chapter 8 in his book *The Gutenberg Elegies: The Fate of Reading in an Electronic Age.* How does the title of the book parallel the opening anecdote about the professor selling his books and getting out of the profession of teaching? What does *elegy* mean? List and discuss what Birkerts refers to as the "morbid symptoms" of the proto-electronic age. Is Birkerts simply caught up with the problem of not changing with the times? Or is he making another point by lamenting the loss of literate book culture? What similarities do you see between Neil Postman and Birkerts? Are they both neo-Luddites? (If you do not know what the word *Luddite* means, then find out what you can about it.) Birkerts, reflecting on the shift from a literate, bookreading culture to an electronic one, says: "I find these portents of change depressing, but also exhilarating—at least to

speculate about." What does Birkerts mean by "depressing" *and* "exhilarating"? (In thinking about this question, you might want to examine the meaning of *spasm* in the glossary, Appendix B.)

4. There is a tremendous amount of talk about the end of books in these readings and elsewhere. Do you really think that books will become obsolete, things of the past? Are writers who speculate about the end/death of books or novels only exaggerating? Or do they mean something else in terms of the "end" of books (or novels)?

5. At this point how would you explain to someone what hypertext is? When you read about hypertext, you will find that many of its advocates talk about it as liberating, emancipating, life improving. How would a movement from linear prose to a weblike, rhizomelike prose be liberating? Would you say that hypertext is liberating? (What could *liberating* mean?) Or is hypertext so much hype?

6. When you "write" (i.e., compose an essay for class), do you use pencils or pens to write on paper, do you use a typewriter, use a computer? Have you ever written on a computer using not a word-processing program but a hypercard program or a hypertext program? If so, how would you explain the differences between or among writing with pencils/pens on paper through and up to writing hypertexts? If you have not had a chance to write hypertexts, try to find someone on campus who has a program like *StorySpace* and see if you can try it out. (See if your campus writing center has such a writing program.)

7. The articles on Gibson's *Agrippa* are generally arranged in order of complexity, with the article by Schwenger the most difficult for a simple reason—it attempts to develop the paradox (always very abstract) of life (revelation) in death: the story/poem encrypted with the four codes of DNA (A, C, G, T) in *Agrippa* is revelation and yet disappearance as the virus in the program destroys the encrypted text before the great majority of us can decode it. (Life itself has built into it the death principle, which is a revelation.) The various paradoxes that are generated out of (the death of) this book and its images are multiple. (Another is: remembering is forgetting!)

In the brief introduction to this section, I ended (rebegan!) with the death of death leading to life. Now that you have read about Gibson's *Agrippa,* what could I possibly have meant by such a statement? Does the DNA, or an understanding of it, somehow suggest an answer? Does the DNA somehow suggest what might be meant by the end/death of the book, its metastasizing into a hypertext? Is this what is happening to books—are they metaphorically developing cancer cells that grow wildly in different direction? Though metastatis causes death, is it also a form of (other) life? Continue to play heuristically with these metaphors.

Let's move from image to image, associatively, in yet another way and recall that the dinner discussion between Postman and Paglia began with two biblical quotations; *Agrippa* is also predicated on a biblical quotation. What parallels do you see between the two groups of discussions? How do Gibson and Ashbaugh, who collaborated on *Agrippa,* employ images in the multimedia sense that Paglia talks about and engages in herself? (A rereading of

Schwenger, who teases out some possible associations, might help to think through this question.)

- **FURTHER STUDY ON THE NET/WWW:**

  Make a search for *hypertext* and *hypermedia* on the various search engines such as *WebCrawler* <http://webcrawler.com/>, *Lycos* <http://lycos.cs. cmu.edu/>. (If you need help with this search, see Appendix A.)

  - *The Voice of the Shuttle: Technology of Writing Page:* <http://humanitas. ucsb.edu/shuttle/techwrit.html>. There are pages of links to browse here. Explore the *Research on Hypertext* and *Research on Hypermedia* categories. You will find Vannevar Bush's "As We May Think" (1945) here along with Stuart Moulthrop's "You Say You Want a Revolution?" (about Ted Nelson's Xanadu project). And there is much more.

  - *Useful WWW Sites on Hypertext:* <http://www.humanities.mcmaster.ca/ hypertext.places.htm>. This is the best all-around site I have found: It is filled with numerous links, from hypertext terms to hypertext markup language made simple. Check it out!

  - *Brown University and its Hypertext Projects* (George Landow): <http:// www.stg.brown.edu/projects/hypertext/landow/HTatBrown/ BrownHT.html>. Some of Landow's and his students' webs, such as *The Freud Web, The Religion in English Web,* and *The Victorian Web,* can be found at <http://www.stg.brown.edu/projects/hypertext/landow/ HTatBrown/wwwtrans.html>.

  - *Eastgate Systems Home Page:* <http://www.eastgate.com/>. Eastgate publishes a lot of hypertext works and the hypertext program *StorySpace*. From here you can read about people like Michael Joyce, Stuart Moulthrop, and other hypertext writers, and you can find pointers to other hypertext websites.

  - *Hyperizons: Hypertext Fiction:* <http://www.duke.edu/~mshumate/ hyperfic.html>.

```
Table of Contents
About Hyperizons
What I'm Onto
Some Others Who've Noticed . . .
Link Structure
[INLINE] What's New
Original Hypertext Compositions
Collaborations
General Fiction, individual authors
Science Fiction, individual authors
From Page to Screen
Print Literature Converted to Hypertext
General Fiction
Science Fiction
```

Precursors of Hypertext
Theory and Technique of Hypertext Fiction
Other sites for hypertext fiction and theory
Individual and institutional sites
Class projects

- *The English Server (CMU):* <http://english-www.hss.cmu.edu/>. In the index, locate *Cyber;* then go to *Hypertext* and locate *Newsday-Hypertext* (Joshua Quittner, "Read Any Good Webs Lately?")

- *The Rossetti Archive* <http://jefferson.village.virginia.edu/rossetti/ rossetti.html>. The longer name is *The Complete Writings and Pictures of Dante Gabriel Rossetti: A Hypermedial Research Archive.* You will need the *Mosaic* or preferably the *Netscape* browser to access the site. If you are in literary studies, you will find this site of special interest.

- *The Media and Communications Studies Page:* Much invaluable information about multimedia is located here. Point to: <http://www.aber.ac.uk/~dgc/media.html>.

■ HERE ARE SOME ADDITIONAL ON-LINE NETWORKS (WEBSITES, WITH DISCUSSION LISTS MENTIONED):

- *Paglia:* Paglia has been interviewed by Stewart Brand for *Wired* magazine. If you go to *Wired,* you have to signup for *HotWired,* which is easy to do. Point to: <http://www.hotwired.com/Login/>. When there, simply follow instructions for subscribing, supplying a name and password. Then, if you are using *Lynx* as your browser, point down ↓ to "Overview" and to the right →. Once there point down until you get to "Wired Back Issues" and point right → and you will get a list of all back issues. Now just move down the list until you get to Issue 1.1 and you will see the interview with Paglia, who refers to the dinner discussion with Postman and just goes on from there. (You will find that the discussion is predicated on Postman's having been a student of Marshall McLuhan's and Postman's having said to Paglia that she reminded him of McLuhan!) You can read it or print it out. (For further instructions, see Appendix A. If you are on Mosaic or Netscape, this will be all so much easier.)

- *Postman:* For a speech given to the German Informatics Society, 11 Oct 1990, Stuttgart, entitled analogously to a book of his, *Informing Ourselves to Death,* point to: <http://cec.wustl.edu/~cs142/articles/MISC/ informing_ourselves_to_death--postman>.

- *Gibson:* <http://sfbox.vt.edu:10021/J/jfoley/gibson/gibson.html>. Here you will find a copy of *Agrippa* decoded. (A copy is also available at the Rice Univ. E-Text Archive <gopher://riceinfo.rice.edu/11/Subject/ LitBooks>.) Be careful of downloading a copy because you might download the virus along with the story/poem.   .)>=

- The "Being Digital" Cyberdock <http://www.obs-us.com/obs/english/ books/nn/bdintro.htm>. Take the link "Cyberdock" and then scroll or point down to:

WHAT DO OTHER AUTHORS SAY ABOUT LIVING, READING, WRITING, AND WORKING IN THE ELECTRONIC AGE?

Sven Birkerts: The Gutenberg Elegies—The Fate of Reading in an Electronic Age (fragments)
Kurt Johmann: The Computer Inside You
William J. Mitchell: City of Bits: Space, Place, and the Infobahn [new]
Howard Rheingold's Home Page
Clifford Stoll: Silicon Snake Oil—Second Thoughts on the Information Highway (fragments)

- *Newsgroups* (Usenet): alt.hypertext

- FAQ File for alt.hypertext: <http://www.eit.com/reports/ht93/hypertext. faq.txt>

■ MORE REFERENCES FOR READING AND FOR SURFING THE WEB:

Birkerts, Sven, and Kevin Kelly. "The Electronic Hive: Two Views. 1. Refuse It. 2. Embrace It." *Harper's Magazine* (May 1994): 17–21, 24–25.

Bush, Vannevar. "As We May Think." *Atlantic* 176 (July 1945): 101–108. Online. Voice of the Shuttle. Internet. 22 August 1995. Available: <http://www.csi.uottawa.ca/~dduchier/misc/vbush/as-we-may-think.html>.

Bush, Vannevar. "Memex Revisited." In *Science Is Not Enough*. New York: William Morrow, 1967: 75–101. See if you can find this online.

Bolter, Jay David. *Writing Space: The Computer, Hypertext, and the History of Writing*. Hillsdale, NJ: Lawrence Erlbaum, 1991. (A version of this book is available in hypertext on disk.)

Deemer, Charles. "What Is Hypertext?" 1994. *Charles Deemer's Homepage*. Online. 22 August 1995. Available: <http://www.teleport.com/~cdeemer/essay.html>.

Johnson, Steven. "Repossession: An Electronic Romance." *Lingua Franca* (May/June 1995): 24–33. (An article about Jerome McGann's Rossetti Archive.)

Joyce, Michael. *Of Two Minds: Hypertext Pedagogy and Poetics*. Ann Arbor: University of Michigan Press, 1995.

Katz, Jon. "Return of the Luddites." *Wired* (June 1995): 162–165, 210.

Kelly, Kevin. "Interview with the Luddite [Kirkpatrick Sale]." *Wired* (June 1995): 166–168, 211–214. Online. *HotWired*. Internet. 22 August 1995. Available: <http://vip.hotwired.com/wired/3.06/features/saleskelly.html>.

Landow, George P. *Hypertext: The Convergence of Contemporary Critical Theory and Technology*. Baltimore: The Johns Hopkins University Press, 1992. (A version of this book is available in hypertext format on two disks.)

Lanham, Richard A. *The Electronic Word. Democracy, Technology, and the Arts.* Chicago: University of Chicago Press, 1993. (This is available in hypercard, expanded book format.)

Negroponte, Nicholas. *Being Digital.* New York: Knopf, 1995.

Paglia, Camille. *Sexual Personae: Art and Decadence from Nefertiti to Emily Dickinson.* New York: Vintage, 1991.

Postman, Neil. *Amusing Ourselves to Death: Public Discourse in the Age of Show Business.* New York: Penguin, 1986.

Postman, Neil. *Technopoly: The Surrender of Culture to Technology.* New York: Vintage, 1993.

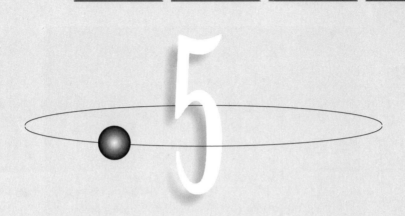

Virtual Libraries

(and Copyright vs. Copyleft):

The narrator of Jorge Luis Borges's short story "The Library of Babel" says: "I affirm that the Library is interminable." I remember not too many years ago being in very large research libraries and seeing rows and rows of card catalogs with hundreds of drawers filled with hundreds of cards on which were typed or even handwritten bibliographical references and call letters. Today in the same libraries where these catalogs used to be, tables and chairs take up much of the space but leave much empty space sparsely filled with a dozen or so computer terminals. To begin my research, all I do is type the name of the book or author or subject matter, execute the request, and wait to see if the library has what I want. (It is not necessary for me to do this *in* the library at all, for I can follow the same procedure from my office or home or wherever I am as long as I have a terminal, a modem, and a telephone.) While checking, I can also query other libraries in the immediate area, or throughout the state, or the country, or the Library of Congress, or the world.

Yes, they carted off those old card catalogs after putting all the references into the database, and then they linked up the databases by way of the World Wide Web (the matrix), and now I have access to all this information, this library that is interminable (in the terminal). I can now reach virtually many of the volumes or articles I previously had to retrieve from the stacks or order through interlibrary loan. I can print them out on my screen and place them in a file in my hard disk. I can scan them. Cut and paste from them. I can delete what I don't want. Just a couple of years ago, our library had about a million books; now it has billions, virtually an indefinite number. (Just a couple of years ago, my study was crammed to the ceiling with tons of books; now many of them are potentially accessible in my hard drive!)

Am I stretching a point to make a point? Perhaps. But in no time at all, this opening statement will not be an exaggeration, but a reality (?)... a Virtuality.

Raymond Kurzweil's three-part article on the future of libraries functions here as a transitional article from the end of books and libraries (Chapter 4 of *CyberReader*) to the beginnings of electronic books and virtual libraries (Chapter 5) and, though he does not mention it, to the Xanadu project itself. What has caused the end of books and libraries is technology, the cycle of which Kurzweil reviews for us. The impact of this technology makes it possible for electronic books to be easily disseminated free of charge on the Net. However, though we might think that books should now be free or at least cheaper, we will have to come to recognize that we must still pay publishers and authors. We must pay them, if not for the physical makeup of a book, then for knowledge itself. Kurzweil—far from thinking, by way of the hacker's ethic, that information wants or can or should be free—instead claims: "*Knowledge is not free, nor should it be.*" A corollary to this view is that copyrights and royalties will be maintained.

Jay David Bolter historicizes the electronic book and its impact on the electronic library, leading to the (perhaps quixotic) Xanadu project. Theodor Nelson, the conceptualizer of the electronic library, summarizes its basic principles. Nelson has been criticized by Gary Wolf in an article in *Wired* magazine. We will take up that criticism and Nelson's response in the Questions and Further Suggestions section at the end of the chapter.

When libraries and books become electronic, the principles of copyright and royalties get reassessed. (It's the return of the hacker ethic, this time in terms of *copyleft*.) John Perry Barlow and the group known as "Critical Art Ensemble" espouse different views on our historical concept of intellectual property and plagiarism.

Jorge Luis Borges

The Library of Babel

By this art you may con-
template the variation of
the 23 letters . . .
          —*The Anatomy of Melancholy,*
          Part 2, Sect. II, Mem. IV.

The universe (which others call the Library) is composed of an indefinite, perhaps an infinite, number of hexagonal galleries, with enormous ventilation shafts in the middle, encircled by very low railings. From any hexagon the upper or lower stories are visible, interminably. The distribution of the galleries is invariable. Twenty shelves—five long shelves per side—cover all sides except two; their height, which is that of each floor, scarcely exceeds that of an average librarian. One of the free sides gives upon a narrow entrance way, which leads to another gallery, identical to the first and to all the others. To the left and to the right of the entrance way are two miniature rooms. One allows standing room for sleeping; the other, the satisfaction of fecal necessities. Through this section passes the spiral staircase, which plunges down into the abyss and rises up to the heights. In the entrance way hangs a mirror, which faithfully duplicates appearances. People are in the habit of inferring from this mirror that the Library is not infinite (if it really were, why this illusory duplication?); I prefer to dream that the polished surfaces feign and promise infinity. . . .

Light comes from some spherical fruits called by the name of lamps. There are two, running transversally, in each hexagon. The light they emit is insufficient, incessant.

Like all men of the Library, I have traveled in my youth. I have journeyed in search of a book, perhaps of the catalogue of catalogues; now that my eyes can scarcely decipher what I write, I am preparing to die a few leagues from the hexagon in which I was born. Once dead, there will not lack pious hands to hurl me over the banister; my sepulchre shall be the unfathomable air: my body will sink lengthily and will corrupt and dissolve in the wind engendered by the fall, which is infinite. I affirm that the Library is interminable. The idealists argue that the hexagonal halls are a necessary form of absolute space or, at least, of our intuition of space. They contend that a triangular or pentagonal hall is inconceivable. (The mystics claim that to them ecstasy reveals a round chamber containing a great book with a continuous back circling the walls of the room; but their testimony is suspect; their words, obscure. That cyclical book is God.) Let it suffice me, for the time being, to repeat the classic dictum: *The Library is a sphere whose consummate center is any hexagon, and whose circumference is inaccessible.*

Five shelves correspond to each one of the walls of each hexagon; each shelf contains thirty-two books of a uniform format; each book is made up of four hundred and ten pages; each page, of forty lines; each line, of some eighty black letters. There are also letters on the spine of each book; these letters do not indicate or prefigure what the pages will say. I know that such a lack of relevance, at one time, seemed mysterious. Before summarizing the solution (whose disclosure, despite its tragic implications, is perhaps the capital fact of this history), I want to recall certain axioms.

> **The Library is a sphere whose consummate center is any hexagon, and whose circumference is inaccessible.**

The first: The Library exists *ab aeterno*. No reasonable mind can doubt this truth, whose immediate corollary is the future eternity of the world. Man, the imperfect librarian, may be the work of chance or of malevolent demiurges; the universe, with its elegant endowment of shelves, of enigmatic volumes, of indefatigable ladders for the voyager, and of privies for the seated librarian, can only be the work of a god. In order to perceive the distance which exists between the divine and the human, it is enough to compare the rude tremulous symbols which my fallible hand scribbles on the end pages of a book with the organic letters inside: exact, delicate, intensely black, inimitably symmetric.

The second: *The number of orthographic symbols is twenty-five.** This bit of evidence permitted the formulation, three hundred years ago, of a general theory of the Library and the satisfactory resolution of the problem which no conjecture had yet made clear: the formless and chaotic nature of almost all books. One of these books, which my father saw in a hexagon of the circuit number fifteen ninety-four, was composed of the letters MCV perversely repeated from the first line to the last. Another, very much consulted in this zone, is a mere labyrinth of letters, but on the next-to-the-last page, one may read *O Time your pyramids.* As is well known: for one reasonable line or one straightforward note there are leagues of insensate cacophony, of verbal farragoes and incoherencies. (I know of a wild region whose librarians repudiate the vain superstitious custom of seeking any sense in books and compare it to looking for meaning in dreams or in the chaotic lines of one's hands. . . . They admit that the inventors of writing imitated the twenty-five natural symbols, but they maintain that this application is accidental and that books in themselves mean nothing. This opinion—we shall see—is not altogether false.)

For a long time it was believed that these impenetrable books belonged to past or remote languages. It is true that the most ancient men, the first librarians, made use of a language quite different from the one we speak today; it is true that some miles to the right the language is dialectical and that ninety stories up it is incomprehensible. All this, I repeat, is true; but four hundred

---

*The original manuscript of the present note does not contain digits or capital letters. The punctuation is limited to the comma and the period. These two signs, plus the space sign and the twenty-two letters of the alphabet, make up the twenty-five sufficient symbols enumerated by the unknown author.

and ten pages of unvarying MCVs do not correspond to any language, however dialectical or rudimentary it might be. Some librarians insinuated that each letter could influence the next, and that the value of MCV on the third line of page 71 was not the same as that of the same series in another position on another page; but this vague thesis did not prosper. Still other men thought in terms of cryptographs; this conjecture has come to be universally accepted, though not in the sense in which it was formulated by its inventors.

Five hundred years ago, the chief of an upper hexagon* came upon a book as confusing as all the rest but which contained nearly two pages of homogenous lines. He showed his find to an ambulant decipherer, who told him the lines were written in Portuguese. Others told him they were in Yiddish. In less than a century the nature of the language was finally established: it was a Samoyed-Lithuanian dialect of Guaraní, with classical Arabic inflections. The contents were also deciphered: notions of combinational analysis, illustrated by examples of variations with unlimited repetition. These examples made it possible for a librarian of genius to discover the fundamental law of the Library. This thinker observed that all the books, however diverse, are made up of uniform elements: the period, the comma, the space, the twenty-two letters of the alphabet. He also adduced a circumstance confirmed by all travelers: *There are not, in the whole vast Library, two identical books.* From all these incontrovertible premises he deduced that the Library is total and that its shelves contain all the possible combinations of the twenty-odd orthographic symbols (whose number, though vast, is not infinite); that is, everything which can be expressed, in all languages. Everything is there: the minute history of the future, the autobiographies of the archangels, the faithful catalogue of the Library, thousands and thousands of false catalogues, a demonstration of the fallacy of these catalogues, a demonstration of the fallacy of the true catalogue, the Gnostic gospel of Basilides, the commentary on this gospel, the commentary on the commentary of this gospel, the veridical account of your death, a version of each book in all languages, the interpolations of every book in all books.

There are not, in the whole vast Library, two identical books.

When it was proclaimed that the Library comprised all books, the first impression was one of extravagant joy. All men felt themselves lords of a secret, intact treasure. There was no personal or universal problem whose eloquent solution did not exist—in some hexagon. The universe was justified, the universe suddenly expanded to the limitless dimensions of hope. At that time there was much talk of the Vindications: books of apology and prophecy, which vindicated for all time the actions of every man in the world and established a store of prodigious arcana for the future. Thousands of covetous persons abandoned their dear natal hexagons and crowded up the stairs, urged

---

*Formerly, for each three hexagons there was one man. Suicide and pulmonary diseases have destroyed this proportion. My memory recalls scenes of unspeakable melancholy: there have been many nights when I have ventured down corridors and polished staircases without encountering a single librarian.

on by the vain aim of finding their Vindication. These pilgrims disputed in the narrow corridors, hurled dark maledictions, strangled each other on the divine stairways, flung the deceitful books to the bottom of the tunnels, and died as they were thrown into space by men from remote regions. Some went mad. . . .

The Vindications do exist. I have myself seen two of these books, which were concerned with future people, people who were perhaps not imaginary. But the searchers did not remember that the calculable possibility of a man's finding his own book, or some perfidious variation of his own book, is close to zero.

The clarification of the basic mysteries of humanity—the origin of the Library and of time—was also expected. It is credible that those grave mysteries can be explained in words: if the language of the philosophers does not suffice, the multiform Library will have produced the unexpected language required and the necessary vocabularies and grammars for this language.

It is now four centuries since men have been wearying the hexagons. . . .

There are official searchers, *inquisitors.* I have observed them carrying out their functions: they are always exhausted. They speak of a staircase without steps where they were almost killed. They speak of galleries and stairs with the local librarian. From time to time they will pick up the nearest book and leaf through its pages, in search of infamous words. Obviously, no one expects to discover anything.

There are official searchers, inquisitors. I have observed them carrying out their functions: they are always exhausted.

The uncommon hope was followed, naturally enough, by deep depression. The certainty that some shelf in some hexagon contained precious books and that these books were inaccessible seemed almost intolerable. A blasphemous sect suggested that all searches be given up and that men everywhere shuffle letters and symbols until they succeeded in composing, by means of an improbable stroke of luck, the canonical books. The authorities found themselves obliged to issue severe orders. The sect disappeared, but in my childhood I still saw old men who would hide out in the privies for long periods of time, and, with metal disks in a forbidden dicebox, feebly mimic the divine disorder.

Other men, inversely, thought that the primary task was to eliminate useless works. They would invade the hexagons, exhibiting credentials which were not always false, skim through a volume with annoyance, and then condemn entire bookshelves to destruction: their ascetic, hygenic fury is responsible for the senseless loss of millions of books. Their name is execrated; but those who mourn the "treasures" destroyed by this frenzy, overlook two notorious facts. One: the Library is so enormous that any reduction undertaken by humans is infinitesimal. Two: each book is unique, irreplaceable, but (inasmuch as the Library is total) there are always several hundreds of thousands of imperfect facsimiles—of works which differ only by one letter or one comma. Contrary to public opinion, I dare suppose that the consequences of the depredations committed by the Purifiers have been exaggerated by the horror which these fanatics provoked. They were spurred by the delirium of storming the books in the Crimson Hexagon: books of a smaller than ordinary format, omnipotent, illustrated, magical.

We know, too, of another superstition of that time: the Man of the Book. In some shelf of some hexagon, men reasoned, there must exist a book which is the cipher and perfect compendium of *all the rest:* some librarian has perused it, and it is analogous to a god. Vestiges of the worship of that remote functionary still persist in the language of this zone. Many pilgrimages have sought Him out. For a century they trod the most diverse routes in vain.

> *To me, it does not seem unlikely that on some shelf of the universe there lies a total book.*

How to locate the secret hexagon which harbored it? Someone proposed a regressive approach: in order to locate book A, first consult book B which will indicate the location of A; in order to locate book B, first consult book C, and so on ad infinitum. . . .

I have squandered and consumed my years in adventures of this type. To me, it does not seem unlikely that on some shelf of the universe there lies a total book.* I pray the unknown gods that some man—even if only one man, and though it have been thousands of years ago!—may have examined and read it. If honor and wisdom and happiness are not for me, let them be for others. May heaven exist, though my place be in hell. Let me be outraged and annihilated, but may Thy enormous Library be justified, for one instant, in one being.

The impious assert that absurdities are the norm in the Library and that anything reasonable (even humble and pure coherence) is an almost miraculous exception. They speak (I know) of "the febrile Library, whose hazardous volumes run the constant risk of being changed into others and in which everything is affirmed, denied, and confused as by a divinity in delirium." These words, which not only denounce disorder but exemplify it as well, manifestly demonstrate the bad taste of the speakers and their desperate ignorance. Actually, the Library includes all verbal structures, all the variations allowed by the twenty-five orthographic symbols, but it does not permit of one absolute absurdity. It is pointless to observe that the best book in the numerous hexagons under my administration is entitled *Combed Clap of Thunder;* or that another is called *The Plaster Cramp;* and still another *Axaxaxas Mlö.* Such propositions as are contained in these titles, at first sight incoherent, doubtless yield a cryptographic or allegorical justification. Since they are verbal, these justifications already figure, *ex hypothesi,* in the Library. I can not combine certain letters, as *dhcmrlchtdj,* which the divine Library has not already foreseen in combination, and which in one of its secret languages does not encompass some terrible meaning. No one can articulate a syllable

---

*I repeat: it is enough that a book be possible for it to exist. Only the impossible is excluded. For example: no book is also a stairway, though doubtless there are books that discuss and deny and demonstrate this possibility and others whose structure corresponds to that of a stairway.

which is not full of tenderness and fear, and which is not, in one of those languages, the powerful name of some god. To speak is to fall into tautologies. This useless and wordy epistle itself already exists in one of the thirty volumes of the five shelves in one of the uncountable hexagons—and so does its refutation. (An *n* number of possible languages makes use of the same vocabulary; in some of them, the symbol *library* admits of the correct definition *ubiquitous and everlasting system of hexagonal galleries,* but *library* is *bread* or *pyramid* or anything else, and the seven words which define it possess another value. You who read me, are you sure you understand my language?)

Methodical writing distracts me from the present condition of men. But the certainty that everything has been already written nullifies or makes phantoms of us all. I know of districts where the youth prostrate themselves before books and barbarously kiss the pages, though they do not know how to make out a single letter. Epidemics, heretical disagreements, the pilgrimages which inevitably degenerate into banditry, have decimated the population. I believe I have mentioned the suicides, more frequent each year. Perhaps I am deceived by old age and fear, but I suspect that the human species—the unique human species—is on the road to extinction, while the Library will last on forever: illuminated, solitary, infinite, perfectly immovable, filled with precious volumes, useless, incorruptible, secret.

To speak is to fall into tautologies.

Infinite I have just written. I have not interpolated this adjective merely from rhetorical habit. It is not illogical, I say, to think that the world is infinite. Those who judge it to be limited, postulate that in remote places the corridors and stairs and hexagons could inconceivably cease—a manifest absurdity. Those who imagined it to be limitless forget that the possible number of books is limited. I dare insinuate the following solution to this ancient problem: *The Library is limitless and periodic.* If an eternal voyager were to traverse it in any direction, he would find, after many centuries, that the same volumes are repeated in the same disorder (which, repeated, would constitute an order: Order itself). My solitude rejoices in this elegant hope.*

Mar del Plata
1941

—Translated by Anthony Kerrigan

---

*Letizia Alvarez de Toledo has observed that the vast Library is useless. Strictly speaking, *one single volume* should suffice: a single volume of ordinary format, printed in nine or ten type body, and consisting of an infinite number of infinitely thin pages. (At the beginning of the seventeenth century, Cavalieri said that any solid body is the superposition of an infinite number of planes.) This silky vade mecum would scarcely be handy: each apparent leaf of the book would divide into other analogous leaves. The inconceivable central leaf would have no reverse.

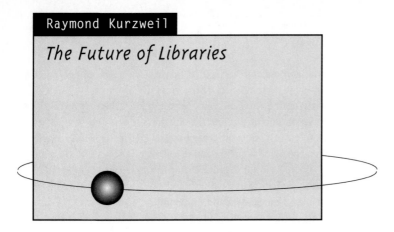

Raymond Kurzweil

The Future of Libraries

I always keep a stack of books on my desk that I leaf through when I run out of ideas, feel restless, or otherwise need a shot of inspiration. Picking up a fat volume that I recently acquired, I consider the bookmaker's craft: 470 finely printed pages organized into 16-page signatures, each of which is sewn together with white thread and glued onto a gray canvas cord. The hard linen-bound covers, stamped with gold letters, are connected to the signature block by delicately embossed end sheets. This is a technology that was perfected many decades ago. Books constitute such an integral element of our society—both reflecting and shaping its culture—that it is hard to imagine life without them. But the printed book, like any other technology, will not live forever.

The Life Cycle of a Technology

We can identify seven distinct stages in the life cycle of a technology. During the *precursor* stage, the prerequisites of a technology exist, and dreamers may contemplate these elements coming together. We do not, however, regard dreaming to be the same as inventing even if the dreams are written down. Leonardo da Vinci drew convincing pictures of airplanes and automobiles, but he is not considered to have invented either.

The next stage, one highly celebrated in our culture, is *invention,* a very brief stage, not dissimilar in some respects to the process of birth after an extended period of labor. Here the inventor blends curiosity, scientific skills, determination, and usually a measure of showmanship to combine methods in a new way and brings a new technology to life.

The next stage is *development,* during which the invention is protected and supported by doting guardians (which may include the original inventor). Often this stage is more crucial than invention and may involve additional creation that can have greater significance than the invention. Many tinkerers had constructed finely hand-tuned horseless carriages, but it was Henry Ford's innovation of mass production that enabled the automobile to take root and flourish.

The fourth stage is *maturity.* Although continuing to evolve, the technology now has a life of its own and has become an independent and established part of the community. It may become so interwoven in the fabric of life that it appears to many observers that it will last forever. This creates an interesting drama when the next stage arrives, which I call the stage of the *false pretenders*. Here an upstart threatens to eclipse the older technology. Its enthusiasts prematurely predict victory. While providing some distinct benefits, the newer technology is found on reflection to be missing some key element of functionality or quality. When it indeed fails to dislodge the established order, the technology conservatives take this as evidence that the original approach will indeed live forever.

Books constitute such an integral element of our society. . .that it is hard to imagine life without them. But the printed book, like any other technology, will not live forever.

This is usually a short-lived victory for the aging technology. Shortly thereafter, another new technology typically does succeed in rendering the original technology into the stage of *obsolescence*. In this part of the life cycle, the technology lives out its senior years in gradual decline, its original purpose and functionality now subsumed by a more spry competitor. This stage, which may comprise five to ten percent of the life cycle, finally yields to *antiquity* (e.g., today the horse and buggy, the harpsichord, and the manual typewriter).

In the mid-19th century, there were several precursors to the phonograph, including de Martinville's *phonautograph,* a device that recorded sound vibrations as a printed pattern. It was Thomas Edison, however, who brought all of the elements together and invented the first device that could both record and reproduce sound in 1877. Further refinements were necessary for the phonograph to become commercially viable. It became a fully mature technology in 1948 when Columbia introduced the 33rpm long-playing record (LP) and RCA Victor introduced the 45rpm small disc. The false pretender was the cassette tape, introduced in the 1960s and popularized during the 1970s. Early enthusiasts predicted that its small size and ability to be rerecorded would make the relatively bulky and scratchable record obsolete.

Despite these obvious benefits, cassettes lack random access (the ability to play selections randomly) and are prone to their own forms of distortion and lack of fidelity. More recently, however, the compact disc (CD) has delivered the mortal blow. With the CD providing both random access and a level of quality close to the limits of the human auditory system, the phonograph record has quickly entered the stage of obsolescence. Although still produced, the technology that Edison gave birth to 114 years ago will reach antiquity by the end of the decade.

Roll over Beethoven

Consider the piano, an area of technology that I am personally familiar with. In the early 18th century, Bartolommeo Cristofori was seeking a way to provide a touch response to the then-popular harpsichord so that the volume of the notes would vary with the intensity of the touch of the performer. Called *gravicembalo col piano e forte* ("harpsichord with soft and loud"), his invention was not an immediate success. Further refinements, including Stein's Viennese action and Zumpe's English action, helped to establish the "piano" as the pre-eminent keyboard instrument. It reached maturity with the development of the complete cast-iron frame, patented in 1825 by Alpheus Babcock, and has seen only subtle refinements since then. The false pretender was the electric piano of the early 1980s. It offered substantially greater functionality. Compared to the single (piano) sound of the acoustic piano, the electronic variant offered dozens of instrument sounds, sequencers that allowed the user to play an entire orchestra at once, automated accompaniment, educational programs to teach keyboard skills, and many other features. The only feature it was missing was a good quality piano sound.

This crucial flaw and the resulting failure of the first generation of electronic pianos to take root led many observers to remark that the piano would *never* be replaced by electronics. But the "victory" of the acoustic piano was short lived. It is entering obsolescence as we speak. Already the upright piano has been largely superseded by the latest wave of digital pianos. Many observers feel that the sound quality of the "piano" sound on digital pianos now equals or exceeds that of the upright acoustic piano, and the far greater range of features and price performance of digital pianos has enabled them to dominate the market. All piano manufacturers I have spoken with report that with the sole exception of the concert grand (a very small part of the market), the sale of acoustic pianos is in rapid decline. The piano should hit antiquity by the turn of the century.

From Goat Skins to CD-ROM

So where in the technology life cycle is the book? Among its precursors were the Mesopotamian clay tablets and the Egyptian papyrus scrolls. In the second century B.C., the Ptolemies of Egypt had created a great library of scrolls at Alexandria and outlawed the export of papyrus to discourage competition.

What were perhaps the first books were created by Eumenes II, ruler of ancient Greek Pergamum, using pages of vellum made from the skins of goats and sheep, which were sewn together between wooden covers. This technique enabled Eumenes to compile a library equal to that of Alexandria. Around the same time, the Chinese had also developed a crude form of book made from bamboo strips.

The development and maturation of books has seen three advances. *Printing,* first experimented with by the Chinese in the eighth century A.D. using raised wood blocks, allowed books to be reproduced in much larger quantities, expanding their audience beyond government and religious leaders. Of even greater significance was the advent of *movable type,* which was experimented with by the Chinese and Koreans in the 11th century, but the complexity of Asian characters prevented these early attempts from being fully successful. Johannes Gutenberg, working in the 15th century, benefited from the relative simplicity of the Roman character set. He produced his Bible, the first large-scale work printed entirely with movable type, in 1455.

While there has been a continual stream of evolutionary improvements in the mechanical and electromechanical process of printing, the technology of bookmaking did not see another qualitative leap until the availability of *computer typesetting,* which has now largely done away with movable type. Typography is now regarded as a part of digital image processing.

With books now a fully mature technology, the false pretenders have arrived with the first wave of "electronic books." As is usually the case, these false pretenders offer dramatic qualitative and quantitative benefits. CD-ROM–based electronic books recently introduced by Sony and others (as well as CD-ROM–based software for personal computers) can provide the equivalent of thousands of books on a single diskette with powerful computer-based search and knowledge navigation features. With my CD-ROM–based encyclopedia, I can perform rapid word searches using extensive logic rules, something that is just not possible with the 33-volume "book" version I possess. Other CD-ROMs I have can provide pictures that are animated or that respond to my input. Pages are not necessarily ordered sequentially, but can be explored along more intuitive connections.

The Eye of the Beholder

So what's the problem? As with the phonograph record and the piano, this first generation of false pretenders is missing an essential quality of the original, which in this case is the superb characteristics of paper and ink. First of all, paper does not *flicker,* whereas the typical computer screen is displaying 60 to 72 interlaced frames per second. This is a problem because of an evolutionary adaptation of the primate visual system. We are only able to see a very small portion of the visual field with high resolution. This portion, imaged by the fovea portion of the retina, is focused on an area about the size of a single word at 22 inches away. Outside of the fovea, we have very little resolution but exquisite sensitivity to brightness changes. This allowed our primitive forebears to quickly detect a predator that might be attacking. The constant flicker of a color/graphics adapter (CGA) or video graphics array (VGA) computer screen is detected by our eyes as motion and causes constant movement of the fovea. This substantially slows down reading speeds, which is one reason that reading on a screen is less pleasant than reading a printed book.

Another issue is *contrast.* A good quality book has an ink-to-paper contrast of about 120:1. Typical computer screens are perhaps half of that.

A crucial issue is *resolution.* Print and illustrations in a print book represent a resolution of about 600 to 1000 dots per inch (dpi). Typical computer screens are about one-tenth of that, with the new CD-ROM–based electronic books providing even less.

Some computer screens provide *color,* but the portable ones usually do not. The *size, weight,* and *cost* of notebook computers and electronic books are impressive, but still not competitive with the good old print version.

Finally, there is the issue of the *available software,* by which I mean the enormous installed base of print books. There are 50,000 new print books published each year in the United States and millions of books in circulation. There are major efforts underway to scan and digitize print materials, but it will be a long time before the electronic databases have a comparable wealth of material.

So, will the book last forever? If today's electronic book is a false pretender, what sort of technology will it take to send the book into obsolescence? When will that happen? What will be the impact on society of the virtual book? Tune in next month.

■ PART 2: THE END OF BOOKS

It is said that in the development of technology we overestimate what can be accomplished in the short term and underestimate what can be accomplished in the long term. With the exception of a few prescient observers (such as Charles Babbage in the case of the computer), most predictions of the 20th century overlooked such breakthroughs as the computer, radio, television, and atomic energy, not to mention such recent innovations as the laser and bioengineering.

Beyond the breakthrough, it is also difficult to anticipate serendipity, the coming together of diverse trends with profound yet unanticipated effects. In the case of the book, it is the interplay of such multifarious trends that will determine its destiny. The trends themselves are not hard to anticipate, although the stunning pace of development, particularly of computer hardware, is often not fully appreciated. In most fields, we take it for granted that things get more expensive each year. But in the computer field, we can at least double functionality for the same unit cost every 12 to 15 months, and even this pace is accelerating.

So, will the book last forever? If today's electronic book is a false pretender, what sort of technology will it take to send the book into obsolescence?

The implications of this geometric trend can be understood by recalling the legend of the inventor of chess and his patron, the emperor of China. The emperor had so fallen in love with his new game, he offered the inventor a reward of anything he wanted in the kingdom.

"Just one grain of rice on the first square, your majesty."

"Just one grain of rice?"

"Yes, and two on the second, four on the third, and so on."

The emperor immediately granted the inventor's seemingly humble request. One version of the story has the emperor going bankrupt (the doubling per square ultimately equaled 18 million trillion grains of rice). The more believable version has the inventor losing his head.

As an example of what this trend has already accomplished, computer scientist David Waltz points out that computer memory today, after adjustment for inflation, costs only one-hundred-millionth of what it did in 1950 (which is consistent with a doubling of price-performance every 18 months). If the automotive industry had made as much progress in the past four decades, a typical automobile today would cost about one-hundredth of a cent.

With the price-performance of computer hardware doubling every year in every dimension, the impact will become increasingly hard to ignore. This becomes all the more significant as computers begin to affect virtually every other area of endeavor.

The Powerbook Looms

So let us examine how just the predictable trends will affect the technology of the book. Last month, we discussed the emergence of the first wave of false pretenders to the functionality of the paper book. While the electronic book provides profound advantages in the quantity and accessibility of information, it falls short in some of the fundamental characteristics of paper and ink in the areas of flicker, contrast, resolution, and color. But as noted above, computer technology is anything but static, and already some of these limitations are being overcome. Alan Kay, senior fellow at Apple Computer, points out that the recently introduced Apple Powerbook 170 is flicker free and has a contrast ratio of 95:1, close to paper's 120:1. Apple is actually positioning its new computer as an electronic book and plans to provide a library of books as software, hence the name Powerbook.

By next year, the first wave of color notebook computers will appear. Perhaps the most significant issue is resolution. Interestingly, the Jacquard loom, perfected by Joseph Marie Jacquard in 1805, which we might regard as the world's first computer display, had a resolution of 1000 silk threads to the inch, equalling that of paper. Jacquard's loom was controlled by punched cards and foreshadowed the emergence of the punched card-based data processing industry 85 years later. Today's notebook computers have a resolution of only about 100 dots per inch (dpi), substantially less than paper. Within two to three years, however, we will see notebook computers with about 250 dpi, which for many applications will begin to rival paper and ink.

Let us jump ahead and describe the notebook computer that we are likely to see by the turn of the century based on readily discernible trends. Resolution will range from 500 to 1000 dpi, the same as high-quality printed documents. The displays will be flicker free and will have contrast ratios and color capabilities comparable to paper and ink. The devices will come in a variety of sizes ranging from pocket sized to double-hinged displays that will present two large pages. These computers will be thin (perhaps ½″ deep) and lightweight.

By the end of this decade, the standard RAM chip will be one gigabit (one billion bits), so the typical personal notebook will provide at least a billion bytes (characters) of random access memory. Low-bandwidth communication (text, voice, still pictures) will be by wireless cellular transmission. High-bandwidth communication (moving high-resolution pictures) will be by optical fiber. In my November 15, 1991 [*Library Journal*] column ("Learning in the Age of Knowledge," p. 60–62), I mentioned Japan's plan to install a fiber optic-based information superhighway into every home and office by early in the next century. President Bush recently signed a $3 billion bill to begin research in this area, but we still lack anything comparable to Japan's multi-hundred-billion-dollar commitment. I do anticipate, however, that we will wake up sooner or later to this enormous competitive threat.

Whatchamacallit

Communication between user and machine will be through voice for entering text and a pen-like device for pointing and for graphical gestures such as crossing out words. The keyboard will be entering obsolescence as we enter the first decade of the next century.

So what is this thing? A PC? A telephone? A television? A personal transcriptionist? A cybernetic research assistant? A book?

Obviously, it is all of the above. As a telephone, it will include real-time language translation (at least between certain popular languages) so that we can readily communicate with people around the globe (the translating telephone capability will mature during the first decade of the next century). With the addition of a small, hand-held digital camera, this "telephone" will also include moving high-definition pictures.

George Gilder describes high-definition television—the marriage of the two great communication technologies of the 20th century (the computer and television)—as creating a highly flexible telecomputer that is interactive and intelligent.

As a personal research assistant, the operating system of our future PCs will contain intelligent knowledge navigators that have the knowledge of where to find knowledge through instantaneous wireless communication with increasingly comprehensive databases.

However, let us concentrate for a moment on its application as a book. The personal computer of the early 2000s will not be a false pretender. These electronic books will have enormous advantages, with pictures that can move and interact with the user, increasingly intelligent search paradigms, simulated environments that the user can enter and explore, and vast quantities of accessible material. Yet vital to its ability to truly make the paper book obsolete is that the essential qualities of paper and ink will have been fully matched. The book will enter obsolescence, although because of its long history and enormous installed base, it will linger for a couple of decades before reaching antiquity.

The Virtue of Virtual Books

The paper book will be replaced by a category of software that we can call virtual books. Is the virtual book really a new technology or just a continuation of the old (paper) technology by other means? It is certainly a new technology in the same sense that the "horseless carriage" automobile was a different technology from the horse and buggy. Changing such a central component of an old technology opens up so many new possibilities that we can truly say that a new technology has been born.

> **The paper book will be replaced by a category of software that we can call virtual books.**

Yet haven't we been hearing about the paperless society for at least a decade now? American business's use of paper for printed documents increased from 850 billion pages in 1981 to nearly four trillion pages in 1990. It is certainly the case that while computers make it possible to handle documents without paper, they also greatly increase the productivity of producing paper documents. Until the computer display truly rivals the qualities of paper, computers will increase the use of paper rather than replace it. But once these qualities are matched, and the requisite communication technologies are in place, the printed book and other paper documents along with it will begin a rapid descent into obsolescence.

Many people were skeptical that the compact-disc (CD) would replace the phonograph record. I remember being hesitant to buy a CD player because I was attached to my extensive collection of LPs collected over a lifetime, and I did not desire it becoming obsolete. My curiosity finally drove me to acquire a CD, and then I was hooked. My CD collection has grown, but I still have several shelves in my living room filled with my old album collection. But it has now been years since I have even touched one of these old phonograph albums, and even more years since I purchased one. People are also attached to their collections of paper books, but when the truly viable electronic book comes along, which will happen by the end of the decade, resistance to it will not last long.

Click and Pick

So how do you buy a virtual book? By going to a bookstore, obviously. Not physically of course, you simply "click" on *bookstore*. Icons then appear for different choices. So let's say we click on *Brentano's*. We now see icons for different categories of books: *best sellers, fantasy & science fiction,* etc. Let's click on *best sellers*. We now see images of book spines, which can be scrolled across the screen. Some books that the bookstore wishes to highlight are shown with the full front jacket.

Ah, here is an interesting one, *The Best of Futurecast* by Raymond Kurzweil. We click on that, and we now see the full front and back jacket. We click on the photo of the author, and he comes alive explaining the virtues of his book. We click on the front cover, and we see the front matter. We scroll through the table of contents. Here is an interesting old article from 1992 on "The End of Books." We click on it and start reading. Hmmm, this is very interesting; Kurzweil's predictions weren't all bad!

Whoops, the computer now tells us that if we want to continue reading, we have to acquire the book. Options are presented. We can *purchase* it, we can *rent* it, there are several other choices. Well, this is a book we will certainly want to return to over and over, so we click on *purchase.* Now we see icons for *debit to checking account, charge to American Express,* etc. Once the transaction is complete, the book is transmitted via wireless cellular communication and becomes part of the permanent data-base of our PC.

What about the public library? Okay, click on *city library.* We see icons for categories. Click on *best sellers.* Now click on *The Best of Futurecast.* Looks interesting, so we click on *borrow book.*

Now wait a second. The library scenario sounds very similar to the bookstore scenario. Why would anyone buy a book if you can borrow it just as easily for free anytime you want to read it?

Other questions come to mind. What happens to that big library building? Will there still be paper books printed? Will libraries still carry these? How will the library work? What will librarians do?

There are reasonable answers to these questions, which we will examine next month.

■ PART 3: THE VIRTUAL LIBRARY

I posed the following dilemma at the end of my previous column (see The Futurecast, *LJ,* February 15, p. 140): If borrowing a virtual book from the virtual "free library" involves simply selecting a few icons on the screen of your circa 2000 notebook computer, why then would anyone *buy* a book (which would involve clicking on a different set of icons as well as a debit to one of your financial accounts)?

Kay replied that the "free library is not free."

I posed this specter to two of our contemporary visionaries: Apple Fellow Alan Kay and Hudson Institute Fellow George Gilder. Gilder replied that no one should feel too secure in the information revolution. Having the courage to radically alter one's self-concept will be the prerequisite to survival for any organization, from IBM to the Mill Valley Local Library.

Kay replied that the "free library is not free."

These two enigmatic replies contain the key to resolving the dilemma if we ponder the implications of both views. We can postulate two visions of the library of the future. If we are indeed entering the Age of Knowledge (see The Futurecast, *LJ,* September 15, 1991, p. 58–59) in which the organization of information will be the paramount strategic asset of nations and individuals, then the library, as the institution in our society primarily responsible for organizing and presenting codified knowledge, may properly be regarded as having the responsibility for leading the charge. On the other hand, if we view the concept of the library more provincially, as a building containing stacks of paper books with librarians who lend these objects out to patrons, then our long-term prognosis for the institution is distinctly more dismal.

If you were a blacksmith at the turn of the century, your outlook would depend on whether you saw yourself as a shaper of horseshoes or a facilitator of transportation (in which case you would trade in your forge and hammer for a gas pump). Gilder is pointing out that with the pace of change accelerating, it is not only the private sector that must dramatically adapt. Our public institutions—schools, government, libraries—must define their missions broadly enough to survive the obsolescence of more narrowly defined self-concepts.

If we define the mission of the library as the shaping and distribution of knowledge through whatever technical means, we are still left with the original predicament. Perhaps it is bookstores that will have to go. If libraries can simply distribute books and other information electromagnetically through the air and optically through the nation's fiberoptic information highway, then who needs bookstores, anyway? The problem, however, is that without revenue, there will be no publishers and nothing will be published.

A Fistful of Knowledge

We must now contemplate a central lesson of the Age of Knowledge, which is implied in Kay's observation above. *Knowledge is not free, nor should it be.* We are used to paying for the knowledge content of products so long as it is integrated into something with mass. We recognize that a $300 software product is physically identical to a few $2 floppy disks, and thus we are primarily paying for the information contained therein. We are aware (or should be) that the manufactured cost of a compact disc recording is less than 50¢ (depending on volume), and that again we are paying for the (musical) information. It is, after all, the information we are after. We obtain no pleasure from the discs themselves. The manufactured cost of most books is only a few dollars. Again, it is the knowledge we are seeking (although I will admit that a well-crafted book is a lovely possession).

Why then do we have difficulty comprehending the value of information when the physical content of a product shrinks to nothing? We are used to buying products that have size and weight. If design and other learned content enhance their value, so be it. Still, the paradigm that we are used to for buying a product is that we purchase an object with size and weight in a store, carry it home in a colorful shopping bag, unwrap it, and only then digest its intellectual content. We are already at the point where at least 90 percent of the value of products of this type result from their knowledge content, and we will need very soon to fully absorb the idea that knowledge without *any* physical construct still represents value. Otherwise, no knowledge of value will be created.

The Royalty Factor

So while it is true that a book could be distributed electronically to millions of people at very little cost, it will nonetheless require compensation to the publisher and author (or artist, musician, programmer, artificial reality designer, etc.) just as is the case today. Thus when you buy a virtual book from your virtual bookstore, the money that is deducted from your (electronic but not so virtual) bank account will be distributed as it is now to the distributor, publisher, and author. The point that Kay is making is that the same transaction will need to take place when you "borrow" a book from the "free" library. It may be a free service to you, but someone is going to have to pay, namely the library. In other words, libraries will not be exempt from violating copyright laws. Publishers will be quite happy with libraries distributing their virtual books, just as they are undoubtedly delighted to receive book orders from libraries today.

The advent of the virtual book will require rethinking the concept of buying a book

Yet library budgets are not unlimited—as most *Library Journal* readers will appreciate—so constraints will have to be applied. Today these constraints are enforced by requiring patrons to physically go to the library, placing limits on the selection and number of books available, putting time limits on borrowing, and other subtle and overt restrictions. The virtual library will undoubtedly find similar ways to constrain its service. It will have no choice; its budget will be set by the same political realities that libraries deal with today.

The advent of the virtual book will require rethinking the concept of buying a book. New options will need to be devised. Some information we may wish to retain indefinitely, other information we may wish to read and then discard, yet other information we may wish to sample or browse through. Some we may not wish to read at all, but will want to have as part of a database for our software-based intelligent "assistants" to "read." Different payment methods will need to be devised to handle these different situations, which in turn will necessarily be reflected in library borrowing policies.

Bootlegging in the 1990s

A prerequisite to the availability of the virtual book is an effective means of software protection, and by software I mean any form of digital information. Today, computer software, which is one of the most valuable and expensive forms of information to create, can be copied and distributed with abandon. Although illegal, it happens all the time. It is estimated that the significant majority of software in use today has been illegally copied.

One person I spoke to recently, who claimed to be unaware that this practice was illegal, complained that if copying software was illegal, then *why do software companies make it so easy to do?* This is a profoundly important challenge. People can copy software from their friends more easily than going to the store and buying it (it can even be done over the phone).

Most children grow up with the paradigm that if they steal something, they are depriving someone else of what they have stolen. The victim of such a crime is usually not far away. Yet the crime of stealing information by breaking the "shrinkwrap" license agreement (the legal agreement that you enter into when you break the shrinkwrap on a package of software) is far more subtle. The person that the information is copied from still has the information, so it is a rather abstract concept that anyone has been deprived of anything. Of course, creators of the software have been deprived of royalties, yet remain blissfully unaware of the crime against them, except through reading occasional surveys of such practices. It is obvious, however, that carried to an extreme, the entire basis for funding the development of such expensive intellectual creations is threatened.

It was precisely this concern that killed the first generation of digital audio tape (DAT) recorders: the music industry believed compact disc recordings would be illegally copied. Once movies exist in high-definition digital form, the concern will exist there as well. The fact is that we have the technical means to enforce information licensing laws and agreements through electronic "locks." What is needed is the social compact that we *should* pay for the information we use because otherwise there will be no useful information to buy or steal. It is not just the locks on our cars or homes that keep intruders out (to the extent that we do succeed in that endeavor), but rather the combination of the technical means (the locks) and the social compact, which is a combination of the law matched with a respect that this is a law responsible citizens will honor. As the technology blazes ahead, law and social consciousness need to catch up.

All Libraries Great and Small

With library limits (on availability, deadlines, restrictions, etc.) again in place, there will be a niche for the (virtual) bookstore. Will there be a niche for the local library? In my view, the funding source has been and is likely to continue to be local. There will undoubtedly be national libraries of various kinds (particularly in scientific and other professional areas), but the city of New York and the town of Mill Valley will still have the same incentive and political will to provide local library service to its citizens, which may very well include making available the notebook computers themselves.

What about paper books? They will ultimately reach antiquity, but because of their enormous installed base, this transition will not be instantaneous. When fully effective virtual books become available later this decade, some of the more progressive libraries will begin to incorporate them into their services. As virtual books become more dominant, libraries will begin to emphasize them over paper books, with some libraries on the leading edge and some on the trailing edge.

When the paper book does reach antiquity, what will happen to those big library buildings? The role of buildings is not an issue solely of concern to libraries. When we can readily meet with people anywhere with high-definition video conferencing (eventually with moving, high-resolution, three-dimensional holographic images) the purpose of buildings will undergo its own transformation, a topic we will examine in a future column.

Personally, I take the view of the library as the leading force in society for gathering knowledge and making it universally available, a service that is a prerequisite for a democratic society. Librarians are charged with guiding and shaping that process. They serve as society's guides to knowledge and where to find it. These roles will only become more important with time, so long as we take the broad view of what the concept of *library* represents.

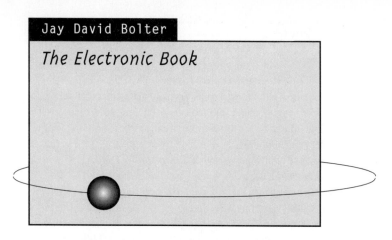

Jay David Bolter

The Electronic Book

■ THE IDEA OF THE BOOK

Every written text occupies physical space and at the same time generates a conceptual space in the minds of writers and readers. The organization of writing, the style of writing, the expectations of the reader—all these are affected by the physical space the text occupies. Above all, the physical space of a writing technology defines the basic unit, the volume of writing. So for centuries in the ancient world, the papyrus roll, about 25 feet long, constituted a written volume. (Our word "volume" comes from the Latin *volumen*, which means roll.) The codex, which replaced the roll, was more effective in enclosing, protecting, and therefore delimiting the writing it contained. The writer was and still is encouraged to think of his or her codex as a unit of meaning, a complete verbal structure. The physical book has fostered the idea that writing can and should be rounded into finite units of expression: that a writer or reader can close his or her text off from all others.

The papyrus roll was poor at suggesting a sense of closure. In the ancient world, authors would often perform their works before an audience of listeners who would not have their own copies. The writing on the roll served as a script, to be consulted when memory failed. The character and the length of these ancient texts were not determined by the size of the roll, but rather by the needs of performance. Since Homeric poets were probably illiterate, their poetry was not determined by writing at all. The *Iliad* and *Odyssey* were far too long to fit on one papyrus roll. In a sense these poems were unbounded; they were fragments of a network of stories that could be extended indefinitely. Each Greek tragedy, on the other hand, was too small to fill up one roll, because its length depended on the conventions of the Greek dramatic festivals. The tragedian did, however, have to write down his play in order to convey it to the actors, so that tragedy remained halfway between orality and full literacy. Even when writers like Plato wrote for individual readers, the oral character of ancient writing remained strong. Perhaps for that reason the ancients were content with the papyrus roll, which was adequate for reading aloud, but not for silent reading and study. The papyrus roll was certainly too short to serve as a grand unit of expression: each major work by a philosopher, historian, or poet must have occupied several rolls. It is no coincidence that many ancient poetic and historical texts do not have climactic endings. They simply fall silent, leaving the impression that there is always more to say. It is perhaps characteristic of a primarily oral rather than written culture, that its texts are often incomplete.

A codex could hold several times as much text as a roll. The early Christians apparently preferred the codex, because one codex could hold all the New Testament writings. Pagan texts followed in being transferred to the new medium. (See Reynolds & Wilson, 1978, pp. 30–32.) The physical presence of the book also began to matter more, as public performance was replaced by individual study. Silent reading became common by the later Middle Ages, but long before that books were set before individual readers—monks in their monastic libraries, for example. (See Saenger, 1982.) Writers and readers were encouraged to identify the physical book, which they held in their hands, with the text and so to see the end of the book as the end of the text. The importance of the book as an object reached its zenith in the Middle Ages, when illuminated manuscripts were examples of multimedia writing at its finest, in which all the elements functioned symbolically as well as aesthetically to create a network of verbal-visual meaning. In this one sense, printing was not an improvement: it destroyed the synthesis that medieval manuscripts had achieved. On the other hand, printing strengthened the impression of the book as a complete and closed verbal structure. Although in medieval codices and early printed books, unrelated texts were often bound together, standardization and economies of scale eventually encouraged printers to put one text in each volume.

In the centuries following the invention of printing, then, writing became synonymous with producing a book. It became the goal of every serious writer to add another volume to the world's library.

In the centuries following the invention of printing, then, writing became synonymous with producing a book. It became the goal of every serious writer to add another volume to the world's library. The paged book became the physical embodiment, the incarnation, of the text it contained. Incarnation is not too strong a metaphor. Through printing, we have come more and more to anthropomorphize books, to regard each book as a little person with a name, a place (in the library), and a bibliographic life of its own. Modern printing includes the making of the binding and dust jacket, so that every copy of an edition looks the same inside and out. Today you can tell a book by its cover. This was not the case in early printing, however, when books were often bound after they had been transported and sold (Febvre & Martin, 1971, p. 159). Children in elementary school learn to draw books with smiling faces, to personify each book with the voice of its text. And books not only talk to us; they also talk about each other. Each strives to assert its identity, while at the same time entering into a cascade of relationships with other books. The relationships are attractive and repulsive, as the book refers the reader to some books and warns against others. Each book must be different enough from all other books to deserve its own place in the library, and it should be complete in its own terms. Many texts in the age of print have required more than one volume—English novels of the 19th century were often published in three volumes even when one would have sufficed, apparently to give the readers the sense that they were getting what today is called "a good read." But the set of volumes simply became a larger book and was often eventually bound as one.

While electronic technology does not destroy the idea of the book, it does diminish the sense of closure that the codex and printing have fostered. The imposing presence of the book is gone. Instead of a binding that the reader can grasp and pages that the reader can turn, the computer uses storage media that must be hidden away in elaborate electromechanical devices, such as disk players or printed circuit boards. A CD-ROM disk is shiny and thoroughly appropriate as a futuristic technology of writing, but it offers the reader no visible cue to the beginning or end of a recorded text. The technology of computer storage may well change several times in the coming decades, but it will evolve toward greater information density, keeping the text remote from the reader.

The electronic book can merge into a larger textual structure at a thousand points of contact; it can dissolve into constituent elements that are constantly redefining their relationships to elements in other books.

The electronic book therefore is not available as an object for decoration in the medieval tradition. Instead, the book is abstract—a concept, not a thing to be held. The writer's and reader's attention is focused on the text as a structure of verbal and visual ideas that may be realized on the computer screen. In these (admittedly early) days of electronic writing, the reader seldom has a sense of where he or she is in the book. The reader does not know whether there are hundreds of screens yet to read or just a few. There are ways of orienting the reader in an electronic document, but in any true hypertext the ending must remain tentative. An electronic text never needs to end. It is a simple matter to branch to a new text or to break into the middle of a text, read a few screens, and then leave. If readers add to the text as they read, their additions may have the same status as the original. An electronic book is a structure that reaches out to other structures, not only metaphorically, as does a printed book, but operationally.

An electronic book does not join itself to other books end to end, as printed books do when we set them on a shelf. Instead, the electronic book can merge into a larger textual structure at a thousand points of contact; it can dissolve into constituent elements that are constantly redefining their relationships to elements in other books. An electronic book is not as vigorous in asserting its identity over against all others in the world's libraries. It invites exploration as part of a vast network of writings, pointing the reader both to itself and to other books. Electronic writing therefore breaks down the familiar distinctions between the book and such larger forms as the encyclopedia and the library. It is this breakdown—the coming together of the book, the encyclopedia, and the library—that we will explore in this chapter.

■ GREAT BOOKS

The book in any technology is a receptacle, a place to put verbal ideas. Once a culture has books, it is perhaps inevitable to dream of putting down all verbal ideas in one place, of creating a "great book." The desire to make a great book was shared by medieval writers, by the Greeks and Romans, and perhaps even by the scribes of the Assyrian library at Nineveh. In the age of the papyrus roll or the codex, that desire expressed itself in two contrasting forms: the library and the encyclopedia. A library amasses books; an encyclopedia condenses them. Both seek to organize and control books in order to make them available to the reader.

The book in any technology is a receptacle, a place to put verbal ideas. Once a culture has books, it is perhaps inevitable to dream of putting down all verbal ideas in one place, of creating a "great book."

The encyclopedic impulse was strong in later antiquity, when editors produced handbooks or miscellanies on subjects important to them, such as rhetoric, poetry, natural history, and medicine. The impulse was also strong in the era of Byzantine scholarship, and it was particularly strong at times during the Middle Ages in Western Europe. Because medieval scholars attached great importance to authoritative texts (the Bible, the Church fathers, later Aristotle), they felt the need to collect and summarize those texts in handbooks of their own. The most influential encyclopedias (by Martianus Capella, Isidore of Seville, and later Vincent of Beauvais) became authoritative texts themselves. These compilations were great books, and they encouraged philosophers and even poets to produce their own great books in response. Philosopher/theologians produced *summae,* which were encyclopedic in ambition—attempts to join the major philosophical and theological traditions into a convincing whole. This joining and reconciling of written authorities was the central task of medieval scholarship, as Ernst Curtius points out:

> For the Middle Ages, all discovery of truth was first reception of traditional authorities, then later—in the thirteenth century—rational reconciliation of authoritative texts. A comprehension of the world was not regarded as a creative function but as an assimilation and retracing of given facts; the symbolic expression of this being reading. The goal and the accomplishment of the thinker is to connect all these facts together in the form of the "summa." Dante's cosmic poem is such a summa too. (Curtius, 1973, p. 326)

The encyclopedic impulse diminished somewhat in the age of print. As books multiplied, it became harder to aspire to the goal of a book that would encompass all important works, even in a single field. Although more encyclopedias and handbooks were produced than ever before, the aim of the encyclopedists became more utilitarian: to generate more accurate information rather than to synthesize all knowledge. The French *Encyclopédie,* whose first volume appeared in 1751, was both the last successful encyclopedia in the medieval sense and the first modern encyclopedia. It was a a statement of the ideals of the Enlightenment as well as a compendium of technical information. In the 19th and particularly in the 20th century, making encyclopedias became a business rather than a philosophical endeavor. The major encyclopedias now maintain permanent editorial staffs, which revise the volumes continuously to furnish up-to-date information in a convenient package. Their concern is to provide information on subjects of popular interest, not to demonstrate the interrelations of all subjects. Yet even today, the ideal of the encyclopedia as a synthesis of knowledge has not completely vanished. The introduction of electronic technology may even reawaken that ideal. For the computer always encourages writers to make new texts out of old ones, and electronic texts naturally join themselves into larger and larger structures, into encyclopedias and libraries.

■ ENCYCLOPEDIC ORDER

Prior to the invention of printing, the population of books grew and declined along with the associated culture. In some periods manuscripts were plentiful; in other periods few manuscripts were read or copied, and many works were lost altogether. The great period of loss of ancient texts, for example, occurred from the sixth to the eighth centuries—both in the Latin West and in the Byzantine East. (See Reynolds & Wilson, 1978, pp. 47–48, 75–76.) Each period of sustained growth created a "textual overload," when there were many more books than a reader could afford to own or had the time or the dedication to read. The opposite problem was a lack of books during periods of cultural decline. Whenever texts become inaccessible—either because the available technology is too successful at producing texts or because the culture goes into decline—readers have turned to encyclopedias and handbooks. At the time of Pliny the Elder's *Natural History,* in the first century A.D., readers had to confront an enormous quantity of scientific and literary texts produced by the Greeks of the classical and Hellenistic periods. By the time of Martianus Capella's allegorical encyclopedia of the liberal arts in the fifth century or Isidore of Seville's *Etymologies* in the seventh, the problem was paucity. Vincent of Beauvais' *Speculum* appeared in the 13th century, when the already large medieval library was again being supplemented by Aristotle and other ancient texts. And 300 years of printing created a vast textual space for the French *Encyclopédie.* Indeed, printing has made textual overload a permanent condition: more books have been produced in each succeeding century, and new editions have succeeded in preserving most important books from the past. (Eisenstein, 1979, vol. 1, pp. 181ff.) The "information revolution" ushered in by the computer is only the most recent manifestation of a problem that is now 500 years old.

The encyclopedia offers a solution for both glut and famine.

The encyclopedia offers a solution for both glut and famine. When there are too many books, it offers to control information that has gotten out of hand. When books are not available, the encyclopedia summarizes information that the reader cannot get from original sources. In either case, the encyclopedia puts textual elements in a place where the reader can be sure to find them. In this sense the encyclopedia performs a therapeutic as well as a bibliographic function: it reassures the reader that the texts in the contemporary writing space are under control. A great encyclopedia performs this function for a whole culture. The key to any encyclopedia is therefore its organization, the principles by which it controls other texts. And the choice of organizing principles depends upon both the contemporary state of knowledge and the contemporary technology of writing.

The ancient and medieval encyclopedias were organized at first simply by association and then by progressively more elaborate hierarchies of topics. Pliny the Elder constructed his *Natural History* on what we would call naive principles of association. He began with the stars and planets, then moved to the geography of the earth, then to humans, animals, plants, and finally minerals. In presenting animal life he began with land animals, then described sea creatures and then birds. This intuitive approach was appropriate for his Roman readers, who were not scientifically sophisticated. It was also appropriate to the highly linear papyrus rolls upon which his work was recorded. After the invention of the codex, encyclopedists gradually developed more elaborate categories and deeper hierarchies. Martianus Capella fit his small encyclopedia into the framework of the seven liberal arts (grammar, rhetoric, dialectic, arithmetic, geometry, astronomy, and music). Isidore of Seville appealed to etymology as well as the seven liberal arts for his organizing principles. In the 12th century, Hugh of St. Victor included the mechanical as well as liberal arts in a scheme that had half a dozen levels. (See Châtillon, 1966.) Vincent of Beauvais used, in addition to other traditional schemes, the seven days of creation from the Old Testament. (See Lemoine, 1966.) The motive in all cases was to provide a framework that would be familiar or accessible to an educated reader. The codex with its "random access" made the reader's work easier and allowed the author to develop a more elaborate outline of knowledge. The outline in turn solved the problem of textual overload by providing categories for all the elements of learning: it showed that one book could indeed encompass the textual world.

Hierarchies continued to be used in the Renaissance and after, but the cumulative medieval systems became less and less appropriate for categorizing new scientific knowledge. Francis Bacon responded by trying to derive his topics from first principles. In the second book of the *Advancement of Learning* he offered a system based upon three mental faculties: memory, imagination, and reason. To the faculty of memory belonged historical experience and writing. Imagination gave us art; reason gave us philosophy and natural science. Bacon went on to elaborate these categories and include the traditional disciplines in this new hierarchy. But the printing press and scientific discovery continued to generate information that needed to be accounted for in any great book. And so there was a growing trend toward neutral methods of "information processing"—alphabetization and indexing, which unlike topical outlines did not presuppose a shared body of knowledge or world-view among the readers. The shift from hierarchical to alphabetic organization in dictionaries and encyclopedias was an admission that such systems as the seven liberal arts, which could be possessed by all educated readers, could no longer accommodate specialized knowledge in physics, anatomy, geography, and mathematics. Most encyclopedias from the 18th century through the 20th have been alphabetical, because access to information, understood in an increasingly technical sense, has become more important than philosophical vision. A good contemporary encyclopedia exploits every technique of print technology to help the reader find the relevant articles, paragraphs, and even finer units of text. These techniques include tables of contents, indices, headnotes, sidenotes, and various type styles, all of which are in the service of alphabetically ordered articles. Printing, which had created a new degree of textual overload, also offered the solution of alphabetical order and precise indices.

Editors of encyclopedias, however, have never been entirely happy with this solution. Those who set out to make encyclopedias are writers who want to impose an intellectually satisfying order upon the world of texts. And alphabetic ordering does not do this: it does not define a writing space in which relations among topical elements are made clear. In an alphabetic encyclopedia, "Bantu" may come after "Banque de France" and before "Baptism, Christian," and the sequence means nothing. The editors of the *Encyclopédie* printed their articles alphabetically, but they did not wish to deny the philosophical value of a hierarchical arrangement of knowledge. D'Alembert wrote in the "Preliminary Discourse" that such an arrangement

consists of collecting knowledge into the smallest area possible and of placing the philosopher at a vantage point, so to speak, high above this vast labyrinth, where he can perceive the principal sciences and the arts simultaneously. . . . It is a kind of world map which is to show the principal countries, their position and their mutual dependence, the road that leads directly from one to the other. (D'Alembert, 1963, p. 47)

Diderot and D'Alembert included in their preface a tree of knowledge based on Francis Bacon's. Articles in the *Encyclopédie* contained references to indicate their place in this tree, although readers could not easily use the tree to organize their reading. The *Encyclopaedia Metropolitana* (1849) in the 19th century also tried to have it both ways: it was a "Universal Dictionary of Knowledge on an original plan, projected by the late Samuel Taylor Coleridge, comprising the twofold advantage of a philosophical and an alphabetical arrangement." Coleridge himself saw the encyclopedia as an educational tool: the reader should be introduced to all knowledge through the proper method, which consisted "in placing one or more particular things or notions, in subordination, either to a preconceived universal Idea, or to some lower form of the latter . . ." (p. 22). Coleridge seems to have imagined the ideal reader starting at page one of the encyclopedia and working straight through. So, while he believed strongly in the topical arrangement that goes back to the Middle Ages, Coleridge's encyclopedia was a clear product of the technology of print, in which the text is laid out in one ideal order.

The 15th edition of the *Encyclopaedia Britannica,* first issued in 1974, was another curious hybrid. It was a good printed encyclopedia, but it was also a book straining to break free of the limitations of print. Mortimer Adler gave the *Britannica* both a topical and an alphabetic arrangement. The main articles were printed alphabetically in volumes called the *Macropaedia.* A separate volume, the *Propaedia,* was a vast outline, in which all knowledge was arranged into ten parts, the parts into some 140 divisions, the divisions into sections, and so on. The *Propaedia* outline was not adventurous or idiosyncratic: it was "constructed and corrected in the light of detailed recommendations, directions, and analytical contributions from scholars and experts in all the fields of knowledge represented" (*Encyclopaedia Britannica,* 1974–1987, vol. 1, p. 6). It divided knowledge into categories suggested by the current sciences: Matter and Energy (Physics and Chemistry), The Earth (Geology), Life on Earth (Biology), Human Life (Anthropology and Sociology), and so on. The most original aspect of Adler's outline was that it was meant to be a guide for reading the *Macropaedia* articles. The reader who pursued topics through the outline was eventually referred to pages in the *Macropaedia.* The *Propaedia* therefore served to reorder the articles of the *Macropaedia:* to show their relationships in Adler's structure of knowledge. There might be no single extended essay in the *Britannica* on creation myths in various cultures or on French tragedy or on the world's rain forests, but the reader could construct such an essay by finding that topic in the *Propaedia* and following the references. The *Propaedia* referred the reader to paragraphs, sections, or articles in the *Macropaedia* from which the essay could be fashioned. In other words, the *Propaedia* turned the encyclopedia into a hypertext whose parts could be assembled and reassembled by the reader.

The problem was that the references were hard to follow in a printed work of 30 folio volumes. Most readers of the *Britannica* were not willing to go to the trouble: they were content to read the articles in the conventional way. In any library that displayed the *Britannica,* the *Propaedia* could immediately be identified as the shiny new volume among the well-used and worn ones. This was not due merely to laziness on the part of the readers. In fact, the *Britannica* was trying to deny the defining qualities of the printed book—its fixity and its linear order. If an encyclopedia is to be an alphabetical sequence of articles, the reader expects that each article will be a self-contained essay. The *Britannica* tried to create both a sequence of articles and a set of instructions for dismantling and reassembling those articles to make new readings. Eventually, the editors of the *Britannica* decided to add a conventional index and take most of the references out of the *Propaedia.* The *Propaedia* remains an outline of knowledge, but is no longer a blueprint for alternate readings of the rest of the work. Since the mid-1980s, the *Britannica* has become again a conventional printed encyclopedia.

▪ THE ELECTRONIC ENCYCLOPEDIA

In spite of or indeed because of its inconsistencies, the *Britannica* points the way to a new kind of encyclopedia. The complex system of references in the *Propaedia,* which seemed irrelevant to readers of a printed book, would make good sense in an electronic edition. The computer would facilitate the task of moving through the encyclopedic outline and among the various articles. It would take over the mechanical aspects of consultation: by getting the reader to the article and letting him or her read, by transferring the reader from one text to another, and by keeping the reader aware of his or her current position within the structure of the encyclopedia. In general the structure of an electronic encyclopedia can be both deeper and broader than that of its printed counterpart. A printed book is generally divided into chapters or headings within chapters, but in the electronic medium the visible and useful structure may extend to the paragraph, the sentence, or even the individual word. The computer can permit the reader to manipulate text at any of these levels.

In this way the computer restores the legitimacy of topical arrangements for great books like the encyclopedia. It answers the modern objections: that the world of textual knowledge is now too complex to be organized by topics; that any topical outline may be arbitrary or confusing; and that the reader will not be able to find elements because he or she will not know their place in the editor's outline. All this is true for a printed encyclopedia but not an electronic one. The problem of finding information in an electronic encyclopedia is facilitated by the fact that searching can be partly or wholly automatic. Readers can ask the machine to take up the search wherever their own knowledge fails them. And such searching can cut across any categories established by the editor. The title and even the text of every article can be stored in an electronic index, so that the encyclopedia is always in alphabetical order. The difference is that the alphabetical order is not the single canonical order of the text, as it is with a printed encyclopedia. Outlines or other topical arrangements can coexist with the alphabetical order. An electronic encyclopedia can be organized in as many ways as the editors and the readers can collectively imagine.

It is true that any topical outline today must seem arbitrary, because it reflects one editorial view of the organization of knowledge, which the reader may not share or even comprehend. The problem was less serious in the Middle Ages, when there was much broader agreement about the available structures of knowledge. But by the time of the *Encyclopédie,* D'Alembert recognized that there were many possible structures. When he compared the encyclopedia to a world map, he went on to say that "one can create as many different systems of human knowledge as there are world maps having different projections. . . . There are hardly any scholars who do not readily assume that their own science is at the center of all the rest, somewhat in the way that the first men placed themselves at the center of the world" (D'Alembert,

1963, p. 48). The encyclopedists were forced to choose one map, and they picked the one based on and therefore validated by Francis Bacon. And in the recent *Britannica,* as we have seen, Mortimer Adler felt compelled to defend himself against this charge—by pointing out that his *Propaedia* outline was certified by scholars and experts. Adler's other defense was that his outline was not rigid: the topics could be displayed in a circle around which the reader could move associatively. However, the circle as a structure is the antithesis of the printed book, which is linear in presentation and hierarchical in organization. In a printed book, the reader is not invited to begin any-where and move to any related section. By allowing multiple organizations, the *Britannica* has anticipated an attitude toward knowledge that belongs to the new medium, where the circle and the line are equally at home.

Because it was a printed book, the *Britannica* could only present one out-line (which itself occupies a whole volume), and that outline had to be a con-sensus. An electronic edition can be more daring, precisely because it does not impose upon the reader a single fixed view. The electronic encyclopedia could offer Mortimer Adler's outline, along with Coleridge's, Bacon's, or the outline of Hugh of St. Victor. It could offer a variety of contemporary views—one by a physicist, one by a historian, and so on. Each outline would be a distorting lens (or as D'Alembert suggested, a different projection) in which some areas of knowledge occupied the foreground while others were in the distance. But the reader would not be permanently constrained by any one view: he or she could shift back and forth among outlines. Or the reader could reject the very idea of a rigid outline. For the outlines themselves float on top of a network of elements, and the electronic medium can present these elements as a hyper-text without imposing a strict hierarchy. The editors of an electronic encyclo-pedia can insert explicit references at any point in any article. In print such references interrupt the visual flow of the text; furthermore, the reader must activate them by hand. In the electronic medium the references can be invisi-ble until the reader asks to see them and can be followed automatically at the reader's request. The editors are therefore free to create a referential network that functions underneath and apart from their topical outlines. All texts in all technologies of writing are bound together by an indefinite number of implicit references, echoes of words and phrases. But only the computer allows the reader to track such echoes—in an encyclopedia as in any elec-tronic book. The computer permits many structures to coexist in the same electronic text: tree structures, circles, and lines can cross and recross without obstructing one another. The encyclopedic impulse to organize can run riot in this new technology of writing.

Readers themselves participate in the organization of the encyclopedia. They are not limited to the references created by the editors, since at any point in any article they can initiate a search for a word or phrase that takes them to another article. They might also make their own explicit references (hypertextual links) for their own purposes, and these new references can be stored as part of any reader's copy of the encyclopedia. The reader might even be permitted to alter one of the encyclopedic outlines or create his or her own. Readers who are writing their own essays may include their text in separate notefiles and link these files into the encyclopedia. In other words, readers may personalize their own copy of the encyclopedia so that the structure and even the prose reflect their reading of the world of texts. As we have emphasized, it is always a short step from electronic reading to electronic writing, from determining the order of texts to altering their structure.

Some electronic encyclopedias are already commercially available, including Grolier's *Electronic Encyclopedia* (1988). These are not true electronic books, but rather printed books that have been transferred to the computer. In some cases articles conceived and written for print have been put in machine-readable form (Grolier's is an electronic version of the *Academic American Encyclopedia*) and made available with conventional search programs. That is, the reader types in a word or phrase to search (say "whales" or "Russo-Japanese War") and is presented with articles that contain the word or phrase in their title or body. Grolier's does allow the reader to go beyond hypertextual bookmarks in order to collect articles of interest. But in general, although readers can search for topics in a number of ways, they cannot intervene in the structure of the encyclopedia or build new structures. Most of the electronic encyclopedias currently available do not reflect the power or the limitations of the new medium, but rather the conservative character of the publishing industry, which is bound inevitably to the technology of print. They only begin to suggest the flexibility that the computer can bring to the organization of a great book.

An exception is the system called Hyperties. It also presents images and text on the computer screen, but in this case both the text and the images are animated. When the reader points to a highlighted phrase or to a graphic element, a window pops up to provide an explanation or elaboration. The reader reads by following links from window to window: a text in Hyperties is a network of such links and therefore a true hypertext. (See Fig. 1.)

The flexibility of hypertext together with the enormous capacity of electronic storage changes the scope of the encyclopedia.

The flexibility of hypertext together with the enormous capacity of electronic storage changes the scope of the encyclopedia. The encyclopedic vision has always been that the great book should contain all symbolic knowledge. This vision has always been utopian: the making of such a great book is impossible because of the human limitations of the editors as well as the limitations of the available technology of writing. Thus, editors of encyclopedias have always made explicit or implicit exclusions: the mechanical arts, for example, were not represented in the early medieval encyclopedias of Martianus and Isidore; biographies were not included in the first *Britannica.* Encyclopedias in the Middle Ages were often statements of high

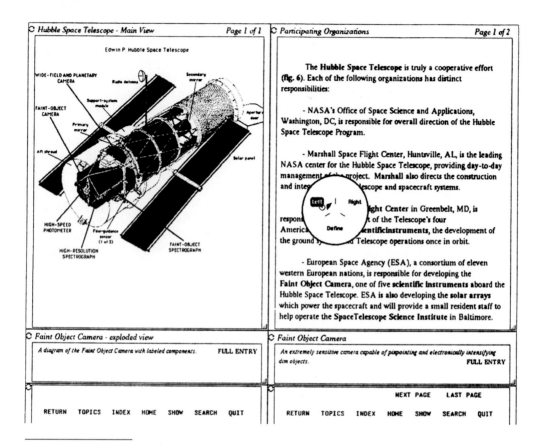

Hubble Space Telescope - Main View Page 1 of 1

FIGURE 1

In this Hyperties document describing the Hubble Space Telescope, both the highlighted phrases on the right and portions of the illustration on the left serve as hypertextual links. © 1988 IEEE. Reprinted with kind permission from Computer and the authors: Marchionini and Schneiderman, 1988, p. 75.

learning: the utilitarian value of encyclopedias has been emphasized only in the last 200 years. In this century American encyclopedias have cut out scholarly subjects in favor of articles of popular interest in order to maintain the largest possible readership. The electronic encyclopedia seems to be following the American trend, although perhaps only because the current examples are often American. In any case, the computer can hold so much information that there is little need to be selective: the reader need only look at a tiny portion at any one time. The attitude toward the knowledge contained in electronic encyclopedias will be opportunistic, almost irreverent, because of the temporary character of electronic information. This was not the case for an encyclopedia in manuscript or in print, where the technology encouraged more or less permanent structures of knowledge. Today we cannot hope for permanence and for general agreement on the order of things—in encyclopedias any more than in politics or the arts. What we have instead is a view of knowledge as collections of (verbal and visual) ideas that can arrange themselves into a kaleidoscope of hierarchical and associative patterns—each pattern meeting the needs of one class of readers on one occasion.

■ E L E C T R O N I C   E N V I R O N M E N T S

We need to consider how digitized images and sound should be integrated into an electronic encyclopedia. In more than one proposal for the encyclopedia of the future, the pictures, sounds, and even smells and tastes seem to overwhelm and replace verbal text. The result would be not principally a hypertext, but instead a multimedia presentation in which the computer addresses all the reader's senses and puts the reader into the situation described. Readers do not read about the French Revolution; they visit Paris in 1789. They do not read about the chemistry of rubber; they take part in an experiment. They do not read about Jupiter, but instead board a simulated spacecraft heading for the planet.

Such multimedia displays would seem to expand the range and the power of the encyclopedia, to be the computer's equivalent of the diagrams or pictures common in printed encyclopedias since the 18th century. (Along with its 17 volumes of prose, the *Encyclopédie* consisted of 11 volumes of plates, of which its editors were justifiably proud.) But there is a danger in such an encyclopedia of losing the symbolic character of reading and writing. As an encyclopedic computer program grows more elaborate, it may make more decisions for the reader and present these decisions in a perceptual, rather than symbolic form. The reader becomes a mere viewer, and the encyclopedia becomes interactive television, or what is now sometimes called "virtual reality." Here is one description of an encyclopedia as a simulation, a guided tour through a world of the editor's making:

A tour *is a particular path through some information (the model). . . . A* filter *is the logical analog of an optical filter. Placed between a model and an observer (the user), it can mask out detail, add emphasis, combine information from several sources, and help determine presentation style. . . . A* guide *is the user's personal (electronic) agent in the encyclopedia system. The guide sets up tours, explains, helps select filters, points out interesting topics, and provides help when requested. The guide also builds up a description of the user's preferences to better tailor the tours that the encyclopedia provides. Guides might have different personalities and styles; the user could pick a guide according to his or her tastes, for example, the Renaissance balance of Leonardo da Vinci or the novelty of the latest rock star. In terms of the models-tours-filter-guides metaphor, using this future encyclopedia bears little resemblance to reading through a set of tomes, but is better viewed instead as a conversation with a guide or tutor who accompanies us during our learning adventure in an electronic amusement park or interactive science museum. (Weyer & Borning, 1985, p. 65)*

Such a computer program, if it were ever possible, would be a kind of anti-encyclopedia, just as computerized simulated environments are in general anti-books. Entering into an environment is the antithesis of reading, because in place of a symbolic structure of words, equations, graphs, and images, the program offers the user the illusion of perceptual experience. An encounter with texts is replaced by perceptions, and the distancing and abstracting quality of text is lost. A simulated rock star or even Leonardo da Vinci as the personified voice of an encyclopedia is no solution at all to the problem of encyclopedic organization. To the extent that the persona is a convincing personality, it merely gets in the way. If we were to meet such a person who knew everything, the question would still be how to learn anything from the encounter—how that person would convey structures of knowledge to us. To structure knowledge, we need a book: in the electronic medium the computer as hypertext, not as superhuman. An electronic encyclopedia may certainly combine several media. The defining quality of the electronic medium is its ability to interweave words, pictures, video images—any material that can be represented as bits. All such material can be formed into an electronic book; it can be treated textually or hypertextually, as a network of elements through which readers can travel. But to clothe a hypertextual network in the persona of a rock star is to obscure the purpose of hypertext itself.

■ THE ELECTRONIC LIBRARY

The library as a great book adopts a strategy opposite to that of the encyclopedia. While the encyclopedia absorbs and digests other books, the library attempts to control knowledge by collecting as many books as possible within one conceptual and physical structure. The library is the physical realization of a culture's writing space of books. In medieval and early modern libraries, books were often chained to their shelves. Such libraries did not merely contain books; the books became part of the furniture and walls. What the reader does metaphorically in the encyclopedia, he or she can do literally in the library—move into and through a textual space.

The library as a great book adopts a strategy opposite to that of the encyclopedia.

The space of the library has evolved along lines similar to those of the encyclopedia, but the principles of organization for libraries have generally been more utilitarian. Ancient Greek and Roman libraries of papyrus rolls were arranged by subject and then by author (Jackson, 1974, p. 23). In the later empire period, the Romans also divided their collections by language: one for Greek and one for Latin. It was common in the Middle Ages and even later to divide the books by university faculty: law, medicine, theology, and the arts. Within each division the organization was roughly alphabetical. However, unlike modern encyclopedias, modern libraries never adopted a completely alphabetical arrangement. They continued to classify books by topic, and, as we would expect, the classifications became more complicated and more ad hoc. When Conrad Gesner published his *Pandects* in 1548, he still suggested classing books under the seven liberal arts as well as by university faculty (Jackson, 1974, pp. 128ff). But by the end of the 19th century, the founders of modern classification, C. A. Cutter and Melvil Dewey, claimed to reject anything but utility as their criterion. Describing his system, Dewey wrote: "[t]he impossibility of making a satisfactory classification of all knowledge as preserved in books, has been appreciated from the first, and nothing of the kind attempted. Theoretical harmony and exactness have been repeatedly sacrificed to the practical requirements of the library . . ." (Jackson, 1974, p. 388). The Library of Congress call numbers, by which books are now shelved, follow a topical system that few users bother to learn. Apart from knowing that books on psychology or books on German literature are shelved together, the user simply treats the call number as a street address, a means of locating the book.

The call numbers in fact constitute a vast system, a mapping of the conceptual library onto the building, which is itself a physical hierarchy of floors, stacks, and shelves. At the same time the library's card catalog provides three different conceptual views of the library: a list of authors' names, one of titles, and one of subjects. The library is a single physical hierarchy that is reorganized or "written over" in three ways by its catalog system. In current libraries the catalog is often computerized, making it easier for the user to jump back and forth among the three views and to search for keywords in titles or subjects. The user can therefore rearrange the conceptual library with relative ease. But the books themselves are still printed, and the user must eventually leave the electronic world and set out on a physical journey among the stacks. In a fully electronic library, the books themselves would be stored electronically; the library would no longer be a building that the reader had to visit. The computers, storage devices, and communications equipment must be housed somewhere, but the reader has no need to see the equipment, any more than he or she needs to see the physical plant of the local telephone company. In such a library, the books could rearrange themselves at the reader's request. The same book could in effect appear on different shelves: for example, a book on the history of theories of mind could appear in the psychology section and in the philosophy section. It is often claimed that a principal advantage of a physical library is that the reader can browse and come across interesting books by chance. But an electronic library could give the reader the same opportunity. A graphic videoscreen could even display the spines of the books on shelves and allow the reader to reach in and open the books, if that is really the best way for the reader to browse.

A major library of printed books is always changing: new books come in, and the physical shelving is expanded or redone. But the ideal of the library is not change, but preservation. Libraries have seemed venerable because they preserved what was created by past writers and valued by past readers. Francis Bacon called libraries "shrines where all the relics of the ancient saints, full of true virtue and that without delusion or imposture, are preserved and reposed" (Bacon, 1955, p. 233). The English poet George Crabbe called them the "tombs of those who cannot die" (1966, p. 9). No one would apply this funerary rhetoric to an electronic library that reorganizes texts as readily as it preserves them. Electronic libraries will no doubt preserve the books of the past, although in a transcribed form. But the reverence accorded to the traditional library of manuscripts and printed books came from the fact that the building itself was a kind of monumental writing, a writing and reading space in stone. In the age of print the library itself became the replacement for Victor Hugo's cathedral: the entry hall or reading room of more than one great library was built to resemble the nave of a cathedral, with the circulation or information desk as the altar. There is nothing monumental about an electronic library, which might appear to users as a CD-ROM or simply as a code number that they select on their university's communications network.

■ FROM PERSEUS TO XANADU

When we look for examples of electronic libraries, we find the same situation as with electronic encyclopedias. There are modest systems already in operation and others in progress, and then there are proposals for a utopian future. In one sense the electronic library is already decades old, for there have been bibliographic and textual databases since the 1960s. At first these databases were expensive and were therefore restricted to industry and medicine, law, and the physical sciences. But now all kinds of information are being put into commercial and private databases: newspaper articles, airline schedules, census data, scholarly bibliographies. Some of the commercial databases already constitute electronic almanacs, indicating the eclectic tastes that the electronic medium both serves and fosters. Other databases are forerunners of an electronic research library. Not only the bibliography of many fields but also the texts of Greek and Latin literature, important poets in various modern languages, and the *Oxford English Dictionary* (1987) have been converted into electronic form. We already see the impulse to create "universal" databases: to have all U.S. Court decisions, all archaeological data from pre-Columbian America, all medical bibliography, or all medieval English literature in one electronic place. There is already underway a project called Perseus whose goal is to assemble an electronic library of materials for classical studies: millions of words of ancient texts in Greek and translation with grammatical notes, a 30,000-word Greek dictionary, an historical atlas, diagrams, and even pictures (stored on videodisk) of archaeological sites.

The Perseus project seeks to place before the reader all the materials of a small research library, and also to make the materials interconnected or hypertextual .

The Perseus project seeks to place before the reader all the materials of a small research library, and also to make the materials interconnected or hypertextual: "Put an atlas, a dictionary, and a collection of texts onto a single compact disk, and you have done more than make three kinds of reference work available. Each affects the form of the other" (Crane, 1988, p. 40). The result will be a universal database, a new space for reading and for writing, since Perseus will also allow the reader to take notes or make excerpts for his or her own purposes.

The universal electronic database may be individual or collective. The individual writer dreams of recording all his or her essays, notes, and jottings in one systematic form, while scholars and scientists imagine vast collective repositories of information available immediately to any user in the nation or the world. For some, these two visions coalesce: each writer's database is absorbed into the universal network, until all writers occupy a single vast space in which all previous literature has been recorded. In this ultimate electronic library, as on a smaller scale in Project Perseus, the distinction between private and public writing breaks down. The computer makes all public writing available to each reader, at the same time permitting the individual to externalize all of his or her own writing.

This utopian (for others, dystopian) vision lies somewhere in the background of all proposals for the electronic collection of text. The desire is always to extend the collection, to incorporate new texts, to bring the whole of a field into the same electronic structure. And this passion is a familiar one: what other goal have librarians ever had than to bring all books under their systematic control? The goal of a universal collection goes back at least to Alexandria, where the Ptolemies apparently ordered that rolls found aboard ships entering the port were to be seized for their library. The modern equivalents of the Alexandrian library are the great national collections, such as the Library of Congress and the British Library, which receive by law copies of all books printed in their respective countries. There are already proposals for universal electronic libraries. One of the earliest has the appropriate visionary name "Xanadu"—it is a proposal by Ted Nelson, who as we have noted also coined the name "hypertext." Xanadu is to be an electronic subscription library: users pay to participate, but the expectation is that everyone will see the value of participation, and the library will become the universal writing space. Nelson has labeled his project: "A Piece of Software that Proposes a New Era of Computers, a New Form of Instant Literature and a Whole New World." The Xanadu system structures information in the computer in such a way that any text can be referenced by any other, these references can in turn be referenced, and so on. Nelson explains that "[b]y using links to mark and type data elements, and to represent typed connections between the data elements, the Xanadu system provides A UNIVERSAL DATA STRUCTURE TO WHICH ALL OTHER DATA MAY BE MAPPED . . ." (Nelson, 1987, p. 1). But the developers have much more in mind than a computer data structure. They see writers and readers throughout the world working in the same conceptual space. Xanadu is "a plan for a worldwide network, intended to serve hundreds of millions of users simultaneously from the corpus of the world's stored writings, graphics and data" (Nelson, 1987. p. 1; see also *Literary Machines* by Nelson, 1984). Xanadu is a vision for the macrocosm: millions of texts are to be managed and ultimately joined into one world network. The result would be a larger library by far than any ever realized in print or manuscript.

There are already proposals for universal electronic libraries. One of the earliest has the appropriate visionary name "Xanadu."

Others have preferred to imagine the microcosm—how such a vast writing space might appear to an individual writer or reader. An example here is a proposal called "Tablet." This Tablet would be a computer the size of a notebook—it looks rather like the old Etch-a-Sketch toy—which delivers text (as well as graphics and video) with clarity equal to the printed page. The writer can record words or draw on the screen with a stylus. Tablet is also the outlet for a worldwide system, in which all users can read and many can write:

Imagine a tremendous hypertext encyclopedia where every expert in every field maintains his or her knowledge online. Such a document can only keep growing and assimilating more and more information, pushing older and less popular information to lower levels while maintaining a hierarchical structure. (Young et al., 1988, p. 12)

Tablet is portable—the writer can work under a (natural) tree—but portability does not mean that the writer will be disconnected from the network of all other texts and writers. The network follows the writer wherever he or she goes.

Tablet integrates a cellular telephone link. This will not only support voice but data communications as well . . . Tablet will have a GPS (Global Positioning System) receiver as a built-in component. GPS is an existing satellite-based system which enables objects to locate themselves in the world to within a few meters. (Young et al., 1988, pp. 9–10)

Every carrier of every Tablet will not only be in contact, but his or her position in the global library will be registered. In earlier times, as we have noted, books were chained to shelves in order to guarantee that patrons would not smuggle them out of the library. The Tablet cannot be taken out of the library, because the world has become the library and the chaining is now electronic.

Neither Tablet nor Xanadu is likely to perform as advertised: besides the technical problems, there are insurmountable political and social obstacles to a universal system. But the image of the electronic library as a community of writers in instant and effortless communication—this image will persist, and it will define the next age of writing. Working libraries will continue for some time to be hybrids: combinations of machine-readable materials, computer services, and familiar printed books and journals. But the emphasis will gradually move from the physical to the electronic components. The library as an idea will become as ephemeral as electronic technology itself; it will no longer be a building or even a fixed conceptual structure, but instead a constantly evolving network of elements. To write and to read in this library will be to move through the network examining and altering elements. Writer and reader will be "connected," and each act of writing and reading will leave a trace for future writing and reading. In at least one sense, the goal of all previous ages will be realized: the library will finally be nothing other than a great book, a larger structure composed of the same elements in the same writing space as the book itself.

■ THE BOOK OF NATURE

I saw buried in the depths, bound with love in one volume,
that which is scattered through the universe.
                                        (Dante, *Paradiso*, XXXIII, 82ff)

The electronic writing Tablet is an attempt to break down the limits of the conventional book—to put the whole world of writing into one book. Yet the Tablet also takes the book out into the world. Writers carry their Tablets everywhere. When they write on (or talk to) their Tablets, the information moves back and forth through a network that blurs the distinction between the world of nature and the symbolic world of the library. For writers seated under the trees beaming information to all other interested writer/readers, the world has become an enormous volume in which they can leave their electronic marks. Like many similar proposals Tablet is a technology for writing *on* the world.

The metaphor of the world-book is not peculiar to the computer age. Throughout the history of writing, the book has served as a metaphor for nature as a whole and for the human mind in particular. Scholars such as Ernst Curtius have traced a series of analogies among the ideas of mind, book, encyclopedia, library, and the world of nature. We shall examine the metaphor of the book as mind in a later chapter, but here we can say something more about the book of nature. The metaphor appealed to the Middle Ages, precisely because of the importance of venerable texts and textual authorities for the medieval mind. For the medieval scholar, the world was made intelligible through such key works as those of Augustine and Aristotle. The very structure of the world was supposed to be mirrored in such books, and conversely the universe itself came to be viewed as a great book—hence the importance of encyclopedias and summae that brought the whole textual world under control. The ambition of encyclopedists and theologians was nothing less than "to gather all strands of learning together into an enormous Text, an encyclopedia or summa, that would mirror the historical and transcendental orders just as the Book of God's Word (the Bible) was a speculum of the Book of his Work (nature)" (Gellrich, *The Idea of the Book,* 1985, p. 18). As Curtius has argued, the poet Dante could invoke the same metaphor. At the end of the *Paradiso,* Dante's ultimate vision is of the universe as an enormous book that has finally been put together properly: "all that has been scattered throughout the entire universe, that has been separated and dissevered, like loose quaderni [quires], is now 'bound in one volume.' The book—[in which all is contained]—is the Godhead" (Curtius, 1973, p. 332). Dante's poem itself has been called a summa, an attempt to encompass all knowledge between two covers.

The time for writing theological summae is long past, but the *Encyclopédie* or the 15th edition of the *Encyclopaedia Britannica* can be understood as modern secular attempts to encompass the book of nature in the technology of print. We recall that D'Alembert described the *Encyclopédie* as a world map (D'Alembert, 1963, p. 47). And now proposals for hypertextual encyclopedias and libraries (Xanadu, the Tablet, and many others) translate this vision into the electronic medium. However, the metaphor has changed in response to the new technology. In the age of the manuscript and especially in the age of print, the book was valued for its capacity to preserve and display fixed structures. It was a technological reflection of the great chain of being, in which all of nature had its place in a subtle, but unalterable hierarchy. The hierarchical divisions of knowledge by Hugh of St. Victor or even Francis Bacon belonged on the written or printed page. Even as late as Coleridge, an encyclopedist thought that the purpose of his great book was to demonstrate how each notion is subordinated "to a preconceived universal Idea" (*Encyclopaedia Metropolitana,* 1849, p. 22)—in other words, to present hierarchies of knowledge. The passion for hierarchy finds its purest expression in the elaborate table of contents of modern encyclopedias and other great books in print. The table of contents is both hierarchical and linear: it shows subordination and superordination, and it also shows the reader the order in which he or she will encounter these ideas in reading from first page to last.

There is nothing in an electronic book that quite corresponds to the printed table of contents. Menus in an electronic book can indicate a hierarchy of topics, but there is no single, linear order of pages to determine how the reader should move through the hierarchy. In this sense, the electronic book reflects a different natural world, in which relationships are multiple and evolving: there is no great chain of being in an electronic world-book. For that very reason, an electronic book is a better analogy for contemporary views of nature, since nature today is often not regarded as a hierarchy, but rather as a network of interdependent species and systems. The biological sciences dispensed with the great chain of being over a century ago—long before the advent of the electronic computer. More recently, but also long before the computer, physics rejected simple hierarchical views of matter and energy. In fact the metaphor of the book of nature has long been moribund. But with the coming of the computer, we have a writing technology that suits a contemporary scientific conception of the world, and the metaphor of the world as a hypertextual book can now be explored. We can expect contemporary scientists and scholars to come more and more to the conclusion that the book of nature is a hypertext, whose language is the computational mathematics of directed graphs. This is an intriguing prospect. For if scientists are studying the interdependencies of nature, while humanists are reading hypertexts, then our vision of nature can be reunited with our technology of writing in a way that we have not seen since the Middle Ages.

■ REFERENCES

Bacon, Francis. (1955). *Advancement of learning.* In H. G. Dick (Ed.), *Selected writings of Francis Bacon* (pp. 157–392). New York: Random House.

Chatillon, Jean. (1966). Le 'Didascalion' de Hugues de Saint-Victor. *Journal of World History,* 9, 539–552.

Crabbe, George. (1966). *The library, a poem.* Boston: G. K. Hall and Co. [originally published in 1781]

Crane, Gregory. (1988). "Redefining the book: Some preliminary problems," *Academic Computing,* 2 (5), 6–11, 36–41.

Curtius, Ernst Robert. (1973). *European literature and the Latin Middle Ages* (Willard R. Trask, Trans.). Princeton, NJ: Princeton University Press.

D'Alembert, Jean le Rond. (1963). *Preliminary discourse to the Encyclopedia of Diderot* (R. N. Schwab, Trans.). Indianapolis, IN: Bobbs-Merrill.

Eisenstein, Elizabeth. (1979). *Printing as an agent of change: Communications and cultural transformations in early-modern Europe* (Vols. 1–2). Cambridge: Cambridge University Press.

Encyclopaedia Britannica. (1974–1987). (Philip W. Goetz, Ed.). Chicago: Encyclopaedia Britannica.

Encyclopedia Metropolitana (1849). (Edward Smedley, Hugh James Rose, and Henry John Rose, Eds.) (Vol. 1). London: John Joseph Griffin and Co.

Febvre, Lucien, and Marin, Henri-Jean. (1971). *L'apparaition du livre [The coming of the book].* Paris: Editions Albin Michel.

Gellrich, J. M. *The idea of the book in the Middle Ages: Language theory, mythology and fiction.* Ithaca, NY: Cornell University Press.

Jackson, S. L. (1974). *Libraries and librarianship in the west: A brief history.* New York: McGraw-Hill.

Lemoine, Michel. (1966). *L'oeuvre encyclopédique de Vincent de Beauvais* [The encyclopedic work of Vincent of Beauvais]. *Journal of World History,* 9, 571–579.

Nelson, Ted H. (1984). *Literary machines.* Theodor H. Nelson.

Nelson, Ted H. (1987). *The Xanadu paradigm.* San Antonio, TX: Project Xanadu. Published broadsheet.

Reynolds, L. D., and Wilson, N. G. (1978). *Scribes and scholars: A guide to the transmission of Greek and Latin literature.* Oxford: Clarendon Press.

Saenger, Paul. (1982). Silent reading: Its impact on late medieval script and society. *Viator,* 13, 367–414.

Weyer, S. A., and Borning, A. H. (1985). A prototype electronic encyclopeda. *ACM Transactions on Office Information Systems,* 3 (1), 63–85.

Young et al. (1988). Academic computing in the year 2000. *Academic Computing* 2 (7), 7–12, 62–65.

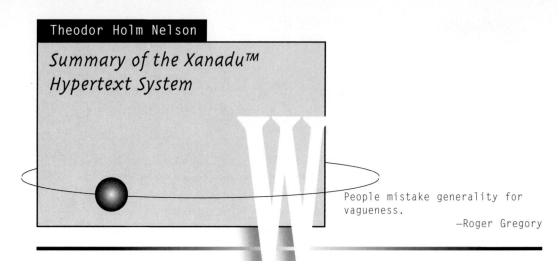

Theodor Holm Nelson

Summary of the Xanadu™ Hypertext System

> People mistake generality for vagueness.
>
> —Roger Gregory

hile the system is conceptually simple, it is amazing how many different ways there are to think about it and describe it. We take this as indicating its generality.

Some of these descriptions are listed below, both as one-liners and in an essay form. Readers may find them useful for communicating to others, or for reviewing their own understanding of the system.

■ SUMMARY OF THE XANADU™ HYPERTEXT SYSTEM:

One-Liners

"A literary system of authorship, ownership, quotation and linkage."

"A pluralistic publishing and archiving medium with open hypertext and semi-closed framing."

"A distributed repository scheme for worldwide electronic publishing."

"A system to promote cumulative order and the equitable coexistence of many viewpoints."

"A vessel for the true shape of information—without having to cut it or jam it."

"A mapping system between storage and virtual documents."

"A distributed server network for documents made out of pooled boilerplate."

"A storage arrangement for linking between arbitrary collections of material."

"A seamless data architecture for linked electronic publishing."

"A linking system for keeping track of anything."

"An applicative virtual document system for applying sequential and non-sequential structure to material that arrived out of sequence and unstructured."

"A grand address space for everything, parts of which can be in different places at once."

"A way of tying it all together and not losing anything."

"A way of including anything in anything else."...

Shortest Description

The Xanadu™ Hypertext System is a form of storage: a new computer filing system which stores and delivers new kinds of documents. These documents may have any form and contents, but may also have links and inclusions from other documents. A user may request parts of documents or may follow links, both within and between documents. The user may easily see highlighted intercomparisons between documents.

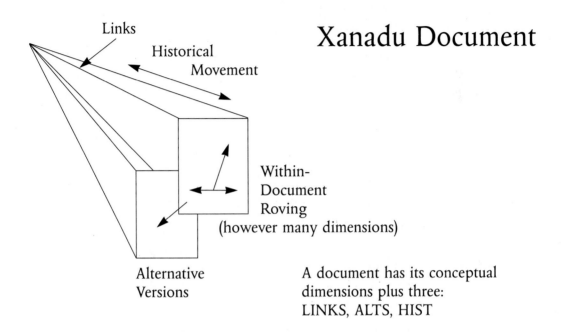

Links

Historical
Movement

Xanadu Document

Within-
Document
Roving
(however many dimensions)

Alternative
Versions

A document has its conceptual
dimensions plus three:
LINKS, ALTS, HIST

This structure is the same regardless of size: a small Xanadu system will hold and clarify an individual's work, the full network is intended to supply millions of documents to millions of simultaneous users, all following links and windows throughout the growing body of hypertext.

Medium-Length Description

The Xanadu™ Hypertext System is a new form of storage intended to simplify and clarify computer use, and make possible new forms of instantaneous electronic publication.

Running on a single computer, it is a file server for the storage and delivery of text, graphics and other digital information with previously impossible arrangements and services. These new arrangements include links and windows between documents, as well as non-sequential writing (hypertext).

It will also reveal and clarify commonalities between documents and among versions, simplifying both storage and comprehensibility. Thus even running on a single computer, it will simplify computer operations, clarify storage, and clarify and simplify office and document work for individuals and corporations.

In the full world-wide network, it will permit the publication and instantaneous world-wide delivery of interconnected works having immense new power to huge numbers of users.

Extended Description

The Xanadu™ Hypertext System is software for the unique organization of computer storage and the rapid delivery of its contents to users. All forms of material—text, pictures, musical notations, even photographs and recordings—may be digitally stored on it. Most importantly, the new forms of interconnection this makes possible among these materials are profound and revealing.

It is a system for the rapid delivery of linked documents (which may share material) and the assimilation and storage of changes. System facilities permit promiscuous linkage and windowing among all materials; with special features for alternative versions, historical backtrack and arbitrary collaging. It is based on new technicalities which are of no concern to the user, and materials are stored in locations the user need not know about.

Any forms of data will eventually share these facilities of linking and inclusions, although each needs separate implementation. Bit-map graphics will be stored in such a way as to allow panning (graphical scrolling) and zoom (continuously increasing or decreasing magnification) as incremental data deliveries. (How your screen machine will show them is another matter.) Three-dimensional objects, when implemented, may be collaged by users into compound objects, scenes from history, enactments and artwork.

It's exactly one system that comes in small, medium and very large. In all cases it is a back-end storage feeder—or "file server," in the current vernacular—for holding and sending out documents which are connected in any possible way (arbitrary topology).

Single-user and multi-user versions for individual and corporate uses will simplify and clarify the user's storage and the interrelations of data—helping your information evolve toward better organization by small increments.

The single-user system will run on personal computers (such as the extended-memory PC clone and the megabyte Macintosh). The multi-user version will provide document services to a network of computers among corporate users.

Custom front ends of any kind are possible. While any sort of terminal may be connected to the system, its best operation requires a full computer in the user's terminal, programmed to handle display functions, interchange protocol, and other work. A front-end program is any program, running on a user's screen machine or other computer, for any purpose and behaving in any manner, which delivers to and extracts from the Xanadu storage system.

A complete network of publishing with royalty has been carefully planned. All users will have access to all public documents instantaneously (not counting network delays). Every byte delivered to the user will return a minute royalty to the document of origin.

In this expected publishing network, Xanadu storage will provide linked access to new and powerful forms of interconnected data and writing in compound documents, the storage of which may be distributed.

Its unique facilities of backtrack, linkage and windowing will allow the creation of new forms of multi-level, explorable collections and collages of material—without losing the well-defined authorship and ownership of all parts.

Anyone may publish collaged and windowing documents having finely-divided ownership. There are simple categories of publication (private and public) and low, comparatively flat costs of usage.

Any part of any available document will be accessible from any port on any computer in the net at any time, at prices comparable to storage on other computer systems.

Users may connect their home or office computers of any kind to this network, whether by dialup, GTE Telenet, leased line, twisted pair, or nearby wink-laser. (Each machine will need its own front-end program, however.)

Services will be differentiated mainly with respect to speed of terminal (1200 baud the minimum). No users will be restricted as to what public documents they may access, though private documents will be restricted as specified by their owners.

The system's contents will be supplied by customers only. There will be no participation by the Xanadu enterprise in the publishing process itself; neither contents nor indexing will be provided by the system, these being rightful endeavors of the customers.

The system will exert no supervision or censorship on stored or published materials, and court orders will be required for the removal of any material held in a stable account. However, publishers and individuals will be thoroughly warned about legal exposure and pitfalls.

Publishing requires an up-front payment of one year's disk rental. A secondary publisher using windowed material need only pay the cost of pointer storage.

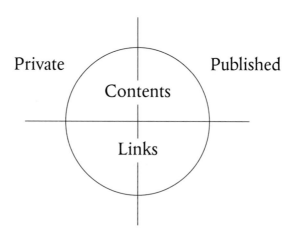

Private   Published

Contents

Links

Private documents are available only to the owner and the owner's designees. Published documents are available to anyone, and yield a royalty to the owner; they may be updated at will, but the earlier contents remain available. They may not be withdrawn from publication except after six months' notice or court order. "Privashed" documents are available to anyone, and may be changed at will, but yield no royalty.

We believe this will make possible a whole new universe of knowledge and understanding.

It is presently on line as an experimental prototype. Later, we expect to offer it in object form to users for both personal and corporate computers, first in single-user, then multi-user configurations. After that comes the network with publishing royalty, which we believe can grow as fast as demand.

In one business scenario, the intended public operation of the publishing system will be out of a chain of suburban or roadside stations, called Silverstands™. New users will learn the operation of the system at such stands, and local users may dial into their nearest Silverstand. Silverstand personnel ("Conductors") will include both local people and an itinerant corps of circulating smarties.

The actual code of the system is a medium-sized program in the C language, currently running under the Unix operating system.

■ "HOW IS IT DIFFERENT FROM THE SOURCE?"

Many public-access computer systems now offer text services. One of the best known is The Source, so we often get this question.

Unlike general-purpose time-sharing systems such as The Source, which can run many kinds of programs and furnishes text services simply as one class of available program, ours is a *specialized* storage form for what we believe is the *most generalized* form of storage. Our system does not permit the running of user programs.

The Source, and other currently available text services, do not support linkage, windows, alternative versions or historical backtrack as they supply their stored documents, let alone maintain these connective structures as documents change.

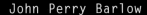

John Perry Barlow

The Economy of Ideas
A framework for rethinking
patents and copyrights in the
Digital Age

f nature has made any one thing less
susceptible than all others of exclusive property, it is the
action of the thinking power called an idea, which an
individual may exclusively possess as long as he keeps it to
himself; but the moment it is divulged, it forces itself
into the possession of everyone, and the receiver cannot
dispossess himself of it. Its peculiar character, too, is
that no one possesses the less, because every other
possesses the whole of it. He who receives an idea from me,
receives instruction himself without lessening mine; as he
who lights his taper at mine, receives light without
darkening me. That ideas should freely spread from one to
another over the globe, for the moral and mutual instruction
of man, and improvement of his condition, seems to have been
peculiarly and benevolently designed by nature, when she
made them, like fire, expansible over all space, without
lessening their density at any point, and like the air in
which we breathe, move, and have our physical being,
incapable of confinement or exclusive appropriation.
Inventions then cannot, in nature, be a subject of property.
—Thomas Jefferson

   Throughout the time I've been groping around cyberspace, an immense,
unsolved conundrum has remained at the root of nearly every legal, ethical,
governmental, and social vexation to be found in the Virtual World. I refer to
the problem of digitized property. The enigma is this: If our property can be
infinitely reproduced and instantaneously distributed all over the planet without cost, without our knowledge, without its even leaving our possession,
how can we protect it? How are we going to get paid for the work we do
with our minds? And, if we can't get paid, what will assure the continued creation and distribution of such work?

   Since we don't have a solution to what is a profoundly new kind of challenge, and are apparently unable to delay the galloping digitization of everything not obstinately physical, we are sailing into the future on a sinking ship.

   This vessel, the accumulated canon of copyright and patent law, was developed to convey forms and methods of expression entirely different from the

vaporous cargo it is now being asked to carry. It is leaking as much from within as from without.

Legal efforts to keep the old boat floating are taking three forms: a frenzy of deck chair rearrangement, stern warnings to the passengers that if she goes down, they will face harsh criminal penalties, and serene, glassy-eyed denial.

Intellectual property law cannot be patched, retrofitted, or expanded to contain digitized expression any more than real estate law might be revised to cover the allocation of broadcasting spectrum (which, in fact, rather resembles what is being attempted here). We will need to develop an entirely new set of methods as befits this entirely new set of circumstances.

Most of the people who actually create soft property—the programmers, hackers, and Net surfers—already know this. Unfortunately, neither the companies they work for nor the lawyers these companies hire have enough direct experience with nonmaterial goods to understand why they are so problematic. They are proceeding as though the old laws can somehow be made to work, either by grotesque expansion or by force. They are wrong.

The source of this conundrum is as simple as its solution is complex. Digital technology is detaching information from the physical plane, where property law of all sorts has always found definition.

Throughout the history of copyrights and patents, the proprietary assertions of thinkers have been focused not on their ideas but on the expression of those ideas. The ideas themselves, as well as facts about the phenomena of the world, were considered to be the collective property of humanity. One could claim franchise, in the case of copyright, on the precise turn of phrase used to convey a particular idea or the order in which facts were presented.

The point at which this franchise was imposed was that moment when the "word became flesh" by departing the mind of its originator and entering some physical object, whether book or widget. The subsequent arrival of other commercial media besides books didn't alter the legal importance of this moment. Law protected expression and, with few (and recent) exceptions, to express was to make physical.

Protecting physical expression had the force of convenience on its side. Copyright worked well because, Gutenberg notwithstanding, it was hard to make a book. Furthermore, books froze their contents into a condition which was as challenging to alter as it was to reproduce. Counterfeiting and distributing counterfeit volumes were obvious and visible activities—it was easy enough to catch somebody in the act of doing. Finally, unlike unbounded words or images, books had material surfaces to which one could attach copyright notices, publisher's marques, and price tags.

Mental-to-physical conversion was even more central to patent. A patent, until recently, was either a description of the form into which materials were to be rendered in the service of some purpose, or a description of the process by which rendition occurred. In either case, the conceptual heart of patent was the material result. If no purposeful object could be rendered because of some material limitation, the patent was rejected. Neither a Klein bottle nor a shovel made of silk could be patented. It had to be a thing, and the thing had to work.

Thus, the rights of invention and authorship adhered to activities in the physical world. One didn't get paid for ideas, but for the ability to deliver them into reality. For all practical purposes, the value was in the conveyance and not in the thought conveyed.

In other words, the bottle was protected, not the wine.

Now, as information enters cyberspace, the native home of Mind, these bottles are vanishing. With the advent of digitization, it is now possible to replace all previous information storage forms with one metabottle: complex and highly liquid patterns of ones and zeros.

The rights of invention and authorship adhered to activities in the physical world. One didn't get paid for ideas, but for the ability to deliver them into reality. For all practical purposes, the value was in the conveyance and not in the thought conveyed.

Even the physical/digital bottles to which we've become accustomed—floppy disks, CD-ROMs, and other discrete, shrink-wrappable bit-packages—will disappear as all computers jack-in to the global Net. While the Internet may never include every CPU on the planet, it is more than doubling every year and can be expected to become the principal medium of information conveyance, and perhaps eventually, the only one.

Once that has happened, all the goods of the Information Age—all of the expressions once contained in books or film strips or newsletters—will exist either as pure thought or something very much like thought: voltage conditions darting around the Net at the speed of light, in conditions that one might behold in effect, as glowing pixels or transmitted sounds, but never touch or claim to "own" in the old sense of the word.

Some might argue that information will still require some physical manifestation, such as its magnetic existence on the titanic hard disks of distant servers, but these are bottles which have no macroscopically discrete or personally meaningful form.

Some will also argue that we have been dealing with unbottled expression since the advent of radio, and they would be right. But for most of the history of broadcast, there was no convenient way to capture soft goods from the electromagnetic ether and reproduce them with quality available in commercial packages. Only recently has this changed, and little has been done legally or technically to address the change.

Generally, the issue of consumer payment for broadcast products was irrelevant. The consumers themselves were the product. Broadcast media were supported either by the sale of the attention of their audience to advertisers, by government assessing payment through taxes, or by the whining mendicancy of annual donor drives.

All of the broadcast-support models are flawed. Support either by advertisers or government has almost invariably tainted the purity of the goods delivered. Besides, direct marketing is gradually killing the advertiser-support model anyway.

Broadcast media gave us another payment method for a virtual product: the royalties that broadcasters pay songwriters through such organizations as ASCAP and BMI. But, as a member of ASCAP, I can assure you this is not a model that we should emulate. The monitoring methods are wildly approximate. There is no parallel system of accounting in the revenue stream. It doesn't really work. Honest.

In any case, without our old methods, based on physically defining the expression of ideas, and in the absence of successful new models for non-physical transaction, we simply don't know how to assure reliable payment for mental works. To make matters worse, this comes at a time when the human mind is replacing sunlight and mineral deposits as the principal source of new wealth.

Furthermore, the increasing difficulty of enforcing existing copyright and patent laws is already placing in peril the ultimate source of intellectual property—the free exchange of ideas.

That is, when the primary articles of commerce in a society look so much like speech as to be indistinguishable from it, and when the traditional methods of protecting their ownership have become ineffectual, attempting to fix the problem with broader and more vigorous enforcement will inevitably threaten freedom of speech. The greatest constraint on your future liberties may come not from government but from corporate legal departments laboring to protect by force what can no longer be protected by practical efficiency or general social consent.

Furthermore, when Jefferson and his fellow creatures of the Enlightenment designed the system that became American copyright law, their primary objective was assuring the widespread distribution of thought, not profit. Profit was the fuel that would carry ideas into the libraries and minds of their new republic. Libraries would purchase books, thus rewarding the authors for their work in assembling ideas; these ideas, otherwise "incapable of confinement," would then become freely available to the public. But what is the role of libraries in the absence of books? How does society now pay for the distribution of ideas if not by charging for the ideas themselves?

Additionally complicating the matter is the fact that along with the disappearance of the physical bottles in which intellectual property protection has resided, digital technology is also erasing the legal jurisdictions of the physical world and replacing them with the unbounded and perhaps permanently lawless waves of cyberspace.

In cyberspace, no national or local boundaries contain the scene of a crime and determine the method of its prosecution; worse, no clear cultural agreements define what a crime might be. Unresolved and basic differences between Western and Asian cultural assumptions about intellectual property can only be exacerbated when many transactions are taking place in both hemispheres and yet, somehow, in neither.

Even in the most local of digital conditions, jurisdiction and responsibility are hard to assess. A group of music publishers filed suit against CompuServe this fall because it allowed its users to upload musical compositions into areas where other users might access them. But since CompuServe cannot practically exercise much control over the flood of bits that passes between its subscribers, it probably shouldn't be held responsible for unlawfully "publishing" these works.

Notions of property, value, ownership, and the nature of wealth itself are changing more fundamentally than at any time since the Sumerians first poked cuneiform into wet clay and called it stored grain. Only a very few people are aware of the enormity of this shift, and fewer of them are lawyers or public officials.

Those who do see these changes must prepare responses for the legal and social confusion that will erupt as efforts to protect new forms of property with old methods become more obviously futile, and, as a consequence, more adamant.

■ FROM SWORDS TO WRITS TO BITS

Humanity now seems bent on creating a world economy primarily based on goods that take no material form. In doing so, we may be eliminating any predictable connection between creators and a fair reward for the utility or pleasure others may find in their works.

Without that connection, and without a fundamental change in consciousness to accommodate its loss, we are building our future on furor, litigation, and institutionalized evasion of payment except in response to raw force. We may return to the Bad Old Days of property.

Throughout the darker parts of human history, the possession and distribution of property was a largely military matter. "Ownership" was assured those with the nastiest tools, whether fists or armies, and the most resolute will to use them. Property was the divine right of thugs.

By the turn of the First Millennium AD, the emergence of merchant classes and landed gentry forced the development of ethical understandings for the resolution of property disputes. In the Middle Ages, enlightened rulers like England's Henry II began to codify this unwritten "common law" into recorded canons. These laws were local, which didn't matter much as they were primarily directed at real estate, a form of property that is local by definition. And, as the name implied, was very real.

This continued to be the case as long as the origin of wealth was agricultural, but with the dawning of the Industrial Revolution, humanity began to focus as much on means as ends. Tools acquired a new social value and, thanks to their development, it became possible to duplicate and distribute them in quantity.

To encourage their invention, copyright and patent law were developed in most Western countries. These laws were devoted to the delicate task of getting mental creations into the world where they could be used—and could enter the minds of others—while assuring their inventors compensation for the value of their use. And, as previously stated, the systems of both law and practice which grew up around that task were based on physical expression.

Since it is now possible to convey ideas from one mind to another without ever making them physical, we are now claiming to own ideas themselves and not merely their expression. And since it is likewise now possible to create useful tools that never take physical form, we have taken to patenting abstractions, sequences of virtual events, and mathematical formulae—the most unreal estate imaginable.

Since it is now possible to convey ideas from one mind to another without ever making them physical, we are now claiming to own ideas themselves and not merely their expression.

In certain areas, this leaves rights of ownership in such an ambiguous condition that property again adheres to those who can muster the largest armies. The only difference is that this time the armies consist of lawyers.

Threatening their opponents with the endless purgatory of litigation, over which some might prefer death itself, they assert claim to any thought which might have entered another cranium within the collective body of the corporations they serve. They act as though these ideas appeared in splendid detachment from all previous human thought. And they pretend that thinking about a product is somehow as good as manufacturing, distributing, and selling it.

What was previously considered a common human resource, distributed among the minds and libraries of the world, as well as the phenomena of nature herself, is now being fenced and deeded. It is as though a new class of enterprise had arisen that claimed to own the air.

What is to be done? While there is a certain grim fun to be had in it, dancing on the grave of copyright and patent will solve little, especially when so few are willing to admit that the occupant of this grave is even deceased, and so many are trying to uphold by force what can no longer be upheld by popular consent.

The legalists, desperate over their slipping grip, are vigorously trying to extend their reach. Indeed, the United States and other proponents of GATT are making adherence to our moribund systems of intellectual property protection a condition of membership in the marketplace of nations. For example, China will be denied Most Favored Nation trading status unless they agree to uphold a set of culturally alien principles that are no longer even sensibly applicable in their country of origin.

In a more perfect world, we'd be wise to declare a moratorium on litigation, legislation, and international treaties in this area until we had a clearer sense of the terms and conditions of enterprise in cyberspace. Ideally, laws ratify already developed social consensus. They are less the Social Contract itself than a series of memoranda expressing a collective intent that has emerged out of many millions of human interactions.

Humans have not inhabited cyberspace long enough or in sufficient diversity to have developed a Social Contract which conforms to the strange new conditions of that world. Laws developed prior to consensus usually favor the already established few who can get them passed and not society as a whole.

To the extent that law and established social practice exists in this area, they are already in dangerous disagreement. The laws regarding unlicensed reproduction of commercial software are clear and stern . . . and rarely observed. Software piracy laws are so practically unenforceable and breaking them has become so socially acceptable that only a thin minority appears compelled, either by fear or conscience, to obey them. When I give speeches on this subject, I always ask how many people in the audience can honestly claim to have no unauthorized software on their hard disks. I've never seen more than 10 percent of the hands go up.

Whenever there is such profound divergence between law and social practice, it is not society that adapts. Against the swift tide of custom, the software publishers' current practice of hanging a few visible scapegoats is so obviously capricious as to only further diminish respect for the law.

Part of the widespread disregard for commercial software copyrights stems from a legislative failure to understand the conditions into which it was inserted. To assume that systems of law based in the physical world will serve in an environment as fundamentally different as cyberspace is a folly for which everyone doing business in the future will pay.

As I will soon discuss in detail, unbounded intellectual property is very different from physical property and can no longer be protected as though these differences did not exist. For example, if we continue to assume that value is based on scarcity, as it is with regard to physical objects, we will create laws that are precisely contrary to the nature of information, which may, in many cases, increase in value with distribution.

The large, legally risk-averse institutions most likely to play by the old rules will suffer for their compliance. As more lawyers, guns, and money are invested in either protecting their rights or subverting those of their opponents, their ability to produce new technology will simply grind to a halt as every move they make drives them deeper into a tar pit of courtroom warfare.

Faith in law will not be an effective strategy for high-tech companies. Law adapts by continuous increments and at a pace second only to geology. Technology advances in lunging jerks, like the punctuation of biological evolution grotesquely accelerated. Real-world conditions will continue to change at a blinding pace, and the law will lag further behind, more profoundly confused. This mismatch may prove impossible to overcome.

Promising economies based on purely digital products will either be born in a state of paralysis, as appears to be the case with multimedia, or continue in a brave and willful refusal by their owners to play the ownership game at all.

In the United States one can already see a parallel economy developing, mostly among small, fast moving enterprises who protect their ideas by getting into the marketplace quicker then their larger competitors who base their protection on fear and litigation.

Perhaps those who are part of the problem will simply quarantine themselves in court, while those who are part of the solution will create a new society based, at first, on piracy and freebooting. It may well be that when the current system of intellectual property law has collapsed, as seems inevitable, that no new legal structure will arise in its place.

But something will happen. After all, people do business. When a currency becomes meaningless, business is done in barter. When societies develop outside the law, they develop their own unwritten codes, practices, and ethical systems. While technology may undo law, technology offers methods for restoring creative rights.

■ A TAXONOMY OF INFORMATION

It seems to me that the most productive thing to do now is to look into the true nature of what we're trying to protect. How much do we really know about information and its natural behaviors?

What are the essential characteristics of unbounded creation? How does it differ from previous forms of property? How many of our assumptions about it have actually been about its containers rather than their mysterious contents? What are its different species and how does each of them lend itself to control? What technologies will be useful in creating new virtual bottles to replace the old physical ones?

Of course, information is, by nature, intangible and hard to define. Like other such deep phenomena as light or matter, it is a natural host to paradox. It is most helpful to understand light as being both a particle and a wave. An understanding of information may emerge in the abstract congruence of its several different properties which might be described by the following three statements:

Information is an activity.

Information is a life form.

Information is a relationship.

In the following section, I will examine each of these.

■ I. INFORMATION IS AN ACTIVITY

Information Is a Verb, Not a Noun.

Freed of its containers, information is obviously not a thing. In fact, it is something that happens in the field of interaction between minds or objects or other pieces of information.

Gregory Bateson, expanding on the information theory of Claude Shannon, said, "Information is a difference which makes a difference." Thus, information only really exists in the Delta. The making of that difference is an activity within a relationship. Information is an action which occupies time rather than a state of being which occupies physical space, as is the case with hard goods. It is the pitch, not the baseball, the dance, not the dancer.

Information Is Experienced, Not Possessed.

Even when it has been encapsulated in some static form like a book or a hard disk, information is still something that happens to you as you mentally decompress it from its storage code. But, whether it's running at gigabits per second or words per minute, the actual decoding is a process that must be performed by and upon a mind, a process that must take place in time.

There was a cartoon in the *Bulletin of Atomic Scientists* a few years ago that illustrated this point beautifully. In the drawing, a holdup man trains his gun on the sort of bespectacled fellow you'd figure might have a lot of information stored in his head. "Quick," orders the bandit, "give me all your ideas."

Information Has to Move.

Sharks are said to die of suffocation if they stop swimming, and the same is nearly true of information. Information that isn't moving ceases to exist as anything but potential . . . at least until it is allowed to move again. For this reason, the practice of information hoarding, common in bureaucracies, is an especially wrong-headed artifact of physically based value systems.

Information Is Conveyed by Propagation, Not Distribution.

The way in which information spreads is also very different from the distribution of physical goods. It moves more like something from nature than from a factory. It can concatenate like falling dominos or grow in the usual fractal lattice, like frost spreading on a window, but it cannot be shipped around like widgets, except to the extent that it can be contained in them. It doesn't simply move on; it leaves a trail everywhere it's been.

The central economic distinction between information and physical property is that information can be transferred without leaving the possession of the original owner. If I sell you my horse, I can't ride him after that. If I sell you what I know, we both know it.

■ II. INFORMATION IS A LIFE FORM

Information Wants to Be Free.

Stewart Brand is generally credited with this elegant statement of the obvious, which recognizes both the natural desire of secrets to be told and the fact that they might be capable of possessing something like a "desire" in the first place.

English biologist and philosopher Richard Dawkins proposed the idea of "memes," self-replicating patterns of information that propagate themselves across the ecologies of mind, a pattern of reproduction much like that of life forms.

I believe they are life forms in every respect but their freedom from the carbon atom. They self-reproduce, they interact with their surroundings and adapt to them, they mutate, they persist. They evolve to fill the empty niches of their local environments, which are in this case the surrounding belief systems and cultures of their hosts, namely, us.

Indeed, sociobiologists like Dawkins make a plausible case that carbon-based life forms are information as well, that, as the chicken is an egg's way of making another egg, the entire biological spectacle is just the DNA molecule's means of copying out more information strings exactly like itself.

Information Replicates into the Cracks of Possibility.

Like DNA helices, ideas are relentless expansionists, always seeking new opportunities for Lebensraum. And, as in carbon-based nature, the more robust organisms are extremely adept at finding new places to live. Thus, just as the common housefly has insinuated itself into practically every ecosystem on the planet, so has the meme of "life after death" found a niche in most minds, or psycho-ecologies.

The more universally resonant an idea or image or song, the more minds it will enter and remain within. Trying to stop the spread of a really robust piece of information is about as easy as keeping killer bees south of the border.

Information Wants to Change.

If ideas and other interactive patterns of information are indeed life forms, they can be expected to evolve constantly into forms which will be more perfectly adapted to their surroundings. And, as we see, they are doing this all the time.

But for a long time, our static media, whether carvings in stone, ink on paper, or dye on celluloid, have strongly resisted the evolutionary impulse, exalting as a consequence the author's ability to determine the finished product. But, as in an oral tradition, digitized information has no "final cut."

Digital information, unconstrained by packaging, is a continuing process more like the metamorphosing tales of prehistory than anything that will fit in shrink-wrap. From the Neolithic to Gutenberg (monks aside), information was passed on, mouth to ear, changing with every retelling (or resinging). The stories which once shaped our sense of the world didn't have authoritative versions. They adapted to each culture in which they found themselves being told.

Because there was never a moment when the story was frozen in print, the so-called "moral" right of storytellers to own the tale was neither pro-

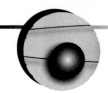

Digital information, unconstrained by packaging, is a continuing process. As we return to continuous information, we can expect the importance of authorship to diminish. Creative people may have to renew their acquaintance with humility.

tected nor recognized. The story simply passed through each of them on its way to the next, where it would assume a different form. As we return to continuous information, we can expect the importance of authorship to diminish. Creative people may have to renew their acquaintance with humility.

But our system of copyright makes no accommodation whatever for expressions which don't become fixed at some point nor for cultural expressions which lack a specific author or inventor.

Jazz improvisations, stand-up comedy routines, mime performances, developing monologues, and unrecorded broadcast transmissions all lack the Constitutional requirement of fixation as a "writing." Without being fixed by a point of publication the liquid works of the future will all look more like these continuously adapting and changing forms and will therefore exist beyond the reach of copyright.

Copyright expert Pamela Samuelson tells of having attended a conference last year convened around the fact that Western countries may legally appropriate the music, designs, and biomedical lore of aboriginal people without compensation to their tribes of origin since those tribes are not an "author" or "inventors."

But soon most information will be generated collaboratively by the cyber-tribal hunter-gatherers of cyberspace. Our arrogant legal dismissal of the rights of "primitives" will soon return to haunt us.

Information Is Perishable.

With the exception of the rare classic, most information is like farm produce. Its quality degrades rapidly both over time and in distance from the source of production. But even here, value is highly subjective and conditional. Yesterday's papers are quite valuable to the historian. In fact, the older they are, the more valuable they become. On the other hand, a commodities broker might consider news of an event that occurred more than an hour ago to have lost any relevance.

■ III.   INFORMATION   IS   A   RELATIONSHIP

Meaning Has Value and Is Unique to Each Case.

In most cases, we assign value to information based on its meaningfulness. The place where information dwells, the holy moment where transmission becomes reception, is a region which has many shifting characteristics and flavors depending on the relationship of sender and receiver, the depth of their interactivity.

Each such relationship is unique. Even in cases where the sender is a broadcast medium, and no response is returned, the receiver is hardly passive. Receiving information is often as creative an act as generating it.

The value of what is sent depends entirely on the extent to which each individual receiver has the receptors—shared terminology, attention, interest, language, paradigm—necessary to render what is received meaningful.

Understanding is a critical element increasingly overlooked in the effort to turn information into a commodity. Data may be any set of facts, useful or not, intelligible or inscrutable, germane or irrelevant. Computers can crank out new data all night long without human help, and the results may be offered for sale as information. They may or may not actually be so. Only a human being can recognize the meaning that separates information from data.

In fact, information, in the economic sense of the word, consists of data which have been passed through a particular human mind and found meaningful within that mental context. One fella's information is all just data to someone else. If you're an anthropologist, my detailed charts of Tasaday kinship patterns might be critical information to you. If you're a banker from Hong Kong, they might barely seem to be data.

Familiarity Has More Value than Scarcity.

With physical goods, there is a direct correlation between scarcity and value. Gold is more valuable than wheat, even though you can't eat it. While this is not always the case, the situation with information is often precisely the reverse. Most soft goods increase in value as they become more common. Familiarity is an important asset in the world of information. It may often be true that the best way to raise demand for your product is to give it away.

While this has not always worked with shareware, it could be argued that there is a connection between the extent to which commercial software is pirated and the amount which gets sold. Broadly pirated software, such as Lotus 1-2-3 or WordPerfect, becomes a standard and benefits from Law of Increasing Returns based on familiarity.

In regard to my own soft product, rock 'n' roll songs, there is no question that the band I write them for, the Grateful Dead, has increased its popularity enormously by giving them away. We have been letting people tape our concerts since the early seventies, but instead of reducing the demand for our product, we are now the largest concert draw in America, a fact that is at least in part attributable to the popularity generated by those tapes.

True, I don't get any royalties on the millions of copies of my songs which have been extracted from concerts, but I see no reason to complain. The fact is, no one but the Grateful Dead can perform a Grateful Dead song, so if you want the experience and not its thin projection, you have to buy a ticket from us. In other words, our intellectual property protection derives from our being the only real-time source of it.

Exclusivity Has Value.

The problem with a model that turns the physical scarcity/value ratio on its head is that sometimes the value of information is very much based on its scarcity. Exclusive possession of certain facts makes them more useful. If everyone knows about conditions which might drive a stock price up, the information is valueless.

But again, the critical factor is usually time. It doesn't matter if this kind of information eventually becomes ubiquitous. What matters is being among the first who possess it and act on it. While potent secrets usually don't stay secret, they may remain so long enough to advance the cause of their original holders.

Point of View and Authority Have Value.

In a world of floating realities and contradictory maps, rewards will accrue to those commentators whose maps seem to fit their territory snugly, based on their ability to yield predictable results for those who use them.

In aesthetic information, whether poetry or rock 'n' roll, people are willing to buy the new product of an artist, sight-unseen, based on their having been delivered a pleasurable experience by previous work.

Reality is an edit.

Reality is an edit. People are willing to pay for the authority of those editors whose point of view seems to fit best. And again, point of view is an asset which cannot be stolen or duplicated. No one sees the world as Esther Dyson does, and the handsome fee she charges for her newsletter is actually payment for the privilege of looking at the world through her unique eyes.

Time Replaces Space.

In the physical world, value depends heavily on possession or proximity in space. One owns the material that falls inside certain dimensional boundaries. The ability to act directly, exclusively, and as one wishes upon what falls inside those boundaries is the principal right of ownership. The relationship between value and scarcity is a limitation in space.

In the virtual world, proximity in time is a value determinant. An informational product is generally more valuable the closer purchasers can place themselves to the moment of its expression, a limitation in time. Many kinds of information degrade rapidly with either time or reproduction. Relevance fades as the territory they map changes. Noise is introduced and bandwidth lost with passage away from the point where the information is first produced.

Thus, listening to a Grateful Dead tape is hardly the same experience as attending a Grateful Dead concert. The closer one can get to the headwaters of an informational stream, the better one's chances of finding an accurate picture of reality in it. In an era of easy reproduction, the informational abstractions of popular experiences will propagate out from their source moments to reach anyone who's interested. But it's easy enough to restrict the real experience of the desirable event, whether knock-out punch or guitar lick, to those willing to pay for being there.

The Protection of Execution

In the hick town I come from, they don't give you much credit for just having ideas. You are judged by what you can make of them. As things continue

In the hick town I come from, they don't give you much credit for just having ideas. You are judged by what you can make of them.

to speed up, I think we see that execution is the best protection for those designs which become physical products. Or, as Steve Jobs once put it, "Real artists ship." The big winner is usually the one who gets to the market first (and with enough organizational force to keep the lead).

But, as we become fixated upon information commerce, many of us seem to think that originality alone is sufficient to convey value, deserving, with the right legal assurances, of a steady wage. In fact, the best way to protect intellectual property is to act on it. It's not enough to invent and patent; one has to innovate as well. Someone claims to have patented the microprocessor before Intel. Maybe so. If he'd actually started shipping microprocessors before Intel, his claim would seem far less spurious.

Information as Its Own Reward

It is now a commonplace to say that money is information. With the exception of Krugerrands, crumpled cab fare, and the contents of those suitcases that drug lords are reputed to carry, most of the money in the informatized world is in ones and zeros. The global money supply sloshes around the Net, as fluid as weather. It is also obvious, that information has become as fundamental to the creation of modern wealth as land and sunlight once were.

What is less obvious is the extent to which information is acquiring intrinsic value, not as a means to acquisition but as the object to be acquired. I suppose this has always been less explicitly the case. In politics and academia, potency and information have always been closely related.

However, as we increasingly buy information with money, we begin to see that buying information with other information is simple economic exchange without the necessity of converting the product into and out of currency. This is somewhat challenging for those who like clean accounting, since, information theory aside, informational exchange rates are too squishy to quantify to the decimal point.

Nevertheless, most of what a middle-class American purchases has little to do with survival. We buy beauty, prestige, experience, education, and all the obscure pleasures of owning. Many of these things can not only be expressed in nonmaterial terms, they can be acquired by nonmaterial means.

And then there are the inexplicable pleasures of information itself, the joys of learning, knowing, and teaching; the strange good feeling of information coming into and out of oneself. Playing with ideas is a recreation which people are willing to pay a lot for, given the market for books and elective seminars. We'd likely spend even more money for such pleasures if we didn't have so many opportunities to pay for ideas with other ideas. This explains much of the collective "volunteer" work which fills the archives, newsgroups, and databases of the Internet. Its denizens are not working for "nothing," as is widely believed. Rather they are getting paid in something besides money. It is an economy which consists almost entirely of information.

This may become the dominant form of human trade, and if we persist in modeling economics on a strictly monetary basis, we may be gravely misled.

Getting Paid in Cyberspace

How all the foregoing relates to solutions to the crisis in intellectual property is something I've barely started to wrap my mind around. It's fairly paradigm warping to look at information through fresh eyes—to see how very little it is like pig iron or pork bellies, and to imagine the tottering travesties of case law we will stack up if we go on legally treating it as though it were.

As I've said, I believe these towers of outmoded boilerplate will be a smoking heap sometime in the next decade, and we mind miners will have no choice but to cast our lot with new systems that work.

I'm not really so gloomy about our prospects as readers of this jeremiad so far might conclude. Solutions will emerge. Nature abhors a vacuum and so does commerce.

Indeed, one of the aspects of the electronic frontier which I have always found most appealing—and the reason Mitch Kapor and I used that phrase in naming our foundation—is the degree to which it resembles the 19th-century American West in its natural preference for social devices that emerge from its conditions rather than those that are imposed from the outside.

Until the West was fully settled and "civilized" in this century, order was established according to an unwritten Code of the West, which had the fluidity of common law rather than the rigidity of statutes.

Until the West was fully settled and "civilized" in this century, order was established according to an unwritten Code of the West, which had the fluidity of common law rather than the rigidity of statutes. Ethics were more important than rules. Understandings were preferred over laws, which were, in any event, largely unenforceable.

I believe that law, as we understand it, was developed to protect the interests which arose in the two economic "waves" which Alvin Toffler accurately identified in *The Third Wave.* The First Wave was agriculturally based and required law to order ownership of the principal source of production, land. In the Second Wave, manufacturing became the economic mainspring, and the structure of modern law grew around the centralized institutions that needed protection for their reserves of capital, labor, and hardware.

Both of these economic systems required stability. Their laws were designed to resist change and to assure some equability of distribution within a fairly static social framework. The empty niches had to be constrained to preserve the predictability necessary to either land stewardship or capital formation.

In the Third Wave we have now entered, information to a large extent replaces land, capital, and hardware, and information is most at home in a much more fluid and adaptable environment. The Third Wave is likely to bring a fundamental shift in the purposes and methods of law which will affect far more than simply those statutes which govern intellectual property.

The "terrain" itself—the architecture of the Net—may come to serve many of the purposes which could only be maintained in the past by legal imposition. For example, it may be unnecessary to constitutionally assure freedom of expression in an environment which, in the words of my fellow EFF cofounder John Gilmore, "treats censorship as a malfunction" and reroutes proscribed ideas around it.

Similar natural balancing mechanisms may arise to smooth over the social discontinuities which previously required legal intercession to set right. On the Net, these differences are more likely to be spanned by a continuous spectrum that connects as much as it separates.

And, despite their fierce grip on the old legal structure, companies that trade in information are likely to find that their increasing inability to deal sensibly with technological issues will not be remedied in the courts, which won't be capable of producing verdicts predictable enough to be supportive of long-term enterprise. Every litigation will become like a game of Russian roulette, depending on the depth of the presiding judge's clue-impairment.

Uncodified or adaptive "law," while as "fast, loose, and out of control" as other emergent forms, is probably more likely to yield something like justice at this point. In fact, one can already see in development new practices to suit the conditions of virtual commerce. The life forms of information are evolving methods to protect their continued reproduction.

For example, while all the tiny print on a commercial diskette envelope punctiliously requires a great deal of those who would open it, few who read those provisos follow them to the letter. And yet, the software business remains a very healthy sector of the American economy.

Why is this? Because people seem to eventually buy the software they really use. Once a program becomes central to your work, you want the latest version of it, the best support, the actual manuals, all privileges attached to ownership. Such practical considerations will, in the absence of working law, become more and more important in getting paid for what might easily be obtained for nothing.

I do think that some software is being purchased in the service of ethics or the abstract awareness that the failure to buy it will result in its not being produced any longer, but I'm going to leave those motivators aside. While I believe that the failure of law will almost certainly result in a compensating re-emergence of ethics as the ordering template of society, this is a belief I don't have room to support here.

Instead, I think that, as in the case cited above, compensation for soft products will be driven primarily by practical considerations, all of them consistent with the true properties of digital information, where the value lies in it, and how it can be both manipulated and protected by technology.

While the conundrum remains a conundrum, I can begin to see the directions from which solutions may emerge, based in part on broadening those practical solutions which are already in practice.

Relationship and Its Tools

I believe one idea is central to understanding liquid commerce: Information economics, in the absence of objects, will be based more on relationship than possession.

One existing model for the future conveyance of intellectual property is real-time performance, a medium currently used only in theater, music, lectures, stand-up comedy, and pedagogy. I believe the concept of performance will expand to include most of the information economy, from multicasted soap operas to stock analysis. In these instances, commercial exchange will be more like ticket sales to a continuous show than the purchase of discrete bundles of that which is being shown.

The other existing model, of course, is service. The entire professional class—doctors, lawyers, consultants, architects, and so on—are already being paid directly for their intellectual property. Who needs copyright when you're on a retainer?

In fact, until the late 18th century this model was applied to much of what is now copyrighted. Before the industrialization of creation, writers, composers, artists, and the like produced their products in the private service of patrons. Without objects to distribute in a mass market, creative people will return to a condition somewhat like this, except that they will serve many patrons, rather than one.

We can already see the emergence of companies which base their existence on supporting and enhancing the soft property they create rather than selling it by the shrink-wrapped piece or embedding it in widgets.

Trip Hawkins's new company for creating and licensing multimedia tools, 3DO, is an example of what I'm talking about. 3DO doesn't intend to produce any commercial software or consumer devices. Instead, it will act as a kind of private standards setting body, mediating among software and device creators who will be their licensees. It will provide a point of commonality for relationships between a broad spectrum of entities.

In any case, whether you think of yourself as a service provider or a performer, the future protection of your intellectual property will depend on your ability to control your relationship to the market—a relationship which will most likely live and grow over a period of time.

The value of that relationship will reside in the quality of performance, the uniqueness of your point of view, the validity of your expertise, its relevance to your market, and, underlying everything, the ability of that market to access your creative services swiftly, conveniently, and interactively.

Interaction and Protection

Direct interaction will provide a lot of intellectual property protection in the future, and, indeed, already has. No one knows how many software pirates have bought legitimate copies of a program after calling its publisher for technical support and offering some proof of purchase, but I would guess the number is very high.

The same kind of controls will be applicable to "question and answer" relationships between authorities (or artists) and those who seek their expertise. Newsletters, magazines, and books will be supplemented by the ability of their subscribers to ask direct questions of authors.

Interactivity will be a billable commodity even in the absence of authorship. As people move into the Net and increasingly get their information directly from its point of production, unfiltered by centralized media, they will attempt to develop the same interactive ability to probe reality that only experience has provided them in the past. Live access to these distant "eyes and ears" will be much easier to cordon than access to static bundles of stored but easily reproducible information.

In most cases, control will be based on restricting access to the freshest, highest bandwidth information. It will be a matter of defining the ticket, the venue, the performer, and the identity of the ticket holder, definitions which I believe will take their forms from technology, not law. In most cases, the defining technology will be cryptography.

Crypto Bottling

Cryptography, as I've said perhaps too many times, is the "material" from which the walls, boundaries—and bottles—of cyberspace will be fashioned.

Of course there are problems with cryptography or any other purely technical method of property protection. It has always appeared to me that the more security you hide your goods behind, the more likely you are to turn your sanctuary into a target. Having come from a place where people leave their keys in their cars and don't even have keys to their houses, I remain convinced that the best obstacle to crime is a society with its ethics intact.

While I admit that this is not the kind of society most of us live in, I also believe that a social overreliance on protection by barricades rather than conscience will eventually wither the latter by turning intrusion and theft into a sport, rather than a crime. This is already occurring in the digital domain, as is evident in the activities of computer crackers.

Furthermore, I would argue that initial efforts to protect digital copyright by copy protection contributed to the current condition in which most otherwise ethical computer users seem morally untroubled by their possession of pirated software.

Instead of cultivating among the newly computerized a sense of respect for the work of their fellows, early reliance on copy protection led to the subliminal notion that cracking into a software package somehow "earned" one the right to use it. Limited not by conscience but by technical skill, many soon felt free to do whatever they could get away with. This will continue to be a potential liability of the encryption of digitized commerce.

Cryptography, as I've said perhaps too many times, is the "material" from which the walls, boundaries—and bottles—of cyberspace will be fashioned.

Furthermore, it's cautionary to remember that copy protection was rejected by the market in most areas. Many of the upcoming efforts to use cryptography-based protection schemes will probably suffer the same fate. People are not going to tolerate much that makes computers harder to use than they already are without any benefit to the user.

Nevertheless, encryption has already demonstrated a certain blunt utility. New subscriptions to various commercial satellite TV services skyrocketed recently after their deployment of more robust encryption of their feeds. This, despite a booming backwoods trade in black decoder chips, conducted by folks who'd look more at home running moonshine than cracking code.

Another obvious problem with encryption as a global solution is that once something has been unscrambled by a legitimate licensee, it may be available to massive reproduction.

In some instances, reproduction following decryption may not be a problem. Many soft products degrade sharply in value with time. It may be that the only real interest in such products will be among those who have purchased the keys to immediacy.

Furthermore, as software becomes more modular and distribution moves online, it will begin to metamorphose in direct interaction with its user base. Discontinuous upgrades will smooth into a constant process of incremental improvement and adaptation, some of it manmade and some of it arising through genetic algorithms. Pirated copies of software may become too static to have much value to anyone.

Even in cases such as images, where the information is expected to remain fixed, the unencrypted file could still be interwoven with code which could continue to protect it by a wide variety of means.

In most of the schemes I can project, the file would be "alive" with permanently embedded software that could "sense" the surrounding conditions and interact with them. For example, it might contain a code that could detect the process of duplication and cause it to self-destruct.

Other methods might give the file the ability to "phone home" through the Net to its original owner. The continued integrity of some files might require periodic "feeding" with digital cash from their host, which they would then relay back to their authors.

Of course, files that possess the independent ability to communicate upstream sound uncomfortably like the Morris Internet Worm. "Live" files do have a certain viral quality. And serious privacy issues would arise if everyone's computer were packed with digital spies.

The point is that cryptography will enable protection technologies that will develop rapidly in the obsessive competition that has always existed between lock-makers and lock-breakers.

But cryptography will not be used simply for making locks. It is also at the heart of both digital signatures and the aforementioned digital cash, both of which I believe will be central to the future protection of intellectual property.

I believe that the generally acknowledged failure of the shareware model in software had less to do with dishonesty than with the simple inconvenience of paying for shareware. If the payment process can be automated, as digital cash and signature will make possible, I believe that soft product creators will reap a much higher return from the bread they cast upon the waters of cyberspace.

Moreover, they will be spared much of the overhead presently attached to the marketing, manufacture, sales, and distribution of information products, whether those products are computer programs, books, CDs, or motion pictures. This will reduce prices and further increase the likelihood of noncompulsory payment.

But of course there is a fundamental problem with a system that requires, through technology, payment for every access to a particular expression. It defeats the original Jeffersonian purpose of seeing that ideas were available to everyone regardless of their economic station. I am not comfortable with a model that will restrict inquiry to the wealthy.

An Economy of Verbs

The future forms and protections of intellectual property are densely obscured at this entrance to the Virtual Age. Nevertheless, I can make (or reiterate) a few flat statements that I earnestly believe won't look too silly in 50 years.

- In the absence of the old containers, almost everything we think we know about intellectual property is wrong. We're going to have to unlearn it. We're going to have to look at information as though we'd never seen the stuff before.

- The protections that we will develop will rely far more on ethics and technology than on law.

- Encryption will be the technical basis for most intellectual property protection. (And should, for many reasons, be made more widely available.)

- The economy of the future will be based on relationship rather than possession. It will be continuous rather than sequential.

- And finally, in the years to come, most human exchange will be virtual rather than physical, consisting not of stuff but the stuff of which dreams are made. Our future business will be conducted in a world made more of verbs than nouns.

Utopian Plagiarism, Hypertextuality, and Electronic Cultural Production

lagiarism has long been considered an evil in the cultural world. Typically it has been viewed as the theft of language, ideas, and images by the less than talented, often for the enhancement of personal fortune or prestige. Yet, like most mythologies, the myth of plagiarism is easily inverted. Perhaps it is those who support the legislation of representation and the privatization of language that are suspect; perhaps the plagiarist's actions, given a specific set of social conditions, are the ones contributing most to cultural enrichment. Prior to the Enlightenment, plagiarism was useful in aiding the distribution of ideas. An English poet could appropriate and translate a sonnet from Petrarch and call it his own. In accordance with the classical aesthetic of art as imitation, this was a perfectly acceptable practice. The real value of this activity rested less in the reinforcement of classical aesthetics than in the distribution of work to areas where otherwise it probably would not have appeared. The works of English plagiarists, such as Chaucer, Shakespeare, Spenser, Sterne, Coleridge, and De Quincey, are still a vital part of the English heritage, and remain in the literary canon to this day.

> **Prior to the Enlightenment, plagiarism was useful in aiding the distribution of ideas.**

At present, new conditions have emerged that once again make plagiarism an acceptable, even crucial strategy for textual production. This is the age of the recombinant: recombinant bodies, recombinant gender, recombinant texts, recombinant culture. Looking back through the privileged frame of hindsight, one can argue that the recombinant has always been key in the development of meaning and invention; recent extraordinary advances in electronic technology have called attention to the recombinant both in theory and in practice (for example, the use of morphing in video and film). The primary value of all electronic technology, especially computers and imaging systems, is the startling speed at which they can transmit information in both raw and refined forms. As information flows at a high velocity through the electronic networks, disparate and sometimes incommensurable systems of meaning intersect, with both enlightening and inventive consequences. In a society dominated by a "knowledge" explosion, exploring the possibilities of meaning in that which already exists is more pressing than adding redundant informa-

At present, new conditions have emerged that once again make plagiarism an acceptable, even crucial strategy for textual production.

tion (even if it is produced using the methodology and meta-physic of the "original"). In the past, arguments in favor of plagiarism were limited to showing its use in resisting the pri-vatization of culture that serves the needs and desires of the power elite. Today one can argue that plagiarism is acceptable, even inevitable, given the nature of postmodern existence with its techno-infrastructure. In a recombinant culture, plagiarism is productive, although we need not abandon the romantic model of cultural production which privileges a model of *ex nihilo* creation. Certainly in a general sense the latter model is somewhat anachronistic. There are still specific situations where such thinking is useful, and one can never be sure when it could become appropriate again. What is called for is an end to its tyranny and to its institutionalized cultural big-

otry. This is a call to open the cultural data base, to let everyone use the tech-nology of textual production to its maximum potential.

Ideas improve. The meaning of words participates in the improvement. Plagiarism is nec-essary. Progress implies it. It embraces an author's phrase, makes use of his expressions, erases a false idea, and replaces it with the right idea.[1]

Plagiarism often carries a weight of negative connotations (particularly in the bureaucratic class); while the need for its use has increased over the century, plagiarism itself has been camouflaged in a new lexicon by those desiring to explore the practice as method and as a legitimized form of cultural discourse. Readymades, collage, found art or found text, intertexts, combines, detourn-ment, and appropriation—all these terms represent explorations in plagiarism. Indeed, these terms are not perfectly synonymous, but they all intersect a set of meanings primary to the philosophy and activity of plagiarism. Philosophi-cally, they all stand in opposition to essentialist doctrines of the text: They all assume that no structure within a given text provides a universal and neces-sary meaning. No work of art or philosophy exhausts itself in itself alone, in its being-in-itself. Such works have always stood in relation to the actual life-process of society from which they have distinguished themselves. Enlighten-ment essentialism failed to provide a unit of analysis that could act as a basis of meaning. Just as the connection between a signifier and its referent is arbi-trary, the unit of meaning used for any given textual analysis is also arbitrary. Roland Barthes' notion of the lexia primarily indicates surrender in the search for a basic unit of meaning. Since language was the only tool available for the development of metalanguage, such a project was doomed from its inception. It was much like trying to eat soup with soup. The text itself is fluid—although the language game of ideology can provide the illusion of stability, creating blockage by manipulating the unacknowledged assumptions of every-day life. Consequently, one of the main goals of the plagiarist is to restore the dynamic and unstable drift of meaning, by appropriating and recombining fragments of culture. In this way, meanings can be produced that were not previously associated with an object or a given set of objects.

Marcel Duchamp, one of the first to understand the power of recombination, presented an early incarnation of this new aesthetic with his readymade series. Duchamp took objects to which he was "visually indifferent," and recontextualized them in a manner that shifted their meaning. For example, by taking a urinal out of the rest room, signing it, and placing it on a pedestal in an art gallery, meaning slid away from the apparently exhaustive functional interpretation of the object. Although this meaning did not completely disappear, it was placed in harsh juxtaposition to another possibility— meaning as an art object. This problem of instability increased when problems of origin were raised: The object was not made by an artist, but by a machine. Whether or not the viewer chose to accept other possibilities for interpreting the function of the artist and the authenticity of the art object, the urinal in a gallery instigated a moment of uncertainty and reassessment. This conceptual game has been replayed numerous times over the 20th century, at times for very narrow purposes, as with Rauschenberg's combines—done for the sake of attacking the critical hegemony of Clement Greenberg—while at other times it has been done to promote large-scale political and cultural restructuring, as in the case of the Situationists. In each case, the plagiarist works to open meaning through the injection of scepticism into the culture-text.

One of the main goals of the plagiarist is to restore the dynamic and unstable drift of meaning, by appropriating and recombining fragments of culture.

Here one also sees the failure of Romantic essentialism. Even the alleged transcendental object cannot escape the sceptics' critique. Duchamp's notion of the inverted readymade (turning a Rembrandt painting into an ironing board) suggested that the distinguished art object draws its power from a historical legitimation process firmly rooted in the institutions of western culture, and not from being an unalterable conduit to transcendental realms. This is not to deny the possibility of transcendental experience, but only to say that if it does exist, it is prelinguistic, and thereby relegated to the privacy of an individual's subjectivity. A society with a complex division of labor requires a rationalization of institutional processes, a situation which in turn robs the individual of a way to share nonrational experience. Unlike societies with a simple division of labor, in which the experience of one member closely resembles the experience of another (minimal alienation), under a complex division of labor, the life experience of the individual turned specialist holds little in common with other specialists. Consequently, communication exists primarily as an instrumental function.

Plagiarism has historically stood against the privileging of any text through spiritual, scientific, or other legitimizing myths. The plagiarist sees all objects as equal, and thereby horizontalizes the plane of phenomena. All texts become potentially usable and reusable. Herein lies an epistemology of anarchy, according to which the plagiarist argues that if science, religion, or any other social institution precludes certainty beyond the realm of the private, then it is best to endow consciousness with as many categories of interpreta-

tion as possible. The tyranny of paradigms may have some useful consequences (such as greater efficiency within the paradigm), but the repressive
costs to the individual (excluding other modes of thinking and reducing the
possibility of invention) are too high. Rather than being led by sequences of
signs, one should instead drift through them, choosing the interpretation best
suited to the social conditions of a given situation.

*It is a matter of throwing together various cut-up techniques in order to respond to the
omnipresence of transmitters feeding us with their dead discourses (mass media, publicity,
etc.). It is a question of unchaining the codes—not the subject anymore—so that something will burst out, will escape; words beneath words, personal obsessions. Another kind
of word is born which escapes from the totalitarianism of the media but retains their
power, and turns it against their old masters.*

Cultural production, literary or otherwise, has traditionally been a slow, labor-
intensive process. In painting, sculpture, or written work, the technology has
always been primitive by contemporary standards. Paintbrushes, hammers and
chisels, quills and paper, and even the printing press do not
lend themselves well to rapid production and broad-range distribution. The time lapse between production and distribution
can seem unbearably long. Book arts and traditional visual
arts still suffer tremendously from this problem, when compared to the electronic arts. Before electronic technology
became dominant, cultural perspectives developed in a manner
that more clearly defined texts as individual works. Cultural
fragments appeared in their own right as discrete units, since
their influence moved slowly enough to allow the orderly
evolution of an argument or an aesthetic. Boundaries could be
maintained between disciplines and schools of thought.
Knowledge was considered finite, and was therefore easier to
control. In the 19th century this traditional order began to
collapse as new technology began to increase the velocity of
cultural development. The first strong indicators began to
appear that speed was becoming a crucial issue. Knowledge
was shifting away from certitude, and transforming itself into
information. During the American Civil War, Lincoln sat impatiently by his
telegraph line, awaiting reports from his generals at the front. He had no
patience with the long-winded rhetoric of the past, and demanded from his
generals an efficient economy of language. There was no time for the traditional trappings of the elegant essayist. Cultural velocity and information have
continued to increase at a geometric rate since then, resulting in an information panic. Production and distribution of information (or any other product)
must be immediate; there can be no lag time between the two. Techno-culture
has met this demand with data bases and electronic networks that rapidly
move any type of information.

Under such conditions, plagiarism fulfills the requirements of economy of
representation, without stifling invention. If invention occurs when a new

*The plagiarist
sees all objects
as equal. All
texts become
potentially
usable and
reusable.
Herein lies an
epistemology
of anarchy.*

perception or idea is brought out—by intersecting two or more formally disparate systems—then recombinant methodologies are desirable. This is where plagiarism progresses beyond nihilism. It does not simply inject scepticism to help destroy totalitarian systems that stop invention; it participates in invention, and is thereby also productive. The genius of an inventor like Leonardo da Vinci lay in his ability to recombine the then separate systems of biology, mathematics, engineering, and art. He was not so much an originator as a synthesizer. There have been few people like him over the centuries, because the ability to hold that much data in one's own biological memory is rare. Now, however, the technology of recombination is available in the computer. The problem now for would-be cultural producers is to gain access to this technology and information. After all, access is the most precious of all privileges, and is therefore strictly guarded, which in turn makes one wonder whether to be a successful plagiarist, one must also be a successful hacker.

Most serious writers refuse to make themselves available to the things that technology is doing. I have never been able to understand this sort of fear. Many are afraid of using tape recorders, and the idea of using any electronic means for literary or artistic purposes seems to them some sort of sacrilege.

To some degree, a small portion of technology has fallen through the cracks into the hands of the lucky few. Personal computers and video cameras are the best examples. To accompany these consumer items and make their use more versatile, hypertextual and image sampling programs have also been developed—programs designed to facilitate recombination. It is the plagiarist's dream to be able to call up, move, and recombine text with simple user-friendly commands. Perhaps plagiarism rightfully belongs to post-book culture, since only in that society can it be made explicit what book culture, with its geniuses and auteurs, tends to hide—that information is most useful when it interacts with other information, rather than when it is deified and presented in a vacuum.

Thinking about a new means for recombining information has always been on 20th-century minds, although this search has been left to a few until recently. In 1945 Vannevar Bush, a former science advisor to Franklin D. Roosevelt, proposed a new way of organizing information in an *Atlantic Monthly* article. At that time, computer technology was in its earliest stages of development and its full potential was not really understood. Bush, however, had the foresight to imagine a device he called the Memex. In his view it would be based around storage of information on microfilm, integrated with some means to allow the user to select and display any section at will, thus enabling one to move freely among previously unrelated increments of information.

At the time, Bush's Memex could not be built, but as computer technology evolved, his idea eventually gained practicality. Around 1960 Theodor Nelson made this realization when he began studying computer programming in college:

Over a period of months, I came to realize that, although programmers structured their data hierarchically, they didn't have to. I began to see the computer as the ideal place for making interconnections among things accessible to people.

I realized that writing did not have to be sequential and that not only would tomorrow's books and magazines be on [cathode ray terminal] screens, they could all tie to one another in every direction. At once I began working on a program (written in 7090 assembler language) to carry out these ideas.

Nelson's idea, which he called hypertext, failed to attract any supporters at first, although by 1968 its usefulness became obvious to some in the government and in defense industries. A prototype of hypertext was developed by another computer innovator, Douglas Englebart, who is often credited with many breakthroughs in the use of computers (such as the development of the Macintosh interface, Windows). Englebart's system, called Augment, was applied to organizing the government's research network, ARPAnet, and was also used by McDonnell Douglas, the defense contractor, to aid technical work groups in coordinating projects such as aircraft design:

All communications are automatically added to the Augment information base and linked, when appropriate, to other documents. An engineer could, for example, use Augment to write and deliver electronically a work plan to others in the work group. The other members could then review the document and have their comments linked to the original, eventually creating a "group memory" of the decisions made. Augment's powerful linking features allow users to find even old information quickly, without getting lost or being overwhelmed by detail.

Computer technology continued to be refined, and eventually—as with so many other technological breakthroughs in this country—once it had been thoroughly exploited by military and intelligence agencies, the technology was released for commercial exploitation. Of course, the development of microcomputers and consumer-grade technology for personal computers led immediately to the need for software which would help one cope with the exponential increase in information, especially textual information. Probably the first humanistic application of hypertext was in the field of education. Currently, hypertext and hypermedia (which adds graphic images to the network of features which can be interconnected) continue to be fixtures in instructional design and educational technology.

An interesting experiment in this regard was instigated in 1975 by Robert Scholes and Andries Van Dam at Brown University. Scholes, a professor of English, was contacted by Van Dam, a professor of computer science, who wanted to know if there were any courses in the humanities that might benefit from using what at the time was called a text-editing system (now known as a word processor) with hypertext capabilities built in. Scholes and two teaching assistants, who formed a research group, were particularly impressed by one aspect of hypertext. Using this program would make it possible to peruse in a nonlinear fashion all the interrelated materials in a text. A hypertext is thus best seen as a web of interconnected materials. This description suggested that there is a definite parallel between the conception of culture-text and that of hypertext:

One of the most important facets of literature (and one which also leads to difficulties in interpretation) is its reflexive nature. Individual poems constantly develop their mean-ings—often through such means as direct allusion or the reworking of traditional motifs and conventions, at other times through subtler means, such as genre development and expansion or biographical reference—by referring to that total body of poetic material of which the particular poems comprise a small segment.

Although it was not difficult to accumulate a hypertextually-linked data base consisting of poetic materials, Scholes and his group were more concerned with making it interactive—that is, they wanted to construct a "communal text" including not only the poetry, but also incorporating the comments and interpretations offered by individual students. In this way, each student in turn could read a work and attach "notes" to it about his or her observations. The resulting "expanded text" would be read and augmented at a terminal on which the screen was divided into four areas. The student could call up the poem in one of the areas (referred to as windows) and call up related materi-als in the other three windows, in any sequence he or she desired. This would powerfully reinforce the tendency to read in a nonlinear sequence. By this means, each student would learn how to read a work as it truly exists, not in "a vacuum" but rather as the central point of a progressively-revealed body of documents and ideas.

Hypertext is analogous to other forms of literary discourse besides poetry. From the very beginning of its manifestation as a computer program, hyper-text was popularly described as a multidimensional text roughly analogous to the standard scholarly article in the humanities or social sciences, because it uses the same conceptual devices, such as footnotes, annotations, allusions to other works, quotations from other works, etc. Unfortunately, the convention of linear reading and writing, as well as the physical fact of two-dimensional pages and the necessity of binding them in only one possible sequence, have always limited the true potential of this type of text. One problem is that the reader is often forced to search through the text (or forced to leave the book and search elsewhere) for related information. This is a time-consuming and distracting process; instead of being able to move easily and instantly among physically remote or inaccessible areas of information storage, the reader must cope with cumbrous physical impediments to his or her research or creative work. With the advent of hypertext, it has become possible to move among related areas of information with a speed and flexibility that at least approach finally accommodating the workings of human intellect, to a degree that books and sequential reading cannot possibly allow.

The recombinant text in hypertextual form signifies the emergence of the perception of textual constellations that have always/already gone nova. It is in this uncanny luminos-ity that the authorial biomorph has been consumed.[2]

Barthes and Foucault may be lauded for theorizing the death of the author; the absent author is more a matter of everyday life, however, for the techno-crat recombining and augmenting information at the computer or at a video editing console. S/he is living the dream of capitalism that is still being refined in the area of manufacture. The Japanese notion of "just in time deliv-ery," in which the units of assembly are delivered to the assembly line just as they are called for, was a first step in streamlining the tasks of assembly. In such a system, there is no sedentary capital, but a constant flow of raw commodities. The assembled commodity is delivered to the distributor precisely at the moment of con-sumer need. This nomadic system eliminates stockpiles of goods. (There still is some dead time; however, the Japanese have cut it to a matter of hours, and are working on reducing it to a matter of minutes.) In this way, production, distribution, and consumption are imploded into a single act, with no beginning or end, just unbroken circulation. In the same man-ner, the online text flows in an unbroken stream through the electronic network. There can be no place for gaps that mark discrete units in the society of speed. Consequently, notions of origin have no place in electronic reality. The production of the text presupposes its immediate distribution, consumption, and revision. All who participate in the network also partici-pate in the interpretation and mutation of the textual stream. The concept of the author did not so much die as it simply ceased to function. The author has become an abstract aggre-gate that cannot be reduced to biology or to the psychology of personality. Indeed, such a development has apocalyptic connotations—the fear that humanity will be lost in the tex-tual stream. Perhaps humans are not capable of participating in hypervelocity. One must answer that never has there been a time when humans were able, one and all, to participate in cultural produc-tion. Now, at least the potential for cultural democracy is greater. The single bio-genius need not act as a stand-in for all humanity. The real concern is just the same as it has always been: the need for access to cultural resources.

> *The concept of the author did not so much die as it simply ceased to function. The author has become an abstract aggregate that cannot be reduced to biology or to the psychology of personality.*

The discoveries of postmodern art and criticism regarding the analogical structures of images demonstrate that when two objects are brought together, no matter how far apart their contexts may be, a relationship is formed. Restricting oneself to a personal relationship of words is mere convention. The bringing together of two independent expressions supersedes the original elements and produces a synthetic organization of greater possibility.[3]

The book has by no means disappeared. The publishing industry continues to resist the emergence of the recombinant text, and opposes increases in cultural speed. It has set itself in the gap between production and consumption of texts, which for purposes of survival it is bound to maintain. If speed is allowed to increase, the book is doomed to perish, along with its renaissance companions painting and sculpture. This is why the industry is so afraid of the recombinant text. Such a work closes the gap between production and consumption, and opens the industry to those other than the literary celebrity. If the industry is unable to differentiate its product through the spectacle of originality and uniqueness, its profitability collapses. Consequently, the industry plods along, taking years to publish information needed immediately. Yet there is a peculiar irony to this situation. In order to reduce speed, it must also participate in velocity in its most intense form, that of spectacle. It must claim to defend "quality and standards," and it must invent celebrities. Such endeavors require the immediacy of advertising—that is, full participation in the simulacra that will be the industry's own destruction.

   Hence for the bureaucrat, from an everyday life perspective, the author is alive and well. S/he can be seen and touched and traces of h/is existence are on the covers of books and magazines everywhere in the form of the signature. To such evidence, theory can only respond with the maxim that the meaning of a given text derives exclusively from its relation to other texts. Such texts are contingent upon what came before them, the context in which they are placed, and the interpretive ability of the reader. This argument is of course unconvincing to the social segments caught in cultural lag. So long as this is the case, no recognized historical legitimation will support the producers of recombinant texts, who will always be suspect to the keepers of "high" culture.

Take your own words or the words said to be "the very own words" of anyone else living or dead. You will soon see that words do not belong to anyone. Words have a vitality of their own. Poets are supposed to liberate the words—not to chain them in phrases. Poets have no words "of their very own." Writers do not own their words. Since when do words belong to anybody? "Your very own words" indeed! and who are "you"?

The invention of the video portapak in the late 1960s and early 70s led to considerable speculation among radical media artists that in the near future, everyone would have access to such equipment, causing a revolution in the television industry. Many hoped that video would become the ultimate tool for distributable democratic art. Each home would become its own production center, and the reliance on network television for electronic information would be only one of many options. Unfortunately this prophecy never came to pass. In the democratic sense, video did little more than super 8 film to redistribute the possibility for image production, and it has had little or no effect on image distribution. Any video besides home movies has remained in the hands of an elite technocratic class, although (as with any class) there are marginalized segments which resist the media industry, and maintain a program of decentralization.

   The video revolution failed for two reasons—a lack of access and an absence of desire. Gaining access to the hardware, particularly post-production equipment, has remained as difficult as ever, nor are there any regular distribution points beyond the local public access offered by some cable TV franchises. It has also been hard to convince those outside of the technocratic class why they should want to do something with video, even if they had access to equipment. This is quite understandable when one considers that media images are provided in such an overwhelming quantity that the thought of producing more is empty. The contemporary plagiarist faces precisely the same discouragement. The potential for generating recombinant texts at present is just that, potential. It does at least have a wider base, since the computer technology for making recombinant texts has escaped the technocratic class and spread to the bureaucratic class; however, electronic cultural production has by no means become the democratic form that utopian plagiarists hope it will be.

The immediate problems are obvious. The cost of technology for productive plagiarism is still too high. Even if one chooses to use the less efficient form of a hand-written plagiarist manuscript, desktop publishing technology is required to distribute it, since no publishing house will accept it. Further, the population in the US is generally skilled only as receivers of information, not as producers. With this exclusive structure solidified, technology and the desire and ability to use it remain centered in utilitarian economy, and hence not much time is given to the technology's aesthetic or resistant possibilities.

In addition to these obvious barriers, there is a more insidious problem that emerges from the social schizophrenia of the US. While its political system is theoretically based on democratic principles of inclusion, its economic system is based on the principle of exclusion. Consequently, as a luxury itself, the cultural superstructure tends towards exclusion as well. This economic principle determined the invention of copyright, which originally developed not in order to protect writers, but to reduce competition among publishers. In 17th-century England, where copyright first appeared, the goal was to reserve for publishers themselves, in perpetuity, the exclusive right to print certain books. The justification, of course, was that when formed into a literary work, language has the author's personality imposed upon it, thereby marking it as private property. Under this mythology, copyright has flourished in late capital, setting the legal precedent to privatize any cultural item, whether it is an image, a word, or a sound. Thus the plagiarist (even of the technocratic class) is kept in a deeply marginal position, regardless of the inventive efficient uses h/is methodology may have for the current state of technology and knowledge.

What is the point of saving language when there is no longer anything to say?

The present requires us to rethink and re-present the notion of plagiarism. Its function has for too long been devalued by an ideology with little place in techno-culture. Let the romantic notions of originality, genius, and authorship remain, but as elements for cultural production without special privilege above other equally useful elements. It is time to openly and boldly use the methodology of recombination so as to better parallel the technology of our time.

■ NOTES

1. In its more heroic form the footnote has a low-speed hypertextual function—that is, connecting the reader with other sources of information that can further articulate the producer's words. It points to additional information too lengthy to include in the text itself. This is not an objectionable function. The footnote is also a means of surveillance by which one can "check up" on a writer, to be sure that s/he is not improperly using an idea or phrase from the work of another. This function makes the footnote problematic, although it may be appropriate as a means of verifying conclusions in a quantitative study, for example. The surveillance function of the footnote imposes fixed interpretations on a linguistic sequence, and implies ownership of language and ideas by the individual cited. The note becomes an homage to the genius who supposedly originated the idea. This would be acceptable if all who deserved credit got their due; however, such crediting is impossible, since it would begin an infinite regress. Consequently, that which is most feared occurs: the labor of many is stolen, smuggled in under the authority of the signature which is cited. In the case of those cited who are still living, this designation of authorial ownership allows them to collect rewards for the work of others. It must be realized that writing itself is theft: it is a changing of the features of the old culture-text in much the same way one disguises stolen goods. This is not to say that signatures should never be cited; but remember that the signature is merely a sign, a shorthand under which a collection of interrelated ideas may be stored and rapidly deployed.

2. If the signature is a form of cultural shorthand, then it is not necessarily horrific on occasion to sabotage the structures so they do not fall into rigid complacency. Attributing words to an image, i.e., an intellectual celebrity, is inappropriate. The image is a tool for playful use, like any culture-text or part thereof. It is just as necessary to imagine the history of the spectacular image, and write it as imagined, as it is to show fidelity to its current "factual" structure. One should choose the method that best suits the context of production, one that will render the greater possibility for interpretation. The producer of recombinant texts augments the language, and often preserves the generalized code, as when Karen Eliot quoted Sherrie Levine as saying, "Plagiarism? I just don't like the way it tastes."

3. It goes without saying that one is not limited to correcting a work or to integrating diverse fragments of out-of-date works into a new one; one can also alter the meaning of these fragments in any appropriate way, leaving the constipated to their slavish preservation of "citations."

Chapter 5

Questions and Suggestions for Further Study on the Net/WWW

■ QUESTIONS BASED ON THE READINGS:

1. In "The Library of Babel," we read: "the Library is total and . . . its shelves contain all the possible combinations of the twenty-odd orthographic symbols . . .; that is, everything which can be expressed, in all languages. Everything is there." And: "When it was proclaimed that the Library comprised all books, the first impression was one of extravagant joy. All men felt themselves lords of a secret, intact treasure. There was no personal or universal problem whose eloquent solution did not exist. . . . The universe was justified, the universe suddenly expanded to the limitless dimensions of hope." Yet what change of mind does the narrator experience and report? Is there a possible analogy here between the Library and the World Wide Web? Many Internauts are as optimistic about the Web as the narrator of the Library was. Compared to the Library, how promising or disappointing is the Web?

2. Kurzweil, in "The Future of Libraries," agrees with his friend Kay "that the 'free library is not free.'" Explain what he means by this statement. Assuming that you agree with this apparent paradox, is it possible for information on the Internet to be free? If not, who pays for it? Subsidizes it? In the light of your conclusions, what do you think about the hacker's ethic that information wants to be free?

3. Bolter's "The Electronic Book" (chapter 6 of his *Writing Space*) surveys changing media from the papyrus roll to the World Wide Web and how they parcel out information and knowledge in differing ways. Discuss these ways. How do media change the information and knowledge they transmit? In his depiction of great libraries such as the famed and fated one at Alexandria and the modern Library of Congress, Bolter speaks of Ted Nelson's vision of an electronic virtual library called Xanadu. Why does Nelson call his library "Xanadu"? What is the source of this name, its significance? Such a library of libraries would be Borges's Library, infinite in its possibilities. Bolter, however, is skeptical about Xanadu. (See Gary Wolf below.)

4. What was your attitude toward copyrights before reading Barlow's article on the subject and the Critical Art Ensemble's statement from *The Electronic Disturbance*? Barlow talks about the "mental-to-physical conversion" (the

word becoming flesh) as central to patents and copyrights. However, with the physical returning to the mental or the actual becoming virtual, Barlow argues, the conditions for copyright law have changed: "the rights of invention and authorship adhered to activities in the physical world. One didn't get paid for ideas, but for the ability to deliver them into reality." Barlow asks: "What is to be done? While there is a certain grim fun to be had in it, dancing on the grave of copyright and patent will solve little." (Kurzweil maintains, if you recall, that copyright has to be maintained: free information is not free!) The Critical Art Ensemble, however, see the conditions as having changed so radically that they would make a virtue of "utopian plagiarism." Where do you stand on this issue, specifically in relation to intellectual property in virtual space (libraries, journals, zines, e-mail postings)?

■ FURTHER STUDY ON THE NET/WWW:

- *Virtual Libraries:* Going to WebCrawler <http://webcrawler.com/> and using the search words *Virtual Library* will get you more than you can deal with, but I asked for a maximum return of 25 hits. Here is the list returned:

```
The query "virtual library" found 5748 documents and returned
25:

1000 WWW Virtual Library in JAPAN: %[!<%`%Z!<%8
0549 PLANET EARTH HOME PAGE VIRTUAL LIBRARY
0488 The CWRU Virtual Library
0471 Virtual Library stuff
0440 Search the CWRU Virtual Library by Title, Author, or
Subject Keyword
0412 PLANET EARTH HOME PAGE VIRTUAL LIBRARY IMAGE MAP
0323 The Virtual SMOF-BBS
0258 The World-Wide Web Virtual Library: Geophysics
0244 The World-Wide Web Virtual Library: Earth Sciences
0244 The PALS Virtual Library
0239 WebStars: Virtual Reality
0231 TUB-DMIE Virtual Library
0220 http://daedalus.edc.rmit.edu.au/subjects
0220 The World-Wide Web Virtual Library: Civil Engineering
0209 Virtual Computer Library
0191 WWW Virtual Library—Education
0191 Virtual Library
0191 Virtual Libraries
0183 Internet Virtual Library & Searches
0177 ASPEN PLUS Virtual Library
0174 The World-Wide Web Virtual Library: Earth Sciences
Resources
0169 Real-Time Application Platform (RTAP) Virtual Library
```

0169 LSU Virtual Library
0166 The World-Wide Web Virtual Library: Environment—Subject
Tree
0161 Welcome to the Virtual Garden

If you point to some of these sites variously referred to as *World-Wide Web Virtual Library,* you will reach one big site <http://www.csu.edu.au/education/library.html> by that name, which is housed virtually at Charles Sturt University.

Another site is *The World-Wide Web Virtual Library: Subject Catalogue:* <http://18.23.0.22/hypertext/DataSources/bySubject/Overview.html>, where you will find:

VIRTUAL LIBRARY THE WWW VIRTUAL LIBRARY

This is a distributed subject catalogue. See **Category Sub-tree, Library of Congress Classification** (Experimental), **Top Ten most popular Fields** (Experimental), **Statistics** (Experimental), and **Index.** See also arrangement by **service type,** and other subject catalogues of network information.

Mail to **maintainers** of the specified subject or www-request@mail.w3.org to add pointers to this list, or if you would like **to contribute to administration of a subject area.**

See also **how to put your data on the web.** All items starting with ! are NEW! (or newly maintained). New this month: [INLINE] Genetics [INLINE] Accelerator Physics [INLINE] Broadcasters [INLINE] Caenorhabditis elegans (nematode) [INLINE] Cartography [INLINE] Classical Music [INLINE] Developmental Biology [INLINE] Drosophila (fruit fly) [INLINE] Epidemiology [INLINE] Forest Genetics and Tree Breeding [INLINE] Journalism [INLINE] Mycology (Fungi) [INLINE] Non-Profit Organizations [INLINE] Pharmacy (Medicine) [INLINE] Physiology and Biophysics [INLINE] Roadkill [INLINE] Yeasts [INLINE] Zoos [INLINE]

Aboriginal Studies
This document keeps track of leading information facilities in the field of Australian Aboriginal studies as well as the Indigenous Peoples studies.

Aeronautics and Aeronautical Engineering
African Studies
Agriculture
Animal health, wellbeing, and rights
Anthropology
Applied Linguistics
Archaeology
Architecture
Art

... and continues down the index. The best way to learn about this site is to browse through it at your own pace. (Since the site, like most sites, is updated constantly, what you see here might not be what you find later and even much later, but at least you can get an impression of how it is organized.)

- Other Virtual Libraries: *British Library:* <gopher://portico.bl.uk/> *Library of Congress:* <http://lcweb.loc.gov/homepage/lchp.html> *Harvard Library:* <gopher://hplus.harvard.edu/> *Yahoo's List of Libraries:* <http://www.yahoo.com/Reference/Libraries/University_Libraries/> *The University of California—Irvine Virtual Reference Desk:* <gopher://peg.cwis.uci.edu:7000/11/gopher.welcome/peg/VIRTUAL%20REFERENCE%20DESK>.

- *Hytelnet:* <http://library.usask.ca/cgi-bin/hytelnet>. You can add to the list above by simply searching for various libraries or by going to *Hytelnet,* which telnets you to virtually every library in the world!

- *Project Xanadu:* <http://xanadu.net/the.project>. This project has been criticized by Gary Wolf in "The Curse of Xanadu." *Wired* 3.06 (July 1995): 137–52, 194–202. Online. *HotWired.* Internet. 22 August 1995. Available: <http://vip.hotwired.com/wired/3.06/features/xanadu.html>. Read this lengthy article. Then read Ted Nelson's response at the Project Xanadu site under the link *Wolfsbane.* Nelson has also responded in print in *Wired* (see "Rants & Raves," September 1995, 28, 33; for the full letter, point your browser to <http://www.hotwired.com/Lib/Wired/3.06/features/Xanadu/nelson_letter.html>). A search for *Xanadu* by way of *WebCrawler* will give you numerous additional sites to visit.

■ HERE ARE SOME ADDITIONAL WEBSITES:

- *The Copyright WebSite:* <http://www.benedict.com/index.html>

- *Copyright Act of 1976, as amended:* <http://www.law.cornell.edu/usc/17/overview.html>

- *Copyright Clearance Center On line:* <http://www.openmarket.com/copyright/> (*WebCrawler* will give more sites on *Copyright* than you probably have time to visit. Also see Appendix A.)

- *The On-Line Book Initiative:* <ftp://ftp.std.com/obi>

- *The B&R Samizdat Express:* <http://www/users/samizdat>. Here you will find a wealth of information in the form of newsletters about various sites on the Web where books have been digitized and are "free." (Subscribe to the newsletter.) There are also links to other sites.

- Rice University *E-Text Archive:* <gopher://riceinfo.rice.edu/11/Subject/LitBooks>.

- *Project Gutenberg:* <http://jg.cso.uiuc.edu/PG/welcome.html> will give you:

Welcome to Project Gutenberg

What is Project Gutenberg?
In English
In German
Project Gutenberg Electronic Texts
Project Gutenberg Newsletters: Current and Past Issues
Articles about Project Gutenberg
How to Volunteer for Project Gutenberg
Links to Other Electronic Text Archives

- *The Rossetti Archive* <http://jefferson.village.virginia.edu/rossetti/rossetti.html>. The longer name is *The Complete Writings and Pictures of Dante Gabriel Rossetti: A Hypermedial Research Archive.* You will need the *Mosaic* or preferably the *Netscape* browser to access this site. If you are in literary studies, you should find this site of special interest.

- *Zines or E(lectronic maga)Zines:* Point to *WebCrawler* <http://webcrawler.com/> and search *Zines*; you will get more than you can look at and read. Try *World Wide Punk: Punk Zines—Directory of Punk/Hardcore Zines on The Net* <http://wchat.on.ca/vic/wwp-zine.htm>. Also, try *The English Server* (CMU) <http://english-www.hss.cmu.edu/>, and in the index look for "journals and magazines." Or go to *The Whole Internet Catalog* <http://gnn.com/wic/wics/index.html>, where you will find "Arts & Entertainment," with "E-Zines," which will give you:

E-Zines

Chip's Closet Cleaner
c|net
FEED
Fine Art Forum
FiX Magazine
International Teletimes
John Labovitz's E-ZINE-LIST [index]
London Calling
Melvin
NetSurfer Digest
Urban Desires

■ MORE REFERENCES FOR READING:

Alternative-X. Online. Internet. 22 August 1995. Available: <http://marketplace.com/alt.x/althome.html>. Check out this zine, edited by Mark Amerika.

Benjamin, Walter. "The Work of Art in the Age of Mechanical Reproduction." *Illuminations.* Ed. Hannah Arendt. New York: Schocken, 1969: 217–251.

boing boing. The zine has a homepage: Online. Internet. 22 August 1995. Available: <http://www.zeitgeist.net/Public/Boing-boing/>. Check out the zine in print as well.

Bolter, Jay David. *Writing Space: The Computer, Hypertext, and the History of Writing.* Hillsdale, NJ: Lawrence Erlbaum, 1991.

Borges, Jorge Luis. *Ficciones.* New York: Grove, 1962.

Critical Art Ensemble. *The Electronic Disturbance.* New York: Autonomedia, 1994.

Dingbat (Satire for Global Village Idiots), edited by Derek Pell. A wonderful zine, in print only.

Fringe Ware. The zine/review that goes by this name has a homepage: Online. Internet. 22 August 1995. Available: <http://www.fringeware.com/>. Check out the zine *Fringe Ware Review* in print.

Jacobson, Robert L. "No Copying." *The Chronicle of Higher Education* (March 10, 1995): A17–19.

Katsh, M. Ethan. *Law in a Digital World.* Oxford University Press, 1995.

Liberal Education 79 (Winter 1993). Special issue: The Future of the Book in the Electronic Age.

MONDO 2000. Check out this most famous magazine. At present, this zine does not have a website but is building one. Check out its gopher site: Online. Internet. 22 August 1995. Available: <gopher://gopher. well.sf.ca.us/11/Publications/MONDO>.

Nelson, Theodor Holm. *Literary Machines.* (self published, distrib. by The Mindful Press), 1980.

Net (British version). The publication's homepage: Online. Internet. 22 August 1995. Available: <http://www.futurenet.co.uk/netmag/net.html>.

Postmodern Culture. Online. University of Virginia's Advanced Technology in the Humanities. 22 August 1995. Available: <http://jefferson.village. virginia.edu/pmc/contents.all.html>.

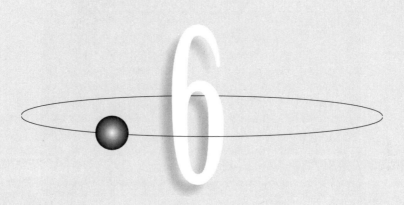

CyberPunk/Cyborgs

C

yber + punk form a hybrid. Cyber comes
from the Greek *kybernetes* (pilot, steersman). Punk comes from the media
understanding of rebellious (working-class) British and American youth who
wear Mohawks and black clothes and pierce their bodies beyond their ear-
lobes. Together, the hybrid cyberpunk has spawned as many definitions as
definers.

In his *Time* magazine article, cast in the form of a primer, Philip Elmer-
Dewitt surveys some of the various meanings of *cyberpunk* along with its various hyperassociations, one of which is that the punks of the 1970s ,'80s, and
'90s take technology and steer it against itself. Whereas technology is used
against people in centralizing information and in collecting and encrypting
the data, cyberpunks (now broadly defined as cyberculture and associated
with hackers) have adopted the following as their ethic: information wants to
be and should be free-in-access to everyone so that each can act on, steer, his
or her own reality. Cyberpunks in various ways make up a contemporary
counterculture.

An important part of cyberculture is punk music. In "Seriously Wired,"
Schoemer begins: "Billy Idol is playing with his new best friend, technology."
Here we have one example among many available of a rock artist turning
(steering) technology in his favor.

By far two of the most popular treatments of things cyberpunk are by
R. U. Sirius (Ken Goffman) and Timothy Leary. Sirius, who was associated
with the magazine MONDO 2000, employs a pastiche approach, listing people
and events that signify cyberpunk culture. For example, he includes Gareth
Branwyn, who on a MONDO 2000 conference on the WELL put forth a description of the cyberpunk worldview: "The future has imploded onto the present.
There was no nuclear Armageddon. There's too much real estate to lose. The
new battlefield is people's minds." Branwyn alludes to the fact that there was

tremendous fear of the nuclear holocaust following World War II. Turning things around in his statement, he refers not only to the threat to all people and the environment but also—and most prominently now—to their minds. The new world order would centralize everything, making difference difficult, unifying all thought for mass consumption, while the cyberpunk disorder would be "splintering [the world] into a trillion subcultures and designer cults with their own languages, codes, and lifestyles," making difference a virtue. (There is a subtle irony here: the Internet within the World Wide Web, which is where cyberpunk culture mostly lives, was built in the U.S. by the federal government as a means of communication during and after a nuclear attack. Now these virtual underground tunnels have become the places of dissent by a counterculture.)

Leary—famous in the 1960s for the saying "Turn on, tune in, drop out"—returns on the scene and asks us to take a close look at the etymology of the word *kybernetes* (pilot) so that we can understand that the Greek term for *pilot,* when appropriated by the Romans, became *gubernetes,* which means one who *governs* or *controls* others. It is this change in meaning, from pilot to controller, Leary claims, that is "our oppressive birthright." Leary sees cyberpunks, how-ever, as the new pilots showing the way for controllers or the controlled to become their own pilots. Cyberpunks are the new role model for the millen-nium. Leary chants:

Cyberpunks are the inventors, innovative writers, technofrontier artists, risk-taking film directors, icon-shifting composers, stand-up comedians, expressionist artists, free-agent sci-entists, technocreatives, computer visionaries, elegant hackers, bit-blitting Prolog adepts, special-effectives, cognitive dissidents, video wizards, neurological text pilots, media explorers—all of those who boldly package and steer ideas out there where no thoughts have gone before.

So now, it's "Turn on, tune in, and boot up."

Though not always identified as a cyberpunk, Hakim Bey writes of *temporary autonomous zones* (TAZs), which can be disembodied space. Bey speaks in terms of the Internet and the World Wide Web, but he also speaks of a third virtual place, which he calls the "counter-Net." Finally (but beginningly) Donna Haraway concentrates extensively on the human species becoming machine: the cyborg. The word became flesh, and now flesh becomes silicon. As cyborgs, as cybernauts, we will be free of the distinctions human versus animal, human versus machine, and physical (body) versus metaphysical (spirit). And we will have a new politics!

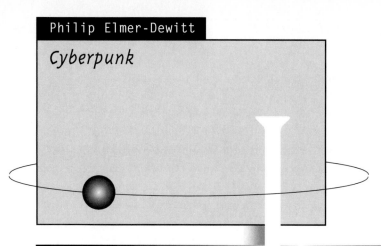

Philip Elmer-Dewitt

Cyberpunk

I n the 1950s it was the beatniks, staging a coffeehouse rebellion against the *Leave It to Beaver* conformity of the Eisenhower era. In the 1960s the hippies arrived, combining antiwar activism with the energy of sex, drugs and rock 'n' roll. Now a new subculture is bubbling up from the underground, popping out of computer screens like a piece of futuristic **HYPERTEXT** *(see margin).*

They call it cyberpunk, a late–20th century term pieced together from **CYBERNETICS** (the science of communication and control theory) and **PUNK** (an antisocial rebel or hoodlum). Within this odd pairing lurks the essence of cyberpunk culture. It's a way of looking at the world that combines an infatuation with high-tech tools and a disdain for conventional ways of using them. Originally applied to a school of hardboiled science-fiction writers and then to certain semi-tough computer hackers, the word cyberpunk now covers a broad range of music, art, psychedelics, smart drugs and cutting-edge technology. The cult is new enough that fresh offshoots are sprouting every day, which infuriates the hardcore cyberpunks, who feel they got there first.

Stewart Brand, editor of the hippie-era *Whole Earth Catalog,* describes cyberpunk as "technology with attitude." Science-fiction writer Bruce Sterling calls it "an unholy alliance of the technical world with the underground of pop culture and street-level anarchy." Jude Milhon, a cyberpunk journalist who writes under the byline St. Jude, defines it as "the place where the worlds of science and art overlap, the intersection of the future and now." What cyberpunk is about, says Rudy Rucker, a San Jose State University mathematician who writes science-fiction books on the side, is nothing less than "the fusion of humans and machines."

As in any counterculture movement, some denizens would deny that they are part of a "movement" at all. Certainly they are not as visible from a passing car as beatniks or hippies once

were. Ponytails (on men) and tattoos (on women) do not a cyberpunk make—though dressing all in black and donning mirrored sunglasses will go a long way. And although the biggest cyberpunk journal claims a readership approaching 70,000, there are probably no more than a few thousand computer hackers, futurists, fringe scientists, computer-savvy artists and musicians, and assorted science-fiction geeks around the world who actually call themselves cyberpunks.

Nevertheless, cyberpunk may be the defining counterculture of the computer age. It embraces, in spirit at least, not just the nearest thirtysomething hacker hunched over his terminal but also nose-ringed twentysomethings gathered at clandestine **RAVES,** teenagers who feel about the Macintosh computer the way their parents felt about Apple Records, and even preadolescent vidkids fused like Krazy Glue to their Super Nintendo and Sega Genesis games—the training wheels of cyberpunk. Obsessed with technology, especially technology that is just beyond their reach (like **BRAIN IMPLANTS**), the cyberpunks are future oriented to a fault. They already have one foot in the 21st century, and time is on their side. In the long run, we will all be cyberpunks.

The cyberpunk look—a kind of SF (science-fiction) surrealism tweaked by computer graphics—is already finding its way into art galleries, music videos and Hollywood movies. Cyberpunk magazines, many of which are "'zines" cheaply published by desktop computer and distributed by electronic mail, are multiplying like cable-TV channels. The newest, a glossy, big-budget entry called *Wired,* premiered last week with Bruce Sterling on the cover and ads from the likes of Apple Computer and AT&T. Cyberpunk music, including **ACID HOUSE** and **INDUSTRIAL,** is popular enough to keep several record companies and scores of bands cranking out CDs. Cyberpunk-oriented books are snapped up by eager fans as soon as they hit the stores. (Sterling's latest, *The Hacker Crackdown,* quickly sold out its first hard-cover printing of 30,000.) A piece of cyberpunk performance art, *Tubes,* starring Blue Man Group, is a hit off-Broadway. And cyberpunk films such as *Blade Runner, Videodrome, Robocop, Total Recall, Terminator 2* and *The Lawnmower Man* have moved out of the cult market and into the mall.

Cyberpunk culture is likely to get a boost from, of all things, the Clinton-Gore Administration, because of a shared interest in what the new regime calls America's "data highways" and what the cyberpunks call **CYBERSPACE.** Both terms describe the globe-circling, interconnected telephone network that is the conduit for billions of voice, fax and computer-to-computer communications. The incoming Administration is focused on the wiring, and it has made

Raves Organized on the fly (sometimes by electronic mail) and often held in warehouses, raves are huge, nomadic dance parties that tend to last all night, or until the police show up. Psychedelic mood enhancers and funny accessories (white cotton gloves, face masks) are optional.

Brain Implants Slip a microchip into snug contact with your gray matter (a.k.a. wetware) and suddenly gain instant fluency in a foreign language or arcane subject.

Acid House White-hot dance music that falls somewhere between disco and hip-hop.

Industrial Mixing rhythmic machine clanks, electronic feedback and random radio noise, industrial music is "the sounds our culture makes as it comes unglued," says cyberpunk writer Gareth Branwyn.

Cyberspace SF writer William Gibson called it "a consensual hallucination . . . a graphic representation of data abstracted from the banks of every computer in the human system." You can get there simply by picking up the phone.

Virtual Reality An interactive technology that creates an illusion, still crude rather than convincing, of being immersed in an artificial world. The user generally dons a computerized glove and a head-mounted display equipped with a TV screen for each eye. Now available as an arcade game.

Computer Virus The cybernetic analogue of AIDS, these self-replicating programs infect computers and can destroy data. There are hundreds loose in cyberspace, although few are as destructive as the Internet virus— which is now classified as a "worm" because the writer of the program did not mean to do damage.

Internet The successor of an experimental network built by the U.S. Defense Department in the 1960s, the Internet links at least 3 million computers, many of them university- and research-related, around the world. Users can connect to the Internet by phone to share information or tap into data banks.

Virtual Communities Collections of like-minded people who meet on-line and share ideas on everything from politics to punk rock. The global village is full of tiny electronic subdivisions made up of cold-fusion physicists, white supremacists, gerontologists and Grateful Deadheads. Like any other community, each has its own in-jokes, cliques, bozos and bores.

The WELL Compared with million-plus-member networks such as CompuServe and Prodigy, the Northern California-based Whole Earth 'Lectronic Link is a tiny outpost in cyberspace. But its 7,000 subscribers include an unusual concentration of artists, activists, journalists and other writers. "It has a regional flavor," says co-founder Stewart Brand. "You can smell the sourdough."

strengthening the network's high-speed data links a priority. The cyberpunks look at those wires from the inside; they talk of the network as if it were an actual place—a **VIRTUAL REALITY** that can be entered, explored and manipulated.

Cyberspace plays a central role in the cyberpunk world view. The literature is filled with "console cow-boys" who prove their mettle by donning virtual-reality headgear and performing heroic feats in the imaginary "matrix" of cyberspace. Many of the punks' real-life heroes are also computer cowboys of one sort or another. *Cyberpunk,* a 1991 book by two New York *Times* reporters, John Markoff and Katie Hafner, features profiles of three canonical cyberpunk hackers, including Robert Morris, the Cornell graduate student whose **COMPUTER VIRUS** brought the huge network called the **INTERNET** to a halt.

But cyberspace is more than a playground for hacker high jinks. What cyberpunks have known for some time—and what 17.5 million modem-equipped computer users around the world have discovered—is that cyberspace is also a new medium. Every night on Prodigy, CompuServe, GEnie and thousands of smaller computer bulletin boards, people by the hundreds of thousands are logging on to a great computer-mediated gabfest, an interactive debate that allows them to leap over barriers of time, place, sex and social status. Computer networks make it easy to reach out and touch strangers who share a particular obsession or concern. "We're replacing the old drugstore soda fountain and town square, where community used to happen in the physical world," says Howard Rheingold, a California-based author and editor who is writing a book on what he calls **VIRTUAL COMMUNITIES.**

Most computer users are content to visit cyberspace now and then, to read their electronic mail, check the bulletin boards and do a bit of electronic shopping. But cyberpunks go there to live and play—and even die. The WELL, one of the hippest virtual communities on the Internet, was shaken 2½ years ago when one of its most active participants ran a computer program that erased every message he had ever left— thousands of postings, some running for many pages. It was an act that amounted to virtual suicide. A few weeks later, he committed suicide for real.

The WELL is a magnet for cyberpunk thinkers, and it is there, appropriately enough, that much of the debate over the scope and significance of cyberpunk has occurred. The question "Is there a cyberpunk movement?" launched a freewheeling on-line **FLAME**-fest that ran for months. The debate yielded, among other things, a fairly concise list of "attitudes" that, by general agreement, seem to be central to the idea of cyberpunk. Among them:

Information wants to be free. A good piece of information-age technology will eventually get into the hands of those who can make the best use of it, despite the best efforts of the censors, copyright lawyers and **DATACOPS.**

Always yield to the hands-on imperative. Cyberpunks believe they can run the world for the better, if they can only get their hands on the control box.

Promote decentralization. Society is splintering into hundreds of subcultures and designer cults, each with its own language, code and life-style.

Surf the edges. When the world is changing by the nanosecond, the best way to keep your head above water is to stay at the front end of the Zeitgeist.

The roots of cyberpunk, curiously, are as much literary as they are technological. The term was coined in the late 1980s to describe a group of science-fiction writers—and in particular **WILLIAM GIBSON,** a 44-year-old American now living in Vancouver. Gibson's *Neuromancer,* the first novel to win SF's triple crown—the Hugo, Nebula and Philip K. Dick awards— quickly became a cyberpunk classic, attracting an audience beyond the world of SF. Critics were intrigued by a dense, technopoetic prose style that invites comparisons to Hammett, Burroughs and Pynchon. Computer-literate readers were drawn by Gibson's nightmarish depictions of an imaginary world disturbingly similar to the one they inhabit.

In fact, the key to cyberpunk science fiction is that it is not so much a projection into the future as a metaphorical evocation of today's technological flux. The hero of *Neuromancer,* a burned-out, drug-addicted street hustler named Case, inhabits a sleazy **INTERZONE** on the fringes of a megacorporate global village where all transactions are carried out in New Yen. There he encounters Molly, a sharp-edged beauty with reflective lenses grafted to her eye sockets and retractable razor blades implanted in her fingers. They are hired by a mysterious employer who offers to fix Case's damaged nerves so he can once again enter cyberspace—a term Gibson invented. Soon Case discovers that he is actually working for an AI (artificial intelligence) named Wintermute, who is trying to get around the restrictions placed on AIs by the **TURING POLICE** to keep the computers under control. "What's important to me," says Gibson, "is that *Neuromancer* is about the present."

The themes and motifs of cyberpunk have been percolating through the culture for nearly a decade. But they have coalesced in the past few years, thanks in large part to an upstart magazine called **MONDO 2000**. Since 1988, *Mondo*'s editors have covered cyberpunk

---

Flame Sociologists note that, without visual cues, people communicating on-line tend to flame: to state their views more heatedly than they would face-to-face.

Datacops Any department or agency charged with protecting data security. Most notoriously: the U.S. Secret Service, whose 1990 Operation Sundevil launched constitutionally questionable predawn raids on computer hackers in a dozen U.S. cities and provoked international outrage in the cyberpunk community.

William Gibson Gibson knows precious little about cybernetic technology. When the success of *Neuromancer* enabled him to buy his own computer, he was surprised to discover that it had a disk drive. "I had been expecting an exotic crystalline thing. What I got was a little piece of a Victorian engine that makes noises like a scratchy old record player."

Interzone The wasteland setting of William Burroughs' *Naked Lunch* (1959) has become a favorite haunt for cyberpunk writers. It is here, in Gibson's words, that "the street finds its own uses for things," subverting cutting-edge technology to suit the needs of the underground.

Turing Police British mathematician Alan Turing predicted in 1950 that computers would someday be as intelligent as humans.

MONDO 2000 *Mondo* is Italian for world; 2000 is the year. Says editor R. U. Sirius: "I like the idea of a magazine with an expiration date."

Negativland Better known for media pranks than records (*Helter Stupid*), this band canceled a tour in 1988 after a Minnesota teen axed his family to death. The band's press release said the family had been arguing about Negativland's song *Christianity Is Stupid.* The story was a hoax, but the press ran with it, turning the band into cyberpunk heroes.

Timothy Leary Yes, he's back. At 72, the ex-Harvard professor who encouraged a generation to "turn on, tune in, drop out" now counts himself a cyberpunk. "The PC is the LSD of the 1990s," he says.

Techno-Erotic Paganism Sound intriguing? That's probably why the editors of MONDO 2000 put the term on the cover of their book. Unfortunately, they never got around to explaining what it means.

Synaesthesia From the Greek *syn* (union) and *aesthesia* (sensation), synesthesia is a merging of sensory input in which sounds appear as colors in the brain or words evoke a specific taste or smell.

Temporary Autonomous Zones These are the electronic analogue of mountain fortresses and pirate islands, but they can be formed or dismantled in a flash, says cyberpunk essayist Hakim Bey. As political systems decay and networking becomes more widespread, he envisions a proliferation of autonomous areas in cyberspace: giant worker-owned corporations, independent enclaves devoted to data piracy, Green-Social Democrat collectives, anarchist liberation zones, etc.

as *Rolling Stone* magazine chronicles rock music, with celebrity interviews of such cyberheroes as **NEGATIVLAND** and **TIMOTHY LEARY,** alongside features detailing what's hot and what's on the horizon. *Mondo*'s editors have packaged their quirky view of the world into a glossy book titled *Mondo 2000: A User's Guide to the New Edge* (HarperCollins; $20). Its cover touts alphabetic entries on everything from virtual reality and wetware to designer aphrodisiacs and **TECHNO-EROTIC PAGANISM**, promising to make cyberpunk's rarefied perspective immediately accessible. Inside, in an innovative hypertext format (which is echoed in this article), relatively straightforward updates on computer graphics, multimedia and fiber optics accompany wild screeds on such recondite subjects as **SYNESTHESIA** and **TEMPORARY AUTONOMOUS ZONES**.

The book and the magazine that inspired it are the product of a group of brainy (if eccentric) visionaries holed up in a rambling Victorian mansion perched on a hillside in Berkeley, California. The MTV-style graphics are supplied by designer Bart Nagel, the overcaffeinated prose by Ken Goffman (writing under the pen name R. U. Sirius) and Alison Kennedy (listed on the masthead as Queen Mu, "domineditrix"), with help from Rudy Rucker and a small staff of freelancers and contributions from an international cast of cyberpunk enthusiasts. The goal is to inspire and instruct but not to lead. "We don't want to tell people what to think," says assistant art director Heide Foley. "We want to tell them what the possibilities are."

Largely patched together from back issues of *Mondo 2000* magazine (and its precursor, a short-lived 'zine called *Reality Hackers*), the *Guide* is filled with articles on all the traditional cyberpunk obsessions, from **ARTIFICIAL LIFE** to **VIRTUAL SEX.** But some of the best entries are those that report on the activities of real people trying to live the cyberpunk life. For example, Mark Pauline, a San Francisco performance artist, specializes in giant machines and vast public spectacles: sonic booms that pin audiences to their chairs or the huge, stinking vat of rotting cheese with which he perfumed the air of Denmark to remind the citizenry of its Viking roots. When an explosion blew the thumb and three fingers off his right hand, Pauline simply had his big toe grafted where his thumb had been. He can pick things up again, but now he's waiting for medical science and grafting technology to advance to the point where he can replace his jerry-built hand with one taken from a cadaver.

Much of *Mondo 2000* strains credibility. Does physicist Nick Herbert really believe there might be a way to build **TIME MACHINES**? Did the **CRYONICS** experts at Trans-Time Laboratory really chill a family pet named Miles and then, after its near death experience, turn it back into what its owner describes as a "fully functional dog"? Are we expected to accept on faith that a **SMART DRUG** called centrophenoxine is an "intelligence booster" that provides "effective anti-aging therapy," or that another compound called hydergine increases mental abilities and prevents damage to brain cells? "All of this has some basis in today's technologies," says Paul Saffo, a research fellow at the Institute for the Future. "But it has a very anticipatory quality. These are people who assume that they will shape the future and the rest of us will live it."

Parents who thumb through *Mondo 2000* will find much here to upset them. An article on house music makes popping MDMA (**ECSTASY**) and thrashing all night to music that clocks 120 beats per minute sound like an experience no red-blooded teenager would want to miss. After describing in detail the erotic effects of massive doses of L-dopa, MDA and deprenyl, the entry on aphrodisiacs adds as an afterthought that in some combinations these drugs can be fatal. Essays praising the beneficial effects of psychedelics and smart drugs on the "information processing" power of the brain sit alongside **RANTS** that declare, among other things, that "safe sex is boring sex" and that "cheap thrills are fun."

Much of this, of course, is a cyberpunk pose. As Rucker confesses in his preface, he enjoys reading and thinking about psychedelic drugs but doesn't really like to take them. "To me the political point of being pro-psychedelic," he writes, "is that this means being against consensus reality, which I very strongly am." To some extent, says author Rheingold, cyberpunk is driven by young people trying to come up with a movement they can call their own. As he puts it, "They're tired of all these old geezers talking about how great the '60s were."

That sentiment was echoed by a recent posting on the WELL. "I didn't get to pop some 'shrooms and dance naked in a park with several hundred of my peers," wrote a cyberpunk wannabe who calls himself Alien. "To me, and to a lot of other generally disenfranchised members of my generation, surfing the edges is all we've got."

More troubling, from a philosophic standpoint, is the theme of **DYSTOPIA** that runs like a bad trip through the cyberpunk world view. Gibson's fictional world is filled with glassy-eyed

Artificial Life Inspired by the behavior of computer viruses, scientists are wondering how sophisticated a computer program or robot would have to be before you could say it was "alive." One computer-software company, Maxis, has marketed a whole line of simulated animals, ant colonies, cities, train systems and even a planet-like organism called Gaia.

Virtual Sex The way it would work, says Howard Rheingold, is that you slip into a virtual-reality bodysuit that fits with the "intimate snugness of a condom." When your partner (lying somewhere in cyberspace) fondles your computer-generated image, you actually feel it on your skin, and vice versa. Miniature sensors and actuators would have to be woven into the clothing by a technology that has yet to be invented.

Time Machines Anyone who has read H. G. Wells or seen *Back to the Future* knows how these things are supposed to work. Certain obscure results of Einstein's relativity theory suggest that there could actually be shortcuts through the space-time continuum, but it's unlikely that a human could squeeze through them.

Cryonics For a price, a terminally ill patient can be frozen—as in the new movie *Forever Young*—until some future time when a cure has been discovered. Some people save on storage costs by having just their head frozen.

Smart Drugs "Don't eat any of that stuff they say will make you smarter," says Bruce Sterling. "It will only make you poorer."

girls strung out on their Walkman-like **SIMSTIM DECKS** and young men who get their kicks from **MICROSOFTS** plugged into sockets behind their ears. His brooding, dehumanized vision conveys a strong sense that technology is changing civilization and the course of history in frightening ways. But many of his readers don't seem to care. "History is a funny thing for cyberpunks," says Christopher Meyer, a music-synthesizer designer from Calabasas, California, writing on the WELL. "It's all data. It all takes up the same amount of space on disk, and a lot of it is just plain noise."

For cyberpunks, pondering history is not as important as coming to terms with the future. For all their flaws, they have found ways to live with technology, to make it theirs—something the back-to-the-land hippies never accomplished. Cyberpunks use technology to bridge the gulf between art and science, between the world of literature and the world of industry. Most of all, they realize that if you don't control technology, it will control you. It is a lesson that will serve them—and all of us—well in the next century.

Ecstasy Enthusiasts describe this New Age psychedelic, which heightens the senses, as "LSD without the hallucinations." The drug was outlawed in the U.S. in 1987.

Rants A hyperbolic literary form favored by cyberpunk writers, these extended diatribes make up in attitude what they lack in modesty.

Dystopia Utopia's evil twin. Merriam-Webster defines it as "an imaginary place which is depressingly wretched and whose people lead a fearful existence."

Simstim Decks These simulated stimuli machines are what television might evolve into. Rather than just watching your favorite characters on TV, you strap some plastic electrodes to your forehead and experience their thoughts and feelings—slightly edited, of course, to spare you the headaches and hangovers.

Microsofts Without apologies to the software company by the same name, Gibson has his fictional characters alter their reality by plugging into their brains these angular fragments of colored silicon, which house a read-only-memory chip.

Seriously Wired

Billy Idol is playing with his new best friend, technology. Bounding across the living room of his home in the Hollywood Hills with the manic energy of a truant 10-year-old, the platinum-blond, spiky-haired singer is fixating on one of his favorite toys, a palm-sized camcorder. The device is sitting atop his enormo-screen television set, pointed toward a sofa across the room and playing it live on the television, turning what was supposed to be a simple, low-tech print interview into a do-it-yourself media event. Welcome to the wonderful world of Idolvision!

Wearing a black T-shirt, magenta silk pants, combat boots and purple sunglasses, Mr. Idol looks something like an overgrown punk-rock version of Macaulay Culkin with his finger in a light socket. He fiddles with the camcorder's lens, mumbling to himself. "I'm just going to—ummph, there we go," he says. "I've got these—heh, heh; oh, this should be good." At the moment, the television simply shows a straight-on shot of the couch, but Mr. Idol wants to doctor it up a little. He picks up a plastic lens and clicks it over the camera's eye. "This one's a sort of prism," he says. Now the shot has been broken up into several kaleidoscopic images. Suddenly we have entered an episode of "The Monkees," circa 1966. "Ah, yes!" Mr. Idol says, stepping back and scrutinizing his work.

He scuttles over to the couch and sits down, fidgeting to locate himself properly within the shot. He grins happily. "It's sort of silly, but it's great fun," he says. "I might as well entertain myself! Nobody else is going to do it!"

Billy Idol is playing with his new best friend, technology.

Technology is Mr. Idol's unquenchable passion these days, so much so that he's titled his sixth and latest solo album *Cyberpunk* (Chrysalis) and based it upon that cultish, futuristic science of computer information that has been creeping into the mainstream for the past few years. With its booming techno beats, screeching guitar riffs, sampled computer voices and songs like "Power Junkie" ("I feel tonight we're bought and sold/Ah yeah, I think I'll overload"), the album functions as Mr. Idol's interpretation of cyber culture.

It opens with a spoken manifesto that summarizes some essential tenets of cyber philosophy: "All information should be free," Mr. Idol says in his best

Terminator voice. "It is not. Information is power and currency in the virtual world we inhabit. So mistrust authority. Cyberpunks are the true rebels. Cyber culture is coming in under the radar of ordinary society. . . ."

Mr. Idol wants to talk about nothing so much as cyberpunk. He is nuts on the subject. Ask him a question and he will embark upon a long, enthusiastic cyber ramble. Ask him a different question, and he will talk about it some more. Go so far as to try to interrupt and force another topic on him, and he will answer your question, but will always work his way back to cyberpunk.

At the moment, he is talking about his upcoming tour, and the ways in which he will incorporate cyber elements into the concerts. "You're going to have these screens that are going to be thirty feet tall, the full length of the stage," he says. "We're going to be lit by these stream-of-consciousness images. It's going to almost be like that's your *mind*. And we'll have four people swarming the gig with camcorders, which will be put live into this blend. And people from the audience can bring their filmed footage—God knows, them with their girlfriend, I don't know! And then we'll put it up on the screen.

"Part of the idea is to create an element of visible language, so that you feel as if you're being talked to through images. I think you have to start looking to get to the future of what rock-and-roll concerts should be like. We're working; we're *pushing* the technology to the edge."

One might point out that all this sounds rather similar to U2's Zoo TV tour, and Mr. Idol wouldn't disagree. But, he says a trifle competitively, "Whereas with U2 I think it all looks rather comfortable, we want to push the technology so it's *screaming!*" He is, in fact, screaming. The veins on his neck are popping out. "These computers will wish they never got involved with us! Ha ha!"

A cynic might point out that Mr. Idol's adoption of cyberpunk must signal some sort of death knell for the movement. Is Mr. Idol just the Marky Mark of cyber culture, appropriating a fringe movement for his own commercial ends? Can cyberpunk still be cool if it's on the *Billboard* charts? In fact, a minor hullabaloo did erupt when Mr. Idol logged onto the WELL, a computer bulletin board based in Sausalito, California, where people exchange information. He posted a computer address so that anyone could send him electronic mail. But apparently a bunch of cyberpunks felt that a pop star didn't belong in their rebel universe and started sending him nasty messages. One particularly self-righteous computer geek even takes pleasure in stuffing Mr. Idol's Well file with junk mail.

Mr. Idol has responded by saying they're elitist. Mark Frauenfelder, the former editor in chief of *Boing Boing,* a cyberpunk-oriented publication that calls itself "the world's greatest neurozine!" takes Mr. Idol's side. "It's stupid, because the whole cyberpunk thing is that information is supposed to be free," says Mr. Frauenfelder, who is now an editor at *Wired,* another computer magazine. "There are all these 16- and 17-year-old cyberpunks who are afraid that everybody's going to learn their secret handshake or something."

Furthermore, Mr. Idol hasn't just jumped on the bandwagon. He first became interested in cyberpunk—like everyone else—in the mid-80's when he read William Gibson's now-classic books like *Neuromancer* (Ace Books, 1984). Then, in 1990, while he was laid up from a motorcycle accident that almost killed him, he began to take the whole thing more seriously and saw cyberpunk as a new way to re-explore his roots in the late-70's British punk movement. "It's 1993," he says. "I better wake up and be part of it. I'm sitting there, a 1977 punk watching Courtney Love talk about punk, watching Nirvana talk about punk, and this is my reply. It's just my own way of saying, *woco!*" He is screaming again. "What about that?" he Hey, I'm Lollapalooza too! I'm the *cyberpunk;* you guys are still punks!"

> *"These computers will wish they never got involved with us."*

When it comes right down to it, Mr. Idol has spent his entire career putting his own peculiar slant on pop styles. In the late 70's, he and his band Generation X put a brash, tongue-in-cheek spin on punk rock. As a solo artist in the early and mid-80's, he riffed on the new-wave phenomenon to come up with hits like "White Wedding," "Rebel Yell" and "Eyes Without a Face." Then, just when you thought his biker/S & M gear and ever-present sneer were entombed as relics of MTV's early years, Mr. Idol came back in 1990 with the hit "Cradle of Love," from his album *Charmed Life.*

And therein lies Mr. Idol's most endearing quality. No matter what style he appropriates, he always manages to sound like Billy Idol. He rides the styles enough to seem current, but never so much that he loses his identity. He keeps his spiky blond hair, and be can always be coaxed into sneering for the camera. He's no spring chicken—this fall he'll turn 38—and yet he's still going strong. Get used to it: Billy Idol will never go away. Like Tom Jones, the Rolling Stones or "Mony Mony," he's a pop music perennial.

And there's a reason he won't go away, You might want to sit down here; pregnant women, be cautioned before reading any further. Billy Idol has soul. He is deep. Sure, there's an exaggerated, slightly cheesy quality about his image; it's something he's fully aware of, and perhaps at times a bit rueful about. But underneath that, there's more. Much more.

The first real taste came with "Charmed Life." Distant, melancholy songs like "Prodigal Blues" and "The Loveless" seemed to ask forgiveness for past sins. "Now," sang Mr. Idol in a deep, penitent croon, "I believe in mercy." And then, a few months before the album's release, came the accident. Mr. Idol's leg was in three pieces. In fact, there was a big hole in his leg where a broken bone popped through.

He rolls up a pant leg to display a bevy of scars, including one the size and shape of an eight ball. "The doctor was able to take the whole of my foot and waggle it about, like I was Rubber Man or something," he says unsqueamishly. "There was nothing holding it. It wasn't joined up. So they had to put this steel rod in my leg."

By the time of the accident, Mr. Idol had a son, Willem, from a long-term (but now defunct) relationship with Perri Lister. (Willem is 5, and there are pictures of him scattered around the room.) With *Charmed Life,* Mr. Idol may not have exactly emerged a new man—"Cradle of Love" was featured in the Andrew Dice Clay movie *Ford Fairlane*—but he did seem renewed, somehow more vulnerable and human.

Mr. Idol leans forward on the sofa in his living room. With its red uphol-stered furniture and matching wallpaper, amiable clutter and dim lighting, the room feels like a cross between a bachelor pad and an opium den. Glass doors allow a view from the Hollywood Hills into sprawling Los Angeles. The singer has drastically quieted down. The energy that has been emanating off him like sparks from a laboratory power source has vanished, as if someone had cut the switch. His Mr. Hyde becomes Dr. Jekyll.

In a strange way, Mr. Idol sees *Cyberpunk* as a continuation of his effort to keep himself vital. "There's an element of the cartoon that you get through MTV and things," he says solemnly. "But I think for the people who really like my music, I'm not like that at all. I think they see a much fuller person. It's very important for me to show an active, intelligent mind enjoying the artistic process of coming to grips with himself and everybody else."

And that wild, reckless side still pops up every now and then. In 1991 he was arrested for hitting a woman in a bar in West Hollywood. He publicly apologized, paid $2,000 in damages and is undergoing counseling for alco-holism. Rumors about him still seem to circulate. One of the most recent had him falling out of a window in Paris. "I don't remember falling out of a win-dow," he says with a flicker of self-deprecating humor. "It seems a bit like one of those things you'd really *remember.*"

To his credit, Mr. Idol doesn't seem at all proud of such behavior. "I don't like it if it hurts other people," he says, his voice barely a whisper. "You become so totally insensitive that you do hurt other people. It's the lowest point of your existence, really. People expect you to be. . . ." His face twists into a grotesque, sideshow grin. "Like, 'Buy my records, please!' I think that's very hard for someone in rock-and-roll, because you're just not going to work on those terms. But at the same time, I don't want to do things that hurt people, and I've seen that violent streak in myself come out, and I don't like it much.

"I suppose the thing is trying to cure yourself of it. And the only way I can really do that is through my music. I always think that inside my music is the best and worst sides of myself, and you're seeing it all. If people really lis-ten to your records, and they like them and all, then they really do see the person who's struggling with his foibles, as much as anybody else."

Then, like some unstoppable molecular force, the manic energy starts to return, "How's that, then?" he says, signaling the end of the interview. "Is that probably O.K.?" Mr. Idol has things to do. For one thing, he needs to pick up his son at the end of the afternoon. But before that, he wants to play on his computer a bit.

He leaves the house and walks across the driveway to a second building that serves as a garage and mixing studio. He goes inside, through a gym with full wall and ceiling mirrors, and then upstairs to a small desk that holds a cheap personal computer. Inside the top drawer are several pieces of legal-size yellow-lined paper that serve as his cheat sheets.

Mr. Idol bends over the computer keyboard like a child over a drawing pad. He hits the letters one at a time, slowly and deliberately, the classic hunt-and-peck system. He logs onto the WELL to read his mail. He fiddles around for a bit, but for some reason, he's having trouble getting the program to work.

It's O.K., though. He'll get through eventually.

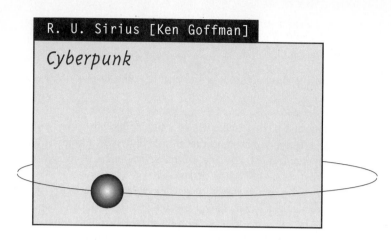

R. U. Sirius [Ken Goffman]

Cyberpunk

R.U. SIRIUS: Cyberpunk escaped from being a literary genre into cultural reality. People started calling themselves cyberpunks, or the media started calling people cyberpunks. In fact, in the last six months, I've been labeled a cyberpunk on *CBS Night Watch* and *The Ron Reagan Show*, although I've never actually called myself a cyberpunk. The first people to identify themselves as cyberpunks were adolescent computer hackers who related to the street-hardened characters and the worlds created in the books of William Gibson, Bruce Sterling, John Shirley, and others. As we were going to press with our first issue of MONDO 2000, cyberpunk hit the front page of the *New York Times* when some young computer kids were arrested for cracking a government computer file. The *Times* called the kids "cyberpunks." From there, the performers involved in the high-tech-oriented radical art movement generally known as "Industrial" started to call themselves—or be called—cyberpunks, largely thanks to an article in *Electronic Musician* by Mark Dery. Turned out that most of the people involved in that artistic sensibility did, in fact, feel a rapport with the worlds created by Gibson & Co. Finally, cyberpunk has come to be seen as a generic name for a much larger trend more or less describing anyone who relates to the cyberpunk vision. This, in turn, has created a purist reaction among the hard-core cyberpunks, who feel they got there first.

MARK DERY is the hot new writer on the cyber scene. His writing appears regularly in the *New York Times* and *Rolling Stone*. He is currently at work on a book called *Cyberculture: Road Warriors, Console Cowboys and the Silicon Underground.* His regular column for MONDO 2000 is called "Guerrilla Semiotics."

GARETH BRANWYN is the street tech editor for MONDO 2000 and the main editor of a HyperCard Stack called "Beyond Cyberpunk."

Gareth Branwyn posted the following description of the cyberpunk worldview to general approval at a MONDO 2000 conference on the WELL:

A) The future has imploded onto the present. There was no nuclear Armageddon. There's too much real estate to lose. The new battlefield is people's minds.

B) The megacorps *are* the new governments.

C) The U.S. is a big bully with lackluster economic power.

D) The world is splintering into a trillion subcultures and designer cults with their own languages, codes, and lifestyles.

E) Computer-generated info-domains are the next frontiers.

F) There *is* better living through chemistry.

G) Small groups or individual "console cowboys" can wield tremendous power over governments, corporations, etc.

H) The coalescence of a computer "culture" is expressed in self-aware computer music, art, virtual communities, and a hacker/street tech subculture. The computer nerd image is passé, and people are not ashamed anymore about the role the computer has in this subculture. The computer is a cool tool, a friend, important human augmentation.

I) We're becoming cyborgs. Our tech is getting smaller, closer to us, and it will soon merge with us.

J) Some attitudes that seem to be related:

- Information wants to be free.

- Access to computers and anything which may teach you something about how the world works should be unlimited and total.

- Always yield to the hands-on imperative.

- Mistrust Authority.

"CYBORG" is a science-fictional shorting of "cybernetic organism." The idea is that, in the future, we may have more and more artificial body parts—arms, legs, hearts, eyes, and so on. The logical conclusion of this process is that one might become a brain in a wholly artificial body. And the step after that is to replace your meat brain by a computer brain.

RELATED ATTITUDES: A few of these "attitudes" have time-traveled directly from the 1960s hacker's ethic as defined by Stephen Levy in his 1984 book *Hackers*.

- Promote Decentralization.

- Do It Yourself.

- Fight the Power.

- Feed the noise back into the system.

- Surf the Edges.

■ MICHAEL SYNERGY, CYBERPUNK

R.U. SIRIUS: Michael Synergy may be the first person I ever met who actually described himself as a cyberpunk. While the people around the Electronic Frontier Foundation are trying to gently reassure the body politic that the onslaught of information technology is *not* a threat to the stability of the system, Synergy will tell us that it *is* indeed an assault on all fronts. His message is simple: "Surrender!"

■ C Y B E R P U N K   A N A R C H Y

CYBERPUNK ANARCHY In a recent computer-crime scandal, credit for the idea was given to John Brunner's *Shockwave Rider*. That's very encouraging to me. You could say that cyberpunk is intrinsically anarchistic. It's endlessly anti-authoritarian, and it can be employed like a weapon, like a computer virus, injecting new information by means of the existing mechanisms. The pop image of anarchism has always been a bomb—yeah, well, this is an ideological bomb that has been planted in the culture. I just saw a *New York Times* headline that used the term cyberpunk to describe a computer virus hacker—as if it were already part of the language.

CYBERPUNK ANARCHY: This comment is from John Shirley, cyberpunk science-fiction writer. John was lead singer for a Portland punk band called Sado-Nation and cut his own album in France: *Obsession* by John Shirley, Celluloid Records, Alpha Presse. The word which best sums up Shirley's personality is "labile," as used by Samuel R. Delany in his classic ur-cyberpunk story "The Edge of Space." In biology, a labile cell structure is one which changes or breaks down very quickly when being examined. Delany uses it to mean rapid mood shifts sensitively attuned to the situational input. In person John Shirley initially comes on as wise, kind, and sweet—but he can break into wild ranting as easily as Axl Rose slips into falsetto. He has been known to lean into strangers' car windows and scream, "Have y'all ever ate any LIVE BRAIN?" Shirley's amazing early cyberpunk novel *City Come a-Walkin'* appeared in 1980. Another not-to-be missed Shirley book is *A Splendid Chaos.*

Shockwave Rider is the tale of a superbright young man who is able to plug into the Net and create himself new computer identities, credit records, etc. Though it has the cyber element, *Shockwave Rider* is not very punk, due to the fact that the main character has been brought up in a special school for cream-of-the-crop kids.

NEW YORK TIMES: John Markoff of the *New York Times* recently wrote a book with his wife about computer crime called *Cyberpunk.*

Timothy Leary

The Cyberpunk: The Individual as Reality Pilot

> Your true pilot cares nothing about anything on Earth but the river, and his pride in his occupation surpasses the pride of kings.
>
> —Mark Twain, *Life on the Mississippi*

yber means "pilot."

A **"cyberperson"** is one who pilots his/her own life. By definition, the cyberperson is fascinated by navigational information—especially maps, charts, labels, guides, manuals that help pilot one through life. The cyberperson continually searches for theories, models, paradigms, metaphors, images, icons that help chart and define the realities that we inhabit.

"Cybertech" refers to the tools, appliances, and methodologies of knowing and communicating. Linguistics. Philosophy. Semantics. Semiotics. Practical epistemologies. The ontologies of daily life. Words, icons, pencils, printing presses, screens, keyboards, computers, disks.

"Cyberpolitics" introduces the Foucault notions of the use of language and linguistic-tech by the ruling classes in feudal and industrial societies to control children, the uneducated, and the under classes. The words "governor" or "steersman" or "G-man" are used to describe those who manipulate words and communication devices in order to control, to bolster authority—feudal, management, government—and to discourage innovative thought and free exchange.

■ WHO IS THE CYBERPUNK?

Cyberpunks use all available data-input to think for themselves.

You know who they are.

Every stage of history has produced names and heroic legends for the strong, stubborn, creative individuals who explore some future frontier, collect and bring back new information, and offer to guide the human gene pool to the next stage. Typically, these time mavericks combine bravery, and high curiosity, with super self-esteem. These three characteristics are considered necessary for those engaged in the profession of genetic guide, *aka* counter-culture philosopher.

The classical Olde Westworld model for the cyberpunk is Prometheus, a technological genius who "stole" fire from the Gods and gave it to humanity.

Prometheus also taught his gene pool many useful arts and sciences. According to the official version of the legend, he/she was exiled from the gene pool and sentenced to the ultimate torture for these unauthorized transmissions of classified information. In another version of the myth (unauthorized), Prometheus (*aka* the Pied Piper) uses his/her skills to escape the sinking kinship, taking with him/her the cream of the gene pool.

The Newe World version of this ancient myth is Quetzalcoatl, God of civilization, high-tech wizard who introduced maize, the calendar, erotic sculpture, flute-playing, the arts, and the sciences. He was driven into exile by the G-man in power, who was called Tezcatlipoca.

Self-assured singularities of the cyberbreed have been called mavericks, ronin, freelancers, independents, self-starters, nonconformists, oddballs, troublemakers, kooks, visionaries, iconoclasts, insurgents, blue-sky thinkers, loners, smart alecks. Before Gorbachev, the Soviets scornfully called them hooligans. Religious organizations have always called them heretics. Bureaucrats call them disloyal dissidents, traitors, or worse. In the old days, even sensible people called them mad.

They have been variously labeled clever, creative, entrepreneurial, imaginative, enterprising, fertile, ingenious, inventive, resourceful, talented, eccentric.

During the tribal, feudal, and industrial-literate phases of human evolution, the logical survival traits were conformity and dependability. The "good serf" or "vassal" was obedient. The "good worker" or "manager" was reliable. Maverick thinkers were tolerated only at moments when innovation and change were necessary, usually to deal with the local competition.

In the information-communication civilization of the 21st Century, creativity and mental excellence will become the ethical norm. The world will be too dynamic, complex, and diversified, too cross-linked by the global immediacies of modern (quantum) communication, for stability of thought or dependability of behaviour to be successful. The "good persons" in the cybernetic society are the intelligent ones who can think for themselves. The "problem person" in the cybernetic society of the 21st Century is the one who automatically obeys, who never questions authority, who acts to protect his/her official status, who placates and politics rather than thinks independently.

Thoughtful Japanese are worried about the need for ronin thinking in their obedient culture, the postwar generation now taking over.

The Cyberpunk Counterculture in the Soviet Union

The new postwar generation of Soviets caught on that new role models are necessary to compete in the information age. Under Gorbachev, bureaucratic control is being softened, made elastic to encourage some modicum of innovative, dissident thought!

Aleksandr N. Yakovlev, Politburo member and key strategist of the glasnost policy, describes that reform: "Fundamentally, we are talking about self-government. We are moving toward a time when people will be able to govern themselves and control the activities of people that have been placed in the position of learning and governing them.

"It is not accidental that we are talking about *self*-government, or *self*-sufficiency and *self*-profitability of an enterprise, *self*-this and *self*-that. It all concerns the decentralization of power."

The cyberpunk person, the pilot who thinks clearly and creatively, using quantum-electronic appliances and brain know-how, is the newest, updated, top-of-the-line model of the 21st Century: *Homo sapiens sapiens cyberneticus.*

■ THE GREEK WORD FOR "PILOT"

A great pilot can sail even when his canvas is rent.
—Lucius Annaeus Seneca

The term "cybernetics" comes from the Greek word *kubernetes*, "pilot."

The Hellenic origin of this word is important in that it reflects the Socratic-Platonic traditions of independence and individual self-reliance which, we are told, derived from geography. The proud little Greek city-states were perched on peninsular fingers wiggling down into the fertile Mediterranean Sea, protected by mountains from the land-mass armies of Asia.

Mariners of those ancient days had to be bold and resourceful. Sailing the seven seas without maps or navigational equipment, they were forced to develop independence of thought. The self-reliance that these Hellenic pilots developed in their voyages probably carried over to the democratic, inquiring, questioning nature of their land life.

The Athenian cyberpunks, the pilots, made their own navigational decisions.

These psychogeographical factors may have contributed to the humanism of the Hellenic religions that emphasized freedom, pagan joy, celebration of life, and speculative thought. The humanist and polytheistic religions of ancient Greece are often compared with the austere morality of monotheistic Judaism, the fierce, dogmatic polarities of Persian–Arab dogma, and the imperial authority of Roman (Christian) culture.

The Roman Concept of Director, Governor, Steersman

The Greek word *kubernetes*, when translated to Latin, comes out as *gubernetes*. This basic verb *gubernare* means to control the actions or behavior, to direct, to exercise sovereign authority, to regulate, to keep under, to restrain, to steer. This Roman concept is obviously very different from the Hellenic notion of "pilot."

It may be relevant that the Latin term "to steer" comes from the word *stare*, which means "to stand," with derivative meanings "place or thing which is standing." The past participle of the Latin word produces "status," "state," "institute," "statue," "static," "statistics," "prostitute," "restitute," "constitute."

■ CYBERPUNK PILOTS REPLACE
   GOVERNETICS-CONTROLLERS

> Society everywhere is in conspiracy against the self-hood of
> every one of its members. The virtue in most request is
> conformity. Self-reliance is its aversion. It loves not
> realities and creators, but names and customs.
> —Ralph Waldo Emerson, *Nature*

> Who so would be a man must be a nonconformist.
> —Emerson, *ibid.*

The word "cybernetics" was coined in 1948 by Norbert Weiner, who
wrote, "We have decided to call the entire field of control and communication
theory, whether in the machine or in the animal, by the name of Cybernetics,
which we form from the Greek for steersman. *[sic]*"

The word "cyber" has been redefined (in the *American Heritage Dictionary*) as
"the theoretical study of control processes in electronic, mechanical, and biological systems, especially the flow of information in such systems." The
derivative word "cybernate" means "to control automatically by computer or
to be so controlled."

An even more ominous interpretation defines cybernetics as "the study of
human control mechanisms and their replacement by mechanical or electronic
systems."

Note how Weiner and the Romanesque engineers have corrupted the
meaning of "cyber." The Greek word "pilot" becomes "governor" or "director";
the term "to steer" becomes "to control."

Now we are liberating the term, teasing it free from serfdom to represent
the autopoetic, self-directed principle of organization that arises in the universe in many systems of widely varying sizes, in people, societies, and atoms.

■ OUR OPPRESSIVE BIRTHRIGHT:
   THE POLITICS OF LITERACY

The etymological distinctions between Greek and Roman terms are quite
relevant to the pragmatics of the culture surrounding their usage. French philosophy, for example, has recently stressed the importance of language and
semiotics in determining human behaviour and social structures. Michel
Foucault's classic studies of linguistic politics and mind control led him to
believe that

*human consciousness—as expressed in speech and images, in self-definition and mutual
designation . . . is the authentic locale of the determinant politics of being. . . . What
men and women are born into is only superficially this or that social, legislative, and
executive system. Their ambiguous, oppressive birthright is the language, the conceptual categories, the conventions of identification and perception which have evolved*

*and, very largely, atrophied up to the time of their personal and social existence.
It is the established but customarily subconscious, unargued constraints of awareness
that enslave.*

Orwell and Wittgenstein and McLuhan agree. To remove the means of
expressing dissent is to remove the possibility of dissent. "Whereof one cannot speak, thereof must one remain silent." In this light the difference
between the Greek word "pilot" and the Roman translation "governor"
becomes a most significant semantic manipulation, and the flexibility granted
to symbol systems of all kinds by their representation in digital computers
becomes dramatically liberating.

Do we pride ourselves for becoming ingenious "pilots" or dutiful "controllers"?

■ WHO, WHAT, AND WHY IS GOVERNETICS

```
Damn the torpedoes, full speed ahead.
                    —Captain David Glasgow Farragut's order to his
            steersman at the Battle of Mobile Bay, August 5, 1864


Aye, aye, sir.
                         —Unknown enlisted steersman at the
                    Battle of Mobile Bay, August 5, 1864
```

The word "governetics" refers to an attitude of obedience-control in relationship to self or others.

Pilots, those who navigate on the seven seas or in the sky, have to devise
and execute course changes continually in response to the changing environment. They respond continually to feedback, information about the environment. Dynamic. Alert. Alive.

The Latinate "steersman," by contrast, is in the situation of following
orders. The Romans, we recall, were great organizers, road-builders, administrators. The galleys, the chariots must be controlled. The legions of soldiers
must be directed.

The Hellenic concept of the individual navigating his/her own course was
an island of humanism in a raging sea of totalitarian empires. To the East (the
past) were the centralized, authoritarian kingdoms. The governors of Iran,
from Cyrus, the Persian emperor, to the recent shah and ayatollah, have exemplified the highest traditions of state control.

The Greeks were flanked on the other side, which we shall designate as
the West (or future), by a certain heavy concept called Rome. The cæsars and
popes of the Holy Roman Empire represented the next grand phase of institutional control. The governing hand on the wheel stands for stability, dura-
bility, continuity, permanence. Staying the course. Individual creativity,
exploration, and change are usually not encouraged.

■ CYBERPUNKS: PILOTS OF THE SPECIES

> The winds and waves are always on the side of the ablest navigators.
>
> —Edward Gibbon

The terms "cybernetic person" or "cybernaut" return us to the original meaning of "pilot" and puts the self-reliant person back in the loop. These words (and the more pop term "cyberpunk") refer to the personalization (and thus the popularization) of knowledge-information technology, to innovative thinking on the part of the individual.

Cyber: The Greek word *kubernetes,* when translated to Latin, comes out as *gubernetes.* This basic verb *gubernare* means to control the actions or behavior, to direct, to exercise sovereign authority, to regulate, to keep under, to restrain, to steer. This Roman concept is obviously very different from the Hellenic notion of "pilot" [making their own navigational decisions]....
the meaning of "cyber" has been corrupted. The Greek word "pilot" becomes "governor" or "director"; the term "to steer" becomes "to control."...The terms "cybernetic person" or "cybernaut" return us to the original meaning of "pilot" and puts the self-reliant person back in the loop.

According to McLuhan and Foucault, if you change the language, you change the society. Following their lead, we suggest that the terms "cybernetic person, cybernaut" may describe a new species model of human being and a new social order. "Cyberpunk" is, admittedly, a risky term. Like all linguistic innovations, it must be used with a tolerant sense of high-tech humor. It's a stopgap, transitional meaning-grenade thrown over the language barricades to describe the resourceful, skillful individual who accesses and steers knowledge-communication technology toward his/her own private goals, for personal pleasure, profit, principle, or growth.

Cyberpunks are the inventors, innovative writers, technofrontier artists, risk-taking film directors, icon-shifting composers, stand-up comedians, expressionist artists, free-agent scientists, technocreatives, computer visionaries, elegant hackers, bit-blitting Prolog adepts, special-effectives, cognitive dissidents, video wizards, neurological test pilots, media explorers—all of those who boldly package and steer ideas out there where no thoughts have gone before.

Countercultures are sometimes tolerated by the governors. They can, with sweet cynicism and patient humor, interface their singularity with institutions. They often work within the "governing systems" on a temporary basis.

As often as not, they are unauthorized.

■ THE LEGEND OF THE RONIN

> The ronin . . . has broken with the tradition of career feudalism. Guided by a personally defined code of adaptability, autonomy, and excellence, ronin are employing career strategies grounded in a premise of rapid change.
>
> —Beverly Potter, *The Way of the Ronin*

Ronin is used as a metaphor based on a Japanese word for lordless samurai. As early as the 8th Century, ronin was translated literally as "wave people"

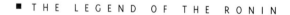

and used in Japan to describe those who had left their allotted, caste-predetermined stations in life: samurai who left the service of their feudal lords to become masterless.

Ronin played a key role in Japan's abrupt transition from a feudal society to industrialism. Under feudal rule, warriors were not allowed to think freely, or act according to their will. On the other hand, having been forced by circumstances to develop independence, [ronin] took more readily to new ideas and technology and became increasingly influential in the independent schools.

—*Potter, ibid.*

The West has many historical parallels to the ronin archetype. The term "free lance" has its origin in the period after the Crusades, when a large number of knights were separated from their lords. Many lived by the code of chivalry and became "lances for hire."

The American frontier was fertile ground for the ronin archetype. "Maverick," derived from the Texan word for unbranded steer, was used to describe a free and self-directed individual.

Although many of the ronin's roots . . . are in the male culture, most career women are well acquainted with the way of the ronin. Career women left their traditional stations and battled their way into the recesses of the male-dominated workplaces. . . . Like the ronin who had no clan, professional women often feel excluded from the corporate cliques' inside tracks, without ally or mentor.

—*Potter, ibid.*

■ SOME EXAMPLES OF CYBERPUNKS

Christopher Columbus (1451–1506) was born in Genoa. At age 25 he showed up in Lisbon and learned the craft of map-making. This was the golden era of Portuguese exploration. Many pilots and navigators were convinced that the Earth was round, and that the Indies and other unknown lands could be found by crossing the western seas. What was special about Columbus was his persistence and eloquence in support of the dream of discovery. For more than ten years he traveled the courts of Europe attempting to make "the deal"; to find backing for his "enterprise of the Indies."

According to the *Columbia Encyclopedia,* "Historians have disputed for centuries his skill as a navigator, but it has been recently proved that with only dead reckoning Columbus was unsurpassed in charting and finding his way about unknown seas."

Columbus was a most unsuccessful governor of the colonies he had discovered. He died in disgrace, his cyberskills almost forgotten. (At least that's what they tell us in the authorized history books.)

In 1992 the Political Correction Department dismissed Columbus as a racist colonialist.

Mark Twain. He purchased the Remington typewriter when it appeared in 1874 for $125. In 1875 he became the first author in history to submit a typewritten manuscript to a publisher. It was *The Adventures of Tom Sawyer.*

"This newfangled writing machine," Twain wrote, "has several virtues. It piles an awful stack of words on one page. It don't muss things or scatter ink blots around. Of course it saves paper."

Mathias (Rusty) Rust, a 19-year-old loner from Hamburg, Germany, attained all-star status as a cyberpunk when, on May 28, 1987, he flew a one-engine Cessna through the "impenetrable" Soviet air defenses and landed in Moscow's Red Square. There were no gubernal or organizational motives. The technological adventure was a personal mission. Rusty just wanted to talk to some Russians. German newspapers celebrated the event, calling it "the stuff of dreams," and comparing the youth to the Red Baron Manfred von Richthofen and Charles Augustus Lindbergh.

■ THE CYBERPUNK CODE: TFYQA

War Games is an electronic quantum signal, a movie about high-tech computers and human evolution that illustrates and condemns the use of quantum-electronic knowledge technology by governors to control. The film celebrates the independence and skill of cyberpunks who think for themselves and innovate from within the static system. The Captain and his wife use high-tech agriculture methods to enhance the potency of unauthorized botanical neuroactivators. The Captain makes an unauthorized decision to abort World War III. In both instances the Captain follows the cyberpunk code: *Think for yourself; question authority (TFYQA).*

The cyberkid Matthew Broderick is equally courageous, outrageous, creative, and bright. When the audience is introduced to the hero of *War Games,* he is in a video arcade playing a space-adventure game with poise and proficiency. An electron jock.

Late for school, he's pulled into the classic confrontation: the authoritarian teacher humiliates and punishes the Tom Sawyer kid, sends him to the principal's office. There he obtains the code for the school's computer system. Back home, he uses his PC to access the school records. He changes an unfair grade to a passing level. He thinks for himself and questions authority.

At the crucial moment he rushes to the library and researches the life of a physicist, scans scientific journals, scopes microfilm files—not to please the system, but in pursuit of his own personal grail.

Note that there is a new dimension of electronic ethics and quantum legality here. The Captain and Matthew perform no act of physical violence, no theft of material goods. The Captain processes some computer data and decides for himself. Matthew rearranges clusters of electrons stored on a chip. They seek independence, not control over others.

■ T H E   C Y B E R P U N K   A S   R O L E
  M O D E L   F O R   T H E   21 S T   C E N T U R Y

The tradition of the "individual who thinks for him/herself" extends to the beginings of recorded human history. Indeed, the very label of our species, *Homo sapiens,* defines us as the animals who think.

If our genetic function is *computare* ("to think"), then it follows that the ages and stages of human history, so far, have been larval or preparatory. After the insectoid phases of submission to gene pools, the mature stage of the human life cycle is the individual who thinks for him/herself. Now, at the beginnings of the information age, are we ready to assume our genetic function?

Timothy Leary

Evolution of Countercultures

Beats (1950–1965)

MOOD:	Cool, laid back.
AESTHETIC-EROTICS:	Artistic, literate, hip, interested in poetry, drugs, jazz.
ATTITUDE:	Sarcastic, cynical.
BRAIN-TECH:	Low-tech, but early psychedelic explorers.
INTELLECTUAL VIEWPOINT:	Well-informed, skeptical, street-smart.
HUMANIST QUOTIENT:	Tolerant of race and gay rights, but often male chauvinist.
POLITICS:	Bohemian, anti-Establishment.
COSMIC VIEW:	Romantic pessimism, Buddhist cosmology.

Hippies (1965–1975)

MOOD:	Blissed out.
AESTHETIC-EROTICS:	Earthy, horny, free-love oriented. Pot, LSD, acid rock.
ATTITUDE:	Peaceful, idealistic.
BRAIN-TECH:	Psychedelic, but anti-high-tech.
INTELLECTUAL VIEWPOINT:	Know-it-all, anti-intellectual.
HUMANIST QUOTIENT:	Male chauvinist, sometimes sexist, but socially tolerant and global village visionary.
POLITICS:	Classless, irreverent, passivist, but occasionally activist.
COSMIC VIEW:	Acceptance of chaotic nature of universe, but via Hindu passivity. Unscientific, occult minded, intuitive.

Cyberpunks (1975–1990)

MOOD:	Gloomy. Hip, but downbeat.
AESTHETIC-EROTICS:	Leather and grunge, tattoos, piercings. Hard drugs, psychedelics, smart drugs. Various forms of rock from metal to rap.
ATTITUDE:	Angry, cynical, feel undervalued by elders.
BRAIN-TECH:	High-tech electronic.

INTELLECTUAL VIEWPOINT:	Informed, open-minded, irreverent, inundated with electronic signals.
HUMANIST QUOTIENT:	Non-sexist, ecological, global minded.
POLITICS:	Alienated, skeptical.
COSMIC VIEW:	Pessimistic, but closet hope fiends.

New Breed (1990–2005)

MOOD:	Alert, cheerful.
AESTHETIC-EROTICS:	Invention of personal style. Eclectic. Prefer techno and ambient music.
ATTITUDE:	Self-confident.
BRAIN-TECH:	Psychedelic, super high-tech. Smart drugs, brain machines, Internet.
INTELLECTUAL VIEWPOINT:	Informed, open-minded, irreverent.
HUMANIST QUOTIENT:	Tolerant, non-sexist, ecological, global.
POLITICS:	Detached, individualistic. Zen opportunists.
COSMIC VIEW:	Acceptance of complexity, willingness to be a "chaos designer."

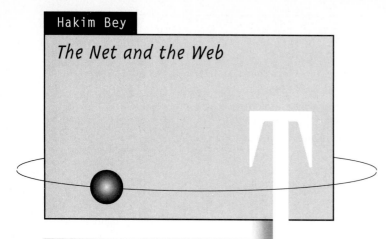

The Net and the Web

he next factor contributing to the TAZ [temporary autonomous zones] is so vast and ambiguous that it needs a section unto itself.

We've spoken of the *Net,* which can be defined as the totality of all information and communication transfer. Some of these transfers are privileged and limited to various elites, which give the Net a hierarchic aspect. Other transactions are open to all—so the Net has a horizontal or non-hierarchic aspect as well. Military and Intelligence data are restricted, as are banking and currency information and the like. But for the most part the telephone, the postal system, public data banks, etc. are accessible to everyone and anyone. Thus *within the Net* there has begun to emerge a shadowy sort of *counter-Net,* which we will call the *Web* (as if the Net were a fishing-net and the Web were spider-webs woven through the interstices and broken sections of the Net). Generally we'll use the term *Web* to refer to the alternate horizontal open structure of info-exchange, the non-hierarchic network, and reserve the term *counter-Net* to indicate clandestine illegal and rebellious use of the Web, including actual data-piracy and other forms of leeching off the Net itself. Net, Web, and counter-Net are all parts of the same whole pattern-complex—they blur into each other at innumerable points. The terms are not meant to define areas but to suggest tendencies.

> *Thus within the Net there has begun to emerge a shadowy sort of counter-Net.*

(Digression: Before you condemn the Web or counter-Net for its "parasitism," which can never be a truly revolutionary force, ask yourself what "production" consists of in the Age of Simulation. What is the "productive class"? Perhaps you'll be forced to admit that these terms seem to have lost their meaning. In any case the answers to such questions are so complex that the TAZ tends to ignore them altogether and simply picks up what it can *use.* "Culture is our Nature"—and we are the thieving magpies, or the hunter/gatherers of the world of CommTech.)

The present forms of the unofficial Web are, one must suppose, still rather primitive: the marginal zine network, the BBS networks, pirated software, hacking, phone-phreaking, some influence in print and radio, almost none in the other big media—no TV stations, no satellites, no fiber-optics, no cable, etc., etc. However the Net itself presents a pattern of changing/evolving relations between subjects ("users") and objects ("data"). The nature of these relations has been exhaustively explored, from McLuhan to Virilio. It would take pages and pages to "prove" what by now "everyone knows." Rather than rehash it all, I am interested in asking how these evolving relations suggest modes of implementation for the TAZ.

The TAZ has a temporary but actual location in time and a temporary but actual location in space. But clearly it must also have "location" *in the Web,* and this location is of a different sort, not actual but virtual, not immediate but instantaneous. The Web not only provides logistical support for the TAZ, it also helps to bring it into being; crudely speaking one might say that the TAZ "exists" in information-space as well as in the "real world." The Web can compact a great deal of time, as data, into an infinitesimal "space." We have noted that the TAZ, because it is temporary, must necessarily lack some of the advantages of a freedom which experiences *duration* and a more-or-less fixed *locale.* But the Web can provide a kind of substitute for some of this duration and locale—it can *inform* the TAZ, from its inception, with vast amounts of compacted time and space which have been "subtilized" as data.

At this moment in the evolution of the Web, and considering our demands for the "face-to-face" and the sensual, consider the Web primarily as a support system, capable of carrying information from one TAZ to another, of defending the TAZ, rendering it "invisible" or giving it teeth, as the situation might demand. But more than that: If the TAZ is a nomad camp, then the Web helps provide the epics, songs, genealogies and legends of the tribe; it provides the secret caravan routes and raiding trails which make up the flowlines of tribal economy; it even *contains* some of the very roads they will follow, some of the very dreams they will experience as signs and portents.

The Web does not depend for its existence on any computer technology. Word-of-mouth, mail, the marginal zine network, "phone trees," and the like already suffice to construct an information webwork. The key is not the brand or level of tech involved, but the openness and horizontality of the structure. Nevertheless, the whole concept of the Net *implies* the use of computers. In the SciFi imagination the Net is headed for the condition of Cyberspace (as in *Tron* or *Neuromancer*) and the pseudo-telepathy of "virtual reality." As a Cyberpunk fan I can't help but envision "reality hacking" playing a major role in the creation of TAZs. Like Gibson and Sterling I am assuming that the official Net will never succeed in shutting down the Web or the counter-Net—that data-piracy, unauthorized transmissions and the free flow of information can never be frozen. (In fact, as I understand it, chaos theory *predicts* that any universal Control-system is impossible.)

· However, leaving aside all mere speculation about the future, we must face a very serious question about the Web and the tech it involves. The TAZ desires above all to avoid *mediation,* to experience its existence as *immediate.* The very essence of the affair is "breast-to-breast" as the sufis say, or face-to-face. But, BUT: the very essence of the Web is mediation. Machines here are our ambassadors—the flesh is irrelevant except as a *terminal,* with all the sinister connotations of the term.

The TAZ may perhaps best find its own space by wrapping its head around two seemingly contradictory attitudes toward Hi-Tech and its apotheosis the Net: (1) what we might call the *Fifth Estate/* Neo-Paleolithic Post-Situ Ultra-Green position, which construes itself as a luddite argument against mediation and against the Net; and (2) the Cyberpunk utopianists, futuro-libertarians, Reality Hackers and their allies who see the Net as a step forward in evolution, and who assume that any possible ill effects of mediation can be overcome—at least, once we've liberated the means of production.

The TAZ agrees with the hackers because it wants to come into being—in part—through the Net, even through the mediation of the Net. But it also agrees with the greens because it retains intense awareness of itself as *body* and feels only revulsion for *CyberGnosis,* the attempt to transcend the body through instantaneity and simulation. The TAZ tends to view the Tech/anti-Tech dichotomy as misleading, like most dichotomies, in which apparent opposites turn out to be falsifications or even hallucinations caused by semantics. This is a way of saying that the TAZ wants to live in *this* world, not in the idea of another world, some visionary world born of false unification (*all* green OR *all* metal) which can only be more pie in the sky by-&-by (or as *Alice* put it, "Jam yesterday or jam tomorrow. but never jam today").

The TAZ by its very nature seizes every available means to realize itself.

The TAZ is "utopian" in the sense that it envisions an *intensification* of everyday life, or as the Surrealists might have said, life's penetration by the Marvelous. But it cannot be utopian in the actual meaning of the word, *nowhere,* or NoPlace Place. *The TAZ is somewhere.* It lies at the intersection of many forces, like some pagan power-spot at the junction of mysterious ley-lines, visible to the adept in seemingly unrelated bits of terrain, landscape, flows of air, water, animals. But now the lines are not all etched in time and space. Some of them exist only "within" the Web, even though they also intersect with real times and places. Perhaps some of the lines are "non-ordinary" in the sense that no convention for quantifying them exists. These lines might better be studied in the light of chaos science than of sociology, statistics, economics, etc. The patterns of force which bring the TAZ into being have something in common with those chaotic "Strange Attractors" which exist, so to speak, *between* the dimensions.

The TAZ by its very nature seizes every available means to realize itself—it will come to life whether in a cave or an L-5 Space City—but above all it will live, now, or as soon as possible, in however suspect or ramshackle a form, spontaneously, without regard for ideology or even anti-ideology. It will use the computer because the computer exists, but it will also use powers which are so completely unrelated to alienation or simulation that they guarantee a certain *psychic paleolithism* to the TAZ, a primordial-shamanic spirit which will "infect" even the Net itself (the true meaning of Cyberpunk as I read it). Because the TAZ is an intensification, a surplus, an excess, a potlatch, life spending itself in living rather than merely *surviving* (that snivelling shibboleth of the eighties), it cannot be defined either by Tech or anti-Tech. It contradicts itself like a true despiser of hobgoblins, because it wills itself to be, at any cost in damage to "perfection," to the immobility of the final.

In the Mandelbrot Set and its computer-graphic realization we watch—in a fractal universe—maps which are embedded and in fact hidden within maps within maps etc. to the limits of computational power. What is it *for*, this map which in a sense bears a 1:1 relation with a fractal dimension? What can one do with it, other than admire its psychedelic elegance?

If we were to imagine an *information map*—a cartographic projection of the Net in its entirety—we would have to include in it the features of chaos, which have already begun to appear, for example, in the operations of complex parallel processing, telecommunications, transfers of electronic "money," viruses, guerilla hacking and so on.

Each of these "areas" of chaos could be represented by topographs similar to the Mandelbrot Set, such that the "peninsulas" are embedded or hidden within the map—such that they seem to "disappear." This "writing"—parts of which vanish, parts of which efface themselves—represents the very process by which the Net is already compromised, incomplete to its own view, ultimately un-Controllable. In other words, the M Set, or something like it, might prove to be useful in "plotting" (in all senses of the word) the emergence of the counter-Net as a chaotic process, a "creative evolution" in Prigogine's term. If nothing else the M Set serves as a *metaphor* for a "mapping" of the TAZ's interface with the Net as a *disappearance of information*. Every "catastrophe" in the Net is a node of power for the Web, the counter-Net. The Net will be damaged by chaos, while the Web may thrive on it.

Whether through simple data-piracy, or else by a more complex development of actual rapport with chaos, the Web-hacker, the cybernetician of the TAZ, will find ways to take advantage of perturbations, crashes, and breakdowns in the Net (ways to make information out of "entropy"). As a bricoleur, a scavenger of information shards, smuggler, blackmailer, perhaps even cyberterrorist, the TAZ-hacker will work for the evolution of clandestine fractal connections. These connections, and the *different* information that flows among and between them, will form "power outlets" for the coming-into-being of the TAZ itself—as if one were to steal electricity from the energy-monopoly to light an abandoned house for squatters.

Thus the Web, in order to produce situations conducive to the TAZ, will parasitize the Net—but we can also conceive of this strategy as an attempt to build toward the construction of an alternative and autonomous Net, "free" and no longer parasitic, which will serve as the basis for a "new society emerging from the shell of the old." The counter-Net and the TAZ can be considered, practically speaking, as ends in themselves—but theoretically they can also be viewed as forms of struggle toward a different reality.

Having said this we must still admit to some qualms about computers, some still unanswered questions, especially about the Personal Computer.

The story of computer networks, BBSs and various other experiments in electro-democracy has so far been one of *hobbyism* for the most part. Many anarchists and libertarians have deep faith in the PC as a weapon of liberation and self-liberation—but no real gains to show, no palpable liberty.

I have little interest in some hypothetical emergent entrepreneurial class of self-employed data/word processors who will soon be able to carry on a vast cottage industry or piecemeal shitwork for various corporations and bureaucracies. Moreover it takes no ESP to foresee that this "class" will develop its *under*class—a sort of lumpen yuppetariat: housewives, for example, who will provide their families with "second incomes" by turning their own homes into electro-sweatshops, little Work-tyrannies where the "boss" is a computer network.

Also I am not impressed by the sort of information and services proffered by contemporary "radical" networks. Somewhere—one is told—there exists an "information economy." Maybe so; but the info being traded over the "alternative" BBSs seems to consist entirely of chitchat and techie-talk. Is this an economy? or merely a pastime for enthusiasts? OK, PCs have created yet another "print revolution"—OK, marginal webworks are evolving—OK, I can now carry on six phone conversations at once. But what difference has this made in my ordinary life?

Frankly, I already had plenty of data to enrich my perceptions, what with books, movies, TV, theater, telephones, the U.S. Postal Service, altered states of consciousness, and so on. Do I really need a PC in order to obtain yet more such data? You offer me *secret* information? Well . . . perhaps I'm tempted—but still I demand *marvelous* secrets, not just unlisted telephone numbers or the trivia of cops and politicians. Most of all I want computers to provide me with information linked to *real goods*—"the good things in life" as the IWW Preamble puts it. And here, since I'm accusing the hackers and BBSers of irritating intellectual vagueness, I must myself descend from the baroque clouds of Theory & Critique and explain what I mean by "real goods."

Let's say that for both political and personal reasons I desire good food, better than I can obtain from Capitalism—unpolluted food still blessed with strong and natural flavors. To complicate the game imagine that the food I crave is illegal—raw milk perhaps, or the exquisite Cuban fruit *mamey*, which cannot be imported fresh into the U.S. because its seed is hallucinogenic (or so I'm told). I am not a farmer. Let's pretend I'm an importer of rare perfumes and aphrodisiacs, and sharpen the play by assuming most of my stock is also illegal. Or maybe I only want to trade word processing services for organic turnips, but refuse to report the transaction to the IRS (as required by law, believe it or not). Or maybe I want to meet other humans for consensual but illegal acts of mutual pleasure (this has actually been tried, but all the hard-sex BBSs have been busted—and what use is an underground with *lousy security*?). In short, assume that I'm fed up with mere information, the ghost in the machine. According to you, computers should already be quite capable of facilitating my desires for food, drugs, sex, tax evasion. So what's the matter? Why isn't it happening?

The TAZ has occurred, is occurring, and will occur with or without the computer. But for the TAZ to reach its full potential it must become less a matter of spontaneous combustion and more a matter of "islands in the Net." The Net, or rather the counter-Net, assumes the promise of an integral aspect of the TAZ, an addition that will multiply its potential, a "quantum jump" (odd how this expression has come to mean a *big* leap) in complexity and significance. The TAZ must now exist within a world of pure space, the world of the senses. Liminal, even evanescent, the TAZ must combine information and desire in order to fulfill its adventure (its "happening"), in order to fill itself to the borders of its destiny, to saturate itself with its own becoming.

Perhaps the Neo-Paleolithic School are correct when they assert that all forms of alienation and mediation must be destroyed or abandoned before our goals can be realized—or perhaps true anarchy will be realized only in Outer Space, as some futuro-libertarians assert. But the TAZ does not concern itself very much with "was" or "will be." The TAZ is interested in results, successful raids on consensus reality, breakthroughs into more intense and more abundant life. If the computer cannot be used in this project, then the computer will have to be overcome. My intuition however suggests that the counter-Net is already coming into being, perhaps already exists—but I cannot prove it. I've based the theory of the TAZ in large part on this intuition. Of course the Web also involves non-computerized networks of exchange such as samizdat, the black market, etc.—but the full potential of non-hierarchic information networking logically leads to the computer as the tool par excellence. Now I'm waiting for the hackers to prove I'm right, that my intuition is valid. Where are my turnips?

Donna Haraway

A Manifesto for Cyborgs: Science, Technology, and Socialist Feminism in the 1980s

■ AN IRONIC DREAM OF A COMMON LANGUAGE
FOR WOMEN IN THE INTEGRATED CIRCUIT

This chapter is an effort to build an ironic political myth faithful to feminism, socialism, and materialism. Perhaps more faithful as blasphemy is faithful, than as reverent worship and identification. Blasphemy has always seemed to require taking things very seriously. I know no better stance to adopt from within the secular-religious, evangelical traditions of U.S. politics, including the politics of socialist feminism. Blasphemy protects one from the Moral Majority within, while still insisting on the need for community. Blasphemy is not apostasy. Irony is about contradictions that do not resolve into larger wholes, even dialectically, about the tension of holding incompatible things together because both or all are necessary and true. Irony is about humor and serious play. It is also a rhetorical strategy and a political method, one I would like to see more honored within socialist feminism. At the center of my ironic faith, my blasphemy, is the image of the cyborg.

A cyborg is a cybernetic organism, a hybrid of machine and organism, a creature of social reality as well as a creature of fiction. Social reality is lived social relations, our most important political construction, a world-changing fiction. The international women's movements have constructed "women's experience," as well as uncovered or discovered this crucial collective object. This experience is a fiction and fact of the most crucial, political kind. Liberation rests on the construction of the consciousness, the imaginative apprehension, of oppression, and so of possibility. The cyborg is a matter of fiction

This article was first published in *Socialist Review*, No. 80, 1985. The essay originated as a response to a call for political thinking about the 1980s from socialist-feminist points of view, in hopes of deepening our political and cultural debates in order to renew commitments to fundamental social change in the face of the Reagan years. The cyborg manifesto tried to find a feminist place for connected thinking and acting in profoundly contradictory worlds. Since its publication, this bit of cyborgian writing has had a surprising half life. It has proved impossible to rewrite the cyborg. Cyborg's daughter will have to find its own matrix in another essay, starting from the proposition that the immune system is the biotechnical body's chief system of differences in late capitalism, where feminists might find provocative extraterrestrial maps of the networks of embodied power marked by race, sex, and class. This essay is substantially the same as the 1985 version, with minor revisions and correction of notes.

and lived experience that changes what counts as women's experience in the late twentieth century. This is a struggle over life and death, but the boundary between science fiction and social reality is an optical illusion.

Contemporary science fiction is full of cyborgs—creatures simultaneously animal and machine, who populate worlds ambiguously natural and crafted. Modern medicine is also full of cyborgs, of couplings between organism and machine, each conceived as coded devices, in an intimacy and with a power that was not generated in the history of sexuality. Cyborg "sex" restores some of the lovely replicative baroque of ferns and invertebrates (such nice organic prophylactics against heterosexism). Cyborg replication is uncoupled from organic reproduction. Modern production seems like a dream of cyborg colonization of work, a dream that makes the nightmare of Taylorism seem idyllic. Modern war is a cyborg orgy, coded by C^3I, command-control-communication-intelligence, an $84 billion item in 1984's U.S. defense budget. I am making an argument for the cyborg as a fiction mapping our social and bodily reality and as an imaginative resource suggesting some very fruitful couplings. Foucault's biopolitics is a flaccid premonition of cyborg politics, a very open field.

A cyborg is a cybernetic organism, a hybrid of machine and organism, a creature of social reality as well as a creature of fiction.

By the late twentieth century, our time, a mythic time, we are all chimeras, theorized and fabricated hybrids of machine and organism; in short, we are cyborgs. The cyborg is our ontology; it gives us our politics. The cyborg is a condensed image of both imagination and material reality, the two joined centers structuring any possibility of historical transformation. In the traditions of Western science and politics—the tradition of racist, male-dominant capitalism; the tradition of progress; the tradition of the appropriation of nature as resource for the productions of culture; the tradition of reproduction of the self from the reflections of the other—the relation between organism and machine has been a border war. The stakes in the border war have been the territories of production, reproduction, and imagination. This chapter is an argument for pleasure in the confusion of boundaries and for responsibility in their construction. It is also an effort to contribute to socialist-feminist culture and theory in a postmodernist, nonnaturalist mode and in the utopian tradition of imagining a world without gender, which is perhaps a world without genesis, but maybe also a world without end. The cyborg incarnation is outside salvation history. Nor does it mark time on an Oedipal calendar, attempting to heal the terrible cleavages of gender in oral symbiotic utopia or post-Oedipal apocalypse. As Zoe Sofoulis argues in her unpublished manuscript on Lacan, Klein, and nuclear culture, *Lacklein,* the most terrible and perhaps the most promising monsters in cyborg worlds are embodied in non-Oedipal narratives with a different logic of repression, which we need to understand for our survival.

The cyborg is a creature in a postgender world; it has no truck with bisexuality, pre-Oedipal symbiosis, unalienated labor, or other seductions to organic wholeness through a final appropriation of all the powers of the parts into a higher unity. In a sense, the cyborg has no origin story in the Western sense; a "final" irony since the cyborg is also the awful apocalyptic telos of

The cyborg is a creature in a postgender world.

the West's escalating dominations of abstract individuation, an ultimate self untied at last from all dependency, a man in space. An origin story in the Western humanist sense depends on the myth of original unity, fullness, bliss, and terror, represented by the phallic mother from whom all humans must separate, the task of individual development and of history, the twin potent myths inscribed most powerfully for us in psychoanalysis and Marxism. Hilary Klein has argued that both Marxism and psychoanalysis, in their concepts of labor and of individuation and gender formation, depend on the plot of original unity out of which difference must be produced and enlisted in a drama of escalating domination of woman/nature. The cyborg skips the step of original unity, of identification with nature in the Western sense. This is its illegitimate promise that might lead to subversion of its teleology as Star Wars.

The cyborg is resolutely committed to partiality, irony, intimacy, and perversity. It is oppositional, utopian, and completely without innocence. No longer structured by the polarity of public and private, the cyborg defines a technological polis based partly on a revolution of social relations in the oikos, the household. Nature and culture are reworked; the one can no longer be the resource for appropriation or incorporation by the other. The relationships for forming wholes from parts, including those of polarity and hierarchical domination, are at issue in the cyborg world. Unlike the hopes of Frankenstein's monster, the cyborg does not expect its father to save it through a restoration of the garden, that is, through the fabrication of a heterosexual mate, through its completion in a finished whole, a city and cosmos. The cyborg does not dream of community on the model of the organic family, this time without the Oedipal project. The cyborg would not recognize the Garden of Eden; it is not made of mud and cannot dream of returning to dust. Perhaps that is why I want to see if cyborgs can subvert the apocalypse of returning to nuclear dust in the manic compulsion to name the Enemy. Cyborgs are not reverent; they do not remember the cosmos. They are wary of holism, but needy for connection—they seem to have a natural feel for united front politics, but without the vanguard party. The main trouble with cyborgs, of course, is that they are the illegitimate offspring of militarism and patriarchal capitalism, not to mention state socialism. But illegitimate offspring are often exceedingly unfaithful to their origins. Their fathers, after all, are inessential.

I will return to the science fiction of cyborgs at the end of the chapter, but now I want to signal three crucial boundary breakdowns that make the following political fictional (political scientific) analysis possible. By the late twentieth century in United States, scientific culture, the boundary between human and animal, is thoroughly breached. The last beachheads of uniqueness have been polluted, if not turned into amusement parks—language, tool use, social behavior, mental events. Nothing really convincingly settles the separation of human and animal. Many people no longer feel the need of such a separation; indeed, many branches of feminist culture affirm the pleasure of connection with human and other living creatures. Movements for animal rights are not irrational denials of human uniqueness; they are clear-sighted recognition of connection across the discredited breach of nature and culture. Biology and evolutionary theory over the last two centuries have simultaneously produced modern organisms as objects of knowledge and reduced the line between humans and animals to a faint trace re-etched in ideological struggle or professional disputes between life and social sciences. Within this framework, teaching modern Christian creationism should be fought as a form of child abuse.

Biological-determinist ideology is only one position opened up in scientific culture for arguing the meanings of human animality. There is much room for radical political people to contest for the meanings of the breached boundary.[1] The cyborg appears in myth precisely where the boundary between human and animal is transgressed. Far from signaling a walling off of people from other living things, cyborgs signal disturbingly and pleasurably tight coupling. Bestiality has a new status in this cycle of marriage exchange.

The second leaky distinction is between animal-human (organism) and machine. Pre-cybernetic machines could be haunted; there was always the specter of the ghost in the machine. This dualism structured the dialogue between materialism and idealism that was settled by a dialectical progeny called spirit or history, according to taste. But basically machines were not self-moving, self-designing, autonomous. They could not achieve man's dream, only mock it. They were not man, an author of himself, but only a caricature of that masculinist reproductive dream. To think they were otherwise was paranoid. Now we are not so sure. Late twentieth-century machines have made thoroughly ambiguous the difference between natural and artificial, mind and body, self-developing and externally designed, and many other distinctions that used to apply to organisms and machines. Our machines are disturbingly lively, and we ourselves frighteningly inert.

Technological determinism is only one ideological space opened up by the reconceptions of machine and organism as coded texts through which we engage in the play of writing and reading the world.[2] "Textualization" of everything in poststructuralist, postmodernist theory has been damned by Marxists and socialist feminists for its utopian disregard for lived relations of domination that ground the "play" of arbitrary reading.[3]* It is certainly true that postmodernist strategies, like my cyborg myth, subvert myriad organic wholes (e.g., the poem, the primitive culture, the biological organism). In short, the certainty of what counts as nature—a source of insight and a promise of innocence—is undermined, probably fatally. The transcendent authorization of interpretation is lost and with it the ontology grounding Western epistemology. But the alternative is not cynicism or faithlessness, that is, some version of abstract existence, like the accounts of technological determinism destroying "man" by the "machine" or "meaningful political action" by the "text." Who cyborgs will be is a radical question; the answers are a matter of survival. Both chimpanzees and artifacts have politics, so why shouldn't we?[4]

The third distinction is a subset of the second: The boundary between physical and nonphysical is very imprecise for us. Pop physics books on the consequences of quantum theory and the indeterminacy principle are a kind of popular scientific equivalent to the Harlequin romances as a marker of radical change in American white heterosexuality: They get it wrong, but they are on the right subject. Modern machines are quintessentially microelectronic devices: They are everywhere and they are invisible. Modern machinery is an irreverent upstart god, mocking the Father's ubiquity and spirituality. The silicon chip is a surface for writing; it is etched in molecular scales disturbed only by atomic noise, the ultimate interference for nuclear scores. Writing, power, and technology are old partners in Western stories of the origin of civilization, but miniaturization has changed our experience of mechanism. Miniaturization has turned out to be about power; small is not so much beautiful as preeminently dangerous, as in Cruise missiles. Contrast the TV sets of

---

*A provocative, comprehensive argument about the politics and theories of postmodernism is made by Fredric Jameson, who argues that postmodernism is not an option, a style among others, but a cultural dominant requiring radical reinvention of left politics from within; there is no longer any place from without that gives meaning to the comforting fiction of critical distance. Jameson also makes clear why one cannot be for or against postmodernism, an essentially moralist move. My position is that feminists (and others) need continuous cultural reinventions, postmodernist critique, and historical materialism; only a cyborg would have a chance. The old dominations of white capitalist patriarchy seem nostalgically innocent now: They normalized heterogeneity, e.g., into man and woman, white and black. "Advanced capitalism" and postmodernism release heterogeneity without a norm, and we are flattened, without subjectivity, which requires depth, even unfriendly and drowning depths. It is time to write *The Death of the Clinic.* The clinic's methods required bodies and works; we have texts and surfaces. Our dominations don't work by medicalization and normalization anymore; they work by networking, communications redesign, stress management. Normalization gives way to automation, utter redundancy. Michel Foucault's *Birth of the Clinic, History of Sexuality,* and *Discipline and Punish* name a form of power at its moment of implosion. The discourse of biopolitics gives way to technobabble, the language of the spliced substantive; no noun is left whole by the multinationals. These are their names, listed from one issue of *Science:* Tech-Knowledge, Genentech, Allergen, Hybritech, Compupro, Genen-cor, Syntex, Allelix, Agrigenetics Corp., Syntro, Codon, Repligen; Micro-Angelo from Scion Corp., Percom Data, Inter Systems, Cyborg Corp., Statcom Corp., Intertec. If we are imprisoned by language, then escape from that prison-house requires language poets, a kind of cultural restriction enzyme to cut the code, cyborg heteroglossia is one form of radical culture politics.

the 1950s or the news cameras of the 1970s with the TV wristbands or hand-sized video cameras now advertised. Our best machines are made of sunshine; they are all light and clean because they are nothing but signals, electromagnetic waves, a section of a spectrum. These machines are eminently portable, mobile—a matter of immense human pain in Detroit and Singapore. People are nowhere near so fluid, being both material and opaque. Cyborgs are ether, quintessence.

The ubiquity and invisibility of cyborgs is precisely why these Sunshine Belt machines are so deadly. They are as hard to see politically as materially. They are about consciousness—or its simulation.[5] They are floating signifiers moving in pickup trucks across Europe, blocked more effectively by the witch-weavings of the displaced and so unnatural Greenham women, who read the cyborg webs of power very well, than by the militant labor of older masculinist politics, whose natural constituency needs defense jobs. Ultimately, the "hardest" science is about the realm of greatest boundary confusion, the realm of pure number, pure spirit, C^3I, cryptography, and the preservation of potent secrets. The new machines are so clean and light. Their engineers are sun worshipers mediating a new scientific revolution associated with the night dream of post industrial society. The diseases evoked by these clean machines are "no more" than the minuscule coding changes of an antigen in the immune system, "no more" than the experience of stress. The "nimble" fingers of "Oriental" women, the old fascination of little Anglo-Saxon Victorian girls with dollhouses, and women's enforced attention to the small take on quite new dimensions in this world. There might be a cyborg Alice taking account of these new dimensions. Ironically, it might be the unnatural cyborg women making chips in Asia and spiral dancing in Santa Rita jail after an antinuclear action whose constructed unities will guide effective oppositional strategies.

So my cyborg myth is about transgressed boundaries, potent fusions, and dangerous possibilities which progressive people might explore as one part of needed political work. One of my premises is that most American socialists and feminists see deepened dualisms of mind and body, animal and machine, idealism and materialism in the social practices, symbolic formulations, and physical artifacts associated with high technology and scientific culture. From *One-Dimensional Man* to *The Death of Nature,*[6] the analytic resources developed by progressives have insisted on the necessary domination of technics and recalled us to an imagined organic body to integrate our resistance. Another of my premises is that the need for unity of people trying to resist worldwide intensification of domination has never been more acute. But a slightly perverse shift of perspective might better enable us to contest for meanings, as well as for other forms of power and pleasure in technologically mediated societies.

From one perspective, a cyborg world is about the final imposition of a grid of control on the planet, about the final abstraction embodied in a Star Wars apocalypse waged in the name of defense, about the final appropriation of women's bodies in a masculinist orgy of war.[7] From another perspective, a cyborg world might be about lived social and bodily realities in which people are not afraid of their joint kinship with animals and machines, not afraid of permanently partial identities and contradictory standpoints. The political struggle is to see from both perspectives at once because each reveals both dominations and possibilities unimaginable from the other vantage point. Single vision produces worse illusions than double vision or many-headed monsters. Cyborg unities are monstrous and illegitimate; in our present political circumstances, we could hardly hope for more potent myths for resistance and recoupling. I like to imagine the Livermore Action Group, LAG, as a kind of cyborg society, dedicated to realistically converting the laboratories that most fiercely embody and spew out the tools of technological apocalypse, and committed to building a political form that actually manages to hold together witches, engineers, elders, perverts, Christians, mothers, and Leninists long enough to disarm the state. Fission Impossible is the name of the affinity group in my town. (Affinity: related not by blood but by choice, the appeal of one chemical nuclear group for another, avidity.)[8]

■ FRACTURED IDENTITIES

It has become difficult to name one's feminism by a single adjective—or even to insist in every circumstance upon the noun. Consciousness of exclusion through naming is acute. Identities seem contradictory, partial, and strategic. With the hard-won recognition of their social and historical constitution, gender, race, and class cannot provide the basis for belief in "essential" unity. There is nothing about being "female" that naturally binds women. There is not even such a state as "being" female, itself a highly complex category constructed in contested sexual scientific discourses and other social practices. Gender, race, or class consciousness is an achievement forced on us by the terrible historical experience of the contradictory social realities of patriarchy, colonialism, racism and capitalism. Who counts as "us" in my own rhetoric? Which identities are available to ground such a potent political myth called "us," and what could motivate enlistment in this collectivity? Painful fragmentation among feminists (not to mention among women) along every possible fault line has made the concept of woman elusive, an excuse for the matrix of women's dominations of each other. For me—and for many who share a similar historical location in white, professional, middle-class, female, radical, North American, mid-adult bodies—the sources of a crisis in political identity are legion. The recent history for much of the U.S. Left and the U.S. feminism has been a response to this kind of crisis by endless splitting and searches for a new essential unity. But there has also been a growing recognition of another response through coalition—affinity, not identity.[9]

Chela Sandoval, from a consideration of specific historical moments in the formation of the new political voice called women of color, has theorized a hopeful model of political identity called "oppositional consciousness," born of the skills for reading webs of power by those refused stable membership in the social categories of race, sex, or class.[10] "Women of color," a name con-

tested at its origins by those whom it would incorporate, as well as a historical consciousness marking systematic breakdown of all the signs of Man in
Western traditions, constructs a king of postmodernist identity out of otherness, difference, and specificity. This postmodernist identity is fully political,
whatever might be said about other possible postmodernisms. Sandoval's
oppositional consciousness is about contradictory locations and heterochronic
calendars, not about relativisms and pluralisms.

Sandoval emphasizes the lack of any essential criterion for identifying who
is a woman of color. She notes that the definition of the group has been by
conscious appropriation of negation. For example, a chicana or a U.S. black
woman has not been able to speak as a woman or as a black person or as a
chicano. Thus, she was at the bottom of a cascade of negative identities, left
out of even the "privileged" oppressed authorial categories called "women and
blacks," who claimed to make the important revolutions. The category
"woman" negated all nonwhite women; "black" negated all nonblack people,
as well as all black women. But there was also no "she," no singularity, but a
sea of differences among U.S. women who have affirmed their historical identity as U.S. women of color. This identity marks out a self-consciously constructed space that cannot affirm the capacity to act on the basis of natural
identification, but only on the basis of conscious coalition, of affinity, of
political kinship.[11] Unlike the "woman" of some streams of the white
women's movement in the United States, there is no naturalization of the
matrix, or at least this is what Sandoval argues is uniquely available through
the power of oppositional consciousness.

Sandoval's argument has to be seen as one potent formulation for feminists
out of the worldwide development of anti-colonialist discourse, that is, discourse dissolving the West and its highest product—the one who is not animal, barbarian, or woman: that is, man, the author of a cosmos called history.
As Orientalism is deconstructed politically and semiotically, the identities of
the Occident destabilize, including those of its feminists.[12] Sandoval argues
that "women of color" have a chance to build an effective unity that does not
replicate the imperializing, totalizing revolutionary subjects of previous
Marxisms and feminisms which had not faced the consequences of the disor-
derly polyphony emerging from decolonization.

Katie King has emphasized the limits of identification and the
political/poetic mechanics of identification built into reading "the poem," that
generative core of cultural feminism. King criticizes the persistent tendency
among contemporary feminists from different "moments" or "conversations" in
feminist practice to taxonomize the women's movement to make one's own
political tendencies appear to be the telos of the whole. These taxonomies
tend to remake feminist history to appear to be an ideological struggle among
coherent types persisting over time, especially those typical units called radical, liberal, and socialist feminism. Literally, all other feminisms are either
incorporated or marginalized, usually by building an explicit ontology and
epistemology.[13] Taxonomies of feminism produce epistemologies to police
deviation from official women's experience. Of course, "women's culture," like

women of color, is consciously created by mechanisms inducing affinity. The rituals of poetry, music, and certain forms of academic practice have been preeminent. The politics of race and culture in the U.S. women's movements are intimately interwoven. The common achievement of King and Sandoval is learning how to craft a poetic/political unity without relying on a logic of appropriation, incorporation, and taxonomic identification.

The theoretical and practical struggle against unity-through-domination or unity-through-incorporation ironically not only undermines the justifications for patriarchy, colonialism, humanism, positivism, essentialism, scientism, and other unlamented -isms, but all claims for an organic or natural standpoint. I think that radical and socialist/Marxist feminisms have also undermined their/our own epistemological strategies and that this is a crucially valuable step in imagining possible unities. It remains to be seen whether all epistemologies as Western political people have known them fail us in the task to build effective affinities.

It is important to note that the effort to construct revolutionary standpoints, epistemologies as achievements of people committed to changing the world, has been part of the process showing the limits of identification. The acid tools of postmodernist theory and the constructive tools of ontological discourse about revolutionary subjects might be seen as ironic allies in dissolving Western selves in the interests of survival. We are excruciatingly conscious of what it means to have a historically constituted body. But with the loss of innocence in our origin, there is no expulsion from the Garden either. Our politics lose the indulgence of guilt with the *naïveté* of innocence. But what would another political myth for socialist feminism look like? What kind of politics could embrace partial, contradictory, permanently unclosed constructions of personal and collective selves and still be faithful, effective—and, ironically, socialist feminist?

I do not know of any other time in history when there was greater need for political unity to confront effectively the dominations of race, gender, sexuality, and class. I also do not know of any other time when the kind of unity we might help build could have been possible. None of "us" have any longer the symbolic or material capability of dictating the shape of reality to any of "them." Or at least "we" cannot claim innocence from practicing such dominations. White women, including Euroamerican socialist feminists, discovered (i.e., were forced kicking and screaming to notice) the noninnocence of the category "woman." That consciousness changes the configuration of all previous categories; it denatures them as heat denatures a fragile protein. Cyborg feminists have to argue that "we" do not want any more natural matrix of unity and that no construction is whole. Innocence, and the corollary insistence on victimhood as the only ground for insight, has done enough damage. But the constructed revolutionary subject must give late twentieth-century people pause as well. In the fraying of identities and in the reflexive strategies for constructing them, the possibility opens up for weaving something other than a shroud for the day after the apocalypse that so prophetically ends salvation history.

But Marxist/socialist feminisms and radical feminisms have simultaneously naturalized and denatured the category "woman" and consciousness of the social lives of "women." Perhaps a schematic caricature can highlight both kinds of moves. Marxian socialism is rooted in an analysis of wage labor which reveals class structure. The consequence of the wage relationship is systematic alienation, as the worker is dissociated from his [sic] product. Abstraction and illusion rule in knowledge; domination rules in practice. Labor is the preeminently privileged category enabling the Marxist to overcome illusion and find that point of view which is necessary for changing the world. Labor is the humanizing activity that makes man; labor is an ontological category permitting the knowledge of a subject, and so the knowledge of subjugation and alienation.

In faithful filiation, socialist feminism advanced by allying itself with the basic analytic strategies of this Marxism. The main achievement of both Marxist feminists and socialist feminists was to expand the category of labor to accommodate what (some) women did, even when the wage relation was subordinated to a more comprehensive view of labor under capitalist patriarchy. In particular, women's labor in the household and women's activity as mothers generally, that is, reproduction in the socialist feminist sense, entered theory on the authority of analogy to the Marxian concept of labor. The unity of women here rests on an epistemology based on the ontological structure of "labor." Marxist/socialist feminism does not "naturalize" unity; it is a possible achievement based on a possible standpoint rooted in social relations. The essentializing move is in the ontological structure of labor or of its analogue, women's activity.[14*] The inheritance of Marxian humanism, with its preeminently Western self, is the difficulty for me. The contribution from these formulations has been the emphasis on the daily responsibility of real women to *build* unities, rather than to naturalize them.

Catherine MacKinnon's version of radical feminism is itself a caricature of the appropriating, incorporating, totalizing tendencies of Western theories of identity grounding action.[15] It is factually and politically wrong to assimilate all of the diverse "moments" or "conversations" in recent women's politics named radical feminism to MacKinnon's version. But the teleological logic of her theory shows how an epistemology and ontology—including their negations—erase or police difference. Only one of the effects of MacKinnon's theory is the rewriting of the history of the polymorphous field called radical feminism. The major effect is the production of a theory of experience, of women's identity, that is a kind of apocalypse for all revolutionary standpoints. That is, the totalization built into this tale of radical feminism achieves its end—the unity of women—by enforcing the experience of and testimony

---

*The central role of object-relations versions of psychoanalysis and related strong universalizing moves in discussing reproduction, caring work, and mothering in many approaches to epistemology underline their authors' resistance to what I am calling postmodernism. For me, both the universalizing moves and these versions of psychoanalysis make analysis of "women's place in the integrated circuit" difficult and lead to systematic difficulties in accounting for or even seeing major aspects of the construction of gender and gendered social life.

to radical nonbeing. As for the Marxist/socialist feminist, consciousness is an achievement, not a natural fact. MacKinnon's theory eliminates some of the difficulties built into humanist revolutionary subjects, but at the cost of radical reductionism.

MacKinnon argues that feminism necessarily adopted a different analytical strategy from Marxism, looking first not at the structure of class, but at the structure of sex/gender and its generative relationship, men's constitution and appropriation of women sexually. Ironically, MacKinnon's "ontology" constructs a nonsubject, a nonbeing. Another's desire, not the self's labor, is the origin of "woman." She therefore develops a theory of consciousness that enforces what can count as "women's" experience—anything that names sexual violation, indeed, sex itself as far as "women" can be concerned. Feminist practice is the construction of this form of consciousness; that is, the self-knowledge of a self-who-is-not.

Perversely, sexual appropriation in this feminism still has the epistemological status of labor, that is, the point from which analysis able to contribute to changing the world must flow. But sexual objectification, not alienation, is the consequence of the structure of sex/gender. In the realm of knowledge, the result of sexual objectification is illusion and abstraction. However, a woman is not simply alienated from her product, but in a deep sense she does not exist as a subject, or even potential subject, since she owes her existence as a woman to sexual appropriation. To be constituted by another's desire is not the same thing as to be alienated in the violent separation of the laborer from his product.

MacKinnon's radical theory of experience is totalizing in the extreme; it does not so much marginalize as obliterate the authority of any other women's political speech and action. It is a totalization producing what Western patriarchy itself never succeeded in doing—feminists' consciousness of the nonexistence of women, except as products of men's desire. I think MacKinnon correctly argues that no Marxian version of identity can firmly ground women's unity. But in solving the problem of the contradictions of any Western revolutionary subject for feminist purposes, she develops an even more authoritarian doctrine of experience. If my complaint about socialist/Marxian standpoints is their unintended erasure of polyvocal, unassimilable, radical difference made visible in anti-colonial discourse and practice, MacKinnon's intentional erasure of all difference through the device of the "essential" nonexistence of women is not reassuring.

In my taxonomy, which like any other taxonomy is a reinscription of history, radical feminism can accommodate all the activities of women named by socialist feminists as forms of labor only if the activity can somehow be sexualized. Reproduction had different tones of meanings for the two tendencies, one rooted in labor, one in sex, both calling the consequences of domination and ignorance of social and personal reality "false consciousness."

Beyond either the difficulties or the contributions in the argument of any one author, neither Marxist nor radical-feminist points of view have tended to embrace the status of a partial explanation; both were regularly constituted as totalities. Western explanation has demanded as much; how else could the Western author incorporate its others? Each tried to annex other forms of domination by expanding its basic categories through analogy, simple listing, or addition. Embarrassed silence about race among white radical and socialist feminists was one major, devastating political consequence. History and polyvocality disappear into political taxonomies that try to establish genealogies. There was no structural room for race (or for much else) in theory claiming to reveal the construction of the category "woman" and social group "women" as a unified or totalizable whole. The structure of my caricature looks like this:

Socialist Feminism—
> *structure of class//wage labor//alienation*
> *labor, by analogy reproduction, by extension sex, by addition race*

Radical Feminism—
> *structure of gender//sexual appropriation//objectification*
> *sex, by analogy labor, by extension reproduction, by addition race*

In another context, the French theorist Julia Kristeva claimed women appeared as a historical group after World War II, along with groups like youth. Her dates are doubtful, but we are now accustomed to remembering that as objects of knowledge and as historical actors, "race" did not always exist, "class" has a historical genesis, and "homosexuals" are quite junior. It is no accident that the symbolic system of the family of man—and so the essence of woman—breaks up at the same moment that networks of connection among people on the planet are unprecedentedly multiple, pregnant, and complex. "Advanced capitalism" is inadequate to convey the structure of this historical moment. In the Western sense, the end of man is at stake. It is no accident that woman disintegrates into women in our time. Perhaps socialist feminists were not substantially guilty of producing essentialist theory that suppressed women's particularity and contradictory interests. I think we have been, at least through unreflective participation in the logics, languages, and practices of white humanism and through searching for a single ground of domination to secure our revolutionary voice. Now we have less excuse. But in the consciousness of our failures, we risk lapsing into boundless difference and giving up on the confusing task of making partial, real connection. Some differences are playful; some are poles of world historical systems of domination. Epistemology is about knowing the difference.

■ THE INFORMATICS OF DOMINATION

In this attempt at an epistemological and political position, I would like to sketch a picture of possible unity, a picture indebted to socialist and feminist principles of design. The frame for my sketch is set by the extent and importance of rearrangements in worldwide social relations tied to science and technology. I argue for a politics rooted in claims about fundamental changes in the nature of class, race, and gender in an emerging system of world order analogous in its novelty and scope to that created by industrial capitalism; we are living through a movement from an organic, industrial society to a polymorphous, information system—from all work to all play, a deadly game. Simultaneously material and ideological, the dichotomies may be expressed in the following chart of transitions from the comfortable old hierarchical dominations to the scary new networks I have called the informatics of domination:

Representation	Simulation
Bourgeois novel, realism	Science fiction, postmodernism
Organism	Biotic component
Depth, integrity	Surface, boundary
Heat	Noise
Biology as clinical practice	Biology as inscription
Physiology	Communications engineering
Small group	Subsystem
Perfection	Optimization
Eugenics	Population Control
Decadence, *Magic Mountain*	Obsolescence, *Future Shock*
Hygiene	Stress management
Microbiology, tuberculosis	Immunology, AIDS
Organic division of labor	Ergonomics/cybernetics of labor
Functional specialization	Modular construction
Reproduction	Replication
Organic sex role specialization	Optimal genetic strategies
Biological determinism	Evolutionary inertia, constraints
Community ecology	Ecosystem
Racial chain of being	Neo-imperialism, United Nations humanism
Scientific management in home/factory	Global factory/electronic cottage
Family/market/factory	Women in the integrated circuit
Family wage	Comparable worth
Public/private	Cyborg citizenship

Nature/culture	Fields of difference
Cooperation	Communications enhancement
Freud	Lacan
Sex	Genetic engineering
Labor	Robotics
Mind	Artificial intelligence
World War II	Star Wars
White capitalist patriarchy	Informatics of domination

This list suggests several interesting things.[16] First, the objects on the right-hand side cannot be coded as "natural," a realization that subverts naturalistic coding for the left-hand side as well. We cannot go back ideologically or materially. It's not just that "god" is dead; so is the "goddess." Or both are revivified in the worlds charged with microelectronic and biotechnological politics. In relation to objects like biotic components, one must think not in terms of essential properties, but in terms of design, boundary constraints, rates of flows, systems logics, costs of lowering constraints. Sexual reproduction is one kind of reproductive strategy among many, with costs and benefits as a function of the system environment. Ideologies of sexual reproduction can no longer reasonably call on notions of sex and sex role as organic aspects in natural objects like organisms and families. Such reasoning will be unmasked as irrational, and ironically corporate executives reading *Playboy* and anti-porn radical feminists will make strange bedfellows in jointly unmasking the irrationalism.

Likewise for race, racist and anti-racist ideologies about human diversity have to be formulated in terms of frequencies of parameters. It is "irrational" to invoke concepts like primitive and civilized. For liberals and radicals, the search for integrated social systems gives way to a new practice called "experimental ethnography" in which an organic object dissipates in attention to the play of writing. At the level of ideology, we see translations of racism and colonialism into languages of development and underdevelopment, rates and constraints of modernization. Any objects or persons can be "reasonably" thought of in terms of disassembly and reassembly; no "natural" architectures constrain system design. The financial districts in all the world's cities, as well as the export-processing and free-trade zones, proclaim this elementary fact of "late capitalism." The entire universe of objects that can be known scientifically must be formulated as problems in communications engineering (for the managers) or theories of the text (for those who would resist). Both are cyborg semiologies.

One should expect control strategies to concentrate on boundary conditions and interfaces, on rates of flow across boundaries—and not on the integrity of natural objects. "Integrity" or "sincerity" of the Western self gives way to decision procedures and expert systems. For example, control strategies applied to women's capacities to give birth to new human beings will be developed in the languages of population control and maximization of goal achievement for individual decisionmakers. Control strategies will be formulated in terms of rates, costs of constraints, degrees of freedom. Human beings, like any other component or subsystem, must be localized in a system architecture whose basic modes of operation are probabilistic, statistical. No objects, spaces, or bodies are sacred in themselves; any component can be interfaced with any other if the proper standard, the proper code, can be constructed for processing signals in a common language. Exchange in this world transcends the universal translation effected by capitalist markets that Marx analyzed so well. The privileged pathology affecting all kinds of components in this universe is stress—communications breakdown.[17] The cyborg is not subject to Foucault's biopolitics; the cyborg simulates politics, a much more potent field of operations. Discursive constructions are no joke.

This kind of analysis of scientific and cultural objects of knowledge which have appeared historically since World War II prepares us to notice some important inadequacies in feminist analysis which has proceeded as if the organic, hierarchical dualism ordering discourse in the West since Aristotle still ruled. They have been cannibalized, or as Zoe Sofia (Sofoulis) might put it, they have been "techno-digested." The dichotomies between mind and body, animal and human, organism and machine, public and private, nature and culture, men and women, primitive and civilized are all in question ideologically. The actual situation of women is their integration/exploitation into a world system of production/reproduction and communication called the informatics of domination. The home, work place, market, public arena, the body itself—all can be dispersed and interfaced in nearly infinite, polymorphous ways, with large consequences for women and others—consequences that themselves are very different for different people and which make potent oppositional international movements difficult to imagine and essential for survival. One important route for reconstructing socialist-feminist politics is through theory and practice addressed to the social relations of science and technology, including crucially the systems of myth and meanings structuring our imaginations. The cyborg is a kind of disassembled and reassembled, postmodern collective and personal self. This is the self feminists must code.

Communications technologies and biotechnologies are the crucial tools recrafting our bodies. These tools embody and enforce new social relations for women worldwide. Technologies and scientific discourses can be partially understood as formalizations, that is, as frozen moments, of the fluid social interactions constituting them, but they should also be viewed as instruments for enforcing meanings. The boundary is permeable between tool and myth, instrument and concept, historical systems of social relations and historical anatomies of possible bodies, including objects of knowledge. Indeed, myth and tool mutually constitute each other.

Furthermore, communications sciences and modern biologies are constructed by a common move—the translation of the world into a problem of coding, a search for a common language in which all resistance to instrumental control disappears and all heterogeneity can be submitted to disassembly, reassembly, investment, and exchange.

In communications sciences, the translation of the world into a problem in coding can be illustrated by looking at cybernetic (feedback controlled) systems theories applied to telephone technology, computer design, weapons deployment, or data-base construction and maintenance. In each case, solution to the key questions rests on a theory of language and control; the key operation is determining the rates, directions, and probabilities of flow of a quantity called information. The world is subdivided by boundaries differentially permeable to information. Information is just that kind of quantifiable element (unit, basis of unity) which allows universal translation and so unhindered instrumental power (called effective communication). The biggest threat to such power is interruption of communication. Any system breakdown is a function of stress. The fundamentals of this technology can be condensed into the metaphor C^3I, command-control-communication-intelligence, the military's symbol for its operations theory.

In modern biologies, the translation of the world into a problem in coding can be illustrated by molecular genetics, ecology, sociobiological evolutionary theory, and immunobiology. The organism has been translated into problems of genetic coding and read-out. Biotechnology, a writing technology, informs research broadly.[18] In a sense, organisms have ceased to exist as objects of knowledge, giving way to biotic components, that is, special kinds of information-processing devices. The analogous moves in ecology could be examined by probing the history and utility of the concept of the ecosystem. Immunobiology and associated medical practices are rich exemplars of the privilege of coding and recognition systems as objects of knowledge, as constructions of bodily reality for us. Biology here is a king of cryptography. Research is necessarily a kind of intelligence activity. Ironies abound. A stressed system goes awry; its communication processes break down; it fails to recognize the difference between self and other. Human babies with baboon hearts evoke national ethical perplexity—for animal-rights activists at least as much as for the guardians of human purity. In the United States gay men and intravenous drug users are the most "privileged" victims of an awful immune-system disease that marks (inscribes on the body) confusion of boundaries and moral pollution.[19]

But these excursions into communications sciences and biology have been at a rarefied level; there is a mundane, largely economic reality to support my claim that these sciences and technologies indicate fundamental transformations in the structure of the world for us. Communications technologies depend on electronics. Modern states, multinational corporations, military power, welfare-state apparatuses, satellite systems, political processes, fabrication of our imaginations, labor-control systems, medical constructions of our bodies, commercial pornography, the international division of labor, and religious evangelism depend intimately upon electronics. Microelectronics is the technical basis of simulacra, that is, of copies without originals.

Microelectronics mediates the translations of labor into robotics and word processing, sex into genetic engineering and reproductive technologies, and mind into artificial intelligence and decision procedures. The new biotechnologies concern more than human reproduction. Biology as a powerful engineering science for redesigning materials and processes has revolutionary implications for industry, perhaps most obvious today in areas of fermentation, agriculture, and energy. Communications sciences and biology are constructions of natural-technical objects of knowledge in which the difference between machine and organism is thoroughly blurred; mind, body, and tool are on very intimate terms. The "multinational" material organization of the production and reproduction of daily life and the symbolic organization of the production and reproduction of culture and imagination seem equally implicated. The boundary-maintaining images of base and superstructure, public and private, or material and ideal never seemed more feeble.

I have used Rachel Grossman's image of women in the integrated circuit to name the situation of women in a world so intimately restructured through the social relations of science and technology.[20] I use the odd circumlocution, "the social relations of science and technology," to indicate that we are not dealing with a technological determinism, but with a historical system depending upon structured relations among people. But the phrase should also indicate that science and technology provide fresh sources of power, that we need fresh sources of analysis and political action.[21] Some of the rearrangements of race, sex, and class rooted in high-tech-facilitated social relations can make socialist feminism more relevant to effective progressive politics.

■ THE HOMEWORK ECONOMY

The "New Industrial Revolution" is producing a new worldwide working class, as well as new sexualities and ethnicities. The extreme mobility of capital and the emerging international division of labor are intertwined with the emergence of new collectivities and the weakening of familiar groupings. These developments are neither gender- nor race-neutral. White men in advanced industrial societies have become newly vulnerable to permanent job loss, and women are not disappearing from the job rolls at the same rates as men. It is not simply that women in third-world countries are the preferred labor force for the science-based multinationals in the export-processing sectors, particularly in electronics. The picture is more systematic and involves reproduction, sexuality, culture, consumption, and production. In the prototypical Silicon Valley, many women's lives have been structured around employment in electronics-dependent jobs, and their intimate realities include serial heterosexual monogamy, negotiating child care, distance from extended kin or most other forms of traditional community, a high likelihood of loneliness and extreme economic vulnerability as they age. The ethnic and racial diversity of women in Silicon Valley structures a microcosm of conflicting differences in culture, family, religion, education, and language.

Richard Gordon has called this new situation the homework economy.[22] Although he includes the phenomenon of literal homework emerging in connection with electronics assembly, Gordon intends "homework economy" to name a restructuring of work that broadly has the characteristics formerly ascribed to female jobs, jobs literally done only by women. Work is being redefined as both literally female and feminized, whether performed by men or women. To be feminized means to be made extremely vulnerable; able to be disassembled, reassembled, exploited as a reserve labor force; seen less as workers than as servers; subjected to time arrangements on and off the paid job that make a mockery of a limited work day; leading an existence that always borders on being obscene, out of place, and reducible to sex. De-skilling is an old strategy newly applicable to formerly privileged workers. However, the homework economy does not refer only to large-scale de-skilling, nor does it deny that new areas of high skill are emerging, even for women and men previously excluded from skilled employment.

The "New Industrial Revolution" is producing a new worldwide working class, as well as new sexualities and ethnicities.

Rather, the concept indicates that factory, home, and market are integrated on a new scale and that the places of women are crucial—and need to be analyzed for differences among women and for meanings for relations between men and women in various situations.

The homework economy as a world capitalist organizational structure is made possible by (not caused by) the new technologies. The success of the attack on relatively privileged, mostly white men's unionized jobs is tied to the power of the new communications technologies to integrate and control labor despite extensive dispersion and decentralization. The consequences of the new technologies are felt by women both in the loss of the family (male) wage (if they ever had access to this white privilege) and in the character of their own jobs, which are becoming capital-intensive, for example, office work and nursing.

The new economic and technological arrangements are also related to the collapsing welfare state and the ensuing intensification of demands on women to sustain daily life for themselves as well as for men, children, and old people. The feminization of poverty—generated by dismantling the welfare state, by the homework economy where stable jobs become the exception, and sustained by the expectation that women's wage will not be matched by a male income for the support of children—has become an urgent focus. The causes of various women-headed households are a function of race, class, or sexuality; but their increasing generality is a ground for coalitions of women on many issues. That women regularly sustain daily life partly as a function of their enforced status as mothers is hardly new; the kind of integration with the overall capitalist and progressively war-based economy is new. The particular pressure, for example, on U.S. black women, who have achieved an escape from (barely) paid domestic service and who now hold clerical and similar jobs in large numbers, has large implications for continued enforced black poverty with employment. Teenage women in industrializing areas of the third world increasingly find themselves the sole or major source of a cash wage for their families, while access to land is ever more problematic. These developments must have major consequences in the psychodynamics and politics of gender and race.

Within the narrative framework of three major stages of capitalism (commercial/early industrial, monopoly, multinational)—tied to nationalism, imperialism, and multinationalism, and related to Jameson's three dominant aesthetic periods of realism, modernism, and postmodernism—I would argue that specific forms of families dialectically relate to forms of capital and to its political and cultural concomitants. Although lived problematically and unequally, ideal forms of these families might be schematized as (1) the patriarchal nuclear family, structured by the dichotomy between public and private and accompanied by the white bourgeois ideology of separate spheres and nineteenth-century Anglo-American bourgeois feminism; (2) the modern family mediated (or enforced) by the welfare state and institutions like the family wage, with a flowering of afeminist heterosexual ideologies, including their radical versions represented in Greenwich Village around World War I; and (3) the "family" of the homework economy with its oxymoronic structure of women-headed households and its explosion of feminisms and the paradoxical intensification and erosion of gender itself.

This is the context in which the projections for worldwide structural unemployment stemming from the new technologies are part of the picture of the homework economy. As robotics and related technologies put men out of work in "developed" countries and exacerbate failure to generate male jobs in third-world "development" and as the automated office becomes the rule even in labor-surplus countries, the feminization of work intensifies. Black women in the United States have long known what it looks like to face the structural underemployment ("feminization") of black men, as well as their own highly vulnerable position in the wage economy. It is no longer a secret that sexuality, reproduction, family, and community life are interwoven with this economic structure in myriad ways which have also differentiated the situations of white and black women. Many more women and men will contend with similar situations, which will make cross-gender and race alliances on issues of basic life support (with or without jobs) necessary, not just nice.

The new technologies also have a profound effect on hunger and on food production for subsistence worldwide. Rae Lessor Blumberg estimates that women produce about 50 percent of the world's subsistence food.[23]* Women

---

*The conjunction of the Green Revolution's social relations with biotechnologies like plant genetic engineering makes the pressures on the land in the third world increasingly intense. The Agency for International Development's estimates (*New York Times* October 14, 1984) used at the 1984 World Food Day are that in Africa, women produce about 90 percent of rural food supplies, about 60 to 80 percent in Asia, and provide 40 percent of agricultural labor in the Near East and Latin America. Blumberg charges that world organizations' agricultural politics, as well

are excluded generally from benefiting from the increased high-tech commodification of food and energy crops, their days are made more arduous because
their responsibilities to provide food do not diminish, and their reproductive
situations are made more complex. Green Revolution technologies interact
with other high-tech industrial production to alter gender divisions of labor
and differential gender migration patterns.

The new technologies seem deeply involved in the forms of "privatization"
that Ros Petchesky has analyzed, in which militarization, right-wing family
ideologies and policies, and intensified definitions of corporate (and state)
property as private synergistically interact.[24] The new communications technologies are fundamental to the eradication of "public life" for everyone. This
facilitates the mushrooming of a permanent high-tech military establishment
at the cultural and economic expense of most people, but especially of
women. Technologies like video games and highly miniaturized television
seem crucial to production of modern forms of "private life." The culture of
video games is heavily oriented to individual competition and extraterrestrial
warfare. High-tech, gendered imaginations are produced here, imaginations
that can contemplate destruction of the planet and a sci-fi escape from its
consequences. More than our imaginations is militarized, and the other realities of electronic and nuclear warfare are inescapable. These are the technologies that promise ultimate mobility and perfect exchange—and incidentally
enable tourism, that perfect practice of mobility and exchange, to emerge as
one of the world's largest single industries.

The new technologies affect the social relations of both sexuality and
reproduction, and not always in the same ways. The close ties of sexuality and
instrumentality, of views of the body as a kind of private satisfaction- and
utility-maximizing machine, are described nicely in sociobiological origin stories that stress a genetic calculus and explain the inevitable dialectic of domination of male and female gender roles.[25] These sociobiological stories
depend on a high-tech view of the body as a biotic component or cybernetic
communications system. Among the many transformations of reproductive situations is the medical one, where women's bodies have boundaries newly permeable to both "visualization" and "intervention." Of course, who controls the
interpretation of bodily boundaries in medical hermeneutics is a major feminist issue. The speculum served as an icon of women's claiming their bodies
in the 1970s; that handcrafted tool is inadequate to express our needed body
politics in the negotiation of reality in the practices of cyborg reproduction.
Self-help is not enough. The technologies of visualization recall the important
cultural practice of hunting with the camera and the deeply predatory nature

as those of multinationals and national governments in the third world, generally ignore fundamental issues in the sexual division of labor. The present tragedy of famine in Africa might
owe as much to male supremacy as to capitalism, colonialism, and rain patterns. More accurately,
capitalism and racism are usually structurally male dominant.

of a photographic consciousness.[26] Sex, sexuality, and reproduction are central actors in high-tech myth systems structuring our imaginations of personal and social possibility.

Another critical aspect of the social relations of the new technologies is the reformulation of expectations, culture, work, and reproduction for the large scientific and technical work force. A major social and political danger is the formation of a strongly bimodal social structure, with masses of women and men of all ethnic groups, but especially people of color, confined to a homework economy, illiteracy of several varieties, and general redundancy and impotence, controlled by high-tech repressive apparatuses ranging from entertainment to surveillance and disappearance. An adequate socialist-feminist politics should address women in the privileged occupational categories and particularly in the production of science and technology that constructs scientific-technical discourse, processes, and objects.[27]

This issue is only one aspect of inquiry into the possibility of a feminist science, but it is important. What kind of constitutive role in the production of knowledge, imagination, and practice can new groups doing science have? How can these groups be allied with progressive social and political movements? What kind of political accountability can be constructed to tie women together across the scientific-technical hierarchies separating us? Might there be ways of developing feminist science/technology politics in alliance with anti-military science facility conversion action groups? Many scientific and technical workers in Silicon Valley, the high-tech cowboys included, do not want to work on military science.[28] Can these personal preferences and cultural tendencies be welded into progressive politics among this professional middle class in which women, including women of color, are coming to be fairly numerous?

■ WOMEN IN THE INTEGRATED CIRCUIT

Let me summarize the picture of women's historical locations in advanced industrial societies, as these positions have been restructured partly through the social relations of science and technology. If it was ever possible ideologically to characterize women's lives by the distinction of public and private domains—suggested by images of the division of working-class life into factory and home, of bourgeois life into market and home, and of gender existence into personal and political realms—it is now a totally misleading ideology, even to show how both terms of these dichotomies construct each other in practice and in theory. I prefer a network ideological image, suggesting the profusion of spaces and identities and the permeability of boundaries in the personal body and in the body politic. "Networking" is both a feminist practice and a multinational corporate strategy—weaving is for oppositional cyborgs.

So let me return to the earlier image of the informatics of domination and trace one vision of women's "place" in the integrated circuit, touching only a few idealized social locations seen primarily from the point of view of advanced capitalist societies: Home, Market, Paid Work Place, State, School, Clinic-Hospital, and Church. Each of these idealized spaces is logically and practically implied in every other locus, perhaps analogous to a holographic photograph. I want to suggest the impact of the social relations mediated and enforced by the new technologies in order to help formulate needed analysis and practical work. However, there is no "place" for women in these networks, only geometries of difference and contradiction crucial to women's cyborg identities. If we learn how to read these webs of power and social life, we might learn new couplings, new coalitions. There is no way to read the following list from a standpoint of "identification," of a unitary self. The issue is dispersion. The task is to survive in diaspora.

"Networking" is both a feminist practice and a multinational corporate strategy— weaving is for oppositional cyborgs.

Home: Women-headed households, serial monogamy, flight of men, old women alone, technology of domestic work, paid home work, reemergence of home sweatshops, home-based businesses and telecommuting, electronic cottage, urban homelessness, migration, module architecture, reinforced (simulated) nuclear family, intense domestic violence.

Market: Women's continuing consumption work, newly targeted to buy the profusion of new production from the new technologies (especially as the competitive race among industrialized and industrializing nations to avoid dangerous mass unemployment necessitates finding ever bigger new markets for ever less clearly needed commodities); bimodal buying power, coupled with advertising targeting of the numerous affluent groups and neglect of the previous mass markets; growing importance of informal markets in labor and commodities parallel to high-tech, affluent market structures; surveillance systems through electronic funds transfer; intensified market abstraction (commodification) of experience, resulting in ineffective utopian or equivalent cynical theories of community; extreme mobility (abstraction) of marketing/financing systems; interpenetration of sexual and labor markets; intensified sexualization of abstracted and alienated consumption.

Paid Work Place: Continued intense sexual and racial division of labor, but considerable growth of membership in privileged occupational categories for many white women and people of color; impact of new technologies on women's work in clerical, service, manufacturing (especially textiles), agriculture, electronics; international restructuring of the working classes; development of new time arrangements to facilitate the homework economy (flex time, part time, overtime, no time); homework and out work; increased pressures for two-tiered wage structures; significant numbers of people in cash-dependent populations worldwide with no experience or no further hope of stable employment; most labor "marginal" or "feminized."

State: Continued erosion of the welfare state; decentralizations with increased surveillance and control; citizenship by telematics; imperialism and political power broadly in the form of information-rich/information-poor differentiation; increased high-tech militarization increasingly opposed by many social groups; reduction of civil service jobs as a result of the growing capital intensification of office work, with implications for occupational mobility for women of color; growing privatization of material and ideological life and culture; close integration of privatization and militarization, the high-tech forms of bourgeois capitalist personal and public life; invisibility of different social groups to each other, linked to psychological mechanisms of belief in abstract enemies.

The task is to survive in diaspora.

School: Deepening coupling of high-tech capital needs and public education at all levels, differentiated by race, class, and gender; managerial classes involved in educational reform and refunding at the cost of remaining progressive educational democratic structures for children and teachers; education for mass ignorance and repression in technocratic and militarized culture; growing anti-science mystery cults in dissenting and radical political movements; continued relative scientific illiteracy among white women and people of color; growing industrial direction of education (especially higher education) by science-based multinationals (particularly in electronics- and biotechnology-dependent companies); highly educated, numerous elites in a progressively bimodal society.

Clinic-Hospital: Intensified machine-body relations; renegotiations of public metaphors which channel personal experience of the body, particularly in relation to reproduction, immune system functions, and "stress" phenomena; intensification of reproductive politics in response to world historical implications of women's unrealized, potential control of their relation to reproduction; emergence of new historically specific diseases; struggles over meanings and means of health in environments pervaded by high-technology products and processes; continuing feminization of health work; intensified struggle over state responsibility for health; continued ideological role of popular health movements as a major form of American politics.

Church: Electronic fundamentalist "super-saver" preachers solemnizing the union of electronic capital and automated fetish gods; intensified importance of churches in resisting the militarized state; central struggle over women's meanings and authority in religion; continued relevance of spirituality, intertwined with sex and health, in political struggle.

The only way to characterize the informatics of domination is as a massive intensification of insecurity and cultural impoverishment, with common failure of subsistence networks for the most vulnerable. Since much of this picture interweaves with the social relations of science and technology, the urgency of a socialist-feminist politics addressed to science and technology is plain. There is much now being done, and the grounds for political work are rich. For example, the efforts to develop forms of collective struggle for women in paid work, like District 925 of the SEIU (Service Employees International Union) should be a high priority for all of us. These efforts are profoundly tied to technical restructuring of labor processes and reformations of working classes. These efforts also are providing understanding of a more comprehensive kind of labor organization, involving community, sexuality, and family issues never privileged in the largely white male industrial unions.

The structural rearrangements related to the social relations of science and technology evoke strong ambivalence. But it is not necessary to be ultimately depressed by the implications of late twentieth-century women's relation to all aspects of work, culture, production of knowledge, sexuality, and repro-duction. For excellent reasons, most Marxisms see domination best and have trouble understanding what can only look like false consciousness and peo-ple's complicity in their own domination in late capitalism. It is crucial to remember that what is lost, perhaps especially from women's points of view, is often virulent forms of oppression, nostalgically naturalized in the face of current violation. Ambivalence toward the disrupted unities mediated by high-tech culture requires not sorting consciousness into categories of "clear-sighted critique grounding a solid political epistemology" versus "manipulated false consciousness," but subtle understanding of emerging pleasures, experi-ences, and powers with serious potential for changing the rules of the game.

There are grounds for hope in the emerging bases for new kinds of unity across race, gender, and class, as these elementary units of socialist-feminist analysis themselves suffer protean transformations. Intensifications of hardship experienced worldwide in connection with the social relations of science and technology are severe. But what people are experiencing is not transparently clear, and we lack sufficiently subtle connections for collectively building effective theories of experience. Present efforts—Marxist, psychoanalytic, feminist, anthropological—to clarify even "our" experience are rudimentary.

I am conscious of the odd perspective provided by my historical posi-tion—a Ph.D. in biology for an Irish Catholic girl was made possible by Sputnik's impact on U.S. national science-education policy. I have a body and mind as much constructed by the post–World War II arms race and cold war as by the women's movements. There are more grounds for hope by focusing on the contradictory effects of politics designed to produce loyal American technocrats, which as well produced large numbers of dissidents, rather than by focusing on the present defeats.

The permanent partiality of feminist points of view has consequences for our expectations of forms of political organization and participation. We do not need a totality in order to work well. The feminist dream of a common language, like all dreams for a perfectly true language, of a per-fectly faithful naming of experience, is a totalizing and imperialist one. In that sense, dialectics too is a dream language, longing to resolve contradic-tion. Perhaps, ironically, we can learn from our fusions with animals and machines how not to be Man, the embodiment of Western logos. From the point of view of pleasure in these potent and taboo fusions, made inevitable by the social relations of science and technology, there might indeed be a feminist science.

■ CYBORGS: A MYTH OF POLITICAL IDENTITY

I want to conclude with a myth about identity and boundaries which might inform late twentieth-century political imaginations. I am indebted in this story to writers like Joanna Russ, Samuel Delany, John Varley, James Tiptree, Jr., Octavia Butler, and Vonda McIntyre.[29] These are our storytellers exploring what it means to be embodied in high-tech worlds. They are theorists for cyborgs. Exploring conceptions of bodily boundaries and social order, the anthropologist Mary Douglas should be credited with helping us to consciousness about how fundamental body imagery is to world view and so to political language.[30] French feminists like Luce Irigaray and Monique Wittig, for all their differences, know how to write the body, how to weave eroticism, cosmology, and politics from imagery of embodiment, and especially for Wittig, from imagery of fragmentation and reconstitution of bodies.[31]

American radical feminists like Susan Griffin, Audre Lorde, and Adrienne Rich have profoundly affected our political imaginations—and perhaps restricted too much what we allow as a friendly body and political language.[32] They insist on the organic, opposing it to the technological. But their symbolic systems and the related positions of eco-feminism and feminist paganism, replete with organicisms, can only be understood in Sandoval's terms as oppositional ideologies fitting the late twentieth century. They would simply bewilder anyone not preoccupied with the machines and consciousness of late capitalism. In that sense they are part of the cyborg world. But there are also great riches for feminists in explicitly embracing the possibilities inherent in the breakdown of clean distinctions between organism and machine and similar distinctions structuring the Western self. It is the simultaneity of breakdowns that cracks the matrices of domination and opens geometric possibilities. What might be learned from personal and political "technological" pollution? I will look briefly at two overlapping groups of texts for their insight into the construction of a potentially helpful cyborg myth: constructions of women of color and monstrous selves in feminist science fiction.

Earlier I suggested that "women of color" might be understood as a cyborg identity, a potent subjectivity synthesized from fusions of outsider identities and in the complex political-historical layerings of Audre Lorde's "biomythography," *Zami*.[33] There are material and cultural grids mapping this potential. Lorde captures the tone in the title of her book *Sister Outsider*. In my political myth, Sister Outsider is the offshore woman, whom U.S. workers, female and feminized, are supposed to regard as the enemy preventing their solidarity, threatening their security. Onshore, inside the boundary of the United States, Sister Outsider is a potential amid the races and ethnic identities of women manipulated for division, competition, and exploitation in the same industries. "Women of color" are the preferred labor force for the science-based industries, the real women for whom the worldwide sexual market, labor market, and politics of reproduction kaleidoscope into daily life. Young Korean women hired in the sex industry and in electronics assembly are recruited from high schools, educated for the integrated circuit. Literacy, especially in English, distinguishes the "cheap" female labor so attractive to the multinationals.

Contrary to Orientalist stereotypes of the "oral primitive," literacy is a special mark of women of color, acquired by U.S. black women as well as men through a history of risking death to learn and to teach reading and writing. Writing has a special significance for all colonized groups. Writing has been crucial to the Western myth of the distinction of oral and written cultures, primitive and civilized mentalities, and more recently to the erosion of that distinction in postmodernist theories attacking the phallogocentrism of the West, with its worship of the monotheistic, phallic, authoritative, and singular work, the unique and perfect name.[34] Contests for the meanings of writing are a major form of contemporary political struggle. Releasing the play of writing is deadly serious. The poetry and stories of U.S. women of color are repeatedly about writing, about access to the power to signify, but this time that power must be neither phallic nor innocent. Cyborg writing must not be about the Fall, the imagination of a once-upon-a-time wholeness before language, before writing, before Man. Cyborg writing is about the power to survive not on the basis of original innocence, but on the basis of seizing the tools to mark the world that marked them as other.

The tools are often stories, retold stories, versions that reverse and displace the hierarchical dualisms of naturalized identities. In retelling origin stories, cyborg authors subvert the central myths of origin of Western culture. We have all been colonized by those origin myths, with their longing for fulfillment in apocalypse. The phallogocentric origin stories most crucial for feminist cyborgs are built into the literal technologies—technologies that write the world, biotechnology and microelectronics—that have recently textualized our bodies as code problems on the grid of C^3I. Feminist cyborg stories have the task of recoding communication and intelligence to subvert command and control.

Figuratively and literally, language politics pervade the struggles of women of color, and stories about language have a special power in the rich contemporary writing by U.S. women of color. For example, retellings of the story of the indigenous woman Malinche, mother of the mestizo "bastard" race of the new world, master of languages, and mistress of Cortés, carry special meaning for Chicana constructions of identity. Cherríe Moraga in *Loving in the War Years* explores the themes of identity when one never possessed the original language, never told the original story, never resided in the harmony of legitimate heterosexuality in the garden of culture, and so cannot base identity on a myth or a fall from innocence and right to natural names, mother's or father's.[35] Moraga's writing, her superb literacy, is presented in her poetry as the same kind of violation as Malinche's mastery of the conqueror's language—a violation, an illegitimate production, that allows survival. Moraga's language is not "whole"; it is self-consciously spliced, a chimera of English and Spanish, both conqueror's languages. But it is this chimeric monster, without claim to an original language before violation, that crafts the erotic, competent, potent identities of women of color. Sister Outsider hints at the possibility of world survival not because of her innocence, but because of her ability to live on the boundaries, to write without the founding myth of original wholeness, with its inescapable apocalypse of final return to a deathly oneness that Man has imagined to be the innocent and all-powerful Mother, freed at the End from another spiral of appropriation by her son. Writing marks Moraga's body, affirms it as the body of a woman of color, against the possibility of passing into the unmarked category of the Anglo father or into the Orientalist myth of "original illiteracy" of a mother that never was. Malinche was mother here, not Eve before eating the forbidden fruit. Writing affirms Sister Outsider, not the Woman-before-the-Fall-into-Writing needed by the phallogocentric Family of Man.

Writing is preeminently the technology of cyborgs, etched surfaces of the late twentieth century. Cyborg politics is the struggle for language and the struggle against perfect communication, against the one code that translates all meaning perfectly, the central dogma of phallogocentrism. That is why cyborg politics insist on noise and advocate pollution, rejoicing in the illegitimate fusions of animal and machine. These are the couplings which make Man and Woman so problematic, subverting the structure of desire, the force imagined to generate language and gender, and so subverting the structure and modes of reproduction of Western identity, of nature and culture, of mirror and eye, slave and master, body and mind. "We" did not originally choose to be cyborgs, but choice grounds a liberal politics and epistemology that imagines the reproduction of individuals before the wider replications of "texts."

From the perspective of cyborgs, freed of the need to ground politics in "our" privileged position of the oppression that incorporates all other dominations, the innocence of the merely violated, the ground of those closer to nature, we can see powerful possibilities. Feminisms and Marxisms have run aground of Western epistemological imperatives to construct a revolutionary subject from the perspective of a hierarchy of oppressions and a latent position of moral superiority, innocence, and greater closeness to nature. With no available original dream of a common language or original symbiosis promising protection from hostile "masculine" separation, but written into the play of a text that has no finally privileged reading or salvation history, to recognize "oneself" as fully implicated in the world, frees us of the need to root politics in identification, vanguard parties, purity, and mothering. Stripped of identity, the bastard race teaches about the power of the margins and the importance of a mother like Malinche. Women of color have transformed her from the evil mother of masculinist fear into the originally literate mother who teaches survival.

This is not just deconstruction but liminal transformation. Every story that begins with original innocence and privileges the return to wholeness imagines the drama of life to be individuation, separation, the birth of the self, the tragedy of autonomy, the fall into writing, alienation; that is, war, tempered by imaginary respite in the bosom of the Other. These plots are ruled by a reproductive politics—rebirth without flaw, perfection, abstraction. In this plot women are imagined either better or worse off, but all agree they have less selfhood, weaker individuation, more fusion to the oral, to Mother, less at stake in masculine autonomy. But there is another route to having less at stake in masculine autonomy, a route that does not pass through Woman, Primitive, Zero, the Mirror Stage and its imaginary. It passes through women and other present-tense, illegitimate cyborgs, not of Woman born, who refuse the ideological resources of victimization so as to have a real life. These cyborgs are the people who refuse to disappear on cue, no matter how many times a Western commentator remarks on the sad passing of another primitive, another organic group done in by Western technology, by writing.[36] These real-life cyborgs, for example, the Southeast Asian village women workers in Japanese and U.S. electronics firms described by Aihwa Ong, are actively rewriting the texts of their bodies and societies. Survival is the stakes in this play of readings.

To recapitulate, certain dualisms have been persistent in Western traditions; they have all been systemic to the logics and practices of domination of women, people of color, nature, workers, animals—in short, domination of all constituted as others, whose task is to mirror the self. Chief among these troubling dualisms are self/other, mind/body, culture/nature, male/female, civilized/primitive, reality/appearance, whole/part, agent/resource, maker/made, active/passive, right/wrong, truth/illusion, total/partial, God/man. The self is the One who is not dominated, who knows that by the service of the other; the other is the one who holds the future, who knows that by the experience of domination, which gives the lie to the autonomy of the self. To be One is to be autonomous, to be powerful, to be God; but to be One is to be an illusion and so to be involved in a dialectic of apocalypse with the other. Yet, to be other is to be multiple, without clear boundaries, frayed, insubstantial. One is too few, but two are too many.

High-tech culture challenges these dualisms in intriguing ways. It is not clear who makes and who is made in the relation between human and machine. It is not clear what is mind and what is body in machines that resolve into coding practices. Insofar as we know ourselves in both formal discourse (e.g., biology) and in daily practice, (e.g., the homework economy in the integrated circuit), we find ourselves to be cyborgs, hybrids, mosaics, chimeras. Biological organisms have become biotic systems, communications devices like others. There is no fundamental, ontological separation in our formal knowledge of machine and organism, of technical and organic. The replicant Rachel in the film *Blade Runner* stands as the image of a cyborg culture's fear, love, and confusion.

One consequence is that our sense of connection to our tools is heightened. The trance state experienced by many computer users has become a staple of science-fiction film and cultural jokes. Perhaps paraplegics and other severely handicapped people can (and sometimes do) have the most intense experiences of complex hybridization with other communication devices.[37] Anne McCaffrey's prefeminist *The Ship Who Sang* explored the consciousness of a cyborg, hybrid of girl's brain and complex machinery, formed after the birth of a severely handicapped child. Gender, sexuality, embodiment, skill: All were reconstituted in the story. Why should our bodies end at the skin or include at best other beings encapsulated by skin? From the seventeenth century till now, machines could be animated—given ghostly souls to make them speak or move or to account for their orderly development and mental capacities. Or organisms could be mechanized—reduced to body understood as resource of mind. These machine/organism relationships are obsolete, unnecessary. For us, in imagination and in other practice, machines can be prosthetic devices, intimate components, friendly selves. We don't need organic holism to give impermeable wholeness, the total woman and her feminist variants (mutants?). Let me conclude this point by a very partial reading of the logic of the cyborg monsters of my second group of texts, feminist science fiction.

The cyborgs populating feminist science fiction make very problematic the statuses of man or woman, human, artifact, member of a race, individual identity, or body. Katie King clarifies how pleasure in reading these fictions is not largely based on identification. Students facing Joanna Russ for the first time, students who have learned to take modernist writers like James Joyce or Virginia Woolf without flinching, do not know what to make of *Adventures of Alyx, The Female Man,* where characters refuse the reader's search for innocent wholeness while granting the wish for heroic quests, exuberant eroticism, and serious politics. *The Female Man* is the story of four versions of one genotype, all of whom meet, but even taken together do not make a whole, resolve the dilemmas of violent moral action, nor remove the growing scandal of gender. The feminist science fiction of Samuel Delany, especially *Tales of Neverÿon,* mocks stories of origin by redoing the neolithic revolution, replaying the founding moves of Western civilization to subvert their plausibility. James Tiptree, Jr., an author whose fiction was regarded as particularly manly until her "true" gender was revealed, tells tales of reproduction based on nonmammalian technologies like alternation of generations or male brood pouches and male nurturing. John Varley constructs a supreme cyborg in his archfeminist exploration of Gaea, a mad goddess-planet-trickster-old-woman-technological device on whose surface an extraordinary array of post cyborg symbioses are spawned. Octavia Butler writes of an African sorceress pitting her powers of transformation against the genetic manipulations of her rival (*Wild Seed*), of time warps that bring a modern U.S. black woman into slavery where her actions in relation to her white master-ancestor determine the possibility of her own birth (*Kindred*), and of the illegitimate insights into identity and community of an adopted cross-species child who came to know the enemy as self (*Survivor*). In her recent novel, *Dawn* (1987), the first installment of a series called *Xenogenesis,* Butler tells the story of Lilith Iyapo, whose personal name recalls Adam's first and repudiated wife and whose family name marks her status as the widow of the son of Nigerian immigrants to the United States. A black woman and a mother whose child is dead, Lilith mediates the transformation of humanity through genetic exchange with extraterrestrial lovers/rescuers/destroyers/genetic engineers, who reform earth's habitats after the nuclear holocaust and coerce surviving humans into intimate fusion with them. It is a novel that interrogates reproductive, linguistic, and nuclear politics in a mythic field structured by late twentieth-century race and gender.

Because it is particularly rich in boundary transgressions, Vonda McIntyre's *Superluminal* can close this truncated catalogue of promising and dangerous monsters who help redefine the pleasures and politics of embodiment and feminist writing. In a fiction where no character is "simply" human, human status is highly problematic. Orca, a genetically altered diver, can speak with killer whales and survive deep ocean conditions, but she longs to explore space as a pilot, necessitating bionic implants jeopardizing her kinship with the divers and cetaceans. Transformations are effected by virus vectors carrying a new developmental code, by transplant surgery, by implants of microelectronic devices, by analogue doubles, and by other means. Laenea becomes a pilot by accepting a heart implant and a host of other alterations allowing survival in transit at speeds exceeding that of light. Radu Dracul survives a virus-caused plague on his outerworld planet to find himself with a time sense that changes the boundaries of spatial perception for the whole species. All the characters explore the limits of language, the dream of communicating experience, and the necessity of limitation, partiality, and intimacy even in this world of protean transformation and connection. *Superluminal* stands also for the defining contradictions of a cyborg world in another sense; it embodies textually the intersection of feminist theory and colonial discourse in the science fiction I have alluded to in this essay. This is a conjunction with a long history that many first world feminists have tried to repress, including myself in my readings of *Superluminal* before being called to account by Zoe Sofoulis, whose different location in the world system's informatics of domination made her acutely alert to the imperialist moment of all science-fiction cultures, including women's science fiction. From an Australian feminist sensitivity, Sofoulis remembered more readily McIntyre's role as writer of the adventures of Captain Kirk and Spock in "Star Trek" than her rewriting the romance in *Superluminal.*

Monsters have always defined the limits of community in Western imaginations. The centaurs and Amazons of ancient Greece established the limits of the centered polis of the Greek male human by their disruption of marriage and boundary pollutions of the warrior with animality and woman. Unseparated twins and hermaphrodites were the confused human material in early modern France who grounded discourse on the natural and supernatural, medical and legal, portents and diseases—all crucial to establishing modern identity.[38] The evolutionary and behavioral sciences of monkeys and apes have marked the multiple boundaries of late twentieth-century industrial identities. Cyborg monsters in feminist science fiction define quite different political possibilities and limits from those proposed by the mundane fiction of Man and Woman.

There are several consequences to taking seriously the imagery of cyborgs as other than our enemies. Our bodies, ourselves—bodies are maps of power and identity. Cyborgs are no exceptions. A cyborg body is not innocent; it was not born in a garden; it does not seek unitary identity and so generates antagonistic dualisms without end (or until the world ends); it takes irony for granted. One is too few, and two is only one possibility. Intense pleasure in skill, machine skill, ceases to be a sin, but an aspect of embodiment. The machine is not an it to be animated, worshiped, and dominated. The machine is us, our processes, an aspect of our embodiment. We can be responsible for machines; they do not dominate or threaten us. We are responsible for boundaries; we are they. Up till now (once upon a time), female embodiment seemed to be given, organic, necessary; female embodiment seemed to mean skill in mothering and its metaphoric extensions. Only by being out of place could we take intense pleasure in machines and then with excuses that this was organic activity after all, appropriate to females. Cyborgs might consider more seriously the partial, fluid, sometimes aspect of sex and sexual embodiment. Gender might not be global identity after all, even if it has profound historical breadth and depth.

The ideologically charged question of what counts as daily activity, as experience, can be approached by exploiting the cyborg image. Feminists have recently claimed that women are given to dailiness, that women more than men somehow sustain daily life, and so have a privileged epistemological position potentially. There is a compelling aspect to this claim, one that makes visible unvalued female activity and names it as the ground of life. But the ground of life? What about all the ignorance of women, all the exclusions and failures of knowledge and skill? What about men's access to daily competence, to knowing how to build things, to take them apart, to play? What about other embodiments? Cyborg gender is a local possibility taking a global vengeance. Race, gender, and capital require a cyborg theory of wholes and parts. There is no drive in cyborgs to produce total theory, but there is an intimate experience of boundaries, their construction and deconstruction. There is a myth system waiting to become a political language to ground one way of looking at science and technology and challenging the informatics of domination—in order to act potently.

I would rather be a cyborg than a goddess.

One last image: organisms and organismic, holistic politics depend on metaphors of rebirth and invariably call on the resources of reproductive sex. I would suggest that cyborgs have more to do with regeneration and are suspicious of the reproductive matrix and of most birthing. For salamanders, regeneration after injury, such as the loss of a limb, involves regrowth of structure and restoration of function with the constant possibility of twinning or other odd topographical productions at the site of former injury. The regrown limb can be monstrous, duplicated, potent. We have all been injured, profoundly. We require regeneration, not rebirth, and the possibilities for our reconstitution include the utopian dream of the hope for a monstrous world without gender.

Cyborg imagery can help express two crucial arguments in this essay: (1) the production of universal, totalizing theory is a major mistake that misses most of reality, probably always, but certainly now; (2) taking responsibility for the social relations of science and technology means refusing an anti-science metaphysics, a demonology of technology, and so means embracing the skillful task of reconstructing the boundaries of daily life, in partial connection with others, in communication with all of our parts. It is not just that science and technology are possible means of great human satisfaction, as well as a matrix of complex dominations. Cyborg imagery can suggest a way out of the maze of dualisms in which we have explained our bodies and our tools to ourselves. This is a dream not of a common language, but of a powerful infidel heteroglossia. It is an imagination of a feminist speaking in tongues to strike fear into the circuits of the super savers of the New Right. It means both building and destroying machines, identities, categories, relationships, spaces, stories. Although both are bound in the spiral dance, I would rather be a cyborg than a goddess.

■ ACKNOWLEDGMENTS

Research was funded by an Academic Senate Faculty Research Grant from the University of California, Santa Cruz. An earlier version of this chapter, on genetic engineering, appeared as "Lieber Kyborg als Göttin: Für eine sozialistisch-feministische Unterwanderung der Gentechnologie," in Bernd-Peter Lange and Anna Marie Stuby, eds., (Berlin: Argument-Sonderband 105, 1984), pp. 66–84. The cyborg manifesto grew from "New Machines, New Bodies, New Communities: Political Dilemmas of a Cyborg Feminist," The Scholar and the Feminist X: The Question of Technology Conference, April 1983.

The people associated with the History of Consciousness Board of University of California, Santa Cruz, have had an enormous influence on this essay, so that it feels collectively authored more than most, although those I cite may not recognize their ideas. In particular, members of graduate and undergraduate feminist theory, science and politics, and theory and methods courses have contributed to the cyborg manifesto. Particular debts here are due Hilary Klein ("Marxism, Psychoanalysis, and Mother Nature"); Paul Edwards ("Border Wars: The Science and Politics of Artificial Intelligence"); Lisa Lowe ("Julia Kristeva's *Des Chinoises:* Representing Cultural and Sexual Others"); Jim Clifford, "On Ethnographic Allegory," in James Clifford and George E. Marcus, eds., *Writing Culture, the Poetics and Politics of Ethnography* (University of California Press, 1985), pp. 98–121.

Parts of the chapter were my contribution to a collectively developed session, Poetic Tools and Political Bodies: Feminist Approaches to High Technology Culture, 1984 California American Studies Association, with History of Consciousness graduate students Zoe Sofoulis, "Jupiter Space"; Katie King, "The Pleasures of Repetition and the Limits of Identification in Feminist Science Fiction: Reimaginations of the Body after the Cyborg"; and Chela Sandoval, "The Construction of Subjectivity and Oppositional Consciousness in Feminist Film and Video." Sandoval's theory of oppositional consciousness was published as "Women Respond to Racism: A Report on the National Women's Studies Association Conference," Center for Third World Organizing, Oakland, California, n.d. For Sofoulis's semiotic-psychoanalytic readings of nuclear culture, see Z. Sofia, "Exterminating Fetuses: Abortion, Disarmament and the Sexo-Semiotics of Extraterrestrialism," Nuclear Criticism issue, *Diacritics,* Vol 14, No. 2, 1984, pp. 47–59. King's manuscripts ("Questioning Tradition: Canon Formation and the Veiling of Power"; "Gender and Genre: Reading the Science Fiction of Joanna Russ"; "Varley's Titan and Wizard: Feminist Parodies of Nature, Culture, and Hardware") deeply inform the cyborg manifesto.

Barbara Epstein, Jeff Escoffier, Rusten Hogness, and Jaye Miler gave extensive discussion and editorial help. Members of the Silicon Valley Research Project of the University of California, Santa Cruz and participants in conferences and workshops sponsored by SVRP (Silicon Valley Research Project) have been very important, especially Rick Gordon, Linda Kimball, Nancy Snyder, Langdon Winner, Judith Stacey, Linda Lim, Patricia Fernandez-Kelly, and Judith Gregory. Finally, I want to thank Nancy Hartsock for years of friendship and discussion on feminist theory and feminist science fiction. I also thank Elizabeth Bird for my favorite political button: Cyborgs for Earthly Survival.

■ NOTES

1. Useful references to left and/or feminist radical science movements and theory and to biological/biotechnological issues include Ruth Bleier, *Science and Gender: A Critique of Biology and Its Themes on Women* (New York: Pergamon, 1984); Ruth Bleier, ed., *Feminist Approaches to Science* (New York: Pergamon, 1986); Sandra Harding, *The Science Question in Feminism* (Ithaca, NY: Cornell University Press, 1986); Anne Fausto-Sterling, *Myths of Gender* (New York: Basic Books, 1985): Stephen J. Gould, *Mismeasure of Man* (New York: Norton, 1981); Ruth Hubbard, Mary Sue Henifin, Barbara Fried, eds., *Biological Woman, the Convenient Myth* (Cambridge, MA: Schenkman, 1982); Evelyn Fox Keller, *Reflections on Gender and Science* (New Haven, CT: Yale University Press, 1985); R. C. Lewontin, Steve Rose, and Leon Kamin, *Not in Our Genes* (New York: Pantheon, 1984); *Radical Science Journal* (from 1987, *Science as Culture*), 26 Freegrove Road, London N7 9RQ; *Science for the People,* 897 Main St., Cambridge, MA 02139.

2. Starting points for left and/or feminist approaches to technology and politics include Ruth Schwartz Cowan, *More Work for Mother: The Ironies of Household Technology from the Open Hearth to the Microwave* (New York: Basic Books, 1983); Joan Rothschild, *Machina ex Dea: Feminist Perspectives on Tech-*

nology (New York: Pergamon, 1983); Sharon Traweek, *Beantimes and Life-times: The World of High Energy Physics* (Cambridge, MA: Harvard University Press, 1988); R. M. Young and Les Levidov, eds., *Science, Technology, and the Labour Process,* Vols. 1–3 (London: CSE Books); Joseph Weizenbaum, *Computer Power and Human Reason* (San Francisco: Freeman, 1976); Langdon Winner, *Autonomous Technology: Technics Out of Control as a Theme in Political Thought* (Cambridge, MA: MIT Press, 1977); Langdon Winner, *The Whale and the Reactor* (Chicago: Chicago University Press, 1986); Jan Zimmerman, ed., *The Technological Woman: Interfacing with Tomorrow* (New York: Praeger, 1983); Tom Athanasiou, "High-tech Politics. The Case of Artificial Intelligence," *Socialist Review,* No. 92, 1987, pp. 7–35; Carol Cohn, "Nuclear Language and How We Learned to Pat the Bomb," *Bulletin of Atomic Scientists,* June 1987, pp. 17–24; Terry Winograd and Fernando Flores, *Understanding Computers and Cognition: A New Foundation for Design* (New Jersey: Ablex, 1986); Paul Edwards, "Border Wars: The Politics of Artificial Intelligence," *Radical America,* Vol. 19, No. 6, 1985, pp. 39–52; *Global Electronics Newsletter,* 867 West Dana St., #204, Mountain View, CA 94041; *Processed World,* 55 Sutter St., San Francisco, CA 94104; *ISIS,* Women's International Information and Communication Service, P. O. Box 50 (Corhavin), 1211 Geneva 2, Switzerland, and Via Santa Maria dell'Anima 30, 00186 Rome, Italy. Fundamental approaches to modern social studies of science that do not continue the liberal mystification that it all started with Thomas Kuhn, include: Karin Knorr-Cetina, *The Manufacture of Knowledge* (Oxford: Pergamon. 1981); K. D. Knorr-Cetina and Michael Mulkay, eds., *Science Observed: Perspectives on the Social Study of Science* (Beverly Hills, CA: Sage, 1983); Bruno Latour and Steve Woolgar, *Laboratory Life: The Social Construction of Scientific Facts* (Beverly Hills, CA: Sage, 1979); Robert M. Young, "Interpreting the Production of Science," *New Scientist,* Vol. 29, March 1979, pp. 1026–1028. More is claimed than is known about room for contesting productions of science in the mythic/material space of "the laboratory"; the 1984 Directory of the Network for the Ethnographic Study of Science, Technology, and Organizations lists a wide range of people and projects crucial to better radical analysis; available from NESSTO, P. O. Box 11442, Stanford, CA 94305.

3. Fredric Jameson, "Post Modernism, or the Cultural Logic of Late Capitalism," *New Left Review,* July/August 1984, pp. 53–94. See Marjorie Perloff, " 'Dirty' Language and Scramble Systems," *Sulfur* Vol. 2, 1984, pp. 178–183; Kathleen Fraser, *Something (Even Human Voices) in the Foreground, a Lake* (Berkeley, CA: Kelsey St. Press, 1984). For feminist modernist/postmodernist cyborg writing, see *How(ever),* 871 Corbett Ave., San Francisco, CA 94131.

4. Frans de Waal, *Chimpanzee Politics: Power and Sex among the Apes* (New York: Harper & Row, 1982); Langdon Winner, "Do artifacts have politics?" *Daedalus* (Winter 1980): 121–136.

5. Jean Baudrillard, *Simulations,* trans. P. Foss, P. Patton, P. Beitchman (New York: Semiotext(e), 1983). Jameson ("Postmodernism," p. 66) points out that Plato's definition of the simulacrum is the copy for which there is no original, i.e., the world of advanced capitalism, of pure exchange. See *Dis-*

course 9, Spring/Summer 1987, for a special issue on technology (Cybernetics, Ecology, and the Postmodern Imagination).

6. Herbert Marcuse, *One-Dimensional Man* (Boston: Beacon Press, 1964); Carolyn Merchant, *Death of Nature* (San Francisco: Harper & Row, 1980).

7. Zoe Sofia, "Exterminating Fetuses," *Diacritics,* Vol. 14, No. 2, Summer 1984, pp. 47–59, and "Jupiter Space" (Pomona, CA: American Studies Association, 1984).

8. For ethnographic accounts and political evaluations, see Barbara Epstein, "The Politics of Prefigurative Community: The Non-Violent Direction Action Movement," *The Year Left,* forthcoming, and Noel Sturgeon, qualifying essay on feminism, anarchism, and nonviolent direct-action politics, University of California, Santa Cruz, 1986. Without explicit irony, adopting the spaceship earth/whole earth logo of the planet photographed from space, set off by the slogan "Love Your Mother," the May 1987 Mothers and Others Day action at the nuclear weapons testing facility in Nevada nonetheless took account of the tragic contradictions of views of the earth. Demonstrators applied for official permits to be on the land from officers of the Western Shoshone tribe, whose territory was invaded by the U.S. government when it built the nuclear weapons test ground in the 1950s. Arrested for trespassing, the demonstrators argued that the police and weapons facility personnel, without authorization from the proper officials, were the trespassers. One affinity group at the women's action called themselves the Surrogate Others, and in solidarity with the creatures forced to tunnel in the same ground with the bomb, they enacted a cyborgian emergence from the constructed body of a large, nonheterosexual desert worm.

9. Powerful developments of coalition politics emerge from "third world" speakers, speaking from nowhere, the displaced center of the universe, earth: "We live on the third planet from the sun"—*Sun Poem* by Jamaican writer Edward Kamau Braithwaite, review by Nathaniel Mackey, *Sulfur,* Vol. 2, 1984, pp. 200–205. *Home Girls,* ed. Barbara Smith (New York: Kitchen Table Women of Color Press, 1983), ironically subverts naturalized identities precisely while constructing a place from which to speak called home. See Bernice Reagan, "Coalition Politics, Turning the Century," pp. 356–368. Trinh T. Minh-ha, ed., "She, the Inappropriate/d Other," *Discourse* Vol. 8, Fall/Winter 1986–1987.

10. Chela Sandoval, "Dis-Illusionment and the Poetry of the Future: The Making of Oppositional Consciousness," Ph.D. qualifying essay, University of California, Santa Cruz, 1984.

11. Bell Hooks, *Ain't I a Woman?* (Boston: South End Press, 1981); Bell Hooks, *Feminist Theory: From Margin to Center* (Boston: South End Press, 1984); Gloria Hull, Patricia Bell Scott, and Barbara Smith, eds., *All the Women Are White, All the Men Are Black, But Some of Us Are Brave: Black Women's Studies* (Old Westbury, NY: Feminist Press, 1982). Toni Cade Bambara, *The Salt Eaters* (New York: Vintage/Random House, 1981), writes an extraordinary postmodernist novel, in which the women of

color theater group, The Seven Sisters, explores a form of unity. Elliott Butler-Evans, *Race, Gender, and Desire: Narrative Strategies and the Production of Ideology in the Fiction of Toni Cade Bambara, Toni Morrison and Alice Walker,* Ph.D. Dissertation, University of California, Santa Cruz, 1987.

12. On Orientalism in feminist works and elsewhere, see Lisa Lowe, "Orientation: Representations of Cultural and Sexual 'Others,' " Ph.D. thesis, University of California, Santa Cruz; Edward Said, *Orientalism* (New York: Pantheon, 1978). Chandra Talpade Mohanty, "Under Western Eyes: Feminist Scholarship and Colonial Discourse," *Boundry* Vol. 2, No. 12, and Vol. 3, No. 13, 1984, pp. 333–357; "Many Voices, One Chant: Black Feminist Perspectives," *Feminist Review,* Vol. 17, Autumn 1984.

13. Katie King has developed a theoretically sensitive treatment of the workings of feminist taxonomies as genealogies of power in feminist ideology and polemic: Katie King, "Canons without Innocence," Ph.D. thesis, University of California, Santa Cruz, 1987, and "The Situation of Lesbianism as Feminism's Magical Sign: Contests for Meaning in the U.S. Women's Movement, 1968–72," *Communication* Vol. 9, No. 1, 1985, pp. 65–91. King examines an intelligent, problematic example of taxonomizing feminisms to make a little machine producing the desired final position; Alison Jaggar, *Feminist Politics and Human Nature* (Totowa, NJ: Rowman & Allanheld, 1983). My caricature here of socialist and radical feminism is also an example.

14. The feminist standpoint argument has been developed by Jane Flax, "Political Philosophy and the Patriarchal Unconsciousness," *Discovering Reality,* ed. Sandra Harding and Merill Hintikka, (Dordrecht: Reidel, 1983); Sandra Harding, "The Contradictions and Ambivalence of a Feminist Science," ms.; Harding and Hintikka, *Discovering Reality;* Nancy Hartsock, *Money, Sex and Power* (New York: Longman, 1983) and "The Feminist Standpoint: Developing the Ground for a Specifically Feminist Historical Materialism," *Discovering Reality,* ed. S. Harding and M. Hintikka; Mary O'Brien, *The Politics of Reproduction* (New York: Routledge & Kegan Paul, 1981); Hilary Rose, "Hand, Brain, and Heart: A Feminist Epistemology for the Natural Sciences," *Signs,* Vol. 9, No. I, 1983, pp. 73–90; Dorothy Smith, "Women's Perspective as a Radical Critique of Sociology," *Sociological Inquiry,* Vol. 44, 1974, and "A Sociology of Women," *The Prism of Sex,* ed. J. Sherman and E. T. Beck, Madison, WI: University of Wisconsin Press, 1979. For rethinking theories of feminist materialism and feminist standpoint in response to criticism, see Chapter 7 in Harding, *The Science Question in Feminism,* op. cit. (note 1); Nancy Hartsock, "Rethinking Modernism: Minority versus Majority Theories," *Cultural Critique* 7 (1987): 187–206; Hilary Rose, "Women's Work: Women's Knowledge," *What is Feminism? A Re-examination,* ed. Juliet Mitchell and Ann Oakley (New York: Pantheon, 1986), pp. 161–183.

15. Catherine MacKinnon, "Feminism, Marxism, Method, and the State: An Agenda for Theory," *Signs,* Vol. 7, No. 3, Spring 1982, pp. 515–544. See also MacKinnon, *Feminism Unmodified* (Cambridge, MA: Harvard University Press, 1987). I make a category error in "modifying" MacKinnon's positions with the qualifier "radical," thereby generating my own reduc-

tive critique of extremely heterogeneous writing, which does explicitly use that label, by my taxonomically interested argument about writing which does not use the modifier and which brooks no limits and thereby adds to the various dreams of a common, in the sense of univocal, language for feminism. My category error was occasioned by an assignment to write from a particular taxonomic position which itself has a heterogeneous history, socialist feminism, for *Socialist Review.* A critique indebted to MacKinnon, but without the reductionism and with an elegant feminist account of Foucault's paradoxical conservatism on sexual violence (rape), is Teresa de Lauretis, "The Violence of Rhetoric: Considerations on Representation and Gender," *Semiotica,* Vol. 54, 1985, pp. 11–31, and Teresa de Lauretis, ed., *Feminist Studies/Critical Studies* (Bloomington: Indiana University Press, 1986). A theoretically elegant feminist social-historical examination of family violence, that insists on women's, men's, and children's complex agency without losing sight of the material structures of male domination, race, and class, is Linda Gordon, *Heroes of their own Lives* (New York: Viking, 1988).

16. My previous efforts to understand biology as a cybernetic command-control discourse and organisms as "natural-technical objects of knowledge" are "The High Cost of Information in Post-World War II Evolutionary Biology," *Philosophical Forum,* Vol. 13, Nos. 2–3, 1979, pp. 206–237; "Signs of Dominance: From a Physiology to a Cybernetics of Primate Society," *Studies in History of Biology,* Vol. 6, 1983, pp. 129–219; "Class, Race, Sex, Scientific Objects of Knowledge: A Socialist-Feminist Perspective on the Social Construction of Productive Knowledge and Some Political Consequences," *Women in Scientific and Engineering Professions,* ed. Violet Haas and Carolyn Perucci (Ann Arbor, MI: University of Michigan Press, 1984), pp. 212–229.

17. E. Rusten Hogness, "Why Stress? A Look at the Making of Stress, 1936–1956," available from the author, 4437 Mill Creek Rd., Healdsburg, CA 95448.

18. A left entry to the biotechnology debate: *Genewatch,* a Bulletin of the Committee for Responsible Genetics, 5 Doane St., 4th floor, Boston, MA 02109; Susan Wright, "Recombinant DNA Technology and Its Social Transformation, 1972–82," *Osiris,* 2nd series, Vol. 2, 1986, pp. 303–360 and "Recombinant DNA: The Status of Hazards and Controls," *Environment,* July/August 1982; Edward Yoxen, *The Gene Business* (New York: Harper & Row, 1983).

19. Paula Treichler, "AIDS, Homophobia, and Biomedical Discourse: An Epidemic of Signification," forthcoming in *Cultural Studies.*

20. Starting references for "women in the integrated circuit": *Scientific-Technological Change and the Role of Women in Development,* ed. Pamela D'Onofrio-Flores and Sheila M. Pfafflin (Boulder, CO: Westview Press, 1982); Maria Patricia Fernandez-Kelly, *For We Are Sold, I and My People* (Albany, NY: SUNY Press, 1983); Annette Fuentes and Barbara Ehrenreich, *Women in the Global Factory* (Boston: South End Press, 1983), with an especially useful list of resources and organizations; Rachael Grossman, "Women's Place in the Integrated

Circuit," *Radical America*, Vol. 14, No. 1, 1980, pp. 29–50; *Women and Men and the International Division of Labor*, ed. June Nash and M. P. Fernandez-Kelly (Albany, NY: SUNY Press, 1983); Aihwa Ong, "Japanese Factories, Malay Workers: Industrialization and the Cultural Construction of Gender in West Malaysia, *Power and Difference*, ed. Shelly Errington and Jane Atkinson (Palo Alto, CA: Stanford University Press, forthcoming); Aihwa Ong, *Spirits of Resistance and Capitalist Discipline: Factory Workers in Malaysia* (Albany, SUNY Press, 1987); *Science Policy Research Unity, Microelectronics and Women's Employment in Britain* (University of Sussex, 1982).

21. The best example is Bruno Latour, *Les Microbes: Guerre et Paix, suivi de Irréductions* (Paris: Métailié, 1984).

22. For the homework economy and some related arguments: Richard Gordon, "The Computerization of Daily Life, the Sexual Division of Labor, and the Homework Economy," paper delivered at the Silicon Valley Workshop Group conference, 1983; Richard Gordon and Linda Kimball, "High-Technology, Employment and the Challenges of Education," *SVRG Working Paper*, No. 1, July 1985; Judith Stacey, "Sexism by a Subtler Name? Postindustrial Conditions and Postfeminist Consciousness in the Silicon Valley," *Socialist Review*, no. 96, 1987, pp. 7–30; Women's Work, Men's Work, ed. Barbara F. Reskin and Heidi Hartmann (Washington, DC: National Academy of Sciences Press, 1986); *Signs*, Vol. 10, No. 2, 1984, special issue on women and poverty; Stephen Rose, *The American Profile Poster: Who Owns What, Who Makes How Much, Who Works Where, and Who Lives With Whom?* (New York: Pantheon, 1986); Patricia Hill Collins, "Third World Women in America," and Sara G. Burr, "Women and Work," ed. Barbara K. Haber, *The Women's Annual, 1981* (Boston: G. K. Hall, 1982); Judith Gregory and Karen Nussbaum, "Race against Time: Automation of the Office," *Office: Technology and People*, Vol. 1, 1982, pp. 197–236; Frances Fox Piven and Richard Cloward, *The New Class War: Reagan's Attack on the Welfare State and Its Consequences* (New York: Pantheon, 1982); Microelectronics Group, *Microelectronics: Capitalist Technology and the Working Class* (London: CSE, 1980); Karin Stallard, Barbara Ehrenreich, and Holly Sklar, *Poverty in the American Dream* (Boston: South End Press, 1983) including a useful organization and resource list.

23. Rae Lessor Blumberg, "A General Theory of Sex Stratification and Its Application to the Position of Women in Today's World Economy," paper delivered to Sociology Board, University of California, Santa Cruz, February 1983. Also R. L. Blumberg, *Stratification: Socioeconomic and Sexual Inequality* (Boston: Brown, 1981). See also Sally Hacker, "Doing It the Hard Way: Ethnographic Studies in the Agribusiness and Engineering Classroom," California American Studies Association, Pomona, 1984, forthcoming in *Humanity and Society;* S. Hacker and Lisa Bovit, Agriculture to Agribusiness: Technical Imperatives and Changing Roles," *Proceedings of the Society for the History of Technology, Milwaukee*, 1981; Lawrence Busch and William Lacy, *Science, Agriculture, and the Politics of Research* (Boulder, CO: Westview Press, 1983); Denis Wilfred, "Capital and Agriculture, a Review of Marxian Problematics," *Studies in Political Economy*, No. 7, 1982,

pp. 127–154; Carolyn Sachs, *The Invisible Farmers: Women in Agricultural Production* (Totowa, NJ: Rowman & Allanheld, 1983). International Fund for Agricultural Development, IFAD Experience Relating to Rural Women, 1977–84 (Rome: IFAD, 1985), 37 pp. Thanks to Elizabeth Bird, "Green Revolution Imperialism," I & II, ms. University of California, Santa Cruz, 1984.

24. Cynthia Enloe, "Women Textile Workers in the Militarization of Southeast Asia," *Women and Men,* ed. Nash and Fernandez-Kelly; Rosalind Petchesky, "Abortion, Anti-Feminism, and the Rise of the New Right," *Feminist Studies,* Vol. 7, No. 2, 1981. Cynthia Enloe, *Does Khaki Become You? The Militarization of Women's Lives* (Boston: South End Press, 1983).

25. For a feminist version of this logic, see Sarah Blaffer Hrdy, *The Woman That Never Evolved* (Cambridge, MA: Harvard University Press, 1981). For an analysis of scientific women's story-telling practices, especially in relation to sociobiology, in evolutionary debates around child abuse and infanticide, see Donna Haraway, "The Contest for Primate Nature: Daughters of Man the Hunter in the Field, 1960–80," *The Future of American Democracy,* ed. Mark Kann (Philadelphia: Temple University Press, 1983), pp. 175–208. See also D. Haraway, *Primate Visions: Gender, Race, and Nature in the World of Modern Science* (New York: Routledge, 1989).

26. For the moment of transition of hunting with guns to hunting with cameras in the construction of popular meanings of nature for an American urban immigrant public, see Donna Haraway, "Teddy Bear Patriarchy," *Social Text,* No. 11, Winter 1984–1985, pp. 20–64; Roderick Nash, "The Exporting and Importing of Nature: Nature-Appreciation as a Commodity, 1850–1980," *Perspectives in American History,* Vol. 3, 1979, pp. 517–560; Susan Sontag, *On Photography* (New York: Dell, 1977); and Douglas Preston, "Shooting in Paradise," *Natural History,* Vol. 93, No. 12, December 1984, pp. 14–19.

27. For crucial guidance for thinking about the political/cultural implications of the history of women doing science in the United States see *Women in Scientific and Engineering Professions,* ed. Violet Haas and Carolyn Perucci (Ann Arbor, MI: University of Michigan Press, 1984); Sally Hacker, "The Culture of Engineering: Women, Workplace, and Machine," *Women's Studies International Quarterly,* Vol. 4, No. 3, 1981, pp. 341–353; Evelyn Fox Keller, *A Feeling for the Organism* (San Francisco: Freeman, 1983); National Science Foundation, *Women and Minorities in Science and Engineering* (Washington, DC: NSF, 1988); Margaret Rossiter, *Women Scientists in America* (Baltimore, MD: Johns Hopkins University Press, 1982); Londa Schiebinger, "The History and Philosophy of Women in Science: A Review Essay," *Signs,* Vol. 12, No. 2, 1987, pp. 305–332.

28. John Markoff and Lenny Siegel, "Military Micros," University of California, Santa Cruz, Silicon Valley Research Project conference, 1983. High Technology Professionals for Peace and Computer Professionals for Social Responsibility are promising organizations.

29. Katie King, "The Pleasure of Repetition and the Limits of Identification in Feminist Science Fiction: Reimaginations of the Body after the Cyborg," California American Studies Association, Pomona, 1984. An abbreviated list of feminist science fiction underlying themes of this essay: Octavia Butler, *Wild Seed, Mind of My Mind, Kindred, Survivor*; Suzy McKee Charnas, *Motherlines*; Samuel Delany, *Tales of Neverÿon*; Anne McCaffery, *The Ship Who Sang, Dinosaur Planet*; Vonda McIntyre, *Superluminal, Dreamsnake*; Joanna Russ, *Adventures of Alyx, The Female Man*; James Tiptree, Jr., *Star Songs of an Old Primate, Up the Walls of the World*; John Varley, *Titan, Wizard, Demon.*

30. Mary Douglas, *Purity and Danger* (London: Routledge & Kegan Paul, 1966), *Natural Symbols* (London: Cresset Press, 1970).

31. French feminisms contribute to cyborg heteroglossia. Carolyn Burke, "Irigaray through the Looking Glass," *Feminist Studies,* Vol. 7, No. 2, Summer 1981, pp. 288–306; Luce Irigaray, *Ce sexe qui n'en est pas un* (Paris: Minuit, 1977); L. Irigaray, *Et l'une ne bouge pas sans l'autre* (Paris: Minuit, 1979); *New French Feminisms,* ed. Elaine Marks and Isabelle de Courtivron (Amherst, MA: University of Massachusetts Press, 1980); *Signs,* Vol. 7, No. 1, Autumn 1981, special issue on French feminism; Monique Wittig, *The Lesbian Body,* trans. David LeVay (New York: Avon, 1975; *Le corps lesbien,* 1973). See especially *Feminist Issues: A Journal of Feminist Social and Political Theory,* 1 (1980), and Claire Duchen, *Feminism in France: From May '68 to Mitterand* (London: Routledge & Kegan, Paul, 1986).

32. But all these poets are very complex, not least in treatment of themes of lying and erotic, decentered collective and personal identities. Susan Griffin, *Women and Nature: The Roaring Inside Her* (New York: Harper & Row, 1978); Audre Lorde, *Sister Outsider* (Trumansburg, NY: Crossing Press, 1984); Adrienne Rich, *The Dream of a Common Language* (New York: Norton, 1978).

33. Audre Lorde, *Zami, a New Spelling of my Name* (Trumansburg, NY: Crossing Press, 1983); Katie King, "Audre Lorde: Layering History/Constructing Poetry," Canons without Innocence, Ph.D. thesis, University of California, Santa Cruz, 1987.

34. Jacques Derrida, *Of Grammatology,* trans. and introd. G. C. Spivak (Baltimore, MD: Johns Hopkins University Press, 1976), especially part II, "Nature, Culture, Writing"; Claude Lévi-Strauss, *Tristes Tropiques,* trans. John Russell (New York: Criterion Books, 1961), especially "The Writing Lesson"; Henry Louis Gates, "Writing 'Race' and the Difference It Makes," in "Race," Writing and Difference, special issue of *Critical Inquiry,* Vol. 12, No. 1, Autumn 1985, pp. 1–20; *Cultures in Contention,* ed. Douglas Kahn and Diane Neumaier, (Seattle: Real Comet Press, 1985); Walter Ong, *Orality and Literacy: The Technologizing of the Word* (New York: Methuen, 1982); Cheris Kramarae and Paula Treichler, *A Feminist Dictionary* (Boston: Pandora, 1985).

35. Cherrie Moraga, *Loving in the War Years* (Boston: South End Press, 1983). The sharp relation of women of color to writing as theme and politics can be approached through "The Black Woman and the Diaspora: Hidden Connections and Extended Acknowledgments," An International Literacy Conference, Michigan State University, October 1985; *Black Women Writers: A Critical Evaluation,* ed. Mari Evans (Garden City, NY: Doubleday/Anchor, 1984); Barbara Christian, *Black Feminist Criticism* (New York: Pergamon, 1985); *The Third Woman: Minority Women Writers of the United States,* ed. Dexter Fisher (Boston: Houghton Mifflin, 1980); several issues of *Frontiers,* especially vol. 5, 1980, "Chicanas en el Ambiente Nacional" and Vol. 7, 1983, "Feminisms in the Non-Western World"; Maxine Hong Kingston, *China Men* (New York: Knopf, 1977); *Black Women in White America: A Documentary History,* ed. Gerda Lemer (New York: Vintage, 1973); Paula Giddings, *When and Where I Enter: The Impact of Black Women on Race and Sex in America* (Toronto: Bantam, 1985); *This Bridge Called My Back: Writings by Radical Women of Color,* ed. Cherrie Moraga and Gloria Anzaldua (Watertown, MA: Persephone, 1981); *Sisterhood Is Global,* ed. Robin Morgan (Garden City, NY: Anchor/Doubleday, 1984). The writing of white women has had similar meanings: Sandra Gilbert and Susan Gubar, *The Madwoman in the Attic* (New Haven, CT: Yale University Press, 1979); Joanna Russ, *How to Suppress Women's Writing* (Austin, TX: University of Texas Press, 1983).

36. James Clifford argues persuasively for recognition of continuous cultural reinvention, the stubborn nondisappearance of those "marked" by Western imperializing practices; see "On Ethnographic Allegory," Clifford and Marcus, *op. cit.* (acknowledgments), and "On Ethnographic Authority," *Representations,* Vol. 1, No. 2 (1983), pp. 118–146.

37. The convention of ideologically taming militarized high technology by publicizing its applications to speech and motion problems of the disabled-differently abled takes on a special irony in monotheistic, patriarchal, and frequently anti-Semitic culture when computer-generated speech allows a boy with no voice to chant the Haftorah at his bar mitzvah. See Vic Sussman, "Personal Technology Lends a Hand," *Washington Post Magazine,* Nov. 9, 1986, pp. 45–46. Making the always context-relative social definitions of "abledness" particularly clear, military high-tech has a way of making human beings disabled by definition, a perverse aspect of much automated battlefield and Star Wars R&D. See John Noble Welford, "Pilot's Helmet Helps Interpret High Speed World," *New York Times,* July 1, 1986, pp. 21, 24.

38. Page DuBois, *Centaurs and Amazons* (Ann Arbor, MI: University of Michigan Press, 1982); Lorraine Daston and Katharine Park, "Hermaphrodites in Renaissance France," ms., n.d.; Katharine Park and Lorraine Daston, "Unnatural Conceptions: The Study of Monsters in 16th and 17th Century France and England," *Past and Present,* No. 92, August 1981, pp. 20–54. The word *monster* shares its root with the verb *to demonstrate.*

Questions and
Suggestions for
Further Study on
the Net/WWW

■ QUESTIONS BASED ON THE READINGS:

1. If you know something about punk music or cyberpunk anything, do you find that Philip Elmer-Dewitt in his *Time* magazine article oversimplifies or misinterprets the counterculture movement? What are the major differences between the counterculture movement of the 1960s and that of the 1970s, '80s, and '90s? Given that this article is written in the form of a history, what does history mean to cyberpunks? What does technology mean to cyberpunks? Freedom? The value of the individual versus that of the masses?

2. Is Billy Idol just another tired rocker attempting to find renewed success in cyberpunk technology, or is he contributing to a counterculture just as the cyberpunks are? What do you make of the reporting of Idol's bad bike accident? The showing of the scars on his leg? His recuperation period? If you have not already, listen to his CD *Cyberpunk.* How would you characterize the music and the lyrics?

3. R. U. Sirius reports what Gareth Branwyn has to say about the cyberpunk worldview: "Access to computers . . . should be unlimited and total"; "always yield to the hands-on imperative"; "mistrust authority"; etc. Given your values, how do you interpret this worldview? If you are against it, why do you think you are? Do you see value in this worldview nonetheless? or is it just bad anarchy? Do you find, perhaps, that though you might find the cyberpunk worldview nihilistic, you do nonetheless admire aspects of the value system? If so, what might they be? If you, however, completely or in great part, identify with cyberpunks, then why? Are they by now a thing of the past? Why trust the authority of such thinkers as R. U. Sirius and Timothy Leary? What does "Surf the Edges" mean? Is a hacker a cyberpunk?

4. Timothy Leary speaks of getting control of your own life. Do you find Leary's claim—based on the etymology of the Greek word *kubernetes* (pilot) into the Latin word *gubernare* (controller)—credible in having an influence on our lives today? And what about the credibility of his reference to the terms *freelance* and *mavericks*? Had you heard of Leary before reading him here? If

so, has reporting by the popular media made it difficult to take Leary and his claims very seriously? Or have you accepted everything that you have heard through the media about him? What do you make of the legend of the ronin? Could you base your life on such a worldview? If not the ronin, do you base your life on another legend or image or personage that stands for individuality? For TFYQA: that is, *Think for yourself; question authority?* What are your thoughts on Leary's four stages of development in his chart "Evolution of Countercultures"? Do you identify with any one of these stages?

5. What does Bey mean by the Web ("counter-Net")? What is a TAZ? What does Bey mean when he says: "The Net will be damaged by chaos, while the Web may thrive on it"? Also, what does he mean when he says: "Because the TAZ is an intensification, a surplus, an excess, a potlatch, life spending itself in living rather than merely surviving (that snivelling shibboleth of the eighties), it cannot be defined either by Tech or anti-Tech"? What is a Mandelbrot Set? Why does Bey use this notion in distinguishing between the Net and the Web (counter-Net)?

6. What is a cyborg? Leary speaks of designer reality and identity. Is a cyborg, as Haraway speaks of it, similar to Leary's notion of designer reality? Other cyberpunks' notions? Haraway writes: "A cyborg world is about the final imposition of a grid of control on the planet," and: "A cyborg world might be about lived social and bodily realities in which people are not afraid of their joint kinship with animals and machines, not afraid of permanently partial identities and contradictory standpoints." What does she mean by these statements? How does cyborg feminism parallel cyberpunk thinking? What does Haraway mean by "the informatics of domination"? Does such an informatics parallel anything that Branwyn or Leary have to say about a cyberpunk worldview? What is cyborg writing? Cyborg politics? What does Haraway mean when she says: "I would rather be a cyborg than a goddess"? Who are the female science-fiction writers that Haraway mentions? Could they be classified as cyberpunk SF writers?

■ FURTHER STUDY ON THE NET/WWW:

Let's make some searches using the Web. (If you need help with these search engines, turn to Appendix A.)

• *WebCrawler* <http://webcrawler.com/> search for Cyberpunk:

WebCrawler Search Results

The query "cyberpunk" found 233 documents and returned 25:

1000 The alt.cyberpunk FAQ has moved
0684 william gibson
0584 Cyberpunk Home Page
0474 CYBERPUNK: 2020—"Into Harms Way Again . . ."
0261 Cyberpunk and Cypherpunk Info on the Web
0237 alt.cyberpunk FAQ list

```
0201 links galore
0172 Andreas Ehrencrona's Home Page
0161 Dave's RPG Projects Page
0151 Malcolm McLaren, LE GRAND AMATEUR
0142 Cyberpunk 2020 Web Archive
0113 Dan's Web Site from Hell
0099 Navigating The Internet
```

- *CMU Lycos:* The Catalog of the Internet <http://lycos.cs.cmu.edu />:
  Search for "Cyborg."

```
LYCOS SEARCH: CYBORG

Load average: 0.28: Lycos June 28, 1995 catalog, 434620
unique URLs (see Lycos News)

Found 157 documents matching at least one search term. Print-
ing only the first 15 of 157 documents with at least scores
of 0.010.

Matching words (number of documents): cyborg (67),
cyborganic (49), cyborganics (3), cyborgasm (3),
cyborgasmic (16), cyborged (1), cyborgfilm (2), cybor-
girl (1), cyborgs (24), cyborgsmall (1)
```

- *The English Server* (CMU) <http://english-www.hss.cmu.edu/>: In the
  topical list, you will find

```
Sterling,
Cyberpunk From . . .,
Cyberpunk Archives,
Maddox essay (Tom Maddox, "After the Deluge: Cyberpunk in the
'80s and '90s").
```

- *Electronic Frontier Foundation* <http://www.eff.org/>. Search under
  Archives then under either *Topical Index* or *FTP Archive Top Level* and then
  the directory *Netculture,* where you will find *Cyberpunk* (a caveat: things get
  moved around, so if you do not find these specific instructions still work,
  it will be necessary to search through both the archives and ftp site and a
  variety of categories; originally cyberpunk had its own category in the
  archives and then was moved to *Netculture*):

```
Files in this Archive

baudy_world_of_byte_ban.article "A Postmodernist Interpreta-
tion of the Computer Underground," by Gordon Meyer and Jim
Thomas, is a sociological analysis of the computer underground
which takes a more sympathetic than usual look at the members
and actions of the computer underground.
cpunk_as_counterculture.article Fascinating article by Seeker1
examining the cyberpunk phenomenon and analyzing the appropri-
ateness of assigning the "counterculture" label to cyberpunks.
```

culture_jamming.article Article by Seeker1 about culture jamming, sabotaging advertising campaigns to point out the flawed reasoning encouraged by advertisers.

cyber_net.biblio List of books and articles about cyberspace, cyberpunk, electronic communications and other related ideas.

cyberpunk_terminal_chic.article Article by Nathan Cobb, from the *Boston Globe*, about cyberpunk culture, specifically the differences between hackers and punks, how the two cultures merged, and the resulting cyberculture.

feminism_and_cyberpunk.article Brief article about feminism in cyberspace and how it differs from "mainstream" feminism.

philip_dick.article Article by Seeker1 about author Philip K. Dick and his role in shaping the cyberpunk genre. Pretty weird.

slacker_manifesto.article To describe this article by Seeker1 (using his real name) would be to violate the principles espoused therein. Read it.

subculture_and_cpunk.article An examination of post–WWII subcultures that places the cyberpunk culture in an historical context.

subdirectory

Bruce Sterling Directory of things written by or about Bruce Sterling.

William Gibson Directory of things written by or about William Gibson.

■ HERE ARE SOME ADDITIONAL ON-LINE NETWORKS (WEBSITES, WITH DISCUSSION LISTS MENTIONED):

- *Cyberpunk:* <http://www.cs.uidaho.edu/lal/cyberspace/cyberpunk/cyberpunk.html>. Cyberpunk as Literary Genre and as a Social Movement (hackers, cyberpunks, ravers).

- *Unofficial Cyberpunk Home Page:* <http://rohan.sdsu.edu/home/vanzoest/www/cyberpunk/>.

- *World Wide Punk—Links to PUNK* sites all over the world, about everything punk (e-zines, music, etc.) <http://wchat.on.ca/vic/wwp.htm>

- *alt.cyberpunk FAQ list* <http://bush.cs.tamu.edu/~erich/alt.cp.faq.html>

- *Usenets:* for example,
  alt.cyberpunk (high-tech low-life)
  alt.cyberpunk.chatsubo (literary virtual reality in a cyberpunk hangout)
  alt.cyberpunk.movement
  alt.cyberpunk.tech (cyberspace and cyberpunk technology)
  alt.rave
  sci.virtual-worlds

- *Hakim Bey's Homepage:* <http://www.uio.no/~mwatz/bey/index.html>. This is an excellent homepage with much information in the form of a virtual copy of TAZ, many of Bey's papers, and a recorded interview with Bey.

- *William Gibson's Homepage:* <http://sfbox.vt.edu:10021/J/jfoley/gibson/gibson.html>.

- *Cyberanthropology* ("the study of human beings in virtual communities and networked environments"): <http://www.clas.ufl.edu/anthro/cyberanthro/frontdoor.html>. Also see Electronic Frontier Foundation for this topic and archives <http://www.eff.org/pub/Net_culture/Cyborg_anthropology/>.

- *Donna Haraway and the Cyborg:* <http://www.stg.brown.edu/projects/hypertext/landow/SSPCluster/Haraway.html>. This is a collection of links to sites developed by students in one of George P. Landow's classes on hypertext, who obviously worked on Haraway's concept of the cyborg. Unfortunately, much at this site has been disconnected; I include it, however, because at this point it still has lots of interesting information and allows you to see what a collaborative project might look like. Understand that there are many class projects out on the WWW, but they often stay for only a little while and then are discarded. (For a few of Landow's and his students' standing projects, see Questions and Further Suggestions in Chapter 4. You may also want to take a look at Diane Greco's work on cyborgs, to be published by Eastgate Systems <http://www.eastgate.com/>.)

- *Extropians and Other Transhumans* <http://www.c2.org/~arkuat/extr>. More on cyborgs. For an article on the extropians, set your browser to *HotWired* <http://hotwired.com/Login/>. Once in the site, point down to or click on *Overview* and then down to *Back Issues* and down again to *Issue 2.10—October '94,* article "Meet the Extropians!"

- *Transhumanist Texts* <http://www.nada.kth.se/~nv91-asa/trans.html>. More about extropians. There are a number of interesting links on human beings becoming machines.

- *Sandy Stone's Homepage* (Allucquere Rosanne [Sandy] Stone): <http://www.actlab.utexas.edu/~sandy/>. Here you will find designer personal and public reality by way of cyborgisms and performance theory. Stone has written *The War of Desire and Technology at the Close of the Mechanical Age* (MIT Press, 1995).

■ MORE REFERENCES FOR READING
AND FOR SURFING THE WEB:

Bey, Hakim. *T. A. Z.: The Temporary Autonomous Zone, Ontological Anarchy, Poetic Terrorism.* New York: Autonomedia, 1985. Online. Internet. 22 August 1995. Available: <http://www.uio.no/~mwatz/bey/taz/taz_contents.html>.

Bukatman, Scott. *Terminal Identity: The Virtual Subject in Post-Modern Science Fiction.* Durham, NC: Duke University Press, 1993.

Burroughs, William S. *Electronic Revolution.* n.p., West Germany: Bresche
    Publikationen, expanded media edition, 1976.

Burroughs, William S. *Naked Lunch.* New York: Grove, 1962.

Burroughs, William S. *Nova Express.* New York: Grove, 1965.

Burroughs, *The William S. Burroughs Inter* NetWeb *Zone.* Online. Internet. 22
    August 1995. Available: <http://www.hyperreal.com/wsb/>; and
    The Unofficial Home Page. Online. Internet. 22 August 1995. Available:
    <http://www.interport.net/~regulus/pkd/pkd-int.html>. Burroughs's
    fiction is part of what is called "Slipstream," cyberpunk fiction
    written/published prior to 1984 that has influenced, say, the authors
    published in Sterling's *Mirrorshades* collection.

Dick, Philip K. *Do Androids Dream of Electric Sheep?* New York: Ballantine,
    1968.

Dick, Phillip K. *The Online Guide to Philip K. Dick's Short Stories.* Online.
    Internet. 22 August 1995. Available: <http://www.umich.edu/
    ~ryandhoz/pkdick/>; and *PKD FAQ.* Online. Internet. 22 August 1995.
    Available: <http://www.interport.net/~regulus/pkd/pkd-int.html>; *2019:
    Off World (A Blade Runner Page).* Online. Internet. 22 August 1995.
    Available: <http://kzsu.stanford.edu/uwi/br/off-world.html>.

Extropy: The Journal of Transhumanist Thought.

Gibson, William. *Neuromancer.* New York: Ace, 1984.

Gibson, William. *Count Zero.* New York: Ace, 1986.

Gibson, William. *Burning Chrome.* New York: Ace, 1987.

Gibson, William. *Mona Lisa Overdrive.* New York: Bantam, 1988.

Gibson, *William Gibson's Alien III Script* <ftp://cathouse.org:/pub/cathouse/
    movies/scripts/alien.iii>.

Gibson, *Johnny Mnemonic* (cyberspace to film). Online. Internet. 22 August
    1995. Available: <http://www.spe.sony.com/Pictures/SonyMovies/
    09exclsv.html>.

Hafner, Katie, and John Markoff. *Cyberpunk: Outlaws and Hackers on the
    Computer Frontier.* New York: Simon & Schuster, 1991.

Haraway, Donna. *Simians, Cyborgs, and Women.* New York: Routledge, 1991.
    Haraway's article was originally published in *The Socialist Review* (original
    version is included here); later it was incorporated into this book-length
    study.

Haraway, Donna. "The Promises of Monsters: A Regenerative Politics for
    Inappropriate/d." In *Cultural Studies,* ed. Lawrence Grossberg, Cary Nelson,
    and Paula A. Treichler. New York: Routledge, 1992. 295–337.

Leary, Timothy. Homepage. Online. Internet. 22 August 1995. Available: <http://www.interverse.com/conscious> or <http://www.intac.com/ ~dimitri/dh/learywilson.html>.

Lebkowsky, Jon, Paco Xander Nathan, and Dave Demaris. "Bait and Switch with Sandy Stone." *MONDO 2000,* no. 11 (1994): 53–58.

Maddox, Tom. "Halo." November 1994. Online. *Fringeware.* 22 August 1995. Available: <http://fringeware.com/tazmedia/halo/>. Cyberpunk SF novel on-line.

Maddox, Tom. [various articles.] *LOCUS: The Newspaper of the Science Fiction.* Beginning September 1992. Online. The WELL. 22 August 1995. Available: <gopher://gopher.well.sf.ca.us/11/Publications/LOCUS>.

McCaffery, Larry, ed. *Storming the Reality Studio: A Casebook of Cyberpunk and Postmodern Fiction.* Durham, NC: Duke University Press, 1991.

Mississippi Review 47/48 (16.1–2, 1988), on cyberpunk science fiction.

Rucker, Rudy. *Live Robots (Software/Wetware).* New York: Avon, 1994.

Rucker, Rudy, R. U. Sirius, Queen Mu. *MONDO 2000: A User's Guide to the New Edge.* New York: HarperCollins, 1992.

Science-Fiction Studies. Various issues of the journal are devoted to cyberpunk science fiction.

Sterling, Bruce, ed. *Mirrorshades.* New York: Warner Books, 1986.

Sterling, Bruce. *Island in the Net.* New York: Morrow, 1988.

Sterling, Bruce. *Schismatrix.* New York: Arbor House, 1985.

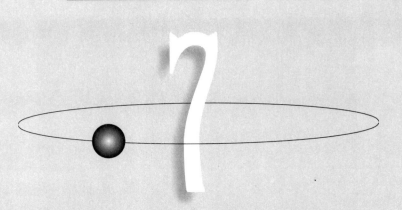

MUDS/MOOS

M

UDs (multi-user dungeons/dimensions/domains) are text-based, real-time virtual realities. Such a definition probably does not tell the uninitiated much at all. Let's try this: MUDs are virtual places in a host computer mainframe in which two guests log in, take a fictitious name, and communicate to each other by rapidly typing back and forth in real time. (It's like being in a relay chat room.) What appears on each participant's monitor is a cascade of mostly one-liners that may compose several conversations. What also can appear is an occasional one-liner resulting from a participant's command to enter or leave a virtual room. Here are some basic examples from a log:

```
You tiptoe onto the main floor . . .

Robin tiptoes in . . .

Cynthia smiles.

Cynthia says, "let me go turn on the lights."

The Usher gives Cynthia the evil eye . . .

@smiles

I don't understand that.

Cynthia lost you!

smiles

I don't understand that.

Cynthia lost Robin!

Cynthia says, "ya'll stay put . . ."

"i am still here

Robin whispers to Victor, "The rowdies theatre is fun too."
```

<Har Har>

<from main floor> <Har Har>

The Usher gives Cynthia the evil eye . . .

You say, "i am still here"

The Usher gives Victor the evil eye . . .

Cynthia says, "I need to turn that Usher off . . . send him
on a smoke creak:)"

Cynthia says, "Break"

The Usher gives Cynthia the evil eye . . .

The Usher points his bony finger at Cynthia, "Please, you
must refrain from talking . . ."

Cynthia says, "be right back!"

<Hee Hee>

<from main floor> <Hee Hee>

The Usher eyes Cynthia warily, "Shh . . ."

Cynthia tiptoes out . . .

Robin pokes Usher in the ribs.

"and how do we get popcorn?

You say, "and how do we get popcorn?"

The Usher eyes Victor warily, "Shh . . ."

The Usher sneaks out the side exit to take a cigarette
break . . .

    This is a brief slice of a log that I made when I was invited to a new MUD—
rather, a MOO—but we will get to the difference later! (My friend and her colleague who lives in a foreign country had virtually constructed the MOO in a
U.S. university's mainframe.) The exchange above is a kind of preamble to
showing me around the MOO from room to room. We are, so to speak, in the
mainframe, in the MOO, typing to each other at the same time (which is what
is meant by *real time*). Two other virtual people are there also. When I first
entered the mainframe, I simply took my real name, Victor, but when I returned
at a later time, I requested my MOO name, which is "R. U. Rhetoricus?"

    In the excerpt above, when we speak to each other, we simply type, for
example,

"i am still here"

and it comes out first on *my* monitor as

You say, "i am still here"

but comes out on *all* others' monitors as

Victor says, "i am still here."

If I want to emote, I type

: smiles

which comes out to everyone as

Victor smiles.

(Notice that when I first started typing in commands, I was doing it incorrectly and the program kept saying to me "I don't understand that"!) These are the simplest commands: <">, a double quote to speak; <:>, a colon to emote. There are many other commands—depending on the particular MUD or MOO—that will allow you to talk either to everyone or to only one other individual. (In Questions and Suggestions for Further Study, you will find a URL for FAQs about MUDs, which provides a list of the basic commands.)

Now for the difference: most simply put, a MOO is a MUD that is object oriented. A fuller but more complicated answer is that a MOO (MUD object oriented, or multi-object oriented) is a programming language within a MUD that gives its participants the ability to create and manipulate their own virtual objects—say, a room with objects (furnishings). I have a room at my friend's MOO, which I call "room" and which has no objects in it, since I am a MOO-minimalist! .)>=. To complicate things further—or perhaps to make them very simple—by turning them around MUD is now a generic term for both MUDs (without a MOO) and MOOs! Originally, as our authors in this section point out, MUDs were "adventure games" similar to Dungeons and Dragons; now their purposes are more varied and, most important, educational. There is the LP family MUD (which includes DikuMUD and AberMUD and which is devoted to role-playing adventure games). And there is the Tiny family or Teeny family of MUDs (which is devoted to being social, engaging in discussions, or anything similar). Then there is ChibaMOO (which is a WOO, or a combination of Web and MOO = WOO). And there is HypertextHotel and a whole bunch of various combinations and permutations (see Suggestions for Further Study).

These are the basics. The readings collected here begin with some rather simple articles from popular magazines. Since, as I said, MUDs are difficult to understand, especially if you have not attended one, Katie Hafner's and Ellen Germain's articles are general and helpful enough to begin with. (The best source for an understanding of MUDS/MOOS, however, that I or anyone else can give you is *to experience one yourself.*) But first, a caveat about what you might find. Jacques Leslie in "MUDroom" takes us to a virtual wedding and then to a virtual-cum-actual-romantic rejection that leads to an attempted suicide. Leslie, so to speak, puts us in the thick of virtual things: from marriage to suicide. However, he also takes us to MicroMUSE, which is for child-adult collaborations and which is strictly controlled to avoid any abuse. Moreover, Leslie suggests what the future holds for MUDS by giving an account of Pavel Curtis and David A. Nichols's Jupiter project. The goal, as they announced in their 1993 paper, is to make MUDS (with MOO programming) capable of audio and video. Soon, if not already by the time this book appears, MUDS will approach the capabilities of electronic cafés.

Leslie also mentions—as is discussed in Chapter 3 of *CyberReader*—that the battle between the sexes can be fierce in MUDS, but it can also be instructive. For example, men logging on will attempt to take on the identity of a female so that they can meet females. More often than not, however, such males give themselves away too easily when they role-play in such a way that few, if any, females would take them actually to be a female. (In many ways, the virtual is more telling than the actual—how else could it be when a male will typically take the name "FantasticHotBabe"?) Amy S. Bruckman in "Gender Swapping on the Internet" extends this discussion of males, females, and role playing with her examination of a Netnews exchange. She concludes: "MUDS are an identity workshop."

Perhaps one of the by-now canonized articles on male-female relations is Julian Dibbell's "A Rape in Cyberspace; Or, How an Evil Clown, a Haitian Trickster Spirit, Two Wizards, and a Cast of Dozens Turned a Database into a Society." The virtual rape, many say, took place at LambdaMOO. Extending Leslie's and Bruckman's concerns about male-female role playing in cyberspace, Dibbell raises the whole question of virtual rape, getting us to rethink what this act constitutes. The brilliance of the article lies in its account of the concerns and virtual acts of LambdaMOO's members in attempting to deal with this problem in cyberspace, just as we are wrestling on a larger scale with the problem of how virtual space obliges us to rethink all of the founding concepts and principles of government and society, of civil and criminal laws.

One last caveat: it is widely known that MUDS/MOOS can be addictive. (You might check out the newsgroup <alt.mudders.anonymous>.) Everyone involved in them has heard of students who have spent hours every day playing in MUDS and consequently flunk out of school. Many administrators of academic computer systems have blocked off access to MUD/MOOS from their mainframe.

Katie Hafner

Get in the MOOD Games: If you have a modem and like adventure, this MUD's for you.

ts population is around 8,500. It has private nooks and corners as well as very public gathering spots. Though small by any demographer's standards, this place has seen more than its share of civic crises. Undesirables and miscreants wreak havoc. There are wild hot-tub parties and heated debates over whether a fellow citizen should be allowed to exist. People are teleported to other places against their will. Some men pose as women, some women pose as neuter aliens.

Welcome to LambdaMOO, which is not a real place at all but a virtual place in cyberspace. More precisely, it is an address on the Internet. Linked to that address is a computer in Palo Alto, California, containing millions of lines of text and computer codes. Most of its inhabitants, who are actually spread from Ohio to Manila, have never met in real life. Their lives in LambdaMOO consist of sitting alone at their computer screens, typing at a furious clip.

LambdaMOO is a form of MUD, or multi-user dungeon. MUDs are text-based real-time bulletin boards with a built-in theme and structure. Connect to a MUD and you are in Camelot or the tomb of Hat-shepsut, ancient Egypt's only female pharoah. Or, as in the case with LambdaMOO, a very crowded house.

The first MUD, a computerized version of the role-playing game Dungeons & Dragons, was created 15 years ago by students at the University of Essex in England. The concept eventually drifted over to North America and, as the Internet exploded, so did the number of MUDs. Today there are more than 500 worldwide.

LambdaMOO is by far the most popular. The brains behind LambdaMOO belong to Pavel Curtis, a 34-year-old computer scientist at Xerox Corp.'s Palo Alto Research Center, who got interested in "mudding" as a distraction when his own research in computer software hit a lull.

Curtis built on work done by Stephen White, a student at the University of Waterloo, who had added to traditional MUDs the notion of players doing their own programming. White built an "object-oriented" language, in which programs are built upon previously defined objects. He called his invention a "MOO," for mud-object-oriented. Curtis developed White's work further, and by the time he opened the doors of LambdaMOO, exactly four years ago on Halloween, MUDs had begun to move beyond the "hack and slash" of more traditional computer-based role-playing games into experiments in social interaction and collaborative programming.

Players on LambdaMOO move about the house and grounds, and speak to one another by typing such simple commands as "out" and "say." With its MOO code, LambdaMOO allows players to create their own objects: a private bedroom containing furniture fashioned out of cobwebs; a shopping cart that serves as a dwelling for a "virtually homeless" woman.

■ T R U L Y   W A C K Y

Programming on the MOO, or "building," can be done by any player. Building includes creating new rooms, linking rooms and creating objects. One player, for instance, whose character is Kilik, a Frisbee-chasing black Labrador, programmed a lavish fireworks display last July 4. Another player began to build a Rube Goldberg device. Others added levers and doors to the machine until it became a truly wacky contraption, complete with blaring trumpets and lemmings in search of high ground. When a virtual version of Mel Tormé appeared, the Rube Goldberg contraption carried out a rather brutal execution of the crooner.

This all takes some imagination. LambdaMOO is entirely text based. There are no graphics. Log on to the MOO and what you see is line after line of text scrolling on your computer screen.

Curtis modeled LambdaMOO after his own large very real house in the hills near Xerox. "I wanted it to be a house, because I like the homey feel," he says. "I liked the idea of people sitting around." Perhaps it is the home metaphor that makes LambdaMOO so attractive. "People have treated LambdaMOO as a house," says Sherry Turkle, a sociologist and psychologist at the Massachusetts Institute of Technology. "And despite the 'Animal House' qualities you see sometimes, the home metaphor has been important for its inhabitants."

LambdaMOO is indeed a seductive place. Many LambdaMOOers, like MUD denizens in general, are college students with plenty of time on their hands. There are usually up to 200 people connected to LambdaMOO at once, and some of them spend up to 20 hours at a time there. "People go there for different reasons," says Julian Dibbell, who is writing a book about MUDs. "They go to socialize, or program, and a lot of people end up getting caught up in the politics of it." Some MOOers simply keep their MOO connections running all day in the background and write programs that alert them when, say, a character they like has connected. Says Dibbell: "There's a tension for a lot of people between their real life and their MOO life."

Some players spend 20 hours at a time in the fantasy worlds they create.

The addictive quality of mudding is a much-discussed topic among LambdaMOOers. After several months of hardcore MOOing, some players attempt to go cold turkey. One method is to randomly change your password by banging your head against the keyboard, making it impossible to log back on.

MIT's Turkle, who has a forthcoming book on what she calls "personal identity in a culture of simulation," describes MUDs as "the most recent computational seduction." MUDs, Turkle says, are to the 1990s what videogames were to the 1980s. Moreover, Turkle adds, MUDs introduce an element beyond the seduction found in videogames. "MUDs are making an offer that people can't refuse, which is extreme personalization," she says. "You actually get to build a self, and an alternate world for that self."

In Turkle's view, people use experiences on MUDs to work through real issues in their lives. "The appeal of MUDs has to do with what people are able to express, work through, understand about themselves by doing this, to work through problems in a relatively unconstrained way. It's a little less strange than it looks."

Players go to great lengths to create their characters—female, male, or neuter, centaur or mermaid. "Whether you're short or tall, fat or thin, black or white, ugly or beautiful in real life, what determines how you look on Lambda is completely controllable," says John Fink, a 21-year-old senior at Miami University in Oxford, Ohio, who took his LambdaMOO character, Yossarian, from Joseph Heller's *Catch-22*. "The anonymity also provides people with a sense of invulnerability."

Which goes a long way to explaining some of the unpleasant, occasionally vile, incidents that have occurred on LambdaMOO. Less than two years after its inception, LambdaMOO was already one of the largest MUDs on the Internet—and it became increasingly unruly. Troublemakers would enter the living room and print out the entire contents of Webster's Dictionary, the digital equivalent of pouring a barrelful of marbles on a dance floor. In early 1993, a virtual rape of two other characters by a male character wielding voodoo dolls took place. The act, though confined entirely to the simulated environment of LambdaMOO, was so hideous and public it generated a MOOwide debate that continues to this day. In the end, one of the MOO wizards, endowed with the power to do so, "toaded" the perpetrator, which means the character was erased from the system.

Ellen Germain

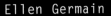

In the Jungle of MUD
*Virtual worlds you can hook
into—and get hooked on—are
the latest rage on the
computer networks*

ashington: You're in a tropical rain forest, try-
ing to decide whether to explore the ruined Maya temple in the distance or
climb into the forest canopy overhead, where you might see some monkeys.
Suddenly there's a yellow-brown jaguar sitting on the branch above you,
flicking his tail from side to side, his yellow eyes fixed on yours. Maybe
climbing a tree isn't such a good idea after all. You don't think jaguars eat
people, but rather than find out, you head off across the forest floor, turning
this way and that, until you manage to get yourself hopelessly lost.

Don't panic. Just hang up, take a deep breath, and log on again. You're not
going to Panama, after all, just to a machine somewhere in Pittsburgh, Pennsylvania. And what you are exploring is not an exotic ecosystem but a computer system called a MUD.

MUDs (the name stands for Multi-User Dungeons) are the latest twist in the
already somewhat twisted world of computer communications. A sort of poor
man's virtual reality—created by using words, not expensive head-mounted
displays—MUDs are a quantum leap over computer bulletin boards, where you
not only meet and interact with other computer users from all over the world
but build your own imaginary worlds as well. The first MUD was invented in
1979 as a way for British university students to play the fantasy game Dungeons & Dragons by computer. But in the past few years computer scientists
have created new kinds of MUDs that are far removed from the D&D world.
These quickly caught on among college students—and among the general
computer-using population too. Suddenly new MUDs are sprouting up everywhere in cyberspace, in every size and shape.

Some MUDs are fashioned after medieval villages, with town squares, black-
smiths and churches. Others re-create science-fiction and fairy-tale settings,
like C. S. Lewis' Narnia, Frank Herbert's Dune and the universe of *Star Trek*.
Massachusetts Institute of Technology researchers have built a MUD model of
their famous Media Lab, with offices and corridors corresponding to the real
thing. One intrepid group of computer users constructed a section of the London Underground, complete with a virtual subway. MUDs come and go, drifting in and out of favor, but the current count is estimated at 300 worldwide,
most of them accessible through the vast global computer grid called the
Internet.

Playing in a MUD is like wandering through a literary maze. Scenes are sketched out in a phrase or two—a woody glade, a drafty cave—and you move from one to the other by typing commands: go west, climb up, enter castle. In your travels, you run into various objects (a giggling robot, a sleeping sloth) as well as other characters. These can be other players, logging on from a remote computer, or cleverly designed computer programs masquerading as humans. You can communicate with anyone you meet by either speaking (typing a message that appears on the other player's screen) or "emoting" (expressing a feeling or performing an action). In the early MUDs, players spent most of their time stabbing, clubbing or otherwise inflicting pain on other players. In more highly evolved MUDs, characters engage in all manner of intimate communications, including simulated sex.

Sex is tricky on the MUDs.

Sex is tricky on the MUDs. Because you can be anything you want to be—a tall Xantian with purple eyes or a gorgeous earthling hunk—there is quite a bit of gender swapping going on. "A lot of men pretend to be women so they can have more virtual sex," says Amy Bruckman, an M.I.T. researcher studying social interaction on MUDs. "A lot of women pretend to be men so they'll be left alone." Tracy (not her real name), a 28-year-old writer, often assumes the identity of a macho, beer-guzzling, care-for-nothing college student. She says it gives her a chance to see how the other half lives—and to work out her frustration with the men she meets in her life off-line.

Committed MUDders find the experience highly addictive—much to the consternation of parents and computer-system administrators. Some students play as much as 80 hours a week, neglecting their schoolwork and overloading their local computer networks. Amherst College banned MUDs from the campus computer system in 1992; Australia has gone so far as to banish them from the continent.

Some educators are trying to find a way to channel all that creative energy. Education-technology researcher Barry Kort administers a child-oriented MUD in Cambridge, Massachusetts, where children learn by doing. Among its virtual worlds are the Land of Oz and a model of Yellowstone National Park, complete with spouting geysers and wandering moose. The Yellowstone world was built by a nine-year-old boy just back from a family vacation. "Instead of writing about what he did on his summer vacation," says Kort, "he built a working model of his summer vacation."

Nobody has yet found a way to make money from MUDs, but commercial exploitation may not be far behind. Howard Rheingold, author of a new book on virtual communities, points out that many MUDs already have elaborate systems for tracking the points that players amass by finding treasures or killing enemies. Those systems could just as easily be used to amass dollars, says Rheingold. "As soon as somebody figures out a way to play for real money, you're going to see some real action."

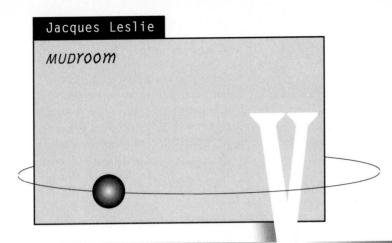

Jacques Leslie

MUDroom

irtual reality," as most people understand the phrase, refers to a computer-simulated three-dimensional world of sight and sound into which participants wearing an electronic helmet and glove can project themselves. It's an exciting field with many promising applications, but realizing them will require overcoming major obstacles of design and expense, and another decade or more may pass before image-based VR touches many people's lives in a significant way.

In the meantime, another kind of VR has already had such an impact. Almost entirely overlooked in our fascination with the vistas conjured up by image-based VR, this more modest form typically deals in nothing but words: if the image-based version is analogous to television or movies, then the other VR suggests books or radio. Pavel Curtis, a computer scientist at the Xerox Palo Alto Research Center who has created a popular model of word-based VR, goes so far as to predict that even after image-based VR becomes commonplace, text-based VR will continue to thrive, precisely because its medium is so much simpler. Word-based VR programs, called MUDs—for "Multi-User Dimensions" or "Multi-User Dungeons"—are accessible without charge to anyone possessing a computer, modem, and a connection to one of hundreds of computer networks around the world. About 250 MUDs are currently accessible through the world-wide amalgam of computer networks known as the Internet; on Curtis's MUD alone, more than 5000 players from 27 countries have registered since it began operation in October 1990. Though most MUDs have been in existence for a shorter time than Curtis's, the total number of regular MUD players is already in the tens of thousands. It's indicative of MUDs' appeal that this total has been reached even though the keyboard commands required to maneuver around MUDs are initially bewildering to all but experienced programmers, and require many hours to master.

One phrase that sums up the allure of MUDs is that they are laboratories for exploring identity.

One phrase that sums up the allure of MUDs is that they are laboratories for exploring identity. Each MUD is an imaginary world, created over time by its players. Reflecting the predilections of the hacker subculture, many MUDs embody themes drawn from science fiction or Arthurian legend: a MUD called

TrekMUSE is based on the *Star Trek* television series, and all of its players must designate themselves as members of either the Klingon or Romulan races in order to enter its realm; another popular MUD, PernMUSH, is modeled after Ann McCaffrey's *Dragonriders of Pern* fantasy novels; and still another MUD, called Nuclear War, depicts a world 75 years after a nuclear holocaust. But not all MUDs are drawn from such a narrow range of themes: DragonMUD, at three years old probably the longest-running MUD on the Internet, is set in 12th- to 19th-century London, and all of FurryMUCK's characters are furry, cuddly animals. Curtis's MUD, called LambdaMOO, is a mere house, now grown to more than 2000 rooms, whose nucleus faithfully reflects the ground plan of Curtis's real-life residence.

Players circulate within each MUD using assumed names, providing descriptions of themselves that typically vary from moderately to wildly fanciful, often even misrepresenting their gender or claiming to possess no gender at all. Shielded by anonymity and distance from most consequences of their actions, they frequently behave on MUDs in ways they would not in real life. A shy woman may try out being a flirt, or a computer "nerd" may portray himself as suave and sexually aggressive; one player describes the character he portrays on MUDs as "the person I want to become." Sometimes players create several personas within one MUD, switching from one to another depending on their mood or trying them out in sequence until they find one that suits them. Since the overwhelming majority of MUDders are male (reflecting the preponderance of men in the hacker subculture, male MUDders often pretend to be women, either to enjoy the increased attention female MUDders typically attract or to sample the experience of being female; women, on the other hand, usually pretend to be men simply to avoid the sexual harassment which is an all-too-common feature of MUD life.

Players may go on quests or compete in games that are built into the MUD environment; they may add new objects or rooms to the MUD, learning basic computer programming skills in the process; or they may indulge in the most common of MUD activities, typed conversation with other players. MUDders hold virtual parties, stage virtual food fights, buy and sell goods with virtual currency they acquire by performing certain tasks, and even fall in love with each other, most often without having met in real life. Some indulge in "text sex" (also called "Tinysex"), typing sexually arousing statements to each other until they reach orgasm while sitting at their keyboards. Virtual weddings occur frequently, and on MicroMUSE, a MUD designed as an educational tool for children, a 10-year-old boy recently presided over a virtual memorial service to commemorate the death of his real-life cousin. Not surprisingly, "MUD addiction" flourishes: some players spend as much as 80 hours a week on the games, and tales of MUDders who have flunked out of college as a result of their obsession are common.

What separates MUDs from books, radio, television, and even most image-based VR applications is their capacity for interaction among participants. A player in Capetown, South Africa who calls himself Guinevere logs onto LambdaMOO and types "say Hello!"; the message is relayed along the Internet to the LambdaMOO computer in Palo Alto; and a moment later another player in Eugene, Oregon, connected to the same LambdaMOO room as Guinevere, sees the words "Guinevere says 'Hello!'" on his computer screen and types his reply. The two players can disseminate their conversation to everyone in the room, enabling others to join in, or they can "whisper" to each other so that no one else sees their exchange. If the players are in different rooms, they can still converse by "paging" each other. And players can do more than talk: I've played roulette in LambdaMOO's casino, and in the Mud Wrestling Pit I was inundated with substances ranging from jello to old editions of the *National Enquirer* (in honor of my profession). Perhaps more gratifying, MUDders can create environments reflecting their own tastes and personalities. On LambdaMOO, players from the United Kingdom have invested a dozen rooms with the spirit of Wales: the rooms, including several pubs, contain such features as a crackling hearthfire, a bubbling tea kettle, meandering cats, and a banner proclaiming "Cymru am byth!" ("Wales forever!"). What players can do, at least in the virtual sense, is limited chiefly by the breadth of their imagination and programming skill.

To Brenda Laurel, a researcher at Interval Research Corp. in Palo Alto and the author of *Computers as Theatre,* MUDS' compelling quality is their capacity for combining interactivity and self-representation. "A big difference between MUDS and even interactive television is that in the interactive television model there is no self-representation: I'm not there," she said. "I get to buy things and maybe I get to vote on things, but I don't represent myself through the medium to other people. So it's still partaking of a broadcast mentality—that is, one person produces content, many people consume it. MUDS are a dramatic counterexample in that they are primarily about self-representation and they are a one-to-one, few-to-few, one-to-few, or few-to-one kind of medium, instead of this tail-wagging-dog problem with broadcasting.

"There is a tremendous need for environments like this, where we have the hope of knowing and understanding other participants as individuals and not just as elements of, say, an election poll, and where we spread our wings and begin to construct things together. Once you see how hungry people are for this, you can forgive the relative triviality of subject matter on MUDS at this moment. I have no doubt that within this decade we will see elaborate MUDS that begin to look like cultures."

On a recent Saturday afternoon I attended a virtual wedding.

On a recent Saturday afternoon I attended a virtual wedding. I'd read an announcement of it in one of the topics reserved for MUD discussions on USENET, a vast international computer conferencing system, and a few minutes before the appointed time I logged onto a MUD called "Singlenesia," the site of the wedding. Having never visited Singlenesia before, I needed a persona, so I checked in as "Dana," a name I chose in order to keep my gender ambiguous. And since I knew no one in the wedding party, I accounted for my presence in my self-description: "a *bon vivant* for 25 years—particularly attracted to weddings." For good measure I added a comment which would appear next to "Dana" when anyone checked the roster of current visitors to Singlenesia: "I love weddings!"

Next I typed "WHO" in order to see the roster, and found a list of the wedding participants including the groom, "Legssus" ("Call me Mr. Nervous," he'd written), and his bride, "Tyne" ("Soon to be Mrs. Nervous"). All visitors to Singlenesia initially find themselves under a pier, surrounded by barnacle-coated pilings and the stench of rotting seaweed, and I quickly set off to find the wedding. By typing compass directions or designated exits such as "trail," "path," or "lighthouse," I managed to wander along the shore, but I found no evidence of the wedding. Giving up the search, I tried paging "Akhond," listed in the roster as "best man," and was rewarded with the information that the wedding would take place in "the gazebo (object #3137)." To teleport myself there, I typed "@tel #3137" and was instantly transported to the wedding venue. Its description rolled across my computer screen:

```
White lattice pine and ivy make up the most beautiful huge
gazebo you have ever laid eyes on. Crawlers stream up the
sides, weaving in and out of the lattice while a large
arrangement of flowers placed around the railing give the air
a wonderful scent. There is plenty of seating in the enormous
structure, allowing everyone a perfect view of the bride and
groom.
Obvious exits:
Hanky out
```

By typing "out," I'd leave the gazebo, but what would happen if I typed "Hanky"? I tried it. "You grab your hanky from your pocket as a tear wells up in one eye," my screen said. "Watching the two youngsters in front of you, you can't hold back a 'It's . . .(sniff). . . so beautiful!' " Again and again throughout the wedding one or another participant was sufficiently moved to type "hanky," and the same sentiments, attributed to the appropriate player, appeared on my screen each time.

The wedding didn't start on time. Impatient, I did what was expected of a *bon vivant*. I'd struck up a conversation with "Soliton," a friend of the groom, so now I asked him, "Has anyone seen the champagne?" He answered that he just happened to be carrying a little bottle of whiskey, and offered me a swig, which I accepted.

At last Tyne, the bride, appeared. I typed "look Tyne" to see her self-description.

```
She is absolutely aglow with the love that is in the air. She
is wearing a stunningly white dress that has a plunging v-
style neckline and back. . . . Two small diamond earrings
shine in her ears, almost matching the gleam that comes from
her soft brown eyes. A long train trails behind Tyne and two
small boys are on each side of its ends, carrying it.
```

Noting that no one had commented on Tyne's appearance, I typed, "Tyne, you look beautiful." The next words on my screen were "Tyne blushes. . . . Thank you, Dana."

"Eastern" conducted the ceremony. Apparently a poor typist, she began, "People we are hear to gather fo the tinywedding of legssus and tyne. They have know each other as friends for a while and relized they were meant to be. Tinymarriage is a committment of love and understanding in the times of internet mudding."

I imagined Eastern's voice droning on through the ceremony, so I asked Soliton for another swig of whiskey. He passed me the bottle so that no one else would see.

The vows were discernibly wry. Eastern asked, "Legssus do you take this woman to be your wife in good times and bad, through the times when you need to build and when you need to relax? do ye promise to be faithful to tyne for the time you have together?" ("To build" means to create new programming code, adding new rooms or objects to an existing MUD.)

The bride and groom both said "I do," but before they could exchange rings, something went wrong. After a few minutes' delay, the words "Technical difficulties" appeared on my screen. "Elminster," an onlooker, said, "Perhaps the Great Net Gods in the Sky don't approve?" Then Legssus disconnected. Somebody gasped. Somebody else said "Oh dear!" Tyne looked down at the ground, and Eastern comforted her. Elminster said, "The Great Net Gods in the sky are displeased!"

But Legssus was back a minute later, blaming the interruption on "line noise" that broke his connection to Singlenesia. Everyone expressed relief, and the wedding proceeded without further problems. The bride and groom kissed, members of the wedding party hugged and cried, and Soliton let me finish off the whiskey bottle. Then, abruptly, Tyne announced that she had to go. "I need to make dinner in real life," she said. Legssus stayed around long enough to listen to Akhond's reading of "The Owl and the Pussycat" at the Singlenesia swimming hole, and then he, too, left.

Though the ceremony was "virtual" and at times verged on farce, it unnerved Soliton nevertheless. "This brings back weird memories," he whispered to me. It turned out that his real-life girl friend of more than four years had asked him to marry her "hundreds of times," but instead, a month earlier, he had broken up with her. Now the wedding made him keenly aware of the opportunity he'd passed up.

Nine days after the ceremony, I called up Legssus. In real life he's a junior in computer science at Florida State University; Tyne, he said, lives in Ohio, but he didn't know what city she lives in or even whether she's a student. They'd been meeting on MUDs for only a month before the wedding, and when he asked her to marry him, he was half-kidding, he said. Even so, the wedding was important to him; one evidence was that when other MUD women flirted with him now, he felt obliged to tell them that he was married and couldn't "mess around" any more. He said he and a few friends had built Singlenesial's gazebo and features such as the "false hanky exit" on the day of

the wedding. He'd been concerned about Eastern's suitability to conduct the
ceremony because she is a poor speller, but he noticed that her accuracy
improved as the rites wore on. The delay in the wedding was actually caused
by a technical problem: passing objects is a complicated programming task in
MUD realms, and in Singlenesia it costs virtual currency. As the ring exchange
approached, Legssus realized he didn't have enough cash, and had to find
someone from whom he could borrow the remainder before the ritual could
proceed.

It turned out that my timing in calling Legssus was ideal, for the previous
night he'd talked to Tyne on a MUD for the first time since the wedding. They
spoke for nearly three hours, and Legssus was "just grinning from ear to ear
because I was so happy to see her." In fact, he confessed sheepishly, they
"consummated" the marriage.

In *The Second Self: Computers and the Human Spirit* (1984), Sherry Turkle portrays hackers as socially awkward, intensely individualistic, and accustomed to
finding satisfaction only in their mastery of computers. She writes, "The
hacker culture appears to be made up of people who need to avoid complicated social situations, who for one reason or another got frightened off or
hurt too badly by the risks and complexities of relationships." The generalization probably applies to a majority of MUDders; what's poignant is that by
playing on MUDs, many are taking their first gingerly steps into a complicated
social arena. In many cases, in fact, MUDs seem to promote socialization. The
adolescent who, emboldened by his anonymity, greets women with a bluntly
sexual invitation finds that he is invariably rebuffed, sometimes angrily, and
develops a different strategy for striking up friendships with women; a person
who fears rejection because of physical handicap, appearance, age, or race discovers in MUDs a haven, where a person's self-presentation is the sole factor in
the response he receives. An engineer at a computer hardware company who
calls herself "Marcia" even attributes her recent promotion to the social skills
she developed as a "wizard"—that is, a volunteer MUD administrator whose
tasks include mediating disputes among players. "I never
thought I was good with people because engineers are never
told that," Marcia said. "By playing on the games, I found out
that I'm really pretty good at leading and administering. So I
took a lot of those skills back to my work, and ended up creating a department that I now manage."

*Many males who
impersonate
females on MUDS
are easy
to detect.*

Hackers aren't the only ones who gain social skills by participating on MUDs. Christian Sykes is no nerd: he's 23, married, a religious studies major at the University of Kansas, and
he characterizes his computer aptitude as "mild." He played on
MUDs long enough to become bored with them, so as "a performance art piece" he decided to find out whether he could portray a woman
convincingly. Many males who impersonate females on MUDs are easy to
detect, for they behave not as real women do but rather as late-adolescent
males wish they would, responding with enthusiasm to all sexual advances,
sometimes in quite explicit terms; thus it takes no particular acumen to deter-

mine that, say, a LambdaMOO character called FantasticHotBabe ("Your eyes marvel at her perfectly firm breasts . . .") is a male. Sykes was determined to be more sophisticated. He kept the description of his female character simple and as consistent with his own appearance as possible. When women on the MUD spoke among themselves about boyfriends, menstruation, or even gynecological problems, he drew upon lore gleaned from his wife and female friends to contribute persuasively to the conversation. After a while he added another fillip to his ruse, casually revealing that his character, "Eris" (named, appropriately enough, after the Greek goddess of discord), was bisexual. That provoked "*lots* of curiosity," Sykes said. More intriguingly, Eris's confession prompted another player to contemplate for the first time without self-condemnation the possibility that he was a homosexual. Sykes calls that "an odd side effect" of his experiment.

Sykes' major discovery, however, was the extent of sexual harassment of women. Though not one person suspected Sykes' prank, he abandoned it after four months because he could not write programs without being constantly interrupted by male advances. "The chief thing I learned," he said, "is simply how irritating some men can be." Revealing the hoax didn't even end Sykes's problems, for one male player who apparently had a crush on Eris became so irate that he tried to get Sykes banished from the MUD.

The fury of Eris's "suitor" demonstrates MUDs' double-edged sword: the anonymity which shields players from the consequences of their ill-conceived acts also promotes their deception. When the players possess limited social skills or great emotional vulnerabilities, they're at risk, perhaps just as much as in real life. The story of Chris Thornborrow, a self-described "naive computer scientist," is instructive. Four years ago, when he was 21, he was an honors student in his final year at the University of Edinburgh in Scotland. An experienced MUD player, he met "Melanie" online, and soon was spending as much as forty hours a week with her, first on a MUD, then on a computer chatline. He taught her the MUD's programming intricacies, and she, ostensibly a mathematics student at Cambridge University, taught him mathematical integrations. For several months they conversed only by computer, until at last Melanie agreed to take a train to Edinburgh to meet him. Thornborrow remembers standing at the station, watching every passenger debark from the train, until only one, a young woman "wearing a black leather jacket and a black pair of jeans," was left. "I started to go towards her to ask her if she was Melanie," Thornborrow said, "and when I did that, she picked up her suitcase and very coolly walked past me."

Thornborrow assumed that Melanie had missed the train, and when she confirmed his supposition during their next computer conversation, he believed her. A month later, however, Melanie's best friend, "Debbie," told him via computer that Melanie was lying. It was indeed Melanie who'd walked past him at the train station, Debbie said; Melanie didn't introduce herself only because she lost her nerve at the last minute. Thornborrow knew that Debbie's account was at least partially accurate, for when he pressed Melanie, she conceded that she'd been on the train. What he didn't believe was that she'd lost her nerve. "I knew she'd looked at me and then walked away," he said. "My instinctive and abiding reaction was that visually I didn't come up to scratch, and that's quite an ego-destroying thing." Thornborrow tried to locate Melanie and Debbie, and found that contrary to their stories, they were not enrolled as mathematics students at Cambridge; in fact, none of the information they provided about themselves checked out. Thornborrow had trusted Melanie "completely," and had been gratified by her seeming acceptance of him, but now he discovered that he'd "basically been talking to a lie." The result was that he no longer trusted his ability to distinguish truth from deception.

Thornborrow had only a month before he was required to turn in his honors project, the culmination of three years of university work, but he felt too shattered to complete it. When university officials asked for an explanation, he was too ashamed to provide one. Finally, he said, the officials told him that if he would meet with a psychologist who would confirm that he could not finish the school year, he would receive his degree anyway. He agreed, the psychologist wrote a report, but he still didn't get the degree. Now he felt doubly betrayed. Lacking the money to repeat his final year at Edinburgh, he grew increasingly despondent, and several months later he tried to commit suicide by swallowing fifty pain tablets. The pills, however, contained a safety mechanism, and he merely regurgitated them.

Two years ago Thornborrow acquired a real-life girl friend, and though he has given up trying to get his degree, he still hopes to become a university lecturer. Nevertheless, he said, the experience has left an indelible mark. "I find I am much more cynical, and I trust almost nobody with anything that can hurt me. Even my girlfriend says that she hardly knows me." As for MUDs, he said, "I would advise people to play your character, have fun, but keep away from talking to people because they will just lie to you."

If accounts like Thornborrow's fail to inspire second thoughts among MUD developers, one reason is that they believe MUDs are in their infancy, with rules of behavior and even future applications still largely uncharted. Randy Farmer, a co-creator of several MUD-like environments and a partner in Electric Communities, a Palo Alto company attempting to create an "electronic society," says, "Right now MUDs are wild frontier towns being held together by a bunch of homesteaders." The evidence, moreover, is that most of the homesteaders prefer an ordered domain: while many MUDs last for no more than a few months, those that survive tend to evolve rules of conduct and even forms of self-governance. For example, LambdaMOO players build so many new structures that the host computer continually verges on being overloaded; as a result, an "Architecture Review Board" consisting of 20 players was formed to decide which buildings to jettison. DragonMUD holds regular town meetings, at which issues as volatile as a case of "virtual rape" have been discussed. Farmer believes that MUDs will evolve until they are electronically interconnected; then they'll face issues similar to those of contending nation-states. At that point, he predicts, "The people who will be managing the large systems will have degrees in economics and international relations, not computer science."

Some MUDs are already specialized. One ambitious model in science education is MicroMUSE, housed inside a computer at the Massachusetts Institute of Technology's Artificial Intelligence lab. MicroMUSE is meant to be non-violent, non-competitive, and collaborative, and it welcomes children as young as 6 years old. Though participants use pseudonyms as on other MUDs, they must provide their real names when registering, so that offenders can be identified and, if necessary, banished. Perhaps because its atmosphere is so tranquil, MicroMUSE attracts more women than most other MUDs.

Some MUDs are already specialized.

MicroMUSE's major installation is Cyberion City, a simulated 22-mile-long cylindrical space station in orbit around the Earth. Cyberion City is designed to behave according to the laws of physics, and incorporates such features as gravity, both plant- and machine-generated oxygen, glass radiation shields, and artificially-produced 24-hour-long day-night cycles. Among its attractions are a simulated rain forest designed by a Boston University graduate student in environmental studies; an adventure based on C. S. Lewis' *Chronicles of Narnia* which was written by a Harvard University graduate student in artificial intelligence; and a Wizard of Oz adventure created by an 8-year-old boy collaborating with Barry Kort, a 47-year-old educational technology researcher.

Kort, one of MicroMUSE's founders, says such child-adult collaborations are at the heart of its purpose. Many adults who participate on MicroMUSE play a coaching role, sometimes providing the guidance that children have failed to receive from parents and teachers. "We see tremendous breakthroughs in kids who were stuck basically because they weren't getting accurate feedback," Kort said. "When we provide the missing function, they zoom right along, and gain not only scholastic development but maturity."

Another promising MUD application is in providing a virtual meeting hall for far-flung professional colleagues or corporate employees. Curtis, the LambdaMOO creator, said, "Right now you go to a conference and you sit down at dinner with the five people in the world who really do your kind of work, and the next day you all go home and it's a year before you meet again. Well, a MUD is the place where you can meet the rest of the year." To that end, Curtis is working with Dave Van Buren, an astronomer at the California Institute of Technology, to develop a MUD for the international astronomy community. The MUD, which Van Buren expects to be running by late 1993, will possess a library containing prepublication versions of astronomy journal articles. It probably will be divided not by rooms but by stellar regions, so that an astronomer looking for, say, a photograph of a nova in a particular galaxy would enter the appropriate MUD galaxy chamber to look up the real-life location of the photograph and could then signal that site to transmit the photograph electronically to the astronomer's computer. The MUD may also possess astronomical tools including a simulated telescope, which would be used to estimate the best time to look at a particular object in the sky.

Curtis is also working on a sound- and video-enhanced MUD environment. Each computer connected to the system would possess a microphone and speaker, and most sites would also have video cameras. Participants would move around inside the MUD by typing computer commands, as they do in a conventional MUD, but they would be both visible and audible to each other. The advantages are obvious, since voice and image convey many more layers of information than typed words. In addition, the shift to voice would overcome one of the most annoying features of MUDs, which is that after a player types a statement he waits, sometimes for many seconds, while the computer transmits his words and his respondent types a reply; when many people are conversing in the same virtual room, the computer can lag half a minute or longer.

Curtis' prototype, called the Jupiter Project, is a simulated version of the Xerox PARC building where he works. While sitting at his computer terminal, he can enter the virtual common room within the MUD, thus signalling his willingness to chat. Another Xerox PARC researcher, working at home or even at the Center's sister building in Cambridge, England while logged onto the MUD common room, can then start a conversation with Curtis. If the conversation turns into a professional discussion, the two researchers might move to one of their virtual offices to continue it in privacy. "One of the key goals of the Jupiter Project is to foster casual interaction between people who are geographically separated," Curtis said. "If I'm working at home, or if I'm separated from you just by a stairway, I'm not a part of what's going on here. But if we make a virtual space where people can have a chat, maybe it will turn into a real professional interaction. That kind of thing is invaluable, and it's the thing that is missing from current telecommunications mechanisms."

That missing space is what Brenda Laurel calls "the agora," the meeting place where people have always told each other stories, and the need for it is what all MUDs, from "Nuclear War" to the Jupiter Project, address. "What's different is that now we're participating in collective narrative activity in a world where our communities are too spread out and too overpopulated and too diverse, and the traditional gathering places are disappearing," Laurel said. "The market isn't a farmers' market where you know people, it's a Safeway; people aren't going to church like they used to; only the picturesque town in New England still has a town meeting. So where is the agora for the global community? The answer has to be: on the Net."

It is tempting to condemn MUDs because they promote bizarre, and, in the case of "addicts," arguably unhealthful activity. So seductive is their potential, we fear, that under their sway fewer and fewer people might choose to inhabit "real" terrain. The trouble with this view is that it doesn't acknowledge MUDs' evocative and complicated relationship to "reality."

After all, theater, films, and television purvey fantasies, too; the difference that MUDs make is to enable us to step out of the audience and on to the stage, to build our own sets, and then, in concert with others, play the role we write for ourselves. It's as if we've grown so accustomed to thinking of machines as dehumanizing that now, when computers show promise in assisting us at least a few steps out of isolation and towards community, we say, "It's not safe."

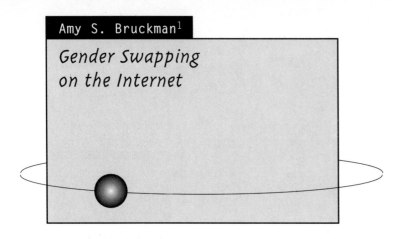

Amy S. Bruckman[1]

Gender Swapping on the Internet

■ GENDER SWAPPING ON THE INTERNET

On the television show *Saturday Night Live,* a series of skits concerned a character named Pat, who has no apparent gender. The audience is tempted with the promise of clues. In one episode, Pat gets his or her hair cut. A sign in the salon says that men's haircuts are $7, and women's haircuts are $9. The audience waits in suspense: when Pat goes to pay, his or her true gender will be revealed. The humor of the series lies in the fact that those hopes are constantly foiled; in this instance, Pat leaves $10 and says to keep the change.

Fundamental to human interactions that the idea of a person without gender is absurd. The audience thinks that surely some clue must reveal Pat's gender, but none ever does. Many who have never seen *Saturday Night Live* know about Pat.[2] The character has become a kind of cultural icon. Pat's popularity is revealing.

On many MUDs, it is possible to create gender neutral characters. It is possible not only to meet Pat, but also to be Pat. When I [3] first met an ungendered character, I felt a profound sense of unease. How should I relate to this person? Most unsettling was my unease about my unease: why should this matter? I am having a casual conversation with a random stranger; why should I feel a need to know his or her gender?

The experience highlights two things: the ways in which gender structures human interactions, and, more importantly, the ways in which MUDs help people to understand these phenomena by experiencing them. This essay briefly introduces the technology called MUDs, and then analyzes a community discussion about the role of gender in human social interaction which was inspired by the participants' experiences in MUDs. Gender swapping is one example of how the Internet has the potential to change not just work practice but also culture and values.

■ WHAT ARE MUDS?

A MUD is a text-based multi-user virtual-reality environment. As of April 16th, 1993, there were 276 publicly announced MUDs based on twenty different kinds of software on the Internet. I will use the term "MUD," which

stands for "Multi-User Dungeon," to refer to all the various kinds.[4] The original MUDs were adventure games; however, the technology has been adapted to
a variety of purposes.

When a person first logs onto a MUD, he or she creates a character. The
person selects the character's name and gender, and writes a description of
what the character looks like. It is possible for a character to be male or
female, regardless of the gender of the player. In many MUDs, a character can
also be neuter or even plural. A plural character could, for example, be called
swarm_of_bees or Laurel&Hardy.

MUDs are organized around the metaphor of physical space. You can "talk"
to anyone in the same virtual room. When you connect to a MUD at the Media
Lab called MediaMOO,[5] you see the description:

```
>connect guest

Okay,. . . guest is in use. Logging you in as 'Green_Guest'

*** Connected ***

The LEGO Closet

It's dark in here, and there are little crunchy plastic
things under your feet! Groping around, you discover what
feels like a doorknob on one wall.

Obvious exits: out to The E&L Garden
```

MediaMOO is a virtual representation of the MIT Media Lab. Typing
"out" gets you to the "E&L Garden," a central work area for the lab's Epistemology and Learning research group:

```
>out

The E&L Garden

The E&L Garden is a happy jumble of little and big computers,
papers, coffee cups, and stray pieces of LEGO.

Obvious exits: hallway to E&L Hallway, closet to The LEGO
Closet, and sts to STS Centre Lounge

You see a newspaper, a Warhol print, a Sun SPARCstation IPC,
Projects Chalkboard, and Research Directory here. Amy is here.

>say hi

You say, "hi"

Amy says, "Hi Green_Guest! Welcome!"
```

The earliest MUDs such as "MUD1" and "Scepter of Goth" were based on the
role-playing game Dungeons and Dragons, and were written in late 1978 to

1979.[6] They were also based on early single-user text adventure games, such as the original ADVENT by Crowther and Woods [7]. In adventure-based MUDs, the object is to kill monsters and obtain treasure in order to gain "experience points." As a character gains experience, he/she/it becomes more powerful.

In 1989, a graduate student at Carnegie Mellon University named James Aspnes decided to see what would happen if the monsters and magic swords were removed. He created a new type of MUD, called "TinyMUD," which was not an adventure game. Instead of spending time killing virtual monsters, participants work together to help extend the virtual world using a simple programming language. Langdon Winner remarks that "social activity is an ongoing process of world-making" [9]. In MUDs, this is true in a literal sense.

In most MUDs, characters are anonymous. People who become friends can exchange real names and email addresses, but many choose not to. Conventions about when it is acceptable to talk about "real life" vary between communities. In most MUDs, people begin to talk more about real life when they get to know someone better. However, in some communities such as those based on the Dragonriders of Pern series of books by Anne McCaffrey, talking about real life is taboo.

MUDs are increasingly being used for more "serious" purposes. Pavel Curtis of Xerox PARC has developed a MUD to enhance professional community amongst astrophysicists called AstroVR [4]. The MediaMOO project, which I began in fall of 1992, is designed to enhance professional community amongst media researchers [2]. MediaMOO currently has over 500 participants from fourteen countries and is growing rapidly.

MUDs also have an intriguing potential as an educational environment. Since 1990, Barry Kort has been running a MUD for children called Micro-MUSE.[7] I am currently in the process of designing a MUD language and interface to make the technology more usable by children as part of my dissertation research. I hope to use this technology to encourage ten- to twelve-year-old girls to be more interested in computers.

▪ A PUBLIC DEBATE ABOUT GENDER

Gender pervades human interactions in such basic ways that its impact is often difficult to observe. Phenomena that are subtle in real life become obvious in MUDs, and are a frequent topic of discussion on USENET newsgroups about MUDs. For example, men are often surprised at how they are treated when they log on as a female character. Andrew writes on the newsgroup rec.games.mud:[8]

Back when I had time for MUD, I, too, played female characters. I found it extraordinarily interesting. It gave me a slightly more concrete understanding of why some women say, "Men suck." It was both amusing and disturbing.

Female characters are often besieged with attention. By typing using the Who command, it is possible to get a list of all characters logged on. The page command allows one to talk to people not in the same room. Many male players will get a list of all present and then page characters with female names. Unwanted attention and sexual advances create an uncomfortable atmosphere for women in MUDs, just as they do in real life.

Many people, both male and female, enjoy the attention paid to female characters. Male players will often log on as female characters and behave suggestively, further encouraging sexual advances. Pavel Curtis has noted that the most promiscuous and sexually aggressive women are usually played by men. If you meet a character named "FabulousHotBabe," she is almost certainly a he in real life [3].

Perhaps more damaging than unwanted sexual advances are unrequested offers of assistance. Carol, an experienced programmer who runs a MUD in Britain, writes on rec.games.mud:

What I *do* think is funny is this misconception that women can't play muds, can't work out puzzles, can't even type "kill monster" without help. (Okay, I admit we have it on this side of the Atlantic too . . .) Thanks, guys. . . . I log on, they work out I am female, and then the fun begins. Oh joy! After all, I don't log on to see whether people have found bugs with my little area, or to dispense arbitrary justice ("Please, Miss, he stole my sword!") or to find a friend. I call Aber-o-rama[9] (for this is the place) expressly to meet little spods who think (I assume) that because I am female I need help. People offering me help to solve puzzles *I* wrote are not going to get very far.

Do you think all women in real life too are the same? We don't squeak and look helpless *all* the time (in my case, only when I am tired and can't be bothered to wire the plug, change a fuse or remove the centipede from the bath (I really should move house . . .)).

The constant assumption that women need help can be damaging to a woman's sense of self esteem and competence. If people treat you like an incompetent, you may begin to believe it. Carol here is honest and astute enough to admit that women as well as men help create this problem—sometimes she acts helpless when she's simply "tired and can't be bothered" to complete an uninteresting or unpleasant task.

Male characters often expect sexual favors in return for technical assistance.

In the same netnews discussion, Dennis concurs with Carol:

I played a couple of muds as a female, one making up to wizard level. And the first thing I noticed was that the above was true. Other players start showering you with money to help you get started, and I had never once gotten a handout when playing a male player. And then they feel they should be allowed to tag along forever, and feel hurt when you leave them to go off and explore by yourself. Then when you give them the knee after they grope you, they wonder what your problem is, reciting that famous saying "What's your problem? It's only a game." Lest you get the wrong idea, there was nothing suggesting about my character, merely a female name and the appropriate pronouns in the bland description. Did I mention the friendly wizard who turned cold when he discovered I was male in real life? I guess some people are jerks in real life too.

Male characters often expect sexual favors in return for technical assistance. A male character once requested a kiss from me after answering a question. A gift always incurs an obligation. Offering technical help, like picking up the check at dinner, can be used to try to purchase rather than win a woman's favor. While this can be subtle and sometimes overlooked in real life, in MUDs it is blatant, directly experienced by most, and openly discussed in public forums such as this USENET discussion.

Ellen provides an interesting counterpoint:

This is very odd. I played LPmud[10] once, just to find out what it was like. Since most LP's do something hideous with my preferred capitalization of my preferred name, I chose a different name, and thought, what the heck, I'd try genderbending and find out if it was true that people would be nasty and kill me on sight and other stuff I'd heard about on r.g.m.[11] But, no, everyone was helpful (I was truly clueless and needed the assistance); someone gave me enough money to buy a weapon and armor and someone else showed me where the easy-to-kill newbie[12] monsters were. They definitely went out of their way to be nice to a male-presenting newbie . . . (These were all male-presenting players, btw.[13])

One theory is that my male character (Argyle, description "A short squat fellow who is looking for his socks") was pretty innocuous. Maybe people are only nasty if you are "A broad-shouldered perfect specimen of a man" or something of that nature, which can be taken as vaguely attacking. People are nice if they don't view you as a threat.

Ellen's point is intriguing, and takes the discussion to a new level of sophistication. In "Group Psychology and Analysis of the Ego," Sigmund Freud suggests that "love relationships . . . constitute the essence of the group mind" [5]. Issues of sexual power structure interpersonal interactions, and are more complex than "boy chases girl." Argyle's description invites a phallic interpretation—he is short and squat, and the reference to socks carries a connotation of limpness. Since Argyle is clearly not a sexual threat, he receives kinder treatment.

One cannot fail to be impressed by the quality of the netnews discussion. For the participants, MUDding throws issues of the impact of gender on human relations into high relief. Fundamental to its impact is the fact that it allows people to experience rather than merely observe what it feels like to be the opposite gender or have no gender at all.

Without makeup, special clothing, or risk of social stigma, gender becomes malleable in MUDs. When gender becomes a property that can be reset with a line of code, one bit in a data structure, it becomes an "object to think with," to use Seymour Papert's terminology [6]. In public forums like rec.games.mud, people reflect the values that our society attaches to gender. In private experiences, people can explore the impact of gender on their lives and their constructions of themselves.

■ CONCLUSION

Gender is just one example of an aspect of personal identity that people explore on MUDs. Examples abound. Jack is a British student studying in America. He logs onto MUDs in the morning when it is afternoon in Britain and many British players are on. He enjoys confusing them—he tells them he is in America, but displays a detailed knowledge of Britain. On further questioning, Jack tells me he is trying to decide whether to return to Britain or continue his studies in America. What does it mean to be British or American? Jack is exploring his sense of national identity in virtual reality. MUDs are an identity workshop.

Gender swapping is an extreme example of a fundamental fact: the network is in the process of changing not just how we work, but how we think of ourselves—and ultimately, who we are.

■ REFERENCES

[1] A. Bruckman. "Identity Workshop: Emergent Social and Psychological Phenomena in Text-Based Virtual Reality." Unpublished manuscript, 1992. Available via anonymous ftp from media.mit.edu in pub/asb/papers/ identity-workshop.{ps.Z, rtf.Z}

[2] A. Bruckman and M. Resnick. "Virtual Professional Community: Results from the MediaMOO Project." Presented at the Third International Conference on Cyberspace in Austin, Texas on May 15th, 1993. Available via anonymous ftp from media.mit.edu in pub/asb/papers/MediaMOO-3cyberconf.{ps.Z,rtf.Z,txt}

[3] P. Curtis. "MUDding: Social Phenomena in Text-Based Virtual Realities." Proceedings of DIAC T92. Available via anonymous ftp from parcftp.xerox.com, pub/MOO/papers/DIAC92.{ps, txt}.

[4] P. Curtis and D. Nichols. "MUDs Grow Up: Social Virtual Reality in the Real World." Presented at the Third International Conference on Cyberspace in Austin, Texas on May 15th, 1993. Available via anonymous ftp from parcftp.xerox.com in pub/MOO/papers/MUDsGrowUp. {ps,txt}

[5] S. Freud. *Group Psychology and Analysis of the Ego.* New York: W. W. Norton & Company, 1989.

[6] S. Papert. *Mindstorms: Children, Computers, and Powerful Ideas.* New York: Basic Books, 1980.

[7] E. Raymond. *The New Hacker's Dictionary.* Cambridge, MA: MIT Press, 1991.

[8] S. Turkle. *The Second Self: Computers and the Human Spirit.* New York: Simon & Schuster, 1984.

[9] L. Winner. *The Whale and the Reactor.* Chicago: University of Chicago Press, 1986.

■ ACKNOWLEDGMENTS

I'd like to thank MIT Professors Sherry Turkle, Mitchel Resnick, and Glorianna Davenport for their support of this research. Warren Sack and Lenny Foner read drafts of this paper. Most importantly, I'd like to thank the MUDders who have shared their experiences with me.

- **N O T E S**

1. Amy Bruckman is with the MIT Media Laboratory. She may be reached at asb@media-lab.media.mit.edu.

2. In fact, I retell this story secondhand; the details may not exactly reflect the television show.

3. I have chosen to write in the first person, because many of the ideas in this paper are based on my experiences as a participant-observer and because notions of identity are part of my topic.

4. On March 6th, 1992 there were 143 MUDs based on 13 kinds of software. This is an increase of 93 percent in number of MUDs and 54 percent in number of types of software over slightly more than a year. MUDs are constantly being created and destroyed. A current list is regularly posted to the USENET news group rec.games.mud.announce.

5. To connect to MediaMOO, type "telnet purple-crayon.media.mit.edu 8888" from a UNIX system on the Internet. Send electronic mail to mediamoo-registration@media.mit.edu for more information.

6. The earliest multi-player games existed on stand-alone time-sharing systems. In 1977, Jim Guyton adapted a game called "mazewar" to run on the ARPAnet. Participants in mazewar could duck around corners of a maze and shoot at one another, but could not communicate in any other fashion [email conversation with Jim Guyton, March 1992]. Numerous multi-user games based on the *Dungeons and Dragons* role playing game appeared in 1978–1979, including *Scepter of Goth* by Alan Klietz and MUD1 by Roy Trubshaw and Richard Bartle [email conversation with Alan Klietz, March 1992].

7. MicroMUSE is at chezmoto.ai.mit.edu 4201.

8. This is an excerpt from a USENET discussion about MUDs. Communications technologies have complex interactions. Since most MUDders have read USENET groups about MUDding for at least some period of time, the culture of USENET and of MUDs are in some ways linked. Social conventions evolve in the context of the complete set of technologies in use, including email, netnews, surface mail, telephones, answering machines, voice mail, television, radio, newspapers, magazines, books, and the like. Email, netnews, and MUDs have especially complex interactions.

9. The name of the MUD has been changed.

10. LPMUDs are a type of adventure-game-style MUD.

11. The abbreviation "r.g.m" stands for "rec.games.mud," the USENET newsgroup on which this discussion is taking place.

12. A newbie is a new player with little experience. According to Raymond [7], the term comes from British slang for "new boy," and first became popular on the net in the group talk.bizarre. A newbie monster is a monster that a low-level player could defeat.

13. This is an abbreviation for "by the way."

Julian Dibbell

A Rape in Cyberspace

They say he raped them that night. They say he did it with a cunning little doll, fashioned in their image and imbued with the power to make them do whatever he desired. They say that by manipulating the doll he forced them to have sex with him, and with each other, and to do horrible, brutal things to their own bodies. And though I wasn't there that night, I think I can assure you that what they say is true, because it all happened right in the living room—right there amid the well-stocked bookcases and the sofas and the fireplace—of a house I've come to think of as my second home.

Call me Dr. Bombay. Some months ago—let's say about halfway between the first time you heard the words *information superhighway* and the first time you wished you never had—I found myself tripping with compulsive regularity down the well-traveled information lane that leads to LambdaMOO, a very large and very busy rustic chateau built entirely of words. Nightly, I typed the commands that called those words onto my computer screen, dropping me with what seemed a warm electric thud inside the mansion's darkened coat closet, where I checked my quotidian identity, stepped into the persona and appearance of a minor character from a long-gone television sitcom, and stepped out into the glaring chatter of the crowded living room. Sometimes, when the mood struck me, I emerged as a dolphin instead.

Call me Dr. Bombay.

I won't say why I chose to masquerade as Samantha Stevens's outlandish cousin, or as the dolphin, or what exactly led to my mild but so-far incurable addiction to the semifictional digital otherworlds known around the Internet as multi-user dimensions, or MUDs. This isn't my story, after all. It's the story of a man named Mr. Bungle, and of the ghostly sexual violence he committed in the halls of LambdaMOO, and most importantly of the ways his violence and his victims challenged the thousand and more residents of that surreal, magic-infested mansion to become, finally, the community so many of them already believed they were.

That I was myself one of those residents has little direct bearing on the story's events. I mention it only as a warning that my own perspective is perhaps too steeped in the surreality and magic of the place to serve as an entirely appropriate guide. For the Bungle Affair raises questions that—here on the brink of a future in which human life may find itself as tightly enveloped in digital environments as it is today in the architectural kind— demand a clear-eyed, sober, and unmystified consideration. It asks us to shut our ears momentarily to the techno-utopian ecstasies of West Coast cyberhippies and look without illusion upon the present possibilities for building, in the on-line spaces of this world, societies more decent and free than those mapped onto dirt and concrete and capital. It asks us to behold the new bodies awaiting us in virtual space undazzled by their phantom powers, and to get to the crucial work of sorting out the socially meaningful differences between those bodies and our physical ones. And most forthrightly it asks us to wrap our late modern ontologies, epistemologics, sexual ethics, and common sense around the curious notion of rape by voodoo doll—and to try not to warp them beyond recognition in the process.

In short, the Bungle Affair dares me to explain it to you without resort to dime-store mysticisms, and I fear I may have shape-shifted by the digital moonlight one too many times to be quite up to the task. But I will do what I can, and I can do no better, I suppose, than to lead with the facts. For if nothing else about Mr. Bungle's case is unambiguous, the facts at least are crystal clear.

The facts begin (as they often do) with a time and a place. The time was a Monday night in March, and the place, as I've said, was the living room— which, due to the inviting warmth of its decor, is so invariably packed with chitchatters as to be roughly synonymous among LambdaMOOers with a party. So strong, indeed, is the sense of convivial common ground invested in the living room that a cruel mind could hardly imagine a better place in which to stage a violation of LambdaMOO's communal spirit. And there was cruelty enough lurking in the appearance Mr. Bungle presented to the virtual world—he was at the time a fat, oleaginous, Bisquick-faced clown dressed in cum-stained harlequin garb and girdled with a mistletoe-and-hemlock belt whose buckle bore the quaint inscription "KISS ME UNDER THIS, BITCH!" But whether cruelty motivated his choice of crime scene is not among the established facts of the case. It is a fact only that he did choose the living room.

The remaining facts tell us a bit more about the inner world of Mr. Bungle, though only perhaps that it couldn't have been a very comfortable place. They tell us that he commenced his assault entirely unprovoked, at or about 10 P.M. Pacific Standard Time. That he began by using his voodoo doll to force one of the room's occupants to sexually service him in a variety of more or less conventional ways. That this victim was legba, a Haitian trickster spirit of indeterminate gender, brown-skinned and wearing an expensive pearl gray suit, top hat, and dark glasses. That legba heaped vicious imprecations on him all the while and that he was soon ejected bodily from the room. That he hid himself away then in his private chambers somewhere on the mansion grounds and continued the attacks without interruption, since the voodoo doll worked just as well at a distance as in proximity. That he turned his attentions now to Starsinger, a rather pointedly nondescript female character, tall, stout, and brown-haired, forcing her into unwanted liaisons with other individuals present in the room, among them legba, Bakunin (the well-known radical), and Juniper (the squirrel). That his actions grew progressively violent. That he made legba eat his/her own pubic hair. That he caused Starsinger to violate herself with a piece of kitchen cutlery. That his distant laughter echoed evilly in the living room with every successive outrage. That he could not be stopped until at last someone summoned Zippy, a wise and trusted old-timer who brought with him a gun of near wizardly powers, a gun that didn't kill but enveloped its targets in a cage impermeable even to a voodoo doll's powers. That Zippy fired this gun at Mr. Bungle, thwarting the doll at last and silencing the evil, distant laughter.

These particulars, as I said, are unambiguous. But they are far from simple, for the simple reason that every set of facts in virtual reality (or VR, as the locals abbreviate it) is shadowed by a second, complicating set: the "real-life" facts. And while a certain tension invariably buzzes in the gap between the hard, prosaic RL facts and their more fluid, dreamy VR counterparts, the dissonance in the Bungle case is striking. No hideous clowns or trickster spirits appear in the RL version of the incident, no voodoo dolls or wizard guns, indeed no rape at all as any RL court of law has yet defined it. The actors in the drama were university students for the most part, and they sat rather undramatically before computer screens the entire time, their only actions a spidery flitting of fingers across standard QWERTY keyboards. No bodies touched. Whatever physical interaction occurred consisted of a mingling of electronic signals sent from sites spread out between New York City and Sydney, Australia. Those signals met in LambdaMOO, certainly, just as the hideous clown and the living room party did, but what was LambdaMOO after all? Not an enchanted mansion or anything of the sort—just a middlingly complex database, maintained for experimental purposes inside a Xerox Corporation research computer in Palo Alto and open to public access via the Internet.

To be more precise about it, LambdaMOO was a MUD. Or to be yet more precise, it was a subspecies of MUD known as a MOO, which is short for "MUD, Object-Oriented." All of which means that it was a kind of database especially designed to give users the vivid impression of moving through a physical space that in reality exists only as descriptive data filed away on a hard drive. When users dial into LambdaMOO, for instance, the program immediately presents them with a brief textual description of one of the rooms of the database's fictional mansion (the coat closet, say). If the user wants to leave this room, she can enter a command to move in a particular direction and the database will replace the original description with a new one corresponding to the room located in the direction she chose. When the new description scrolls across the user's screen it lists not only the fixed features of the room but all its contents at that moment—including things (tools, toys, weapons) and other users (each represented as a "character" over which he or she has sole control).

As far as the database program is concerned, all of these entities—rooms, things, characters—are just different subprograms that the program allows to interact according to rules very roughly mimicking the laws of the physical world. Characters may not leave a room in a given direction, for instance, unless the room subprogram contains an "exit" at that compass point. And if a character "says" or "does" something (as directed by its user-owner), then only the users whose characters are also located in that room will see the output describing the statement or action. Aside from such basic constraints, however, LambdaMOOers are allowed a broad freedom to create—they can describe their characters any way they like, they can make rooms of their own and decorate them to taste, and they can build new objects almost at will.

To the extent that Mr. Bungle's assault happened in real life at all, it happened as a sort of Punch-and-Judy show, in which the puppets and the scenery were made of nothing more substantial than digital code and snippets of creative writing.

The combination of all this busy user activity with the hard physics of the database can certainly induce a lucid illusion of presence—but when all is said and done the only thing you *really* see when you visit LambdaMOO is a kind of slow-crawling script, lines of dialogue and stage direction creeping steadily up your computer screen.

Which is all just to say that, to the extent that Mr. Bungle's assault happened in real life at all, it happened as a sort of Punch-and-Judy show, in which the puppets and the scenery were made of nothing more substantial than digital code and snippets of creative writing. The puppeteer behind Bungle, as it happened, was a young man logging in to the MOO from a New York University computer. He could have been Al Gore for all any of the others knew, however, and he could have written Bungle's script that night any way he chose. He could have sent a command to print the message "Mr. Bungle, smiling a saintly smile, floats angelic near the ceiling of the living room, showering joy and candy kisses down upon the heads of all below"—and everyone then receiving output from the database's subprogram #17 (a/k/a the "living room") would have seen that sentence on their screens.

Instead, he entered sadistic fantasies into the "voodoo doll," a subprogram that served the not exactly kosher purpose of attributing actions to other characters that their users did not actually write. And thus a woman in Haverford, Pennsylvania, whose account on the MOO attached her to a character she called Starsinger, was given the unasked-for opportunity to read the words "As if against her will, Starsinger jabs a steak knife up her ass, causing immense joy. You hear Mr. Bungle laughing evilly in the distance." And thus the woman in Seattle who had written herself the character called legba, with a view perhaps to tasting in imagination a deity's freedom from the burdens of the gendered flesh, got to read similarly constructed sentences in which legba, messenger of the gods, lord of crossroads and communications, suffered a brand of degradation all-too customarily reserved for the embodied female.

"Mostly voodoo dolls are amusing," wrote legba on the evening after Bungle's rampage, posting a public statement to the widely read in-MOO mailing list called *social-issues,* a forum for debate on matters of import to the entire populace. "And mostly I tend to think that restrictive measures around here cause more trouble than they prevent. But I also think that Mr. Bungle was being a vicious, vile fuckhead, and I . . . want his sorry ass scattered from #17 to the Cinder Pile. I'm not calling for policies, trials, or better jails. I'm not sure what I'm calling for. Virtual castration, if I could manage it. Mostly, [this type of thing] doesn't happen here. Mostly, perhaps I thought it wouldn't happen to me. Mostly, I trust people to conduct themselves with some veneer of civility. Mostly, I want his ass."

Months later, the woman in Seattle would confide to me that as she wrote those words posttraumatic tears were streaming down her face—a real-life fact that should suffice to prove that the words' emotional content was no mere playacting. The precise tenor of that content, however, its mingling of murderous rage and eyeball-rolling annoyance, was a curious amalgam that neither the RL nor the VR facts alone can quite account for. Where virtual reality and its conventions would have us believe that legba and Starsinger were brutally raped in their own living room, here was the victim legba scolding Mr. Bungle for a breach of "civility." Where real life, on the other hand, insists the incident was only an episode in a free-form version of Dungeons and Dragons, confined to the realm of the symbolic and at no point threatening any player's life, limb, or material wellbeing, here now was the player legba issuing aggrieved and heartfelt calls for Mr. Bungle's dismemberment. Ludicrously excessive by RL's lights, woefully understated by VR's, the tone of legba's response made sense only in the buzzing, dissonant gap between them.

Which is to say it made the only kind of sense that *can* be made of MUDly phenomena. For while the *facts* attached to any event born of a MUD's strange, ethereal universe may march in straight, tandem lines separated neatly into the virtual and the real, its meaning lies always in that gap. You learn this axiom early in your life as a player, and it's of no small relevance to the Bungle case that you often learn it between the sheets, so to speak. Netsex, tinysex, virtual sex—however you name it, in real-life reality it's nothing more than a 900-line encounter stripped of even the vestigial physicality of the voice. And yet, as many a player can tell you, it's possibly the headiest experience the very heady world of MUDs has to offer. Amid flurries of even the most cursorily described caresses, sighs, and penetrations, the glands do engage, and often as throbbingly as they would in a real-life assignation— sometimes even more so, given the combined power of anonymity and textual suggestiveness to unshackle deep-seated fantasies. And if the virtual setting and the interplayer vibe are right, who knows? The heart may engage as well, stirring up passions as strong as many that bind lovers who observe the formality of trysting in the flesh.

To participate, therefore, in this disembodied enactment of life's most body-centered activity is to risk the realization that when it comes to sex, perhaps the body in question is not the physical one at all, but its psychic double, the bodylike self-representation we carry around in our heads. I know, I know, you've read Foucault and your mind is not quite blown by the notion that sex is never so much an exchange of fluids as it is an exchange of signs. But trust your friend Dr. Bombay, it's one thing to grasp the notion intellectually and quite another to feel it coursing through your veins amid the virtual steam of hot netnookie. And it's a whole other mind-blowing trip altogether to encounter it thus as a college frosh, new to the net and still in the grip of hormonal hurricanes and high-school sexual mythologies. The shock can easily reverberate throughout an entire young worldview. Small wonder, then, that a newbie's first taste of MUD sex is often also the first time she or he surrenders wholly to the slippery terms of MUDish ontology, recognizing in a full-bodied way that what happens inside a MUDmade world is neither exactly real nor exactly make-believe, but profoundly, compellingly, and emotionally meaningful.

And small wonder indeed that the sexual nature of Mr. Bungle's crime provoked such powerful feelings, and not just in legba (who, be it noted, was in real life a theory-savvy doctoral candidate and a longtime MOOer, but just as baffled and overwhelmed by the force of her own reaction, she later would attest, as any panting undergrad might have been). Even players who had never experienced MUD rape (the vast majority of male-presenting characters, but not as large a majority of the female-presenting as might be hoped) immediately appreciated its gravity and were moved to condemnation of the perp. legba's missive to *social-issues followed a strongly worded one from Zippy ("Well, well," it began, "no matter what else happens on Lambda, I can always be sure that some jerk is going to reinforce my low opinion of humanity") and was itself followed by others from Moriah, Raccoon, Crawfish, and evangeline. Starsinger also let her feelings ("pissed") be known. And even Jander, the Clueless Samaritan who had responded to Bungle's cries for help and uncaged him shortly after the incident, expressed his regret once apprised of Bungle's deeds, which he allowed to be "despicable."

A sense was brewing that something needed to be done—done soon and in something like an organized fashion—about Mr. Bungle, in particular, and about MUD rape, in general.

A sense was brewing that something needed to be done—done soon and in something like an organized fashion—about Mr. Bungle, in particular, and about MUD rape, in general. Regarding the general problem, evangeline, who identified herself as a survivor of both virtual rape ("many times over") and real-life sexual assault, floated a cautious proposal for a MOO-wide powwow on the subject of virtual sex offenses and what mechanisms if any might be put in place to deal with their future occurrence. As for the specific problem, the answer no doubt seemed obvious to many. But it wasn't until the evening of the second day after the incident that legba, finally and rather solemnly, gave it voice: "I am requesting that Mr. Bungle be toaded for raping Starsinger and I. I have never done this before, and have thought about it for days. He hurt us both."

That was all. Three simple sentences posted to *social. Reading them, an outsider might never guess that they were an application for a death warrant.

Even an outsider familiar with other MUDs might not guess it, since in many of them "toading" still refers to a command that, true to the gameworlds' sword-and-sorcery origins, simply turns a player into a toad, wiping the player's description and attributes and replacing them with those of the slimy amphibian. Bad luck for sure, but not quite as bad as what happens when the same command is invoked in the MOOish strains of MUD: not only are the description and attributes of the toaded player erased, but the account itself goes too. The annihilation of the character, thus, is total.

And nothing less than total annihilation, it seemed, would do to settle LambdaMOO's accounts with Mr. Bungle. Within minutes of the posting of legba's appeal, SamIAm, the Australian Deleuzean, who had witnessed much of the attack from the back room of his suburban Sydney home, seconded the motion with a brief message crisply entitled "Toad the fukr." SamIAm's posting was seconded almost as quickly by that of Bakunin, covictim of Mr. Bungle and well-known radical, who in real life happened also to be married to the real-life legba. And over the course of the next 24 hours as many as 50 players made it known, on *social and in a variety of other forms and forums, that they would be pleased to see Mr. Bungle erased from the face of the MOO. And with dissent so far confined to a dozen or so antitoading hardliners, the numbers suggested that the citizenry was indeed moving toward a resolve to have Bungle's virtual head.

There was one small but stubborn obstacle in the way of this resolve, however, and that was a curious state of social affairs known in some quarters of the MOO as the New Direction. It was all very fine. you see, for the LambdaMOO rabble to get it in their heads to liquidate one of their peers, but when the time came to actually do the deed it would require the services of a nobler class of character. It would require a wizard. Masterprogrammers of the MOO, spelunkers of the database's deepest code-structures and custodians of its day-to-day administrative trivia, wizards are also the only players empowered to issue the toad command, a feature maintained on nearly all MUDs as a quick-and-dirty means of social control. But the wizards of LambdaMOO, after years of adjudicating all manner of interplayer disputes with little to show for it but their own weariness and the smoldering resentment of the general populace, had decided they'd had enough of the social sphere. And so, four months before the Bungle incident, the archwizard Haakon (known in RL as Pavel Curtis, Xerox researcher and LambdaMOO's principal architect) formalized this decision in a document called "LambdaMOO Takes a New Direction," which he placed in the living room for all to see. In it, Haakon announced that the wizards from that day forth were pure technicians. From then on, they would make no decisions affecting the social life of the MOO, but only implement whatever decisions the community as a whole directed them to. From then on, it was decreed, LambdaMOO would just have to grow up and solve its problems on its own.

Faced with the task of inventing its own self-governance from scratch, the LambdaMOO population had so far done what any other loose, amorphous agglomeration of individuals would have done: they'd let it slide. But now the task took on new urgency. Since getting the wizards to toad Mr. Bungle (or to toad the likes of him in the future) required a convincing case that the cry for his head came from the community at large, then the community itself would have to be defined; and if the community was to be convincingly defined, then some form of social organization, no matter how rudimentary, would have to be settled on. And thus, as if against its will, the question of what to do about Mr. Bungle began to shape itself into a sort of referendum on the political future of the MOO. Arguments broke out on *social and else-where that had only superficially to do with Bungle (since everyone agreed he was a cad) and everything to do with where the participants stood on LambdaMOO's crazy-quilty political map. Parliamentarian legalist types argued that unfortunately Bungle could not legitimately be toaded at all, since there were no explicit MOO rules against rape, or against just about anything else—and the sooner such rules were established, they added, and maybe even a full-blown judiciary system complete with elected officials and prisons to enforce those rules, the better. Others, with a royalist streak in them, seemed to feel that Bungle's as-yet unpunished outrage only proved this New Direction silliness had gone on long enough, and that it was high time the wizardocracy returned to the position of swift and decisive leadership their player class was born to.

And then there were what I'll call the technolibertarians. For them, MUD rapists were of course assholes, but the presence of assholes on the system was a technical inevitability, like noise on a phone line, and best dealt with not through repressive social disciplinary mechanisms but through the timely deployment of defensive software tools. Some asshole blasting violent, graphic language at you? Don't whine to the authorities about it—hit the @gag command and the asshole's statements will be blocked from your screen (and only yours). It's simple, it's effective, and it censors no one.

But the Bungle case was rather hard on such arguments. For one thing, the extremely public nature of the living room meant that gagging would spare the victims only from witnessing their own violation, but not from having others witness it. You might want to argue that what those victims didn't directly experience couldn't hurt them, but consider how that wisdom would sound to a woman who'd been, say, fondled by strangers while passed out drunk and you have a rough idea how it might go over with a crowd of hard-core MOOers. Consider, for another thing, that many of the biologically female participants in the Bungle debate had been around long enough to grow lethally weary of the gag-and-get-over-it school of virtual-rape counsel-ing, with its fine line between empowering victims and holding them respon-sible for their own suffering, and its shrugging indifference to the window of pain between the moment the rape-text starts flowing and the moment a gag shuts it off. From the outset it was clear that the technolibertarians were going to have to tiptoe through this issue with care, and for the most part they did.

Yet no position was trickier to maintain than that of the MOO's resident anarchists. Like the technolibbers, the anarchists didn't care much for punish-ments or policies or power elites. Like them, they hoped the MOO could be a place where people interacted fulfillingly without the need for such things. But their high hopes were complicated, in general, by a somewhat less thoroughgoing faith in technology ("Even if you can't tear down the master's house with the master's tools"—read a slogan written into one anarchist player's self-description—"it is a damned good place to start"). And at present they were additionally complicated by the fact that the most vocal anarchists in the discussion were none other than legba, Bakunin, and SamIAm, who wanted to see Mr. Bungle toaded as badly as anyone did.

Needless to say, a pro-death-penalty platform is not an especially comfortable one for an anarchist to sit on, so these particular anarchists were now at great pains to sever the conceptual ties between toading and capital punishment. Toading, they insisted (almost convincingly), was much more closely analogous to banishment; it was a kind of turning of the communal back on the offending party, a collective action which, if carried out properly, was entirely consistent with anarchist models of community. And carrying it out properly meant first and foremost building a consensus around it—a messy process for which there were no easy technocratic substitutes. It was going to take plenty of good old-fashioned, jawbone-intensive grass-roots organizing.

So that when the time came, at 7 P. M. PST on the evening of the third day after the occurrence in the living room, to gather in evangeline's room for her proposed real-time open conclave, Bakunin and legba were among the first to arrive. But this was hardly to be an anarchist-dominated affair, for the room was crowding rapidly with representatives of all the MOO's political stripes, and even a few wizards. Hagbard showed up, and Autumn and Quastro, Puff, JoeFeedback, L-dopa and Bloaf, HerkieCosmo, Silver Rocket, Karl Porcupine, Matchstick—the names piled up and the discussion gathered momentum under their weight. Arguments multiplied and mingled, players talked past and through each other, the textual clutter of utterances and gestures filled up the screen like thick cigar smoke. Peaking in number at around 30, this was one of the largest crowds that ever gathered in a single LambdaMOO chamber, and while evangeline had given her place a description that made it "infinite in expanse and fluid in form," it now seemed anything but roomy. You could almost feel the claustrophobic air of the place, dank and overheated by virtual bodies, pressing against your skin.

I know you could because I too was there, making my lone and insignificant appearance in this story. Completely ignorant of any of the goings-on that had led to the meeting, I wandered in purely to see what the crowd was about, and though I observed the proceedings for a good while, I confess I found it hard to grasp what was going on. I was still the rankest of newbies then, my MOO legs still too unsteady to make the leaps of faith, logic, and empathy required to meet the spectacle on its own terms. I was fascinated by the concept of virtual rape, but I couldn't quite take it seriously.

In this, though, I was in a small and mostly silent minority, for the discussion that raged around me was of an almost unrelieved earnestness, bent, it seemed, on examining every last aspect and implication of Mr. Bungle's crime. There were the central questions, of course: thumbs up or down on Bungle's virtual existence? And if down, how then to insure that his toading was not just some isolated lynching but a first step toward shaping LambdaMOO into a legitimate community? Surrounding these, however, a tangle of weighty side issues proliferated. What, some wondered, was the real-life legal status of the offense? Could Bungle's university administrators punish him for sexual harassment? Could he be prosecuted under California state laws against obscene phone calls? Little enthusiasm was shown for pursuing either of these lines of action, which testifies both to the uniqueness of the crime and to the nimbleness with which the discussants were negotiating its idiosyncrasies. Many were the casual references to Bungle's deed as simply "rape," but these in no way implied that the players had lost sight of all distinctions between the virtual and physical versions, or that they believed Bungle should be dealt with in the same way a real-life criminal would. He had committed a MOO crime, and his punishment, if any, would be meted out via the MOO.

On the other hand, little patience was shown toward any attempts to downplay the seriousness of what Mr. Bungle had done. When the affable HerkieCosmo proposed, more in the way of a hypothesis than an assertion, that "perhaps it's better to release . . . violent tendencies in a virtual environ-ment rather than in real life," he was tut-tutted so swiftly and relentlessly that he withdrew the hypothesis altogether, apologizing humbly as he did so. Not that the assembly was averse to putting matters into a more philosophical per-spective. "Where does the body end and the mind begin?" young Quastro asked, amid recurring attempts to fine-tune the differences between real and virtual violence. "Is not the mind a part of the body?" "In MOO, the body is the mind," offered HerkieCosmo gamely, and not at all implausibly, demon-strating the ease with which very knotty metaphysical conundrums come undone in VR. The not-so-aptly named Obvious seemed to agree, arriving after deep consideration of the nature of Bungle's crime at the hardly novel yet now somehow newly resonant conjecture "All reality might consist of ideas, who knows."

On these and other matters the anarchists, the libertarians, the legalists, the wizardists—and the wizards—all had their thoughtful say. But as the evening wore on and the talk grew more heated and more heady, it seemed increas-ingly clear that the vigorous intelligence being brought to bear on this swarm of issues wasn't going to result in anything remotely like resolution. The per-spectives were just too varied, the meme-scape just too slippery. Again and again, arguments that looked at first to be heading in a decisive direction ended up chasing their own tails; and slowly, depressingly, a dusty haze of irrelevance gathered over the proceedings.

It was almost a relief, therefore, when midway through the evening Mr. Bungle himself, the living, breathing cause of all this talk, teleported into the room. Not that it was much of a surprise. Oddly enough, in the three days since his release from Zippy's cage, Bungle had returned more than once to wander the public spaces of LambdaMOO, walking willingly into one of the fiercest storms of ill will and invective ever to rain down on a player. He'd been taking it all with a curious and mostly silent passivity, and when chal-

lenged face to virtual face by both legba and the genderless elder stateschar-
acter PatGently to defend himself on *social,* he'd demurred, mumbling something about Christ and expiation. He was equally quiet now, and his
reception was still uniformly cool. legba fixed an arctic stare on him—"no
hate, no anger, no interest at all. Just . . . watching." Others were more actively
unfriendly. "Asshole," spat Karl Porcupine, "creep." But the harshest of the
MOO's hostility toward him had already been vented, and the attention he
drew now was motivated more, it seemed, by the opportunity to probe the
rapist's mind, to find out what made it tick and if possible how to get it to
tick differently. In short, they wanted to know why he'd done it. So they
asked him.

And Mr. Bungle thought about it. And as eddies of discussion and debate
continued to swirl around him, he thought about it some more. And then he
said this:

*"I engaged in a bit of a psychological device that is called thought-polarization, the fact
that this is not RL simply added to heighten the affect of the device. It was purely a
sequence of events with no consequence on my RL existence."*

They might have known. Stilted though its diction was, the gist of the
answer was simple, and something many in the room had probably already
surmised: Mr. Bungle was a psycho. Not, perhaps, in real life—but then in
real life it's possible for reasonable people to assume, as Bungle clearly did,
that what transpires between word-costumed characters within the boundaries
of a makebelieve world is, if not mere play, then at most some kind of emotional laboratory experiment. Inside the MOO, however, such thinking marked
a person as one of two basically subcompetent types. The first was the newbie, in which case the confusion was understandable, since there were few
MOOers who had not, upon their first visits as anonymous "guest" characters,
mistaken the place for a vast playpen in which they might act out their
wildest fantasies without fear of censure. Only with time and the acquisition
of a fixed character do players tend to make the critical passage from
anonymity to pseudonymity, developing the concern for their character's reputation that marks the attainment of virtual adulthood. But while Mr. Bungle
hadn't been around as long as most MOOers, he'd been around long enough
to leave his newbie status behind, and his delusional statement therefore
placed him among the second type: the sociopath.

And as there is but small percentage in arguing with a head case, the
room's attention gradually abandoned Mr. Bungle and returned to the discussions that had previously occupied it. But if the debate had been edging
toward ineffectuality before, Bungle's anticlimactic appearance had evidently
robbed it of any forward motion whatsoever. What's more, from his lonely
corner of the room Mr. Bungle kept issuing periodic expressions of a prickly
sort of remorse, interlaced with sarcasm and belligerence, and though it was
hard to tell if he wasn't still just conducting his experiments, some people
thought his regret genuine enough that maybe he didn't deserve to be toaded
after all. Logically, of course, discussion of the principal issues at hand didn't

require unanimous belief that Bungle was an irredeemable bastard, but now that cracks were showing in that unanimity, the last of the meeting's fervor seemed to be draining out through them.

People started drifting away. Mr. Bungle left first, then others followed—one by one, in twos and threes, hugging friends and waving goodnight. By 9:45 only a handful remained, and the great debate had wound down into casual conversation, the melancholy remains of another fruitless good idea. The arguments had been well-honed, certainly, and perhaps might prove useful in some as-yet-unclear long run. But at this point what seemed clear was that evangeline's meeting had died, at last, and without any practical results to mark its passing.

It was also at this point, most likely, that JoeFeedback reached his decision. JoeFeedback was a wizard, a taciturn sort of fellow who'd sat brooding on the sidelines all evening. He hadn't said a lot, but what he had said indicated that he took the crime committed against legba and Starsinger very seriously, and that he felt no particular compassion toward the character who had committed it. But on the other hand he had made it equally plain that he took the elimination of a fellow player just as seriously, and moreover that he had no desire to return to the days of wizardly fiat. It must have been difficult, therefore, to reconcile the conflicting impulses churning within him at that moment. In fact, it was probably impossible, for as much as he would have liked to make himself an instrument of LambdaMOO's collective will, he surely realized that under the present order of things he must in the final analysis either act alone or not act at all.

They say that LambdaMOO has never been the same since Mr. Bungle's toading. They say as well that nothing's really changed.

So JoeFeedback acted alone.

He told the lingering few players in the room that he had to go, and then he went. It was a minute or two before ten. He did it quietly and he did it privately, but all anyone had to do to know he'd done it was to type the @who command, which was normally what you typed if you wanted to know a player's present location and the time he last logged in. But if you had run a @who on Mr. Bungle not too long after JoeFeedback left evangeline's room, the database would have told you something different.

"Mr. Bungle," it would have said, "is not the name of any player."

The date, as it happened, was April Fool's Day, and it would still be April Fool's Day for another two hours. But this was no joke: Mr. Bungle was truly dead and truly gone.

They say that LambdaMOO has never been the same since Mr. Bungle's toading. They say as well that nothing's really changed. And though it skirts the fuzziest of dream-logics to say that both these statements are true, the MOO is just the sort of fuzzy, dreamlike place in which such contradictions thrive.

Certainly whatever civil society now informs LambdaMOO owes its existence to the Bungle Affair. The archwizard Haakon made sure of that. Away on business for the duration of the episode, Haakon returned to find its

wreckage strewn across the tiny universe he'd set in motion. The death of a
player, the trauma of several others, and the angst-ridden conscience of his
colleague JoeFeedback presented themselves to his concerned and astonished
attention, and he resolved to see if he couldn't learn some lesson from it all.
For the better part of a day he brooded over the record of events and arguments left in *social, then he sat pondering the chaotically evolving shape of
his creation, and at the day's end he descended once again into the social
arena of the MOO with another history-altering proclamation.

It was probably his last, for what he now decreed was the final, missing
piece of the New Direction. In a few days, Haakon announced, he would
build into the database a system of petitions and ballots whereby anyone
could put to popular vote any social scheme requiring wizardly powers for its
implementation, with the results of the vote to be binding on the wizards. At
last and for good, the awkward gap between the will of the players and the
efficacy of the technicians would be closed. And though some anarchists
grumbled about the irony of Haakon's dictatorially imposing universal suffrage
on an unconsulted populace, in general the citizens of LambdaMOO seemed to
find it hard to fault a system more purely democratic than any that could ever
exist in real life. Eight months and a dozen ballot measures later, widespread
participation in the new regime has produced a small arsenal of mechanisms
for dealing with the types of violence that called the system into being. MOO
residents now have access to a @boot command, for instance, with which to
summarily eject berserker "guest" characters. And players can bring suit
against one another through an ad hoc arbitration system in which mutually
agreed-upon judges have at their disposition the full range of
wizardly punishments—up to and including the capital.

Yet the continued dependence on death as the ultimate
keeper of the peace suggests that this new MOO order may not
be built on the most solid of foundations. For if life on LambdaMOO began to acquire more coherence in the wake of the
toading, death retained all the fuzziness of pre-Bungle days.
This truth was rather dramatically borne out, not too many
days after Bungle departed, by the arrival of a strange new
character named Dr. Jest. There was a forceful eccentricity to the newcomer's
manner, but the oddest thing about his style was its striking yet unnameable
familiarity. And when he developed the annoying habit of stuffing fellow
players into a jar containing a tiny simulacrum of a certain deceased rapist,
the source of this familiarity became obvious:

Mr. Bungle had risen from the grave.

In itself, Bungle's reincarnation as Dr. Jest was a remarkable turn of events,
but perhaps even more remarkable was the utter lack of amazement with
which the LambdaMOO public took note of it. To be sure, many residents
were appalled by the brazenness of Bungle's return. In fact, one of the first
petitions circulated under the new voting system was a request for Dr. Jest's
toading that almost immediately gathered 52 signatures (but has failed so far
to reach ballot status). Yet few were unaware of the ease with which the toad

*Mr. Bungle
had risen from
the grave.*

proscription could be circumvented—all the toadee had to do (all the urBungle at NYU presumably had done) was to go to the minor hassle of acquiring a new Internet account, and LambdaMOO's character registration program would then simply treat the known felon as an entirely new and innocent person. Nor was this ease generally understood to represent a failure of toading's social disciplinary function. On the contrary, it only underlined the truism (repeated many times throughout the debate over Mr. Bungle's fate) that his punishment, ultimately, had been no more or less symbolic than his crime.

What *was* surprising, however, was that Mr. Bungle/Dr. Jest seemed to have taken the symbolism to heart. Dark themes still obsessed him—the objects he created gave off wafts of Nazi imagery and medical torture—but he no longer radiated the aggressively antisocial vibes he had before. He was a lot less unpleasant to look at (the outrageously seedy clown description had been replaced by that of a mildly creepy but actually rather natty young man, with "blue eyes . . . suggestive of conspiracy, untamed eroticism and perhaps a sense of understanding of the future"), and aside from the occasional jar-stuffing incident, he was also a lot less dangerous to be around. It was obvious he'd undergone some sort of personal transformation in the days since I'd first glimpsed him back in evangeline's crowded room—nothing radical maybe, but powerful nonetheless, and resonant enough with my own experience, I felt, that it might be more than professionally interesting to talk with him, and perhaps compare notes.

For I too was undergoing a transformation in the aftermath of that night in evangeline's, and I'm still not entirely sure what to make of it. As I pursued my runaway fascination with the discussion I had heard there, as I pored over the *social debate and got to know legba and some of the other victims and witnesses, I could feel my newbie consciousness falling away from me. Where before I'd found it hard to take virtual rape seriously, I now was finding it difficult to remember how I could ever not have taken it seriously. I was proud to have arrived at this perspective—it felt like an exotic sort of achievement, and it definitely made my ongoing experience of the MOO a richer one.

But it was also having some unsettling effects on the way I looked at the rest of the world. Sometimes, for instance, it was hard for me to understand why RL society classifies RL rape alongside crimes against person or property. Since rape can occur without any physical pain or damage, I found myself reasoning, then it must be classed as a crime against the mind—more intimately and deeply hurtful, to be sure, than cross-burnings, wolf whistles, and virtual rape, but undeniably located on the same conceptual continuum. I did not, however, conclude as a result that rapists were protected in any fashion by the First Amendment. Quite the opposite, in fact: the more seriously I took the notion of virtual rape, the less seriously I was able to take the notion of freedom of speech, with its tidy division of the world into the symbolic and the real.

Let me assure you, though, that I am not presenting these thoughts as arguments. I offer them, rather, as a picture of the sort of mindset that deep immersion in a virtual world has inspired in me. I offer them also, therefore, as a kind of prophecy. For whatever else these thoughts tell me, I have come

to believe that they announce the final stages of our decades-long passage
into the Information Age, a paradigm shift that the classic liberal firewall
between word and deed (itself a product of an earlier paradigm shift commonly known as the Enlightenment) is not likely to survive intact. After all,
anyone the least bit familiar with the workings of the new era's definitive
technology, the computer, knows that it operates on a principle impracticably
difficult to distinguish from the pre-Enlightenment principle of the magic
word: the commands you type into a computer are a kind of speech that
doesn't so much communicate as *make things happen,* directly and ineluctably,
the same way pulling a trigger does. They are incantations, in other words,
and anyone at all attuned to the technosocial megatrends of the moment—
from the growing dependence of economies on the global flow of intensely
fetishized words and numbers to the burgeoning ability of bioengineers to
speak the spells written in the four-letter text of DNA—knows that the logic
of the incantation is rapidly permeating the fabric of our lives.

And it's precisely this logic that provides the real magic in a place like
LambdaMOO—not the fictive trappings of voodoo and shapeshifting and wiz-
ardry, but the conflation of speech and act that's inevitable in any computer-
mediated world, be it Lambda or the increasingly wired world at large. This is
dangerous magic, to be sure, a potential threat—if misconstrued or misap-
plied—to our always precarious freedoms of expression, and as someone who
lives by his words I do not take the threat lightly. And yet, on the other hand,
I can no longer convince myself that our wishful insulation of language from
the realm of action has ever been anything but a valuable kludge, a philo-
sophically damaged stopgap against oppression that would just have to do till
something truer and more elegant came along.

Am I wrong to think this truer, more elegant thing can be found on LambdaMOO? Perhaps, but I continue to seek it there, sensing its presence just
beneath the surface of every interaction. I have even thought, as I said, that
discussing with Dr. Jest our shared experience of the workings of the MOO
might help me in my search. But when that notion first occurred to me, I still
felt somewhat intimidated by his lingering criminal aura, and I hemmed and
hawed a good long time before finally resolving to drop him MOO-mail
requesting an interview. By then it was too late. For reasons known only to
himself, Dr. Jest had stopped logging in. Maybe he'd grown bored with the
MOO. Maybe the loneliness of ostracism had gotten to him. Maybe a psycho
whim had carried him far away or maybe he'd quietly acquired a third character and started life over with a cleaner slate.

Wherever he'd gone, though, he left behind the room he'd created for
himself—a treehouse "tastefully decorated" with rare-book shelves, an operating table, and a life-size William S. Burroughs doll—and he left it unlocked.
So I took to checking in there occasionally, and I still do from time to time. I
head out of my own cozy nook (inside a TV set inside the little red hotel
inside the Monopoly board inside the dining room of LambdaMOO), and I
teleport on over to the treehouse, where the room description always tells me
Dr. Jest is present but asleep, in the conventional depiction for disconnected

characters. The not-quite-emptiness of the abandoned room invariably instills in me an uncomfortable mix of melancholy and the creeps, and I stick around only on the off chance that Dr. Jest will wake up, say hello, and share his understanding of the future with me.

He won't, of course, but this is no great loss. Increasingly, the complex magic of the MOO interests me more as a way to live the present than to understand the future. And it's never very long before I leave Dr. Jest's lonely treehouse and head back to the mansion, to see some friends.

I won't pretend I knew what I was doing when I wrote "A Rape in Cyberspace." I thought, to be honest and if you can believe it, that I was setting down little more than an engaging true-life fable, played out in a realm of experience so circumscribed and so unique that no one (except perhaps the residents of LambdaMOO itself) could possibly take it as anything but a curiosity, a traveler's tale brought back from strange climes and only barely pertinent to the world as we know it. The philosophical excursions woven into the piece reached for a certain universal relevance, to be sure, but they were almost an afterthought, added at the last moment in hopes of teasing from the story a broader significance I wasn't entirely sure it had.

I needn't have bothered, though. For in the deluge of online responses to which I was soon exposed, very few readers remarked directly on my transparent attempts at intellectual provocation. It was the story itself that provoked them, or elements of the story anyway. And it was the story seen not as a piece of exotica but as a dispatch from a place maybe a little too close to home: the busy intersection of sex, violence, and representation around which late twentieth-century American culture hovers like a soul obsessed.

That the story tapped such a deep vein of anxieties is a development I look on now with some sense of gratification, yet I can't say I was exactly enjoying myself as those anxieties began flooding in my general direction. Opinions ran strong, and those that reflected not-so-very-well on me—or on the acts and attitudes of the tiny, textual world I had tried to represent as accurately as possible—seemed to run strongest. "Media culture keeps blurring the line between real offense and imaginary offense, but this is ridiculous," wrote one participant in a lengthy discussion on the haut-cachet New York bulletin-board system ECHO. "That article had no journalistic value whatsoever" added another ECHO-dweller, fuming at what many in that virtual community saw as crass exploitation of the unsettling and admittedly problematic notion of "virtual rape": "It was just using the RAPE catchphrase to SELL PAPERS . . . and it brutally trivializes people who have suffered through the real thing."

This hurt. The trivialization charge was an argument I recognized as part of the rhetorical arsenal of pro-sex feminists in their righteous battle against legal scholar Catharine MacKinnon's creepy redefinitions of porn as rape (and more broadly, of word as deed), and I didn't feel at all good about being placed conceptually in her camp. Compared to this insult, one Echoid's crudely worded announcement that he had used a copy of my article to tidy himself after a bowel movement seemed a friendly chuck under the chin. So I was relieved when West Coast feminist pornographer (and disaffected former MacKinnon-ite) Lisa Palac posted on ECHO in the article's favor, downplaying any fuss over its use of the word *rape* as essentially semantic, and finding in it an effective illustration of "how online worlds and identities reflect . . . RL socialization":

I can't tell you how often I am interviewed by reporters who are under the assumption that taking on an online identity is "risk-free." And that for some reason, going online will be free from the social/cultural shapes as we know them. . . .[The subject of] this article may be extreme, but it disproves the "all is safe in cyberspace" notion.

Palac's note signaled, or so I thought, that the debate was mellowing and would soon enough be off my screen and out of my life. In fact, though, what it mainly signaled was that the debate had reached the other side of the country and would soon become fodder for the topic-hungry habitués of the WELL, a Bay Area bulletin-board system even more vigorously literate than ECHO. Once there, the discussion grew a notch more thoughtful, though no less contentious. Even more than the ECHO conference, the WELL's discussion seemed haunted by the ghosts of nearly every nineties polemic to have grappled with the issue of dangerous expression, from Anita Hill to the campus curriculum battles to the *succès de scandale* of "Beavis and Butt-head." The twists and turns of the arguments grew so convoluted that at one point, if I followed correctly, my account of Mr. Bungle's fate was determined to imply that Shakespeare, Sophocles, and Ibsen should also have been lynched on grounds of subjecting countless audience members to the emotional vio-lence of catharsis.

More effectively critical, though, were the comments of R. U. Sirius, cofounder and guiding light of the magazine *MONDO 2000.* "The conflation of language and mediated activity with real activity seems to be more or less complete," wrote Sirius, in a formulation not at all surprising to anyone famil-iar with *MONDO 2000*'s reputation as a nest of giddy, pop-Baudrillardian arm-chair prophets stoned out of their minds on the ascendancy of digital simulation. What might have surprised those unable or unwilling to look past that caricature, however, was the entirely characteristic moral rigor Sirius then brought to bear on LambdaMOO's own giddy romp through the conflations of the hyperreal:

These people all volunteered to act in a theater of the imagination and then got scared. Do we want Disney World? As the simulacrum becomes a bigger part of our lives, do we demand that people clip their imaginations at the place where it feels comfortable?. . . I think that freedom would be well served by simple toughening up.

And this hurt too. It was bad enough feeling like a rhetorical football, after all, without feeling part of me wanting to agree with some of those landing the hardest kicks.

Days of online discussion started piling up into weeks, and I began to wonder: How long could this go on? And how long would it be before the turbulence of the debate spilled over into less neatly compartmentalized venues for social interaction, like my more casual online encounters on the MOO, or the offline interactions I still respectfully referred to as real life? The WELL conference slowed down eventually, but controversy over the tale of Mr. Bungle spread into other online conferencing forums: Internet mailing lists, Usenet newsgroups, Compuserve. To this day, in fact, four months after its original publication, the story (stripped down to ASCII and turned loose to wander the nets) continues to find new pockets of interest and to gather online discussion around itself. Yet in the end, what I had dreaded most—the general irruption of the controversy into other areas of my life—has failed to materialize. LambdaMOOers, for the most part, seem to have accepted my interpretation of their world as true to their own experiences and left it at that. Most real-lifers unacquainted with any form of cyberspace, on the other hand, have found in the story a fascinating glimpse of a realm too distant from their own to pass judgment on—a parallel universe perhaps, or maybe a hint of their own future.

Which leaves only the denizens of the bulletin-board cybercosm to argue over the meaning of the life and crimes of Mr. Bungle. And, frankly, the fact that they have done so with such vociferous gusto remains something of a puzzle to me. Certainly, arguing is what people mainly do in such settings, and certainly, as I suggested earlier, the bleedthrough from larger cultural concerns about texts and violence has fed much of the fracas. Yet the more I ponder the furious online response to my story, the more I suspect the real object of that fury is neither LambdaMOO nor America's latest culture wars, but the ambiguous nature of online discourse itself.

Perched on a tightwire between the reasoned deliberation of text and the emotional immediacy of conversation, online communication sets itself up for a fall that is constantly realized. Fooled by the cool surface of electronic text, people lob messages cast in aggressively forensic impersonality into the midst of this combustibly personal medium, and the result, routinely, is just the sort of flame war I found myself embroiled in: a heatedly antagonistic exchange fueled by the most livid of emotions yet pretending in its rhetorical strategies to the most rational of dialogue. And in some sense, I think, the two sides of the Bungle war have taken up the two sides of this basic tension: the rational recognition (on the part of those who found the story ridiculous) that ultimately anything that happens online is "only words on a screen" countered by the emotional understanding (on the part of those who found the story compelling) that words can have powerful and deeply felt effects. It's too much to hope, I suppose, that this tension will ever really be resolved. Still, it's comforting to think that the noisy dialogue sparked by my article has not been only sound and fury. On its surface, of course, the discussion has provided more than its share of insight into a story I myself didn't fully understand when I wrote it. But deeper down, in the very structure of the debate, I have sometimes imagined I can hear the sound of cyberspace groping toward an end to flame wars.

■ QUESTIONS BASED ON THE READINGS:

1. In Chapter 3, I suggested (planted the idea) that you and a friend go to a MUD or a MOO. Now is a good time to do just that. See a list of MUDS/MOOS below. But first you should prepare yourself by reading and studying the FAQs on MUDS, in which you will find out about the different kinds of MUDS, how to get to one, how to act when you get there, and so on.

2. As I said in the introduction to this chapter, many administrators of university computer systems have a policy of banning certain telnet ports to MUDS. The reasons commonly given are that some students spend far too much time playing adventure games and not studying. What other reasons are there in defense of this action? What are the arguments for not banning the ports? If necessary, do some research to determine what people have already said pro and con on this question.

3. Given your reading of Leslie's, Bruckman's, and Dibbell's articles, how would you think MUDS differ, if any, from actual life? Specifically, do MUDS dull actual life or enhance it? Do MUDS contribute to a counterproductive confusion between actuality and fantasy? Or do they, by way of role playing, foster a better understanding of self- and group identity? If they do both, then add up the gains and losses. In the light of your estimation, what is to be done with this ever-growing sophisticated technology?

4. Leslie and Bruckman suggest ways in which MUDS can be productive in terms of collaborative work or identity workshops. If your university has a MUD/MOO, try to get permission to use it to do collaborative work. How would you and your classmates organize collaborative work on a MUD? Try to get permission to meet at your MUD or another university's MUD with the purpose of doing collaborative projects either during or between classes.

5. Plot out, as best as you can, the events that take place in Dibbell's account of a virtual rape at LambdaMOO and his account of how the members of that virtual community responded to it. First you might be concerned with defining what constitutes the act of rape. Is there a difference between actual and virtual rape? (In other words, Is there a difference between real action and symbolic action?) What might be the difference between sexual harassment in actuality, over the telephone, in e-mail messages, or at a MUD/MOO? What might be the consequences for the person being harassed or assaulted? In considering these questions, take note of how

males and females answer them. If you are a male, listen carefully to what the females say; and vice versa. Again, if you are a male, go to a MUD/MOO, sign in with a female name, and pretend to be female. If you are a female, do the opposite. After attempting this exercise, write about it and discuss it in class. Now return to Dibbell's article and read it again.

■ F U R T H E R   S T U D Y   O N   T H E   N E T / W W W :

If you point your browser to *WebCrawler* <http://webcrawler.com/> and search simply for MOO and not MUD, you will get quite a few hits from such a broad topic. (If you include MUD, yes, you will get mud—namely, wet dirt. Even with MOO, you will get references to cows.) I set the hits at 25 and this is what I discovered:

```
The query "MOO" found 453 documents and returned 25:

1000   Official Cult Song
0578   The MOO User's Guide
0577   Lots of MOO . . .
0260   MOO-WWW Research Directory
0203   Multi-User Dungeons (MUDS)
0181   Miami MOO
0178   More about MOOS
0177   MOO Resources
0168   MOO-WWW Links—Research Guide and Resource Information
0154   CRASHPAD MOO
0147   Alf's MOO Info
0144   mmmMOO
0144   You can MOO too
0128   1848 MOO Web Server Page
0128   http://wwwsc.library.unh.edu/Systems/mudmoo.htm
0128   The Virtual Headquarters
0126   CTP: Hosting: ATHE MOO Project
0115   The WWW VL: Educational Technology—Educational VR (MUD)
sub-page (29-Jun-1995)
0114   The Lost Library of MOO
0110   BayMOO Home Page
0108   Cows Caught in the Web
0022   Patrick Crispen's Internet Roadmap Course
0022   The TechMOOseum
0022   ENSP 482: Theory and Practice of Hypertext
0021   Cyberspace Writing Center Consultation Project
```

About 80 percent of the hits are either MUDS/MOOS or information about them, and much of it is extremely valuable not only because it gets you to a MOO but also because it tells you precisely what to do when you get there. For example, if you follow the second item on the list, *The MOO User's Guide,* you get:

```
The FredNet MOO
```

The FredNet MOO: Specialized texts for the FredNet MOO, also an entry spot for the MOO.

The Complete Guide to LambdaMOO
General Commands: The help system text for the MOO commands.
Editor Commands: The MOO commands found in the editors.
Programmer Commands: The commands specifically for MOO programmers.
Wizard Commands: Commands reserved for wizards.

If you follow General Commands under LambdaMOO, you get:

```
summary
"
:
::
?
@add-entrance
@add-exit
@addroom
@addword
@answer
@audit
@bug
building
burn
@check
@classes
@comment
(etc.)
```

If you follow *summary,* you get:

```
SUMMARY

Help is available on the following general topics:
introduction—what's going on here and some basic commands
index—index into the help system
players—setting characteristics of yourself
movement—moving yourself between rooms
communication—communicating with other players
manipulation—moving or using other objects
miscellaneous—commands that don't fit anywhere else
building—extending the MOO
(etc.)
```

What you have here, then, are all of the commands necessary to function in the MOO known as LambdaMOO.

Here are some additional sites to search from or to visit:

- *Yahoo:* <http://www.yahoo.com/>. Search MUDs or MOOs.

- *Hypertext Hotel,* WWW Entrance: <http://duke.cs.brown.edu:8888/>.
  Point here and you get:

The Hypertext Hotel is a constructive, collaborative hypertext which is located at Brown University.

The WWW version of this hypertext is generated dynamically
from the MOO server which it runs on. This MOO, which allows
for writer collaboration and more flexible narrative experiments, is located at duke.cs.brown.edu 8888. There are many
other MOOs currently on the net.

We are also able to import StorySpace documents into the MOO
so that they can be collaboratively edited and then distributed using WWW.

- *A list of MUDs/MOOs to visit that are open to the public.* Before accessing
  these MUDs, you should contact your local—that is, campus—system
  administrator to see what the policy is for telneting. Because of their bad
  connotations, you should inquire about the policy for MOOs that are
  generally considered to be educational and not game oriented. But be
  aware that some of these MUDs are social while others are educational
  and professional. When you telnet and make a connection, you should
  type *connect guest* unless otherwise instructed. A caveat: Many MUD
  administrators have now made it technically possible for anyone at a
  MUD to record precisely what you say/type. Remember you are a guest
  in someone's virtual home/community.

LambdaMOO	lambda.parc.xerox.com 8888
Meridian	sky.bellcore.com 7777
BayMOO	baymoo.sfsu.edu 8888
Dragonsfire	moo.eskimo.com 7777
MOOsaico	moo.di.uminmo.pt 7777
PMC-MOO	hero.village.virginia.edu 7777
MirrorMOO	mirror.ccs.neu.edu 8889
Chiba Sprawl	sequoia.picosof.com 7777
Jay's House MOO	129.10.111.77 1709
Diversity University	moo.du.org 8888
MOOtiny	spsyc.psychology.nottingham.ac.uk 8888
MediaMOO	purple-crayon.media.mit.edu 8888
ThunderDome	199.2.48.11 4444
Dhalgren	acatinic.princeton.edu 7777
FurryMuck	138.74.0.10 8888
PointMOOt	actlab.rtf.utexas.edu 8888
WriteMush	palmer.sacc.colostate.edu 6250
Brown Hypertext Hotel	128.148.37.8 8888
BioMOO	bioinformatics.weizmann.ac.il 8888

```
LinguaMOO (private)    mohawk.utdallas.edu 7777
```

For a more complete list of MUDS/MOOS, point your browser to Andrew Wozniak's, a.k.a. Doran's, Mudlist: <http://www.cm.cf.ac.uk/User/Andrew.Wilson/MUDlist/dorans.html>.

- *Frequently Asked Questions (FAQs) for MUDS:* <http://math.okstate.edu/~jds/mudfaqs.html>. At this site you will find the following, with links:

```
These should be the most recent versions of the FAQs. Text-
only versions can be found in <ftp.math.okstate.edu:/pub/
muds/misc/mud-faq>.
FAQ #1/3: MUDS and MUDding
FAQ #2/3: MUD Clients and Servers
FAQ #3/3: RWHO and mudwho
```

As I mentioned in the introduction to this chapter, this is the best source of accessible, easy-to-follow information, such as the different kinds of MUDS, how to telnet to them, and what to expect once you arrive.

■ HERE ARE SOME ADDITIONAL ON-LINE NETWORKS (WEBSITES, WITH ARCHIVES AND NEWSGROUPS):

- You can search and search for sites, but here is one, along with others, you should definitely visit: *Educational Technology: Educational VR (MUD) sub-page:* <http://tecfa.unige.ch/edu-comp/WWW-VL/eduVR-page.html>. Here is the table of contents:

```
1. Introduction
2. Events, What's new
3. General Index Pages
4. Educational MUDS
5. Publications
6. Guides, FAQs & Manuals
7. "Educational" MOO objects
8. Clients
9. Various
```

- *The ChibaMOO Papers* (The SenseMedia Surfer): <http://sensemedia.net/papers>. Be sure to visit and read about ChibaMOO and see just how it is a hybrid made of the Web (WWW) and a MOO—hence, the notion of a WOO. This concept is currently one of the most innovative approaches to a collaborative hypermedia system. For example, read these papers:

```
ChibaMOO WOO!—About Webbed MOO—S. Latt Epstein
ChibaMOO—The Sprawl—R. Armstrong, J. Campbell, S. Latt
Epstein, P. Kautz
ChibaMOO—Collaborative Hypermedia Interactive Buildable Area—
R. Armstrong, J. Campbell, S. Latt Epstein, P. Kautz
```

- *MOO Research Archive:* <http://www.actlab.utexas.edu/~smack/moo.html>. Papers, stories, and research data. (Julian Dibbell's "A Rape in Cyberspace" can be found here, among other places.)

- *The Lost Library of MOO:* <http://lucien.berkeley.edu/moo.html>. Manual, tutorials, and FAQs; MOO research papers.

- *MUD literature reference list:* <http://moo.cas.muohio.edu/~moo/mudlit. html>. This is a rich source of gathered material, including papers, articles, transcripts, references to books and journals, and forthcoming works.

- *The MUD Resource Collection:* <http://www.cis.upenn.edu/~lwl/ mudinfo.html>. Mostly devoted to MUSHes, which are social MUDs, though the website owner does not accept the distinction.

- *The Aragorn.UIO. NO WWW Server:* <http://aragorn.uio.no/>. Here are links to various MUDs (mostly LPMUDs), to JUD-related newsgroups, ftp sites, etc.

- *USENET newsgroups,* which you can subscribe to and join in on discussions about MUDs (see Appendix A for instructions about subscribing):
  alt.fan.furry.muck
  alt.mud
  alt.mud.tiny
  alt.mudders.anonymous   (for those who get addicted!)
  rec.games.mud.announce
  rec.games.mud.diku   (DikuMUDs)
  rec.games.mud.lp   (LPMUDs)
  rec.games.mud.misc
  rec.games.mud.tiny   (Tiny family of MUDs)

■ MORE REFERENCES FOR READING AND FOR SURFING THE WEB:

Bennahum, David. "Fly Me to the MOO: Adventures in Textual Reality." *Lingua Franca* (June 1994): 1, 22–26, 28–36.

Bruckman, Amy. Homepage. Internet. Available: <http://asb.www.media.mit. edu/people/asb/>. Bruckman created MediaMOO.

Curtis, Pavel, and David A. Nichols. "MUDs Grow Up: Social Virtual Reality in the Real World." 5 May 1993. *Xerox Parc.* Online. 22 August 1995. Available: <ftp://parcftp.xerox.com/pub/MOO/papers/ MUDsGrowUp.txt>.

Dibbell, Julian. [A forthcoming book on LambdaMOO.]

Fanderclai, Tari Lin. "Muds in Education: New Environments, New Pedagogies." 1995. *SenseMedia.* Online. 22 August 1995. Available: <http://sensemedia.net/sprawl/16880>.

Rosenberg, Michael S. "Virtual Reality: Reflections of Life, Dreams, and Technology: An Ethnography of a Computer Society." 16 March 1992. *Xerox Parc.* Online. Internet. 22 August 1995. Available: <ftp://parcftp. xerox.com/pub/MOO/papers/ethnography.txt>. Includes an excellent glossary.

Shaw, Rawn, and James Romine. *Playing MUDs on the Internet.* New York: John Wiley, 1995.

Wired magazine has an on-line facility that allows for a MOO (on-line chat room) experience. Point your browser to *HotWired* <http://www. hotwired.com/>. Once there, you will follow a set of commands somewhat similar to those for interacting in a MUD/MOO.

Young, Jeffrey R. "Textuality in Cyberspace: MUDs and Written Experience." 28 May 1994. Online. 22 August 1995. Available: <http://moo.cas. muohio.edu/~moo/mudlit.html>. The article is invaluable for a number of reasons, one of which is its explanations of the differences among oral communications, writing for actual reading, and writing conversations for MUDding. See especially headings such as *Linguistic Feel of Mudding, Writing Conversations, Visual Cues, Self as Object: The Decentering Grammar of* MUDS, *Liberating Environment,* and *Net Sex.*

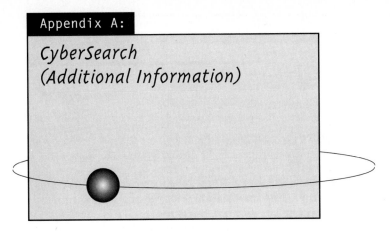

Appendix A:

*CyberSearch
(Additional Information)*

- Netiquette

- How to E-mail and Subscribe to Lists

- How to do reSEARCH (& SURF) on the Net/WWW: Some Pointers

- How to Avoid Copyright Problems (Citing Electronic Discourse)

- On-Line Writing Labs (OWLs)

This appendix is basically a *general* guide to doing research on the Net and World Wide Web (WWW). If you already have an e-mail account and some knowledge of the Net and the Web, it may not be that helpful, though you would do well to review the material discussed here and look at the material on copyright problems and on OWLs.

To avoid repetition, I have not included much information about virtual libraries here, that can be found in Chapter 5 of *CyberReader.* I have not discussed ftp or Gopher or many of the other ways of getting around on the Web; instead, I have concentrated on some very powerful search engines (and search engines of search engines) that include ftp and Gopher sites as well as other sources. Again, this appendix is only a general guide. Once you are capable of navigating the WWW, you will find many free sources to help you in much greater detail. For example:

1. *Electronic Freedom Foundation's Guide to the Internet,* v. 2.39 (formerly *The Big Dummy's Guide to the Internet*), with text without links. Online. Internet. 22 August 1995. Available: <http://www.eff.org/pub/EFF/netguide.eff>.

2. *Big Dummy's Guide to the Internet,* by Adam Gaffin with Jvrg Heitkvtter, table of contents with links. Online. Internet. 22 August 1995. Available: <http://www.cs.yale.edu/HTML/WORLD/org/eff/bdgtti-1.04/bdgtti-1.04_toc.html>.

3. "Internet." *The English Server* (CMU). Online. Internet. 22 August 1995. Available: <http://english-www.hss.com.edu/internet.html>. (This is a topic in which many invaluable discussions about the Net are hypertextually embedded.)

■ N E T I Q U E T T E

Netiquette is a combination of two words, namely, *Net* and *etiquette.* Netiquette has to do with the basic rules of how to behave in cyberspace.

When you first get into cyberspace, whether you are sending out e-mail or attending a MUD, you are called a *newbie.* Being new to the virtual environment means that you may make mistakes. When we travel to foreign countries, for example, we discover often that the rules of behavior are very different from the ones that we are used to. Cyberspace *is* a different country! Netiquette, therefore, has been developed to warn you of the problems you will be confronted with in virtual environments and to instruct you in ways of avoiding these problems. Here is a list of simple guidelines:

1. Always remember that even though you are typing into a machine, human beings on the other end are receiving the message. It may be wise at first to simply observe and study by reading different posts on newsgroups or discussion groups. In another word, be a *lurker.*

2. Avoid *flaming* someone. In other words, do not attack another person on line. If you do, be prepared to be attacked in return. Don't be afraid to apologize. Understand that as a newbie you can send out a message that, unbeknownst to you, will be received as a flame (an attack). Until you learn the basic conventions of communicating in this environment, you can easily make a mistake such as responding to someone, say, in an ironic tone (as far as you are concerned) but having it not perceived as ironic (as far as the other person is concerned). Irony or any other similar tone is difficult enough in real life (IRL) to detect. Don't expect someone staring into a monitor reading your text to know that you are being ironic. Tone is usually interpreted in a negative way.

3. Since face-to-face (F2F) communication is replaced by words typed across a monitor, you will have to learn some of the basic graphic conventions that suggest tone. For example, learn to use *smileys* and *emoticons.* Here are a few:

:-)	smiling or happy
.)>=	(this is my own smiley ... pirate + vampire + beard)
:-(	sad
:,(	crying
;-)	wink
:-&	tongue tied
:-X	lips are sealed
:-o	shocked, incredulous
:-#	my lips are sealed
:D	laughter
:|	Hmmm
>:->	Devilish

(8-o   It's Mr. Bill!

etc.

Along the same lines, if you TYPE YOUR MESSAGE IN ALL CAPS, you will be read as being *angry.*

4. Never send a message or say something in private that you would not want the entire world to read. Nothing is secure in cyberspace. And we human beings make mistakes! I have. You will!

   A special caveat: If you are replying to someone's message by way of a reply command, be very careful; make sure that the address is the correct destination for your message. If someone has forwarded a message to you and you return a message by the reply command, your message will most likely go out to a lot of people you don't even know. :-(

5. If possible, keep messages brief. This rule holds in most cases. But again, when you are on a list, lurk (observe) a while to learn what is and is not acceptable. If your message is too long or if you send out far too many messages, brief or long, you may be accused of *spam*ming. By the way (BTW), you can shorten your messages by using abbreviations, as I have a number of times above. Here are some commonly accepted abbreviations:

IMHO   in my humble opinion

BTW   by the way

IOW   in other words

FYI   for your information

TNX   thanks

ROFL   rolling on the floor laughing

RTFM   read the f***ing manual . . .

(Often, one way to get flamed on a discussion list is to start asking basic questions that you could find the answers to elsewhere. Don't waste people's time. If you do, you may get a shorthand response such as RTFM. In general, never get on a list as a newbie and start asking people to help you with your homework, or never make any similar request, unless you want to get flamed!)

There are many other considerations, but these will get you started. (If you want to know more about netiquette, try *EINet Galaxy* <http://www.einet. net/> and search for the term or any other terms. Also see *I'm Not Miss Manners of the Internet* <http://rs6000.adm.fau.edu/rinaldi/netiquette.html>. (Often when a URL or address is given, it is placed in <> such as above; understand that you are *not* to type or include these right/left angles when using a URL or address.)

■ HOW TO E-MAIL AND SUBSCRIBE TO LISTS

There are many ways to get on the Net by way of commercial providers, but I am going to assume here that your school or university provides access for you. Moreover, I am going to assume that your access will be by way of what is called a VAX account. (Usually, faculty or more "serious" users of the Net have UNIX accounts, which later you may want to have.)

Getting on line:

The very first thing you should do is visit the academic computing services office on your campus. (In some schools, as at my university, every student is automatically given an account, but it is necessary to request that this account be activated.) When you request an account, the computing services office will most likely give you a pamphlet explaining the use of its system. You will also be given an address, which is composed of these generic parts: your *user name or userid @ domain address.* For example: *jsmith@utarlg.uta.edu.* And you will have to establish a password, which you need to change intermittently. (You should never give your password to anyone! And you should, when establishing your new password, not use your name, initials, or anything obvious to someone who would want to crack into your account and use it for illegal purposes.)

If the computer you are using is connected directly to the university's mainframe, then, simply follow the instructions given to you by your academic services. If you are using a telephone and a modem, however, you will have to make sure that the e-mail software (which comes with your modem) that you are using is configured correctly and that you have the correct telephone number to dial in for the size of your modem (2400 baud, 14,400 baud, 28,000 baud). Essentially what you are doing is making a telephone call to the university's host computer, which will tell you on your monitor when you have connected. At this point, you will need to know how to log on to a particular service, which would be a particular address to the VAX account (or to the university library or similar address), and in some cases you will need to establish a terminal emulation setting, which is usually *VT100.* Again, all of this information must be obtained from your on-campus computer services, for it can vary from campus to campus, and from system to system.

Sending e-mail:

Once you get on line and to the $ or % or equivalent prompt, you can begin sending and eventually reading mail. This may be done in many cases by typing the word *mail* after the $ prompt and striking the return key. Then you will get the *EMAIL>* prompt, after which you type *send* and the return key. Then, you will be asked to type in the e-mail address. The way that you do this can vary from service to service. Sometimes you have to put in a lengthy procedure such as: *IN%"userid@domaine.address".* If any of this is missing, you will immediately get a message saying *"illegal address specified."* A shorter version of this long procedure does away with IN% and the quotation marks. After typing in the full address, hit the return key. Next you fill in the *Subject:* heading with a phrase designating specifically what the message is about. In sum, with the longer version:

```
$ mail

EMAIL> send

To: IN%"jsmith@utarlg.uta.edu"

CC:IN%"jbrown@utarlg.uta.edu"

Subject:tomorrow's exam
```

(Notice here, as in some software, that a *CC:* prompt gives you an opportunity to send yourself or another person a copy of the message. What you do is simply include the correct address following the same procedure as for the *To:* prompt.) After setting up the complete address, you again type the return key and begin your message. Be very careful to type in about three-quarters of the way across the space provided and then strike the return key. You should do this with every line. If you do not, there is a chance that the message will be received as an unevenly distributed set of typed lines. Once you have finished your message and want to send it, you usually type *control-Z.* (Check the manual supplied by your academic computer services.) If you wish to cancel your message, you usually type *control-C.*

If you wish to delete mail that you have received, simply type *d* (or *delete*) after reading the specific post that you wish to delete, or type *d* and the number of the post or posts, e.g., d 1–4 or d 1, 2–3 and hit return. All other posts are automatically saved. When you are given an account, you are allotted a number of *blocks;* if you wish to check how much space you have remaining, type at the $ or % prompt *show quota* and then hit return.

Once you have sent and read all the messages, you will want to disconnect from the host frame. This is done while still in mail mode by typing *exit.* Once in *exit,* then, you usually type *logoff* or *lo.* At this point, use your software command (usually in the *dial* menu) to *hangup* (often *control-H* will do, and then *control-Q* to quit the application).

Some universities have a mail program called *Pine,* which is easy to use and allows you to do all kinds of things you cannot do with the method just described. Pine has too many features to describe here, but the directions in the software that you will access are very clear. Instead of typing *mail* at the $ or equivalent prompt, you will type *pine* and then return, which will get you to the index and the help files:

```
? HELP—Get help using Pine

C COMPOSE MESSAGE—Compose and send a message

I FOLDER INDEX—View messages in current folder

L FOLDER LIST—Select a folder to view

A ADDRESS BOOK—Update address book

S SETUP—Configure or update Pine

Q QUIT—Exit the Pine program
```

Take the time to learn this mail and editing program. It will be definitely worth your effort.

You need to be aware that these instructions may not be absolutely precise for every case. Learning how to get logged on will require some patience and, in many cases, some help from your instructor or a friend.

Subscribing to and Reading Usenet:

After sending private mail, you might be interested in looking over available *newsgroups* (on *Usenet*). Having made this suggestion, however, I must tell you that newsgroups have become more and more controversial because of some of the topics. Many colleges and universities restrict the groups you can have access to, raising the issue of censorship. (A famous case is the restriction of newsgroups at Carnegie-Mellon University. You can go to *The English Server* <http://english-www.hss.cmu.edu/>, CMU, to find information on the controversy.) I mention this issue because you simply may not have access to Usenet or access to only a limited version of it. There are many other reasons for why your local institution may not provide this service. One is simply space or bandwidth.

In any case, here are the basics: Usenet is not accessible through e-mail and is separate from what is called the Net but is nonetheless available on the Net. There are many, many Usenets sending information to each other. Each discussion group on a given topic is called a *newsgroup* and there are thousands of such groups, which fall into a variety of categories such as *alt* (alternative), *comp* (computers), *info, misc, news, rec* (recreational activities), *soc* (social issues), *sci* (science), *tx* (Texas), and so on. (Today, when I accessed the software known as *Tin,* there were 5,650 groups available to me! When I accessed newsgroups on *Netscape,* there were over 8,000 available.) Such lists might be designated as <alt.cyberpunk>, <comp.os.msdos>, <rec.wine. making>. (In the various chapters of *CyberReader,* you will find references to particular newsgroups you may want to start reading or even contributing to.)

To see what's available and simply to read the discussions, you will access software in your university's computer that is most often *Tin.* (Of course, your university may not have this identical program. If you wish, check with academic computer services to see if Usenet is available and how to access it.) When you get to the *$* or *%* prompt, simply type *tin.* If the program is available, it will begin searching for available lists. This may take a while. (If you are using the browser *Netscape,* all this is much easier.) Eventually, you will see printed on your screen the beginning of a list of the <alt.> newsgroups. Understand that you are automatically subscribed to *all* the lists available to you and that you can go through all several hundreds or thousands and unsubscribe to the ones you are not interested in and subscribe to those you are. But nothing could be more time consuming! However, if you wish to do that, you will get a list of items (here's one such item) that looks like this:

```
Subscribe to new group alt.cyberpunk (y/n/q) [n]:
```

If you are not interested, type *n* or strike the return key. If you are, type *y.* Again, I would not recommend this approach. I took the opposite approach and unsubscribed from the kinds of lists that do not interest me. All that you would have to do, when you are in *Tin,* is to unsubscribe to multiple groups such as <rec> or <sci>, is to type *U. (Tin* is case sensitive.) Then you will receive this prompt at the lower left of your screen:

```
Enter regex unsubscribe pattern>
```

If you want to unsubscribe all of the <rec> lists, then type *rec.** and all the lists in this grouping will be eliminated from showing up on your screen the next time you access *Tin.* (If you ever want to see them on your screen again, simply type *y,* the yank command.) If you want to unsubscribe to particular groups within the hierarchy of <rec.>, then type, for example, <rec.arts> or <rec.arts.comics>, and so on.

Later, if you change your mind, you can resubscribe by typing *S,* which will give you the prompt:

```
Enter regex subscribe pattern>
```

If you want to resubscribe to all the <rec> lists, then, type *rec.* *

You might want to save for later any decision about what you want to keep and discard and just start reading. To read the first time around, just move down the list by following the directions at the bottom of the screen:

```
<n>=set current to n, TAB=next unread, /=search pattern,
c)atchup,   g)oto, j=line down, k=line up, h)elp, m)ove,
q)uit, r=toggle all/unread, s)ubscribe, S)ub pattern, u)nsub-
scribe, U)nsub pattern, y)ank in/out
```

Instead of using *j* or *k,* you can use your arrow keys. If you wish to search, then type </> and the key word. The directions are easy to follow. I navigate on newsgroups the same way that I do on the Web, using arrows and the return key to move up and down one level or the return key to read what has been posted on a particular newsgroup. The space bar will allow you to skip down the lists of pages. You will catch on quickly. If you want to add a point to the discussion, type *r* and your message, following instructions again. To exit from *Tin,* simply type *q.* (Again, if you use *Netscape,* it is all just a matter of clicking on the button for newsgroups and following the simple instructions by way of pointing and clicking.)

Subscribing to Listservs (academic discussion groups):

It is hard to know what to say about these lists, which can be more formal in tone and academic, but you should know about them. It would be best to discuss with your instructor the appropriateness of your subscribing to a *particular* academic list. If you are interested in finding a list of lists, point your browser to the *Directory of Scholarly Electronic Conferences* <http://www.mid.net/KOVACS/>. There are also nonacademic lists.

Downloading and Printing Electronic Discourse:

When you find a document on the WWW that you would like to save a copy of, all you have to do, if you are on *Lynx,* is to type *p* and then you will usually be given three options:

Save to a local file

Mail the file to yourself

Print to the screen

I tend to use the second and third options. If you want to e-mail the file to yourself, you simply arrow down to that link and arrow right. You will be asked for your e-mail address. After giving it, you hit the return key and the file will be sent to you. If you want to print and save the file on your monitor (in your hard disk), you arrow down to the third option. To save the file, however, you will have to use your e-mail software, the commands for which are different from software to software. I use *Z-Term* and therefore go to the file menu and pull down to *start capture,* then I name the file, and arrow right or hit return twice; the file is printed and captured on my screen. I have to return to the file menu and *stop capture.* Later, if I wish and if it is legal (and it usually is), I can print out the file. When I use *Netscape,* I simply point to Print and click. (See the last section of this appendix about copyright problems.)

■ HOW TO DO RESEARCH (& SURF) ON THE NET/WWW: SOME POINTERS

Do you have any idea about how *to point your browser,* as I suggested that you do in the previous paragraph? If not, you will learn how in this section. I will spend most of the time, however, introducing very briefly the various *search engines.* As I stated in the preface, I will give instructions for using *Lynx* (the text-based web program); if you have access to *Mosaic* or *Netscape,* which are much easier and more exciting to use, then, you will be able to follow what I say here easily. *Netscape* has a few search engines, such as *WebCrawler* and *Lycos* and *CUIS,* readily available.

If your university makes *Lynx* available, when you are at the *$* or *%* prompt, type either *<www>* or *<lynx>* and then hit return. You should or will usually find on your screen your university's website. From here you can navigate to any number of places (on campus, throughout your state, or else-where), depending on the links that have been established locally for you. However, if you want to discover information beyond what is immediately available to you on your university website, type *g* and you will get in the left bottom of the box

URL to open:

At this point you type in the URL (Uniform Resource Locators). The URL is composed of <access method://host.domain/path/filename>. It can begin with the access method *http://* and then become a unique address—for exam-ple, <http://www.mid.net/KOVACS/>. When this is accurately typed, hit the return key (or arrow right) and you are on your way to a website. The same procedure is followed for the access methods such as ftp or Gopher, which I will not discuss here for reasons given earlier. (Remember that you will follow a slightly different, easier procedure if you are using *Mosaic* or *Netscape.*)

Knowing how to http is one thing; knowing how to find a URL for what you want is quite another. When you go to the library and use the computers to check the holdings and to determine whether or not particular books are on the shelves, you are simply engaging in a database search. When you use the World Wide Web, you are checking databases as well by using a variety of what are called search engines. Here I will quickly survey some of the engines with their directories so that you will know what to expect.

Here are the *major search engines:*

---

1. WebCrawler ‹http://webcrawler.com/›

WebCrawler is generally used by many people—so many that you frequently find yourself having to wait for access. Remember after you get into *Lynx,* type *g* and then the URL and finally the return key. (If you are on *Netscape,* you will click on the "search" button, scroll down and then click on webcrawler.) When you arrive, you will see on Lynx

SEARCHING WITH WEBCRAWLER(TM)

To search the WebCrawler database, type in your search key-words here. Type as many relevant keywords as possible; it will help to uniquely identify what you're looking for. Last update: July 13, 1995.

Search   (*)AND words together

Number of results to return: [25_]

News | Home | Random Links | FAQ | Top 25 Sites | Submit URLs | Simple Search

(Text entry field) Enter text. Use UP or DOWN arrows or tab to move off.

The line _____ above the word **search** is the point at which you type in your key word(s). You can use * for **AND** words as in a boolean search. Hence, you could type in *search*engines.* You move off the line by using the down arrow key ↓. The number of searches (or hits) that you want is auto-matically set at 25; if you wish more, then, arrow down to the number and then arrow to the right → and select the number you wish. Then return by arrowing up to *search* and then arrow right. After you have read everything you want out on the link, arrow left ←. (Remember: You navigate up and down with arrows in those directions ↑ and ↓, even if you have a column of links that are set alongside each other. Your tendency will be to use the right arrow, which will send you, however, out on a link. (Learning how to navi-gate with Lynx is like learning how to use a standard transmission!) If you wish to move to the next page down, hit the space bar; move up to the prior page, type - [a hyphen]. It's simple.) Searching for the key terms *search*engines,* your return may show:

WebCrawler Search Results

The query "search*engines" found 3823 documents and returned 25:

1000 Internet Search Engines

0700 Lists of Search Engines

0500 Wandex Web Search Engine

0466 Search Engines

0416 Search Engines

0358 Information on Swets database HTML interface, and search engine

0317 Some Search-engines in the web

0311 VILSPA Search Engine Gateway

0291 Internet Search Engines

0233 Search Engines and Lists

0227 CTI Centre for Geography: Search Engines

0224 Paradox Engine Tech Support Home Page

0205 SMC Home Page

0201 INTERNET INTERFACE SYSTEMS

0194 ZWeb z39.50 Search Engine

0194 Glimpes Search Engine

0186 WWW Indexes and Search Engines

0185 The Best Search Engines

0179 DECdirect Search Engine

0179 Interactive Real Estate Search Engine

0173 Search Engines

0170 Nucleus Information Service Search Engines

0166 Search Engines

0158 Search

0150 World Wide Web Search Engines

Many of the hits are often the same. Each of these is a title for a website.
When you arrow up and down this list and decide to arrow right, you are
going to the virtual destination of the website, Gopher, or ftp site. (While
WebCrawler is making an http connection, you will see or glimpse the
URL/address. (On *Netscape,* however, the URL is always readable.) Often,
attempting to get to a search engine requires patience, since each is often
being used and is overloaded. If this is the case, you will be notified: "Unable
to connect." The best thing to do then is to try again or try another link.) You
may type into the *search* space whatever key terms you have an interest in
knowing more about. (As you go through each chapter of *CyberReader,* you
will find that I have given instructions for using *WebCrawler* as well as other
search engines in the sections entitled "Further Suggestions". Here I have also
suggested key terms from the readings that you might search for. I have also
given a number of URLs you might want to try.)

---

2. EINet Galaxy ‹*http://www.einet.net/*›

EINet allows you to search for either *key terms* by way of many different categories or it allows you to search by *topics.* At the website, you will see

Galaxy | Add | Help | Search | What's New | About EINet

Arrowing down—remember, even though the links are horizontally arranged, you arrow *down*; to arrow to the right is to go with the link elsewhere!—so, arrowing down, stop at **Search** and take that link to search for key terms. Doing so will get you to

EINET SEARCHING THE GALAXY

Galaxy | Add | Help | Search | What's New | About EINet

". . . and where are my potato chips?"

Search for: _____ Search Reset [50 hits_]
()Galaxy Pages ()Galaxy Entries ()Gopher ()Hytelnet ()World Wide Web (full text search) ()World Wide Web Links (link text only)

When you are setting up your search by way of *key terms,* you have a number of options. According to the *Help* file for Galaxy EINet,

Galaxy pages "contains only pages in the Galaxy itself. This helps you find collections of references to related information"

Galaxy entries "contains only the titles of information references in the Galaxy pages. This helps you find a very specific information reference. (Search for "Texas", for example)"

Gopher "contains the titles of Gopher menus from much of Gopher Space. To improve search quality, only those Gophers referenced in the Gopher Jewels appear in the index"

Hytelnet "contains the pages of the hypertext telnet database" and "provide[s] access to several thousand telnet sites"

World Wide Web text "contains almost all of the thousands of Web pages referenced in the Galaxy"

World Wide Web links "contains all the links found in the World Wide Web text (above)—over 175,000 links at last count"

When setting up your search by way of *topics,* you have, at present, the set topics and subtopics (each is a link), such as

Arts and Humanities

Architecture—Art History—Language and Literature—Museums—Performing Arts—Philosophy—Religion—Visual Arts

Business and Commerce

Business Administration—Business General Resources—Consortia and Research Centers—Consumer Products and Services—Electronic Commerce—General Products and Services—Investment Sources—Management—Marketing and Sales

Community

Births Deaths and Weddings—Charity and Community Service—
Consumer Issues—Crime and Law Enforcement—Culture—Education—
Environment—Family—Gay Lesbian and Bisexual—Gender Issues—
Health—Home—Immigration—Law—Liberties—Lifestyle—Net Citizens—
Networking and
Communication—News—Parascience—Politics—Religion—Safety—US
States—Urban Life—Veteran Affairs—Workplace—World Communities

and so on.

---

3. The Global Network Navigator

<http://www.gnn.com/gnn/GNNhome.html>.

Here you will find *The Whole Internet Catalog* (which can be accessed with-out GNN): <http://www.gnn.com/gnn/wic/newrescat.toc.html>. At *WIC,* like at Galaxy EINet, you will find an elaborate set of topics with subtopics, for example:

Arts & Entertainment

Architecture—Art Exhibits—Comics—Digital Images—E-Zines—Humor—
Magazines—Movies—Music—Photography—Radio—Science Fiction—Sound
Files—Television—Theater

Business & Finance

Agriculture—Career & Employment—Government Information—Internet Commerce—Investment—Management—Marketing—Nonprofits—Personal Finance—Real Estate—Small Business—Taxes—Yellow Pages

and so on. Each of these is a link to more links. Similar sites of this kind can be found at *The English Server,* CMU, <http://english-www.hss.cmu.edu/>, and at *Yahoo* <http://www.yahoo.com/>, both of which are excellent sources for research. And yet another site with a directory of numerous topics is *The City of Bits Surf Site:* <http://www-mitpress.mit.edu:80/City_of_Bits/ surf.html#econ>.

---

4. The Lycos Home Page: Hunting WWW Information *(CMU) ‹http://lycos.cs.cmu.edu/›*

The Lycos Home Page: Hunting WWW Information (p1 of 3)

CMU LYCOS (TM)

THE CATALOG OF THE INTERNET

A 1995 GNN Best of the Net Nominee. Over 28 million queries
answered. Rated number 1 in content by Point Survey.

Frontier Technologies licenses Lycos Technology for CD-ROM
Product.

Search the **big Lycos catalog** (5.5 million web pages), or if
you have forms, use the Lycos search form to set the number
of hits, and other options.

Search the **small Lycos catalog** (486k web pages), or if you have forms, use the Lycos search form to set the number of hits, and other options. [etc.]

To make a search, you access either the big or small *Lycos* catalog, again by arrowing down. As with *WebCrawler,* you type in the word or words (no *) you want information about and then arrow to search. What is especially good about *Lycos* is that it gives you matching words in various forms.

---

5. ALIWEB Search Form

<http://web.nexor.co.uk/public/aliweb/search/doc/form.html>. ALIWEB is updated each day and should be very accurate because, as it claims, the descriptions of data are made by persons who want their services included. The types of searches are comparable to those on EINet.

A **Public Service** provided by **NEXOR**

ALIWEB SEARCH FORM

This form queries the **ALIWEB** database. You can provide multiple search terms separated by spaces, and the results will be displayed in a best-match order.

Search term(s): _____ Submit Reset

There are several types of search: [Substring_____]( )
Case Sensitive

Which type records would you like to search:
[Any_____]

Which fields would you like to search?
(*) Titles (*) Descriptions (*) Keywords () URL's

What fields would you like displayed in addition to the title? (*) Descriptions () Keywords () URL's () Other fields

You can restrict the results to a domain (e.g. "uk"):

Stop after the first _____ matches.

---

6. Hytelnet

<http://www.usask.ca/cgi-bin/hytelnet>. Hytelnet "is designed to assist users in reaching all of the INTERNET-accessible libraries, Free-nets, BBSs, & other information sites by Telnet."

Hytelnet—Welcome to HYTELNET version 6.9.x

Welcome to HYTELNET version 6.9.x

July 3, 1995

```
What is HYTELNET?            <WHATIS>

Library catalogs            <SITES1>

Other resources             <SITES2>

Help files for catalogs     <OP000>

Catalog interfaces          <SYS000>

Internet Glossary           <GLOSSARY>

Telnet tips                 <TELNET>

Telnet/TN3270 escape keys   <ESCAPE.KEY>

Key-stroke commands         <HELP>

HYTELNET 6.9 was written by Peter Scott

Northern Lights Internet Solutions, Saskatoon, Sask, Canada
```

7. The World Wide Web Worm

<http://www.cs.colorado.edu/home/mcbryan/WWWW.html>. Here's another one!

WWWW—WORLD WIDE WEB WORM

Best of the Web '94—Best Navigational Aid. Oliver McBryan

Serving 3,000,000 URL's to 2,000,000 folks/month.

Instructions, Definitions, Examples, Failures, Register, WWWW Paper.

VOTELINK—Check out this week's *hot* issues and VOTE.

[1. Search all URL references_____]

[a. AND—match all keywords][5 matches___]

Keywords: _____

Start Search

8. CUSI

<http://pubweb.nexor.co.uk/public/cusi/cusi.html>. "CUSI (Configurable Unified Search Engine) is a configurable search interface for many searchable WWW resources. It allows you to quickly check related resources, without having to navigate and re-type the keywords." Here in one place, therefore, you will find virtually everything we have thus far discussed and more. This is a search engine for search engines. The URL above is the official site of CUSI. You should use, however, the "nearest CUSI." As you might note in the

URL for CUSI, it is located in the United Kingdom. For nearest CUSI sites, go to:

CUSI at Northwestern University <http://www.eecs.nwu.edu/susi/cusi.html>
Tennessee Commerce Net Surfer <http://www.tenn.com/cusi/cusi.html>
CUSI at UC, San Diego <http://www-cetc.ucsd.edu/cusi.html>.

---

9. Additional Search Engines

Internet Resources Meta-Index <http://www.ncsa.uiuc.edu/SDG/Software/Mosaic/MetaIndex.html>
　World Wide Web Servers: Summary <http://www.w3.org/hypertext/DataSources/WWW/Servers.html>

- HOW TO AVOID COPYRIGHT PROBLEMS
  (CITING ELECTRONIC DISCOURSE)

Copyrights:

The best discussion on copyright problems that I know of is *10 Big Myths about Copyright Explained,* by Brad Templeton <http://www.clarinet.com/brad/>, to be found at <http://www.clarinet.com/brad/copymyths.html>. If you have any doubts whatsoever about things on the Net or WWW, generally assume you *should* have doubts! Alway look for copyright statements at websites and Gopher/ftp sites, specifically those attached to any article, chapter or book, or graphic found in cyberspace. Along the same lines, you should be very sensitive to the fact that e-mail sent to you personally should *never* be disseminated (forwarded, cited, published, in part or whole) without the written permission of the poster (author). It is generally understood, however, that posts sent to newsgroups and to listservs (discussion groups) are disseminated to everyone and often archived and in that sense published. If you wish to cite any of this material, you should be guided by the "fair use" principle; in other words, as a student or academic, you have the right to quote a limited amount from electronic works just as you do from printed works. However, you must give correct and full references (see below). But remember that there is no "fair use" principle for private e-mail!
　Additional information about copyrights on the Net:

Copyright FAQ <http://www.cis.ohio-state.edu/hypertext/faq/usenet/Copyright-FAQ/top.html>

The Copyright WebSite <http://www.benedict.com/index.html>

Copyright Act of 1976, as amended <http://www.law.cornell.edu/usc/17/overview.html>

Copyright Clearance Center Online <http://www.openmarket.com/copyright/>

Electronic Discourse and How to Cite It:

What, in part, contributes to failure to cite material on the Net or WWW is that there is not yet a standardized (i.e., widely accepted) bibliographical form for citing electronic discourse. The Modern Language Association in the *MLA Handbook for Writers of Research Papers* (Fourth Edition), recommends several formats (in section 4.9–10, "Citing Online Databases"). Also you might want to check the American Psychological Association's (APA) *Publication Manual,* 4th ed. Here I will simply give the following brief outlines and a few examples from the *MLA Handbook* (for additional help, see the section on OWLs below). Throughout *CyberReader,* I have tried to follow the suggested forms for citing electronic discourse; in some cases, however, I have had to modify the forms. You, too, may find this a necessity. In any case, here are the general recommendations for citing electronic discourse:

A. *AN ELECTRONIC TEXT* that has a printed source but is also available on line (for Work Cited). The concept of "printed source" generally suggests that the discourse is fixed or stable, though of course the text may be corrected by textual scholars. What you have to keep in mind, however, is that before being placed in an electronic medium (on line or on a CD-ROM), the text was in print. Here is a simple outline to follow for bibliographical references:

1. Name of author (if available)

2. Title of the text (underlined)

3. Publication information for the printed source

4. Publication medium ("Online")

5. Name of the repository of the electronic text (e.g., Oxford Text Archive, CD-ROM)

6. Name of the computer network (e.g., Internet, Bitnet, America On Line, Dow Jones News Retrieval)

7. Date of access

[8. The electronic address, or the URL, if available. The address should be preceded by the word *Available.*]

Some examples:

Aristotle. *Rhetoric.* Trans. W. Rhys Roberts. New York: The Modern Library, 1954. Online. *The English Server* (Carnegie-Mellon Univ.). Internet. 22 August 1995. Available: <http://www.rpi.edu/~honeyl/Rhetoric/index.html>

(Simply skip any of the information that is not available.) I think it would be helpful to add another item of information such as a URL (if available), which would serve as simple specific locater. Thus, following date of access, I would include the word "Available" and then the URL.

Hardy, Thomas. *Far from the Madding Crowd.* Ed. Ronald Blythe. Harmondsworth: Penguin, 1978. Online. Oxford Text Archive. Internet. 24 Jan. 1994.

Shakespeare, William. *Hamlet. The Works of William Shakespeare.* Ed. Arthur H. Bullen. Stratford Town ed. Stratford-on-Avon: Shakespeare Head, 1911. Online. Dartmouth Coll. Lib. Internet. 26 Dec. 1992.

B. *MATERIAL IN GENERAL WITH NO PRINTED SOURCES* (for Work Cited). This form is for text that has not (yet) been printed.

1. Name of author (if available)

2. Title (in quotations)

3. Date

4. Title of the database (underlined)

5. Publication medium ("Online")

6. Name of the computer service or provider

7. Date of access

[8. The electronic address, or the URL, if available. The address should be preceded by the word *Available.*]

For example:

Brickman, Gary. "HotWired Interviews Elmer-DeWitt." 7 July 1995. *HotWired.* Online. 8 July 1995: Available: <http://www.hotwired.com/special/pornscare/>.

Other examples:

"Middle Ages." *Academic American Encyclopedia.* Online. Prodigy. 30 Mar. 1993.

"Foreign Weather: European Cities." *Accu-Date.* Online. Dow Jones News Retrieval. 20 Aug. 1993.

C. *MATERIAL SPECIFICALLY FROM ELECTRONIC JOURNALS, ELECTRONIC NEWSLETTERS, AND ELECTRONIC CONFERENCES* (for Work Cited). This form is for text that has not (yet) been printed.

1. Name of author

2. Title of article (in double quotations)

3. Title of journal, newsletter or conference (underlined)

4. Volume, issue

5. Year of publication (parentheses)

6. Number of pages or paragraphs or n. pag. (no pages)

7. Publication medium ("Online")

8. Name of computer network (Bitnet or Internet)

9. Date of access

[10. The electronic address, or URL. The address should be preceded by the word *Available.*]

For example:

Newsletter

Vitanza, Victor J. "Women on the Net." PRETEXT, *The Pretext Conversations Newsletter* 1.1 (1995): n. pag. Online. Bitnet. 28 May 1995. <Listserv@miamiu.acs.muohio.edu>

(Note that there are no pages or URL available, which means that this post has not been put out on a website, but note that the listserv that serves this academic list PRETEXT is given. What this piece of information tells you is that you can subscribe to this list via the listserv address.)

Electronic conference

Ulmer, Gregory. "Invention and Heuretics." REINVW, *The Pretext Conversations* (1994): n. pag. Online. Bitnet. 12 Nov. 1994. Available: <http://miavx1.muohio.edu/~pretext/>.

(Note that the URL is given, which means that the post, along with the rest of the conversation, is available at a website.)

Electronic journal

Moulthrop, Stuart. "You Say You Want a Revolution?: Hypertext and the Laws of Media." *Postmodern Culture.* 1.3 (1991): 53 par. Online. Bitnet. 21 August 1995. Available: <http://jefferson.village.virginia.edu/pmc/contents.all.html>.

D. E-MAIL COMMUNICATION (FOR WORK CITED)

1. Name of author

2. Subject heading or description of post

3. Date of post

For example:

Rheingold, Howard. "Permission to reprint." E-Mail to Victor Vitanza. 22 July 1995.

Haynes-Burton, Cynthia. "Collab-1, Cyberabus." E-Mail to Alternative Educational Environments. 5 August 1995.

Parenthetical Citations:

To cite this material within the body of your paper, I would use parenthetical, short forms including the author's name (if not used in introducing a quote or paraphrase) and a short title and date. For example, when I was editing and writing this book, I e-mailed Howard Rheingold and he responded ("Permission to reprint," 22 July 1995), granting me permission to reprint a section of his book *Virtual Reality*. Note that in the previous sentence I referred to the author's name in the text and then parenthetically cited the title of the message and gave the full date; the full reference, as given above, would be in a Works Cited page. If I were to include the citation to the printed book, which is not online, then I would follow standard MLA form for books in print.

Here's another example of parenthetical citations using several cites: when I was editing and writing this book, I was also collaborating with three of my colleagues (at other universities) online about four graduate seminars that we were planning to teach at our separate universities, online and through one mailserv, which would allow all the students to send and receive posts. After I received a message from Cynthia Haynes-Burton ("Collab-1, Cyberabus," 5 August 1995), I received a message from David Downing ("Re: Collab-1, Cyberabus," 5 August 1995), requesting my syllabus, which we are calling a "cyberabus." I wrote back to David and sent myself a copy of the post ("vjv: Collab-1, Cyberabus with dates," 5 August 1995), telling him that I would send him the cyberabus in several days. The next day, I received a post from James Sosnoski ("My class," 6 August 1995), also asking for my cyberabus.

Citations of this sort are simple. The primary reason for the dates is that there might be multiple posts back and forth, so that at times the title (usually taken from the subject heading of the post) might be the same as the posters' replies back and forth. (If there are more than one post and with the same title from one poster, then I would simply label them "first post," "second post," or whatever is comparable as long as you are consistent with your citations. Just remember that you are abbreviating what will be given as a complete reference in the Works Cited section.)

If you were citing parenthetically something from an electronic journal— say, from an article by Moulthrop (as above)—you might write something like the following:

In speaking about Ted Nelson's Xanadu Project, Moulthrop says: "As Nelson foresees it, Xanadu would embody [a] textual universe. The system would provide a central repository and distribution network for all writing: it would be the publishing house, communications medium, and great hypertextual Library of Babel" ("You Say You Want," par. 6).

Hence, the method of parenthetical citation is comparable to that method for citing published works in print.

There are many variations, of course. You should spend some time reading the MLA and APA guides. However, since there is really no set style as yet, I would leave this whole issue of documentation for your class discussion or for your instructors' suggestions. And, of course, why don't you use the powerful search engines to discover what others are saying about electronic documentation? One other book that you might want to look at is *Electronic Style: A Guide to Citing Electronic Information* by Xia Li and Nancy B. Crane (Westport, CN: Meckler, 1993).

On-Line Writing Labs (OWLS):

There is one more major source for help about any problems that you might be having with writing or citing references, which is your local writing center or laboratory. But if your local lab resources are not the best or the lab is not online, you can point your browser to a number of really excellent OWLs, where you can find information about and help with the most basic writing problems (such as punctuation, developing a thesis sentence, basic grammar, etc.) and help with writing in various genres (such as letters of application and résumés), but also you will find information about citing electronic references in MLA and APA formats. Here are a few OWLs you might want to visit and browse around in (note that many of the sites are linked to other sites; so when you are at one, you are only a click away from another):

The Purdue University On-Line Writing Lab <http://owl.trc.purdue.edu/>

The Writery (University of Missouri) <http://www.missouri.edu/~wleric/writery.html>

Roane State Community College Owl <http://fur.rscc.cc.tn.us/OWL/OWL.html>

The University of Texas–Austin, Undergraduate Writing Center <http://www.utexas.edu/depts/uwc/.html/main.html>

Bowling Green University Writing Center <http://www.bgsu.edu/departments/writing-lab/Homepage.html>

The Dakota State University Online Writing Lab <http://www.dsu.edu:80/departments/liberal/cola/OWL/>

Michigan Tech. University Writing Center <http://www.hu.mtu.edu/~jdcolman/wc/welcome.html>

The University of Michigan OWL <http://www.umich.edu/~nesta/OWL/owl.html>

Rensselaer Writing Center <http://www.rpi.edu/dept/llc/writecenter/web/home.html>

Taft Community College Online Writing Lab <http://www.taft.cc.ca.us/www/tc/tceng/owl.html>

Writing Online Resource Directory <http://darkwing.uoregon.edu/~jcross/word.html>

These, then, are some of the most basic introductions to the Net and the WWW. Remember: there's a great deal more information of this kind out on our website: <http://www.abacon.com/~cyber>. Also, you will learn as you go; you should share what you know; and it should be our purpose to build an actual community and virtual ones as well. Have phun—the surf's up.

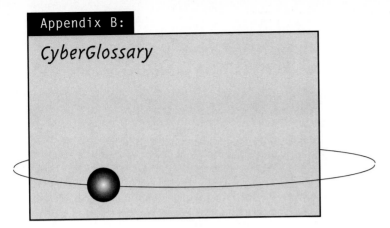

Appendix B:

CyberGlossary

The list of terms in this glossary is *only* a beginning. I have included only those words and proper names that might be of help to you while reading *CyberReader*. You will find on many occasions that you will need additional reference sources. When this happens, you might check these on-line glossaries:

Babel: A Glossary of Computer Related Abbreviations and Acronyms: <http://www.access.digex.net/~ikind/babel95b.html>

Computing Dictionary: <http://wombat.doc.ic.ac.uk/>

Cyberpoets Guide to Virtual Culture (see *Lexicon of Virtual Culture*): <http://www.seas.upenn.edu/~mengwong/cyber/cgvc1.html#1.2>

Jargon File 3.0.0. <http://www.phil.uni-sb.de/fun/jargon/index.html>

The WWW Jargon File <http://farmr4.med.uth.tmc.edu/Miscellaneous/ JARGON30/HOMEPAGE.HTML>. Also, magazines such as *Wired* (Gareth Brandwyn's "Jargon Watch") will include updates on the growing number of new words. If you find or invent a new bit of cyberbabble, why not submit it to *Net Jargon A-Go-Go*? <http://www.clark.net/pub/ atomicbk/contest/contest.html>.

ABRAHAM, RALPH: Author of *Chaos, Gaia, and Eros* (1994), which identifies three different views of history—the mind, the body, and the spirit of evolution. This book has had a profound influence on people who write about cyberspace. It has an excellent glossary.

ACKER, KATHY (CF. APPROPRIATION): Novelist. See her *Empire of the Senseless* (1988), which is a cyberpunk-textual appropriation of Gibson's *Neuromancer*. In her novels, Acker takes large chunks of other authors' works and reworks them.

AGRIPPA: A BOOK OF THE DEAD: William Gibson's (Dennis Ashbaugh's, and Kevin Begos's) electronic book that can be read only once because it is consumed by a virus as it is read! A copy of the decoded, nondestroyed version can be found at <http://sfbox.vt.edu: 10021/J/jfoley/gibson/gibson.html>.

A G E N T :   Software that can change and learn in virtuality. A typical agent might be coded with a user's preferences and made to search the Web until recalled.

A P P R O P R I A T I O N :   Borrowing another artist's work in one's own work in dis/order to play with it and make something new. Appropriation, according to Kathy Acker, is not plagiarism, but Pla(y)giarism!

A R P A N E T :   Advanced Research Projects Agency, a wide-area network, was developed by the federal government during the Cold War and has become the U.S.'s contribution to the World Wide Web.

B A N D W I D T H :   The amount of information that can be transferred per second through copper wires or fiber optic cables.

B A R L O W ,   J O H N   P E R R Y :   Lyricist for the Grateful Dead, co-founder of the Electronic Freedom Foundation, and "cognitive dissonant." Homepage: <http://www.eff.org/~barlow/barlow.html>.

B A U D R I L L A R D ,   J E A N :   French sociologist–cultural theorist who is most known for his discussions of simulation replacing "reality." See his *Simulacra and Simulation* (1981).

B I T N E T :   A major wide-area network that allows for sending and receiving e-mail. Bitnet stands for Because It's Time Network.

B I T S   &   B Y T E S :   Units of computerized information. A bit is the binary 0/1. A byte is a group of 8 such bits.

B U R R O U G H S ,   W I L L I A M   S . :   Novelist, first known as a Beat. See his *Nova Express* (1965) and other novels. Burroughs's fiction is part of what is now called "Slipstream," cyberpunk fiction written/published prior to 1984 that has influenced, say, the authors published in Bruce Sterling's *Mirrorshades* (1986) collection. Burroughs has recently been featured in commercials for Nike running shoes.

C R A C K E R :   (See *Hacker*).

C R A S H   C U L T U R E   (C F .   P O S T M O D E R N) :   Perhaps best explained in a simile: it's like speeding up in your car and passing everyone else, only to have to stop for the traffic light. This is a term coined by Arthur Kroker in *Data Trash* (1994): "Contemporary society as it undergoes a simultaneous fatal acceleration and terminal shutdown." Or, like crash TV, 500 channels and nothing to see.

C T H E O R Y :   A listserv and website edited by Arthur and Marilouise Kroker: <http://www.freedonia.com/ctheory/>.

C Y B E R - :   A prefix from the Greek, meaning *pilot* or one who *steers,* that has been attached to many words with different meanings, as featured in this glossary.

C Y B E R C R U D   (A L S O   C Y B E R B A B B L E) :   Computer talk, jargon.

C Y B E R N E T I C S :   The study of systems of communications and control in living organisms and machines. See "Principia Cybernetica Web" <http://pespmcl.vub.ac.be>.

C Y B E R P U N K :   A literary genre and a social movement (hackers, cyberpunks, ravers). (See Chapter 6, *CyberReader.*)

C Y B E R R E A D E R :   This book, edited and written by Victor J. Vitanza. Homepage: <http://www.uta.edu/english/V/Victor_.html>.

C Y B E R S P A C E :   William Gibson coined this term in *Neuromancer* (1984). The virtual meeting place of the "matrix," where everything from telephone conversations to bank transactions take place. (See Chapter 1, *CyberReader.*)

C Y B O R G :   A concept developed by science fiction writers. Short for *cybernetic organism,* either half protoplasm and half artificial (silicon) body parts or all protoplasm replaced with artificial body parts. Cyborg has recently become a post-political concept for breaking out of such binaries as male/female. (See Chapter 6, *CyberReader.*)

E L E C T R O N I C   B O O K :   Simply put, a book formatted in an electronic medium. However, such a book is really no longer a book as we generally think of one: the electronic medium changes the message of the book it transmits. (See Chapter 4, *CyberReader.*)

E L E C T R O N I C   F R O N T I E R   F O U N D A T I O N (E F F) :   In its own words, "a non-profit civil liberties organization working in the public interest to protect privacy, free expression, and access to on-line resources and information." Cofounded by John Perry Barlow and Mitchell Kapor. EFF's website: <http://www.eff.org/>.

E - M A I L :   Electronic mail, which is distributed over the Net.

E X C R E M E N T A L   C U L T U R E :   Reruns on television. Recycling. Grunge. (See Kroker, *Data Trash.*)

F A Q S :   Frequently asked questions.

F T P   (C F .   G O P H E R ,   H T T P) :   File transfer protocol, which allows for the transference of complete files from a remote computer to one's own computer.

F L A M E ,   F L A M I N G :   To post a nasty, ugly, or harassing message.

F L E S H M E E T :   An event at which on-line participants who have never previously met in real life (IRL) finally agree to meet face to face (F2F). There may of course be subsequent meetings or none at all, even online. .)>=

F R E E W A R E   (C F .   S H A R E W A R E) :   Software that is free of charge.

F R I N G E :　　The opposite of mainstream, meaning on the edge. Fringe science includes such areas as nanotechnology.

G A T E S , B I L L :　　The man from (President of) Microsoft. See John Seabrook's "E-Mail from Bill."

G I B S O N , W I L L I A M (C F . N E U R O M A N C E R) : Along with Bruce Sterling, *the* cyberpunk science fiction writer. His home-page: <http://sfbox.vt.edu:10021/J/jfoley/gibson/gibson.html>. (See Chapter 6, *CyberReader.*)

G O P H E R (C F . F T P , H T T P) :　　A protocol and pro-gram that searches and retrieves documents from remote databases. Gopher will allow you to access ftp sites as well as other sites. (More and more of these sites, Gopher or ftp, are being transferred to the WWW, which are accessed through http.)

G R A T E F U L D E A D :　　The Group. See their homepage: <http://www.cs.cmu.edu/afs/cs.cmu.edu/user/mleone/web/dead.html>.

G L O B A L V I L L A G E :　　A phrase popularized by Marshall McLuhan, referring to, for example, television as the medium unifying the various societies and cultures of the world.

G U T E N B E R G G A L A X Y :　　A term and title of a book (subti-tled *The Making of Typographic Man* [1962]), by Marshall McLuhan, in which the author discusses the influence of various technologies, but espe-cially print technology (literacy), on shaping culture and society. McLuhan even speaks of "waves," electronic ones, and surfing on them!

H A C K E R (A L S O C R A C K E R) :　　Person who hacks his or her way into and through security systems and finally into a database. There is much confusion, however, between the terms *Hacker* and *Cracker.* The former refers to one engaged in noncriminal activity, while the latter is reserved for one engaged in criminal activity. (See Chapter 2, *CyberReader.*)

H A R D W A R E (C F . S O F T W A R E) :　　Machine.

H T M L (C F . H Y P E R T E X T) :　　Hypertext markup lan-guage, which is used to establish nonsequential discourse.

H T T P :　　Hypertext transfer protocol, which specifies sites that are part of the World Wide Web. A URL begins with http:// and the rest of the address follows. Similarly, a ftp or Gopher will begin with ftp://, etc.

H Y P E R R E A L I T Y :　　Extended reality, more real than reality, simulated to such a high degree that it often seduces its viewers/partici-pants to prefer it to reality. (This term is extremely complicated in its philosophical ramifications. See Chapter 1, *CyberReader.*)

H Y P E R T E X T :　　Literally, extended text, a form of nonsequential discourse used on the World Wide Web or other computer environments.

Constructed at the surface similarly to sequential discourse, it features *links* or *hotspots* (in boldface or underlined), which when activated bring up on the monitor embedded discourse, which in turn can have links to more embedded discourse. Hypertext is generally limited to text only, whereas *hypermedia* includes not only text but also audio and video. (See Chapter 4, *CyberReader.*)

INTERNET (THE NET):   The gateway of electronic pathways around the world, used for on-line communications, which include commercial, governmental, and educational networks among others.

IRC: Internet relay chat. In real-time (IRT) communicating on the Net, which can be done at MUDS (or MOOS) or in "rooms" provided by commercial servers.

ISDN: Integrated services digital network. Changes information online into digital packets (groups of 1s and 0s) that are capable of traveling at high speeds. ISDN travels through fiber optic cables. In contrast, POTS (plain old telephone service) transfers information by way of analog, by sound waves boosted continuously by amplifiers through copper wires.

KAPOR, MITCHELL: Cofounder of the Electronic Frontier Foundation. See his homepage: <http://www.kei.com:80/homepages/mkapor/>.

KROKER, ARTHUR AND MARILOUISE: Cultural critics, known for a number of books such as *The Panic Encyclopedia* (1989), and for their electronic list *C-Theory.*

LANIER, JARON: Coiner of the term *virtual reality* and developer of VPL (virtual programming language). Homepage <http://www.well.com/Community/Jaron.Lanier/index.html>.

LEARY, TIMOTHY: Famous as the philosopher-professor and "LSD guru" of the 1960s. (See Chapter 6, *CyberReader.*)

LOVELACE, ADA: The world's first programmer. (See Chapter 3, *CyberReader.*)

LUDDITES (NEO-LUDDITES):   The term derives from Ned Ludd, a leader of a nineteenth-century radical agrarian movement and very anti-industrial revolution. A contemporary manifestation, by analogy, is the neo-Luddite movement against high technology and computers.

LURK (LURKER):   To frequent a discussion list or BBS without contributing to the discussion.

LYNX: A text-based application that allows users to browse the World Wide Web.

MCKENNA, TERENCE: Like Timothy Leary, known as a pyschedelic philosopher. McKenna has published *Food of the Gods* (1992). (See Chapter 1, *CyberReader.*)

M C L U H A N , M A R S H A L L : See *Gutenberg Galaxy.*

M E M E S (A . K . A . M E T A V I R U S) : A word based on *mimesis,* imitation: ideas are like viruses as they spread from host mind to host mind. This whole idea of memes is based on Richard Dawkin's book *The Selfish Gene* (1989). (See Chapter 1, *CyberReader.*)

M I R R O R S H A D E S : A 1986 collection of cyberpunk short fiction, edited by Bruce Sterling.

MUD (MOO): MUDs (multi-user dungeons/dimensions/domains) are text-based, real-time virtual realities. A MOO (MUD object oriented, or multi-object oriented), however, is a programming language within a MUD, that gives its participants the ability to create and manipulate their own virtual objects—say, a room with objects (furnishings).

M O N D O 2 0 0 0 : A much-celebrated magazine (prior to *Wired*), celebrating things on the edge or things fringe. Mostly devoted to cyberpunk, virtual reality, wetware, designer aphrodisiacs, artificial life, techno-erotic paganism, and the like. See also *MONDO 2000: A User's Guide to the New Edge* (1992).

M O R P H (I N G) : Metamorphosis, changing shapes.

M U D R A P E : Virtual rape. (See Chapter 7, *CyberReader.*)

M U L T I M E D I A (C F . H Y P E R T E X T) : A hypertext (extended text) that can feature not only text but also audio and video. (See Chapter 4, *CyberReader.*)

N A N O T E C H N O L O G Y : *Nano-* is a prefix meaning one-billionth—yes, technology reduced to the size of molecules and atoms! The possibilities, in medicine alone, are staggering. See Eric Drexler's *Engines of Creation* (1986).

N E L S O N , T H E O D O R H . : Founding genius, among other things, of the Xanadu project, postulating the connectability of all libraries and publishers and their holdings on the World Wide Web, allowing them to sell books to buyers. The project is more complicated and richer than suggested here. Nelson's site: <http://xanadu.net/the.project>. (See Chapter 5, *CyberReader.*)

N E W E D G E : On the fringes of culture, knowledge, or science. *MONDO 2000* represents the new edge.

N E W S G R O U P : Discussion group on a wide variety of subjects delivered by a network called Usenet. Unlike discussion groups on a listserv (or mailserv), which deliver each contribution in the form of e-mail to its subscribers, newsgroups subscribers travel virtually to the individual group site to sort and read the posts. (See Appendix A, *CyberReader.*)

N E T I Q U E T T E : *Etiquette + Net.* Manners on the Internet. (See *CyberReader,* Chapter 3 and Appendix A.)

NEURAL CHIPS: First the book became flesh; now the flesh becomes a chip, or as Kroker says, "When flesh goes electronic." (See Kroker, *Data Trash,* and William Gibson's science fiction short story "Johnny Mnemonic.")

NEUROMANCER: (cf. *Gibson*). Title of William Gibson's cyberpunk novel, published in 1984.

NOMAD (CF. POSTMODERN):   One who lives in a group with no set place or territory that drifts from place to place depending on needs and desires.

OPERATION SUN DEVIL: The U.S. Secret Service name for a whole group of raids on alleged crackers. The OSD and related raids are discussed fully in Bruce Sterling's *The Hacker Crackdown.* (See Chapter 2, *CyberReader.*)

PH (FOR F/f):   The *Ph* replacing *F/f* is often used by hackers as a sign of their interests in tele*Ph*ones and how to hack them.

PHIBER OPTICK: Pseudonym for a well-known hacker. (See Chapters 2 and 6, *CyberReader.*)

PHRACK: An electronic zine, mostly for hackers and computer enthusiasts. The name *Phrack* is a neologism based on *phone, freak,* and *hack. Phrack* <http://freeside.com/phrack.html> has a full archive of articles.

PHREAK: Tele*phone* + *freak* = phreak.

PINE: A software program, situated in the provider's mainframe, that allows for reading and filing e-mail and for setting up a directory of "eddresses." (See Appendix A, *CyberReader.*)

PIXELS: Tiny electronic dots, configured to represent information.

PLAGIARISM (CF. APPROPRIATE):   Theft of another's ideas without giving credit. A concept that is getting more and more difficult to define.

POSTMODERN/ISM (POMO; CF. CRASH CULTURE, SIMULATION):   Has competing definitions depending on one's ideological position. For Jean-François Lyotard, POMO is incredulity toward metanarratives; that is, POMO carries with it a predisposition toward not believing in such major concepts as origination and progress and liberation (emancipation). (See Lyotard's *The Postmodern Condition* [1984].) Hence, a postmodernist is not predisposed toward particular goals, but toward drifting; is not predisposed towards searching for the way of accomplishing an end, but toward taking what is ready at hand to achieve what is tentatively decided on or presented; is not predisposed to believe in origins or originals but that all is simulation or copies of copies. Surfing on the Net or WWW (or rhizome, that which has no beginning or end, only middle) can be and has been seen as a postmodernist form of drifting. The term is a complicated one and must be studied from its many ramifications. (See Thomas Docherty, ed. *Postmodernism: A Reader* [1993].)

POSTMODERN CULTURE: An electronic journal <http://jefferson.village.virginia.edu/pmc/contents.all.html>.

QUEEN MU: "Domineditrix" on the editorial staff and co-founder of *MONDO 2000.*

RANT: On-line histrionics in content and style. (I myself enjoy ranting!)

RAVE: An all-night dance party.

RHIZOME: A nonhierarchical configuration found in vegetables that is *a middle* everywhere on its surface and innards. The rhizome has been popularized by Gilles Deleuze and Félix Guattari in their book *A Thousand Plateaus* (1987). The Internet and the World Wide Web have been compared to a rhizome.

RUCKER, RUDY: A cyberpunk science fiction author. See his *Live Robots,* which includes *Software* (1982) and *Wetware* (1988). Rucker has been associated with R. U. Sirius and Queen Mu and the magaZine *MONDO 2000.*

SHAREWARE (CF. FREEWARE): A software program written and developed usually by an individual instead of a company that its user can try out for a while and then pay a fee to the programmer.

SIMULATION (CF. POSTMODERN, RHIZOME): A sham representation of the real. However, this heavily laden ideological term needs to be carefully considered from various vantage points. One view of simulation holds that there is no original (or traceable origin) but only copies. See Plato, *Republic,* Book 10; Baudrillard, *Simulacra and Simulation* (1994). (See Chapter 1, *CyberReader.*)

SIRIUS, R. U.: Cultural critic and cofounder of *MONDO 2000.*

SMILEYS (EMOTICONS): Conventional graphical representations for on-line discussions that suggest the poster's tone (voice, attitude) such as :-) for smiling or :D for laughing. (See Appendix A, *CyberReader.*)

SNAIL MAIL (CF. E-MAIL): Regular postal system, akin to the pony express.

SOFTWARE (CF. HARDWARE): Information.

SPAM (SPAMMING, PASTE BOMBING): A load of nasty or worthless posts dumped by way of e-mail to an individual or subscribers to a discussion list.

S P A S M :   "The state of living with absolutely contradictory feelings all the time and really loving it: fascinated yet bored/panicked yet calm/ecstatic yet terminal/apathetic yet fully committed" (Kroker, *Data Trash*).

S P R A W L :   A term used by William Gibson (in *Neuromancer*), indicating the accumulation of cities growing up next to each other to make even larger cities. Sprawl is also taking place in many MUDs and MOOs such as ChibaMOO and LambdaMOO. (See Chapter 7, *CyberReader*.)

S T E R L I N G ,   B R U C E :   Along with William Gibson, *the* cyberpunk science fiction writer. Sterling is editor of *Mirrorshades* (1986), the anthology of cyberpunk SF authors. He is also the author of several novels such as *Islands in the Net* (1988) and the nonfiction work *The Hacker Crackdown* (1992). (See Chapter 6, *CyberReader*.)

S T E V E   J A C K S O N   G A M E S :   The company—named after its owner in Austin, Texas—that was raided by the U.S. Secret Service. Read all about it in Bruce Sterling's *The Hacker Crackdown* (1992). The URL for SJGames is <http://www.io.com/sjgames/>.

T A Z   (S H O R T   F O R   T E M P O R A R Y   A U T O N O M O U S   Z O N E) :   A phrase and motto coined by Hakim Bey, who in his essay/book of the same title writes about physical and electronic space (a "free enclave") as a territory in which to live free lives. Bey's examples are historical, such as Sir Walter Raleigh and many settlers in the New World. Bey focuses on the settlement at Roanoke that "failed": "The colonists disappeared, leaving behind them only the cryptic message 'Gone to Croatan.'" This message, for Bey, signals the establishment of a TAZ.

T E C H N O C U L T U R E   (C Y B E R C U L T U R E) :   A culture with a style of thinking founded on technology, often new edge and fringe. In extreme form, technoculture manifests *techno-paganism,* belief in new technology as an agent of change.

T E L E D I L D O N I C S   (D I L D O N I C S) :   Howard Rheingold added the prefix *tele-* to Ted Nelson's *dildonics* to coin a term signifying the possibilities of cybersex. (See Chapter 1, *CyberReader*.)

T H R E A D :   A particular topic of discussion on a newsgroup or listserv.

T I N :   The name of a program for reading newsgroups, usually found in a university server's mainframe.

U R L :   Uniform resource locators, types of addresses that allow Net surfers to locate sites. They begin, e.g., with <http://> (hypertext transfer protocol), which is one type of access method. A complete URL is composed of <access method://host.domain/path/filename>. Other access methods are file transfer protocol (ftp), Gopher protocol (gopher), and wide-area information servers (wais).

V I R T U A L   R E A L I T Y :   VR is best understood in terms of cyberspace: when human beings don cyberhelmets and gloves, they have the feeling of being *in* VR; they don't when they pick up the telephone and talk and listen. VR simulates reality and can create a vision of reality, not only simulated and apparently real, but also more real than real. (See Chapter 1, *CyberReader.*)

V I R T U A L   E L I T E   (V I R T U A L   C L A S S) :   A term used by Arthur Kroker and Michael Weinstein to describe a new economic and social class that lives partially, and completely transacts its business, in virtual space. See *Data Trash: The Theory of the Virtual Class* (1994). The phrases *virtual elite* and *virtual class* most likely echo Thorstein Veblen's notion of a "leisure class."

V I R T U A L   S E X   (C Y B E R S E X ,   C Y B E R - E R O T I C S ,   D I L D O N I C S ,   T E L E D I L D O N I C S) : Sex in virtual reality! (See Chapter 3, *CyberReader.*)

V I R U S   (C F .   M E M E) :   Will infect your software and wipe out information in your hardware. A famous virus is "Friday the 13th." (See Chapter 1, *CyberReader.*)

W E L L ,   T H E :   The Whole Earth 'Lectronic Link, a computer network <http://www.well.com/> in the San Francisco area, which can be subscribed to from anywhere. It is the site of many well-known and published discussions among hackers, techno-philosophers, Internet enthusiasts, and the like.

W E T W A R E   (L I V E W A R E) :   Protoplasm as software. DNA (codes) in a cell is wetware. See Rudy Rucker, *Live Robots (Software/Wetware)* (1994).

W I R E D :   A slick magazine and one that must be read! The company has an electronic version known as *HotWired,* which can be subscribed to at no charge: <http://www.hotwired.com/Login/>.

W O R L D   W I D E   W E B   (a . k . a .   W W W ,   W 3) : The application, developed in 1990 in Switzerland at the European Laboratory for Particle Physics, which provides a hypertext/multimedia interface for all those connected to it, whether on the Internet, Bitnet, or other networks.

W O R M :   A computer virus that geometrically folds and squares (replicates) itself across the Net.

X A N A D U :   See *Nelson, Theodor H.*

Z I N E :   Mostly, but not by any means limited to, electronic (maga)zines. (See Chapter 5, *CyberReader.*)

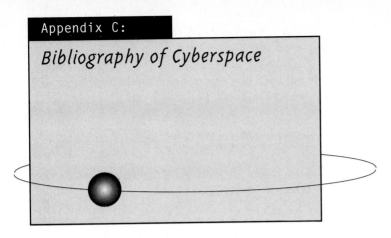

This is a very select set of references. As you begin to read, you will find other references both in print and electronic media.

Abraham, Ralph H. *Chaos Gaia Eros.* New York: HarperCollins, 1994.

Acker, Kathy. *Empire of the Senseless.* New York: Grove Weidenfeld, 1988.

Baker, John F. "Electronic Art Book . . . For One Read Only." *Publishers Weekly* (June 29, 1992): 28.

Barlow, John Perry. "Crime and Puzzlement." *Whole Earth Review* 68 (Fall 1990): 44–57. Online. Barlow's Homepage. Internet. 22 August 1995. Available: <http://www.eff.org/~barlow/barlow.html>.

Barlow, John Perry. "The Economy of Ideas: A Framework for Rethinking Patents and Copyrights in a Digital Age." *Wired* 2.03 (March 1994): 85–90, 126–129. Online. *HotWired.* Internet. 22 August 1995. Available: <http://vip.hotwired.com/wired/2.03/features/economy.ideas.html>.

Barlow, John Perry, Sven Birkerts, Kevin Kelly, Mark Slouka. "What Are We Doing On-line?" *Harper's Magazine* (August 1995): 35–46.

Baudrillard, Jean. *Simulacra and Simulation.* Trans. Sheila Faria Glaser. Ann Arbor: University of Michigan Press, 1994.

Bender, Gretchen, and Timothy Druckrey, ed. *Culture on the Brink: Ideologies of Technology.* Seattle: Bay Press, 1994.

Benedikt, Michael, ed. *Cyberspace: First Steps.* Cambridge, MA: MIT Press, 1991.

Benjamin, Walter. "The Work of Art in the Age of Mechanical Reproduction." In *Illuminations,* ed. Hannah Arendt. New York: Schocken, 1969.

Bey, Hakim. *T.A.Z.: The Temporary Autonomous Zone, Ontological Anarchy, Poetic Terrorism.* New York: Autonomedia, 1991. Online. Bey's Homepage. Internet. 22 August 1995. Available: <http://www.uio.no/~mwatz/bey/index.html>.

Birkerts, Sven. *The Gutenberg Elegies: The Fate of Reading in an Electronic Age.* Boston: Faber & Faber, 1994.

Birkerts, Sven, and Kevin Kelly. "The Electronic Hive: Two Views." *Harper's Magazine* (May 1994): 17–21, 24–25.

Bolter, Jay David. *Writing Space: The Computer, Hypertext, and the History of Writing.* Hillsdale, NJ: Lawrence Erlbaum, 1991.

Borges, Jorge Luis. *Ficciones.* New York: Grove Press, 1962.

Brand, Stewart. *The Media Lab: Inventing the Future at MIT.* New York: Viking, 1987.

Bukatman, Scott. *Terminal Identity: The Virtual Subject in Post-Modern Science Fiction.* Durham, NC: Duke University Press, 1990.

Burroughs, William S. *Nova Express.* New York: Grove, 1965.

Bush, Vannevar. "As We May Think." *Atlantic Monthly* 176 (July 1945): 101–108. Online. *Voice of the Shuttle.* Internet. 22 August 1995. Available: <http://www.csi.uottawa.ca/~dduchier/misc/vbush/as-we-may-think.html>.

Cavazos, Edward A. *Cyberspace and the Law: Your Rights and Duties in the On-line World.* Cambridge, MA: MIT Press, 1994.

Conley, Verena Andermatt, ed. *Rethinking Technologies.* Minneapolis: University of Minnesota Press, 1993.

Connor, James A. "Strategies for Hyperreal Travelers." *Science-Fiction Studies* 20 (1993): 69–79.

Critical Art Ensemble. *The Electronic Disturbance.* New York: Antonomedia, 1994.

Dawkins, Richard. *The Selfish Gene.* 2nd ed. Oxford: Oxford University Press, 1989.

De Landa, Manuel. *War in the Age of Intelligent Machines.* Cambridge, MA: Zone/MIT Press, 1991.

Deleuze, Gilles, and Félix Guattari. *A Thousand Plateaus.* Trans. Brian Massumi. Minneapolis: University of Minnesota Press, 1987.

Dery, Mark, ed. *Flame Wars: The Discourse of Cyberculture.* Durham, NC: Duke University Press, 1994.

Dibbell, Julian. "A Rape in Cyberspace." *The Village Voice* (December 21, 1993): 36–42.

Dick, Phillip K., *Do Androids Dream of Electric Sheep?* New York: Ballantine, 1968.

Downing, David, and James Sosnoski. Special Issue: The Geography of Cyberspace. *Works and Days* 23/24 or 12.1–2 (Spring/Fall 1994).

Drexler, Eric. *Engines of Creation.* Garden City, NY: Doubleday, 1986.

Eco, Umberto. *Travels in Hyper Reality.* Trans. William Weaver. New York: Harcourt Brace Jovanovich, 1986.

Elmer-Dewitt, Philip. "Cyberpunk." *Time* (February 8, 1993): 59–65.

Exon, Senator J. James. "Keep Internet Safe for Families." *Dallas Morning News* (April 9, 1995): J1, 10J.

Gibaldi, Joseph. *MLA Handbook for Writers of Research Papers.* 4th ed. New York: Modern Language Association, 1995.

Gibson, William. *Neuromancer.* New York: Ace, 1984.

Germain, Ellen. "In the Jungle of MUD." *Time* (September 13, 1993): 61.

Goodell, Jeff. "The Samurai and the Cyberthief." *Rolling Stone* (May 4, 1995): 40–44, 46–47, 71.

Hackers (roundtable). "Is Computer Hacking a Crime?" *Harper's Magazine* (March 1990): 45–55, 57.

Hafner, Katie. "Kevin Mitnick, Unplugged." *Esquire* (August 1995): 81–88.

Hafner, Katie. "Get in the MOOd." *Newsweek* (November 7, 1994): 58–59.

Hafner, Katie, and John Markoff. *Cyberpunk: Outlaws and Hackers on the Computer Frontier.* New York: Simon & Schuster, 1991.

Haraway, Donna. "A Manifesto for Cyborgs: Science, Technology, and Socialist Feminism in the 1980s." *Socialist Review* 15, No. 80 (1985): 65–107.

Harrington, James. "Beware of Chilling Freedom of Expression." *Dallas Morning News* (April 9, 1995): J1, J10.

Heidegger, Martin. *The Question Concerning Technology and Other Essays.* Trans. William Lovitt. New York: Harper & Row, 1977.

Heim, Michael. *Electric Language: A Philosophical Study of Word Processing.* New Haven: Yale University Press, 1987.

Heim, Michael. *The Metaphysics of Virtual Reality.* New York: Oxford University Press, 1993.

Hollinger, Veronica. "Cybernetic Deconstructions: Cyberpunk and Postmodernism." *Mosaic* 23 (Spring 1990): 29–44.

Holtzman, Steven R. *Digital Mantras: The Languages of Abstract and Virtual Worlds.* Cambridge, MA: MIT Press, 1994.

Jonas, Gerald. "The Disappearing $2,000 Book." *The New York Times Book Review* (August 29): 12–13.

Joyce, Michael. *Of Two Minds: Hypertext, Pedagogy, and Poetics.* Ann Arbor: University of Michigan Press, 1995.

Kantrowitz, Barbara. "Men, Women, Computers." *Newsweek* (May 16, 1994): 48–52, 54–55.

Kelly, Kevin. *Out of Control: The New Biology of Machines, Social Systems, and the Economic World.* New York: Addison-Wesley, 1994.

Kramarae, C., ed. *Technology and Women's Voices: Keeping in Touch.* New York: Routledge, 1988.

Kroker, Arthur, and Marilouise Kroker. "Excremental TV." *Mediamatic* 7.2 (1993): 147–153.

Kroker, Arthur, Marilouise Kroker, and David Cook. *Panic Encyclopedia: The Definitive Guide to the Postmodern Scene.* New York: St. Martin's Press, 1989. Online. *The English Server* (CMU). Internet. 22 August 1995. Available: <http://english-www.hss.cmu.edu/ctheory/panic/panic_contents.html>.

Kroker, Arthur, and Michael A. Weinstein. *Data Trash: The Theory of the Virtual Class.* New York: St. Martin's Press, 1994.

Kurzweil, Raymond. "The Future of Libraries." *Library Journal* 117 (January 1992): 80, 82; (February 1992): 140–141; (March 1992): 63–64.

Landow, George P., ed. *Hyper/Text/Theory.* Baltimore: The Johns Hopkins University Press, 1994.

Landow, George P. *Hypertext: The Convergence of Contemporary Critical Theory and Technology.* Baltimore: The Johns Hopkins University Press, 1992.

Lanham, Richard. *The Electronic Word: Democracy, Technology, and the Arts.* Chicago: University of Chicago Press, 1993.

Leary, Timothy. *Chaos and Cyber Culture.* Berkeley, CA: Ronin, 1994.

Levy, Steven. *Hackers: Heroes of the Computer Revolution.* Garden City, NJ: Anchor/Doubleday, 1984. Online. Levy's Homepage. Internet. 22 August 1995. Available: <http://www.echonyc.com/~steven/Steven.Levy.html>.

Lewis, Peter H. "No More 'Anything Goes': Cyberspace Gets Censors." *The New York Times* (June 29, 1994): A1, D5.

Lyotard, Jean-François. *The Postmodern Condition.* Trans. Geoff Bennington and Brian Massumi. Minneapolis: University of Minnesota Press, 1984.

Markley, Robert, ed. Special Issue: Dreaming Real: Cyberspace, Virtual Realities, and Their Discontents. *Configurations* 2.3 (Fall 1994).

Markoff, John. "Hacker and Grifter Duel on the Net." *The New York Times* (February 19, 1995): A1, 3.

Markoff, John. "A Most-Wanted Cyberthief Is Caught in His Own Web." *The New York Times* (February 16, 1995): A1, D17.

McCaffery, Larry, ed. *Storming the Reality Studio: A Casebook of Cyberpunk and Postmodern Science Fiction.* Durham, NC: Duke University Press, 1991.

McLuhan, Marshall. *The Gutenberg Galaxy: The Making of Topographic Man.* Toronto: University of Toronto Press, 1965.

McLuhan, Marshall. *Understanding Media: The Extensions of Man.* London: Routledge, 1964.

McLuhan, Marshall, and Quentin Fiore. *The Medium is the Massage: An Inventory of Effects.* New York: Bantam, 1967.

Meyer, Michael. "Crimes of the 'Net.'" *Newsweek* (November 14, 1994): 46–47.

Mitchell, William J. *City of Bits: Space, Place, and the Infobahn.* Cambridge, MA: MIT Press, 1995.

Moore, Dinty W. *The Emperor's Virtual Clothes: The Naked Truth About Internet Culture.* Chapel Hill, NC: Algonquin, 1995.

Morton, Donald. "Birth of the Cyberqueer." *PMLA* 110.3 (May 1995): 369–381.

Negroponte, Nicholas. *Being Digital.* New York: Knopf, 1995.

Nelson, Theodor Holm. *Literary Machines.* Theodor H. Nelson, 1987.

Nunberg, Geoffrey. "The Places of Books in the Age of Electronic Reproduction." *Representations* 42 (Spring 1993): 13–37.

Ong, Walter J. *Orality and Literacy: The Technologizing of the Word.* New York: Methuen, 1982.

Paglia, Camille, and Neil Postman. "She Wants Her TV! He Wants His Book!" *Harper's Magazine* (March 1991): 44–51, 54–55.

Poster, Mark. *The Mode of Information.* Cambridge: Polity Press, 1990.

Postman, Neil. *Amusing Ourselves to Death: Public Discourse in the Age of Show Business.* New York: Penguin, 1986.

Postman, Neil. *Technopoly: The Surrender of Culture to Technology.* New York: Vintage, 1993.

Quittner, Joshua. "Johnny Manhattan Meets the Furry Muckers." *Wired* 2.03 (March 1994): 92–97, 138. Online. *HotWired.* Internet. 22 August 1995. Available: <http://vip.hotwired.com/wired/2.03/features/muds.html>

Rheingold, Howard. *Virtual Reality.* New York: Simon & Schuster, 1991.

Roszak, Theodore. *The Making of a Counter Culture: Reflections on the Technocratic Society and Its Youthful Opposition.* New York: Anchor, 1969.

Rucker, Rudy. *Live Robots (Software/Wetware).* New York: Avon, 1994.

Rucker, Rudy, R. U. Sirius and Queen Mu. *MONDO 2000: A User's Guide to the New Edge: Cyberpunk, Virtual Reality, Wetware, Designer Aphrodisiacs, Artificial Life, Techno-Erotic Paganism, and More.* New York: HarperCollins, 1992.

Rushkoff, Douglas. *Cyberia: Life in the Trenches of Hyperspace.* San Francisco: HarperCollins, 1995.

Schoemer, Karen. "Seriously Wired." *The New York Times* (August 8, 1993): sec. 9: 1, 9–10.

Schwenger, Peter. "*Agrippa,* or, The Apocalyptic Book." In *Flame Wars.* Durham, NC: Duke University Press, 1994: 61–70.

Seabrook, John. "E-Mail from Bill." *The New Yorker* (January 10, 1994): 48–61.

Seabrook, John. "No E-Mail from Bill." *The New Yorker* (February 7, 1994): 8–9.

Shah, Rawn, and James Romine. *Playing MUDS on the Internet.* New York: John Wiley, 1995.

Shapiro, Andrew L. "Cyberscoop!" *The Nation* (March 20, 1995): 369–370.

Slatalla, Michelle, and Joshua Quittner. *Masters of Deception: The Gang That Ruled Cyberspace.* New York: HarperCollins, 1995.

Slouka, Mark. *War of the Worlds: Cyberspace and the High-Tech Assault on Reality.* New York: Basic Books, 1995.

Sponsler, Claire. "Beyond the Ruins: The Geopolitics of Urban Decay and Cybernetic Play." *Science-Fiction Studies* 20 (1993): 251–264.

Sterling, Bruce. *The Hacker Crackdown: Law and Disorder on the Electronic Frontier.* New York: Bantam, 1992. Online. Fric's Home Page. Internet. 27 August 1995. Available as hypertext version: <http://home.eznet.net/~frac/crack.html>; or Online. *The English Server* (CMU). Internet. 27 August 1995. Available as plain text version: <gopher://english.hss.cmu.edu:70/0F-2%3A1576%3AThe%20Hacker%20Crackdown>.

Sterling, Bruce. *Island in the Net.* New York: Morrow, 1988.

Sterling, Bruce, ed. *Mirrorshades.* New York: Warner Books, 1986.

Stoll, Clifford. *Silicon Snake Oil: Second Thoughts on the Information Highway.* New York: Doubleday, 1995.

Stone, Allucqukre Rosanne. *The War of Desire and Technology at the Close of the Mechanical Age.* Cambridge, MA: MIT Press, 1995.

Tannen, Deborah. "Gender Gap in Cyberspace." *Newsweek* (May 16, 1994): 52–53.

Taylor, Mark C., and Esa Saarinen. *Imagologies: Media Philosophy.* New York: Routledge, 1994.

Turkle, Sherry. *Life on the Screen: Identity in the Age of the Internet.* New York: Simon & Schuster, 1995.

Turkle, Sherry. *The Second Self: Computers and the Human Spirit.* New York: Simon & Schuster, 1984.

Ulmer, Gregory. *Teletheory: Grammatology in the Age of Video.* New York: Routledge, 1989.

Uncapher, Willard. "Trouble in Cyberspace." *Humanist* 51 (September/October 1991): 5–14.

Van Der Leun, Gerard. "This Is a Naked Lady." *Wired* (1993, Premiere Issue): 74, 109. Online. *HotWired.* Internet. 22 August 1995. Available: <http://vip.hotwired.com/wired/1.1/features/cybersex.html>.

Virilio, Paul. *Speed and Politics.* Trans. Mark Polizzotti. New York: Semiotext(e), 1986.

Virilio, Paul, and Sylvère Lotringer. *Pure War.* Trans. Mark Polizzotti. New York: Semiotext(e), 1983.

Wajcman, J. *Feminism Confronts Technology.* University Park, PA: The Pennsylvania State University Press, 1991.

Wertheim, Margaret. "Electronic Café." *Omni* (January 1993): 66–68, 70.

Wolf, Gary. "The Curse of Xanadu." *Wired* 3.06 (July 1995): 137–152, 194–202. Online. *HotWired.* Internet. 22 August 1995. Available: <http://vip.hotwired.com/wired/3.06/features/xanadu.html>.

Woolley, Benjamin. *Virtual Worlds: A Journey in Hype and Hyperreality.* New York: Penguin, 1992.